Table of Contents

3

Part 1
Introduction

"There are worse crimes than burning books. One of them is not reading them."
Joseph Brodsky, Soviet-Russian-American poet, essayist, and Nobel Laureate in Literature, and Poet Laureate Consultant to the Library of Congress, and National Book Critics Award winner (1940-1996)

Banned Books:
Challenging Our Freedom to Read

Robert P. Doyle

Banned Books: Challenging Our Freedom to Read
Robert P. Doyle

Sponsored by the American Booksellers
Association, the American Booksellers Foundation
for Free Expression, the American Library
Association, the American Society of Journalists
and Authors, the Association of American
Publishers, and the National Association of
College Stores.

Endorsed by the Center for the Book in the
Library of Congress.

American Library Association
Chicago, Illinois

2010 Design and publication composition by
Silvio Design, Inc., Chicago.

Printed by McNaughton & Gunn, Inc.
Saline, Michigan

This publication was composed using
QuarkXPress, and Adobe Photoshop for the
Macintosh. The typeface used is MetaPlus.

ISBN 0-8389-8279-4
ISSN 0888-0123
LCCN 88-659709

In the spring of 1982, thousands of onlookers in Anaheim, California stared in disbelief at the sight of three well-respected twentieth-century women behind bars. Their individual imprisonment would have been improbable enough; even more baffling was imagining what the "three prisoners" could have in common. What crimes were committed by an African-American poetess, a German-Jewish adolescent, and an All-American Hollywood star?

The crowds surrounding the padlocked cells that day nearly thirty years ago found themselves gazing at Maya Angelou, Anne Frank, and Doris Day. In actuality, the crowd was captivated not by these three authors in person, but rather by a display of their books. The three imprisoned authors apparently did have a crime in common—they were guilty, at least in the opinion of some individuals, of creating controversial content. Maya Angelou's *I Know Why the Caged Bird Sings* was objectionable because it preaches "bitterness and hatred against whites" *The Diary of Anne Frank* because it was "a real downer" and *Doris Day: Her Own Story* because a group found the content shocking "in light of Miss Day's All-American image."

To call attention to the practice of book banning, The American Booksellers Association (ABA) had included these three titles in a selection of recently banned books displayed in a series of cages at their annual convention. Up until that day when they witnessed the display of books behind bars, the members of the professional association—the authors, publishers, booksellers, librarians, and journalists attending the convention—were all unaware that so many books and such familiar titles were removed from bookstore and library shelves because an individual or group thought the printed matter unfit for others to read. To the spectators the implication was clear—it was readers who were being caged, not just books.

As a result of the attention to the display and the conversations and questions it provoked, the first Banned Books Week was held several months later in the fall of 1982. It was then, and is still, sponsored by the following organizations and endorsed by the Center for the Book of the Library of Congress:

- American Booksellers Association
- American Booksellers Foundation for Free Expression
- American Library Association
- American Society of Journalists and Authors
- Association of American Publishers
- National Association of College Stores

This coalition selected the first full week of September as Banned Books Week to coincide with the beginning of the school year, because so many of the challenges occur in schools throughout the country. The ABA and the cosponsoring National Association of College Stores (NACS) sent out a promotional packet to members that included a list of more than five hundred banned books, a poster titled "Caution! Some People Consider These Books Are Dangerous," a sample press release, and background information for booksellers. The American Library Association (ALA) endorsed the week and publicized the event to its members.

With an enthusiastic response from the local and national press, book censorship became a front-page story for dozens of newspapers, radio, and television stations. During that first Banned Books Week in 1982, the press and the library community frequently posed the questions, "Why was the book banned?" "Where was it banned?" "When was it banned?" "What can we do?" Without annotations or explanations, the list of banned books distributed that first year left many of the questions unanswered.

The following year, working for ALA's Office of Intellectual Freedom, I prepared the first annotated list of banned books for the Banned Books Week celebration. Titled "A List of Books Some People Consider Dangerous," that first list in 1983 contained 404 titles compared to this year's list of more than 1,800. The increase in the number of challenges and bannings is more the result of better reporting of such incidents, rather than an indication of their proliferation. Each entry in the list includes a brief explanation of the reasons, location, and dates for the challenged, restricted, or banned titles, and the information is cumulative, offering a chronological history for each title.

Each year, the list is updated, revised, and published in an abbreviated version as a brochure. Every third year, an updated edition of *Banned Books* is published in book form.

The intent of Banned Books Week is three-fold: to draw attention to the importance of the freedom to read, to publicize threats to that freedom, and to provide information to combat ignorance and lack of awareness. The provocative title, Banned Books Week, has sometimes generated controversy, but rarely has it failed to attract attention—its primary reason for being.

Occasionally, individuals have misinterpreted the name as a celebration of the legal prohibition of books; worse, others have thought the book community was actively engaged in banning or advocating the removal of books from publication, purchase, or library circulation. Banned Books Week has even been accused of being fraudulent because, in many cases, the banning is requested but doesn't actually take place.

Suggestions to rename the week inevitably arise from time to time, but mostly they carry the same potential confusion and dilute its central message—that readers are banished when a book is banned and the threat of banning can be as dangerous as the actuality.

Now in its twenty-ninth year, Banned Books Week continues to uphold one of the world's greatest visions of the right to free expression—the First Amendment to the U.S. Constitution. Judge Oliver Wendell Holmes, Jr., an eloquent spokesperson for the role of free speech in a democracy, characterized it as "freedom for the thought that we hate." Resisting the temptation to curb such thought, lest our own be curbed as well, is the basis for this book and the annual week of celebrations from which it draws its name.

Robert P. Doyle

The better informed you are about a subject, the better you can reach—and teach—others. You'll find a robust supply of re-designed information in this new edition.

Even flawless information is no substitute for insight and interpretation. Along with ready reference tools and practical tips, we've seeded this book with ideas for further thought and reflection. Read on to use this book in ways designed to ignite your intellect and inspire your imagination.

How to Use This Book

Part 1 Introduction

How It All Began

If you're new to the subject of Banned Books Week, this surprising story will fill you in on the background and bring you up to date on the current state of book-banning in America.

How to Use This Book

Start here to get your bearings. Take a quick look at this content overview to find your way around the re-designed publication and see what's in it for you.

Part 2 Insight

The Challenge of Censorship

This introduction establishes a framework for understanding literary censorship and the danger it poses to our First Amendment freedom to read.

Part 3 Interpretations

The First Amendment

Study the singular beauty of this unprecedented and inspiring document to grasp the power of the original words penned on paper in 1791.

The Freedom of Expression

Discover the principles beneath the ongoing interpretation of the law that protects our uniquely American freedom of expression. Gain an overview of the issues that have come to symbolize First Amendment rights.

The Freedom to Read

As you read this section, consider the role of libraries in a democratic society. Think about the contributions of librarians and publishers to intellectual freedom and the educational process.

Part 4 Information

First Amendment Timeline

Get a sense of the First Amendment unfolding over time. From the ratification of the U.S. Constitution in 1787 to present-day Supreme Court opinion, a chronology puts it all in order. This well-researched, concise timeline will help you put the significant events in perspective.

First Amendment Court Cases

This section describes some noted legal precedents concerning freedom of speech. Use these to launch further research, and you'll have ample information to support your programs, presentations, articles, and displays.

First Amendment Glossary and Acronyms

Straightforward, precise, and relevant, you'll want to keep this glossary close at hand. Familiarize yourself with these definitions and soon you'll be using these essential words and phrases like an expert.

First Amendment Bibliography

Once you've mastered the vocabulary, you'll want to dig deeper for more information. Review this annotated bibliography to find the best books—history, analysis, commentary, case studies—for further critical study of the issues surrounding the First Amendment.

First Amendment Quotations

Summing up the value of the First Amendment can be difficult for the layperson, especially compared to these eloquent and memorable expressions by notable individuals. Don't hesitate to use these quotes to elevate your celebration and illustrate your displays. Incorporate an unconventional utterance into in your press materials or even print an erudite expression on your T-shirts or tote bags.

Part 5 Ideas

Celebration Guide

This guide features activities for celebrating Banned Books Week. From sponsoring a community-wide forum on censorship to organizing a reading and discussion series, you'll discover innovative ideas to draw attention to your bookstore or library. You'll read success stories of activities from the field and learn new approaches to connecting with your community members. Information on where to order T-shirts, lapel buttons, books, educational materials— even copies of the U.S. Constitution.

Communication Guide

This guide features strategies for communicating when dealing with concerns about library resources. You'll find basic, best-practice techniques for addressing challenges and resolving complaints. You'll learn about developing key messages when responding to a challenge, plus ideas and simple PR tips for dealing with the media or speaking to other audiences—community groups, trustees, and staff.

This year a number of resources are available at the American Library Association's Web site. For example, display ideas, a First Amendment timeline, a list of concerned national organizations, and downloadable images are all available at www.ala.org/bbooks. In addition, *Books Challenged or Banned in 2009–2010* is available at www.ala.org/bbooks.

This list makes it easier for you to identify material that has been challenged within the past year. Reprints of this list are available for distribution to bookstore customers and library patrons.

Part 6 Incidents

Top Ten Challenged Books of 2009

It should come as no surprise to find that Harper Lee, J.D. Salinger, and Alice Walker are among the Top Ten once again. To find out who the other contenders are, along with the top categories of objection, take a look at the Top Ten page.

Challenged or Banned Books

This extensive list includes books banned or considered controversial from 387 B.C. to 2010. Redesigned with the reader in mind, the entries are easy to scan visually to find the information you need. New entries added since the last edition are clearly marked. Browsing through this list leads to valuable ideas for creating an exhibit or preparing for discussions, presentations, and writings.

It should be noted that this bibliography is limited to documented challenges to free speech and expression. Surveys indicate that approximately 85 percent of such challenges to library materials receive no media attention and remain unreported. Moreover, this list is limited to books and does not include challenges to magazines, newspapers, films, broadcasts, plays, performances, electronic publications, or exhibits.

Indices

The three indices to the comprehensive Challenged or Banned Books list can help customize an exhibit or program by identifying challenged books by title, location, and category. For example, if you want to create an exhibit of books banned or challenged in your state or city, use the geographic index to find the titles. Or, if you want to have a program on children's literature or gay literature, check the topical index. Using these tools will help create an event targeted for your audience or community. Please note that the bibliography entries are numbered sequentially and the entry number (not the page number) is used in all three indices.

Part 2

Insight

"A point of view can be a dangerous luxury when substituted for insight and understanding."
Herbert Marshall McLuhan, Canadian sociologist (1911–80), from *The Gutenberg Galaxy: The Making of Typographic Man.* Toronto: University of Toronto Pr., 1962, p. 216.

Even in the digital era, books are an unsurpassed medium for advancing ideas and influencing others. It's no wonder that books continue to be an irresistible target for the undeniably human urge to censor.

Insight offers a perspective on the desire to censor literary expression and the danger of disregarding it.

The Challenge of Censorship

Censorship is nothing new; it has always been with us. The urge to censor is primordial. The instinct isn't limited just to those in positions of power who are driven to control access to information. The truth is, almost everyone wants to censor something at some point in time. Adults often censor to protect children, and children sometimes to protect their parents. If you believe something to be true, you may have the impulse to suppress or censor expression to the contrary, finding it to be inaccurate or harmful.

Recognizing the difference between an individual restricting his or her own choices and action by a governmental or public body is at the root of any discussion of censorship. The first is an exercise of freedom, while the second is its reverse. We may use the word "censor" to describe both actions, but it is the action of the government that is the concern of this book.

Censorship is everywhere. It isn't restricted by geography or ideology, nor limited to certain religious practices or political beliefs. Although it may be more commonly found where narrow viewpoints are the norm, it surprisingly still appears in open societies and circumstances.

Censorship is current. It didn't disappear with the end of the Inquisition or other repressive regimes. But unless it somehow comes up in conversation, people tend to dismiss it as a thing of the past. Censorship? It couldn't possibly still be happening today, not in a society as tolerant, diverse, and sophisticated as ours, could it? It seems remote until it happens in our hometown, or to someone we know, or we overhear a conversation at work or school.

Censorship is captivating. Even when we oppose it, we're intrigued by it. It prompts our curiosity, and in its own way, creates bestsellers. Challenging, restricting, removing, banning, or burning a book arouses as much fascination as fear, maybe more. Contrary to the censors' original intent to limit exposure, banning generates interest, increases sales, and provokes discussion.

In the United States, the freedom to choose what we read, to select from a full array of possibilities, is more pronounced than in most societies. Firmly rooted in the First Amendment to the U.S. Constitution, this right protects freedom of speech and freedom of the press in our country. Despite constitutional guarantees, however, these precious rights are vulnerable to erosion. Our freedom is only as secure as we make it. And what makes those rights secure is the body of law developed gradually over time—through the dedicated efforts of readers, publishers, booksellers, librarians, and others.

Books aren't the only form of expression subjected to censoring, but they may well be the most significant. Even in the digital age, we endow books with a certain aura of permanence and authority that gives weight to their content. Gossip and news are transitory by nature, easier to ignore than to ban. Movies and plays often have limited life spans, where ticket sales for box office hits peak and then plummet after a few short weeks or months. But books stick around. Their popularity endures. They're not so susceptible to the whims of fashion. We can find them in library stacks and bookstore shelves, making their ideas accessible to a growing audience for years to come. So it comes as no surprise that attempts to censor books are more robust and often take the form of "challenges"—the formal, written requests to remove them from library shelves or otherwise restrict public access.

As noted earlier, censorship pressures come from all quarters and all political persuasions. No matter how well intentioned, the practice of censorship limits the freedom of others to choose what they read, see, or hear. Sex, profanity, and racism remain the primary categories of objections, and most challenges occur in schools and school libraries.

Challenges are often motivated by the desire to protect children, but deciding what we get to read has broader consequences; if the government can restrict access for one reason, it can extend it to another. Supreme Court Justice William Brennan, in *Texas v. Johnson*, said, "If there is a bedrock principle underlying the First Amendment, it is that the Government may not prohibit the expression of an idea simply because society finds the idea itself offensive or disagreeable." Individuals can choose for themselves and their children, but if governmental or public agencies are called on to make that choice, we all ultimately forfeit our own right to choose.

The challenges documented in this publication are not merely expressing a point of view or exercising the right to choose; rather, they are formal requests for removal of materials from schools or libraries, restricting access to them by others. Even when the eventual outcome allows the book to stay on the library shelves, the censorship attempt is real. Someone has tried to limit another person's ability to choose.

Challenges are as important to document as actual bannings that result in removing a book from the shelves of a library or bookstore or from the curriculum at a school. Challenges—or attempts to censor—can eventually lead to a narrowing down of the range of books available for us to read. The constant pressure from those determined to censor our reading materials can have a chilling effect on publishers and editors who might decide that certain topics are simply too incendiary, so that some books may never make their way into print. Even librarians, booksellers, and educators might find it easier to avoid controversy and aggravation by staying away from certain authors or subjects altogether.

Readers everywhere can take heart from the fact that challenges are often met with successful resistance, keeping reading materials on the shelves where they belong. The everyday vigilance of ordinary people prevents censorship from encroaching upon our hard-won freedoms. The freedom to read, as promised by the First Amendment, is ours to use or to lose. This book is one small part of the ongoing endeavor to preserve our freedom to read and to promote understanding of the precarious nature of our irreplaceable right to learn.

Part 3
Interpretation

"All human knowledge takes the form of interpretation."
Walter Benjamin, German-Jewish philosopher, sociologist, literary critic, translator and essayist (1892–1940), from *Briefe* 126 (December 9, 1923).

In spite of the permanence of written documents, the meaning of words on paper changes over time. No matter how precise or powerful the language, every expression of thought—from the Bill of Rights to a scientific theory to a lullaby— is open to interpretation.

Interpretation traces the American notion of freedom of expression beginning with the momentous First Amendment doctrine.

"Congress shall respecting an e religion, or pro exercise thereo the freedom of press; or the ri peaceably to as to petition the a redress of gri

The First Amendment of the Bill of Rights to the United States Constitution 1791

make no law
stablishment of
hibiting the free
f; or abridging
speech, or of the
ght of the people
semble, and
Government for
evances."

The Freedom of Expression

The Freedom of Expression

Freedom of expression is a uniquely American tradition, at least to the degree it is practiced here. Whether born out of the founders' desire to make sure they wouldn't have to leave their new land when and if the new government became as oppressive as their old one — or simply a political strategy to get the new Constitution adopted by states unwilling to surrender their sovereignty — it put notions into law that hadn't been there before.

Governments were thought to reign supreme and criticizing them to be a crime. And for much of the First Amendment's history, its protection primarily extended to political expression, and even then was reluctantly employed by the courts. Development of First Amendment law has been a process of each decision building upon the cumulative pattern of earlier ones, each lending weight and voice to what has become a solid foundation for the right of writers and speakers to express themselves freely without fear of repercussion.

As Supreme Court Justice John Marshall Harlan continued in his opinion for the majority in a 1971 case about the right to protest, albeit profanely, during the Vietnam War:

"The constitutional right of free expression is powerful medicine in a society as diverse and populous as ours. It is designed and intended to remove governmental restraints from the arena of public discussion, putting the decision as to what views shall be voiced largely into the hands of each of us, in the hope that use of such freedom will ultimately produce a more capable citizenry and more perfect polity and in the belief that no other approach would comport with the premise of individual dignity and choice upon which our political system rests. . . . That the air may at times seem filled with verbal cacophony is, in this sense, not a sign of weakness but of strength."
U.S. Supreme Court Justice John Marshall Harlan, *Cohen v. California*, 403 U.S. 15, 91 S.Ct. 1780, 29 L.Ed.2d 284 (1971).

Both the Supreme Court and the rest of the country generally ignored these constitutional rights until well into the twentieth century. And the first time the Court cited the First Amendment in defending freedom of speech, it was in a dissenting opinion. But even dissenting opinions are part of the process that builds the body of law. A series of dissents authored by Justices Oliver Wendell Holmes, Jr., and Louis D. Brandeis in the 1920s began to change what the award-winning journalist Anthony Lewis called "the old, crabbed view of what the First Amendment protects." Lewis went on to say:

"It was an extraordinary change, really a legal revolution. And it showed the power of words to change minds. Holmes and Brandeis had only two votes of nine. But their rhetoric was so powerful, so convincing, that it changed the attitude of the country and the Court."
from *Freedom for the Thought That We Hate: A Biography of the First Amendment*

It was in one of these opinions that Holmes coined the phrase we still use today to describe the fundamental nature of free speech—"freedom for the thought we hate." Supporting expression of ideas with which we agree is easy; much harder, and more important, is supporting expression of ideas we condemn. Jailing of socialists and unionists, the burning of German-language books during World War I and detention of Japanese-Americans during World War II, treatment of communist sympathizers during the Cold War, and even the rights of Nazis to march in Skokie, Illinois, in the 1970s were all issues that came to symbolize First Amendment rights. Most recently, the threat of terrorism in the wake of September 11, 2001, has led to suppression or suspension of some of these rights, not by the courts, but by other units of government.

Fighting for the freedom to read is not an isolated act. It is part of all these other battles waged, most of which were eventually won in front of the Court, though victory often followed earlier defeats. The right to publish and to read "the thought that we hate" has been the basis for resisting demands to remove books and reading materials from libraries, schools, bookstores, and other public places. It has finally and firmly been embraced by the Supreme Court.

The Court's first key decision to apply this reasoning came in *Stromberg v. California* in 1931. Even though this decision established the principles the Court still observes, case law continues to evolve. The amendment did not come with specific instructions, but was rather "a sweeping command," as Justice Holmes termed it, left to each generation and set of circumstances to define and refine.

Much of the attention to defining the parameters of free speech occurred in cases involving the press, often dealing with the protection of journalists and their sources. The role of a free press in limiting the government's power to put its own spin on information became a particular area of interest, and was largely upheld by the Court, though stopping short of making journalists a special or privileged class.

In fact, sexual rather than political content is what ultimately brought books and their banning to the attention of the Court. In the early twentieth century, literary classics such as D. H. Lawrence's *Lady Chatterley's Lover*, Theodore Dreiser's *An American Tragedy*, and James Joyce's *Ulysses* were found to be obscene and frequently banned, bans upheld by local, state, and federal district courts. In one such case in 1933, the presiding judge set a new test for obscenity, judging a work by its effect on an average reader. Applying that test, Judge John M. Woolsey found *Ulysses* was not obscene, and the test was widely adopted.

An obscenity case before the Supreme Court in 1948 was the last to allow a lower court ban on a serious book to stand, and even then in a split 4-4 decision. Subsequent decisions attempted to separate free speech and obscenity, guaranteeing one while placing the other outside the amendment's protection. Two great friends of the freedom that libraries claim for their readers were Justices William O. Douglas and Hugo Black, both contending that this freedom is one that individual citizens are capable of exercising without governmental support or interference. Douglas said he had "the same confidence in the ability of our people to reject noxious literature as I have in their capacity to sort out the true from the false in theology, economics, politics or any other field."

This tradition of First Amendment law, handed down by the U.S. Supreme Court, has built a strong foundation for the freedom to read. While it may seem secure in legal precedent, at least at the national level, it remains subject to local pressure and the continuing evolution of ideas under our societal blueprint, the U.S. Constitution. Librarians, booksellers, lawyers, judges, journalists, readers, and writers have all helped define this precious freedom. This book looks at many of the examples in which they've succeeded, some in which they've failed. All are part of the beautiful and textured fabric of the First Amendment, embroidered with words, phrases, and ideas from some of the world's bravest hearts and best minds.

An opinion authored by Justice Robert H. Jackson in 1943 in reference to saluting the flag makes it clear that all First Amendment cases have much in common, whether they address literary, political, or other forms of expression:

"Compulsory unification of opinion achieves only the unanimity of the graveyard. ...We can have intellectual individuals and the rich cultural diversity that we owe to exceptional minds only at the price of occasional eccentricity and abnormal attitudes. When they are so harmless to others or to the State as those we deal with here, the price is not too great. But freedom to differ is not limited to things that do not matter much. That would be a mere shadow of freedom. The test of its substance is the right to differ as to things that touch the heart of the existing order."
West Virginia Board of Education v. Barnette (1943)

The Freedom to Read

Just like the courts, the American book community did not become serious advocates of First Amendment freedoms as they applied to library materials until well into the twentieth century. The first expressions of concern were in the 1920s and 1930s and were typically related to the exclusion of political ideas, whether through library policies about what could be placed on shelves or tariffs on imports or ideas in specific publications. Responses were isolated and sporadic, and neither unanimously held nor widely publicized.

Efforts to ban John Steinbeck's *The Grapes of Wrath* in the late 1930s brought about adoption by the American Library Association (ALA) of *The Library's Bill of Rights*, which focused on unbiased book selection and open meeting rooms and didn't even mention censorship or book banning. The document evolved, however, through the general climate of political repression in the 1950s and civil rights issues of the 1960s, eventually becoming *The Library Bill of Rights*, the profession's basic policy statement on intellectual freedom and library materials.

The role of ALA has evolved as well, with expanded services to librarians who find themselves on the front lines of censorship issues. While ALA's Committee on Intellectual Freedom provided a forum for philosophical discussion and policy formation, creation of the Office for Intellectual Freedom (OIF) in 1967 and the Freedom to Read Foundation in 1969 positioned the association to provide support to librarians through continuing education, publications, court cases, and even direct financial support.

The approach throughout has been one that seeks to both reflect the views of the profession and offer leadership for the positions taken. The Freedom to Read statement, originally adopted in 1953, has been maintained as a bedrock document, subject to minor revision and interpretation, but steering clear of major shifts and swings. Like the Constitution itself, it is a living document, meant to be applied to changing realities but holding fast to basic principles.

The freedom to read is essential to our democracy. It is continuously under attack. Private groups and public authorities in various parts of the country are working to remove books from sale, to censor textbooks, to label "controversial" books, to distribute lists of "objectionable" books or authors, and to purge libraries. These actions apparently rise from a view that our national tradition of free expression is no longer valid; that censorship and suppression are needed to avoid the subversion of politics and the corruption of morals. We, as citizens devoted to the use of books and as librarians and publishers responsible for disseminating them, wish to assert the public interest in the preservation of the freedom to read.

We are deeply concerned about these attempts at suppression. Most such attempts rest on a denial of the fundamental premise of democracy: that the ordinary citizen, by exercising critical judgment, will accept the good and reject the bad. The censors, public and private, assume that they should determine what is good and what is bad for their fellow-citizens.

We trust Americans to recognize propaganda, and to reject it. We do not believe they need the help of censors to assist them in this task. We do not believe they are prepared to sacrifice their heritage of a free press in order to be "protected" against what others think may be bad for them. We believe they still favor free enterprise in ideas and expression

We are aware, of course, that books are not alone in being subjected to efforts at suppression. We are aware that these efforts are related to a larger pattern of pressures being brought against education, the press, films, radio and television. The problem is not only one of actual censorship. The shadow of fear cast by these pressures leads, we suspect, to an even larger voluntary curtailment of expression by those who seek to avoid controversy.

Such pressure toward conformity is perhaps natural to a time of uneasy change and pervading fear. Especially when so many of our apprehensions are directed against an ideology, the expression of a dissident idea becomes a thing feared in itself, and we tend to move against it as against a hostile deed, with suppression.

And yet suppression is never more dangerous than in such a time of social tension. Freedom has given the United States the elasticity to endure strain. Freedom keeps open the path of novel and creative solutions, and enables change to come by choice. Every silencing of a heresy, every enforcement of an orthodoxy, diminishes the toughness and resilience of our society and leaves it the less able to deal with stress.

Now as always in our history, books are among our greatest instruments of freedom. They are almost the only means for making generally available ideas or manners of expression that can initially command only a small audience. They are the natural medium for the new idea and the untried voice from which come the original contributions to social growth. They are essential to the extended discussion which serious thought requires, and to the accumulation of knowledge and ideas into organized collections.

We believe that free communication is essential to the preservation of a free society and a creative culture. We believe that these pressures towards conformity present the danger of limiting the range and variety of inquiry and expression on which our democracy and our culture depend. We believe that every American community must jealously guard the freedom to publish and to circulate, in order to preserve its own freedom to read. We believe that publishers and librarians have a profound responsibility to give validity to that freedom to read by making it possible for the readers to choose freely from a variety of offerings.

The freedom to read is guaranteed by the Constitution. Those with faith in free people will stand firm on these constitutional guarantees of essential rights and will exercise the responsibilities that accompany these rights. We therefore affirm these propositions:

1. It is in the public interest for publishers and librarians to make available the widest diversity of views and expressions, including those which are unorthodox or unpopular with the majority.

Creative thought is by definition new, and what is new is different. The bearer of every new thought is a rebel until that idea is refined and tested. Totalitarian systems attempt to maintain themselves in power by the ruthless suppression of any concept which challenges the established orthodoxy. The power of a democratic system to adapt to change is vastly strengthened by the freedom of its citizens to choose widely from among conflicting opinions offered freely to them.

To stifle every nonconformist idea at birth would mark the end of the democratic process. Furthermore, only through the constant activity of weighing and selecting can the democratic mind attain the strength demanded by times like these. We need to know not only what we believe but why we believe it.

2. Publishers, librarians and booksellers do not need to endorse every idea or presentation contained in the books they make available. It would conflict with the public interest for them to establish their own political, moral or aesthetic views as a standard for determining what books should be published or circulated.

Publishers and librarians serve the educational process by helping to make available knowledge and ideas required for the growth of the mind and the increase of learning. They do not foster education by imposing as mentors the patterns of their own thought. The people should have the freedom to read and consider a broader range of ideas than those that may be held by any single librarian or publisher or government or church. It is wrong that what one can read should be confined to what another thinks proper.

3. It is contrary to the public interest for publishers or librarians to determine the acceptability of a book on the basis of the personal history or political affiliations of the author.

A book should be judged as a book. No art or literature can flourish if it is to be measured by the political views or private lives of its creators. No society of free people can flourish which draws up lists of writers to whom it will not listen, whatever they may have to say.

4. There is no place in our society for efforts to coerce the taste of others, to confine adults to the reading matter deemed suitable for adolescents, or to inhibit the efforts of writers to achieve artistic expression.

To some, much of modern literature is shocking. But is not much of life itself shocking? We cut off literature at the source if we prevent writers from dealing with the stuff of life. Parents and teachers have a responsibility to prepare the young to meet the diversity of experiences in life to which they will be exposed, as they have a responsibility to help them learn to think critically for themselves. These are affirmative responsibilities, not to be discharged simply by preventing them from reading works for which they are not yet prepared. In these matters taste differs, and taste cannot be legislated; nor can machinery be devised which will suit the demands of one group without limiting the freedom of others.

5. It is not in the public interest to force a reader to accept with any book the prejudgment of a label characterizing the book or author as subversive or dangerous.

The ideal of labeling presupposes the existence of individuals or groups with wisdom to determine by authority what is good or bad for the citizen. It presupposes that individuals must be directed in making up their minds about the ideas they examine. But Americans do not need others to do their thinking for them.

6. It is the responsibility of publishers and librarians, as guardians of the people's freedom to read, to contest encroachments upon that freedom by individuals or groups seeking to impose their own standards or tastes upon the community at large.

It is inevitable in the give and take of the democratic process that the political, the moral, or the aesthetic concepts of an individual or group will occasionally collide with those of another individual or group. In a free society individuals are free to determine for themselves what they wish to read, and each group is free to determine what it will recommend to its freely associated members. But no group has the right to take the law into its own hands, and to impose its own concept of politics or morality upon other members of a democratic society. Freedom is no freedom if it is accorded only to the accepted and the inoffensive.

7. It is the responsibility of publishers and librarians to give full meaning to the freedom to read by providing books that enrich the quality and diversity of thought and expression. By the exercise of this affirmative responsibility, they can demonstrate that the answer to a bad book is a good one, the answer to a bad idea is a good one.

The freedom to read is of little consequence when expended on the trivial; it is frustrated when the reader cannot obtain matter fit for that reader's purpose. What is needed is not only the absence of restraint, but the positive provision of opportunity for the people to read the best that has been thought and said. Books are the major channel by which the intellectual inheritance is handed down, and the principal means of its testing and growth. The defense of their freedom and integrity, and the enlargement of their service to society, requires of all publishers and librarians the utmost of their faculties, and deserves of all citizens the fullest of their support.

The Freedom to Read Statement

We state these propositions neither lightly nor as easy generalizations. We here stake out a lofty claim for the value of books. We do so because we believe that they are good, possessed of enormous variety and usefulness, worthy of cherishing and keeping free. We realize that the application of these propositions may mean the dissemination of ideas and manners of expression that are repugnant to many persons. We do not state these propositions in the comfortable belief that what people read is unimportant. We believe rather that what people read is deeply important; that ideas can be dangerous; but that the suppression of ideas is fatal to a democratic society. Freedom itself is a dangerous way of life, but it is ours.

This statement was originally issued in May of 1953 by the Westchester Conference of the American Library Association and the American Book Publishers Council, which in 1970 consolidated with the American Educational Publishers Institute to become the Association of American Publishers.

Adopted June 25, 1953; revised January 28, 1972, January 16, 1991, by the ALA Council and the AAP Freedom to Read Committee.

A Joint Statement by: American Library Association & Association of American Publishers.

The American Library Association affirms that all libraries are forums for information and ideas, and that the following basic policies should guide their services.

1. Books and other library resources should be provided for the interest, information, and enlightenment of all people of the community the library serves. Materials should not be excluded because of the origin, background, or views of those contributing to their creation.

2. Libraries should provide materials and information presenting all points of view on current and historical issues. Materials should not be proscribed or removed because of partisan or doctrinal disapproval.

3. Libraries should challenge censorship in the fulfillment of their responsibility to provide information and enlightenment.

4. Libraries should cooperate with all persons and groups concerned with resisting abridgment of free expression and free access to ideas.

5. A person's right to use a library should not be denied or abridged because of origin, age, background, or views.

6. Libraries which make exhibit spaces and meeting rooms available to the public they serve should make such facilities available on an equitable basis, regardless of the beliefs or affiliations of individuals or groups requesting their use.

Adopted June 18, 1948; amended February 2, 1961, and January 23, 1980, by the ALA Council.

inclusion of "age" reaffirmed January 23, 1996, by the ALA Council.

Part 4
Information

"Whenever the people are well informed, they can be trusted with their own government."
Thomas Jefferson (1743–1826) third U.S. President (1801–9) and principal author of the Declaration of Independence to Richard Price, 1789.

In a democratic society, people have the right to think freely, to express their thoughts, and to read the books they choose. When these freedoms are protected by constitutional guarantees, individuals with open access to information are empowered to learn and share their newfound knowledge to effect positive change for the community.

Information chronicles the milestones shaping the First Amendment as it emerges over the generations—in the courts, in the literature, and in the language.

First Amendment Timeline

Every challenge to the First Amendment has helped shape
the current interpretation of Americans' rights.

1787
The U.S. Constitution is ratified on the unwritten condition by many
states that a Bill of Rights be added soon afterward.

1788
The Constitution goes into effect; nine states have ratified it, with
others to follow. Several states gave their approval on the unwritten
condition that a Bill of Rights be added soon afterward.

1791
The First through Tenth Amendments are adopted, comprising
the Bill of Rights.

1798
Fearing war with France, Congress passes the unpopular
Sedition Act of 1798, curtailing First Amendment freedoms.
Numerous newspaper editors were fined and jailed under the Act.

1868
The Fourteenth Amendment is adopted, as one of the Civil War
Amendments. The due process clause of this amendment has served
as the basis for the Supreme Court to apply selectively, against actions
by state governments, the checks and guarantees contained in the
Bill of Rights. Up to this time, the free speech rights of the citizen of a
state were safeguarded solely by the constitution and laws of the state.

1885
Mark Twain's *The Adventures of Huckleberry Finn* is banned in
Concord, Mass. The book continues to be one of the most frequently
challenged or banned books in the United States.

1917
The Court defines freedom of speech quite narrowly in the years around
World War I, upholding the Espionage Act of 1917 in several cases.

1919

U.S. Supreme Court Justice Oliver Wendell Holmes, Jr., announces in *Schenck v. U.S.* (249 U.S. 47) a "clear and present danger" test to judge whether the First Amendment protects speech. Using the test, the Supreme Court affirmed the wartime convictions of the defendants charged with interfering in armed forces recruitment by mailing new recruits leaflets urging them to resist conscription.

Justice Holmes demonstrates the limits of his "clear and present danger" test by dissenting in *Abrams v. U.S.*, 250 U.S. 616, which affirmed the convictions of several Russian immigrants who distributed circulars that denounced President Wilson and urged workers to unite in support of the Bolshevik Revolution. In his dissent, he argues that the "silly leaflet" of the immigrants posed no real danger to the United States or its war effort, and thus failed to present a "clear and present danger" that the government might be justified in trying to suppress.

1920

Roger N. Baldwin creates the American Civil liberties Union (ACLU).

1923

Writer Upton Sinclair is arrested in Los Angeles after trying to read the Bill of Rights in public at a dockworkers strike. He is later charged with "discussing, arguing, orating and debating certain thoughts and theories, which . . . were detrimental and in opposition to the orderly conduct of affairs of business, affecting the rights of private property. . . ."

1925

When science teacher John Scopes challenges a Tennessee law forbidding him from teaching the theory of evolution, one of the most noted trials in U.S. history follows. Though Scopes lost the "monkey trial," his conviction was overturned later on a technicality. It is forty-three years before the U.S. Supreme Court rules on the same issue. In 1968, in *Epperson v. Arkansas* (393 U.S. 97), the Court said that rules that require that only Biblical or religious theories of the origin of man be taught violate the U.S. Constitution.

1925
The U.S. Supreme Court, in *Gitlow v. New York* (268 U.S. 652), decides that rights protected under the First Amendment are among the personal "liberties" protected by the due process clause of the Fourteenth Amendment from impairment by states. Nevertheless, the Court declined to apply Justice Holmes's "clear and present danger" test and upheld the defendant's convictions under New York statutes for publishing a manifesto advocating, advising, or teaching the overthrow of organized government by force or violence.

1931
In *Near v. Minnesota ex rel. Olson* (283 U.S. 697), the U.S. Supreme Court interprets the First and Fourteenth Amendments to forbid as "prior restraints" a lawsuit authorized by a state statute to enjoin future publication of a newspaper. The case extended the definition of "prior restraints" to include more than simply official pre-publication review that involves either licensing or censoring of particular content.

1931
The U.S. Supreme Court invalidates California's "anti-red flag" law in *Stromberg v. California* (283 U.S. 359). The Court found the California statute that made it a felony to display a red flag "as a sign, symbol or emblem of opposition to organized government" repugnant to the Constitution.

1939
The American Library Association adopts the *Library Bill of Rights*, the profession's basic policy statement on intellectual freedom involving library materials.

1942
In *Chaplinsky v. New Hampshire* (315 U.S. 568), the high court upholds a New Hampshire statute as a valid regulation of "fighting words," i.e., words "which by their very utterance inflict injury or tend to incite an immediate breach of peace." Fighting words, like certain other limited classes of speech, e.g., the lewd and obscene, "are no

essential part of any exposition of ideas and are of such slight social value as a step to truth that any benefit that may be derived from them is clearly outweighed by the social interest in order and morality."

1943

The Bill of Rights is included for the first time in the handbooks given to immigrants to study for their citizenship tests.

In *West Virginia State Board of Education v. Barnette*, the U.S. Supreme Court overturns a law requiring schoolchildren to salute the U.S. flag, holding that the government cannot compel or coerce an individual's speech against his conscience. Justice Jackson, writing for the majority, stated that "[i]f there is any fixed star in our constitutional constellation, it is that no official, high or petty, can prescribe what shall be orthodox in politics, nationalism, religion or other matters of opinion or force citizens to confess by word or act their faith therein."

1951

During the era of McCarthyism and Communist witch-hunting, the Court weakens free speech rights by ruling that speakers can be punished for advocating overthrow of the government, even if the likelihood of such an occurrence is remote.

1953

The Freedom to Read statement is issued by the Westchester Conference of the American Library Association and the American Publishers Council, which in 1970 consolidated with the American Educational Publishers Institute to become the Association of American Publishers. The statement was subsequently endorsed by American Booksellers Association, American Booksellers Foundation for Free Expression, American Civil Liberties Union, American Federation of Teachers AFL-CIO, Anti-Defamation League of B'nai B'rith, Association of American University Presses, Children's Book Council, Freedom to Read Foundation, International Reading Association, Thomas Jefferson Center for the Protection of Free

Expression, National Association of College Stores, National Council of Teachers of English, P.E.N.-American Center, People for the American Way, Periodical and Book Association of America, Sex Information and Education Council of the U.S., Society of Professional Journalists, Women's National Book Association, and YWCA of the USA.

1957

The appeal taken in *Roth v. U.S.* (354 U.S. 476) directly raises before the U.S. Supreme Court the question of whether obscenity is speech protected under either the First or Fourteenth Amendments. U.S. Justice Brennan answered that it is not, and set forth the standard for judging obscenity as "whether to the average person, applying contemporary standards, the dominant theme of the material taken as a whole appeals to the prurient interest." The "Hicklin test," which judged obscenity by the effect of isolated excerpts upon the most susceptible persons in a community, was thus rejected.

The Court, in *Yates v. United States* (354 U.S. 298), draws a distinction between advocacy of an abstract doctrine such as Marxism and advocacy directed at promoting unlawful action. The decision construed certain federal statutes regulating subversive political activity to permit advocacy and teaching of the forcible overthrow of the government, even with evil intent, so long as the advocacy and teaching is divorced from any effort to instigate action.

1961

In *Scales v. U.S.* (367 U.S. 203), the Court further construes the statutes at issue in Yates v. United States, upholding a clause that criminalizes knowing membership in any organization that advocates the overthrow of the government by force or violence. The clause presses the limits of constitutionality, the Court observed. However, "active" members who also have a "guilty knowledge and intent"—going beyond "merely an expression of sympathy with an alleged criminal enterprise"—"unaccompanied by any significant action" or "any commitment to undertake such action" engage in illegal advocacy.

1962

The U.S. Supreme Court, in *Engel v. Vitale* (370 U.S. 421), rules that public school use of a prayer composed by state officials and recommended as part of a program for moral and spiritual training violated the First Amendment prohibition against governmental establishment of religion. The Court found irrelevant the fact that the prayer may have been denominationally neutral or that its observance by students was voluntary.

1964

In the first libel case to reach the Supreme Court, *New York Times v. Sullivan*, (376 U.S. 254), the justices rule 9-0 that a public official may not recover damages for a defamatory statement, unless he can prove the statement was made with "actual malice."

1967

The American Library Association establishes the Office for Intellectual Freedom. The office's goal is to educate librarians and the general public on the importance of intellectual freedom.

1968

Though the Supreme Court has made clear in a series of opinions that symbolic speech may be protected by the First Amendment, in *United States v. O' Brien* (391 U.S. 367), it identified the limits that could be placed on symbolic speech. After he burned his draft card during a public protest, Paul O'Brien was found guilty of violating federal statutes forbidding the destruction of Selective Service documents. The Court affirmed O'Brien's conviction, stating that the draft card statutes furthered an important governmental objective unrelated to the suppression of speech, were narrowly tailored to achieve the government's legitimate objective of assuring the efficient functioning of the selective service system, and left open ample alternative means for protest. Laws that did not meet this stringent test would be struck down as unconstitutional.

1969

The Freedom to Read Foundation is created. The Foundation assists groups or individuals in litigation by securing counsel, or providing funding and by participating directly or as a "friend of the court" in important and possibly precedent-setting litigation.

1969

Reversing the conviction of a Ku Klux Klan member, the U.S. Supreme Court, in *Brandenberg v. Ohio* (395 U.S. 444), overrules its earlier decision, which had upheld criminal syndicalism statutes that proscribe advocacy of violent means to effect political and economic change. Constitutional guarantees do not permit a state to forbid such speech, except where advocacy of the use of force "is directed to inciting or producing imminent lawless action and is likely to incite or produce such action."

1971

Efforts by the U.S. federal government to stop the publication of the "Pentagon Papers," bring to a head conflicting claims of free speech and national security. The Court ruling in *New York Times Company v. United States* (403 U.S. 713) reaffirmed the heavy presumption that a "prior restraint" of free expression is constitutionally invalid. Because the government failed to meet the "heavy burden of showing justification" for such a restraint, newspapers were not enjoined from releasing the secret history of American involvement in Vietnam.

1973

Striving to remove confusions concerning a test for obscenity requiring that the material be "utterly without redeeming social value," the Supreme Court in *Miller v. California* (413 U.S. 15) reformulated the test. The Court's test, which still stands, involves three parts. First, the average person, applying contemporary community standards, finds that the work, taken as a whole, appeals to the prurient interests. Second, that the work depicts sexual conduct in a patently offensive way. Third, the work, taken as a whole, lacks serious literary, artistic, political or scientific value.

1977

When neo-Nazi Frank Collin and his National Socialist Party of America are denied a permit to march in Skokie, a Chicago suburb with thousands of Holocaust survivors, the ACLU fights for their First Amendment rights. The protracted legal battle concluded after the U.S. Supreme Court refused, in *Smith v. Collin* (439 U.S. 916), to review the proceedings, resulting in Collin eventually obtaining a permit. The Party's march, however, was held in Chicago's Marquette Park.

1978

In proceedings on a complaint about an afternoon radio broadcast of comic George Carlin's seven "dirty words" monologue, the Supreme Court in *Federal Communications Commission v. Pacifica Foundation* (438 U.S. 726), upholds an FCC order as to "possible" sanctions against the radio station, which found the monologue as broadcast "indecent" but not obscene.

1979

When the Progressive, an alternative newspaper in Madison, Wis., prepares to run a cover story that explains how to build a hydrogen bomb, the government takes quick action to prevent publication. After a seven-month showdown, the government backs down and the article runs.

1981

Banned Books Week: Celebrating the Freedom to Read is created. The week is sponsored by the American Booksellers Association, the American Booksellers Foundation for Free Expression, the American Library Association, the American Society of Journalists and Authors, the Association of American Publishers, and the National Association of College Stores. These groups sponsor this week to draw attention to the danger that exists when restraints are imposed on the availability of information in a free society.

1982

In *Island Trees Union Free School District No. 26 v. Pico* (457 U.S. 853), a divided U.S. Supreme Court recognizes that a board of education's discretion to remove books from junior and senior high school libraries is more limited that its discretion with respect to classrooms and the curriculum. The plurality opinion by Justice William Brennan declared that "local school boards may not remove books from school library shelves simply because they dislike the ideas contained in those books and seek by their removal to prescribe what shall be orthodox in politics, nationalism, religion or other matters of opinion."

1982

The U.S. Supreme Court added child pornography as another category of speech excluded from First Amendment protection. The ruling came in the case *New York v. Ferber* (458 U.S. 747), when the Court upheld the constitutionality of a New York statute prohibiting persons from promoting a sexual performance by a child under the age of sixteen by distributing material, which need not be legally obscene, that depicts such a performance.

1989

Burning the U.S. flag is a protected form of symbolic political speech, the Supreme Court rules in *Texas v. Johnson* (491 U.S. 397). Because a principal function of free speech is to invite dispute, any interest asserted by the state in preventing breaches of the peace from outraged onlookers was found to be insufficient to support the defendant's conviction under a Texas statute prohibiting "desecration of a venerated object."

1990

The Supreme Court, in *U.S. v. Eichmann and U.S. v. Haggerty* (496 U.S. 310), strikes down convictions under the Flag Protection Act of 1989, passed by Congress in response to the Court's flag desecration decision that year.

1990

The constitutionally protected right to receive obscenity, and information generally, in the privacy of one's home does not extend to child pornography, the U.S. Supreme Court rules in *Osborne v. Ohio* (495 U.S. 103). The Court found that Ohio reasonably concluded that the state will decrease the production of child pornography, thereby protecting child victims, if it penalizes those who possess and view the product.

1992

The U.S. Supreme Court clarifies that "fighting words" is not a category of speech that is wholly outside of First Amendment protection. In *R.A.V. v. St. Paul* (505 U.S. 377), the Court overturned a St. Paul ordinance punishing the placement of certain symbols that were "likely to arouse anger, alarm, or resentment on the basis of race, religion, or gender" after a teenager was convicted of violating the ordinance by burning a cross in the yard of a black family. The Court reversed the teen's conviction on the grounds that the ordinance unconstitutionally criminalized some hurtful expression (specifically that aimed at racial and religious minorities) and not other hurtful expression (that aimed at other unprotected groups) based on the political preferences of legislators.

1997

The first U.S. Supreme Court decision regarding the Internet, *American Library Association v. U.S. Department of Justice* and *Reno v. American Civil Liberties Union* (521 U.S. 844), strikes down provisions of the Communications Decency Act regulating "indecent" and "patently offensive" speech. Intended to protect minors, the Act was found to unconstitutionally limit adults' reading on the Internet to only "what is fit for children." The rare 9-0 decision by the Court sets forth the rule that the First Amendment applies, without limitation or restriction, to all content published on the Internet.

1998

In response to the U.S. Supreme Court's decision in *Reno v. ACLU*, Congress enacts the Child Online Protection Act (COPA), which criminalizes the online transmission of material considered harmful to minors for commercial purposes. Artists, writers, and publishers immediately challenge the new law, and the courts prohibit its enforcement. The law is eventually declared unconstitutional and overturned after a decade of litigation.

2003

The U.S. Supreme Court upholds the Children's Internet Protection Act in *United States v. American Library Association* (539 U.S. 194), a law requiring public schools and libraries receiving certain kinds of federal funding to install Internet filtering software on their computers. The Court upholds the law as a constitutional condition imposed on institutions in exchange for government funding because the law's provisions entitle adult patrons to ask the institution to disable the filtering software, noting that, "[w]hen a patron encounters a blocked site, he need only ask a librarian to unblock it or (at least in the case of adults) disable the filter."

2004

The U.S. Supreme Court upholds a lower court's preliminary injunction preventing enforcement of the Child Online Protection Act (COPA). The Court reasons that the use of filtering software by parents is an alternative less restrictive of First Amendment rights than COPA, which criminalized online transmission of speech protected for adults. The Court noted that parents' use of filtering was likely a more effective means of restricting children's access to materials considered harmful to minors.

2010

Challenges to library materials continue. Among the challenged titles in the past year are *The Perks of Being a Wallflower*, by Stephen Chbosky; *The Chocolate War*, by Robert Cormier; *Anne Frank: The Diary of a Young Girl*, by Anne Frank; *Aura*, by Carlos Fuentes; *The Bean Trees*, by Barbara Kingsolver; *To Kill a Mockingbird*, by Harper Lee; *Merriam-Webster Collegiate Dictionary; Twilight* series, by Stephenie H. Meyer; *Song of Solomon*, by Toni Morrison; and *And Tango Makes Three*, by Justin Richardson and Peter Parnell. Librarians, teachers, parents, trustees, students, and administrators continue to work to defend library collections.

In *Citizens United v. Federal Election Commission*, the U.S. Supreme Court holds that corporate funding of independent political broadcasts in candidate elections cannot be limited by the government, overturning existing laws restricting what and when profit-making and nonprofit corporations may say during federal election campaigns. Writing on behalf of the majority, Justice Kennedy wrote that "[i]f the First Amendment has any force, it prohibits Congress from fining or jailing citizens, or associations of citizens, for simply engaging in political speech." The opinion was immediately criticized for holding that corporations are, for constitutional purposes, persons entitled to First Amendment rights as well as increasing the power of corporations and special interests to influence elections.

This timeline was compiled using a variety of sources including, but not limited to: Patrick, John J. *Oxford Companion to the Supreme Court of the United States*. New York: Oxford University Pr., 1994;

Spaeth, Harold J., and Edward Conrad Smith. *The Constitution of the United States*. New York: HarperPerennial, 1991; and

Weber, Laura, and Charles Apple. "The Evolving 1st Amendment." *Chicago Tribune*, Friday, July 4, 1997.

First Amendment Court Cases

This section contains summaries of frequently cited First Amendment cases. Arranged by topic, they cover case law issued by a variety of courts: the Supreme Court of the United States, the Court of Appeals of different Federal circuits, the District Court of several Federal districts, as well as the highest court of several states and particular appellate courts of action.

The standard citation is given to indicate where to find the complete text of a decision. For example, *Kreimer v. Bureau of Police for Morristown*, 958 F.2 1242 (3d Cir. 1992), gives the names of the main parties in the case ("Kreimer," who sued the "Bureau of Police for Morristown"), the abbreviated title of the case reporter where the decision is published ("F.2d" for *Federal Reporter, Second Series*) — which is preceded by the particular volume number ("958") of the reporter and followed by the page number 1242 where the decision begins — and, in parentheses, the name of court that issued the decision ("3d Cir." for Circuit of Appeals for the Third Circuit) and the year ("1992"). Other conventions may apply, depending on which case reporter is involved.

Abbreviations

U.S.	*United States Reports*
S.Ct.	*Supreme Court Reporter*
L.Ed.	*United States Supreme Court Reports Lawyers' Edition*
L.Ed.2d	*United States Supreme Court Reports Lawyers' Edition, Second Series*
F.2d	*Federal Reporter, Second Series*
F.3d	*Federal Reporter, Third Series*
F.Supp.	*Federal Supplement*
F.Supp.2d	*Federal Supplement, Second Series*
N.W.	*North Western Reporter*
N.W.	*North Western Reporter, Second Series*
N.Y.S.	*New York Supplement*
N.Y.S.	*New York Supplement, Second Series*
P.	*Pacific Reporter*

Foundations of Free Expression: Historic Cases

Schenck v. United States

249 U.S. 47, 39 S.Ct. 247, 63 L.Ed.2d (1919)

Justice Oliver Wendell Holmes, Jr., stated in this case his famous aphorism about "falsely shouting fire in a theatre" and set forth a "clear and present danger test" to judge whether speech is protected by the First Amendment. "The question," he wrote, "is whether the words are used in such circumstances and are of such a nature as to create a clear and present danger that they will bring about the substantive evils that Congress has the right to prevent. It is a question of proximity and degree." The Supreme Court affirmed the convictions of the defendants for conspiring to violate certain federal statutes by attempting to incite subordination in the armed forces and interfere with recruitment and enlistment. During wartime, the defendants mailed to new recruits and enlisted men leaflets that compared military conscription to involuntary servitude and urged them to assert their constitutional rights.

Near v. Minnesota

283 U.S. 697, 51 S.Ct. 625, 75 L.Ed. 1357 (1931)

In this case, the Supreme Court interpreted the First and Fourteenth Amendments to forbid "previous restraints" upon publication of a newspaper. "Previous restraints"—or in current terminology, "prior restraints"—suppress the freedom of the press to publish without obstruction, and recognize that lawsuits or prosecutions for libel are "subsequent punishments." The Court invalidated as an infringement of constitutional guarantees a Minnesota statute allowing specified government officials or private citizens to maintain a lawsuit in the name of the State to suppress a public nuisance and enjoin the publication of future issues of a "malicious, scandalous and defamatory newspaper, magazine or other periodical," unless the publisher can prove "the truth was published with good motives and for justifiable ends."

Brandenburg v. Ohio

395 U.S. 444, 89 S.Ct. 1827, 23 L.Ed.2d 430 (1969)

The Supreme Court established the modern version of the "clear and present danger" doctrine, holding that states only could restrict speech that "is directed to inciting or producing imminent lawless action, and is likely to incite or produce such action."

The Right to Read Freely

Evans v. Shelma Union High School District of Fresno County

222 P. 801 (Ca. 1924)

The California State Supreme Court held that the King James version of the Bible was not a "publication of a sectarian, partisan, or denominational character" that a State statute required a public high school library to exclude from its collections. The "fact that the King

James Version is commonly used by Protestant Churches and not by Catholics" does not "make its character sectarian," the court stated. "The mere act of purchasing a book to be added to the school library does not carry with it any implication of the adoption of the theory or dogma contained therein, or any approval of the book itself, except as a work of literature fit to be included in a reference library."

Rosenberg v. Board of Education of City of New York

92 N.Y.S.2d 344 (Sup. Ct. Kings County 1949)

After considering the charge that *Oliver Twist* and the *Merchant of Venice* are "objectionable because they tend to engender hatred of the Jew as a person and as a race," the Supreme Court, Kings County, New York, decided that these two works cannot be banned from the New York City schools, libraries, or classrooms, declaring that the Board of Education "acted in good faith without malice or prejudice and in the best interests of the school system entrusted to their care and control, and, therefore, that no substantial reason exists which compels the suppression of the two books under oconsideration."

Todd v. Rochester Community Schools

200 N.W.2d 90 (Mich. Ct. App. 1972)

In deciding that *Slaughterhouse-Five* could not be banned from the libraries and classrooms of the Michigan schools, the Court of Appeals of Michigan declared: "Vonnegut's literary dwellings on war, religion, death, Christ, God, government, politics, and any other subject should be as welcome in the public schools of this state as those of Machiavelli, Chaucer, Shakespeare, Melville, Lenin, Joseph McCarthy, or Walt Disney. The students of Michigan are free to make of *Slaughterhouse-Five* what they will."

Minarcini v. Strongsville (Ohio) City School District

541 F.2d 577 (6th Cir. 1976)

The Strongsville City Board of Education rejected faculty recommendations to purchase Joseph Heller's *Catch-22* and Kurt Vonnegut's *God Bless You, Mr. Rosewater* and ordered the removal of *Catch-22* and Vonnegut's *Cat's Cradle* from the library. The U.S. Court of Appeals for the Sixth Circuit ruled against the School Board, upholding the students' First Amendment right to receive information and the librarian's right to disseminate it. "The removal of books from a school library is a much more serious burden upon the freedom of classroom discussion than the action found unconstitutional in *Tinker v. Des Moines School District*."

Right to Read Defense Committee v. School Committee of the City of Chelsea

454 F.Supp. 703 (D. Mass. 1978)

The Chelsea, Massachusetts, School Committee decided to bar from the high school library a poetry anthology, *Male and Female Under 18*, because of the inclusion of an "offensive" and "damaging" poem,

"The City to a Young Girl," written by a fifteen-year-old girl. Challenged in U.S. District Court, Joseph L. Tauro ruled: "The library is 'a mighty resource in the marketplace of ideas.' There a student can literally explore the unknown, and discover areas of interest and thought not covered by the prescribed curriculum. The student who discovers the magic of the library is on the way to a life-long experience of self-education and enrichment. That student learns that a library is a place to test or expand upon ideas presented to him, in or out of the classroom. The most effective antidote to the poison of mindless orthodoxy is ready access to a broad sweep of ideas and philosophies. There is no danger from such exposure. The danger is mind control. The committee's ban of the anthology *Male and Female* is enjoined."

Salvail v. Nashua Board of Education
469 F.Supp. 1269 (D.N.H. 1979)

MS magazine was removed from a New Hampshire high school library by order of the Nashua School Board. The U.S. District Court decided for the student, teacher, and adult residents who had brought action against the school board, the Court concluding: "The Court finds and rules that the defendants herein have failed to demonstrate a substantial and legitimate government interest sufficient to warrant the removal of *MS* magazine from the Nashua High School library. Their action contravenes the plaintiffs' First Amendment rights, and as such it is plainly wrong."

Loewen v. Turnipseed
488 F.Supp. 1138 (N.D. Miss. 1980)

When the Mississippi Textbook Purchasing Board refused to approve *Mississippi: Conflict and Change* for use in Mississippi public schools, on the grounds that it was too concerned with racial matters and too controversial, the authors filed suit. U.S. District Judge Orma R. Smith ruled that the criteria used were not justifiable grounds for rejecting the book. He held that the controversial racial matter was a factor leading to its rejection, and thus the authors had been denied their constitutionally guaranteed rights of freedom of speech and the press.

Kreimer v. Bureau of Police for Morristown
958 F.2d 1242 (3d Cir. 1992)

In detailed analysis, the court of appeals held that a municipal public library was a limited public forum, meaning open to the public for the specified purposes of exercising their First Amendment rights to read and receive information from library materials. Such exercise could not interfere with or disrupt the library's reasonable rules of operation. The court then upheld three library rules which: (1) required patrons to read, study, or otherwise use library materials while there; (2) prohibited noisy or boisterous activities which might disturb other patrons; and (3) permitted the removal of any patron whose offensive bodily hygiene was a nuisance to other patrons.

Case v. Unified School District No. 233
908 F.Supp. 864 (D. Kan. 1995)

When the Olathe, Kansas, School Board voted to remove the book *Annie on My Mind*, a novel depicting a lesbian relationship between two teenagers, from the district's junior and senior high school libraries, the federal district court in Kansas found they violated the students' rights under the First Amendment to the United States Constitution and the corresponding provisions of the Kansas State Constitution. Despite the fact that the school board testified that they had removed the book because of "educational unsuitability," which is within their rights under the *Pico* decision, it became obvious from their testimony that the book was removed because they disapproved of the book's ideology. In addition, it was found that the school board had violated its own materials selection and reconsideration policies, which weighed heavily in the judge's decision.

Campbell v. St. Tammany Parish School Board
64 F.3d 184 (5th Cir. 1995)

A public school district removed the book *Voodoo and Hoodoo*, a discussion of the origins, history, and practices of the voodoo and hoodoo religions that included an outline of some specific practices, from all district library shelves. Parents of several students sued and the district court granted summary judgment in their favor. The court of appeals reversed, finding that there was not enough evidence at that stage to determine that board members had an unconstitutional motivation, such as denying students access to ideas with which board members disagreed; the court remanded the case for a full trial at which all board members could be questioned about their reasons for removing the book. The court observed that "in light of the special role of the school library as a place where students may freely and voluntarily explore diverse topics, the school board's non-curricular decision to remove a book well after it had been placed in the public school libraries evokes the question whether that action might not be an attempt to 'strangle the free mind at its source.'" The court focused on some evidence that school board members had removed the book without having read it or having read only excerpts provided by the Christian Coalition. The parties settled the case before trial by returning the book to the libraries on specially designated reserve shelves.

Sund v. City of Wichita Falls, Texas
121 F.Supp. 2d 530 (N.D. Texas 2000)

City residents who were members of a church sought removal of two books, *Heather Has Two Mommies* and *Daddy's Roommate*, because they disapproved of the books' depiction of homosexuality. The Wichita Falls City Council voted to restrict access to the books if 300 persons signed a petition asking for the restriction. A separate group of citizens filed suit after the books were removed from the children's section and placed on a locked shelf in the adult area of the library. Following a trial on the merits, the district court permanently enjoined the city from enforcing the resolution permitting the removal of the two books. It held that the city's resolution constituted impermissible content-based and viewpoint-based discrimination; was not narrowly tailored to serve a compelling state interest; provided no standards or review process; and improperly delegated governmental authority over the selection and removal of the library's books to any 300 private citizens who wish to remove a book from the children's area of the library.

Counts v. Cedarville School District
295 F.Supp.2d 996 (W.D. Ark. 2003)
The Cedarville, Arkansas, School Board voted to restrict students' access to the Harry Potter books, on the grounds that the books promoted disobedience and disrespect for authority and dealt with witchcraft and the occult. As a result of the vote, students in the Cedarville school district were required to obtain a signed permission slip from their parents or guardians before they would be allowed to borrow any of the Harry Potter books from school libraries. The district court overturned the board's decision and ordered the books returned to unrestricted circulation, on the grounds that the restrictions violated students' First Amendment right to read and receive information. In so doing, the court noted that while the board necessarily performed highly discretionary functions related to the operation of the schools, it was still bound by the Bill of Rights and could not abridge students' First Amendment right to read a book on the basis of an undifferentiated fear of disturbance or because the board disagreed with the ideas contained in the book.

See also:
Board of Education, Island Trees Union Free School District No. 26 v. Pico, 457 U.S. 853, 102 S.Ct. 2799, 73 L.Ed.2d 435 (1982)

Smith v. Board of School Commissioners of Mobile (Ala.) County, 827 F.2d 684 (11th Cir. 1987)

Mozert v. Hawkins County Board of Education, 827 F.2d 1058 (6th Cir. 1987)

Virgil v. School Board of Columbia County, 862 F.2d 1517 (11th Cir. 1989)

American Library Association v. U.S. Department of Justice and Reno v. American Civil Liberties Union, 521 U.S. 844, 117 S.Ct. 2329, 138 L.Ed.2d 874 (1997)

Mainstream Loudoun, et al. v. Board of Trustees of the Loudoun County Library, 24 F.Supp.2d 552 (E.D. Va. 1998)

Freedom of Expression in Schools

Tinker v. Des Moines Independent Community School District
393 U.S. 503, 89 S.Ct. 733, 21 L.Ed.2d 731 (1969)
In this seminal case considering the First Amendment rights of students who were expelled after they wore black armbands to school in symbolic protest of the Vietnam War, the Supreme Court held that students "do not shed their constitutional rights at the schoolhouse gate" and that the First Amendment protects public school students' rights to express political and social views.

Zykan v. Warsaw (Indiana) Community School Corporation and Warsaw School Board of Trustees
631 F.2d 1300 (7th Cir. 1980)
A student brought suit seeking to reverse school officials' decision to "limit or prohibit the use of certain textbooks, to remove a certain book from the school library, and to delete certain courses from the curriculum." The district court dismissed the suit. On appeal, the Court of Appeals for the Seventh Circuit ruled that the school board has the right to establish a curriculum on the basis of its own discretion, but it is forbidden to impose a "pall of orthodoxy." The right of students to file complaints was recognized, but the court held that the students' claims "must cross a relatively high threshold before entering upon the field of a constitutional claim suitable for federal court litigation."

Board of Education, Island Trees Union Free School District No. 26 v. Pico
457 U.S. 853, 102 S.Ct. 2799, 73 L.Ed.2d 435 (1982)
In 1975, three school board members sought the removal of several books determined objectionable by a politically conservative organization. The following February, the board gave an "unofficial direction" that the books be removed from the school libraries, so that board members could read them. When the board action attracted press attention, the board described the books as "anti-American, anti-Christian, anti-Semitic, and just plain filthy." The nine books that were the subject of the lawsuit were Slaughterhouse-Five, by Kurt Vonnegut, Jr.; The Naked Ape, by Desmond Morris; Down These Mean Streets, by Piri Thomas; Best Short Stories of Negro Writers, edited by Langston Hughes; Go Ask Alice; Laughing Boy, by Oliver LaFarge; Black Boy, by Richard Wright; A Hero Ain't Nothin' But a Sandwich, by Alice Childress; and Soul on Ice, by Eldrige Cleaver.

The board appointed a review committee that recommended that five of the books be returned to the shelves, two be placed on restricted shelves, and two be removed from the library. The full board voted to remove all but one book.

After years of appeals, the U.S. Supreme Court upheld (5–4) the students' challenge to the board's action. The Court held that school boards do not have unrestricted authority to select library books and that the First Amendment is implicated when books are removed arbitrarily. Justice Brennan declared in the plurality opinion: "Local school boards may not remove books from school library shelves simply because they dislike the ideas contained in those books and seek by their removal to prescribe what shall be orthodox in politics, nationalism, religion, or other matters of opinion."

Smith v. Board of School Commissioners of Mobile (Ala.) County
827 F.2d 684 (11th Cir. 1987)
Parents and other citizens brought a lawsuit against the school board, alleging that the school system was teaching the tenets of an anti-religious religion called "secular humanism." The complainants asked that forty-four different elementary through high school level textbooks be removed from the curriculum. After an initial ruling in a federal district court in favor of the plaintiffs, the U.S. Court of Appeals for the Eleventh Circuit ruled that as long as the school was motivated by a secular purpose, it didn't matter whether the curriculum and texts shared ideas held by one or more religious groups. The court found that the texts in question promoted important secular values (tolerance, self-respect, logical decision making) and thus the use of the textbooks neither unconstitutionally advanced a nontheistic religion nor inhibited theistic religions.

Mozert v. Hawkins County Board of Education
827 F.2d 1058 (6th Cir. 1987)
Parents and students brought this action challenging the mandatory use of certain textbooks on the ground that the texts promoted values offensive to their religious beliefs. The U.S. Court of Appeals for the Sixth Circuit rejected the plaintiffs' claim, finding that the Constitution does not require school curricula to be revised substantially in order to accommodate religious beliefs.

Hazelwood School District v. Kuhlmeier
484 U.S. 260, 108 S.Ct. 562, 98 L.Ed.2d 592 (1988)
After a school principal removed two pages containing articles, among others, on teenage pregnancy and the impact of divorce on students from a newspaper produced as part of a high school journalism class, the student staff filed suit claiming violation of their First Amendment rights. The principal defended his action on the grounds that he was protecting the privacy of the pregnant students described, protecting younger students from inappropriate references to sexual activity and birth control, and protecting the school from a potential libel action.

The Supreme Court held that the principal acted reasonably and did not violate the students' First Amendment rights. A school need not tolerate student speech, the Court declared, "that is inconsistent with its 'basic educational mission,' even though the government could not censor similar speech outside the school." In addition, the Court found the newspaper was part of the regular journalism curriculum and subject to extensive control by a faculty member. The school, thus, did not create a public forum for the expression of ideas, but instead maintained the newspaper "as supervised learning experience for journalism students." The Court concluded that "educators do not offend the First Amendment by exercising editorial control over the style and content of student speech in school-sponsored expressive activities so long as their actions are reasonably related to legitimate pedagogical concerns." The Court strongly suggested that supervised student activities that "may fairly be characterized as part of the school curriculum," including school-sponsored publications and theatrical productions, were subject to the authority of educators. The Court cautioned, however, that this authority does not justify an educator's attempt "to silence a student's personal expression that happens to occur on the school premises."

Virgil v. School Board of Columbia County
862 F.2d 1517 (11th Cir. 1989)
This case presented the question of whether the First Amendment prevents a school board from removing a previously approved textbook from an elective high school class because of objections to the material's vulgarity and sexual explicitness. The U.S. Circuit Court of Appeals concluded that a school board may, without contravening constitutional limits, take such action when the removal decision was "reasonably related" to the "legitimate pedagogical concern" of denying students access to "potentially sensitive topics." The written "stipulation concerning Board Reasons" cites explicit sexuality and excessively vulgar language in two selections contained in *Volume 1, The Humanities: Cultural Roots and Continuities* as the basis for removal of this textbook. The two selections are Chaucer's *The Miller's Tale* and Aristophanes' *Lysistrata*.

Romano v. Harrington
725 F.Supp. 687 (E.D. N.Y. 1989)
The U.S. District Court found in favor of a faculty adviser to a high school newspaper who claimed a violation of the First and Fourteenth Amendments when fired following the newspaper's publication of a student's article opposing the federal holiday for Martin Luther King Jr. The court held that educators may exercise greater editorial control over what students write for class than what they voluntarily submit to extracurricular publications.

Cohen v. San Bernardino Valley College
92 F.3d 968 (9th Cir. 1996)
A tenured English professor was disciplined for violating the college's sexual harassment policy against creating a "hostile learning environment" for his in-class use of profanity, and discussions of sex, pornography, obscenity, cannibalism, and other controversial topics in a confrontational, devil's advocate style. The court held the policy unconstitutionally vague as applied to Cohen's in-class speech, calling it a "legalistic ambush." In-class speech did not fall within the policy's core definition of sexual harassment and Cohen, who had used this apparently sound and proper teaching style for years, did not know the policy would be applied to him or his teaching methods.

Morse v. Frederick
551 U.S. 393 (2007)
In this case, the Supreme Court ruled that a principal did not violate the First Amendment rights of a student when the principal punished the student for displaying a banner across the street from the school that read "Bong Hits 4 Jesus." The Court held that school officials can prohibit students from displaying messages that promote illegal drug use, explaining that while students do have some right to political speech even while in school, this right does not extend to pro-drug messages that may undermine the school's important mission to discourage drug use, and that the highly protective standard set by *Tinker* would not always be applied. Justice Alito stressed that the decision applied only to pro-drug messages and not to broader political speech.

See also:
Evans v. Shelma Union High School District of Fresno County, 222 P. 801 (Ca. 1924)

West Virginia State Board of Education v. Barnette, 319 U.S. 624 (1943)

Rosenberg v. Board of Education of City of New York, 92 N.Y.S.2d 344 (Sup. Ct. Kings County 1949)

Todd v. Rochester Community Schools, 200 N.W.2d 90 (Mich. Ct. App. 1972)

Minarcini v. Strongsville (Ohio) City School District, 541 F.2d 577 (6th Cir. 1976)

Right to Read Defense Committee v. School Committee of the City of Chelsea, 454 F.Supp. 703 (D. Mass. 1978)

Salvail v. Nashua Board of Education, 469 F.Supp. 1269 (D.N.H. 1979)

Loewen v. Turnipseed, 488 F.Supp. 1138 (N.D. Miss. 1980)

Case v. Unified School District No. 233, 908 F.Supp. 864 (D. Kan. 1995)

Campbell v. St. Tammany Parish School Board, 64 F.3d 184 (5th Cir. 1995)

Counts v. Cedarville School District, 295 F.Supp.2d 996 (W.D. Ark. 2003)

Minors' First Amendment Rights

American Amusement Machine Association, et al. v. Teri Kendrick, et al.
244 F.3d 572 (7th Cir. 2001); cert. denied, 534 U.S. 994; 122 S. Ct. 462; 151 L.Ed.2d 379 (2001).
Enacted in July 2001, an Indianapolis, Indiana, city ordinance required video game arcade owners to limit access to games that depicted certain activities, including amputation, decapitation, dismemberment, bloodshed, or sexual intercourse. Only with the permission of an accompanying parent or guardian could children seventeen years old and younger play these types of video games. On March 23, 2001, a three-judge panel of the Seventh Circuit Court of Appeals reversed and remanded the trial court's decision stating that "children have First Amendment rights." On Monday, October 29, 2001, the U.S. Supreme Court denied certiorari thus, leting the Appeals court's decision stand.

Interactive Digital Software Association, et al. v. St. Louis County, Missouri, et al.
329 F.3d 954 (8th Cir. 2003)
St. Louis County passed an ordinance that banned selling or renting violent video games to minors, or permitting them to play such games, without parental consent, and video game dealers sued to overturn the law. The court of appeals found the ordinance unconstitutional, holding that depictions of violence alone cannot fall within the legal definition of obscenity for either minors or adults, and that a government cannot silence protected speech for children by wrapping itself in the cloak of parental authority. The court ordered the lower court to enter an injunction barring enforcement of the law, citing the Supreme Court's recognition in *Erznoznik v. Jacksonville*, 422 U.S. 205, 213–14, 45 L.Ed.2d 125, 95 S. Ct. 2268 (1975) that "speech that is neither obscene as to youths nor subject to some other legitimate proscription cannot be suppressed solely to protect the young from ideas or images that a legislative body thinks unsuitable for them. In most circumstances, the values protected by the First Amendment are no less applicable when the government seeks to control the flow of information to minors."

See also:
West Virginia State Board of Education v. Barnette, 319 U.S. 624 (1943)

Ginsberg v. New York, 390 U.S. 629 (1968)

Tinker v. Des Moines Independent Community School District, 393 U.S. 503, 89 S.Ct. 733, 21 L.Ed.2d 731 (1969)

Board of Education, Island Trees Union Free School District No. 26 v. Pico, 457 U.S. 853, 102 S.Ct. 2799, 73 L.Ed.2d 435 (1982)

Free Press

New York Times Company v. United States
403 U.S. 713, 91 S.Ct. 2140, 29 L.Ed.2d 822 (1971)
In the "Pentagon Papers" case, the U.S. government attempted to enjoin the *New York Times* and the *Washington Post* from publishing classified documents concerning the Vietnam War. Applying the doctrine of prior restraint from *Near v. Minnesota*, the Court found that the claims that publication of the documents would interfere with foreign policy and prolong the war were too speculative, and could not overcome the strong presumption against prior restraint.

Hustler Magazine, Inc. v. Falwell
485 U.S. 46, 108 S.Ct. 876, 99 L.Ed.2d 41 (1988)
Hustler magazine published a parody of a liquor advertisement in which Rev. Jerry Falwell described his "first time" as a drunken encounter with his mother in an outhouse. A unanimous Supreme Court held that a public figure had to show actual malice in order to recover for intentional infliction of emotional distress as a result of a parody in a magazine. The Court held that political cartoons and satire such as this parody "have played a prominent role in public and political debate. And although the outrageous caricature in this case "is at best a distant cousin of political cartoons," the Court could see no standard to distinguish among types of parodies that would not harm public discourse, which would be poorer without such satire.

Simon & Schuster, Inc. v. Members of New York State Crime Victims Board
502 U.S. 105, 112 S.Ct. 501, 116 L.Ed.2d 476 (1991)
The Supreme Court struck down New York's "Son of Sam Law," which required book publishers to turn over to the state any proceeds from a book written by any person convicted of a crime, related to, or about that crime. The Court said the law impermissibly singled out income only from the prisoner's expressive activity, and then only expressive activity relating to his crime, without necessarily compensating any victims of those crimes. The Court agreed that many important books—including the Autobiography of *Malcolm X, Thoreau's Civil Disobedience*, and works by Martin Luther King—perhaps might not have been published with such a law in place.

See also:
The New York Times v. Sullivan, 376 U.S. 254, 84 S.Ct. 710, 11 L.Ed.2d 686 (1964)

Gertz v. Robert Welch, Inc., 418 U.S. 323, 94 S.Ct. 2997, 41 L.Ed.2d 789 (1974)

The Right to Dissent

West Virginia State Board of Education v. Barnette
319 U.S. 624, 87 L.Ed. 1628, 63 S.Ct. 1178 (1943)
In 1940, the West Virginia Board of Education issued regulations requiring every schoolchild to participate daily in a salute to the flag of the United States. The Barnette children, all members of the Jehovah's Witnesses, refused to participate in the flag salute, consistent with the tenets of their religious beliefs, and were expelled from school. The Supreme Court struck down the regulation on the grounds that the First Amendment barred any rule compelling an individual to salute the flag or participate in the Pledge of Allegiance. In strong language, the Court affirmed the right to dissent: "But freedom to differ is not limited to things that do not matter much. That would be a mere shadow of freedom. The test of its substance is the right to differ as to things that touch the heart of the existing order. If there is any fixed star in our constitutional constellation, it is that no official, high or petty, can prescribe what shall be orthodox in politics, nationalism, religion, or other matters of opinion, or force citizens to confess by word or act their faith therein. If there are any circumstances which permit an exception, they do not now occur to us."

Texas v. Johnson
491 U.S. 397, 109 S.Ct. 2533, 105 L.Ed.2d 342 (1989)
In this case the Supreme Court held that burning the U.S. flag was a protected form of symbolic political speech, concluding that there is no legitimate government interest in protecting the U.S. flag where the sole act in question is destroying the flag in its symbolic capacity. "A bedrock principle underlying the First Amendment is that Government may not prohibit the expression of an idea simply because society finds the idea itself offensive or disagreeable."

U.S. v. Eichman and U.S. v. Haggerty
496 U.S. 310, 110 S.Ct. 2404, 110 L.Ed.2d 287 (1990)
The Supreme Court struck down a federal statute designed to allow the government to punish persons who burn U.S. flags. The Court held that the plain intent of the statute was to punish persons for political expression and that burning the flag inextricably carries with it a political message.

City of Ladue v. Gilleo
512 U.S. 43, 114 S.Ct. 2038, 129 L.Ed. 2d 36 (1994)
A federal court struck down a local ordinance banning

the placement of signs on private property, in a challenge brought by a woman who had posted a sign on her lawn protesting the Persian Gulf War. The Court said lawn signs were a "venerable means of communication that is both unique and important," for which "no adequate substitutes exist."

R.A.V. v. St. Paul
505 U.S. 377, 112 S.Ct. 2538, 120 L.Ed.2d 305 (1992)

St. Paul, Minnesota, passed an ordinance that banned "hate speech," any expression, such as a burning cross or swastika, that might arouse anger, alarm, or resentment in others on the basis of race, color, religion, or gender. The Supreme Court struck the ordinance down as unconstitutionally discriminating based on the content of expression: the law banned only fighting words that insult, based on race, religion, or gender, while abusive invective aimed at someone on the basis of political affiliation or sexual orientation would be permissible. The law thus reflected only the city's special hostility towards certain biases and not others, which is what the First Amendment forbids.

See also:

Tinker v. Des Moines Independent Community School District, 393 U.S. 503, 89 S.Ct. 733, 21 L.Ed.2d 731 (1969)

The Right to Free Association and the Freedom of Religion

Concerned Women for America, Inc. v. Lafayette County
883 F.2d 32 (5th Cir. 1989)

The county library that had permitted various groups to use its auditorium had created a designated public forum and thus could not deny access to groups whose meetings had political or religious content. Such a denial would be based on the content of speech and would be permissible only as the least restrictive means to serve a compelling interest. Preventing disruption or interference with general use of the library could be such an interest; library officials' first step to controlling such disruptions would be to impose reasonable regulations on the time, place, or manner of the auditorium's use, provided the regulations apply regardless of the subject matter of the speech.

Lamb's Chapel v. Center Moriches Union Free School Dist.
508 U.S. 384, 113 S.Ct. 2141, 124 L.Ed.2d 352 (1993)

The Court held that a school district that opened its classrooms after hours to a range of groups for social, civic, and recreational purposes, including films and lectures about a range of issues such as family values and child rearing, could not deny access to a religious organization to discuss the same, permissible issues from a religious point of view. Whether or not the classrooms were public fora, the school district could not deny use based on the speaker's point of view on an otherwise permissible topic.

Right to Privacy and Anonymity

Stanley v. Georgia
394 U.S. 55, 22 L.Ed.2d 542, 89 S.Ct. 1243 (1969)

A man found to possess obscene materials in his home for his private use was convicted of possessing obscene materials in violation of the state laws of Georgia. The Supreme Court overturned the conviction, holding that the Constitution protects the right to receive information and ideas, regardless of their social worth, and to be generally free from governmental intrusions into one's privacy on the grounds that the government "cannot constitutionally premise legislation on the desirability of controlling a person's private thoughts."

McIntyre v. Ohio Election Commission
514 U.S. 334, 115 S.Ct. 1511, 131 L.Ed.2d 426 (1995)

The Supreme Court struck down a state law banning distribution of anonymous campaign literature, emphasizing the long tradition of anonymous and pseudonymous political and literary speech and recognizing the right to exercise First Amendment rights anonymously as an "honorable tradition of advocacy and dissent."

Tattered Cover, Inc. v. City of Thornton
44 P.3d 1044 (Colo. Sup. Ct. 2002)

The Colorado Supreme Court reversed a court decision that required Denver's Tattered Cover Book Store to turn over information about books purchased by one of its customers. As part of an investigation, officers of the City of Thornton (Colo.) discovered two books on the manufacture of amphetamines in a suspect's residence and found a Tattered Cover mailer in the garbage. The officers, seeking to tie the books to the suspect directly, served a Drug Enforcement Agency subpoena on the Tattered Cover. The subpoena demanded the title of the books corresponding to the order and invoice numbers of the mailer, as well as information about all other books ever ordered by the suspect. The Tattered Cover then brought suit to litigate the validity of the search warrant. The court began its opinion by stating that both the First Amendment to the U.S. Constitution and Article II, Section 10, of the Colorado Constitution protect an individual's fundamental right to purchase books anonymously, free from governmental interference.

When Is Speech Unprotected?
Obscenity and Indecency

Butler v. Michigan
352 U.S. 380, 1 L.Ed.2d 412, 77 S.Ct. 524 (1957)

A man convicted of selling "a book containing obscene, immoral, lewd, lascivious language, or descriptions, tending to incite minors to violent or depraved or immoral acts, manifestly tending to the corruption of the morals of youth" to a police officer appealed his conviction to the Supreme Court. The Court overturned the conviction and struck down the law, holding that the state's attempt to quarantine the general reading public against books not too rugged for grown men and women to read in order to shield juvenile innocence "is to burn the house to roast the pig." Famously, the Court ruled that the state of Michigan could not "reduce[s] the adult population of Michigan to reading only what is fit for children."

Ginsberg v. New York
390 U.S. 62, 20 L.Ed.2d 195, 88 S. Ct. 1274 (1968)
The Supreme Court upheld a New York State statute barring retailers from selling sexually explicit publications to minors under the age of seventeen. Noting that the statute did not interfere with the right of adults to purchase and read such materials, it found that it was not constitutionally impermissible for New York to restrict minors' rights to such publications in light of the state's interest in safeguarding children's welfare and supporting parents' claim to authority in the rearing of their children.

Miller v. California
413 U.S. 15, 93 S.Ct. 2607, 37 L.Ed.2d 419 (1973)
In this case, the U.S. Supreme Court mapped out its famous three-part definition of obscenity. First, the average person, applying contemporary community standards, must find that the work, taken as a whole, appeals to prurient interests; second, that it depicts or describes, in a patently offensive way, sexual conduct as defined by state law; and third, that the work, taken as a whole, lacks serious literary, artistic, political, or scientific value. The Court ruled that community standards and state statutes that describe sexual depictions to be suppressed could be used to prosecute Miller, who operated one of the largest West Coast mail order businesses dealing in sexually explicit materials.

New York v. Ferber
458 U.S. 747, 102 S.Ct. 3348, 73 L.Ed.2d 1113 (1982)
In July 1982, the U.S. Supreme Court added child pornography as another category of speech excluded from First Amendment protection. The other categories excluded are obscenity, defamation, incitement, and "fighting words." The ruling came in the case when the U.S. Supreme Court affirmed a conviction against Ferber for showing a movie depicting two young boys masturbating. The film itself was not seen as obscene for adults, but the Court made the distinction between what was obscene if children were the participants compared with if adults were the leading actors.

American Booksellers Assoc., Inc. v. Hudnut
771 F.2d 323 (7th Cir. 1985) (Easterbrook, J.), aff'd., 475 U.S. 1001, 106 S.Ct. 1172, 89 L.Ed.2d 291 (1986)
The city of Indianapolis passed a statute outlawing pornography, defined as the graphic, sexually explicit subordination of women, presenting women as sex objects, or as enjoying pain, humiliation, or servility. The court of appeals struck the law down, saying it impermissibly established an "approved" view of women and how they react in sexual encounters. The law therefore allowed sexually explicit words and images that adhered to that approved view, but banned sexually explicit words and images that did not adhere to the approved view. The court called this "thought control," saying the "Constitution forbids the state to declare one perspective right and silence opponents."

National Endowment for the Arts, et al. v. Finley, et al.
524 U.S. 569, 118 S.Ct. 2168, 141 L.Ed.2d 500 (1998)
In 1990, homoerotic photographs by Robert Mapplethorpe and blasphemous ones by Andres Serrano created a furor on Capitol Hill, because both artists had received grants from the National Endowment for the Arts (NEA). As a consequence, the NEA governing statute was amended to require the NEA to consider "decency" and "respect" for American "values" when selecting future grant recipients. Shortly thereafter, performance artists Karen Finley, John Fleck, Holly Hughes, and Tim Miller were denied fellowships, because of the "decency and respect" clause, they alleged. They made this allegation in a federal court lawsuit seeking to have the clause declared unconstitutional; and they were successful at the district court and court of appeals level. The U.S. Supreme Court ruled, however, that the statute is constitutional "on its face." Writing for the court, Justice Sandra Day O'Connor did not "perceive a realistic danger that it will be utilized to preclude or punish the expression of particular views," nor did she think that the statute would "significantly compromise First Amendment values."

John D. Ashcroft, Attorney General, et al. v. Free Speech Coalition, et al.
535 U.S. 234, 122 S.Ct. 1389, 152 L.Ed.2d 403 (2002)
The U.S. Supreme Court affirmed the Ninth Circuit's judgment invalidating the Child Pornography Prevention Act of 1996 on the grounds that the act's ban on any depiction of pornographic images of children, including computer-generated images, was overly broad and unconstitutional under the First Amendment. Supreme Court Justice Anthony M. Kennedy wrote: "First Amendment freedoms are most in danger when the government seeks to control thought or to justify its laws for that impermissible end. The right to think is the beginning of freedom, and speech must be protected from the government because speech is the beginning of thought."

See also:
Stanley v. Georgia, 394 U.S. 55, 22 L.Ed.2d 542, 89 S.Ct. 1243 (1969)

Libel

The New York Times v. Sullivan

376 U.S. 254, 84 S.Ct. 710, 11 L.Ed.2d 686 (1964)
To protect "uninhibited, robust, and wide-open" debate on public issues, the Supreme Court held that no public official may recover "damages for a defamatory falsehood relating to his official conduct unless he proves that the statement was made with 'actual malice'—that is, with knowledge that it was false or with reckless disregard of whether it was false or not." The Court stated that the First and Fourteenth Amendments require that critics of official conduct have the "fair equivalent" to the immunity protection given to a public official when he is sued for defamatory speech uttered in the course of his duties.

Gertz v. Robert Welch, Inc.

418 U.S. 323, 94 S.Ct. 2997, 41 L.Ed.2d 789 (1974)
The Court applied the rule in the New York Times case to public figures, finding that persons who have special prominence in society by virtue of their fame or notoriety, even if they are not public officials, must prove "actual malice" when alleging libel. Gertz was a prominent lawyer who alleged that a leaflet defamed him.

See also:
Hustler Magazine, Inc. v. Falwell, 485 U.S. 46, 108 S.Ct. 876, 99 L.Ed.2d 41 (1988)

The First Amendment and New Technologies:
Broadcast and Cable Communications

FCC V. Pacifica Foundation

438 U.S. 726, 57 L.Ed.2d 1073, 98 S.Ct. 3026 (1978)
In a case that considered the First Amendment protections extended to a radio station's daytime broadcast of comedian George Carlin's "Seven Filthy Words" monologue, the Supreme Court held that Section 326 of the Telecommunications Act, which prohibits the FCC from censoring broadcasts over radio or television, does not limit the FCC's authority to sanction radio or television stations broadcasting material that is obscene, indecent, or profane. Though the censorship ban under Section 326 precludes editing proposed broadcasts in advance, the ban does not deny the FCC the power to review the content of completed broadcasts. In its decision, the Court concluded that broadcast materials have limited First Amendment protection because of the uniquely pervasive presence that radio and television occupy in the lives of people, and the unique ability of children to access radio and television broadcasts.

Denver Area Educational Telecommunications Consortium, Inc. v. FCC

518 U.S. 727, 116 S.Ct. 2374, 135 L.Ed.2d 288 (1996)
In a decision that produced six opinions, the Supreme Court upheld a federal law permitting cable system operators to ban "indecent" or "patently offensive" speech on leased access channels. The Court also struck down a similar law for nonleased, public access channels, and struck down a law requiring indecent material to be shown on separate, segregated cable channels. The case is significant in that the Court affirmed that protecting children from some speech is a compelling state interest.

United States, et al. v. Playboy Entertainment Group, Inc.

529 U.S. 803, 120 S.Ct. 1878, 146 L.Ed.2d 865 (2000)
On May 22, 2000, in a 5–4 decision, the U.S. Supreme Court upheld a U.S. District Court decision that Section 505 of the Telecommunications Act of 1996 violated the First Amendment when it sought to restrict certain cable channels with sexually explicit content to late night hours unless they fully scrambled their signal bleed. In an opinion written by Justice Anthony Kennedy, the Court ruled that the government may have a legitimate interest in protecting children from exposure to "indecent material." Section 505, however, is a content-based speech restriction and, therefore, must be the least restrictive means for meeting the governmental interest. The Court found that Section 505 is not the least restrictive means.

Telecommunications

Sable Communications of California, Inc. v. FCC

492 U.S. 115, 106 L.Ed. 2d 93, 109 S.Ct. 2829 (1989)
The Supreme Court overturned a Telecommunications Act ban on indecent telephone messages, concluding the law violates the First Amendment because the statute's denial of adult access to such messages far exceeds that which is necessary to serve the compelling interest of preventing minors from being exposed to the messages. Unlike broadcast radio and television, which can intrude on the privacy of the home without prior warning of content and which is uniquely accessible to children, telephone communications require the listener to take affirmative steps to receive the communications. The failure of the government to show any findings that would justify a conclusion that there are no constitutionally acceptable less restrictive means to achieve the government's interest in protecting minors, such as scrambling or the use of access codes, demonstrates that a total ban on such communications goes too far in restricting constitutionally protected speech. To allow the ban to stand would have the effect of "limiting the content of adult telephone communications to that which is suitable for children to hear."

The Internet

American Library Association v. U.S. Department of Justice and Reno v. American Civil Liberties Union

521 U.S. 844, 117 S.Ct. 2329, 138 L.Ed.2d 874 (1997)
In a 9–0 decision, the U.S. Supreme Court on June 26, 1997, declared unconstitutional a federal law making it

a crime to send or display indecent material online in a way available to minors. The decision in the consolidated cases completed a successful challenge to the so-called Communications Decency Act by the Citizens Internet Empowerment Coalition, in which the American Library Association and the Freedom to Read Foundation played leading roles. The Court held that speech on the Internet is entitled to the highest level of First Amendment protection, similar to the protection the Court gives to books and newspapers.

Mainstream Loudoun, et al. v. Board of Trustees of the Loudoun County Library
24 F.Supp.2d 552 (E.D. Va. 1998)

Adopted in 1997, the Loudoun County, Virginia, Library Board's "Policy on Internet Sexual Harassment" was designed to prevent adult and minor Internet users from accessing illegal pornography and to avoid the creation of a sexually hostile environment. To accomplish these goals, the board contracted with Log-On Data Corporation, a filtering software manufacturer that offers a product called "X-Stop." Though Log-On Data Corp. refused to divulge the method by which X-Stop filters sites, it soon became apparent that the software blocks some sites that are not prohibited by the policy. Shortly after the adoption of the policy, People for the American Way Foundation commenced litigation on behalf of several Loudoun County residents and members of a nonprofit organization, claiming the policy violates the right to free speech under the First Amendment. The suit was predicated on the theory that the policy is unnecessarily restrictive because it treats adults and children similarly, and precludes access to legitimate as well as pornographic material. On November 23, 1998, Judge Leonie Brinkema declared that the highly restrictive Loudoun County Internet policy was invalid under the free speech provisions of the First Amendment.

United States, et al. v. American Library Association, Inc. et al.
539 U.S. 194, 123 S.Ct. 2297, 156 L.Ed.2d 221 (2003)

The Supreme Court upheld the Children's Internet Protection Act, which requires libraries receiving federal funds for Internet access to install filters so that both adult and child patrons cannot access materials considered obscene, child pornography, or "harmful to minors." Chief Justice Rehnquist announced the judgment of the Court that the law, on its face, is constitutional. Speaking for a plurality of four justices, Rehnquist held that CIPA was a valid exercise of Congress's spending power and did not impose an unconstitutional condition on public libraries that received federal assistance for Internet access because Congress could reasonably impose limitations on its Internet assistance, and because any concerns over filtering software's alleged tendency to erroneously "overblock" access to constitutionally protected speech were dispelled by the ease with which library patrons could have the filtering software disabled. Justices Kennedy and Breyer concurred with the judgment, holding that CIPA, while raising First Amendment concerns, did not violate the First Amendment as long as adult library users could request that the Internet filter be disabled without delay.

First Amendment Glossary and Acronyms

Absolutism

The position that the right to free speech is absolutely inviolable and cannot be infringed by any governmental action that would inhibit the exercise of free speech. It requires a determination whether the action at issue is "speech" (and therefore protected) or "conduct" (and therefore subject to reasonable governmental regulation).

Actual Malice

In *New York Times Co. v. Sullivan* (1964), the Supreme Court defined actual malice as a state of mind in which a person or publication makes an untrue and defamatory statement about a person "with knowledge that it was false or with reckless disregard of whether it was false or not." In order to recover damages for libel or defamation, a public official or public figure must be able to show by clear and convincing evidence that the defendant acted with actual malice.

Amendment

The process of formally altering or adding to a document or record. In the United States, an amendment is a change or addition to the Constitution. Proposed by a two-thirds vote of both houses of Congress or by a convention called by Congress at the request of two-thirds of the state legislatures. Ratified by approval of three-fourths of the states.

Amicus Curiae

The legal Latin phrase, literally translated as "friend of the court," that refers to someone, not a party to a case, who volunteers to offer information on a point of law or some other aspect of the case to assist the court in deciding a matter before it. The information may be a legal opinion in the form of a brief, a testimony that has not been solicited by any of the parties, or a learned treatise on a matter that bears on the case. The decision whether to admit the information lies with the discretion of the court.

Anti-Federalist

An opponent of the ratification of the U.S. Constitution.

Arbitrary Distinctions

Inappropriate categorizations of persons, classes of persons, conduct, or things based on criteria irrelevant to the purpose for which the distinctions are made. For example, a rule intended to regulate the length of time an item may be borrowed should not be based on an irrelevant consideration (arbitrary distinction), such as a personal characteristic of the borrower (height or age).

Assembly

A group of persons gathered together for a common reason, or a legislative, religious, educational, or social purpose.

Bill of Rights

The first ten amendments to the U.S. Constitution. Ratified in 1791, these amendments limit governmental power and protect basic rights and liberties of individuals.

Boycott

To abstain from or act together in abstaining from using, buying, or dealing with, as an expression of protest or disfavor or as a means of coercion.

Brief

A written legal document used in various legal adversary systems that is presented to a court arguing why the party to the case should prevail.

Captive Audience

A person or group of people forcibly subjected to view or hear expression in the use of public facilities or places where they are reasonably unable to avoid seeing or hearing the expression. The government has the ability to limit speech when it is impractical for the listener to escape that speech.

Censor

To edit, expurgate, stifle, repress.

Censorship

Official prohibition or restriction of any type of expression believed to threaten the political, social, or moral order. A change in access status of library materials, made by a governing body or its representatives. Such changes include exclusion, restriction, removal, labeling, or age/grade level changes.

Certiorari (writ of certiorari)

Certiorari, meaning in Latin to "be more fully informed," is the procedure used by the Supreme Court and appellate courts to review the cases they hear. After receiving an appeal, the court decides whether to grant certiorari and review the lower court's case. If it grants certiorari, or "cert," then the higher court reviews the case. If the court denies cert, then the lower court ruling stands. In the Supreme Court, the votes of four justices are required to grant certiorari.

Child Pornography

Special category of sexual material that the U.S. Supreme Court has said can be prohibited in the interest of preventing commerce in the abusive use of children as subjects of pornography.

Chilling Effect

Term of art to describe the self-censorship that occurs when someone fears the actions of another; the idea that vague and overly broad rules regulating speech are likely to result in people censoring themselves, even censoring acceptable speech, since they cannot be sure whether their speech is illegal or not.

Clear and Present Danger
In *Schenck v. United States* (1919), Justice Oliver Wendell Holmes, Jr., articulated this test, which said that the government may suppress speech that presents a clear and present danger, as long as the government can show that that danger is both real and imminent.

Commercial Speech
Speech (as advertising) that proposes a commercial transaction.

Compelling Government Interest
A term used by courts when assessing the burden of government regulation or action upon the exercise of a fundamental right, such as freedom of speech. For such a rule to withstand constitutional challenge, the government must show more than a merely important reason for the rule. The reason for the rule must be compelling; that is, it must be so important that it outweighs even the most valued and basic freedom it negatively affects.

Constitution
The system of fundamental laws and principles that prescribe the nature, functions, and limits of a government or another institution. The fundamental law of the United States, framed in 1787, ratified in 1789, and variously amended since that time.

Content-based Laws and Regulations
Statutory restrictions on speech that prohibit some categories of expression while allowing others. In contrast, viewpoint-based laws and regulations restrict expression because of the regulator's favoring of one opinion or side of an issue over another. For example, a ban on the publication of confidential information is content-based; however, a ban on all picketing except that by labor unions is viewpoint-based.

Content Neutrality
The opposite of content-based laws, content-neutral laws and regulations apply to all categories of speech and do not expressly prohibit any particular subject matter of expression. For example, although a law might be able to regulate whether pamphlets could be distributed in a public school, it could not discriminate against only Christian or Muslim pamphlets. Such content-neutral regulations that interfere with speech are examined under a balancing test, comparing the state's interest in prohibiting the activity in question and the level of interference with the speaker, which is often determined by looking at available avenues of communication.

Copyright Laws
The legal right granted to an author, composer, playwright, publisher, or distributor to exclusive publication, production, sale, or distribution of a literary, musical, dramatic, or artistic work.

Defamation
Communication to third parties of false statements about a person that injures the reputation of or deters others from associating with that person.

Dissenting Opinion
Opinion disagreeing with the majority opinion; in the context of a legal action, an opinion that dissents from the majority decision rendered by a panel of judges.

Diversity
The state of being different; a point or respect in which things differ.

Due Process
The principle, encapsulated in the Fifth and Fourteenth Amendments, that neither the federal or state and local governments may deprive one of life, liberty, or property without appropriate legal procedures and safeguards. In the United States, this principle gives individuals a varying ability to enforce their rights against alleged violations by the government, but normally not against private citizens.

Editorial
An article in a publication expressing the opinion of its editors or publishers or commentary on television or radio expressing the opinion of the station or network.

Editorializing
To express an opinion in or as if in an editorial.

Equal Access Act
Passed by Congress to end growing discrimination against student religious groups that began to occur in public schools.

Equal and Equitable Access to Information and Services
Approach to operating that ensures that everyone the library serves is entitled to the same level of access to information and services and that all have the opportunity to avail themselves if they so choose. Equal access refers to uniform access to information and services. Equitable access refers to just and fair access taking into consideration the facts and circumstances of the individual case. Access to information and services is equal and equitable when there is a level playing field.

Established Church
A church that a government officially recognizes as a national institution and to which it accords support.

Establishment Clause
A clause in the First Amendment to the U.S. Constitution forbidding Congress from establishing a state religion.

Expression of Concern
An inquiry that has judgmental overtones.

Extralegal Pressure

Threat of legal action or pressure by community members or organized groups that results in the banning of materials. The term also refers to requests from law enforcement without proper court order and actions taken by persons in positions of authority (e.g., mayor, elected officials, school officials) to remove or restrict access to materials or services without following established policies and procedures.

Fair Use

The U.S. Copyright Act has a fair-use exemption, allowing a defendant to a copyright-infringement claim to escape liability on the theory that it is only equitable that he should be able to use the original work in some manner. Fair-use inquiries are examined case by case and depend on four factors:

1. The purpose and the character of the use.
2. The nature of the original copyrighted work.
3. The amount of the original work used in the secondary work.
4. The economic impact of the use.

Federalist

An advocate of federalism who was a member or supporter of the Federalist Party. One who supported ratification of the U.S. Constitution.

Fighting Words

Those words "which by their very utterance inflict injury or tend to incite an immediate breach of the peace." Such words must be uttered as a direct personal insult in a face-to-face confrontation and are calculated or highly likely to result in an immediate violent physical reaction.

FOIA

Freedom of Information Act.

Founding Fathers

Delegates to the Constitutional Convention.

The Fourth Estate

A name often given to the public press.

Free Exercise Clause

The clause in the First Amendment to the U.S. Constitution prohibiting Congress from making any law prohibiting the free exercise of religion.

Fundamentalism

A usually religious movement or point of view characterized by a return to fundamental principles by rigid adherence to those principles, and often by intolerance of other views and opposition to secularism.

Gag Order

A court order prohibiting or limiting communication about a case. Gag orders have been imposed on the press, attorneys, jurors, and others. These orders are presumptively unconstitutional when applied to the press. Judges have greater ability to impose such orders on trial participants.

Government Neutrality

The state or policy of the government being neutral.

Harmful to Minors

Phrase used to describe sexual materials that are protected speech for adults but are deemed obscene for minors by state law. Many states have passed such "harmful to minors" obscenity statutes. The U.S. Supreme Court has held that these statutes must be quite narrow and must not limit the ability of adults to access protected speech. Consequently, applying these statutes to material on the Internet has proven to be complicated, as current technology makes it difficult to discern between adult and minor viewers.

Hate Speech

Speech intended to degrade, intimidate, or incite violent or prejudicial action against an individual or group of persons based upon their race, ethnicity, national origin, religion, sexual orientation, or disability. This category of speech receives considerable constitutional protection because the government cannot prescribe which thoughts we can think or which political philosophies we can advocate. The U.S. Supreme Court has said that the "fighting words" doctrine is not a tool to cleanse public debate or regulate words that give offense.

Immigration

The act of entering and settling in a country or region to which one is not native.

Implied

Insinuated, expressed indirectly, hinted at.

Indecency

"Indecent" speech usually receives First Amendment protection, except when it is broadcast over the airwaves. In *FCC v. Pacifica* (1978), the Supreme Court held that the Federal Communications Commission could regulate indecent speech because broadcast media are both uniquely pervasive and uniquely accessible to children. For regulatory purposes, the FCC defines indecency as "language or material that, in context, depicts or describes, in terms patently offensive as measured by contemporary community standards for the broadcast medium, sexual or excretory activities or organs" (16 FCCR 7999, 8000).

Intrusion

Uninvited entry, infringement upon, the act of intruding or infringing on others.

Lawsuit
A civil action brought before a court in which a party (plaintiff) has claimed to receive damages from a defendant's action, and the plaintiff seeks a legal or equitable remedy. The defendant is required to respond to the complaint of the plaintiff.

Libel
A written libel or oral slander defames an individual and has the effect of ruining that person's reputation, standing in the community, or ability to associate with others. Because of the adverse economic consequences that false accusations can have, the courts can award damages to compensate an individual injured by those false accusations. By contrast, truthful yet harmful accusations incur no similar damage and are not actionable.

Limited Public Forum
A public place purposefully designated by the government as a place dedicated to a particular type of expression. As in a traditional public forum, only reasonable content-neutral time, place, and manner restrictions may be imposed on speech, within the scope of the designated purpose of the forum. In a limited public forum, the government may exclude entire categories of speech that do not fall within the designated purpose of the forum, but may not discriminate against particular viewpoints or restrict speech appropriate to the forum.

Lobbyist
A person who is employed by an individual, organization, association, or business to represent its interests before the legislature. The term derives from the fact that lobbyists usually frequent the areas (lobbies) adjacent to the chambers of the senate and the house, either seeking to buttonhole legislators as they walk to and from the chambers or await legislative action, which might affect their clients' interests. Individual citizens may also "lobby" their legislators on matters of concern to them.

Magna Carta
The charter of English political and civil liberties granted by King John at Runnymede in June 1215. It serves as a piece of legislation that guarantees basic rights.

Marketplace of Ideas
One of the main theories of free speech. The theory was first given form by U.S. Supreme Court Judge Oliver Wendell Holmes, Jr., when dissenting in *Abrams v. United States*, 250 U.S. 616, 40 S.Ct. 17, 63 L.Ed. 1173 (1919), stating that, "the best test of truth is the power of the thought to get itself accepted in the competition of the market."

Materially Interfere
A term used by the courts to describe the necessary level on intrusion, inconvenience, or disruption of an accepted or protected activity caused by certain conduct to justify regulation of that conduct. A material interference is much more than mere annoyance—it must be an actual obstacle to the exercise of a right.

Miller Test
The Miller test is the list of criteria used to determine whether particular material is obscene. The Supreme Court held in *Miller v. California* (1973) that material is obscene if:

1. The average person, applying contemporary community standards, would find that the work, taken as a whole, appeals to the prurient interest, which means arousing sexual desire.
2. The work depicts or describes, in a patently offensive way, sexual conduct specifically defined by the applicable state law.
3. The work, taken as a whole, lacks serious literary, artistic, political, or scientific value. Court battles often focus on this third prong of the test.

Morals
Of or concerned with the judgment of the goodness or badness of human action and character.

Neutrality
Unbiased; tolerance attributable to a lack of information.

News
Information about recent events or happenings, especially as reported by newspapers, periodicals, and radio or television presentation of such information, as in a newspaper or on a newscast.

Non-partisan
Not supporting the interests or policies of any particular political party.

Nudity
The state of wearing no clothing. Obscenity and nudity are not synonymous. Although obscene materials, which depict a very narrow category of hardcore sexual acts that have a tendency to incite lustful thoughts, can be illegal, it is unconstitutional to prohibit the circulation or exposure of materials that depict or contain nudity. In 1975, the U.S. Supreme Court issued an opinion in *Erznoznik v. City of Jacksonville*, 422 U.S. 205, that struck down a law that banned nudity in movies shown in drive-in theaters when the screen was visible from the street.

Objectivity
Judgment based on observable phenomena and uninfluenced by emotions or personal prejudices.

Obscenity

For a work to be obscene, a court or jury must determine that (1) the average person, applying contemporary community standards, would find that the work, taken as a whole, appeals to the prurient interest; (2) the work depicts or describes, in a patently offensive way, sexual conduct specifically defined by the applicable law; (3) the work, taken as a whole, lacks serious literary, artistic, political, or scientific value.

Open Meetings Act

Ensures that public business is conducted in public view by prohibiting secret deliberations and actions on matters that should be discussed in a public forum.

Opinion

A belief or conclusion held with confidence but not substantiated by positive knowledge or proof.

Oral Arguments

Spoken presentations to a judge or appellate court by a lawyer (or parties when representing themselves) of the legal reasons why they should prevail. Oral argument at the appellate level accompanies written briefs, which also advance the argument of each party in the legal dispute. Oral arguments can also occur during motion practice when one of the parties presents a motion to the court for consideration before trial, such as when the case is to be dismissed on a point of law, or when summary judgment may lie because there are no factual issues in dispute.

Oral Complaint

An oral challenge to the presence and/or appropriateness of the material in question.

Petition

In law, a request to the government to grant a particular right, or to take a specific action.

Picket

A person or group of persons stationed outside a place of employment, usually during a strike, to express grievances, protest, and discourage entry by nonstriking employees and/or customers. Picketing can also be used to promote interests other than those of workers, such as protests against racial discrimination or particular government actions or decisions.

Plaintiff

The party that files a lawsuit (against a defendant).

Police Power

In law, the right of a government to make laws necessary for the health, morals, and welfare of the populace.

Political Speech

Any form of speech directly linked to the government; speech that conveys opinions and ideas about government and political and social issues. Such speech performs a valuable function as a check and balance of the government. Speaking out against government intervention or financial contributions is considered an example of political speech, as a method of expressing a political ideology.

Pornography

In legal terms, pornography and obscenity are not synonyms, and the U.S. Supreme Court has recognized that erotic messages, nudity, and depictions of sexual behavior are forms of speech protected by the First Amendment of the U.S. Constitution. The court's obscenity decisions comprehend that sex is a subject in well-regarded literature and art and a mysterious force that commands great human attention; as a result, the court has held that society's concerns about obscenity should not be a vehicle to interfere with serious artistic or scientific expression. As a result, materials cannot be prohibited or restricted solely because they contain erotic messages.

Prior Restraint

Prohibition on expression (especially by a publication) before the expression actually takes place.

Protected Speech

Speech that is protected from government censorship or regulation to one extent or another, depending upon the nature of the speech and the nature of the regulation. In law, it is speech that is interpreted as protected by the U.S. Supreme Court under the First Amendment. The Court has never held that the Constitution establishes an absolute right to free speech.

Public Attack

A publicly disseminated statement challenging the value of the material, presented to the media and/or others outside the institutional organization in order to gain public support for further action.

Shield Laws

Laws giving journalists the ability to protect the identities of confidential sources without fear of prosecution.

Slander

A spoken false or malicious statement or report about someone. See *Libel*.

Substantial Objectives

Goals related to the fundamental mission of a government institution and not merely incidental to the performance of that mission. Providing free and unrestricted access to a broad selection of materials representing various points of view is a substantial objective of a public library.

Symbolic Speech
A "message" or conduct intended to convey a particular message, which is likely to be understood by those viewing it.

Tax-exempt
Not subject to being taxed.

Time, Place, and Manner
The U.S. Supreme Court has repeatedly ruled that right to free speech is not absolute and that the state and federal governments may place reasonable restrictions on the time, place, and manner of individual expression. The government cannot, however, impose speech restrictions simply because it disagrees with the message of the speaker. In other words, any government regulation of speech must be content neutral and advance a significant government interest, and must be narrowly tailored so as to not restrict any more speech than is necessary to advance that interest. An example of a "manner" regulation is a restriction on the size of signs carried by picketers.

Tort Liability
A tort is a wrong done to someone, a civil cause of action for which a standard remedy is monetary damages or an injunction. Examples of tort claims include defamation, invasion of privacy and intentional infliction of emotional distress. Liability means that one owes another for the harm he or she has caused.

Unprotected Speech
Speech that may be limited because the First Amendment does not protect it. The U.S. Supreme Court has identified nine areas of unprotected speech in its decisions: (1) obscenity, (2) defamation, (3) expression intended and likely to incite imminent lawless action, (4) fighting words, (5) unwarranted invasion of privacy, (6) deceptive or misleading advertisements or those for illegal products or services, (7) clear and immediate threats to national security, (8) copyright violations, and (9) expression on school grounds that causes a material and substantial disruption of school activities.

USA Patriot Act
Uniting and Strengthening America by Providing Appropriate Tools Required to Intercept and Obstruct Terrorism (USA PATRIOT) Act of 2001

U.S. Courts of Appeals
(or circuit courts)
The intermediate appellate courts of the U.S. federal court system. A court of appeals decides appeals from the district courts within its federal judicial circuit, and in some instances from other designated federal courts and administrative agencies. There currently are thirteen U.S. courts of appeals. The eleven "numbered" circuits and the D.C. Circuit are geographically defined. The thirteenth court of appeals is the U.S. Court of Appeals for the Federal Circuit, which has nationwide jurisdiction over certain appeals based on subject matter.

Written Complaint
A formal written complaint filed with the institution (library, school, etc.) challenging the presence and/or appropriateness of specific material.

This First Amendment Glossary and Acronyms was compiled using a variety of sources including, but not limited to:

Doyle, Robert P., and Robert N. Knight
***Trustee Facts File*. Third edition.**
Chicago: Illinois Library Association, 2004.

First Amendment Center
www.firstamendmentcenter.org

Peck, Robert S.
Libraries, the First Amendment, and Cyberspace: What You Need to Know
Chicago: American Library Association, 1999.

First Amendment Bibliography

Article 19 Freedom of Expression Handbook: International and Comparative Law, Standards and Procedures
London: ARTICLE 19, Int. Centre Against Censorship, 1996.
The handbook brings together, by topic, summaries and analysis of relevant international jurisprudence as well as decisions from national courts around the world that declare strong protections of the rights to freedom of expression and access to information. The handbook's aims are: (1) to enable lawyers around the world to use international and comparative freedom of expression law in cases before national courts and to assess whether their client's case would be advanced by filing an application with an international body; (2) to inform journalists, writers, and human rights campaigners and provide access to information under international and comparative law and standards, and to provide them with examples of how courts from a diversity of legal traditions have protected and promoted freedom of expression, often in the face of repressive government practices; (3) to provide a resource for academics, lawyers, and others interested in comparative and international freedom of expression law and jurisprudence. Updates to the handbook are available at www.article19.org.

Bollinger, Lee C., and Geoffrey R. Stone
Eternally Vigilant: Free Speech in the Modern Era
Chicago: Univ. of Chicago Pr., 2002
While freedom of speech has been guaranteed us for centuries, the First Amendment as we know it today is largely a creation of the past eighty years. *Eternally Vigilant* brings together a group of distinguished legal scholars to reflect boldly on its past, its present shape, and what forms our understanding of it might take in the future.

Boyer, Paul S.
Purity in Print: Book Censorship in America from the Gilded Age to the Computer Age. Second ed.
Madison: Univ. of Wisconsin Pr., 2002
The first edition of Purity in Print documented book censorship in America from the 1870s to the 1930s, embedding it within the larger social and cultural history of the time. In this second edition, Boyer adds two new chapters carrying his history forward to the beginning of the twenty-first century.

Brown, Jean E.
Preserving Intellectual Freedom: Fighting Censorship in Our Schools
Urbana, Ill.: National Council of Teachers of English, 1995
The author sheds light on the ways in which censorship arises; how it affects curricula, students, and teachers; and how it can be fought. The book also takes a comprehensive look at the provisions and implications of the 1988 U.S. Supreme Court decision in *Hazelwood v. Kuhlmeir*, which held that a high school principal's censorship of a student newspaper did not violate students' First Amendment rights, because the paper was not a public forum.

Chmara, Theresa
Privacy and Confidentiality Issues: A Guide for Libraries and Their Lawyers
Chicago: ALA, 2009
Because libraries are on the front lines of patron privacy and confidentiality controversies that raise First Amendment questions, it is critical that libraries and their counsel become familiar with the constitutional rights of patrons. Set up in a frequently-asked-questions format, Chmara discusses: what First Amendment rights exist in libraries; how to create a library policy to best protect patrons' confidentiality and privacy; the appropriate responses to requests for patron records; and, how to deal with the nuances of Internet use privacy.

Cloonan, Martin, and Reebee Garofalo, eds.
Policing Pop
Philadelphia: Temple Univ. Pr., 2003
A fascinating survey of the ways in which pop music has been censored and restricted, this book also makes an eloquent argument for the political and social importance of popular music. The essays collected here focus on the forms of censorship as well as specific instances of how the state and other agencies have attempted to restrict the types of music produced, recorded and performed within a culture. Several show how even unsuccessful attempts to exert the power of the state can cause artists to self-censor. Others point to material that taxes even the most liberal defenders of free speech. Taken together, these essays demonstrate that censoring agents target popular music all over the world, and they raise questions about how artists and the public can resist the narrowing of cultural expression.

Coetzee, J. M.
Giving Offense: Essays on Censorship
Chicago: Univ. of Chicago Pr., 1996
South African writer J. M. Coetzee presents a coherent, unorthodox analysis of censorship from the perspective of a writer who has lived and worked under its shadow.

Cole, David, and James X. Dempsey
Terrorism and the Constitution: Sacrificing Civil Liberties in the Name of National Security
New York: New Pr., 2002
Tracing the history of government intrusions on constitutional rights in response to threats from abroad, Cole and Dempsey warn that a society in which civil liberties are sacrificed in the name of national security is in fact less secure than one in which they are upheld. In a vivid and important critique of our government's response to threats—real and perceived—from communists in the 1950s, Central American activists in the 1980s, Palestinians in the

1990s, and now Islamic terrorists in the twenty-first century, the authors warn that many of our government's anti-terrorism efforts sacrifice civil liberties without effectively protecting national security.

Curtis, Michael Kent
Free Speech, "the People's Darling Privilege:"
Struggles for Freedom of Expression in
American History
Durham, N.C.: Duke Univ. Pr., 2001
Modern ideas about the protection of free speech in the United States did not originate in twentieth-century U.S. Supreme Court cases, as many have thought. Free Speech, "The People's Darling Privilege" refutes this misconception by examining popular struggles for free speech that stretch back through American history. Curtis focuses on struggles in which ordinary and extraordinary people, men and women, black and white, demanded and fought for freedom of speech during the period from 1791—when the Bill of Rights and its First Amendment bound only the federal government to protect free expression—to 1868, when the Fourteenth Amendment sought to extend this mandate to the states. A review chapter is also included to bring the story up to date. Curtis analyzes three crucial political struggles: the controversy that surrounded the 1798 Sedition Act, which raised the question of whether criticism of elected officials would be protected speech; the battle against slavery, which raised the question of whether Americans would be free to criticize a great moral, social, and political evil; and the controversy over anti-war speech during the Civil War. Many speech issues raised by these controversies were ultimately decided outside the judicial arena—in Congress, in state legislatures, and, perhaps most importantly, in public discussion and debate.

Feldman, Stephen M.
Free Expression and Democracy in America: A History
Chicago: Univ. of Chicago Pr., 2008
Charting the course of free expression alongside the nation's political evolution, from the birth of the Constitution to the quagmire of the Vietnam War, Feldman argues that our level of freedom is determined not only by the Supreme Court, but also by cultural, social, and economic forces. Along the way, Feldman pinpoints the struggles of excluded groups—women, African Americans, and laborers—to participate in democratic government as pivotal to the development of free expression.

Finan, Chris
From the Palmer Raids to the PATRIOT Act: A History of
the Fight for Free Speech in America
New York: Beacon, 2007
From the 1919 anti-subversive raids launched by Attorney General A. Mitchell Palmer, to early film censorship, to book banning, to the red scare, to the

attack on comic books, Finan takes us on a censorship tour of the twentieth century. He carefully examines how anti-NAACP legislation, television censorship, and the PATRIOT Act repeatedly put the right to think and speak out to the test.

Finkin, Matthew W., and Robert Post
For the Common Good: Principles of American
Academic Freedom
New Haven, Conn.: Yale Univ. Pr., 2009
Debates about academic freedom can become fierce. This book offers a concise explanation of the history and meaning of American academic freedom, and it attempts to intervene in contemporary debates by clarifying the fundamental functions and purposes of academic freedom in America.

Foerstel, Herbert N.
Banned in the Media
Westport, Conn.: Greenwood, 1998
Herbert Foerstel traces the history of media censorship in the United States, from colonial times to the present day, keeping an eye on the future. This comprehensive reference guide to media censorship provides in-depth coverage of each media format—newspapers, magazines, motion pictures, radio, television, and the Internet. Each format is examined in-depth, from its origins and history through its modern development, and features discussion of landmark incidents and cases.

Foerstel, Herbert N.
Banned in the U.S.A.: A Reference Guide to Book
Censorship in Schools and Public Libraries.
Westport, Conn.: Greenwood, 2002
Almost every aspect of book censorship is examined in this comprehensive source. Included in this readable survey of major book-banning incidents are legal cases surrounding censorship, interviews with the most censored authors, and an annotated list and discussion of the fifty most frequently challenged books for 1996 through 2000.

Foerstel, Herbert N.
Free Expression and Censorship in America:
An Encyclopedia.
Westport, Conn.: Greenwood, 1997
This comprehensive encyclopedia includes analysis of the First Amendment implications of major political issues of the 1990s including abortion, campaign finance, violence on television, homosexuality, and the Internet.

Foerstel, Herbert N.
Freedom of Information and the Right to Know:
The Origins and Applications of the Freedom of
Information Act.
Westport, Conn.: Greenwood, 1999

Foerstel examines the Freedom of Information Act (FOIA) and explores its importance as a tool in guaranteeing an informed citizenry and an open government.

Foerstel, Herbert N.
Refuge of a Scoundrel: The PATRIOT Act in Libraries
Westport, Conn.: Greenwood, 2004
The USA PATRIOT Act may be the most complex and controversial federal statute in American history, argued to undercut American civil liberties in countless ways, including a dramatic extension of domestic surveillance. The author convincingly proves that under this act and FBI guidelines, libraries and bookstores—long subject to FBI surveillance—are more vulnerable than ever before.

Garbus, Martin
Tough Talk: How I Fought for Writers, Comics, Bigots, and the American Way
New York: Times Books, 1998
As one of America's leading First Amendment attorneys, Martin Garbus's clients have included Lenny Bruce, Daniel Ellsberg, Kathy Boudin, Jeffrey Toobin, William B. Shockley, Peter Matthiessen, Spike Lee, Prodigy, Robert Redford, Chuck D, Al Goldstein, and major publishers. What is clear from the many accounts of Garbus's battles for freedom of speech is that the struggle to be free or to remain free will never end. Garbus also shows how one person (or a few) can make a huge difference in the free society we enjoy today.

Hajdu, David
The Ten-Cent Plague: The Great Comic-Book Scare and How It Changed America
New York: Farrar, Straus and Giroux, 2008
Hajdu turns to the writers and artists whose careers were ruined when censorship and other legal restrictions gutted the comics industry, and young kids who were coerced into participating in book burnings by overzealous parents and teachers.

Haynes, Charles, et al.
The First Amendment in Schools: A Guide from the First Amendment Center
Alexandria, Va.: Association for Supervision and Curriculum Development, 2003
A rich resource, the book includes: an explanation of the origins of the First Amendment; a concise, chronological history of fifty legal cases, including many landmark decisions, involving the First Amendment in public schools; and answers to frequently asked questions about the practice of the First Amendment in schools, covering specific issues of religious liberty, free speech, and press as they affect school prayer, use of school facilities, dress and speech codes, student press, book selection, and curriculum.

Heins, Marjorie
Not in Front of the Children: "Indecency," Censorship, and the Innocence of Youth
New York: Hill & Wang, 2001
Heins investigates the origins of conjecture regarding child and adolescent innocence and the history of "harm to minors" censorship beginning with the "virtuous thoughts" espoused by Plato's Republic on through to the installation of Internet filters in schools and libraries. With legal and social examples taken from cultures around the world, the author provides evidence that the "harm to minors" argument lies on unstable ground.

Heins, Marjorie
Sex, Sin, and Blasphemy: A Guide to America's Censorship Wars
New York: New Pr., 1998
Heins has been on the front lines of the "wars" as director of the Arts Censorship Project of the American Civil Liberties Union. She uses many examples to identify the legal themes and strategies of the adversaries, to elucidate the importance of artistic free expression, and to explain why suppression will not solve the problems that beset society.

Hentoff, Nat
Free Speech for Me but Not for Thee: How the American Left and Right Relentlessly Censor Each Other
New York: HarperCollins, 1993
Hentoff explores not only the "traditional" sources of censorship—religious fundamentalists and political right-wingers—but also censorship from the left, e.g., feminists who tried to prevent a pro-life women's group from participating in Yale University's Women's Center. He also takes on proponents of "hate speech" regulations as enemies of free expression.

Hentoff, Nat
Living the Bill of Rights: How to Be an Authentic American
New York: HarperCollins, 1998
Through portrayals of the famous (Supreme Court Justices William O. Douglas and William Brennan) and the not so famous (Anthony Griffin, a black lawyer and ACLU volunteer who defended the First Amendment rights of the Ku Klux Klan), Nat Hentoff pays tribute to American citizens whose lives embody the values and principles of the U.S. Constitution.

Hentoff, Nat
The War on the Bill of Rights and the Gathering Resistance. Rev. ed.
New York: Seven Stories Pr., 2004
This concise manifesto by a longtime defender of constitutional liberties is a blistering attack on the Bush administration, and on U.S. Attorney General John Ashcroft in particular, who Hentoff says has "subverted

more elements of the Bill of Rights than any attorney general in American history." Hentoff berates the U.S. Congress for its "supine" acquiescence to the USA PATRIOT Act, and the media for slack coverage of these issues, and raises the specter of J. Edgar Hoover's goon squads.

Index on Censorship is Britain's leading organization promoting freedom of expression. Since 1972, the magazine and its Web site provide up-to-the-minute news and information on free expression from around the world.

Intellectual Freedom Manual. Eighth ed.
Compiled by the Office for Intellectual Freedom, American Library Association.
Chicago: ALA, 2010
Completely revised, the manual is designed to answer practical questions that confront librarians in applying the principles of intellectual freedom to library service. It provides guidance on developing a materials selection policy and public library Internet use policy, dealing with the political strategies of organized pressure groups, and promoting access to all types of information for all types of users. New features include new interpretations to the *Library Bill of Rights*, a new chapter, "Interactivity and the Internet," and coverage of the latest USA PATRIOT Act debates and extensions. It is an indispensable reference tool.

Jones, Barbara M.
Protecting Intellectual Freedom in Your Academic Library
Chicago: ALA, 2009
Jones uses her experience and expertise to offer an intellectual freedom title tailored to the academic library environment. This title presents a number of scenarios in which intellectual freedom is at risk and includes case studies that provide narrative treatment of common situations tailored to your library type; easy and motivating ways to prepare new hires for handling intellectual freedom issues; sidebars throughout the book that offer sample policies, definitions of key terms, and analysis of important statutes and decisions; and, detailed information on how to handle challenges to materials in your collection.

Jones, Derek, ed.
Censorship: A World Encyclopedia. 4 vols.
Chicago: Fitzroy Dearborn, 2001
This work provides a wide-ranging view of censorship, spanning ancient Egypt to present times and covering art, literature, music, newspapers and broadcasting, and the visual arts, among many other topics. In addition, the work provides country surveys and discussions of major controversies for specific movies, books, and television shows. Nearly 600 contributors wrote the 1,550 entries, arranged alphabetically

by subject. Entries are enhanced by occasional illustrations, a name-subject index, and an alphabetical and thematic list of entries at the beginning of each volume.

Karolides, Nicholas J., Margaret Bald, and Dawn B. Sova
120 Banned Books: Censorship Histories of World Literature
New York: Checkmark Books, 2005
This reference book contains extensive information about books that have been banned, suppressed, or censored for religious, political, sexual, or social reasons across twenty centuries and in many countries. Each entry contains the author's name, original date, and place of publication and literary form, as well as a plot summary. A separate section of each entry provides details of the censorship history of the work, followed by a list of further readings for a more in-depth examination of the challenges.

- Bald, Margaret
  Literature Suppressed on Religious Grounds. Rev. ed.
  New York: Facts on File, 2006.

- Karolides, Nicholas J.
  Literature Suppressed on Political Grounds. Rev. ed.
  New York: Facts on File, 2006.

- Sova, Dawn B.
  Literature Suppressed on Sexual Grounds. Rev. ed.
  New York: Facts on File, 2006.

- Sova, Dawn B.
  Literature Suppressed on Social Grounds. Rev. ed.
  New York: Facts on File, 2006.

The aim of this four-volume set is to spotlight some 400 works that have been censored, banned, or condemned because of their political, social, religious, or sexual content. The entries, which include a summary, censorship history, and brief bibliography, range widely from Aristotle through Galileo and on up to Adolf Hitler and Judy Blume. Such well-known prohibited works as de Sade's *120 Days of Sodom,* the *Communist Manifesto,* and *Huckleberry Finn* are included here, but so are many other works that are now less controversial, e.g., Milton's *Areopagitica* and *Uncle Tom's Cabin.* Some of the censorship histories span several pages, while others are quite concise.

Lane, Frederick S.
American Privacy: The Four-Hundred-Year History of Our Most Contested Right
Boston: Beacon, 2009
A sweeping story of the right to privacy as it sped along colonial postal routes, telegraph wires, and today's fiber-optic cables on a collision course with presidents and programmers, librarians, and letter writers.

Leone, Richard, and Greg Anrig, eds.
The War on Our Freedoms: Civil Liberties in an Age of Terrorism
New York: Century Foundation, 2003
In each generation, for different reasons, America witnesses a tug of war between the instinct to suppress and the instinct for openness. Today, with the perception of a mortal threat from terrorists, the instinct to suppress is in the ascendancy. Part of the reason for this is the trauma that our country experienced on September 11, 2001, and part of the reason is that the people who are in charge of our government are inclined to use the suppression of information as a management strategy. The essays lift the veil on what is happening and why the implications are dangerous and disturbing and ultimately destructive of American values and ideals.

Lewis, Anthony
Freedom for the Thought That We Hate: A Biography of the First Amendment
New York: Basic Books, 2008
Two-time Pulitzer Prize–winner Anthony Lewis describes how our free-speech rights were created in five distinct areas— political speech, artistic expression, libel, commercial speech, and unusual forms of expression such as T-shirts and campaign spending. It is a story of hard choices, heroic judges, and the fascinating and eccentric defendants who forced the legal system to come face to face with one of America's great founding ideas.

Minow, Mary, and Thomas A. Lipinski
The Library's Legal Answer Book
Chicago: ALA, 2003
Containing answers to more than 600 legal questions, the work tackles topics and concerns as diverse as copyright, Web page design, filters and other restrictions on Internet access, privacy, library spaces as "public forums," professional liability, ADA compliance, library employment, and lobbying by nonprofit organizations, foundations, associations, and others. An index and the occasional case study enhance the guide's usability and thoroughness.

Newsletter on Intellectual Freedom
Chicago: ALA
This ALA bimonthly publication reports censorship incidents across the country, summarizes recent court cases on the First Amendment, and includes a bibliography on intellectual freedom. It is the best source of information on the continuing battle to defend and extend First Amendment rights.

Nuzum, Eric D.
Parental Advisory: Music Censorship in America
New York: Perennial, 2001
This thorough history of music censorship—case by case and fight by fight—focuses on the 1950s to the present, but includes incidents dating back to the nineteenth century. Part one is organized thematically, with chapters on the main hot-potato issues that music (especially rock, heavy metal, and gangsta rap) has drawn fire for: "excessive" violence, sex, and drugs; political protests perceived as threatening; and religious "blasphemy." Part two is a nearly year-by-year chronology, beginning in 1865, of notable censorship cases.

O'Harrow, Robert
No Place to Hide: Behind the Scenes of Our Emerging Surveillance Society
New York: Free Pr., 2005
The author details the post-9/11 marriage of private data and technology companies and government anti-terror initiatives to create something entirely new: a security-industrial complex. Drawing on his years of investigation, O'Harrow shows how the government now depends on burgeoning private reservoirs of information about almost every aspect of our lives to promote homeland security and fight the war on terror. In this new world of high-tech domestic intelligence, the author contends there is literally no place to hide.

Peck, Robert
Libraries, the First Amendment, and Cyberspace
Chicago: ALA, 2000
This handbook answers the questions librarians have about the First Amendment and provision of library services. It addresses basic First Amendment principles and their applicability to libraries and the Internet. Information on the application of the First Amendment to children and schools is also included. Appendixes include copies of ALA policies and guidelines.

Phillips, Peter, and Project Censored
Censored 2010: The Top 25 Censored Stories
New York: Seven Stories Pr., 2010
This annual publication of Project Censored presents a report card for the American press, listing the least-reported news stories of the past year. In addition to summarizing the year's twenty-five most censored stories, the volume includes Censored Déjà Vu, censored stories from past years that have since reached the mainstream media; Censored Resource Guide, a directory of media and anti-censorship organizations; and reprints of the top ten censored stories.

Ravitch, Diane
The Language Police: How Pressure Groups Restrict What Students Learn
New York: Knopf, 2003
Ravitch describes in copious detail how pressure groups from the political right and left have attempted to wrest control of the language and content of textbooks and standardized exams. According to the author—a former U.S. Assistant Secretary of Education—the result is often at the expense of the truth (in the case of history), of

literary quality (in the case of literature), and of education in general.

Reichman, Henry F.
Censorship and Selection: Issues and Answers for Schools. Third ed.
Chicago: ALA, 2001
The manual contains clear, concise, and useful information on the issues and solutions to censorship. Though its focus is primarily for schools, information is sufficiently general so libraries will find it useful. Censorship and Selection addresses how to develop viable policies ranging from how to handle complaints to the selection of learning materials. Specific recommendations for how to plan for potential crises also are included.

Robbins, Louise S.
Censorship and the American Library: The American Library Association's Response to Threats to Intellectual Freedom, 1939-1969
Westport, Conn.: Greenwood, 1996
This volume presents a study of the development of the American Library Association's intellectual freedom policies from 1939, when ALA first articulated its commitment to providing diverse viewpoints to library users, to its establishment of the Freedom to Read Foundation in 1969.

Scales, Pat. R.
Protecting Intellectual Freedom in Your School Library
Chicago: ALA, 2009
Scales uses case studies to illustrate real-life scenarios that school librarians are apt to confront, countering each situation with a recommended course of action that focuses on protecting students' First Amendment rights, intellectual freedom, and privacy. Scales includes useful documents, or links to documents, that support suggested resolutions. The section Internet Access provides useful information about dealing with the technology department to unblock sites by explaining the harmful to minors clause in the Children's Internet Protection Act (CIPA).

Scales, Pat. R.
Teaching Banned Books: 12 Guides for Young Readers
Chicago: ALA, 2001
This book can serve as a springboard for class discussions, staff development for administrators and teachers, and for parent groups. It can also reinforce the courage of those who work with young people to provide avenues for them to practice this important right.

Simmons, John S., and Eliza Dresang
School Censorship in the 21st Century: A Guide for Teachers and School Library Media Specialists
Newark, Del.: International Reading Association, 2001
This book offers insights into the nature of current censorship challenges, the historical and cultural context in which they occur in the United States, and the resources that exist for meeting these increasingly complex challenges.

Smith, Robert Ellis
Ben Franklin's Web Site: Privacy and Curiosity from Plymouth Rock to the Internet
Providence, R.I.: Privacy Journal, 2004
Smith explores the hidden niches of American history to discover the tug between Americans' yearning for privacy and their insatiable curiosity. The book describes Puritan monitoring in colonial New England, then shows how the attitudes of the founders placed the concept of privacy in the Constitution. This panoramic view continues with the coming of tabloid journalism in the nineteenth century, and the reaction to it in the form of a new right—the right to privacy.

Stone, Geoffrey R.
Perilous Times: Free Speech in Wartime from the Sedition Act of 1787 to the War on Terrorism
New York: Norton, 2004
Stone investigates how the First Amendment and other civil liberties have been compromised in America during wartime. He delineates the consistent suppression of free speech in six historical periods from the Sedition Act of 1798 to the Vietnam War, and ends with a coda that examines the state of civil liberties in the Bush era. Full of fresh legal and historical insight, *Perilous Times* magisterially presents a dramatic cast of characters who influenced the course of history over a two-hundred-year period: from the presidents— Adams, Lincoln, Wilson, Roosevelt, and Nixon—to the Supreme Court justices—Taney, Holmes, Brandeis, Black, and Warren—to the resisters—Clement Vallandingham, Emma Goldman, Fred Korematsu, and David Dellinger. Filled with dozens of rare photographs, posters, and historical illustrations, *Perilous Times* is resonant in its call for a new approach in our response to grave crises.

Sova, Dawn
Banned Plays: Censorship Histories of 125 Stage Dramas
New York: Facts on File, 2004
Censorship has been around as long as public performance, says Sova, and so she takes her sample of banned plays from the entire 2,500 years of theater. Plays are listed alphabeticallyby title, and include production dates, characters, plot summary, censorship history, and lists of further reading. Appendices contain biographical sketches of the playwrights, categorizations of the profiled plays based on the reasons they were censored, and a list of a further one hundred banned or censored plays.

Sova, Dawn
Forbidden Films: Censorship Histories of 125 Motion Pictures
New York: Facts on File, 2001
Since the earliest days of the film industry, mainstream films have been banned for their sexual, religious, social, and political content. *Forbidden Films* traces the efforts to censor 125 films, ranging from the silent *Birth of a Nation* to *Schlindler's List*. Entries are arranged alphabetically by film title and include production details such as country and date of production, distribution, format, running time, director, writer, awards, genre, and cast. A summary of the film's plot is followed by a description of its censorship history. Each entry concludes with a short bibliography for further reading.

Wartzman, Rick
Obscene in the Extreme: The Burning and Banning of John Steinbeck's the Grapes of Wrath
New York: PublicAffairs, 2008
During May of 1939, as the Nazis were burning books throughout Germany, the people of Bakersfield, California, did exactly the same thing with John Steinbeck's new bestseller. As a pretext, the growers cited, among other things, Steinbeck's use of foul language (bastard, bitch) and vivid scenes such as Rose of Sharon, having lost her baby, offering her milk-filled breast to a starving man. One lone librarian, Gretchen Knief, led the charge against the censors, but the book—by then a Pulitzer Prize winner—remained banned. Detailed portraits of the local businessmen, politicians, and labor leaders caught up in the struggle enliven the text.

Teaching Students about the First Amendment:

The following bibliography was compiled by Pat R. Scales, retired school librarian & author of *Teaching Banned Books: 12 Guides for Young Readers;* and *Protecting Intellectual Freedom in Your School Library: Scenarios from the Front Lines.*

Fiction

Blume, Judy, ed.
Places I Never Meant to Be. Illus. by Jane Wattenberg
New York: Simon Pulse, 2001
This collection of twelve short stories, written by writers whose works have been banned or challenged, have a central theme: the main characters find themselves in places they never meant to be.

Brande, Robin
Evolution, Me & Other Freaks of Nature
New York: Knopf, 2009
Mena Reece, a high school freshman, knows firsthand that it's lonely to stick up for one's rights, but when a favorite science teacher faces off with censors over a unit on evolution, she finds a few "open-minded" friends who are willing to join forces to stand by their teacher.

Bryant, Jen
Ringside 1925: Views From the Scopes Trial
Knopf, 2008
A series of poems, in the voices of real and fictional characters, tells the story of the famous Scopes Monkey Trial that took place in Dayton, Tennessee in 1925, and caused a few young people to think about the First Amendment and academic freedom.

Christian, Peggy
The Bookstore Mouse. Illus. by Gary A. Lippincott
San Diego: Harcourt Brace, 1995
Cervantes, a mouse who lives in an antiquarian bookstore, embarks on a great adventure while trying to elude Milo the cat. When Cervantes discovers the power of words, he finds a special way to deal with Milo, and they both live a more enlightened life.

Cushman, Karen
The Loud Silence of Francine Green
New York: Clarion, 2006
Francine Green has always been taught to keep her ideas and beliefs to herself, but she suddenly finds her voice and the need to express it when outspoken and opinionated Sophie Bowman transfers into her class and challenges her to think about issues like free speech, the atom bomb, the existence of God, and the way people treat one another.

Crutcher, Chris
The Sledding Hill
New York: HarperCollins, 2005
Fourteen-year-old Eddie takes direction from the ghost of a deceased friend as he battles a conservative minister who is leading a censorship war at his school.

Facklam, Margery
The Trouble with Mothers
New York: Clarion, 1989
Eighth-grader Luke Troy is devastated when his mother, a teacher, writes a historical novel that is considered pornography by some people in the community where they live.

Garden, Nancy
The Year They Burned the Books
New York: Farrar, Straus & Giroux, 1999
Jamie, a high school senior who is struggling to come to terms with her own sexuality, gets into a battle with a group of townspeople who want to censor a new health education curriculum in her school.

Hentoff, Nat
The Day They Came to Arrest the Book
New York: Dell, 1985
Students in a high school English class protest the study of Huckleberry Finn until the editor of the school newspaper uncovers other cases of censorship and in a public hearing reveals the truth behind the mysterious disappearance of certain library books and the resignation of the school librarian.

Krisher, Trudy
Fallout
New York: Holiday House, 2006
Set in North Carolina during the McCarthy Era, Genevieve has been taught to keep her opinions to herself, but she finds her voice when she forms an unlikely friendship with Brenda, a newcomer from California.

Lasky, Kathryn
Memoirs of a Bookbat
San Diego: Harcourt Brace, 1994
Fourteen-year-old Harper Jessup, an avid reader, runs away because she feels that her individual rights are threatened when her parents, born-again fundamental-ists, lodge a public promotion of book censorship.

Meyer, Carolyn
Drummers of Jericho
San Diego: Harcourt Brace, 1995
When a fourteen-year-old Jewish girl joins the high school marching band and discovers that the band will play hymns and stand in the formation of a cross, she objects and major issues of individual rights are raised.

Peck, Richard
The Last Safe Place on Earth
New York: Delacorte, 1995
The Tobin family is satisfied that Walden Woods is a quiet, safe community to rear three children. Then, seven-year-old Marnie begins having nightmares after a teenage babysitter tells her that Halloween is "evil," and Todd and Diana, sophomores in high school, witness an organized group's attempt to censor books in their school library.

Selzer, Adam
How to Get Suspended and Influence People
New York: Delacorte Press, 2006
Leon Harris proves just how gifted and talented he is when he produces a "sex education" video called *La Dolce Pubert*, but the school administration isn't amused and suspends Leon, which causes a community debate over censorship.

Winerip, Michael
Adam Canfield, The Last Reporter
Boston: Candlewick Press, 2009
The school board has shut down the Harris Elementary/Middle School newspaper, The Slash, because of their coverage of past stories on a crooked principal, suspicious state test scores, and a dirty school election. Adam Canfield, the famed editor of the newspaper, is determined to find a way to get the banned newspaper going again. Companion books include: *Adam Canfield of the Slash; Adam Canfield Watch Your Back*.

Nonfiction

Burns, Kate
Fighters Against Censorship
Farmington Hills, Mich.: Lucent Books, 2004
Spanning ancient to modern day, seven people are featured in this volume: James Madison, Theodore Schroeder, Emma Goldman, Pete Seeger, Tommy Smothers, Larry Flynt, and Mitchell Kapor. Part of the *History Makers* collective biography series.

Conway, John Richard
A Look at the First Amendment: Freedom of Speech and Religion
Berkeley Heights, N.J.: Enslow Publishers, 2009
In clear and concise language, the author chronicles First Amendment cases, beginning with the 1735 court case that established freedom of the press and continuing with discussion of more recent issues related to the separation of church and state.

Day, Nancy
Censorship, or Freedom of Expression?
Minneapolis: Lerner Publishing, 2005
Peppered with anecdotal accounts of how people

respond to censorship, there is an examination of current issues related to movies, books, art, newspapers, the Internet, and government infringement on individual rights.

Egendorf, Laura K., ed.
Censorship
Farmington Hills, Mich.: Greenhaven Press, 2002
Illustrated with political cartoons, this collection of articles by various people of authority discuss freedom of speech in our democracy; censorship issues in schools; whether or not pornography should be censored; and, whether the government should regulate art and pop art. Part of the *Examining Issues Through Political Cartoons* series.

Feinman, Myke
The Crystal Skull Files: A First Amendment Fable for All Ages
Streator, Ill.: Ink & Feathers Comics, 1998
There is comedy, suspense, and lessons to be learned in this continuation of the *Freedom Mystique* series. Art is done in Bigfoot Popeye style.

Gottfried, Ted
Censorship
Tarrytown, NY: Benchmark Books, 2005
Case studies explain current and often-volatile issues related to the Internet, book censorship, hate speech, and motion picture ratings. A center section called "You Be the Judge" asks readers to debate specific real-life scenarios. Part of the "Open for Debate" series.

Haynes, Charles C., Sam Chaltain & Susan M. Glisson
First Freedoms: A Documentary History of First Amendment Rights in America
New York: Oxford University Press, 2006
Documents, essays by First Amendment scholars, and timelines trace American social history and discuss the five rights—religion, speech, press, assembly, and petition—covered under the First Amendment. There are thirty-seven chapters covering events from the seventeenth century to the debate over the USA PATRIOT Act of 2001.

Krull, Kathleen
A Kids' Guide to America's Bill of Rights: Curfews, Censorship, and the 100-Pound Giant
Illus. by Anna DiVito
New York: HarperCollins, 1999
Anecdotes, case studies, humorous illustrations, and sidebars mask the history lesson of this kid-friendly discussion of the first ten amendments of the U.S. Constitution. Scenarios are presented that make these amendments applicable to daily life.

Lerner, Alicia Cafferty and Adrienne Wilmoth Lerner
Freedom of Expression
Farmington Hills, Mich.: Greenhaven Press, 2009
A collection of articles, speeches, and position papers that focuses on global issues related to censorship issues that artists, journalists, and everyday citizens face.

Meltzer, Milton
The Bill of Rights: How We Got It and What It Means
New York: Crowell, 1990
This book presents a comprehensive discussion of the history of the Bill of Rights and makes specific references to contemporary challenges to the ten amendments.

Sherrow, Victoria
Censorship in Schools
Springfield, N.J.: Enslow Publishers, 1996
This documented text clearly defines censorship and traces the development of censorship in schools throughout history. A detailed discussion of problems of free expression in schools today includes censorship of literature, textbooks, student newspapers, etc.

First Amendment Quotations

"The burning of an author's books, imprisonment for opinion's sake, has always been the tribute that an ignorant age pays to the genius of its time."
Joseph Allen (1749–1827), American politician, nephew of U.S. President Samuel Adams, Massachusetts Constitutional Convention, 1788.

"Freedom of thought and freedom of speech in our great institutions of learning are absolutely necessary . . . the moment that either is restricted, liberty begins to wither and die and the career of a nation after that time is downwards."
John Peter Altgeld, Governor of Illinois, 1893–1897 (1847–1902).

"Intellectual freedom, the essence of equitable library services, provides for free access to all expressions of ideas through which any and all sides of a question, cause, or movement may be explored. Toleration is meaningless without tolerance for what some may consider detestable. Librarians must not permit their own preferences to limit their degree of tolerance in collection development, because freedom is indivisible."
American Library Association, Office for Intellectual Freedom. *Intellectual Freedom Manual.* Eighth edition. Chicago: American Library Association, 2010, p. 108.

"The use of 'religion' as an excuse to repress the freedom of expression and to deny human rights is not confined to any country or time."
Margaret Atwood. Letter. *Index on Censorship*, 1995.

"The freedom to share one's insights and judgments verbally or in writing is, just like the freedom to think, a holy and inalienable right of humanity that, as a universal human right, is above all the rights of princes."
Carl Friedrich Bahrdt. *On Freedom of the Press and Its Limits*, 1787.

"The oppression of any people for opinion's sake has rarely had any other effect than to fix those opinions deeper, and render them more important."
Hosea Ballou, American Universalist clergyman and theological writer (1771–1852).

"To permit every interest group, especially those who claim to be victimized by unfair expression, their own legislative exceptions to the First Amendment so long as they succeed in obtaining a majority of legislative votes in their favor demonstrates the potentially predatory nature of what defendants seek through this Ordinance and defend in this lawsuit.

"It ought to be remembered by defendants and all others who would support such a legislative initiative that, in terms of altering sociological patterns, much as alteration may be necessary and desirable, free speech, rather than being the enemy, is a long-tested and worthy ally. To deny free speech in order to engineer social change in the name of accomplishing a greater good for one sector of our society erodes the freedoms of all and, as such, threatens tyranny and injustice for those subjected to the rule of such laws. The First Amendment protections presuppose the evil of such tyranny and prevent a finding by this Court upholding the Ordinance."
Judge Sarah Evans Barker, *American Booksellers Association, Inc., et al. v. William H. Hudnut III*, 598 F.Supp. 1316 (S.D. Ind. 1984

"Thought that is silenced is always rebellious. Majorities, of course, are often mistaken. This is why the silencing of minorities is necessarily dangerous. Criticism and dissent are the indispensable antidote to major delusions."
Alan Barth. *The Loyalty of Free Men*. London: Gollancz, 1951.

"As long as I don't write about the government, religion, politics, and other institutions, I am free to print anything."
Pierre-Augustin Caron de Beaumarchais, French writer (1732–1799).

"I'm in favour of free expression provided it's kept rigidly under control."
Alan Bennett, British playwright (1934–).

"Political correctness is really a subjective list put together by the few to rule the many—a list of things one must think, say, or do. It affronts the right of the individual to establish his or her own beliefs."
Mark Berley. *Argos*, Spring 1998.

"In order to get the truth, conflicting arguments and expression must be allowed. There can be no freedom without choice, no sound choice without knowledge."
David Knipe Berninghausen. *Arrogance of the Censor, USA Today* 110, no. 2442 (March 1982): 61

"The layman's constitutional view is that what he likes is constitutional and that which he doesn't like is unconstitutional."
U.S. Supreme Court Justice Hugo L. Black. *New York Times*, February 26, 1971.

"I fear more harm from everybody thinking alike than from some people thinking otherwise."
Charles G. Bolte, U.S. publisher and vice president, Carnegie Endowment for International Peace (1920–1994).

"Censorship is the mother of metaphor."
Jorge Luis Borges, Argentine novelist and poet (1899–1986).

"Without free speech no search for truth is possible . . . no discovery of truth is useful. Better thousand-fold abuse of free speech than denial of free speech. The abuse dies in a day, but the denial slays the life of the people, and entombs the hope of the race."
Charles Bradlaugh, British freethinker and reformer (1833–1891).

"Correctly applied (the clear and present danger test), . . . will preserve the right of free speech from suppression by tyrannous majorities and from abuse by irresponsible, fanatical minorities."
U.S. Supreme Court Justice Louis Dembitz Brandeis, *Schaefer v. U.S.*, 251 U.S. 466, 40 S.Ct. 259, 64 L.Ed. 360 (1920).

"Those who won our independence by revolution were not cowards. They did not fear political change. They did not exalt order at the cost of liberty. . . . If there be time to expose through discussion the falsehood and fallacies, to avert the evil by the processes of education, the remedy to be applied is more speech, not enforced silence."
U.S. Supreme Court Justice Louis Dembitz Brandeis, *Whitney v. California*, 274 U.S. 357, 47 S.Ct. 641, 71 L.Ed. 1095 (1927).

"Experience teaches us to be most on our guard to protect liberty when the government's purpose is beneficent. The greatest dangers to liberty lurk in insidious encroachments by men of zeal, well-meaning but without understanding."
U.S. Supreme Court Justice Louis Dembitz Brandeis, dissenting, *Olmstead v. United States*, 277 U.S. 438, 48 S.Ct. 564, 72 L.Ed. 944 (1928).

"Debate on public issues should be uninhibited, robust, and wide-open and that . . . may well include vehement, caustic, and sometimes unpleasantly sharp attacks on government and public officials."
U.S. Supreme Court Justice William J. Brennan Jr., *New York Times v. Sullivan*, 376 U.S. 254, 84 S.Ct. 710, 11 L.Ed.2d 686 (1964).

"If there is a bedrock principle underlying the First Amendment, it is that the Government may not prohibit the expression of an idea simply because society finds the idea itself offensive or disagreeable."
U.S. Supreme Court Justice William J. Brennan Jr., *Texas v. Johnson*, 491 U.S. 397, 109 S.Ct. 2533, 105 L.Ed.2d 342 (1989).

"Everybody favors free speech in the slack moments when no axes are being ground."
Heywood Broun, U.S. journalist (1888–1939). *New York World*, October 23, 1926.

"Censorship is the tool of those who have the need to hide actualities from themselves and others. Their fear is only their inability to face what is real. Somewhere in their upbringing they were shielded against the total facts of our experience. They were only taught to look one way when many ways exist."
Charles Bukowski, U.S. writer and poet (1920–1994).

"The only thing necessary for the triumph of evil is for good men to do nothing."
Edmund Burke, British orator, philosopher, and politician (1729–1797).

"Freedom of expression is the matrix, the indispensable condition, of nearly every other form of freedom."
U.S. Supreme Court Justice Benjamin Nathan Cardozo, *Palko v. Connecticut*, 302 U.S. 319, 58 S.Ct. 149, 82 L.Ed. 288 (1937).

"If we don't believe in freedom of expression for people we despise, we don't believe in it at all."
Noam Chomsky, U.S. professor of linguistics (1928–).

"From a comparative perspective, the United States is unusual if not unique in the lack of restraints on freedom of expression. It is also unusual in the range and effectiveness of methods employed to restrain freedom of thought. . . . Where the voice of the people is heard, elite groups must insure their voice says the right things."
Noam Chomsky. *Index on Censorship*, July/August 1986.

"Everyone is in favor of free speech. Hardly a day passes without it being extolled, but some people's idea of it is that they are free to say what they like, but if anyone says anything back, that is an outrage."
Sir Winston Churchill, British statesman and author (1874–1965).

"You see these dictators on their pedestals, surrounded by the bayonets of their soldiers and the truncheons of their police. Yet in their hearts there is unspoken—unspeakable!—fear. They are afraid of words and thoughts! Words spoken abroad, thoughts stirring at home, all the more powerful because they are forbidden. These terrify them. A little mouse—a little tiny mouse!—of thought appears in the room, and even the mightiest potentates are thrown into panic."
Sir Winston Churchill.

"The public library is the most dangerous
place in town."
John Anthony Ciardi, U.S. poet and critic
(1916–1986).

"The fact is that censorship always defeats its own
purpose, for it creates, in the end, the kind of society
that is incapable of exercising real discretion.…
In the long run it will create a generation incapable
of appreciating the difference between
independence of thought and subservience."
Henry Steele Commager, U.S. historian (1902–1998).

"The irony of book-banning attempts is that the
publicity often causes people to read the books for
the wrong reasons. If a book is controversial,
perhaps the best place for it is the classroom where,
under the guidance of a teacher, the book can be
discussed and evaluated, where each student will
be free to proclaim how he or she feels about the
book and, in fact, can even refuse to read the book.
The point is that free choice must be involved."
Robert Cormier. In Banned in the USA: A Reference
Guide to Book Censorship in Schools and Public
Libraries, edited by Herbert N. Foerstel.
Westport, Conn.: Greenwood Pr., 2002, p. 123.

"The library is not a shrine for the worship of books.
It is not a temple where literary incense must be
burned or where one's devotion to the bound
book is expressed in ritual. A library, to modify the
famous metaphor of Socrates, should be the
delivery room for the birth of ideas—a place where
history comes to life."
Norman Cousins, U.S editor and essayist
(1915–1990).

"What censorship accomplishes, creating an
unreal and hypocritical mythology, fomenting an
attraction for forbidden fruit, inhibiting the
creative minds among us and fostering an illicit
trade. Above all, it curtails the right of the
individual, be he creator or consumer, to satisfy his
intellect and his interest without harm. In our
law-rooted society, we are not the keeper of our
brother's morals—only of his rights."
Judith Crist. Censorship: For and Against, 1971.

"Freedom of the press is not just important to
democracy, it is democracy."
Walter Leland Cronkite, U.S. journalist and radio
and television news broadcaster (1916–2009).

"Students throughout the totalitarian world risk
life and limb for freedom of expression; many
American college students are demanding that big
brother restrict their freedom of speech on
campus. This demand for enhanced censorship is

not emanating only from the usual corner—
the know-nothing fundamentalist right—it is coming
from the radical, and increasingly not-so-radical
left as well."
Alan Morton Dershowitz. Shouting Fire: Civil
Liberties in a Turbulent Age. Boston: Little,
Brown, 2002.

"The function of free speech under our system
of government is to invite dispute. It may indeed
best serve its high purpose when it invites a
condition of unrest, creates dissatisfaction with
conditions as they are, or even stirs people to anger.
Speech is often provocative and challenging.
It may strike at prejudices and preconceptions
and have profound unsettling effects as it passes
for acceptance of an idea."
U.S. Supreme Court Justice William Orville Douglas,
Terminello v. Chicago, 337 U.S. 1, 69 S.Ct. 894,
93 L.Ed. 1131 (1949).

"It is our attitude toward free thought and free
expression that will determine our fate. There must
be no limit on the range of temperate discussion,
no limits on thought. No subject must be taboo.
No censor must preside at our assemblies."
U.S. Supreme Court Justice William Orville
Douglas, address, Author's Guild, December 3, 1952,
on receiving the Richard E. Lauterbach Award
for Distinguished Service in the Field of Civil
Liberties.

"Restriction of free thought and free speech is the
most dangerous of all subversions. It is the one
un-American act that could most easily defeat us."
U.S. Supreme Court Justice William Orville Douglas,
address, Author's Guild, December 3, 1952, on
receiving the Richard E. Lauterbach Award for
Distinguished Service in the Field of Civil Liberties.

"One has the right to freedom of speech whether he
talks to one person or to 1,000."
U.S. Supreme Court Justice William Orville Douglas,
United States v. Auto. Workers, 352 U.S. 567, 77 S.Ct.
529, 1 L.Ed.2d 563 (1957

"[T]he ultimate welfare of the single human
soul (is) the ultimate test of the vitality of the
First Amendment."
U.S. Supreme Court Justice William Orville
Douglas, Gillette v. United States, 401 U.S. 437, 91
S.Ct. 828, 28 L.Ed.2d 168 (1971).

"A government that can give liberty in its
constitution ought to have the power to protect
liberty in its administration."
Frederick Douglass, U.S. abolitionist and journalist
(1818–1895).

"When books are challenged, restricted, removed, or banned, an atmosphere of suppression exists.... The fear of the consequences of censorship is as damaging as, or perhaps more damaging than, the actual censorship attempt. After all, when a published work is banned, it can usually be found elsewhere. Unexpressed ideas, unpublished works, unpurchased books are lost forever."
Robert P. Doyle. *Banned Books: 1998 Resource Guide*. Chicago: American Library Association, 1998, p. ii.

"Free speech has been on balance an ally of those seeking change. Governments that want stasis start by restricting speech.... Change in any complex system ultimately depends on the ability of outsiders to challenge accepted views and the reigning institutions. Without a strong guarantee of freedom of speech, there is no effective right to challenge what is."
Judge Frank Hoover Easterbrook, *American Booksellers Association, Inc., et al. v. William H. Hudnut III*, 771 F.2d 323 (7th Cir. 1985).

"It is evident that any restriction of academic freedom acts in such a way to hamper the dissemination of knowledge among the people and thereby impedes national judgment and action."
Albert Einstein, U.S. (German-born) physicist (1879–1955).

"Don't join the book burners. Don't think you are going to conceal thoughts by concealing evidence that they ever existed."
Dwight David "Ike" Eisenhower, speech at Dartmouth College, June 14, 1953.

"The libraries of America are and must ever remain the home of free, inquiring minds. To them, our citizens—of all ages and races, of all creeds and political persuasions—must ever be able to turn with clear confidence that there they can freely seek the whole truth, unwarped by fashion and uncompromised by expediency. For in such whole and healthy knowledge alone are to be found and understood those majestic truths of man's nature and destiny that prove, to each succeeding generation, the validity of freedom."
Dwight David "Ike" Eisenhower, letter to the American Library Association's Annual Conference, Los Angeles, 1953.

"Censorship is advertising paid by the government."
Federico Fellini, Italian film director (1920–1993).

"If the human body's obscene, complain to the manufacturer, not me."
Larry Flynt, publisher, *Hustler* Magazine (1942–).

"Students in school as well as out of schools are 'persons' under our Constitution. They are possessed of fundamental rights which the state must respect.... It can hardly be argued that either students or teachers shed their constitutional rights to freedom of speech or expression at the schoolhouse gate."
U.S. Supreme Court Justice Abraham Fortas, *Tinker et al. v. Des Moines Independent Community School District et al.*, 393 U.S. 503, 89 S.Ct. 733, 21 L.Ed.2d 731 (1969).

"Liberty is always dangerous, but it is the safest thing we have."
Harry Emerson Fosdick, U.S. clergyman (1878–1969).

"Freedom of the press is not an end in itself but a means to the end of [achieving] a free society."
U.S. Supreme Court Justice Felix Frankfurter, *Pennekamp et al. v. Florida*, 328 U.S. 331, 66 S.Ct. 1029, 90 L.Ed. 1295 (1946).

"Whoever would overthrow the liberty of a nation must begin by subduing the freeness of speech."
Benjamin Franklin, U.S. author, diplomat, inventor, physicist, politician, and printer (1706–1790).

"They that can give up essential liberty to obtain a little temporary safety deserve neither liberty nor safety."
Benjamin Franklin. *Historical Review of Pennsylvania*, 1759.

"If all printers were determined not to print anything till they were sure it would offend nobody, there would be very little printed."
Benjamin Franklin, 1730.

"We state these propositions neither lightly nor as easy generalizations. We here stake out a lofty claim for the value of the written word. We do so because we believe that it is possessed of enormous variety and usefulness, worthy of cherishing and keeping free. We realize that the application of these propositions may mean the dissemination of ideas and manners of expression that are repugnant to many persons. We do not state these propositions in the comfortable belief that what people read is unimportant. We believe rather that what people read is deeply important; that ideas can be dangerous; but that the suppression of ideas is fatal to a democratic society. Freedom itself is a dangerous way of life, but it is ours."

The Freedom to Read Statement's concluding paragraph

Concerned about threats to free communication of ideas, more than thirty librarians, publishers, and others conferred at Rye, New York, May 2–3, 1953. A committee was appointed to prepare a statement to be made public. The American Library Association Council endorsed this officially on June 25, 1953, and it was subsequently endorsed by the American Book Publishers Council (ABPC), American Booksellers Association, Book Manufacturers' Institute, and other national groups. In the light of later developments, a somewhat revised version was prepared after much consultation, and was approved in 1972 by the ALA Council, Association of American Publishers (successor to ABPC and American Educational Publishers Institute), and subsequently by many other book industry, communications, educational, cultural, and public service organizations. The statement was revised in 1991, 2000, and 2004 and is available at http://www.ala.org/oif/policies/freedomtoread.

"What progress we are making. In the Middle Ages they would have burned me. Now they are content with burning my books." Sigmund Freud, Austrian psychologist (1856–1939).

"To suppress free speech in the name of protecting women is dangerous and wrong." Betty Friedan (Betty Naomi Goldstein), U.S. women's rights activist and author (1921–2006).

"We must learn to welcome and not to fear the voices of dissent. We must dare to think about 'unthinkable things' because when things become unthinkable, thinking stops and action becomes mindless." James William Fulbright, U.S. senator D-Ark. (1905–1995).

"Whenever I notice that my name isn't on the list of banned and challenged authors, I feel faintly like I'm letting the side down. Although I suspect all I'd have to do to get on the list is to write a book about naked, bisexual, hard-swearing wizards who drink a lot while disparaging the Second Amendment, and I'd be home and dry." Neil Gaiman, *Badger Herald: Student Newspaper, Serving the University of Wisconsin-Madison Community*, September 27, 2004.

"Freedom is not worth having if it does not include the freedom to make mistakes." Mohandas Karamchand "Mahatma" Gandhi, Indian ascetic, peace activist (1896–1948).

"The First Amendment was designed to protect offensive speech, because nobody ever tries to ban the other kind." Mike Godwin, staff counsel, Electronic Freedom Foundation (1956–).

"The First Amendment does not require silence in the face of outrage. On the contrary, freedom demands a constant assertion of values." Richard Goldstein, media critic, *Village Voice*.

"When there is official censorship it is a sign that speech is serious. When there is none, it is pretty certain that the official spokesmen have all the loudspeakers." Paul Goodman. *Growing Up Absurd*. New York: Vintage Books, 1960.

"Censorship is never over for those who have experienced it. It is a brand on the imagination that affects the individual who has suffered it, forever." Nadine Gordimer, South African novelist (1923–).

"Books won't stay banned. They won't burn. Ideas won't go to jail. In the long run of history, the censor and the inquisitor have always lost. The only sure weapon against bad ideas is better ideas. The source of better ideas is wisdom." Alfred Whitney Griswold. *Essays on Education*. New Haven: Yale University Pr., 1954.

"[O]ne man's vulgarity is another's lyric." U.S. Supreme Court Justice John Marshall Harlan, *Cohen v. California*, 403 U.S. 15, 91 S.Ct. 1780, 29 L.Ed.2d 284 (1971).

"Where they have burned books, they will end in burning human beings." Christian Johann Heinrich Heine, German critic and poet (1797–1856). *Almansor*, 1823.

"I cannot and will not cut my conscience to fit this year's fashions." Lillian Florence Hellman (1905–1984), subpoenaed to appear before the House Un-American Activities Committee, 1952.

"To prohibit the reading of certain books is to declare the inhabitants to be either fools or slaves." Claude Adrien Helvetius. *De l' Homme*, vol. 1, sec. 4.

"Our Constitution was not intended to be used by . . . any group to foist its personal religious beliefs on the rest of us." Katherine Houghton Hepburn, U.S. actress (1907–2003).

"The only difference between the expression of an opinion and an incitement in the narrower sense is the speaker's enthusiasm for the result. Eloquence may set fire to reason."
U.S. Supreme Court Justice Oliver Wendell Holmes, Jr., *Gitlow v. People of State of New York*, 268 U.S. 652, 45 S.Ct. 625, 69 L.Ed. 1138 (1924).

"The best test of truth is the power of the thought to get itself accepted in the competition of the market.... We should be eternally vigilant against attempts to check the expression that we loathe."
U.S. Supreme Court Justice Oliver Wendell Holmes, Jr., dissenting, *Abrams v. United States*, 250 U.S. 616, 40 S.Ct. 17, 63 L.Ed. 1173 (1919).

"The right to be heard does not automatically include the right to be taken seriously."
Vice President Hubert Horatio Humphrey (1911–1978), speech to National Student Association, Madison, Wis., August 23, 1965.

"The vast number of titles which are published each year—all of them are to the good, even if some of them may annoy or even repel us for a time. For none of us would trade freedom of expression and of ideas for the narrowness of the public censor. America is a free market for people who have something to say, and need not fear to say it."
Vice President Hubert Horatio Humphrey (1911–1978), as reported by the *New York Times*, March 9, 1967, p. 42. Humphrey addressed the National Book Awards ceremony in New York City, March 8, 1967, where during his speech more than fifty people walked out to protest the U.S. role in Vietnam.

"Fear of corrupting the mind of the younger generation is the loftiest form of cowardice."
Holbrook Jackson, English writer and critic (1874–1948).

"Did you ever hear anyone say 'That work had better be banned because I might read it and it might be very damaging to me?'"
Joseph Henry Jackson, American critic, travel writer (1894–1955).

"The First Amendment grew out of an experience which taught that society cannot trust the conscience of a majority to keep its religious zeal within the limits that a free society can tolerate. I do not think it any more intended to leave the conscience of a majority to fix its limits. Civil government cannot let any group ride roughshod over others simply because their consciences tell them to do so."
U.S. Supreme Court Justice Robert H. "Bob" Jackson, *Douglas et al. v. City of Jeannette et al.*, 319 U.S. 157, 63 S.Ct. 877, 87 L.Ed. 1324 (1943).

"If there is any fixed star in our constitutional constellation, it is that no official, high or petty, can prescribe what shall be orthodox in politics, nationalism, religion, or other matters of opinion or force citizens to confess by word or act their faith therein."
U.S. Supreme Court Justice Robert H. "Bob" Jackson, *West Virginia State Board of Education v. Barnette*, 319 U.S. 624, 63 S.Ct. 1178, 87 L.Ed. 1628 (1943).

"The very purpose of the Bill of Rights was to withdraw certain subjects from the vicissitudes of political controversy, to place them beyond the reach of majorities and officials and to establish them as legal principles to be applied by the courts."
U.S. Supreme Court Justice Robert H. "Bob" Jackson, *West Virginia State Board of Education v. Barnette*, 319 U.S. 624, 63 S.Ct. 1178, 87 L.Ed. 1628 (1943).

"The First Amendment says nothing about a right not to be offended. The risk of finding someone else's speech offensive is the price each of us pays for our own free speech. Free people don't run to court—or to the principal—when they encounter a message they don't like. They answer it with one of their own."
Jeff Jacoby. "A Little Less Freedom of Speech," Townhall.com, January 26, 2004.

"A democratic society depends upon an informed and educated citizenry."
Thomas Jefferson, U.S. President (1743–1826).

"If the book be false in its facts, disprove them; if false in its reasoning, refute it. But for God's sake, let us hear freely from both sides."
Thomas Jefferson, *A Bookman's Weekly*.

"Books and ideas are the most effective weapons against intolerance and ignorance."
Lyndon Baines Johnson, U.S. President (1908–1973), commenting as he signed into law a bill providing increased federal aid for library service, February 11, 1964.

"The First Amendment is often inconvenient. But that is beside the point. Inconvenience does not absolve the government of its obligation to tolerate speech."
U.S. Supreme Court Justice Anthony McLeod Kennedy, *International Society for Krishna Consciousness, Inc., and Brian Rumbaugh, Petitioners v. Walter Lee; Superintendent of Port Authority Police v. International Society for Krishna Consciousness, Inc., et al.*, 505 U.S. 672, 112 S.Ct. 2711, 120 L.Ed.2d 541 (1992).

"The Constitution exists precisely so that opinions and judgments, including aesthetic and moral judgments about art and literature, can be formed, tested, and expressed. What the Constitution says is that these judgments are for the individual to make, not for the Government to decree, even with the mandate or approval of a majority. Technology expands the capacity to choose; and it denies the potential of this revolution if we assume the government is best positioned to make these choices for us."
U.S. Supreme Court Justice Anthony McLeod Kennedy, *United States, et al. v. Playboy Entertainment Group, Inc.*, 529 U.S. 803, 120 S.Ct. 1878, 146 L.Ed.2d 865 (2000).

"We are not afraid to entrust the American people with unpleasant facts, foreign ideas, alien philosophies, and competitive values. For a nation that is afraid to let its people judge the truth and falsehood in an open market is a nation that is afraid of its people."
John Fitzgerald Kennedy, U.S. President (1917–1963), remarks made on the twentieth anniversary of the Voice of America at H.E.W. Auditorium, February 26, 1962.

"People hardly ever make use of the freedom they have, for example, freedom of thought; instead they demand freedom of speech as a compensation."
Soren Aabye Kierkegaard, Danish philosopher (1813–1855).

"A library's role never has been, is not currently and will not be in the future to keep people from the information they need and want. If the United States is to continue to be a nation of self-governors, the people must have available and accessible the information they need to make decisions."
Judith F. Krug, "Intellectual Freedom 2002: Living the Chinese Curse," Luminary Lectures at the Library of Congress, May 23, 2002.

"The first step in liquidating a people is to erase its memory. Destroy its books, its culture, its history. Then have somebody write new books, manufacture a new culture, invent a new history. Before long the nation will begin to forget what it is and what it was. The world around it will forget even faster."
Milan Kundera. In "Memories of a Wistful Amnesiac," by Walter Goodman. *New Leader* 63, no. 23 (December 15, 1980), p. 26ff.

"I am absolutely convinced that the most important perspective is that people are obligated to respect opposing views. . . . If we are a poor respecter of other people's thoughts, our thoughts are not going to be well-received at another time."
James Albert Smith "Jim" Leach (1942–), former member of the U.S. House of Representatives from Iowa. *Washington Post*, March 20, 2003.

"Why should freedom of speech and freedom of the press be allowed? Why should a government which is doing what it believes to be right allow itself to be criticized? It would not allow itself to be criticized? It would not allow opposition by lethal weapons. Ideas are much more fatal things than guns."
Vladimir Ilyich Lenin (1870–1924), speech in Moscow, 1920. In *A New Dictionary of Quotations on Historical Principles from Ancient and Modern Sources*, edited by H. L. Mencken. New York: Knopf, 1991, p. 966.

"Where all men think alike, no one thinks very much."
Walter Lippmann, U.S. author and journalist (1889–1974).

"Censorship, like charity, should begin at home; but unlike charity, it should end there."
Clare Booth Luce, U.S. diplomat, dramatist, journalist, and politician (1903–1987).

"Every American librarian worthy of the name is today the champion of a cause. It is, to my mind, the noblest of all causes for it is the cause of man, or more precisely the cause of the inquiring mind by which man has come to be. But noblest or not, it is nevertheless a cause—a struggle—not yet won: a struggle which can never perhaps be won for good and all. There are always in any society, even a society founded in the love of freedom, men and women who do not wish to be free themselves and who fear the practice of freedom by others—men and women who long for the comfort of a spiritual and intellectual authority in their own lives and who would feel more comfortable if they could also impose such an authority on the lives of their neighbors. As long as such people exist—and they show no sign of disappearing from the earth, even the American earth—the fight to subvert freedom will continue. And as long as the fight to subvert freedom continues, libraries must be strong points of defense."
Archibald MacLeish. *Champion of a Cause*. Chicago: American Library Association, 1971, pp. 228–29.

"A popular government, without popular information, or the means of acquiring it, is but a prologue to a farce or a tragedy; or perhaps both. Knowledge will forever govern ignorance; and a people who mean to be their own governors, must arm themselves with the power which knowledge gives."
U.S. President James Madison, letter to W. T. Barry, August 4, 1782. In *The Complete Madison*. New York: Harper, 1953, p. 337.

"It is impossible for ideas to compete in the marketplace if no forum for their presentation is provided or available."
Thomas Mann, German writer (1875–1955).

"Thanks to television, for the first time the young are seeing history made before it is censored by their elders."
Margaret Mead, U.S. anthropologist (1901–1978).

"One cannot and must not try to erase the past merely because it does not fit the present."
Golda Meir, Israeli political leader (1898–1978).

"If all mankind minus one were of one opinion, and only one person were of the contrary opinion, mankind would be no more justified in silencing that one person, than he, if he had the power, would be justified in silencing mankind."
John Stuart Mill. *On Liberty*. Girard, Kan.: Haldeman-Julius Co., 1925.

"Who can compute what the world loses in the multitude of promising intellects combined with timid characters, who dare not follow out any bold, vigorous, independent train of thought, lest it should land them in something which would admit of being considered irreligious or immoral?... No one can be a great thinker who does not recognize that as a thinker it is his first duty to follow his intellect to whatever conclusions it may lead."
John Stuart Mill. *On Liberty*. Girard, Kan.: Haldeman-Julius Co., 1925.

"As good almost kill a man as kill a good book; who kills a man kills a reasonable creature, God's image; but he who destroys a good book kills reason itself."
John Milton. *Aeropagitica*. Christchurch, New Zealand: Caxton Pr., 1941.

"Give me the liberty to know, to utter, and to argue freely according to conscience, above all liberties."
John Milton. *Aeropagitica*. Christchurch, New Zealand: Caxton Pr., 1941.

"To forbid us anything is to make us have a mind for it."
Michel Eyquem de Montaigne. *Essays*, 1595.

"You have not converted a man because you have silenced him."
John Morley, 1st Viscount Morley of Blackburn, English politician and writer (1838–1923).

"Senator Smoot (Republican, Ut.)
Is planning a ban on smut
Oh rooti-ti-toot for Smoot of Ut.
And his reverent occiput.
Smite. Smoot, smite for Ut.,
Grit your molars and do your dut.,
Gird up your l--ns,
Smite h-p and th-gh,
We'll all be Kansas
By and By."
Frederic Ogden Nash, "Invocation," 1931.

"When voices of democracy are silenced, freedom becomes a hollow concept. No man or woman should be sentenced to the shadows of silence for something he or she has said or written."
Allen H. Neuharth, U.S. journalist (1924–).

"When information which properly belongs to the public is systematically withheld by those in power, the people will soon become ignorant of their own affairs, distrustful of those who manage them, and—eventually—incapable of determining their own destinies."
Richard Milhous Nixon. *Washington Post*, January 23, 1996, p. D16.

"Censorship of anything, at any time, in any place, on whatever pretense, has always been and always be the last resort of the boob and the bigot."
Eugene Gladstone O'Neill, American playwright (1888–1953).

"The First Amendment forbids any law 'abridging the freedom of speech.' It doesn't say, 'except for commercials on children's television' or 'unless somebody says 'cunt' in a rap song or 'chick' on a college campus.'"
P. J. O'Rourke. *Parliament of Whores: A Lone Humorist Attempts to Explain the Entire U.S. Government*. New York: Vintage Books, 1992.

"Who controls the past controls the future, and who controls the present controls the past."
Eric Arthur Blair, pen name George Orwell, English essayist, novelist, and satirist (1903–1950).

"That is what pluralism is: a nation where people who are different from one another are all entitled to the same rights and opportunities; the same standing before the law; the same respect, given to and received from each other.

"The First Amendment's value is linked directly to its use. To preserve it, it must be shared. Unless it is everyone's, it can be no one's."
Jean Hammond Otto. U.S. journalist (1925–).

"It is shared values, not shared opinions, that keep a diverse and pluralistic nation from splintering. It is tolerance for our differences that binds us. It is the First Amendment that protects the individual mind and conscience against the authority of government and the tyranny of the majority."
Jean Hammond Otto. *Social Education*, October 1990, p. 356.

"He that would make his own liberty secure, must guard even his enemy from opposition; for if he violates this duty he establishes a precedent that will reach to himself."
Thomas Paine. *Dissertation on First Principles of Government*. London: D. I. Eaton, 1795.

"A censor is an expert in cutting remarks. A censor is a man who knows more than he thinks you ought to."
Dr. Laurence Johnston Peter. *Peter's Quotations: Ideas for Our Time*. New York: Morrow, 1977, p. 97.

"Now that eighteen-year-olds have the right to vote, it is obvious that they must be allowed the freedom to form their political views on the basis of uncensored speech before they turn eighteen, so that their minds are not a blank when they first exercise the franchise. And since an eighteen-year-old's right to vote is a right personal to him rather than a right to be exercised on his behalf by his parents, the right of parents to enlist the aid of the state to shield their children from ideas of which the parents disapprove cannot be plenary either. People are unlikely to become well-functioning, independent-minded adults and responsible citizens if they are raised in an intellectual bubble."
Judge Richard Allen Posner, *American Amusement Machine Association, et al., Plaintiffs-Appellants v. Teri Kendrick, et al.*, 244 F.3d 954 (7th Cir. 2001).

"A free press is a cornerstone of our democracy. In the First Amendment to the Constitution, our Founding Fathers affirmed their belief that competing ideas are fundamental to freedom. We Americans cherish our freedom of expression and our access to multiple sources of news and information."
Ronald Wilson Reagan, U.S. President (1911–2004), message of the President for National Newspaper Week, October 10–16, 1982.

"Indeed, perhaps we do the minors of this country harm if First Amendment protections, which they will with age inherit fully, are chipped away in the name of their protection."
Judge Lowell A. Reed Jr., *American Civil Liberties Union, et al. v. Janet Reno*, 931 F.Supp.2d 473 (E.D. Pa. 1999).

"Where, after all, do universal human rights begin? In small places, close to home—so close and so small that they cannot be seen on any maps of the world. Yet they are the world of the individual persons; the neighborhood he lives in; the school or college he attends; the factory, farm, or office where he works. Such are the places where every man, woman and child seeks equal justice, equal opportunity, equal dignity without discrimination. Unless these rights have meaning there, they have little meaning anywhere. Without concerned citizen action to uphold them close to home, we shall look in vain for progress in the larger world."
Anna Eleanor Roosevelt, U.S. diplomat and reformer (1884–1962).

"If in other lands the press and books and literature of all kinds are censored, we must redouble our efforts here to keep it free. Books may be burned and cities sacked, but truth, like the yearning for freedom, lives in the hearts of humble men and women. No people in all the world can be kept eternally ignorant or eternally enslaved."
Franklin Delano Roosevelt, U.S. President (1882–1945), speech before the National Education Association, 1938.

"Free societies . . . are societies in motion, and with motion comes tension, dissent, friction. Free people strike sparks, and those sparks are the best evidence of freedom's existence."
(Ahmed) Salman Rushdie, British (Indian-born) author (1947–).

"What is freedom of expression? Without the freedom to offend, it ceases to exist."
(Ahmed) Salman Rushdie.

"Men fear thoughts as they fear nothing else on earth—more than ruin—more even than death. . . . Thought is subversive and revolutionary, destructive and terrible, thought is merciless to privilege, established institutions, and comfortable habit. Thought looks into the pit of hell and is not afraid. Thought is great and swift and free, the light of the world, and the chief glory of man."
Bertrand Arthur William Russell, English author, mathematician, and philosopher (1872–1970).

"Intellectual freedom is essential to human society. Freedom of thought is the only guarantee against an infection of people by mass myths, which, in the hands of treacherous hypocrites and demagogues, can be transformed into bloody dictatorships."
Andrei Dmitrievich Sakharov, Russian physicist (1921–1989).

"The First Amendment cases of the 1990s and the twenty-first century will pit powerful emotional interests—such as privacy or nationalism—against our intellectual commitment to the value of information and the right of the public to freely receive information."
Bruce W. Sanford, U.S. attorney (1945–).

"All truth passes through three stages: first it is ridiculed, second it is violently opposed, third it is accepted as being self-evident."
Arthur Schopenhauer, German philosopher (1788–1860).

"All censorships exist to prevent anyone from challenging current conceptions and existing institutions. All progress is initiated by challenging current conceptions, and executed by supplanting existing institutions. Consequently the first condition of progress is the removal of censorship."
George Bernard Shaw. Preface to *Mrs. Warren's Profession*. Studio City, Calif.: Players Pr., 1991.

"The war between the artist and writer and government or orthodoxy is one of the tragedies of humankind. One chief enemy is stupidity and failure to understand anything about the creative mind. For a bureaucratic politician to presume to tell any artist or writer how to get his mind functioning is the ultimate in asininity. The artist is no more able to control his mind than is any outsider. Freedom to think requires not only freedom of expression but also freedom from the threat of orthodoxy and being outcast and ostracized."
Helen Foster Snow, U.S. writer promoting American-Chinese understanding (1907–1997).

"The ultimate result of shielding men from the effects of folly is to fill the world with fools."
Herbert Spencer, British philosopher (1820–1903).

"Our nation's understanding and appreciation of the First Amendment is not passed along genetically. It must be reaffirmed and defended, over and over. Keep fighting and keep winning."
Paul Steinle, U.S. journalist.

"The interest in encouraging freedom of expression in a democratic society outweighs any theoretical but unproven benefit of censorship."
U.S. Supreme Court Justice John Paul Stevens, *Janet Reno, Attorney General of the United States, et al., Appellants v. American Civil Liberties Union et al.*, 521 U.S. 844, 117 S.Ct. 2329, 138 L.Ed.2d 874 (1997).

"The sound of tireless voices is the price we pay for the right to hear the music of our own opinions."
Adlai Ewing Stevenson II, U.S. politician (1900–1965).

"Freedom rings where opinions clash."
Adlai Ewing Stevenson II.

"You see, boys forget what their country means by just reading 'the land of the free' in history books. When they get to be men, they forget even more. Liberty is too precious a thing to be buried in books, Miss Saunders. Men should hold it up in front of them every single day of their lives and say 'I'm free—to think and speak. My ancestors couldn't, I can. And my children will.'"
James Stewart in Frank Capra's film *Mr. Smith Goes to Washington*.

"Censorship reflects a society's lack of confidence in itself. It is the hallmark of an authoritarian regime."
U.S. Supreme Court Justice Potter Stewart, dissenting, *Ginzberg v. United States*, 383 U.S. 463, 86 S.Ct. 942, 16 L.Ed.2d 31 (1966).

"The ultimate expression of free speech lies not in the ideas with which we agree, but in those ideas that offend and irritate us."
Charles "Chuck" Sumner Stone, U.S. journalist (1924–).

"Once a government is committed to the principle of silencing the voice of opposition, it has only one way to go, and that is down the path of increasingly repressive measures, until it becomes a source of terror to all its citizens and creates a country where everyone lives in fear."
Harry S Truman, message to Congress, August 8, 1950.

"There is no more fundamental axiom of American freedom than the familiar statement: In a free country we punish men for crimes they commit but never for the opinions they have."
Harry S Truman, U.S. President (1884–1972).

"Censorship is telling a man he can't have a steak just because a baby can't chew it."
Mark Twain [Samuel Langhornne Clemens], U.S. author and humorist (1835–1910).

"In America, as elsewhere, free speech is confined to the dead."
Mark Twain.

"It is by the goodness of God that in our country we have those three unspeakably precious things: freedom of speech, freedom of conscience, and the prudence never to practice either."
Mark Twain, *Pudd' nhead Wilson's Calendar*.

"Everyone has the right to freedom of opinion and expression; this right includes freedom to hold opinions without interference and to seek, receive, and impart information and ideas through any media regardless of frontiers."
United Nations Universal Declaration of Human Rights, Article 19.

"The basis of the First Amendment is the hypothesis that . . . free debate of ideas will result in the wisest governmental policies."
U.S. Supreme Court Justice Fred Moore Vinson, *Dennis et al. v. United States*, 341 U.S. 494, 71 S.Ct. 857, 95 L.Ed. 1137 (1951).

"I may disagree with what you have to say, but I shall defend to the death your right to say it."
François Marie Arouet, pen name Voltaire, French writer (1694–1778).

"It is the characteristic of the most stringent censorships, that they give credibility to the opinions they attack."
Voltaire [François Marie Arouet]. *Poeme sur le desastre de Lisbonne*, 1756.

"If I open my mouth to speak, must I always be correct, and by whose standards."
Alice Malsenior Walker. *In Search of Our Mothers' Gardens*. San Diego: Harcourt, 1983.

"Teachers and students must always remain free to inquire, to study and to evaluate, to gain new maturity and understanding; otherwise our civilization will stagnate and die."
Chief Justice of the United States Earl Warren, *Sweezy v. New Hampshire*, 354 U.S. 234, 77 S.Ct. 1203, 1 L.Ed.2d 1311 (1957).

"I believe in censorship. I made a fortune out of it."
Mae West, U.S. movie actress (1893–1980).

"There were a lot of things the censors wouldn't let me do in the movies that I did on stage. They wouldn't even let me sit on a guy's lap and I'd been on more laps than a napkin."
Mae West, *Index on Censorship*.

"The books that the world calls immoral are the books that show the world its own shame."
Oscar Fingal O'Flahertie Wills Wilde, Irish dramatist, novelist, and poet (1854–1900).

"An idea that is not dangerous is unworthy of being called an idea at all."
Oscar Fingal O'Flahertie Wills Wilde.

"I believe in America because in it we are free— free to choose our government, to speak our minds, to observe our different religions. Because we are generous with our freedom, we share our rights with those who disagree with us."
Wendell Lewis Willkie, U.S. politician (1892–1944).

"To suppress minority thinking and minority expression would tend to freeze society and prevent progress. . . . Now more than ever we must keep in the forefront of our minds the fact that whenever we take away the liberties of those whom we hate, we are opening the way to loss of liberty for those we love."
Wendell Lewis Willkie. *One World*. New York: Limited Editions Club, 1944.

"I have always been among those who believed that the greatest freedom of speech was the greatest safety, because if a man is a fool the best thing to do is to encourage him to advertise the fact by speaking."
Woodrow Wilson, U.S. President (1856–1924).

"The wisest thing to do with a fool is to encourage him to hire a hall and discourse to his fellow citizens. Nothing chills nonsense like exposure to the air."
Woodrow Wilson, 1908. *In First Amendment: What Americans Have Said about Freedom of Expression*, edited by Louis Edward Inglehart. Reston, Va.: Newspaper Association of America, p. 14.

"The trouble with free speech is that it insists on living up to its name."
Jonathan Yardley. *Washington Post*, June 17, 1996, p. CO2.

"Every dogma has its day, but ideals are eternal."
Israel Zangwill, English novelist (1864–1926).

Part 5
Ideas

"Every now and then a man's mind is stretched by a new idea or sensation, and never shrinks back to its former dimensions."

Oliver Wendell Holmes Sr., American physician, professor, lecturer, and author (1809–1894) from *The Autocrat of the Breakfast-Table*.

Where ideas proliferate, encountering opposing points of view is inevitable. An open dialogue in an atmosphere of tolerance and respect for the opinions and rights of all individuals—authors, parents, students, and others—is essential to cultivate understanding and intellectual growth.

Ideas presents innovative activities for annual celebration of Banned Books Week and effective strategies for ongoing communication about challenges and concerns.

Celebration Guide

As authors, booksellers, librarians, and publishers we are passionate about books. We've chosen to lead lives that surround us with books. And we are dedicated to bringing books into the lives of others.

We witness daily the myriad ways that books influence the lives of their readers—from a child just learning how to make sense of letters on a page to a teenager discovering a whole new world to a seasoned professional reinventing her career to a recent retiree who finally finds time to reread his favorite books to his grandchildren.

The power and pleasure of reading can last a lifetime, but the freedom to read can be eroded in a single day unless we all join together to protect our rights.

Join together with your fellow readers, co-workers, family, and friends to preserve our Freedom to Read. Spread the message by planning a celebration with activities and events that connect with your community.

Go ahead and get started.
Show your passion. Inspire your readers.
Celebrate Banned Books Week.

Activate
Silver screen drama & courtroom action

Pass the popcorn.
Hold a film festival.
The first group of titles below includes classic dramas whose plots deal with censorship of various kinds, while the second lists documentaries that chronicle incidents of real-life censorship. The last group lists print and online resources with even more related topics for discovery. Whether you schedule open screenings at the library or simply post resource lists for patrons to watch on DVD, these films provide for lively post-viewing discussion.

Classics

1984 is the George Orwell classic about Big Brother and the subordination of the individual to the state (1955).

Fahrenheit 451 shows a futuristic fascist society where the fireman's job is to burn books (1966).

Inherit the Wind is a fictionalized account of the famous Scopes "monkey trial" starring Spencer Tracy as Clarence Darrow and Matthew Harrison Brady as William Jennings Bryan (1960).

The Seven Minutes, based on the Irving Wallace novel of the same title, tells the story of a bookseller arrested for distributing an "obscene" novel (1971).

South Park: Bigger, Longer and Uncut tells the story of the boys seeing an R-rated movie and being pronounced "corrupted," leading their parents to pressure the United States to wage war against Canada (1999).

Storm Center, a Bette Davis classic, is the story of a small town librarian (Davis) who refuses to remove a book on Communism. The flaming conclusion should generate discussion and interest (1965).

Documentaries

Damned in the USA focuses on censorship controversies in America involving pornography, art and blasphemy.

Dissent: The ACLU Freedom Files tells the story of Muslim hip-hop poet Amir Sulaiman and groups of protesters at the Democratic and Republican national conventions in 2004.

Jailed for Their Words is a powerful, hour-long documentary tracing the dramatic story of Montana's draconian WWI sedition law, the harshest law of its kind in the nation, and the model for a U.S. law passed shortly after.

Skokie, a 1981 television movie directed by Herbert Wise, is based on the real-life National Socialist Party of America controversy of Skokie, Illinois.

Surveillance: The ACLU Freedom Files chronicles warrantless wiretapping of phone calls and monitoring of emails to the creation of a national identity card, with the government using "national security" as justification, stirring intense opposition from many groups across the political spectrum.

This Film is Not Yet Rated, an independent documentary about the Motion Picture Association of America's rating system and its effect on American culture.

Youth Speak: The ACLU Freedom Files features young people in America being treated as if the Bill of Rights doesn't apply to them and shows them fighting back.

Print and Online Resources

American Film Institute, **www.afi.com**, searchable database of American feature films prior to 1972, listing twenty-two films under the subject "censorship."

Banned Films: Movies, Censors, and the First Amendment, by Edward de Grazia and Roger K. Newman (New York: Bowker, 1982) provides 122 examples of American and foreign films banned in the U.S. including *The Birth of a Nation, The Exorcist,* and *Carnal Knowledge.*

Forbidden Films: Censorship Histories of 125 Motion Pictures, by Dawn Sova (New York: Facts on File, 2001) traces the efforts to censor 125 films, ranging from the silent *Birth of a Nation* to *Schlindler's List*. Entries are arranged alphabetically by film title and include production details such as country and date of production, distribution, format, running time, director, writer, awards, genre, and cast. A summary of the film's plot is followed by a description of its censorship history. Each entry concludes with a short bibliography for further reading.

Spout.com. This site hosts a user-created censorship movie list, where members used the tag censorship to describe ninety-one movies that are about, contain, or are related to censorship. **www.spout.com/members/ o/tags/censorship/MemberTagFilms.aspx**

Video Sourcebook (Gale, edition 46, 2010). Includes subject index for more than 160,000 items, *Books Under Fire; Censorship in a Free Society; Censorship or Selection: Choosing Books for Public Schools; The Designated Mourner; Dirty Pictures; Free Press, Fair Trial: Inside the Anonymous Source; Is It Easy to Be Young?; It' s Only Rock and Roll; Legacy of the Hollywood Blacklist; Life and Liberty . . . .For All Who Believe; See Evil;* and *What Johnny Can' t Read.* The *Sourcebook* gives complete ordering information, program description, release date, and other information.

Captivate
Readers, authors, & read-outs

A perilous past.
Organize a reading and discussion series. Your series could focus on books banned in the past year, or it might examine banned books throughout history or by topic (religion, politics, sex, etc.).

Famous phrases.
Invite authors and readers to speak out. At the Ossining (New York) Public Library, actor Alan Arkin and author Sol Stein participated in an evening of celebrity readings. Arkin read from *Catch-22* to a crowd of 250. At the Merrick (New York) Public Library patrons were invited to speak out against censorship by writing their own comments on sheets of newsprint beneath some famous quotes about censorship.

A realistic approach.
Hold a book discussion group with teenagers and their parents. Select banned titles that deal realistically with teens' issues. Have several people read each book. At the book discussion, have the teens discuss the book, followed by parents' reactions to the books and discussion by the teens. End the sessions with a brief description of the book selection policies and procedures for teens, stressing the importance of free access for young adults.

The rewards of reading.
Reward patrons who check out banned books during the week. The staff at the Dallas, Texas, Public Library gave library patrons gift certificates redeemable at a local bookstore each time a banned book was checked out.

A global perspective.
Form a banned books book club. The Malverne, N.Y. Public Library celebrated Banned Books Week by starting a Banned Books Book Club. Patrons were asked to discuss books from around the world that have been banned in the author's country of origin. The reading list included: *One Day in the Life of Ivan Denisovich*, by Aleksandr Isayevich Solzhenitzyn for Russia; *This Earth of Mankind*, by Ananta Pramoedya Toer for Indonesia; *Spycatcher*, by Peter Wright for England; *Madame Bovary*, by Gustave Flaubert for France; *Brave New World*, by Aldous Huxley for England; *The Sorrows of Young Werther*, by Goethe for Germany; *Blood Wedding*, by Federico Garcia Lorca for Spain; and *Ulysses*, by James Joyce for Ireland.

Tips for Organizing a Read-out

Nanette Perez
Program Officer, ALA Office for
Intellectual Freedom

In celebration of Banned Books Week, the American Library Association hosts a "Read-out"—an event featuring the continuous reading of books banned and challenged. The tradition began in 2002 on the steps of the entrance of ALA Headquarters in Chicago, Ill. In later years, it was held in Pioneer Plaza, along Chicago's Magnificent Mile, and in Chicago's Bughouse Square, one of the most celebrated outdoor free-speech centers in the nation.

Over the years, dozens of frequently challenged authors have attended and helped shed light on the ongoing and troubling efforts to ban books and ideas. Local celebrities read from their favorite banned/challenged books. Entertainers performed passages from a banned/challenged book and musicians performed censored music as a way to enhance the event.

The following are some tips on how to host a Read-out of your own:

● **Set a date and time.**
The ALA Read-out kicks off Banned Books Week on the first Saturday of the week, but any day of the week will work. If you cannot host one during Banned Books Week, no need to worry. Any day of the year is a good day to exercise your freedom to read banned and challenged books.

● **Find a location.**
Judith F. Krug, founder and former director of the Office for Intellectual Freedom, insisted that the ALA Read-out be held outdoors to entice passersby to participate. You can host a Read-out on the steps of your local public library or outside your favorite bookstore. Parks work as well. The most important part of finding a location is asking for permission to use the space and acquiring any necessary permits. Also, find a space for a "green room"—an area to accommodate readers while they are not on stage. We reserve a space for a green room with snacks and beverages for our featured authors and guests to enjoy and relax before the event begins.

● **Set a budget.**
You'll need funds to rent equipment, purchase refreshments for the event, and print flyers to market the event. Libraries and bookstores with larger budgets might invite our-of-town speakers, while those with more limited resources can focus on local celebrities or prominent citizens.

● **Get co-sponsors.**
The McCormick Freedom Project and the Newberry Library have co-sponsored ALA's Read-out. Co-sponsors can help market, fund, and set up the event. This is a great way for them to promote their mission, too. Consider asking local restaurants to co-sponsor the event by having them donate food for the green room.

● **Invite banned/challenged authors.** If your local library or school has faced a challenge to a particular book, why not invite the author to attend? Many authors have their own Web page or blog with information on how to contact them. All you need to do is search for them online. You may also contact their publisher for information on how to contact them. If you can afford to fly an author in, you may want to host a book signing after the event. Book signings not only allow people to meet their favorite banned/challenge author, but help the author get their ideas out there, too.

● **Invite local celebrities to read from their favorite banned/challenged book.**
Invite the mayor, local authors, city council members, or any other prominent member of your community. Ask them to pick one of their favorite banned/challenged books from *Banned Books* and explain why it's their favorite book and why it should not be banned or challenged.

● **Invite performers and/or musicians.**
Ask a local theater troupe to perform a selection from a banned/challenged book or play.
You may also invite a musician to perform censored music as a way to boost audience energy.

● **Find an emcee.**

Ask a fun, lively person to be the master of ceremonies. The ALA Executive Director, Keith Michael Fiels, has been our emcee as well as frequently challenged/banned author, Chris Crutcher. They both helped make the event more successful.

● **Rent a stage, audio equipment, chairs, etc.**

If you plan to host the event outside, you must have the right kind of audio equipment as you will compete with outdoor noise like traffic, etc. We rent a tent in case of inclement weather as well as chairs for our audience members.

● **Create a schedule of the day's event.**

Our event lasts three hours, and we typically ask that each person limit their time to eight minutes. We also ask them what time would suit them best for their schedule. When your program features a banned/challenged author, extend their time allottment to address the audience.

● **Promote the event.**

Promotion of the event is crucial to having a successful Read-out.

● A month or two before your Read-out, place ads in your local newspaper inviting people to come to the event.

● Make flyers and ask businesses to display them near the check-out counter or window. Place flyers on any community space available like bulletin boards in nearby coffee shops.

● If you have a Facebook account, create an event page to virally market the Read-out.

● If you use Twitter, send tweets to your followers.

● Send invitations through various e-lists.

● Post information on the event on online and print calendars in your area. You will need to check the deadlines of your local publications first.

● Invite local public school students to the Read-out. Suggest to high school English teachers to have their students attend and report on the event as a way for them to earn extra credit.

● Post your event on www.bannedbooksweek.org.

- **Invite local media to cover the event.**
The Read-out is a celebration of the freedom to read. With media attention, your message will reach a much wider audience, making more people aware of the importance of the freedom to read. Chicago Access Network Television records ALA's Read-out and airs it at various times after the event.

- **Ask for volunteers.**
Volunteers help make the event a success by helping set up, direct folks to places they need to be, and cleaning up afterwards.

- **Decorate the space for the event.**
We use banners and balloons to liven up the space.

- **Have fun!**
This is the most important aspect of hosting a Read-out. Even the best-laid plans sometimes encounter obstacles, so be flexible and follow through to ensure a successful event that everyone will enjoy.

- **Follow up after the event.**
Remember to send thank you letters to everyone who participated. You may also create a "goodie bag" containing fun stuff for participants to take home as a way to thank them. Consider using the "I Read Banned Books" tote bag as a give away. Tote bags and other Banned Books Week "goodies" are available for purchase through the ALA Store online at www.alastore.ala.org/.

If you're not organizing a Read-out of your own, please consider joining us in Chicago. For more information on ALA's Banned Books Week Read-out, please visit www.ala.org/bbooks.

Communicate

On the air, online, in print, & in lights

Keep in touch.
Visit our Web site at http://www.ala.org/bbooks.

Pressing issues.
Ask the student or community newspaper to devote an issue to Banned Books Week. Suggest editorials on the importance of the Bill of Rights, the Constitution, and students' rights.

Survey the situation.
Use readership surveys to point out the hazards of censorship. A serendipitous combination of promotions for a weeklong literacy celebration at the Carroll County Public Library, Maryland, and Banned Books Week resulted in an unprompted editorial in the local newspaper. As part of the literacy celebration, the library surveyed prominent citizens in the community on books that influenced their lives. When the list was published in the newspaper, it coincided with publicity on Banned Books Week from the People for the American Way. The editor noted that many of the "influential" books also were on the banned books list. His editorial "Literature's Worst Obscenity Is Banning, Burning Books" gave the library an added P.R. effort.

Airborne ideas.
Blow up Banned Books Week balloons. Print your message on helium strength balloons. Use for decoration and/or distribute at schools, shopping areas, programs, etc.

Provocative programs.
Schedule provocative speakers to focus on intellectual freedom issues. The Merrick Library, New York, scheduled the Honorable James Buchanan, former chairman of People for the American Way, to speak during Banned Books Week. Also during the week, a librarian from a nearby community spoke on her experience with the Secret Service.
The ALA Office for Intellectual Freedom can provide suggestions for speakers: phone: 800-545-2433, ext. 4223; e-mail: oif@ala.org.

Light up our rights.
Enlist the help of a local business that has an electronic bulletin board on its property.
The Algona, Iowa Public Library partnered with the Iowa State Bank to run a weeklong info-notice about Banned Books Week.

Powerful partners.
Work with other libraries in your area to develop a "united front" for Banned Books Week. Have each library responsible for one event, and schedule them to complement each other. A letter to the editor from four or five libraries, especially representing different constituencies, will be more effective than your library going it alone. Develop information packets that are available at all participating libraries, and say so in your press releases.

Now hear this.
Use the public address system in your school or library to communicate about Banned Books Week. A First Amendment quote at the beginning of the day, or at peak times, would certainly give your patrons something to think about. This idea was submitted by Shannon Van Kirk who successfully used a public address announcement at the St. Cecilia Academy in Nashville, Tenn.

Pumpkin power.
Prepare a speech. Many parents believe that Halloween promotes "evil" and should not be celebrated in schools. Research the origin of Halloween and prepare a persuasive speech about why it should or should not be celebrated by children.

On the air.
Dedicate one day's programming on your National Public Radio (NPR) station to Banned Books Week. For example, "Today's programming on [the name of the radio station] is made possible in part by [your name], who is celebrating this Banned Books Week by re-reading their favorite banned or frequently challenged book.

Wit and wisdom.
Get a daily dose of freedom from this thought-provoking desktop calendar. Each day's page features words of wisdom about the freedoms guaranteed to Americans in the First Amendment. You'll find memorable words to liven up your own written communication with quotes from everyone from Napoleon Bonaparte, Henry David Thoreau, and Thurgood Marshall to Woody Allen, Maureen Dowd, and Bill Gates. Price: $20. The Freedom Forum, 1207 18th Ave. S., Nashville, TN 37212; http://www. freedomforum.org/; e-mail: puborder@freedomforum.org. There are also several publications available to download free of charge.

Express yourself freely.
Purchase a variety of promotional materials (T-shirts, bumper stickers, and buttons) from the American Booksellers Foundation for Free Expression and speak your mind every time you use them. Contact the American Booksellers Foundation for Free Expression, 275 Seventh Ave., Ste. 1504, New York, NY 10001; phone: (212) 587-4025, ext. 12; fax: (212) 587-2436; e-mail: amyl@abffe.com; http://www.abffe.org.

Reach and teach.
Publicize the Bill of Rights with camera-ready art available from the Newspaper Association of America (NAA) Foundation, 4401 Wilson Blvd., Ste. 900, Arlington, VA 22203, fax: (571) 366-1195. The foundation's pamphlet "First Things First: Using the Newspaper to Teach the Five Freedoms of the First Amendment" available for download at www.naafoundation.org.

Create
Artifacts, apparel, & actors

Bag it.
Print the message of Banned Books Week on bags to use during the week. The Camden County (New Jersey) College Library Learning Resource Center and the Merrick (New York) Library used the bag to enclose all materials checked out that week.

Great give-aways.
Give away gags imprinted with the titles of banned books. The gags also could be worn as arm-bands as in mourning, e.g., "Censorship = the death of ideas."

Wear it.
Wear a bright red "I read banned books." button sold by the American Society of Journalists and Authors, 1501 Broadway, Suite 302, New York, NY 10036; phone: (212) 997-0947; fax: (212) 937-2315; http://www.asja.org. 1—10, $1 each; 11--50, 75¢ each; 51—100, 50¢ each; 101—1000, 40¢ each; 1001+, 30¢ each. Or wear the First Amendment on a T-shirt. Cranberry lettering on unbleached cotton, sizes L, XL, XXL; $10 each. Add $3.00 postage and handling each.

Air it.
Create radio spots. Improve the spot with music! Ask the radio station's technician/engineer/ disc jockey to help you select music and dub it into the radio spot. For example, one library used the theme from Dragnet for an effective attention-grabbing spot.

On the road.
Commission a local storyteller or theater group to prepare a dramatic rendition of banned or challenged books. Provide printed lists of appropriate material (books, videotapes, etc.) and take the show on the road—to schools, libraries, and community centers.

A little drama.
Present "Banned." Sigma Tau Delta, the International Honor Society at the University of Northern Colorado, created a collaboration of six directors and their individual ideas about censorship. It presents literature, poetry, musical lyrics, and drama that has been banned, censored or deemed dangerous by certain individuals.

Photoshop yourself.
Create an interesting photo for publicity. The North Salem Free Library in North Salem, New York, dressed three library employees in "prison garb" borrowed from the local barbershop chorus. The "prisoners" were shown reading banned books.

Present the past.
Organize a slide presentation to introduce Banned Books Week. Create slides that help teach and explain the meaning of freedom. The slides can show books written by or about persons who valued intellectual freedom. Examples could include: Thomas Jefferson, Benjamin Franklin, Maya Angelou, John Peter Zenger, Henry Thoreau, Judy Blume, James Baldwin, and Susan B. Anthony. Slides also could include clip art and book jackets. A mini slide show could easily be shown during a class or at a library, where it would be effective for large group presentations.

Table it.
Distribute and place table tent cards that promote the freedom to read in cafeterias, reading rooms and study halls in schools and libraries. The cards could even be personalized with a statement or story.

Sell well.
Create a yearlong public awareness campaign like the one developed at the After-Words new and used bookstore in Chicago. A shelf of banned books is on permanent display in a prominent area. In each of these books—and in many other banned books throughout the store—are custom-made bookmarks with the author and title of the book, reasons why the book was banned, and in what year. These citations are referenced from the Banned Books Week Resource Book. According to the owner, Beverly Dvorkin these "banned books" sell very, very well.

A quotable calendar.
Print a Banned Books Week calendar. The Merrick (New York) Library observed Banned Books Week by printing a calendar showing activities in the library, as well as holidays, events, etc. Each month of the calendar was illustrated with a quotation by a prominent artist, poet, philosopher, scientist, or statesman on the importance of the freedom to read. This Resource Book is a good source for quotations and clip art for your calendar.

Familiar favorites.
Distribute materials to high school students. The Paulsboro, New Jersey, High School librarian compiled a list of challenged and banned books that the students would recognize. These were distributed to English, History, and Civics classes along with a copy of the First Amendment and the editorial from the Banned Books Week kit.

Map it.
Use a periodical index to locate as many articles as possible regarding book challenges in schools in the United States in the past five years. Draw a map of the United States and color in the states where you found challenges. Which state has the most challenges? How have each of the cases been resolved?

Music with a message.
Write a ballad or a legend. Ballads and legends are often written about heroic people. For example, research John Peter Zenger's historic fight for First Amendment rights or select your favorite First Amendment advocate and write a ballad or a legend about him.

Educate
Imagination & intelligence

A thematic approach.

Include a study of banned books in your school's curriculum. Ruth Bauerle, Assistant Professor of English at Ohio Wesleyan University, planned a fall semester seminar on "Banned Books: From Judy Blume to Molly Bloom." The coursework consisted of six reading units and several individual and/or group projects. The six-week seminar began with a background lecture on laws (Constitution, court cases) governing "censorship," and case histories of book withdrawals from libraries.

The reading units were followed by class discussion of the controversial elements in each book, the positive or negative merits in each work, and whether each book met the court test of having social value. Role-playing was used in the first reading unit with students assuming the roles of a parent complaining about the book, a parent defending the right to read, the high school librarian, the high school English teacher, school board members, and high school students for and against the book.

The unit "themes" and titles were:

1) Young adult fiction—Judy Blume's *Are You There God? It's Me, Margaret*; *Deenie*; and *Tiger Eyes* and J. D. Salinger's *The Catcher in the Rye*.

2) Studs Terkel's *Working* was the second unit. As part of the study of this work, students were asked to "test" the common complaint of many dictionaries—including (or excluding) "bad" language. Students listed dirty, profane, and obscene expressions and then looked the words up in a variety of dictionaries.

3) National security censorship readings included: Victor Marchetti and John D. Marks, *The CIA and the Cult of Intelligence*; Philip Agee, *Inside the Company: CIA Diary*; and Frank Snepp, *Decent Interval*.

4) The fourth reading unit was on censored black writers. Bauerle explains this somewhat "illogical" grouping—the books were challenged or banned due to their content, not the color of the author—stating that the books provide realistic portrayals of the black experience and may have been censored because of the sordidness of that experience. Readings included Ralph Ellison, *Invisible Man*; Maya Angelou, *I Know Why the Caged Bird Sings*; Richard Wright, *Native Son*; and Gordon Park, *The Learning Tree*.

5) The class examined school texts (elementary - high school) for slanting, factual completeness, omissions in science and social science, e.g., creationism vs. evolution; controversial topics—women, minorities, Vietnam War, Watergate.

6) "Literary classics" that have been banned was the final unit and James Joyce's *Ulysses* was used. Group projects included interviewing librarians, county school superintendents, curriculum supervisors, and principals to see what censorship problems or complaints they've encountered and how the complaint was handled.

Individual projects included: researching a particular author or book (What has been the writer's experience with censorship? What was the writer's reaction? How many times has the book been challenged? Why was the book banned?). Students also could study a single censorship incident, e.g., the Island Trees case, the Louisiana creationism case, the Scopes trial, the Kanahwa County, the West Virginia controversy. In addition, students could examine positions taken by particular advocacy groups—People for the American Way, the ACLU, the American Family Association, the Family Research Council, the American Library Association, the American Booksellers Association, the Association of American Publishers, etc.

Critical inquiry.
Teach a Banned Books Course. Rebecca Godin, Alternative Community School, Ithaca, N.Y., uses First Amendment rights as a centerpiece for a course called "Banned Books." Each student under eighteen takes home a parent permission slip along with a syllabus describing course expectations, a list of books recommended for independent reading, assignments, and discussion topics. Although the course focuses on books banned in public schools, First Amendment issues in the arts and in society at large are explored.

Can citizens always exercise their First Amendment rights in our country today? Can students always exercise their First Amendment rights? Can these rights be taken too far? Should pornography be outlawed? Should violence and sex be limited on television or in the movies? Should rock music be censored? Should we allow advertisements for all products, even those that are harmful? Discussing these questions helps students find their own voices and sharpen their critical inquiry.

Some of the works discussed are *Howl*, by Allen Ginsberg, *The Catcher in the Rye*, some of Whitman's *Leaves of Grass, Soul on Ice,* by Eldridge Cleaver, Alice Walker's *The Color Purple*, and excerpts from the *Bible*. From the list of books banned in public schools and elsewhere, students choose one book to read independently for their position paper. They write a synopsis, then an analysis of why the book was banned, using the 1957 Supreme Court Roth-decision (*Lady Chatterley' s Lover*) triple test for prurient interest: (1) What is its effect on the average person? (2) Does it appeal to prurient or lustful interests? (3) Does it offend in the light of community standards?

The best approaches for teaching sexually explicit literature are the same ones used in any good teaching: critical thinking, enthusiasm, humor, and trust in each student's intelligence.

Initiate
Issues & inspiration

Editorial expertise.
Write an editorial for your local newspaper. For ideas on framing important issues for a general audience, read the following op-ed piece for publication written by Pat R. Scales, retired school librarian & author of *Teaching Banned Books: 12 Guides for Young Readers;* and *Protecting Intellectual Freedom in Your School Library: Scenarios from the Front Lines.*

Editorial: The Censorship War By Pat R. Scales
According to statistics gathered by the ALA Office for Intellectual Freedom and the National Coalition Against Censorship, book challenges are at an epidemic level in school and public libraries across the United States. What is amiss in this "land of the free?"

Is this "censorship war" about fear? control? power? How does this battle affect the education of our children? What kind of messages are we sending to them regarding their constitutional rights?

When I was in library school, there was a course called "Censorship." This course surveyed books such as *Portnoy's Complaint, Of Mice and Men,* and *The Catcher in the Rye.* This was in the days before Judy Blume, Robert Cormier, Stephen King, R.L. Stein, Katherine Paterson, and Alvin Schwartz. It was in the days when public libraries had more challenges than school libraries.

Most library school students took this censorship course for personal enjoyment. They never realized that fighting censorship could become a very real part of their job.

Today, the battle is raging, and public librarians and school media specialists are stumbling in their fight to win the war. Their enemies are organized groups of people, from the right and the left, who are determined to gain power over what students read and learn.

In some cities, library boards are under pressure to place ratings on books. In other places, students' names are tagged, at parental request, for restricted use of certain library materials. Frightened librarians are limiting young students to the "easy" books section, and they are requiring older students to bring written parental permission to read books such as Judy Blume's *Forever*, Katherine Paterson's *Bridge to Terabithia*, Mark Twain's *The Adventures of Huckleberry Finn*, Harper Lee's *To Kill a Mockingbird*, and Alice Walker's *The Color Purple.*

Professionals are self-censoring in the selection process, making every effort to make "safe" book choices. These practices, however, aren't eliminating the problem; they are only amplifying the issue.

The problem is obvious. Censors want to control the minds of the young. They are fearful of the educational system because students who read learn to think. Thinkers learn to see. Those who see often question.

The answer is the classroom. As educators, we cannot, for the sake of the students, allow ourselves to be bullied into diluting the curriculum into superficial facts. We must talk about the principles of intellectual freedom. We must challenge students to think about the intent of our forefathers when they wrote the *Bill of Rights.*

We must teach students about their First Amendment rights rather than restrict their use of particular books and materials. As educators, we must encourage students to express their own opinions while respecting the views of others.

Teachers, through interdisciplinary units of study, can lead students toward understanding the implications of the First Amendment for all Americans. As librarians and library media specialists, we must realize that our professional role extends beyond removing all restrictions and barriers from the library collection.

We can go into the classroom and engage students in activities and discussion that will enable them to think about their personal rights and responsibilities provided by the Constitution. The appropriate time to make this connection is when students are already engaged in a study of the Constitution.

Ask students to read and react to a contemporary young adult novel like Richard Peck's *The Last Safe Place on Earth*, Julian Thompson's *The Trials of Molly Sheldon*, or Stephanie Tolan's *Save Halloween* that deals with censorship issues. Invite them to apply the situations in the novel to real life.

Encourage them to debate the conflict presented in each novel. Provide a forum in which they can express their views regarding the subject of intellectual freedom. And, help them understand their personal options regarding the use of books and materials that might offend them. Above all, grant them the opportunity to think, to speak, and to be heard.

Classrooms and schools that foster this type of open atmosphere are sending a clear message: The First Amendment is important in school as well as in society at large.

The Censorship War Memorial, an exhibit prepared for Banned Books Week by Jill Sekula, a student in Education at Bowling Green State University, Ohio, lists books challenged or banned. The bottom of the "wall" reads "Dedicated to those wounded or killed in the war against Free Speech in the United States, which has been taking place since our country was born and will continue until we stop the madness."

Motivate

Quizzes, contests, & competition

Poster child.
Sponsor a poster contest for children illustrating the concept of free speech. Display the posters in your bookstore or library during Banned Books Week—Celebrating the Freedom to Read.

Say what you mean.
Co-sponsor an essay contest with the state library association, local school, or community group. Possible topics include "What the First Amendment means to me" or "What does freedom to read mean?" Contestants can include eighth-graders, junior or senior high students. Use local newspaper editors/journalists or university faculty as judges, and award banned books as prizes.

Brain teaser.
Sponsor a contest. Possibilities include matching quotes and titles of the banned books; matching titles and authors; selecting banned authors or titles from lists or displays of books. Make sure your selections reflect the literary quality of the works and inspire contestants to read them. Award banned books to the winners.

Run with it.
Kick off Banned Books Week with a fun run in your community. Print "Banned Books Week-The Censorship Challenge" race T-shirts for participants, volunteers and for sale to spectators. Keep the race distance short (under 3 miles) to involve as many people as possible. Check with your local running club on how to promote and organize the event. Or pick up a copy of the *Road Runners Club of America Handbook*, available for $28.50 member rate or $33.50 for nonmember (postage included) from RRCA, 1501 Lee Hwy., Ste. 140, Arlington, VA 22209;

phone: (703) 525-3890; e-mail: office@rrca.oeg; http://www.rrca.org.

Retail bounty.
Hunt for banned books throughout the business community. The Bernardsville, N.J., Public Library worked with local retail businesses of all kinds to develop a "treasure" hunt of banned books, hiding the titles in plain sight in the display windows and areas of the stores. Patrons were invited to make the rounds of the stores and list all titles they discovered. Participating businesses included flower shops, paint stores, jewelry stores, travel agencies, and many others.

That's the ticket.
Run a raffle that can be entered only by visiting your Banned Books display. The Honolulu, Hawaii, Community College bookstore donated a backpack for the raffle; students checked out the display and entered the contest.

Stop the presses.
Assign a research paper for students, such as: "Censorship and the Democratic Society"; "Banned Authors"; "The Various Forms of Censorship." Make arrangements for the local or school newspaper to print the best paper.

A winning quiz.
Plan a quick quiz. In Bound Brook, N.J., middle school and high school librarian Lillian Keating planned a contest to commemorate the week—a daily quiz from a list of books that have been challenged or removed from libraries. The winner of the quiz received a gift certificate to a local bookstore.

Quiz questions
The high school questions:

Monday
What is a popular book in many high school English classes by Harper Lee that has been banned or challenged?

Tuesday
What is the part of the Bill of Rights that guarantees the freedom of religion, speech, press, assembly, and petition?

Wednesday
Who is the author of *The Chocolate War*, a novel about peer pressure which was banned and challenged?

Thursday
What was one of the most challenged titles in 1995? *The Adventures of _____.*

Friday
John _____, one of America's most famous novelists, has had many titles, banned and challenged, and continues to be challenged frequently.

The middle school questions:

Monday
What was S. E. Hinton's famous novel? *The _____.*

Tuesday
A Light in the Attic and *Where the Sidewalk Ends* are frequently challenged. Who is the author?

Wednesday
Who wrote *Matilda*, a book found offensive for its disrespect for adults? _____

Thursday
What is the title of a spooky series that is often challenged? You may have read the stories when you were younger. _____

Friday
Who is the popular author of novels for young adults, such as *Forever and Deenie?* _____

Quiz answers
The high school answers:

Monday	*To Kill a Mockingbird*
Tuesday	First Amendment
Wednesday	Robert Cormier
Thursday	*The Adventures of Huckleberry Finn*
Friday	Steinbeck

The middle school answers:

Monday	*The Outsiders*
Tuesday	Shel Silverstein
Wednesday	Roald Dahl
Thursday	*Scary Stories to Tell in the Dark*
Friday	Judy Blume

Participate
Debate, discussion, & dialogue

A capitol idea.
Sponsor a day at the state capitol for students, teachers, community leaders, seniors, or other people to learn about the democratic process—work with organizations such as the League of Women Voters.

Memo to the mayor.
Encourage your governor, city council, and/or mayor to proclaim "Banned Books Week—Celebrating the Freedom to Read" in your state or community. For example, the state of Ohio and city of St. Louis did for the purpose of "informing our citizens as to the nature and magnitude of the threat censorship poses to our First Amendment rights of freedom of speech and press, the cornerstone of American liberty."

Speak-up sessions.
Sponsor a community forum. The forums serve both educational and participatory purposes. They allow the public to examine various aspects of the Constitution, its evolution, the underlying values involved, and its significance in contemporary society and to the individual citizen. By encouraging the audience to speak out on the constitutional issues, these sessions emphasize the citizen's role in the continuing development of the law. Organizers may choose from several different model formats, for example, mock legislative hearing, town hall meeting (Socratic discussion), mock trial, and debate.
For planning assistance use *Speaking & Writing Truth: Community Forums on the First Amendment*, by Robert S. Peck and Mary Manemann, published by the American Bar Association. The guide contains information on planning mock legislative hearings, mock trials or debates and provides detailed suggestions on getting started and six First Amendment issues with scripts and legal memoranda.

Sign on the line.
Reenact the signing of the Constitution. Follow with a discussion of the First Amendment and the rights it ensures.

Illuminate the issues.
Examine the role of the free press in contemporary society by hosting a community discussion. The Society of Professional Journalists' Project Sunshine will help with suggestions on topics and speakers for your area. For more information, contact Society of Professional Journalists' Project Sunshine, Eugene S. Pulliam National Journalism Center, 3909 N. Meridian St., Indianapolis, IN 46208; phone: 317-927-8000; fax: 317-920-4789; e-mail: spj@spj.org; http://www.spj.org.

At the forefront.
Join the Freedom to Read Foundation. The Foundation is dedicated to the legal and financial defense of intellectual freedom, especially in libraries. Since its establishment in 1969, the Foundation has stood at the forefront of nearly all major battles to defend the right to read. Your contribution will help the Freedom to Read Foundation preserve First Amendment freedoms by challenging those who would remove or ban materials from library collections, and establishing, through the courts, legal precedents on behalf of intellectual freedom principles. For more information, contact the Freedom to Read Foundation, 50 East Huron Street, Chicago, IL 60611; phone: 800-545-2433, ext. 4226; e-mail: ftrf@ala.org.

In the storefront.

Brown and Clark Booksellers in Mashpee, Massachusetts, held a "Whodunit/Duzzit" forum on censorship and book banning. Four local authors made presentations on self-censorship by authors, the role of "bestseller" lists and chain stores, and the future of electronic books. Coffee and snacks, e.g., *Chocolate War* Brownies and *Uncensored Salsa*, were served after the program. The bookstore had both in-store and window displays profiling banned books.

Get it in writing.

Petition your neighbors and politicians to challenge censorship and cooperate with all persons or groups that resist abridgment of free expression and free access to ideas. In Connecticut, several hundred signatures were obtained on a petition protesting censorship, which was then sent to the governor, state representatives, and members of the U.S. Congress.

Artists and authors.

Work with the local arts council to develop a proposal for Banned Books Week (BBW). Present the proposal well in advance of BBW to potential supporting agencies that might provide some funds for BBW programs and activities, especially if BBW is community-wide in focus, and multi-disciplinary in nature. The Hartland Art Council in Michigan successfully combined an "Authors Live at the Library" program with a banned books theme.

A battle at the border.

Support the legal battle of the Little Sisters Bookstores and other gay and lesbian Canadian stores. Since the 1980s, the stores have been waging an expensive legal battle with the Canadian government for seizing and confiscating books at the Canadian borders. To raise funds, they have published *Forbidden Passages: Writings Banned in Canada*, excerpts from a number of the confiscated materials. In the United States, the book can be obtained from Cleis Press, 2246 Sixth St., Berkeley, CA 94710; phone: 800-780-2279; phone: 510-845-8001; fax: 510- 845-8001; http://www.cleispress.com.

Be the book.

March in a community parade. Staff at the Parlin-Ingersoll Library in Canton, Illinois, celebrated Banned Books Week by marching in the Friendship Festival parade dressed as famous banned books, with Dawn Ward as *Charlotte's Web*. Other Banned Books Week activities included the creation of a Banned Book Club, book discussions for children, and the distribution of an annotated list of banned books with the "hot books" logo.

Material matters.

Contact the Constitutional Rights Foundation (601 South Kingsley Drive, Los Angeles, CA 90005; phone: 213-487-5590; fax: 213-386-0459; http://www.crf-usa.org for a catalog of materials on the U.S. Constitution and Bill of Rights, or visit the Web site for a series of free online lessons.

Ask around.

Conduct a poll. The *Goosebumps* and *Fear Street* series, by R. L. Stine, are among the most censored books in the United States today. Conduct a poll of twenty-five adults asking them if and why they feel scary stories are harmful to children and teenagers. Then, poll twenty-five teenagers, asking them the same question. Make a visual contrasting the results of each poll.

Communication Guide

Introduction

Library policies and decisions often are challenged by individuals and groups concerned about the availability of a wide variety of library materials to everyone.

Addressing these challenges requires a balance of carefully crafted library policy, knowledge and understanding of intellectual freedom principles, and sensitivity to community needs and concerns. It also requires effective communication. The following suggestions were prepared to help if such challenges arise.

Communicating Effectively

A few simple communication techniques can go a long way toward defusing emotion and clearing up misunderstanding. The library staff should be trained in procedures for handling complaints and understanding the importance of treating all people with respect. The goal is to resolve complaints informally whenever possible.

One on one

- Greet the person with a smile. Communicate your openness to receive inquiries and that you take them seriously. Listen more than you talk.

- Practice "active listening." Take time to really listen and acknowledge the individual's concern. This can be as simple as "I'm sorry you're upset. I understand your concern."

- Stay calm and courteous. For example, upset parents are not likely to be impressed by talk about the First Amendment or *Library Bill of Rights*. Talk about freedom of choice, the library's role in serving all people and the responsibility of parents to supervise their own children's library use. Avoid library jargon such as intellectual freedom.

- Distribute facts, policy, and other background materials in writing to all interested parties. Avoid giving personal opinions.

- Be prepared to give a clear and non-intimidating explanation of the library's procedure for registering a complaint and be clear about when a decision can be expected.

Dealing with the media

When a challenge occurs, realize it may attract media attention. How effectively you work with the media may well determine how big the story becomes and will help to shape public opinion.

Some suggestions:

Have one spokesperson for the library. Make sure that reporters, library staff, and the members of the board know who this is. Make it clear that no one other than this spokesperson should express opinions on behalf of the library.

Prepare carefully for any contacts with the media. Know the most important message you want to deliver and be able to deliver it in twenty-five words or less. You will want to review your library's borrowing and collection development policies and the American Library Association's *Library Bill of Rights*.

Practice answering difficult questions out loud. You may wish to invest in a session with a professional media consultant. The American Library Association offers this training at Annual Conferences.

Keep to the high ground—no matter what. Don't mention the other side by name, either personal or corporate. Be careful to speak in neutral terms. Name calling and personalization are great copy for reporters but create barriers to communication.

Do not let yourself be put on the defensive. Stay upbeat, positive—"Libraries are vital to democracy. We are very proud of the service our library provides." If someone makes a false statement, gently but firmly respond: "That's absolutely incorrect. The truth is the vast majority of parents find the library an extremely friendly, safe place for their children. We receive many more compliments from parents than we do complaints."

Be prepared to tell stories or quote comments from parents and children about how the library has helped them.

Be strategic in involving others. For instance, board members, friends of libraries, community leaders, teachers, and other supporters can assist by writing letters to the editor or an opinion column, or meeting with a newspaper editorial board or other members of the media.

More tips

The following tips apply both when dealing with the media and when speaking to other audiences—community groups, trustees, staff:

- Never repeat a negative. Keep your comments upbeat and focused on service.

- Keep it simple. Avoid professional jargon. Try to talk in user-friendly terms your audience can relate to: Freedom of choice—not the *Library Bill of Rights*. "People with concerns" or "concerned parents"—not censors.

- Ask questions. Find out what the approach is, whether there will be someone with an opposing view present. If you do not feel qualified to address the question or are uncomfortable with the approach, say so. Suggest other angles ("The real issue is freedom of choice. . .")

- Be clear whom you represent—yourself or your library.

- Know your audience. Make sure you know which newspaper, radio, or TV station you're dealing with and who the audience is—whether they're parents, seniors, teenagers; their ethnic background, religious affiliation, and anything else that will help you focus your remarks.

- Anticipate the standard "Who-What-When-Where and Why" questions and develop your answers beforehand. Keep your answers brief and to the point. Avoid giving too much information. Let the reporter ask the questions.

- Beware of manipulation. Some reporters may ask leading questions, something like, "Isn't it true that . . . ?" Make your own statement.

- Don't rush. Pause to think about what you want to say and the best way to say it. Speak deliberately. It will make you sound more thoughtful and authoritative.

- Don't be afraid to admit you don't know. "I don't know" is a legitimate answer. Reporters do not want incorrect information. Tell them you'll get the information, and call back.

- Provide handouts with copies of relevant policies, statistics, other helpful information. You also may want to provide a written copy of your statement.

- Never say "No comment." A simple "I'm sorry I can't answer that" will suffice.

- Remember, nothing is "off the record." Assume that anything you say could end up on the front page or leading the news broadcast.

It's not just what you say

How you look and the tone of your voice can be as important as what you say—especially on radio and TV or before a live audience.

You want to sound and look professional, but also friendly and approachable. Studies have shown audiences are more likely to trust and believe you if they like how you look and sound.

Smile when you're introduced, if someone says something funny, if you want to show your enthusiasm for all the good things that your library is doing. On the flip side, be sure not to smile when you—or others—are making a serious point.

Dress and make up appropriately. There are many articles and books on what works for TV and speaking appearances.

On radio, use your voice as a tool to express your feelings—concern, enthusiasm, and empathy. A smile can be "heard" on the radio.

Don't panic if you misspeak. Simply say, "I'm sorry, I forgot what I was going to say." Or, "I'm sorry I was confused. The correct number is..." To err is human, and audiences are very forgiving of those who confess—but don't agonize over—their mistakes.

Sample questions and answers

The following questions provide sample language to use when answering questions from the media and other members of the public. You will want to personalize your remarks for your library and community. Remember, keep it simple. Keep it human.

What is the role of libraries in serving children?

The same as it is for adults. Libraries provide books and other materials that will meet a wide range of ages and interests. Many libraries have special areas for children and teenagers. They also have many special programs, such as preschool story-hour, movies, puppet shows, and term paper clinics. In fact, more children participate in summer reading programs at libraries than play Little League baseball!

Why don't libraries restrict certain materials based on age like movie theaters or video stores?

Movie theaters and video stores are private businesses and can make their own policies. Libraries are public institutions. They cannot limit access on the basis of age or other characteristics. Our library does provide copies of movie reviews and ratings, and we encourage parents to use them in guiding their children's library use.

How do libraries decide what to buy?

Every library has its own policies that are approved by its own board. Our library has adopted the *Library Bill of Rights*. We also have a mission statement that says our goal is to serve a broad range of community needs. Librarians are taught as part of their professional education to evaluate books and other materials and to select materials based on library policies.

What is the *Library Bill of Rights*?

The *Library Bill of Rights* is a policy statement adopted by the American Library Association to protect the right of all library users to choose for themselves what they wish to read or view. The policy is more than fifty years old and has been adopted voluntarily by most libraries as a way of ensuring the highest quality library service to their communities.

Does that mean a child can check out *Playboy* or other materials intended for adults?
We believe in freedom of choice for all people, but we also believe in common sense. It would be extremely unusual for a young child to check out that type of adult material. And there are librarians to provide assistance. We also provide suggested reading lists to help them make appropriate choices. Our goal is to provide the best possible service for young people, and we are very proud of what we offer. If you haven't been to our library recently, we encourage you to come down and see for yourself!

What should I do if I find something I don't approve of in the library?
Libraries offer a wide range of materials, and not everyone is going to like or approve of everything. If you have a concern, simply ask to speak to a librarian. We do want to know your concerns, and we're confident we have or can get materials that meet your needs. The library also has a formal review process if you wish to put your concern in writing.

What does the library do if someone complains about something in its collection?
We take such concerns very seriously. First, we listen. We also have a formal review process in which we ask you to fill out a special form designed to help us understand your concerns. Anyone who makes a written complaint will receive a written response.

What can parents do to protect their children from materials they consider offensive?
Visit the library with your child. If that's not possible, ask to see the materials your child brings home. Set aside a special shelf for library materials. If there are materials on it you don't approve of, talk with your children about why you would rather they not read or view them. Most libraries provide suggested reading lists for various ages. And librarians are always glad to advise children and parents on selecting materials we think your child would enjoy and find helpful.

I pay tax dollars to support the library. Why shouldn't I be able to control what my kids are exposed to?
You can control what your children are exposed to simply by going with them to visit the library or supervising what they bring home. The library has a responsibility to serve all taxpayers, including those you may not agree with—or who may not agree with you. We believe parents know what's best for their children, and each parent is responsible for supervising his or her child.

Key messages
When responding to a challenge, you will want to focus on three key points:

- Libraries provide ideas and information across the spectrum of social and political views.

- Libraries are one of our great democratic institutions. They provide freedom of choice for *all* people.

- Parents are responsible for supervising their own children's library use.

These simple, but sometimes overlooked essentials are the bulwark against challenges.

Public Libraries
An ounce of prevention is worth a pound of cure. Make sure all library staff and board members understand the library's policies and procedures for dealing with challenges. Provide customer service and other human relations training that will help staff deal effectively with sensitive matters.

Tips for directors

- Make sure you have an up-to-date selection policy, reviewed regularly by the appropriate governing board, which includes a request for reconsideration form. It should apply to all library materials equally. If you do not have such a policy, samples are available from your regional library system, the state library, and the ALA Library and Research Center.

- As a public institution, the library must develop and implement all policies within the legal framework that applies to it. Have your policies reviewed regularly by the library's legal counsel for compliance with federal and state constitutional requirements, federal and state civil rights legislation, and other applicable federal and state legislation, including confidentiality legislation and applicable case law.

- Have the request for reconsideration form available at your major service desks and at all your branch facilities.

- Work with your trustees to ensure that they know and understand the library's policies. Institute formal education procedures so all library trustees have the same information.

- Model the behavior you want your staff to practice. When confronted by an individual or representative of an organization that wants an item or items removed or reclassified, listen closely and carefully to what is being said (and what is not). Respect that person's right to have an opinion, and empathize. Keep the lines of communication open to the greatest possible extent.

- Work with your frontline staff (children's librarians, reference librarians, circulation, branch, bookmobile and support staff) to make sure they understand the library's policies. Help them to understand that they are responsible for implementing the library's policy, not their personal beliefs, while they are on duty. Make this a part of customer service training for your staff.

- Have an ongoing public relations program to communicate the many ways your library serves all members of the community, especially families.

- Build a solid working relationship with your local media before controversy arises. Provide them with upbeat, positive stories about what the library is doing, especially in the area of children's services.

- Put key contacts on your library mailing list. The time to build these relationships is before you need them.

- Hit the talk circuit. Every social, fraternal and religious organization that meets regularly needs speakers for its meetings. This is your opportunity to reach leaders and opinion makers in your community and to build a support network.

Tips for trustees

- First, remember your role. As a library trustee, you have a responsibility to speak your mind and to argue forcibly for your point of view within the forum of the board. Once the board has made a decision, it is your responsibility to support the decision of the majority. If you disagree for whatever reason, do not speak out publicly. If, for reasons of conscience, you feel you cannot be silent, it is best to resign from the board before making your opposition public.

- Work with your library director to ensure the necessary policies are in place and reviewed regularly and thoroughly. Review and affirm your library's selection policy annually and make sure it is followed carefully.

- Insist that the entire board understands the library's collection policy and that it be involved in reviewing and reaffirming this policy annually.

- Be an effective advocate for the library. Use your contacts in the community to educate and mobilize others in support of the library.

- Bring what you hear back to the library director. Your roots in the community may be much deeper and of longer duration than those of the director. The things that people will tell you but they won't tell a director can provide valuable feedback.

- Be involved with the professional state and national organizations serving library trustees.

- Remember the roots of the word "trustee." The community has placed its trust in you to act as an effective steward for the library. This means representing the interests of the entire community, not just a vocal minority.

Tips for children's and young adult librarians

- Make sure you and your staff are familiar with the library's collection policy and can explain it in a clear, easily understandable way.

- Take time to listen to and empathize with a parent's concern. Explain in a non-defensive way the need to protect the right of all parents to determine their own children's reading.

- Keep your director informed of any concerns expressed, whether you feel they have been successfully resolved or not.

- Join professional organizations to keep abreast of issues and trends in library service to children and families.

- Encourage parents or guardians to participate in choosing library materials for their young people and to make reading aloud a family activity. Host storytelling, book discussion groups and other activities that involve adults and youth.

- Offer "parent education" programs/workshops throughout the year. National Library Week in April, Teen Read Week in October, and Children's Book Week in November provide timely opportunities. Suggested topics: how to select books and other materials for youth; how to raise a reader; how books and other materials can help children and teens cope with troubling situations; the importance of parents being involved in their children's reading and library use; concepts of intellectual freedom.

- Reach out to the media. Offer to write a newspaper column or host a radio or TV program discussing good books and other materials for children and teens. Give tips for helping families get the most from libraries.

- Build bridges. Offer to speak to parent and other groups on what's new at the library, good reading for youth, how to motivate children and teens to read, how to make effective use of the library, and other topics of special interest.

- Participate in statewide sponsored summer reading programs, e.g., in Illinois—the IREAD (Illinois Reading Enrichment and Development) summer reading program. This program builds the whole family's enthusiasm for reading by involving parents and children of all ages in a variety of summer reading programs and events. Reading programs encourage children to develop an appreciation of reading that will serve them throughout their lives, and their parents will become familiar with the library and its collection.

School Libraries

School librarians play a key role in making sure that students have the broad range of resources and ideas they need to develop critical thinking skills. Challenges to materials provide a "teachable moment" that can help you build understanding and support for the principles of intellectual freedom, including First Amendment rights, student rights of access and professional ethics.

Applying the principles of intellectual freedom

- Connect academic freedom with intellectual freedom. Academic freedom guarantees the teacher's right to teach and to select classroom and library resources for instruction.

- Make sure everyone involved understands the right of people in a democratic society to express their concerns and that all people have the right to due process in the handling of their complaints.

- Explain the obligation of the school district to provide intellectual and physical access to resources that provide for a wide range of abilities and differing points of view.

- Define intellectual and physical access when appropriate. Intellectual access includes the right to read, receive and express ideas and the right to acquire skills to seek out, explore and examine ideas. Physical access includes being able to locate and retrieve information unimpeded by fees, age limits, separate collections or other restrictions.

- Emphasize the need to place the principles of intellectual and academic freedom above personal opinion, and reason above prejudice, when selecting resources.

- Connect intellectual freedom and access. The freedom to express beliefs or ideas becomes meaningless when others are not allowed to receive or have access to those beliefs or ideas.

- Stress the need for teachers and librarians to be free to present students with alternatives and choices if students are to learn and use critical thinking and decision-making skills.

Protecting students and staff with a materials selection policy

- Update your materials selection policy. Include a formal reconsideration process for textbooks, gift materials, electronic and other resources used in classrooms, laboratories and libraries. Seek board of education approval.

- Be sure to include the educational goals of the school district and to relate the selection policy to these goals.

- Emphasize the positive role of the selection policy in clarifying the use of educational resources and in ensuring stability and continuity regardless of staff change.

- To ensure uniformity and fairness in dealing with complaints, delegate the responsibility for dealing with complaints and requests for reconsideration to the principal in each school.

- Inform all your school staff (including nurses, secretaries, cafeteria workers and custodians) about the materials selection policy and reconsideration process. Review the policy with staff at the beginning of each school year.

- Distribute a copy of the policy with a simple statement that explains its importance in protecting students, teachers and librarians against censorship.

Preparing for challenges

- Develop rationales for the use of required materials in each department and/ or grade.

- Introduce the rationales at Parent's Night or open houses or through the school newsletter to help parents understand what materials are being taught and why.

- Work with administrators, teachers and librarians to prepare a list of alternative materials for instructional activities.

- Prepare a packet of materials, including the school district's educational goals and materials selection policy, to give to those registering concerns.

- Review all policies dealing with access to ensure that school rules are conducive to free and open access to the library.

- Prepare an audiocassette, CD or DVD that explains principles of intellectual and academic freedom contained in the materials selection policy and reconsideration process for staff members to listen to at home or in their car.

- Inform staff and board members that complaints and requests for reconsideration made by them will get the same due process as from a parent or community member.

- Engage students in discussions and activities related to intellectual freedom. An educated and informed student body can provide a strong support group for the school when educational resources are challenged.

- Remind school administrators that to ignore or override a board-approved materials selection policy can place them in legal jeopardy.

- Unite with other groups in your community that are concerned with intellectual freedom issues. Make them aware of the rights of children and young adults. Educate administrators, teachers and other school personnel to the importance of the school library and the role it plays in the education of the student as part of in-service training.

Helping everyone understand the reconsideration process

- Be clear that materials under reconsideration will not be removed from use, or have access restricted, pending completion of the reconsideration process.

- Emphasize that parents can request only that their child be denied access to materials being reconsidered.

- Develop a time frame to guide the reconsideration process. For example, the building principal should act within 20 working days.

- Emphasize that the reconsideration process is to collect information in order to make thoughtful decisions.

- Keep careful and accurate records of all requests for reconsideration, even those settled informally.

- Report all requests for reconsideration to the superintendent and other staff members. It is important to demonstrate the ability and commitment to protect the rights of students and staff and still provide due process for those registering their concern.

- Provide clear instruction to the appointed reconsideration committee. Have the committee focus on principles rather than attempt to define or interpret materials or parts of materials.

- Keep the request for reconsideration form uncomplicated and non-threatening.

- Direct the reconsideration committee to prepare a report presenting both majority and minority opinions. Present the report to the principal when the process is completed.

- Keep staff and administrators informed about the reconsideration process and progress toward resolution. Rumors and speculation can distort everyone's perceptions of the situation.

- Explain the benefits of a board-approved materials selection policy, which guides staff in the selection of materials and minimizes the arbitrary and personal element. Such a policy also clarifies to the community how the school decides what materials will be used.

- Inform the ALA's Office for Intellectual Freedom of all challenges to materials in your library's collection.

Part 6
Incidents

"You don't have to burn books to destroy a culture. Just get people to stop reading them."
Ray Bradbury, U.S. science fiction writer (1920–)

To reach their readers, authors and publishers count on librarians, educators, and booksellers to make books openly available to everyone — patrons, students, and customers. But when censors successfully intervene, readers are denied access to the books that some people consider dangerous.

Incidents documents the accumulation of book-by-book attempts to erode our freedom to read in libraries and schools across America.

(out of 460 Challenges)

ttyl; ttfn; l8r, g8r series

Lauren Myracle

Reasons:
Drugs, Nudity, Offensive Language, Sexually Explicit, Unsuited to Age Group

And Tango Makes Three

Peter Parnell and Justin Richardson

Reason:
Homosexuality

The Perks of Being a Wallflower

Stephen Chbosky

Reasons:
Anti-Family, Drugs, Homosexuality, Offensive Language, Religious Viewpoint, Sexually Explicit, Suicide, Unsuited to Age Group

To Kill A Mockingbird

Harper Lee

Reasons:
Offensive Language, Racism, Unsuited to Age Group

Twilight series

Stephenie Meyer

Reasons:
Religious Viewpoint, Sexually Explicit, Unsuited to Age Group

Catcher in the Rye

J.D. Salinger

Reasons:
Offensive Language,
Sexually Explicit,
Unsuited to Age Group

My Sister's Keeper

Jodi Picoult

Reasons:
Drugs, Homosexuality,
Offensive Language, Religious
Viewpoint, Sexism, Sexually
Explicit, Suicide, Unsuited
to Age Group, Violence

The Earth, My Butt, and Other Big, Round Things

Carolyn Mackler

Reasons:
Offensive Language,
Sexually Explicit,
Unsuited to Age Group

The Color Purple

Alice Walker

Reasons:
Offensive Language,
Sexually Explicit,
Unsuited to Age Group

The Chocolate War

Robert Cormier

Reasons:
Nudity, Offensive Language,
Sexually Explicit,
Unsuited to Age Group

[1] As compiled by the Office for Intellectual Freedom, American Library Association. The Office for Intellectual Freedom does not claim comprehensiveness in recording challenges. Research suggests that for each challenge reported there are as many as four or five which go unreported.

Challe
or Bar
Books

enged
nned
s

This "List of Challenged or Banned Books" is a compilation of actual or attempted bannings, over the centuries, worldwide. All entries are books published in the English language and emphasis is on recent U.S. incidents involving popular titles. This list of books was compiled from the following sources:

1. Bald, Margaret
Literature Suppressed on Religious Grounds, **Rev. ed.**
New York, N.Y.: Facts on File, 2006.

2. Geller, Evelyn
Forbidden Books in American Public Libraries, 1876–1939: A Study in Cultural Change
Westport, Conn.: Greenwood Pr., 1984.

3. Green, Jonathon
The Encyclopedia of Censorship
New York, N.Y.: Facts On File, 1990.

4. Haight, Anne Lyon, and Chandler B. Grannis
Banned Books, 387 B.C. to 1978 A.D., **4th ed.**
New York, N.Y.: Bowker Co., 1978.

5. *Index on Censorship*
London: Writers and Scholars International, Ltd., published bimonthly.

6. Jones, Derek, ed.
Censorship: A World Encyclopedia. **4 vols.**
Chicago: Fitzroy Dearborn, 2001.

7. Karolides, Nicholas J.
Literature Suppressed on Political Grounds, **Rev. ed.**
New York, N.Y.: Facts on File, 2006.

8. Karolides, Nicholas J., Margaret Bald, and Dawn B. Sova. *120 Banned Books: Censorship Histories of World Literature*, **Rev. ed.**
New York, N.Y.: Checkmark Books, 2005.

9. *Limiting What Students Shall Read: Books and Other Learning Materials in Our Public Schools: How They Are Selected and How They Are Removed*
Report on a survey sponsored by Association of American Publishers, American Library Association, Association for Supervision and Curriculum Development. Washington, D.C.: Association of American Publishers, 1981.

10. Nelson, Randy F.
"Banned in Boston and Elsewhere." In
The Almanac of American Letters.
Los Altos, Calif.: William Kaufmann, Inc., 1981.

11. *Newsletter on Intellectual Freedom*
Chicago, Ill.: American Library Association, Intellectual Freedom Committee, published bimonthly.

12. O'Neil, Robert M.
Classrooms in the Crossfire: The Rights and Interests of Students, Parents, Teachers, Administrators, Librarians, and the Community
Bloomington, Ind.: Indiana University Pr., 1981.

13. Sova, Dawn B.
Literature Suppressed on Sexual Grounds, **Rev. ed.**
New York, N.Y.: Facts on File, 2006.

14. Sova, Dawn B.
Literature Suppressed on Social Grounds, Rev. ed.
New York, N.Y.: Facts on File, 2006.

15. Tebbel, John
A History of Book Publishing in the United States
New York, N.Y.: Bowker Co., 1981.

This compilation is admittedly incomplete because it is impossible to document and record all prohibitions against free speech and expression. In fact, this list is limited to books and therefore does not include prohibitions against magazines, newspapers, films, broadcasts, plays, performances, exhibits, or access to electronic resources. The professional, economic, or emotional consequences of the curtailment of an author's free expression also are not documented.

At the 1986 American Library Association (ALA) Annual Conference, the ALA Intellectual Freedom Committee adopted the following operative definitions of some terms frequently used to describe the various levels of incidents that may or may not lead to censorship. This terminology is employed by the *Newsletter on Intellectual Freedom*.

Expression of Concern

An inquiry that has judgmental overtones.

Oral Complaint

An oral challenge to the presence and/or appropriateness of the material in question.

Written Complaint

A formal, written complaint filed with the institution (library, school, etc.) challenging the presence and/or appropriateness of specific material.

Public Attack

A publicly disseminated statement challenging the value of the material, presented to the media and/or others outside the institutional organization in order to gain public support for further action.

Censorship

A change in the access status of material, made by a governing authority or its representatives. Such changes include: exclusion, restriction, removal, or age/grade level changes.

New designates incidents added since the previous edition of this publication in May 2007.

In this bibliography, the following postal code abbreviations for states are used:

State or Territory	Abbreviation
Alabama	AL
Alaska	AK
Arizona	AZ
Arkansas	AR
California	CA
Colorado	CO
Connecticut	CT
Delaware	DE
District of Columbia	DC
Florida	FL
Georgia	GA
Hawaii	HI
Idaho	ID
Illinois	IL
Indiana	IN
Iowa	IA
Kansas	KS
Kentucky	KY
Louisiana	LA
Maine	ME
Maryland	MD
Massachusetts	MA
Michigan	MI
Minnesota	MN
Mississippi	MS
Missouri	MO
Montana	MT
Nebraska	NE
Nevada	NV
New Hampshire	NH
New Jersey	NJ
New Mexico	NM
New York	NY
North Carolina	NC
North Dakota	ND
Ohio	OH
Oklahoma	OK
Oregon	OR
Pennsylvania	PA
Puerto Rico	PR
Rhode Island	RI
South Carolina	SC
South Dakota	SD
Tennessee	TN
Texas	TX
Utah	UT
Vermont	VT
Virginia	VA
Washington	WA
West Virginia	WV
Wisconsin	WI
Wyoming	WY

1 **Abelard, Pierre**
Introduction to Theology

1121 The Catholic Church condemned and burned his work in 1121. In 1140, he was charged with heresy, confined to a monastery, and forbidden to continue writing.

1559 Listed on the *Index Librorum Prohibitorum* (Index of Prohibited Books). Also listed in 1564 along with all of his writings. The French theologian, poet, and teacher is best known for his tragic love affair with Heloise, his pupil, and for the love letters he wrote to her after he entered a monastery and she became a nun.

1930 U.S. Customs lifted ban on *The Love Letters of Heloise and Abelard*.

Source: 1, pp. 163–65; 4, p. 6; 6, pp. 2–3.

2 **Abernathy, Rev. Ralph D.**
And the Walls Came Tumbling Down

1989 CO Burned in protest in Denver because it alleges that Martin Luther King, Jr. was involved with three women. E. Napoleon Walton, publisher of the *Denver Cosmopolitan Advertiser*, stated, "[Abernathy] has his freedom of speech, and we have our freedom to burn it."

Source: 11, Jan. 1990, p. 19.

3 **Abrahams, Roger D.**
African Folktales: Traditional Stories of the Black World

1991 TX Dallas school administrators told teachers to rip an offending page from the school textbooks because the story, which refers to male genitals and bodily functions, didn't fit the curriculum. Instructors were also asked to avoid teaching the first two chapters of another book that dealt in part with circumcision and puberty.

Source: 11, Nov. 1991, p. 197.

4 **Adams, Carmen**
The Band

1998 IA Challenged, but retained at the Madison Elementary School in Cedar Rapids.

Source: 11, May 1998, pp. 87–88.

5 **Adler, C. S.**
Down by the River

1983 WA Removed from the Evergreen School District of Vancouver along with twenty-nine other titles. The American Civil Liberties Union of Washington filed suit contending that the removals constituted censorship, a violation of plaintiff's rights to free speech and due process, and the acts were a violation of the state Open Meetings Act because the removal decisions were made behind closed doors.

Source: 11, Nov. 1983, pp. 185–86.

6 **Adler, C. S.**
The Shell Lady's Daughter

2007 WY Challenged, but retained at the Campbell County junior high school libraries in Gillette despite "objectionable subjects: sexual relations between teenagers, sexual thoughts, promiscuity, masturbation, deceiving parents, suicide by overdosing on sleeping pills, suicide by drowning oneself and self-inflicted pain." The book won the 1983 Best Young Adult Book of the Year from the American Library Association.

Source: 11, Nov. 2007, p. 241; Mar. 2008, pp. 79–80.

7 **Adler, David**
I Know I'm a Witch

1998 IL Retained on the shelves at Prairieview Elementary School in Elgin despite a parent's complaint that the material gives children the impression that witchcraft is "fun and harmless."

Source: 11, May 1998, p. 87.

8 **Adler, Margo**
Drawing Down the Moon

1997 TX Removed from the Kirby Junior High School in Wichita Falls because of "Satanic" themes.

Source: 11, July 1997, p. 95.

9 **Adoff, Arnold, ed.**
Poetry of Black America

1996 FL Challenged at the Fort Walton Beach school libraries because it "promotes violence" and contains "expletives and a reference to abortion."

Source: 11, July 1996, p. 133.

10 **Adoff, Arnold**
The Cabbages Are Chasing the Rabbits

1992 IN Challenged at the Deer Ridge Elementary School because the book could breed intolerance for hunters in children's minds.

Source: 11, May 1992, p. 94.

11   Affabee, Eric
Wizards, Warriors & You

1992 OH Removed from the Fairfield elementary school libraries because of "wizardry themes." The series of books were initially challenged because they "promote violence and acceptance and involvement in occult practices."
Source: 11, Sept. 1992, p. 138; Nov. 1992, p. 185.

12   Agee, Philip
Inside the Company: CIA Diary

1974 U.S. Customs stopped delivery of imported copies of Agee's book.
Source: 4, p. 99.

13   Agrippa, Henricus Cornelius
Of the Vanitie and Uncertaintie of Artes and Sciences

1531 Banned in Rome, Italy.
1531 Denounced and banned by the theological faculty of the Sorbonne in Paris, France.
1531 Banned in Cologne, Germany.
1531 Denounced and banned by the theological faculty of Louvain.
Source: 1, pp. 222–23.

14   Aho, Jennifer S., and John W. Petras
Learning about Sex: A Guide for Children and Their Parents

1980 KS Challenged, but retained at the Hays Public Library.
1981 RI Challenged, but retained at the Great Bend Public Library.
1994 NV Challenged, but retained at the Washoe County Library System in Reno because, "Nobody in their right mind would give a book like that to children on their own, except the library."
Source: 11, Nov. 1980, p. 138; Nov. 1981, p. 169; Sept. 1994, p. 147; Nov. 1994, pp. 200–201.

15   Al-Shaykh, Hanan
The Story of Zahra

1980 Banned in Saudi Arabia and other Arab countries more than twenty-five years after its publication for offending religious authorities by its explicit portrayal of sexuality and its indictment of social hypocrisy in contemporary Arab society.
Source: 1, p. 322.

16   Alderman, Ellen
In Our Defense: The Bill of Rights in Action

1998 WI Challenged, but retained at the Wisconsin Rapids high school despite two social studies teachers' objections to descriptions of violence in one chapter and explicit sexual details in another.
Source: 11, Mar. 1999, p. 47.

17   Alderson, Sue Ann, and Ann Blades
Ida and the Wool Smugglers

1991 MD Challenged in the Howard County school libraries. The mother in the picture book was considered neglectful because she sent her daughter to the neighbors when she knew the smugglers were in the vicinity.
Source: 11, Sept. 1991, p. 178.

18   Alexander, Lloyd
The Prydain Chronicles

1993 MA Challenged as required reading at the North bridge Middle School. The complainants said that the series of fantasy novels contains religious themes that are pagan in nature and young minds would be drawn to the allure of witchcraft and black magic that runs through the books.
Source: 11, Mar. 1994, p. 54.

19   Alexander, Lloyd
The Wizard in the Tree

1995 IN After hearing impassioned pleas from parents against book banning, a Duneland School Committee in Chesterton voted to keep the elementary school library book on the shelves. The book came under attack by a parent because a character in the story uses the words "slut" and "damn."
Source: 11, Sept. 1995, p. 157.

20   Alexander, Rae Pace
Young and Black in America

1983 MN After the Minnesota Civil Liberties Union sued the Elk River School Board, the Board reversed its decision to restrict this title to students who have written permission from their parents.
Source: 11, Sept. 1982, pp. 155–56; May 1983, p. 71; Sept. 1983, p. 153.

21 Alexie, Sherman
The Absolutely True Diary of a Part-Time Indian

2008 OR New — Suspended from a Crook County High School classroom in Prineville after a parent complained it was offensive. The *New York Times* best seller and a National Book Award winner will remain out of the classroom until the school district can revamp its policies. The book is about a boy growing up on the Spokane Indian Reservation who decides to attend an all white school. The protagonist in Alexie's book discusses masturbation.

2009 IL New — Retained on the summer reading list at Antioch High School despite objections from several parents who found its language vulgar and racist. In response to concerns, however, the district will form a committee each March to review future summer reading assignments. The committee, which will include parents, would decide whether parents should be warned if a book contains possibly objectionable material.

Source: 11, Mar. 2009, p. 41; Sept. 2009, p. 171.

22 Alinsky, Saul
Rules for Radicals

1987 MI — Challenged at the Plymouth-Canton school system in Canton because the book holds "Lucifer or the Devil up as a role model."

Source: 11, May 1987, p. 109.

23 Allan, Nicholas
Where Willy Went

2007 AZ New — Challenged at the Chandler Public Library along with complaints about the *Phoenix New Times,* comedian George Carlin's audio book, *When Will Jesus Bring the Pork Chops?,* and a fairy tale DVD narrated by Robin Williams. A parent requested that Allan's children's picture book be moved from the children's area to a restricted parenting collection because Willy is a sperm and the book is about sex.

Source: 11, Nov. 2007, pp. 239–40.

24 Allard, Harry, and James Marshall
The Stupids Have a Ball

1993 IA — Challenged in the Iowa City elementary school libraries because the book reinforces negative behavior and low self-esteem, since the Stupids rejoice in their children's behavior.

Source: 11, Jan. 1994, p. 35.

25 Allard, Harry, and James Marshall
The Stupids Step Out

1985 WA — Removed from the Silver Star Elementary School in Vancouver because "it described families in a derogatory manner and might encourage children to disobey their parents."

1985 WI — Challenged at the Cunningham Elementary School in Beloit because it "encourages disrespectful language."

1993 PA — Challenged, removed, and then returned to the shelves in the Horsham schools. The book was challenged because it "makes parents look like boobs and undermines authority."

Source: 11, May 1985, p. 91; Nov. 1985, p. 204; July 1993, p. 101.

26 Allard, Harry
Bumps in the Night

1989 OR — Challenged at the South Prairie Elementary School in Tillamook because a medium and seances are in the story.

Source: 11, Jan. 1990, pp. 4–5.

27 Allard, Harry
The Stupids Die

1998 MI — Pulled from the Howard Miller Library in Zeeland along with the three other Allard books in the series because of complaints that children shouldn't refer to anyone as "stupid."

Source: 11, Sept. 1998, p. 140.

28 Allen, Donald, ed.
The New American Poetry, 1945-1960

1976 CO — Banned for use in Aurora High School English classes on the grounds of "immorality."

Source: 11, May 1977, p. 79; 15, pp. 128–32, 238.

29 Allende, Isabel
The House of the Spirits

1994 CA — Retained in the Paso Robles High School despite objections to accounts of sexual encounters and violence.

1997 VA — Retained on the Stonewall Jackson High School's academically advanced reading list in Brentsville after being challenged for sexual explicitness.

1998 MD — Challenged as obscene on the Montgomery County reading lists and school library shelves.

1999 CA — Challenged on the tenth-grade reading list at La Costa Canyon High School in Encinitas because the work "defames" the Catholic faith and contains "pornographic passages."

2000 CA Retained on the summer reading lists for honors high school students at the Fairfield Unified School District despite objections that the book is "immoral and sexually depraved."

2000 CA Retained on the summer reading lists for honors high school students at the Suisun City Unified School District despite objections that the book is "immoral and sexually depraved."

2003 CA Challenged, but retained in the advanced English classes in Modesto. The seven-member Modesto City School Board said administrators should instead give parents more information about the books their children read, including annotations of each text. Parents can opt their children out of any assignment they find objectionable.

Source: 11, Sept. 1994, p. 167; Nov. 1994, p. 201; Nov. 1997, pp. 169–70; Jan. 1998, p. 29; Mar. 1998, p. 56; May 1998, p. 70; Nov. 1999, p. 164; Nov. 2000, p. 195; Mar. 2001, p. 76; Jan. 2004, pp. 27–28.

30 Allington, Richard
Once Upon a Hippo

2000 GA Challenged, but retained in the Gwinnett County schools. A parent challenged a story in the book *The Hot Hippo*, by Mwenye Hadithi because of a reference to a character called Ngai, described as the "god of everything and everywhere."

Source: 11, May 2000, pp. 76–77; July 2000, p. 124.

31 Allison, Dorothy
Bastard out of Carolina

1996 ME Removed from the Mt. Abram High School English classes in Salem because the language and subject matter (incest and rape) were inappropriate for fifteen-year-olds.

Source: 11, Mar. 1996, p. 49; Nov. 1996, p. 196; Mar. 1997, p. 39.

32 Alvarez, Julia
How the Garcia Girls Lost Their Accents

2002 VA Challenged, along with seventeen other titles in the Fairfax County elementary and secondary libraries, by a group called Parents Against Bad Books in Schools. The group contends the books "contain profanity and descriptions of drug abuse, sexually explicit conduct, and torture."

2006 IL Retained on the Northwest Suburban High School District 214 reading list in Arlington Heights along with eight other challenged titles. A board member, elected amid promises to bring her Christian beliefs into all board decision-making, raised the controversy

based on excerpts from the books she'd found on the Internet.

2007 NC Removed from Johnston County school libraries after a parent challenged its sexual content and profane language. The county school's staff then launched a district-wide book title review.

Source: 11, Jan. 2003, p. 10; July 2006, pp. 210–11; Mar. 2008, pp. 59–60.

33 Alvarez, Julia
In the Time of the Butterflies

2000 NY Withdrawn from inclusion at the Paul D. Schreiber High School in Port Washington because of a drawing of a homemade bomb. The text preceding and following the hand written diagram does not provide details or instructions. The novel was nominated for the National Book Critics Circle Award in 1995 and named a Best Book for Young Adults by the American Library Association.

Source: 11, Jan. 2001, pp. 13–14.

34 Alyson, Sasha, ed.
Young, Gay & Proud!

1989 MI Challenged at the public libraries of Saginaw because the book promoted acts in violation of Michigan law and "appears to qualify as obscene material."

Source: 11, May 1989, p. 78.

35 *American Heritage Dictionary*

1976 AK Removed in school libraries in Anchorage due to "objectionable language."

1976 IN Removed in school libraries in Cedar Lake due to "objectionable language."

1977 MO Removed in school libraries in Eldon due to "objectionable language."

1982 CA Removed in school libraries Folsom due to "objectionable language."

1993 NV Challenged, but retained in the Churchill County school libraries. The controversy began after another dictionary was removed due to "objectionable language." It was removed from, and later returned to, classrooms in Washoe County.

Source: 11, Sept. 1976, p. 115; Nov. 1976, p. 145; Jan. 1977, p. 7; July 1977, p. 101; Mar. 1983, p. 39; Mar. 1994, p. 71.

36 *American Jewish Yearbook*

1983 Banned from the 1983 Moscow, Russia International Book Fair along with more than fifty other books because it is "anti-Soviet."

Source: 11, Nov. 1983, p. 201.

37   **Ames, Lee J.**
Draw 50 Monsters, Creeps, Superheroes, Demons, Dragons, Nerds, Dirts, Ghouls, Giants, Vampires, Zombies and Other Curiosa

1994   MI   Challenged, but retained at the Battle Creek Elementary School library despite protests from a parent who said the book is satanic.
Source: 11, Nov. 1994, p. 200.

38   **Anaya, Rudolfo A.**
Bless Me, Ultima

1992   CA   Challenged at the Porterville high schools because the book contains "many profane and obscene references, vulgar Spanish words and glorifies witchcraft and death."

1996   TX   Retained on the Round Rock Independent High School reading list after a challenge that the book was too violent.

1999   CA   Removed from the Laton Unified School District because it contains violence and profanity that might harm students. The novel is considered by many critics to be the finest work by the New Mexico writer, widely respected as one of the leading Hispanic writers in the U.S. It was chosen by teachers who thought it would be welcomed by the district's students, who are 80 percent Hispanic.

2000   NY   Challenged at the John Jay High School in Wappingers Falls because the book is "full of sex and cursing."

2005   CO   Pulled by the Norwood Schools superintendent after two parents complained about profanity in the book. The superintendent confiscated all of the copies of the book and gave them to the parents, who "tossed them in the trash." The superintendent later apologized. Students organized an all-day sit-in at the school gym. President George W. Bush awarded Anaya the National Media of Arts in 2002. First Lady Laura Bush has listed the book as ninth on a list of twelve books that she highly recommends.

2008   CA   Banned from the Orestimba High School's
New   English classes in Newman by the superintendent after complaints that the book is profane and anti-Catholic. Teachers claimed that the superintendent circumvented the district's policies on book challenges and set a dangerous precedent. The book is about a boy maturing, asking questions about evil, justice, and the nature of God.
Source: 11, Jan. 1993, p. 29; May 1996, p. 99; Sept. 1999, pp. 120–21; Mar. 2000, p. 51; Mar. 2005, p. 55; Jan. 2009, p. 7; Mar. 2009, pp. 39-40.

39   **Ancona, George**
Cuban Kids

2006   FL   Banned in the Miami-Dade County Public Schools. The picture book shows a child with a rifle and children saluting the Cuban flag with the caption, "We will be like Che!"
Source: 11, Nov. 2006, p. 288.

40   **Anders, Jim**
The Complete Idiot's Guide to Sex on the Net

1999   TX   Challenged, but retained at the Will Hampton Branch of the Austin Public Library despite complaints from at least three parents that the book is "obscene."
Source: 11, Nov. 1999, p. 172.

41   **Andersen, Hans Christian**
The Little Mermaid

1994   TX   An edition with illustrations of bare-breasted mermaids was challenged in the Bedford School District because it was "pornographic" and contained "satanic pictures."
Source: 11, Nov. 1994, pp. 188–89.

42   **Andersen, Hans Christian**
Wonder Stories Told for Children

1835   Banned in Russia by Nicholas I during the "censorship terror." Ban removed in 1849.

1954   IL   Stamped in Illinois "For Adult Readers" to make it "impossible for children to obtain smut."
Source: 4, pp. 41–42.

43   **Anderson, Christopher**
Madonna—Unauthorized

1993   CO   Challenged at the Loveland High School library because the book has obscenities and sexual references, and one photo with Madonna posing topless.
Source: 11, July 1993, p. 97.

44   **Anderson, Janice**
The Life and Times of Renoir

1997   PA   Restricted at the Pulaski Elementary School library because of nude paintings in the book.
Source: 11, May 1997, p. 61.

45   Anderson, Jean
The Haunting of America

1985 FL   Challenged at the Sikes Elementary School media center in Lakeland because the collection of historical ghost stories, "would lead children to believe in demons without realizing it."
Source: 11, July 1985, p. 133.

46   Anderson, Jill
Pumsy

1989 OK   The Putnam City Elementary School counselors are forbidden to use this story of a fictional dragon because it propagates the principles of "secular humanism" and "new age religion" and that its use would "drive a wedge between children and parents."
Source: 11, July 1989, p. 129.

47   Anderson, Laurie Halse
Twisted

2009 KY
New   Withdrawn from classroom use and the approved curriculum at the Montgomery County High School, but available at the high school library and student book club. Some parents have complained about five novels that contain foul language and cover topics — including sex, child abuse, suicide, and drug abuse—deemed unsuited for discussion in coed high school classes. They also contend that the books don't provide the intellectual challenge and rigor that students need in college preparatory classes. The titles appeared on suggested book lists compiled by the Young Adult Library Services Association, a division of the American Library Association, for twelve- to eighteen-year-olds who are "reluctant readers." The superintendent removed the book because it wasn't on the pre-approved curriculum list and couldn't be added by teachers in the middle of a school year without permission.
Source: 11, Jan. 2010, pp. 16–17; Mar. 2010, p. 56.

48   Anderson, Lee, et al.
Windows on Our World series

1987 AL   Removed from Alabama's list of approved texts—and from the state's classrooms—because the book promotes the "religion of secular humanism." U.S. District Court Judge W. Brevard Hand ruled on March 4, 1987, that thirty-nine history and social studies texts used in Alabama's 129 school systems "discriminate against the very concept of religion and theistic religions in particular, by omissions so serious that a student learning history from them would not be apprised of relevant facts about America's history. References to religion are isolated and the integration of religion in the history of American society is ignored." The series includes: *At Home, At School; In Our Community; Ourselves and Others; Our Home; The Earth; America: Past and Present;* and *Around Our World.* On August 26, 1987, the U.S. Court of Appeals for the Eleventh Circuit unanimously overturned Judge Hand's decision by ruling that the information in the book was "essentially neutral in its religious content." The fact that the texts omitted references to religion was not "an advancement of secular humanism or an active hostility toward theistic religion."
Source: 11, Jan. 1987, p. 6; May 1987, pp. 75, 104–7; Sept. 1987, pp. 166–67; Nov. 1987, pp. 217–18; Jan. 1988, p. 17; Mar. 1988, p. 40.

49   Anderson, Robert, et al.
Elements of Literature

1994 VA   Retained in the Fairfax County schools despite complaints that it might "plant seeds" of violence or disobedience in students. The anthology contains stories such as Edgar Allen Poe's "TheTell-Tale Heart" and John Steinbeck's "The Pearl."
Source: 11, Nov. 1994, pp. 201–2.

50   Anderson, Sherwood
Dark Laughter

1930 MA   Blacklisted in Boston.
Source: 2, p. 137; 4, p. 62.

51   Andrews, V. C.
Dark Angel

1994 GA   Removed from Oconee County school libraries "due to the filthiness of the material." The school board voted unanimously at a later date to rescind its controversial book-banning order, but then rescinded that action and ordered the removal of the book.
Source: 11, Sept. 1994, pp. 145–46; Nov. 1994, pp. 187–88, 200; Jan. 1995, p. 6.

52   Andrews, V. C.
Darkest Hour

1994 GA   Removed from Oconee County school libraries "due to the filthiness of the material." The school board voted unanimously at a later date to rescind its controversial book-banning order but then rescinded that action and ordered the removal of the book.

Source: 11, Sept. 1994, pp. 145–46; Nov. 1994, pp. 187–88, 200; Jan. 1995, p. 6.

53 **Andrews, V. C.**
Dawn

1994 GA Removed from Oconee County school libraries "due to the filthiness of the material." The school board voted unanimously at a later date to rescind its controversial book-banning order but then rescinded that action and ordered the removal of the book.

Source: 11, Sept. 1994, pp. 145–46; Nov. 1994, pp. 187–88, 200; Jan. 1995, p. 6.

54 **Andrews, V. C.**
Flowers in the Attic

1983 RI Challenged at the Richmond High School because the book contains offensive passages concerning incest and sexual intercourse.

1994 GA Removed from Oconee County school libraries "due to the filthiness of the material." The school board voted unanimously at a later date to rescind its controversial book-banning order but then rescinded that action and ordered the removal of the book.

Source: 11, Sept. 1983, p. 153; Jan. 1984, pp. 9-10; Sept. 1994, pp. 145–46; Nov. 1994, pp. 187–88, 200; Jan. 1995, p. 6.

55 **Andrews, V. C.**
Garden of Shadows

1994 GA Removed from Oconee County school libraries "because the book encouraged sexual activity and the result of reading or seeing it might be 'incestuous relationships' and 'aggressive sexual behavior.'" The book was removed despite a recommendation from a committee of parents and teachers to retain it. The action stemmed from a complaint filed in May 1994 when eight other V. C. Andrews books were removed.

Source: 11, Nov. 1994, p. 188; Jan. 1995, p. 6; July 1996, p. 117.

56 **Andrews, V. C.**
If There Be Thorns

1983 RI Challenged at the Richmond High School because the book contains offensive passages concerning incest and sexual intercourse.

Source: 11, Sept. 1983, p. 153; Jan. 1984, pp. 9–10.

57 **Andrews, V. C.**
My Sweet Audrina

1985 CA Rejected for purchase by the Hayward school trustees because of "rough language" and "explicit sex scenes."

1990 WA Challenged at the Lincoln Middle School in Pullman because it deals with themes related to sexual violence.

1994 GA Removed from Oconee County school libraries "due to the filthiness of the material." The school board voted unanimously at a later date to rescind its controversial book-banning order but then rescinded that action and ordered the removal of the book.

Source: 11, July 1985, p. 111; July 1990, p. 145; Sept. 1994, pp. 145–46; Nov. 1994, pp. 187–88, 200; Jan. 1995, p. 6.

58 **Andrews, V. C.**
Petals on the Wind

1983 RI Challenged at the Richmond High School because the book contains offensive passages concerning incest and sexual intercourse.

1984 GA Removed from Oconee County school libraries "due to the filthiness of the material." The school board voted unanimously at a later date to rescind its controversial book-banning order but then rescinded that action and ordered the removal of the book.

Source: 11, Sept. 1983, p. 153; Jan. 1984, pp. 9–10; Mar. 1984, p. 53; Sept. 1994, pp. 145–46; Nov. 1994, pp. 187–88, 200; Jan. 1995, p. 6.

59 **Andrews, V. C.**
Seeds of Yesterday

1994 GA Removed from Oconee County school libraries "due to the filthiness of the material." The school board voted unanimously at a later date to rescind its controversial book-banning order but then rescinded that action and ordered the removal of the book.

Source: 11, Sept. 1994, pp. 145–46; Nov. 1994, pp. 187–88, 200; Jan. 1995, p. 6.

60 **Andrews, V. C.**
Twilight's Child

1994 GA Removed from Oconee County school libraries "due to the filthiness of the material." The school board voted unanimously at a later date to rescind its controversial book-banning order but then rescinded that action and ordered the removal of the book.

Source: 11, Sept. 1994, pp. 145–46; Nov. 1994, pp. 187–88, 200; Jan. 1995, p. 6.

61   **Andry, Andrew C., and Steven Schepp**
How Babies Are Made

1981   FL   Moved from the children's section to the adult section of the Tampa-Hillsborough County Public Library by order of the Tampa City Council.

1987   WA   Placed on restricted shelves at the Evergreen School District elementary school libraries in Vancouver in accordance with the school board policy to restrict student access to sex education books in elementary school libraries.
Source: 11, Jan. 1982, p. 4; May 1987, p. 87.

62   **Angelou, Maya**
And Still I Rise

1982   LA   Challenged at the Northside High School library in Lafayette.

1987   WA   Challenged at the Longview school system because some "students could be harmed by its graphic language."
Source: 11, May 1982, p. 83; May 1987, p. 91; Sept. 1987, p. 195.

63   **Angelou, Maya**
I Know Why the Caged Bird Sings

1983   AL   Four members of the Alabama State Textbook Committee called for its rejection because Angelou's work preaches "bitterness and hatred against whites."

1987   NC   Removed from the required reading list for Wake County High School juniors in Raleigh because of complaints about a scene in which eight-year-old Maya is raped.

1988   ME   Challenged at Mount Abram Regional High School in Strong because parents objected to a rape scene.

1990   WA   Rejected as required reading for a gifted ninth-grade English class in Bremerton because of the book's "graphic" description of molestation.

1991   CA   Removed from a Banning eighth grade class after several parents complained about explicit passages involving child molestation and rape.

1992   CA   Challenged at the Amador Valley High School in Pleasanton because of sexually explicit language.

1993   FL   Challenged in the Haines City High School library and English curriculum because of objections to a passage that describes the author's rape when she was eight years old.

1993   MS   Temporarily banned from the Caledonia Middle School in Columbus on the grounds that it is too sexually explicit to be read by children.

1993   TX   Challenged in the Hooks High School in a freshman honors history class.

1994   CO   Challenged as part of the Ponderosa High School curriculum in Castle Rock because it is "a lurid tale of sexual perversion."

1994   IA   Retained as required reading for all of Dowling High School's sophomores in Des Moines. The book became an issue after a parent objected to what he said were inappropriately explicit sexual scenes.

1994   TX   Challenged at the Westwood High School in Austin because the book is pornographic, contains profanity, and encourages premarital sex and homosexuality. The superintendent later ruled that parents must first give their children permission to be taught potentially controversial literature.

1995   AZ   Removed from the curriculum pending a review of its content at the Gilbert Unified School. Complaining parents said the book did not represent "traditional values."

1995   FL   Challenged, but retained in the Volusia County County Schools. The complainants wanted the book removed because "it is sexually explicit and promotes cohabitation and rape."

1995   LA   Removed from the Southwood High School Library in Caddo Parish because the book's language and content were objectionable. Eventually, the book was returned after students petitioned and demonstrated against the action.

1995   TN   Challenged, but retained on the Beech High School reading list in Hendersonville.

1995   TX   Challenged at the Danforth High School in Wimberley.

1995   TX   Challenged at the Carroll School in Southlake because it was deemed "pornographic" and full of "gross evils."

1996   AL   Challenged, but retained on an optional reading list at the East Lawrence High School in Moulton. The book was challenged because the School Superintendent decided, "the poet's descriptions of being raped as a little girl were pornographic."

1996   TX   Retained on the Round Rock Independent High School reading list after a challenge that the book was too violent.

1997   CA   Challenged at the Folsom Cordova School District because it contains sexually explicit passages.

1997   GA   Challenged as an Advanced Placement English class reading assignment at the Wayne Count High School due to the novel's sexual explicitness.

1997 MN Removed from the ninth-grade reading list at Richfield High School because some parents say it is too explicit.

1997 NC Removed from the curriculum at the Turrentine Middle School after complaints by parents about profanity and sexual references.

1997 OH Removed from the high school reading list at Lakota High School in Union Township because of Angelou's brief description of being raped at age eight and other sexual content.

1997 WA Retained in the Mukilteo school district's high school curriculum after objections to the work's "explicit sexual content."

1998 FL Banned from the Dolores Parrott Middle School in Brooksville school library and classrooms because of a passage in which Angelou tells of being molested and raped as an eight-year-old. Removed from the Brooksville eighth-grade reading list because of the book's strong sexual content.

1998 MD Removed from the ninth-grade English curriculum in Anne Arundel County by the school superintendent after parents complained the book "portrays white people as being horrible, nasty, stupid people—if a child didn't have negative feelings about white people, this could sow the seeds." Returned to the Anne Arundel County approved reading list for ninth-grade English classes, overriding some parents' complaints that the book is too sexually explicit.

1998 NC Removed from the Turrentine Middle School's reading list in Alamance.

1999 NH Removed from the seventh- and eighth-grade reading list at the Unity Elementary School because the "book is too sexually explicit."

2000 MD Challenged on the Poolesville High School reading list due to the book's sexual content and language.

2002 MT Challenged as required reading for freshman English classes. At issue are scenes in which the author explores her sexuality through intercourse as a teenager and the depiction of a rape and molestation of an eight-year-old girl; homosexuality is another theme explored in the book that has drawn criticism.

2002 VA Challenged, along with seventeen other titles in the Fairfax County elementary and secondary libraries, by a group called Parents Against Bad Books in Schools. The group contends the books "contain profanity and descriptions of drug abuse, sexually explicit conduct, and torture."

2006 MD Removed as required reading in Annapolis freshman English curriculum because the book's rape scenes and other mature content are too advanced for ninth-graders. The freshman English class syllabus is sent home to parents to read at the beginning of each year. It warns them of the book's mature themes and allows parents to ask to have their children read another book instead.

2006 WI Retained in the Fond du Lac High School sophomore advanced English class. Parents objected to teens reading Angelou's account of being brutally raped by her mother's boyfriend and an unwanted pregnancy later in life. Parents will receive notification and be allowed to decide whether or not they approve of its use by their children, according to recommendations agreed upon by a review committee and parents who objected to the use of the book.

2007 ID Challenged in the Coeur d'Alene School District. Some parents say that the book, along with five others, should require parental permission for students to read them.

2007 PA Challenged in the Manheim Township schools due to sexual references. The book was retained in the ninth-grade English curriculum, but it was decided to teach the book later in the school year, after a public forum was held with parents to discuss that book and the entire literary canon of the English department.

2009 CA New Restricted to students with parental permission at the Ocean View School District middle school libraries in Huntington Beach because the "book's contents were inappropriate for children."

2009 CA New Challenged in the Newman-Crows Landing School District on a required reading list presented by the Orestimba High English Department. A trustee questioned the qualifications of Orestimba staff to teach a novel depicting African American culture.

Source: 6, p. 60; 11, Mar. 1983, p. 39; Jan. 1989, p. 8; Mar. 1989, p. 38; Nov. 1990, p. 211; Mar. 1992, p. 42; July 1992, p. 109; July 1993, p. 107; Jan. 1994, p. 34; July 1994, p. 130; Jan. 1995, pp. 11, 14; Mar. 1995, p. 56; May 1995, pp. 67, 72; Sept. 1995, pp. 158–59; Nov. 1995, pp. 183, 186–87; Jan. 1996, pp. 14, 30; Mar. 1996, pp. 47, 63; May 1996, pp. 84, 99; July 1996, p. 120; Sept. 1996, pp. 152–53; Nov. 1996, pp. 197–98; Jan. 1997, p. 26; May 1997, pp. 65–66; July 1997, p. 98; Jan. 1998, pp. 13, 14, 29; Mar. 1998, pp. 41–42; May 1998, pp. 69, 72; July 1998, p. 120; Sept. 1998, pp. 143–44; Nov. 1998, p. 182; Jan. 1999, p. 20; May 1999, p. 69; July 1999, pp. 93–94; Nov. 2000, p. 196; Nov. 2002, p. 258; Jan. 2003, p. 10; May 2006, pp. 132–33; Jan. 2007, pp. 30–31; July 2007, pp. 149–50; Sept. 2007, p. 181; Jan. 2010, pp. 7, 14–15; May 2010, p. 103.

64 Annas, Pamela, and Robert Rosen
Literature in Society: Introduction to Fiction, Poetry and Drama

1994 PA Pulled from the senior literature class at the Hempfield Area School District after it was determined that some passages were "vulgar."

Source: 11, Jan. 1995, pp. 13–14; Mar. 1995, p. 44.

65 Anonymous
Arabian Nights or The Thousand and One Nights

1927   U.S. Customs held up 500 sets of the translation by the French scholar Mardrus, which were imported from England. Continued until 1931

1985   Confiscated in Cairo, Egypt on the grounds that it contained obscene passages which posed a threat to the country's moral fabric. The public prosecutor demanded the book, which contains stories such as "Ali Baba and the 40 Thieves" and "Aladdin and His Magic Lamp," be "burned in a public place" and said that it was the cause of "a wave of incidents of rape which the country has recently experienced."

1985   Judged inappropriate for Jewish pupils by the Israeli director of the British Consul Library in Jerusalem, Israel.

Source: 4, p. 28; 5, June 1985, p. 50; Aug. 1985, p. 51; Oct. 1985, p. 65; 8, pp. 317–18; 11, July 1985, p. 120.

66 Anonymous
Caroline

1991   OR   Removed from the Multnomah County Library because the novel contains graphic descriptions of sexual acts.

Source: 11, Jan. 1992, p. 6.

67 Anonymous
The Fifteen Plagues of a Maidenhead

1707   James Reade and Angell Carter were prosecuted in England for publishing the work and charged with "obscene libel." They were acquitted after the defense counsel asserted that the court had no right to try the case because the defendants were not guilty of breaking any existing law. While the court disliked the tone and content of the book, calling it "bawdy," it acknowledged that no common law or statute existed that "could warrant an indictment against even the filthiest book."

Source: 13, p. 71.

68 Anonymous
Go Ask Alice

1974   MI   Removed from school libraries in Kalamazoo due to "objectionable" language and explicit sexual scenes.

1975   MI   Removed from school libraries in Saginaw due to "objectionable" language and explicit sexual scenes.

1975   NY   Removed from school libraries in Levittown due to "objectionable" language and explicit sexual scenes.

1975   NY   Challenged at the Marcellus School District.

1977   NJ   Removed from school libraries in Trenton due to "objectionable" language and explicit sexual scenes.

1977   TX   Removed from school libraries in Eagle Pass due to "objectionable" language and explicit sexual scenes.

1979   UT   Challenged at the Ogden School District.

1980   NJ   Removed from school libraries in North Bergen due to "objectionable" language and explicit sexual scenes.

1982   FL   Challenged at the Safety Harbor, St. Petersburg Middle School Library where written parental permission was required to check out the title.

1983   CO   Challenged at the Pagosa Springs schools because a parent objected to the "graphic language, subject matter, immoral tone, and lack of literary quality found in the book."

1983   MN   Challenged at the Osseo School District in Brooklyn Park where a school board member found the book's language "personally offensive."

1984   MS   Challenged at the Rankin County School District because it is "profane and sexually objectionable."

1986   GA   Challenged at the Central Gwinnett High School library because "it encourages students to steal and take drugs."

1986   GA   The Gainesville Public Library prohibits young readers from checking out this book along with forty other books. The books, on subjects ranging from hypnosis to drug abuse to breast-feeding and sexual dysfunction, are kept in a locked room.

1986   MI   Removed from the school library shelves in Kalkaska because the book contains "objectionable language."

1988   ME   Challenged at the King Middle School in Portland.

1993   NJ   Removed from the Wall Township Intermediate School library by the Superintendent of Schools because the book contains "inappropriate" language and "borders on pornography." Responding to an anonymous letter in 1987, the superintendent ordered the book removed from all reading lists and classroom book collections. "I thought we'd got rid of them all about five years ago," he said.

1993   NY   Challenged as a required reading assignment at the Johnstown High School because of numerous obscenities.

1993   WV   Removed from an English class at Buckhannon-Upshur High School because of graphic language in the book.

1994   MA   Banned from a ninth-grade reading list at

Shepherd Hill High School in Dudley because of "gross and vulgar language and graphic description of drug use and sexual conduct."

1995 AK Challenged at the Houston Junior and Senior High School in Wasilla.

1995 OH Banned from the Jonathan Alder School District in Plain City.

1995 VA Removed from a supplemental reading list for sophomore English students in Warm Springs because of its "profanity and indecent situations."

1998 R Confiscated by a Tiverton middle school principal, while the class was reading it. The book was later returned by the school board.

1999 TX Removed from the Aledo Middle School library and restricted at the high school library to students with parental permission. A parent complained about the references to drug use, vulgar language, and descriptions of sex.

2000 PA Retained as optional reading for eighth graders at Rice Avenue Middle School in Girard. A grandmother found the book offensive because it contains "filth and smut" that she didn't want her granddaughters reading.

2008 SC Challenged as a reading assignment at
New Hanahan Middle School in Berkeley County because of blatant, explicit language using street terms for sex, talk of worms eating body parts, and blasphemy. The anonymously written 1971 book is about a fifteen-year-old girl who gets caught up in a life of drugs and sex before dying from an overdose. Its explicit references to drugs and sex have been controversial since it was first published.

Source: 8, pp. 456–57; 11, Jan. 1975, p. 6; Mar. 1975, p. 41; May 1975, p. 76; July 1977, p. 100; May 1977, p. 73; May 1979, p. 49; Mar. 1980, p. 32; July 1982, p. 142; Mar. 1983, p. 52; Mar. 1984, p. 53; May 1984, p. 69; July 1986, p. 117; Sept. 1986, pp. 151–52; Nov. 1986, p. 207; Jan. 1987, p. 32; Mar. 1989, p. 39; May 1993, p. 71; July 1993, pp. 109–10; Mar. 1994, p. 54; Sept. 1994, p. 150; July 1995, p. 94; Jan. 1996, p. 12; Mar. 1996, p. 50; Sept. 1998, p. 144; Sept. 1999, pp. 119–20; May 2000, p. 92; May 2008, pp. 98–99.

69   Anonymous
Life: How Did It Get Here?

1992 MA Challenged at the Jones Library in Amherst because it is religious propaganda. "The book lists no authors or editors; there is no accountability for its statements."

Source: 11, Sept. 1992, p. 162.

70   Anonymous.
Marisha II

1991 OR Removed from the Multnomah County Library

because the novel contains graphic descriptions of sexual acts.

Source: 11, Jan. 1992, p. 6.

71   Anthony, Piers
Question Quest

2000 CA Removed from the mandatory reading program at the Norman L. Sullivan Middle School in Bonsall due to sexually explicit language.

Source: 11, May 2000, p. 76.

72   Apollinaire, Guillaume
Memoirs of a Young Rakehill

1964 *The Debauched Hospodar* and *Memoirs of a Young Rakehill* were seized by New Zealand Customs officers. The New Zealand Indecent Publications Tribunal concluded that, "we classify the translation of two novels written by Guillaume Apollinaire as indecent unless circulation is restricted to persons professionally engaged in the study of abnormal psychology, who desire to use them for that purpose."

Source: 13, p. 162.

73   Archer, Jerome W., and A. Schwartz
A Reader for Writers

1976 NY Removed from the Island Trees Union Free School District High School library in 1976 along with nine other titles because they were considered "immoral, anti-American, anti-Christian, or just plain filthy." Returned to the library after the U.S. Supreme Court ruling on June 25, 1982 in *Board of Education, Island Trees Union Free School District No. 26 et al. v. Pico et al.,* 457 U.S. 853 (1982).

Source: 11, Nov. 1982, p. 197.

74   Aristophanes
Lysistrata

1930 U.S. Customs lifts ban. In successful challenge to the Comstock Act of 1873, which empowered the Postmaster General to rule on obscenity of literature sent through the mail, *Lysistrata* was declared mailable.

Source: 4, p. 2.

75   Aristotle
The Metaphysics

1210 The bishops of the Provincial Council of Paris, France forbade the public or private teaching of the natural philosophy and metaphysics of

Aristotle. The ban, which applied to instruction of the arts faculty of the University of Paris, was imposed under penalty of excommunication and confirmed in 1215.

1231 Pope Gregory IX in Rome, Italy prohibited the reading of the works of Aristotle until they were purged of heresy.

Source: 1, p. 205.

76 Arms, Karen, and Pamela S. Camp
Biology

1980 NC Text was rejected by the superintendent of the city-county school system on the basis that it might violate a school policy forbidding the teaching of specific methods of birth control in Winston-Salem.

1985 TX Bowing to pressure from opponents of the textbook planned for use in a high school honors course, the Garland Independent School District's central textbook selection committee withdrew its recommendation because the text includes "overly explicit diagrams of sexual organs, intricate discussion of sexual stimulation, and the implication of abortion as a means of birth control."

Source: 11, Nov. 1980, p. 128; July 1985, p. 114.

77 Armstrong, William Howard
Sounder

1996 NY Challenged, but retained in the Rockingham County schools. A parent had problems with the use of the word "nigger" on page twenty-one and a reference to the main character, a black sharecropper, as "boy."

Source: 11, Sept. 1996, p. 169; Nov. 1996, p. 212.

78 Asher, Don
Blood Summer

1979 AR Returned to publisher because it failed to meet literary standards in Little Rock.

Source: 11, Sept. 1979, p. 104.

79 Asimov, Isaac
In the Beginning: Science Faces God in the Book of Genesis

1981 CA Officials of the Christian Research Center requested San Diego school administrators to keep this title out of all high school libraries because Asimov "subjects the Bible to merciless and unremitting destructive attack."

Source: 11, Jan. 1982, p. 8.

80 Asturias, Miguel Angel
The Green Pope

1954 Banned in Guatemala along with *Strong Wind* (1950) and *The President* (1946) for its exposure of the effects of American imperialism.

Source: 7, pp. 467–68.

81 Atkins, Catherine
Alt Ed

2007 OR New — Challenged as an optional reading in a bullying unit at the Lake Oswego Junior High School because the novel is "peppered with profanities, ranging from derogatory slang terms to sexual encounters and violence." Students are given a list of book summaries and a letter to take to their parents. Four of the eight optional books offered are labeled as having "mature content/language."

Source: 11, July 2007, p. 149.

82 Atkins, Catherine
When Jeff Comes Home

2006 TX Restricted to students with parental permission in the Irving schools. The book is about a boy's recovery after being kidnapped and sexually abused by a man. The publisher recommends the book for readers thirteen and older, while *School Library Journal* suggested it for readers in grades ten and above. It was named a best book for young adults by the American Library Association in 2000.

Source: 11, Mar. 2006, pp. 72–73.

83 Atwood, Margaret
The Handmaid's Tale

1990 CA Challenged as a book assignment at the Rancho Cotati High School in Rohnert Park because it is too explicit for students.

1992 IA Challenged in the Waterloo schools because of profanity, lurid passages about sex, and statements defamatory to minorities, God, women, and the disabled.

1993 MA Removed from the Chicopee High School English class reading list because it contains profanity and sex.

1998 WA Challenged for use in the Richland high school English classes along with six other titles because the "books are poor-quality literature and stress suicide, illicit sex, violence, and hopelessness."

1999 FL Challenged because of graphic sex, but retained on the advanced placement English list at Chamberlain High School in Tampa.

2000 PA — Downgraded from "required" to "optional" on the summer reading list for eleventh graders in the Upper Moreland School District due to "age-inappropriate" subject matter.

2001 TX — Challenged, but retained in the Dripping Springs senior Advanced Placement English courses as an optional reading assignment. Some parents were offended by the book's descriptions of sexual encounters.

2006 TX — The Judson school district board overruled Superintendent Ed Lyman's ban of the novel from an Advanced Placement English curriculum. Lyman had banned the book after a parent complained it was sexually explicit and offensive to Christians. In doing so, he overruled the recommendation of a committee of teachers, students, and parents. The committee appealed the decision to the school board.

Source: 11, Jan. 1991, p. 15; July 1992, p. 126; May 1993, p. 73; Mar. 1999, p. 40; Sept. 1999, p. 121; Nov. 1999, p. 173; Sept. 2000, p. 145; July 2001, p. 174; May 2006, pp. 154–55.

84 Auel, Jean
Clan of the Cave Bear

1988 MI — Challenged at the Berrien Springs High School for use in classrooms and libraries because the novel is "vulgar, profane, and sexually explicit."

1992 OR — Banned from the Cascade Middle School library in Eugene after a parent complained about a rape scene.

1993 CA — Challenged, but retained on the Moorpark High School recommended reading list in Simi Valley despite objections that it contains "hard-core graphic sexual content."

Source: 11, Jan. 1989, p. 28; July 1992, p. 107; Jan. 1994, p. 14; Mar. 1994, p. 70; May 1994, p. 99.

85 Auel, Jean
The Mammoth Hunters

1993 CA — Challenged, but retained from the Moorpark High School recommended reading list in Simi Valley despite objections that it contains "hard-core graphic sexual content."

Source: 11, Mar. 1994, p. 70; May 1994, p. 99.

86 Auel, Jean
Plains of Passage

1993 CA — Challenged, but retained from the Moorpark High School recommended reading list in Simi Valley despite objections that it contains "hard-core graphic sexual content."

Source: 11, Mar. 1994, p. 70; May 1994, p. 99.

87 Auel, Jean
Valley of the Horses

1985 PA — Banned from the Stroudsburg High School library because it was "blatantly graphic, pornographic, and wholly unacceptable for a high school library."

1985 TX — Challenged at the Bastrop Public Library because "the book violates Texas obscenity laws."

1993 CA — Challenged, but retained on the Moorpark High School recommended reading list in Simi Valley despite objections that it contains "hard-core graphic sexual content."

Source: 11, May 1985, pp. 75, 79; Mar. 1986, pp. 33, 64; Jan. 1994, p. 145; Mar. 1994, p. 70; May 1994, p. 99.

88 Avent, Sue
Spells, Chants and Potions

1992 VA — Pulled, but later placed on reserve to children with parental permission at the Forrest Elementary School library in Newport News.

1997 PA — Challenged at the Muncy school library because of the book's "magical thinking."

Source: 11, July 1992, p. 108; Sept. 1992, p. 139; May 1997, p. 61.

89 Averroes (Ibn Rushd)
Commentaries

1210 — The ban applied to instruction at the University of Paris, France.

1210 — Church authorities in Rome, Italy banned his writings on the works of Aristotle between 1210 and 1277 for proposing that philosophy could claim truth outside established religious source.

1231 — In 1231, Pope Gregory IX prohibited the reading of the works of Aristotle until they were purged of heresy.

Source: 1, pp. 50–51.

90 Avi
The Fighting Ground

2000 NH — Retained as part of the John Fuller School curriculum in Conway, despite a complaint by a resident calling himself a concerned Christian.

2008 FL
New — Banned from the Bay District school's library shelves in Panama City after a parent noted several profanities uttered by some soldiers. The award-winning book, intended for the fourth-grade reading level, is about a twenty-four-hour period in the life of a thirteen-year-old boy during the Revolutionary War.

Source: 11, Jan. 2001, p. 37; Mar. 2001, p. 75; July 2008, p. 140.

91   Aylesworth, Thomas G.
Servants of the Devil: A History of Witchcraft

1989 OK Removed from the Cleveland middle school libraries because witchcraft is a "religion" and that the First Amendment bars the teaching of religion in schools.
Source: 11, July 1989, p. 128.

92   Babbitt, Natalie
The Devil's Storybook

1986 TN Returned to the Claxton Elementary School library shelves. The complaint against the book objected to "the total theme of the book," which makes "hell and the devil innocent and alluring."

2004 PA Challenged at the Chestnut Ridge Middle School in Washington Township. The complainants wanted the school district to seek parental approval before elementary- and middle-school students could check out books related to the occult.
Source: 11, Mar. 1987, p. 50; May 2004, pp. 117–18.

93   Babbitt, Natalie
The Imp in the Basket

1991 PA Challenged as required reading in the Annville-Cleona School District because of the story's references to demon possession.
Source: 11, July 1991, p. 130.

94   Babinski, Edward T.
Leaving the Fold: Testimonials of Former Fundamentalists

1995 SC Challenged, but retained at the Anderson County Library, because the book presented fundamentalism in a negative light.
Source: 11, Jan. 1996, p. 30.

95   Bach, Alice
When the Sky Began to Roar

1987 NE Removed from the East Junior-Senior High School library in Lincoln because the book "creates despair, disrespect for parents, and a sense of hopelessness."

1988 NE Challenged at the Seward Public Library because it is "obscene."
Source: 11, May 1987, p. 87; May 1988, p. 85.

96   Bacon, Francis
Advancement of Learning

1640 All works by Bacon were banned by the Inquisition in Spain and placed on the Sotomayor's Index. Book IX of Bacon's work, dedicated to the king, was placed on the *Index Librorum Prohibitorum* (List of Prohibited Books) in Rome, Italy, where it remained in the 1948 edition of the list.
Source: 1, p. 5; 4, p. 17.

97   Bailey, Jacqui, and Jan McCafferty
Sex, Puberty, and All That Stuff: A Guide to Growing Up

2008 CT Retained in the Windsor Library after being
New   challenged as inappropriate for its descriptions of sexual development. The book is designed for students from grades five through ten.
Source: 11, Nov. 2008, pp. 253–54.

98   Bailey, Thomas A., and David M. Kennedy
The American Pageant: A History of the Republic

1966 MD The John Birch Society's chapter in Glen Burnie condemned the textbook and demanded that it be banned in the Anne Arundel County public schools.

1981 MS Removed from the Mississippi state-approved textbook list.

1984 WI Returned to the Racine Unified School District curriculum just one week after the school board voted to ban it. Opponents of the book on the board charged that the social studies volumes contained "judgmental writing" and, in the words of one board member, "a lot more funny pictures of Republicans and nicer pictures of Democrats." Opponents also said that one text did not present an adequate analysis of the Vietnam War.
Source: 7, pp. 34–36; 11, May 1981, p. 67; July 1981, p. 93; Sept. 1984, p. 158.

99   Baker, Keith
Who Is the Beast?

1994 PA Temporarily removed from the Marple schools following a verbal request from a parent who said its message offended his family's religious beliefs.
Source: 11, July 1994, p. 116.

100   Baldwin, James
Another Country

1963 LA Considered obscene, the book was banned from the New Orleans Public Library. After a year of litigation, it was restored.
Source: 4, p. 97; 8, pp. 406–7.

101 Baldwin, James
Blues for Mr. Charlie

1980 SD Challenged in Sioux Falls because it's "pornographic" and it "tears down Christian principles."
Source: 11, May 1980, p. 61.

102 Baldwin, James
Go Tell It on the Mountain

1994 NY Challenged as required reading in the Hudson Falls schools because the book has recurring themes of rape, masturbation, violence, and degrading treatment of women.

1998 VA Challenged as a ninth-grade summer reading option in Prince William County because the book "was rife with profanity and explicit sex."
Source: 11, Nov. 1994, p. 190; Jan. 1995, p. 13; Mar. 1995, p. 55; Nov. 1998, p. 183.

103 Baldwin, James
If Beale Street Could Talk

1989 OR Removed from the St. Paul High School library because the book contains obscene language and explicit descriptions of sexual activity.
Source: 11, July 1989, p. 128.

104 Baldwin, James
Tell Me How Long the Train's Been Gone

1983 AL Four members of the Alabama State Textbook Committee called for its rejection because Baldwin's work preaches "bitterness and hatred against whites."
Source: 11, Mar. 1983, p. 39.

105 Balian, Lorna
Humbug Potion: An A-B-Cipher

1991 OR Challenged for promoting satanism and witchcraft, but retained at the Multnomah County Library.
Source: 11, Jan. 1992, p. 6.

106 Balzac, Honore de
Droll Stories

1850 All works banned in Russia.
1914 *Droll Stories* banned by Canadian Customs.
1930 U.S. Customs lifts ban. U.S. declares the Concord Book Catalog as obscene because it features *Droll Stories*.
1953 Banned in Ireland until 1967. The novel attracted the attention of censors for its excretory references and graphic sexual descriptions.
Source: 4, p. 39; 6, p. 411; 12, p. 140; 13, pp. 62–63

107 Banks, Lynne Reid
The Indian in the Cupboard

1993 FL The school librarian at the Suwannee County Elementary School routinely erased words from books deemed objectionable. In this instance, the words "heck" and "hell" were removed.

1995 MN Removed from the Bemidji school district voluntary reading list and from the school library shelves because it contains subtle stereotypes inconsistent with district diversity goals.
Source: 11, May 1993, pp. 69–70; Nov. 1995, p. 183.

108 Banks, Lynne Reid
Return of the Indian

1995 MN Removed from the Bemidji school district voluntary reading list and from the school library shelves because it contains subtle stereotypes inconsistent with district diversity goals.
Source: 11, Nov. 1995, p. 183.

109 Bannerman, Helen
Little Black Sambo

1956 Removed from classrooms and school library shelves by the Toronto, Ontario, Canada board of education after the board received complaints from several groups that "the popular book was a cause of mental suffering to Negroes in particular and children in general."

1959 NY Removed from a school library in New York City after a black resident challenged the book as racially derogatory. The book was eventually restored to library shelves.

1964 NE Removed from the open shelves of the Lincoln school system on the orders of the School Superintendent because of the inherent racism of the book. The superintendent relocated the book on the "Reserved" shelves, with a note explaining that while it was not "a part of the instructional program, it will be available to those who want to read it as optional material."

1971 AL Banned in Montgomery schools because the book is "inappropriate" and "not in keeping with good human relations."

1972 Attacked in English schools and libraries because it symbolized "the kind of dangerous and obsolete books that must go."

1972 In Hamilton, Ontario, Canada, teachers ordered students to tear from school readers the pages that contained the story.

1972		The Montreal-based Canadian National Black Coalition mobilized efforts to remove the book from school and library shelves.
1972		The book was banned entirely in New Brunswick, Canada.
1972	TX	Removed from the Dallas school libraries because it "distorts a child's view of black people."

Source: 3, p. 173; 11, Apr. 1956, pp. 3–4; July 1963, p. 51; Jan. 1965, p. 12; 14, pp. 212–14.

110 Banville, John
The Untouchable

| 1998 | CT | Challenged at the Bristol Public Library because of references to sexual relations between men and boys. |

Source: 11, May 1998, p. 69.

111 Baraka, Imamu Amiri
The Toilet

| 1969 | | Expurgated at Eastern High School to eliminate all "four-letter words or vernacular." |

Source: 11, May 1969, p. 51.

112 Bargar, Gary W.
What Happened to Mr. Foster?

| 1982 | SC | Challenged at the Greenville County Library because the novel's principal character is a homosexual. |

Source: 11, Jan. 1983, p. 9.

113 Barker, Clive
Tapping the Vein, Book 2

| 1991 | OR | Removed from the Multnomah County Library because of its graphic violence, language, and sexual content. |

Source: 11, Jan. 1992, p. 6.

114 Barnes, Derrick
The Making of Dr. Truelove

| 2007 New | VA | Removed from the Liberty High School in Bedford County because of "sexually explicit content." Administrators pulled the book from the shelf after a parental complaint. While the school system's general policy on content challenges calls for a formal committee's review of the book, that policy was not followed. |

Source: 11, Jan. 2008, pp. 14, 35.

115 Barnes, Djuna
Ryder

| 1984 | | Seized by the British Customs Office as "indecent and obscene." |

Source: 11, Jan. 1985, p. 16.

116 Barron, T. A.
The Great Tree of Avalon: Child of the Dark Prophecy

| 2008 New | NY | Restored by the Lackawanna School Board along with several other books following accusations of censorship by some parents and teachers. The books were pulled from the middle school library recommended list because of concerns that the books deal with the occult. |

Source: 11, May 2008, pp. 115–16.

117 Barth, Edna
Witches, Pumpkins and Grinning Ghosts

| 1992 | AZ | Challenged at the Neely Elementary School in Gilbert because the book "interests little minds into accepting the devil with all of his evil works." |
| 1992 | OR | Challenged in the Salem-Keizer school libraries because it would encourage children to experiment with witchcraft. |

Source: 11, May 1992, p. 78; July 1992, pp. 124–25.

118 Baskin, Julia, Lindsey Newman, Sophie Pollitt-Cohen, and Courtney Toombs
The Notebook Girls

| 2006 | NJ | Challenged, but retained at the Cape May County Library. The book is comprised of the entries four New York City high-school students made in a shared journal in the aftermath of the September 11 terrorist attacks. |

Source: 11, Jan. 2007, p. 29.

119 Bass, Herbert J.
Our American Heritage

| 1987 | AL | Removed from Alabama's list of approved texts—and from the state's classrooms—because the book promotes the "religion of secular humanism." U.S. District Court Judge W. Brevard Hand ruled on March 4, 1987, that thirty-nine history and social studies texts used in Alabama's 129 school systems "discriminate against the very concept of religion and theistic religions in particular, by omissions so serious that a student learning |

history from them would not be apprised of relevant facts about America's history. . . . References to religion are isolated and the integration of religion in the history of American society is ignored." Other texts removed included: *History of a Free People*, by Henry W. Bragdon; *Teen Guide*, by Valerie Chamberlain; *America Is*, by Frank Freidel; *Today's Teen*, by Joan Kelly; *A History of Our American Republic*, by Glenn M. Linden; *Caring, Deciding and Growing*, by Helen McGinley; *Homemaking: Skills for Everyday Living*, by Frances Baynor Parnell; *People and Our Country*, by Norman K. Risjord; *Contemporary Living*, by Verdene Ryder; *Exploring Our Nation's History*, by Sidney Schwartz; *These United States*, by James P. Shenton; *The American Dream*, by Lew Smith; *Social Studies Series* published by Scott, Foresman; and *The Rise of the American Nation* by Lewis Paul Todd. On August 26, 1987, the U.S. Court of Appeals for the Eleventh Circuit unanimously overturned Judge Hand's decision by ruling that the information in the book was "essentially neutral in its religious content." The fact that the texts omitted references to religion was not "an advancement of secular humanism or an active hostility toward theistic religion."

Source: 11, Jan. 1987, p. 6; May 1987, pp. 75, 104–7; Sept. 1987, pp. 166–67; Nov. 1987, pp. 217–18; Jan. 1988, p. 17; Mar. 1988, p. 40.

---

120 Baudelaire, Charles
The Flowers of Evil

1949 Ban lifted in France.
Source: 4, p. 46; 13, pp. 74–75.

---

121 Bauer, Marion Dane, ed.
Am I Blue?: Coming Out from the Silence

2000 IA Challenged, but retained at the Fairfield Middle School and High School libraries despite objections to sexually explicit passages, including a sexual encounter between two girls.
Source: 11, Mar. 2000, p. 62; May 2000, p. 91.

---

122 Bauer, Marion Dane
On My Honor

1989 IA Retained at the Orchard Hill Elementary School in Cedar Falls after being challenged because the 1986 Newbery Honor Book contained "two swear words and one vulgarity."
1992 TX Challenged at the Alamo Heights School District Elementary School because the book

uses the words "hell," "damn" and "frigging."
1995 PA Challenged in fourth to sixth grade reading classes in Grove City because it was "depressing." The criteria used to select the Newbery Award winning book along with a list of other books that focus on "divorce, death, suicide and defeat," was contested.
Source: 11, Mar. 1990, p. 47; May 1990, p. 107; Jan. 1993, p. 13; Sept. 1995, p. 137.

---

123 Bauman, Robert
The Gentleman from Maryland: The Conscience of a Gay Conservative

1993 OR Challenged at the Deschutes County Library in Bend because it "encourages and condones" homosexuality.
Source: 11, Sept. 1993, pp. 158–59.

---

124 Bayle, Pierre
Historical and Critical Dictionary

1754 Burned in France.
1757 Placed by the Vatican on the *Index Librorum Prohibitorum* (Index of Prohibited Books) in Rome, Italy, where it remained through the first two-thirds of the twentieth century.
Source: 1, pp. 135–36.

---

125 Beard, Charles
Rise of American Civilization

1937 LA This Pulitzer Prize winner was seized and destroyed by New Orleans police.
Source: 15, Vol. III, p. 650.

---

126 Beaumarchais, Pierre Augustin Caron de
Barber of Seville

1773 For two years, forbidden to be performed in France.
Source: 4, p. 32.

---

127 Beaumarchais, Pierre Augustin Caron de
Marriage of Figaro

1778 Suppressed for six years by Louis XVI at court in Paris, France and in public performances on the ground of profound immorality. The author was imprisoned in St. Lazare.
Source: 4, p. 32.

---

128 Bechdel, Alison
Fun Home: A Family Tragicomic

2006 MO Challenged, but retained in the adult fiction

section of the Marshall Public Library despite being deemed "pornographic" by some members of the community.

Source: 11, Nov. 2006, p. 289; Jan. 2007, pp. 9–10; May 2007, p. 115; July 2007, pp. 163–64.

129   Beck, Robert E., ed.
Literature of the Supernatural

1986   CO   Challenged at the Jefferson County school libraries in Lakewood because parents objected to many of the stories because they "promoted the occult, sexual promiscuity, and anti-Americanism, and that they attacked other traditional American values." The textbook is a collection of stories written by such authors as Edgar Allen Poe, O. Henry, Ray Bradbury, Dante, and Shakespeare. The Jefferson County School Board refused to ban the book.

Source: 11, May 1986, p. 82; Sept. 1986, p. 173; Nov. 1986, p. 224.

130   Behan, Brendan
Borstal Boy

1958   Banned by the Irish Republic's Censorship of Publications Board. The Irish Censorship Board was not required to give any public explanation for its decisions, but it was generally assumed that the novel was banned because of its treatment of adolescent sexuality and its extensive use of expletives. In fact, Behan does not write graphically about sex and his characters discuss the topic more than they practice it. There can be little doubt that the book was banned essentially because of its attempted subversion of Irish power, structures, religious, social, and political.

1959   Banned in Australia.
1959   Banned in New Zealand.

Source: 6, pp. 203–4.

131   Beiderwell, Bruce, and Jeffrey M. Wheeler, eds.
The Literary Experience

2007   MI   Retained in the Grand Rapids Advanced
New   Placement English classes despite considerations of returning the 1,846 page anthology to its publisher or clipping out about seventy pages with objectionable material, including a drama, "Topdog/Underdog" by Suzan-Lori Parks that contained profanity and descriptions of sexual activity.

Source: 11, Jan. 2008, p. 29.

132   Beisner, Monika
Secret Spells and Curious Charms

1992   OR   Retained by the Salem-Keizer School Board after complaints that the book was a how-to book for satanism.

Source: 11, May 1992, p. 94.

133   Belair, Richard L.
Double Take

1982   LA   Challenged in Livingston due to "objectionable" language.

Source: 11, May 1982, p. 83.

134   Bell, Alan P., and Martin S. Weinberg
Homosexualities: A Study of Diversity among Men and Women

1993   OR   Challenged at the Deschutes County Library in Bend because it "encourages and condones" homosexuality.

Source: 11, Sept. 1993, pp. 158–59.

135   Bell, Ruth, et al.
Changing Bodies, Changing Lives

1981   WI   Placed in a restrictive circulation category at the Muskego High School library.
1982   ME   Challenged in the York school systems.
1982   WI   Challenged in Amherst school system.
1984   MO   Challenged at the William Chrisman High School in Independence because it is "filthy."
1984   OR   Removed from the Sandy Union High School library due to "foul language and disregard for a wholesome balance about human sexuality."
1984   WV   Challenged at the Boone-Madison Public Library.
1986   ME   Challenged at the Gray-New Gloucester High School library because the book contains first person accounts of teenagers' sexual experiences.
1992   AK   Removed from the Kenai Peninsula Borough School District libraries in Homer because the book was too explicit.
1992   WI   Challenged at the Eau Claire Memorial High School library because of its graphic language and because the book condones abortion, homosexuality, and incest.
1994   PA   Challenged at the Council Rock School District in Bucks County because of passages that "undermine parental authority and depict sexual relations in explicit and vulgar language."

Source: 11, July 1981, p. 92; May 1982, p. 100; July 1982, p. 124; July 1984, pp. 104, 106; Sept. 1984, p. 138; Nov. 1984, p. 186; Jan. 1985, pp. 27–28; July 1986, pp. 135–36; Sept. 1992, p. 140; Mar. 1993, p. 41; Mar. 1995, p. 44.

136 Bellairs, John
The Figure in the Shadows

1990 AZ Restricted at the Dysart Unified School District libraries in El Mirage because of two uses of profanity and because of its link to magic.
Source: 11, Jan. 1991, p. 11.

137 Belpre, Pura
Perez and Martina

1988 OR Challenged at the Multnomah County Library in Portland because the death of a mouse in the story could upset children.
Source: 11, Jan. 1989, p. 3.

138 Benchley, Peter
Jaws

1978 KS Removed from all school libraries in Gardner due to a sexually explicit section.
1979 UT Challenged at the Ogden School District and placed in a restricted circulation category.
1980 NC Removed from all elementary and middle school libraries in Clinton due to "objectionable" language.
1986 GA Challenged in the Gwinnett County public schools because of "obscene language."
Source: 11, May 1978, p. 56; May 1979, p. 49; Sept. 1980, p. 99; Mar. 1987, p. 65.

139 Benjamin, Carol Lea
The Wicked Stepdog

1994 MT Challenged by a parent at Newman Elementary School in Billings because of objectionable language including the words "boobs," "ass," and "smoldering kisses." Despite an appeal from parents at a meeting where the offending words were emblazoned on pickets in the audience, two trustees upheld a decision not to remove the book from the district's library shelves.
Source: 11, July 1994, p. 110; Sept. 1994, p. 166.

140 Bennett, James
Blue Star Rapture

1999 IL Challenged, but retained on the Downers Grove High School reading lists despite parents' complaints that the book is "obscene" and "vulgar."
Source: 11, Jan. 2000, p. 28.

141 Bentham, Jeremy
An Introduction to the Principles of Morals and Legislation

1819 Placed on the *Index Librorum Prohibitorum* (Index of Prohibited Books) in Rome, Italy by the Catholic Church, remaining listed through its last edition in effect until 1966.
Source: 1, pp. 166–67.

142 Berendt, John
Midnight in the Garden of Good and Evil: A Savannah Story

2008 ND New Banned for just four days from the Beulah High School library. Two school employees followed school policy to request removing the book after their son brought it home from an accelerated-reading program, in which students pick from a couple of hundred titles. The parents said the 1994 runaway nonfiction best seller was too pornographic and at odds with student behavior promoted in the school handbook. The board reversed its decision at the encouragement of the board president, who said the board moved too fast and unleashed a possible court case it would never win. He said there might be more palatable alternatives, like creating a list of restricted books that parents have to approve before their children can check them out. A decision to review school policies and investigate less restrictive means to control library books was approved by the school board.
Source: 11, Mar. 2009, pp. 55–56.

143 Berger, Melvin
The Supernatural: From ESP to UFOs

1993 TN Challenged, but retained at the Cleveland Public Library along with seventeen other books, most of which are on sex education, AIDS awareness, and some titles on the supernatural.
Source: 11, Sept. 1993, p. 146.

144 Berger, Thomas
Little Big Man

1986 WA Retained on a list of supplementary texts for honor history classes at Juanita High School in Bellevue despite claims that the book is "full of sexual material and questionable messages and should be banned."
Source: 11, Sept. 1986, p. 173.

145 Bergson, Henri
Creative Evolution

1907 The Vatican condemned "modernist" views, and in 1914, it placed Bergson's work on the *Index Librorum Prohibitorum* (Index of Prohibited Books) in Rome, Italy where it remained through the last edition, published until 1966.
Source: 1, pp. 62–63.

146 Berkeley, George
Alciphron, or the Minute Philosopher

1897 Placed on the *Index Librorum Prohibitorum* (Index of Prohibited Books) in Rome, Italy. It was retained on the Index of Pope Leo XII in 1897 and remained listed through the last edition, compiled in 1948 and in print until 1996.
Source: 1, p. 11.

147 Betancourt, Jeanne
Sweet Sixteen and Never. . .

1991 MD Challenged in the Howard County schools because of the book's graphic depiction of teenage romance.
Source: 11, Mar. 1992, p. 40.

148 *The Bible*

1624 Martin Luther's translation of 1534 was burned by Papal authority in Germany.
1926 Soviet officials stated, "The section [in libraries] on religion must contain solely anti-religious books," and the Bible was not published again in the USSR until 1956.
1978 Banned in Ethiopia as "contradictory to the ongoing revolution."
1986 Translations of the Old and New Testament were banned in Turkey.
1992 MN In 1952 and 1953 Fundamentalists in the U.S. attacked the Revised Standard Version because of changes in terminology. Challenged by an atheist "seeking to turn the tables on the religious right," but retained at the Brooklyn Center Independent School District. The challenger stated "the lewd, indecent, and violent contents of that book are hardly suitable for young students."
1993 AK Challenged as "obscene and pornographic," but retained at the Noel Wien Library in Fairbanks.
1993 PA Challenged, but retained in the West Shore schools near Harrisburg despite objections that it "contains language and stories that are inappropriate for children of any age, including

tales of incest and murder. There are more than three hundred examples of 'obscenities' in the book."
2001 FL Challenged, but retained in the Marion-Levy Public Library System in Ocala.
Source: 4, pp. 3–5; 5, Sept. /Oct. 1978, p. 66; July/Aug. 1986, p. 46; 6, pp. 229–32; 8, pp. 208–12; 11, Jan. 1993, p. 8; Mar. 1993, p. 55; Mar. 1993, p. 55; July 1993, p. 123; Jan. 1994, p. 36; May 2001, p. 123.

149 Billington, Ray
Limericks: Historical and Hysterical

1988 CA Removed, but later returned to the Tokay High School library in Lodi because it was "really inappropriate and there ought to be better books on limericks available."
Source: 11, May 1989, p. 75.

150 Bing, Leon
Do or Die

1993 WY Challenged at the Sweetwater County Library in Green River because the book tells young people how to become involved in a gang. The book was retained.
Source: 11, Jan. 1994, p. 14; Mar. 1994, p. 70.

151 Bird, Malcolm
The Witch's Handbook

1991 OR Challenged for promoting witchcraft, but retained at the Multnomah County Library.
Source: 11, Jan. 1992, p. 6.

152 Birdseye, Tom
Attack of the Mutant Underwear

2006 FL Removed from the Pinellas school district's Battle of the Books program because officials found it unsuitable for younger readers. The book is on the Sunshine State Young Reader's Award list of books for third, fourth, and fifth-graders.
Source: 11, Nov. 2006, pp. 290–91.

153 Bishop, Claire H.
The Five Chinese Brothers

1994 WA Challenged at the Spokane School District library because it is too violent.
1998 CA Challenged, but retained at the Colton elementary schools despite a parent's protest that it contains descriptions of violent plots to execute five brothers. Other books have been unsuccessfully challenged in recent years in the Colton School District, including John Steinbeck's *Of Mice and Men* for its use of

profanity and Stephen King's *Misery* for violence.

Source: 11, Jan. 1995, p. 9; Mar. 1999, p. 47.

---

154   Blank, Joan
A Kid's First Book about Sex

1986 IN   Challenged at the Hammond Public Library because "the book promotes immorality and promiscuity. It promotes no moral values whatsoever."

Source: 11, Jan. 1987, p. 30.

---

155   Blank, Joan
Laugh Lines

1990 CA   Removed from the McKinleyville Elementary School library for its "demeaning manner" toward individuals who read the riddles and cannot figure out the answers, rather than for its political or sexual content.

Source: 11, Mar. 1991, p. 42.

---

156   Blatty, William P.
The Exorcist

1975 IA   Challenged at the Grinnell-Newburg school system as "vulgar and obscene by most religious standards."

1976 CO   Banned for use in Aurora High School English classes on the grounds of "immorality."

Source: 11, Mar. 1975, p. 41; May 1975, p. 87; May 1976, p. 70; May 1977, p. 79.

---

157   Block, Francesca Lia, and Suza Scalora
The Rose and the Beast: Fairy Tales Retold

2002 VA   Challenged, along with seventeen other titles in the Fairfax County elementary and secondary libraries, by a group called Parents Against Bad Books in Schools. The group contends the books "contain profanity and descriptions of drug abuse, sexually explicit conduct, and torture."

Source: 11, Jan. 2003, p. 10.

---

158   Block, Francesca Lia
Baby Be-Bop

1998 WI   Removed from the Barron School District because of the book's use of vulgar language and sexually explicit passages. The ACLU of Wisconsin filed suit against the school district on Feb. 16, 1999. The books were then returned to the library while a federal court considered the lawsuit. On October 8, 1999, it

was agreed that the novel will remain available to students as part of the school district's settlement of the federal lawsuit.

2000 CA   Removed from the mandatory reading program at the Norman L. Sullivan Middle School in Bonsall due to sexually explicit language.

2009 WI
New   Four Wisconsin men belonging to the Christian Civil Liberties Union (CCLU) sought $30,000 apiece for emotional distress they suffered from the West Bend Community Memorial Library for displaying a copy of the book. The claim states that, "specific words used in the book are derogatory and slanderous to all males" and "the words can permeate violence and put one's life in possible jeopardy, adults and children alike." The CCLU called for the public burning of this title. Four months later, the library board unanimously voted 9–0 to maintain, "without removing, relocating, labeling, or otherwise restricting access," this and other challenged books in the young adult section at the West Bend Community Memorial Library.

Source: 8, pp. 415–16; 11, Jan. 1999, p. 9; Mar. 1999, p. 37; May 1999, p. 68; Jan. 2000, p. 28; May 2000, p. 76; July 2009, pp. 128, 132, 134; Sept. 2009, pp. 169–70.

---

159   Block, Francesca Lia
Girl Goddess #9: Nine Stories

2002 VA   Challenged, along with seventeen other titles in the Fairfax County elementary and secondary libraries, by a group called Parents Against Bad Books in Schools. The group contends the books "contain profanity and descriptions of drug abuse, sexually explicit conduct, and torture."

Source: 11, Jan. 2003, p. 10.

---

160   Block, Francesca Lia
I Was a Teenage Fairy

2002 VA   Challenged, along with seventeen other titles in the Fairfax County elementary and secondary libraries, by a group called Parents Against Bad Books in Schools. The group contends the books "contain profanity and descriptions of drug abuse, sexually explicit conduct, and torture."

Source: 11, Jan. 2003, p. 10.

---

161   Block, Francesca Lia
Witch Baby

2002 VA   Challenged, along with seventeen other titles in the Fairfax County elementary and secondary libraries, by a group called Parents Against Bad Books in Schools. The group contends the books "contain profanity and descriptions of drug abuse, sexually explicit conduct, and torture." On March 10, 2003, the school board determined the book is suitable for elementary- and middle-school collections and placed a young-adult sticker on its spine.

Source: 11, Jan. 2003, p. 10; May 2003, p. 117.

---

162   Bloom, Harold, ed.
Modern Critical Views: James Baldwin

2000 PA Removed in the Southern Columbia School District in Elysburg because of concerns about sexual references and foul language in a single passage.

Source: 11, July 2000, p. 104.

---

163   Blumberg, Rhoda
Devils and Demons

1988 OR Challenged at the Newberg Public Library because the book was too graphic and the topic was negative and degrading.

Source: 11, Jan. 1990, pp. 4–5.

---

164   Blume, Judy
Are You There God? It's Me, Margaret

1980 AZ Challenged in many libraries but removed from the Gilbert elementary school libraries, and ordered that parental consent be required for students to check out this title from the junior high school library.

1982 AL Challenged in the Tuscaloosa school system.

1982 MN Restricted in Zimmerman to students who have written permission from their parents.

1982 WI Challenged in the Fond du Lac school systems because the book is "sexually offensive and amoral."

1983 MN After the Minnesota Civil Liberties Union sued the Elk River School Board, the Board reversed its decision to restrict this title to students who have written permission from their parents.

1983 OH Challenged at the Xenia school libraries because the book "is built around just two themes: sex and anti-Christian behavior."

1985 MT Challenged as profane, immoral, and offensive, but retained in the Bozeman school libraries.

Source: 9; 11, Jan. 1981, p. 9; Sept. 1982, pp. 155–56; Mar. 1983, pp. 34, 39; May 1983, p. 71; Sept. 1983, pp. 139, 153; Nov. 1983, p. 197; July 1985, p. 112.

---

165   Blume, Judy
Blubber

1980 MD Removed from all library shelves in the Montgomery County elementary schools.

1981 AZ Temporarily banned in Sunizona.

1983 IA Challenged in the Des Moines schools due to "objectionable" subject matter.

1983 OH Challenged at the Xenia school libraries because the book "undermines authority since the word 'bitch' is used in connection with a teacher."

1983 OH Challenged at the Akron School District libraries.

1983 TX Challenged at the Smith Elementary School in Del Valle because it contained the words "damn" and "bitch" and showed children cruelly teasing a classmate.

1984 IL Banned, but later restricted to students with parental permission at the Peoria School District libraries because of its strong sexual content and language, and alleged lack of social or literary value.

1984 NJ Restricted at the Lindenwold elementary school libraries because of "a problem with language."

1984 PA Removed from the Hanover School District's elementary and secondary libraries, but later placed on a "restricted shelf" at middle school libraries because the book was "indecent and inappropriate."

1984 WY Challenged at the Casper school libraries.

1985 MT Challenged as profane, immoral, and offensive, but retained in the Bozeman school libraries.

1986 WI Challenged at the Muskego Elementary School because "the characters curse and the leader of the taunting (of an overweight girl) is never punished for her cruelty."

1991 OH Challenged at the Perry Township elementary school libraries because in the book, "bad is never punished. Good never comes to the fore. Evil is triumphant."

1998 AL Banned at Clements High School in Athens because of objections to two uses of the word "damn" and "bitch" in the novel. The decision was later reversed.

1999 TX Removed from an elementary school in Arlington because educators objected to "verbal, physical, and sexual abuse of student upon student."

Source: 9; 11, May 1980, p. 51; Mar. 1982, p. 57; May 1982, p. 84; July 1982, pp. 124, 142; May 1983, pp. 73, 85–86; July 1983, p. 121; Sept. 1983, pp. 139, 153; Nov. 1983, p. 197; Nov. 1984, p. 185; Jan. 1985, pp. 8–9; Mar. 1985, pp. 33, 42, 58; July 1985, p. 112; Jan. 1987, p. 31; Mar. 1992, p. 41; July 1992, p. 124; Mar. 1999, p. 35; May 1999, p. 83; Jan. 2000, p. 8.

---

166   Blume, Judy
Deenie

1980 AZ Removed from the Gilbert elementary school libraries, and ordered that parental consent be required for students to check out this title from the junior high school library.

1980 UT Removed from the Utah State Library bookmobile because the book contains "the vilest sexual descriptions" and if given to "the wrong kid at the wrong time (would) ruin his life."

1982 CA Challenged in the Cotati-Rohnert Park School District because the novel allegedly undermines parental moral values.

1982 FL Challenged in Orlando.

1983 MN After the Minnesota Civil Liberties Union sued the Elk River School Board, the Board reversed its decision to restrict this title to students who have written permission from their parents.

1984 IL Banned, but later restricted to students with parental permission at the Peoria School District libraries because of its strong sexual content and language, and alleged lack of social or literary value.

1984 PA Removed from the Hanover School District's elementary and secondary libraries, but later placed on a "restricted shelf" at middle school libraries because the book was "indecent and inappropriate."

1984 WY Challenged at the Casper school libraries.

1985 GA Banned from district elementary school libraries in Gwinnett County as "inappropriate."

1985 GA Returned to the elementary and junior high school library shelves in Clayton County after school officials determined that the book is appropriate for young readers.

1985 MT Challenged as profane, immoral, and offensive, but retained in the Bozeman school libraries.

1996 NC Challenged by a parent in the Cornelius Elementary School library in Charlotte due to the novel's sexual content.

2003 FL Challenged by a parent in the Spring Hill Elementary School District in Hernando County due to passages that talk frankly about masturbation. The board decided to retain the title, but require students to have written parental permission to access the novel.

Source: 9; 11, Nov. 1980, p. 128; Jan. 1981, p. 9; July 1982, p. 125; Sept. 1982, pp. 155–56; Jan. 1983, p. 21; May 1983, p. 71; Sept. 1983, p. 153; Jan. 1985, pp. 8–9; Mar. 1985, pp. 33, 42, 58; July 1985, p. 112; Sept. 1985, p. 151; Nov. 1985, p. 193; Jan. 1986, pp. 8–9, 21; May 1996, p. 83; Jan. 2003, pp. 8–9; Mar. 2004, pp. 48–49; May 2004, pp. 95–96.

---

167 **Blume, Judy**
Forever

1982 FL Challenged at the Orlando schools.

1982 MO Challenged at the Park Hill South Junior High School library where it was housed on restricted shelves because the book promotes "the stranglehold of humanism on life in America."

1982 PA Challenged at the Midvalley Junior-Senior High School in Scranton because it contains "four-letter words and talked about masturbation, birth control, and disobedience to parents."

1983 OH Challenged at the Akron School District libraries.

1983 WI Challenged at the Howard-Suamico High School because "it demoralizes marital sex."

1984 IA Challenged at the Cedar Rapids Public Library because it is "pornography and explores areas God didn't intend to explore outside of marriage."

1984 NE Challenged and eventually moved from the Holdrege Public Library young adult section to the adult section because the "book is pornographic and does not promote the sanctity of life, family life."

1986 VA Placed on a restricted shelf at Patrick County School Board.

1986 WY Challenged at the Campbell County school libraries because it is "pornographic" and would encourage young readers "to experiment with sexual encounters."

1987 CA Challenged at the Moreno Valley Unified School District libraries because it "contains profanity, sexual situations, and themes that allegedly encourage disrespectful behavior."

1987 ME Challenged at the Marshwood Junior High School classroom library in Eliot because the "book does not paint a responsible role of parents;" its "cast of sex-minded teenagers is not typical of high schoolers today;" and the "pornographic sexual exploits (in the book) are unsuitable for junior high school role models."

1988 FL West Hernando Middle School principal recommended that Blume's novel be removed from school library shelves because it is "inappropriate."

1992 IL Placed on reserve at the Herrin Junior High School library and can be checked out only with a parent's written permission because the novel is "sexually provocative reading."

1993 IL Removed from the Frost Junior High School library in Schaumburg because "it's basically a sexual 'how-to-do' book for junior high students. It glamorizes [sex] and puts ideas in their heads."

1993 WI Placed on the "parental permission shelf" at the Rib Lake high school libraries after Superintendent Ray Parks filed a "request for reconsideration" because he found the book "sexually explicit." It was subsequently confiscated by the high school principal. A federal jury in Madison, awarded $394,560 to a former Rib Lake High School guidance counselor after finding that his contract was not renewed in retaliation for speaking out against the district's material selection policy. The counselor criticized the decision of the Rib Lake High School principal to restrict student access to the novel.

1994 IA Removed from Mediapolis School District libraries because it "does not promote abstinence and monogamous relationships [and] lacks any aesthetic, literary, or social value." Returned to the shelves a month later but accessible only to high school students.

1995 FL Removed from the Fort Clarke Middle School library in Gainesville after a science teacher objected to its sexually explicit content and a reference to marijuana.

1995 IN Restricted to a reserve section of the Delta High School Library in Muncie. Parents must give their permission in writing before their children can check out the book.

1996 IA Challenged at the Wilton School District for junior and senior high school students because of its sexual content.

1997 IL Banned from middle school libraries in the Elgin School District U46 because of sex scenes. The decision was upheld in June 1999 after an hour of emotional school board discussion. After a four-year absence, the book was returned in 2002 to the shelves of the district's middle school libraries.

2005 AR Challenged in the Fayetteville Middle and Junior High School libraries. The complainant also submitted a list of more than fifty books, citing the books as too sexually explicit and promoting homosexuality.

Source: 8, pp. 334–35; 9; 11, July 1982, pp. 124, 142; May 1982, p. 84; May 1983, pp. 85–86; Mar. 1984, p. 39; May 1984, p. 69; Mar. 1985, p. 59; Sept. 1985, p. 167; Mar. 1986, p. 39; Mar. 1987, pp. 66–67; July 1987, p. 125; Nov. 1987, p. 239; Mar. 1988, p. 45; May 1992, p. 80; May 1993, p. 70; July 1993, pp. 98, 104–5; Sept. 1993, pp. 146–47; May 1994, pp. 83, 86; July 1994, p. 109; Mar. 1995, p. 56; July 1995, p. 93; Nov. 1995, p. 183; May 1996, p. 97; May 1997, pp. 60–61; Sept. 1999, p. 119; Mar. 2002, p. 105; May 2002, pp. 135–36; Sept. 2005, p. 215.

---

168   Blume, Judy
Here's to You, Rachel Robinson

1999 NY Challenged, but retained at the Granville School library in Catskill despite a parent's objection to three words.

Source: 11, Sept. 1999, p. 131.

---

169   Blume, Judy
Iggie's House

1984 WY Challenged at the Casper school libraries.

Source: 11, Mar. 1985, p. 42.

---

170   Blume, Judy
It's Not the End of the World

1984 NJ Restricted at the Lindenwold elementary school libraries because of "a problem with language."

1984 PA Removed from the Hanover School District's elementary and secondary libraries, but later placed on a "restricted shelf" at middle school libraries because the book was "indecent and inappropriate."

1984 WY Challenged at the Casper school libraries.

1985 MN Challenged at the Orchard Lake Elementary School library in Burnsville.

1998 GA Restricted to fourth- and fifth-graders at W. C. Britt Elementary School in Gwinnett County due to concerns about profanity.

Source: 11, Nov. 1984, p. 185; Jan. 1985, p. 9; Mar. 1985, p. 42; Nov. 1985, p. 203; May 1998, pp. 69–70.

---

171   Blume, Judy
The One in the Middle Is the Green Kangaroo

1984 WY Challenged at the Casper school libraries.

Source: 11, Mar. 1985, p. 42.

---

172   Blume, Judy
Otherwise Known as Sheila the Great

1984 WY Challenged at the Casper school libraries.

Source: 11, Mar. 1985, p. 42.

---

173   Blume, Judy
Starring Sally J. Freedman as Herself

1984 PA Removed from the Hanover School District's elementary and secondary libraries, but later placed on a "restricted shelf" at middle school libraries because the book was "indecent and inappropriate."

1984 WY Challenged at the Casper school libraries.

1985 MT Challenged as profane, immoral, and offensive, but retained in the Bozeman school libraries.

Source: 11, Jan. 1985, p. 9; Mar. 1985, p. 42; July 1985, p. 112.

---

174   Blume, Judy
Superfudge

1984 WY Challenged at the Casper school libraries.

1985 MT Challenged as profane, immoral, and offensive, but retained in the Bozeman school libraries.

Source: 11, Mar. 1985, p. 42; July 1985, p. 112.

175 Blume, Judy
Then Again, Maybe I Won't

1980 AZ Challenged in many libraries but removed from the Gilbert elementary school libraries, and ordered that parental consent be required for students to check out this title from the junior high school library.

1982 AL Challenged in Tuscaloosa because the book is "sexually offensive and amoral."

1982 FL Challenged in Orlando.

1982 MD Challenged in the Harford County school systems.

1983 MN After the Minnesota Civil Liberties Union sued the Elk River School Board, the Board reversed its decision to restrict this title to students who have written permission from their parents.

1984 IL Banned, but later restricted to students with parental permission at the Peoria School District libraries because of its strong sexual content and language, and alleged lack of social or literary value.

1984 LA Removed from all school library collections in St. Tammany Parish because its "treatment of immorality and voyeurism do not provide for the growth of desirable attitudes," but later reinstated.

1984 WY Challenged at the Casper school libraries.

1985 MT Challenged as profane, immoral, and offensive, but retained in the Bozeman school libraries.

1988 IA Challenged in the Des Moines elementary schools because of sexual content.

1989 OR Challenged at the Salem-Keizer School District because it is a "dismal tale of a young boy's inability to cope and his very inappropriate responses to the changes taking place in his life."

1990 PA Challenged at the elementary library in Tyrone because the book deals with masturbation and erections, and that it explains how to drink whiskey, vodka, and gin.

Source: 9; 11, July 1982, p. 124; Sept. 1982, pp. 155–56; May 1983, p. 71; Sept. 1983, p. 153; May 1984, p. 69; July 1984, p. 121; Jan. 1985, p. 8; Mar. 1985, pp. 33, 42, 58; July 1985, p. 112; Jan. 1990, pp. 4–5; July 1990, p. 127; Mar. 1991, p. 62.

176 Blume, Judy
Tiger Eyes

1984 IN Challenged at the Daleville Elementary School library due to alleged sexual innuendo in the book.

1984 PA Removed from the Hanover School District's elementary and secondary libraries, but later placed on a "restricted shelf" at middle school libraries because the book was "indecent and inappropriate."

1984 WY Challenged at the Casper school libraries.

1999 LA Pulled from the Many Junior High library shelves because of descriptions of a girl's sexual encounters, getting drunk at school, and the use of profanities.

Source: 11, Jan. 1985, p. 9; Mar. 1985, pp. 42, 59; Jan. 2000, p. 11.

177 Boccaccio, Giovanni
The Decameron

1497 Burned and prohibited in Italy also in 1559.

1800s Banned in France

1906 OH Declared to be an "obscene, lewd and lascivious book of indecent character" by a jury in Cincinnati.

1926 Banned in U.S. until 1931.

1934 MI Seized by Detroit police.

1935 MA Still banned in Boston.

1950s Attemps to get the work destroyed, some of them successful, continued until the 1950s

Source: 6, pp. 257–58; 8, pp. 327–29; 9, p. 7; 10, p. 140.

178 Bode, Janet, and Stan Mack
Heartbreak and Roses: Real Life Stories of Troubled Love

1996 LA Pulled from the Ouachita Parish School library in Monroe because of sexual content. The Louisiana chapter of the ACLU filed a lawsuit in the federal courts on October 3, 1996, claiming that the principal and the school superintendent violated First Amendment free speech rights and also failed to follow established procedure when they removed the book. The three-year-old school library censorship case headed to court after the Ouachita Parish School Board made no decision to seek a settlement at a special meeting April 12, 1999. On August 17, 1999, the Ouachita Parish School Board agreed to return the book to the library and to develop a new book-selection policy that follows state guidelines for school media programs.

Source: 11, Sept. 1996, pp. 151–52; Jan. 1997, p. 7; July 1999, p. 93; Jan. 2000, p. 27.

179 Bode, Janet
View from Another Closet

1982 MI Challenged at the Niles Community Library because the book is "a devious attempt to recruit our young people into the homosexual lifestyle."

Source: 11, Jan. 1983, p. 8.

180 Bogart, Bonnie
Ewoks Join the Fight

1987 CA Challenged at the La Costa Public Library because "every page except for three has some sort of violence—somebody gets knocked down or the Death Star is destroyed."
Source: 11, July 1987, p. 125.

181 Bonner, Cindy
Lily

1994 PA Removed temporarily from the Richland Middle School Library while a "Parental Guidance" program that gives parents more control over what their children read in school is explored. A local parent complained that it was "sexually explicit" and had "no moral guidance."
Source: 11, Jan. 1995, p. 8; Mar. 1995, p. 41.

182 Booth, Jack
Impressions series

1987 WA Challenged in the Oak Harbor school system because it "undermines parental authority, is filled with morbid, frightening imagery and involves children in witchcraft and sorcery." In addition, opponents claimed, "the series promotes Eastern and other religions to the exclusion of Christianity."

1988 OR Challenged at the Talent Elementary School in Phoenix because it "promotes witchcraft and secular humanism and lacks Christian values."

1989 CA Temporarily banned at the Hacienda La Puente Unified School District in Hacienda Heights because of morbid imagery.

1989 CA Removed from the East Whittier School District because parents complained that some stories were evil and morbid.

1989 ID Challenged in the Coeur d'Alene elementary schools.

1990 AK Challenged in the Fairbanks schools.

1990 CA Challenged in the Stockton schools.

1990 CA Challenged in the Redondo Beach schools.

1990 CA Challenged in the Yucaipa schools.

1990 CA Challenged in the Winters schools.

1990 CA Challenged in the Shingletown schools.

1990 CA Challenged in the Campbell schools.

1990 CA Challenged in the Saratoga schools.

1990 ID Challenged in the Boise schools.

1990 IL Challenged in the Wheaton schools. U.S. District Court Judge James B. Moran dismissed a lawsuit filed against Wheaton-Warrenville School District by parents who claimed school officials failed to implement rules allowing their children to be excluded from using the series.

1990 IL Challenged in the Palatine schools.

1990 IL Challenged in the Barrington schools.

1990 IL Challenged in the Arlington Heights schools.

1990 NM Challenged in the Albuquerque schools.

1990 NM Challenged in the Santa Fe schools.

1990 NY Challenged in the Lakewood schools.

1990 SD Challenged in the Box Elder schools.

1990 TN Challenged in the Nashville schools.

1991 CA Challenged in the Eureka schools.

1991 CA Challenged in the Grass Valley schools. U.S. District Court Judge William Shubb dismissed a lawsuit in California alleging that the series violated the state and federal constitutions by promoting the "religion of witchcraft and neo-paganism."

1991 ME Challenged in the Gardiner schools.

1991 OH Challenged in the Willard schools because the series of readers "undermines absolute truth and value, teaches situational ethics and a lack of respect for authority, and curiosity in the occult." The first editions of the series were challenged because there was too much of a Canadian emphasis.

1991 OR Challenged in the Newport schools.

1991 OR Removed in the North Marion School District in Aurora.

1992 IL U.S. District Court Judge James B. Moran dismissed a lawsuit filed against Wheaton-Warrenville School District by parents who claimed school officials failed to implement rules allowing their children to be excluded from using the series.

1992 MD Challenged in Frederick County schools.
Source: 11, Jan. 1988, p. 13; Jan. 1989, p. 3; Jan. 1990, p. 11; Mar. 1990, p. 46; May 1990, pp. 85-86; Sept. 1990, pp. 160–61; Nov. 1990, p. 210; Jan. 1991, pp. 14, 16, 17, 29; Mar. 1991, pp. 46–48; July 1991, pp. 107, 131–32; Sept. 1991, pp. 178–79; Jan. 1992, p. 9; Mar. 1992, pp. 32, 45; July 1992, pp. 110–11, 117; Sept. 1992, p. 163; Jan. 1993, pp. 11, 18.

183 Bopp, Joseph B.
Herbie Capleenies

1982 OR Removed from the Hermiston Elementary School library because of the main character's activities, which included machine-gunning his boring friends and making naked snowwomen.
Source: 11, July 1982, p. 124.

184 Borland, Hal
When the Legends Die

1995 WY Removed from the Lincoln County High School curriculum because of "considerable obscenities." The parent complained that there were 57 swear words in 40 consecutive pages.
Source: 11, July 1995, p. 100.

185 Borten, Helen
Halloween

1992 AZ Challenged at the Neely Elementary School in Gilbert because the book shows the dark side of religion through the occult, the devil, and satanism.
Source: 11, May 1992, p. 78; July 1992, p. 124.

186 Bossert, Jill
Humor 2

1992 WA Challenged at the Sno-Isle Regional Library System in Marysville because the jokes in the book deal with adult subjects.
Source: 11, Nov. 1992, p. 185.

187 Boston Women's Health Book Collective
Our Bodies, Ourselves

1975 FL Removed from high school libraries in Pinellas County.
1975 VT Removed from high school libraries in Townshend.
1977 WV Removed from high school libraries in Morgantown.
1978 MT Removed from high school libraries in Helena.
1982 MI Challenged in Three Rivers Public Library because it "promotes homosexuality and perversion."
1982 WI Challenged in Amherst due to its "pornographic" nature.
1984 MO Challenged at the William Chrisman High School in Independence because the book is "filthy." The controversial feminist health manual was on a bookshelf in the classroom and was the personal property of the teacher.
Source: 9; 11, July 1975, p. 105; Sept. 1975, p. 138; July 1977, p. 100; Mar. 1979, p. 27; May 1982, p. 100; Mar. 1983, p. 29; July 1984, p. 106; 15, Vol. IV, p. 714.

188 Boswell, Robert
Mystery Ride

1994 OR Expurgated by an apparent self-appointed censor at the Coquille Public Library along with several other books. Most were mysteries and romances in which single words and sexually explicit passages were whited out by a vandal who left either dots or solid ink pen lines where the words had been.
Source: 11, Sept. 1994, p. 148.

189 Bowden, Mark
Black Hawk Down: A Story of Modern War

2008 LA New Removed from a classroom at Central Lafourche High School in Raceland for violating the district policy on cursing. The book is the story of a failed Special Forces mission in Somalia.
Source: 11, Jan. 2009, pp. 9–10.

190 Bower, William C.
The Living Bible

1981 NC Burned in Gastonia because it is "a perverted commentary of the King James Version."
Source: 11, July 1981, p. 105.

191 Boyle, T. Coraghessan
The Tortilla Curtain

2010 CA New Challenged on the Santa Rosa High School reading list. A review committee approved the continued use of the book with the following guidelines: "The teacher must appropriately prepare students for parts of the book that may be considered provocative; limit the book to juniors and seniors; should a parent object to the book, board policy is currently in place that allows a student to be excused from the book assignment, and provides for an alternative assignment without penalty to the student."
Source: 11, Mar. 2010, pp. 55–56.

192 Bradbury, Ray
Fahrenheit 451

1992 CA Expurgated at the Venado Middle School in Irvine. Students received copies of the book with scores of words—mostly "hells" and "damns"—blacked out. The novel is about book-burning and censorship. After receiving complaints from parents and being contacted by reporters, school officials said the censored copies would no longer be used.
2006 TX Challenged at the Conroe Independent School District because of the following: "discussion of being drunk, smoking cigarettes, violence, 'dirty talk,' references to the Bible, and using God''s name in vain." The novel went against the complainants' "religious beliefs."
Source: 6, p. 279; 8, pp. 446–47; 11, July 1992, pp. 108–9; Nov. 2006, p. 293.

193 Bradbury, Ray
The Martian Chronicles

1982 FL Challenged at the Haines City High School due to several instances of profanity and the use of God's name in vain in the work.

1987 NC Challenged at the Newton-Conover High School as a supplemental reading due to profanity.

1993 TN Challenged as required reading at the Gatlinburg-Pittman High School due to profanity.

1998 NJ Pulled and replaced with a newer version at the Herbert Hoover Middle School in Edison because a chapter contains the words "the niggers are coming." The new abridged edition of the book omits the inflammatory story, titled "Way Up in the Air."

Source: 11, Jan. 1983, p. 22; May 1987, p. 103; Sept. 1993, p. 149; May 1998, pp. 71–72; July 1998, p. 109.

194 Bradbury, Ray
The Veldt

2006 OR Retained on the Beaverton School District's reading list. The short story was challenged by a middle-school parent who thought its language and plot were inappropriate for students. Her biggest concern is that the story offers no consequences for the children's actions. The short story is part of Bradbury's *The Illustrated Man* anthology. It is twenty pages long and was published in 1951 as the first in the collection of eighteen science fiction stories.

Source: 11, Nov. 2006, p. 319.

195 Bradford, Richard
Red Sky at Morning

1979 WA Challenged in Omak due to "profane language."

1987 MT Challenged at the Big Sky High School in Missoula because the "language was inappropriate for freshman."

2007 MT New Challenged, but retained on the reading list for freshman English classes in Billings School District 2 despite concerns that the book contains excessive profanity and includes sexually suggestive passages that the complainant thought were not appropriate for fourteen-year-olds. The book has been used in the district for more than twenty years.

Source: 11, July 1979, p. 75; July 1987, p. 150; July 2007, pp. 164–65.

196 Brancato, Robin
Winning

1986 CO Challenged at the Greeley-Evans School District in Greeley because the book contained "obscenities, allusions to sexual references, and promoted contempt for parents and acceptance of drug use."

Source: 11, Sept. 1986, p. 171.

197 Brannen, Sarah
Uncle Bobby's Wedding

2008 CO New Challenged at the Douglas County Libraries in Castle Rock because "some material may be inappropriate for young children." The children's book features two gay guinea pigs. A resident requested that the book be removed from the library and placed in a special area or labeled "some material may be inappropriate for young children."

Source: 11, Sept. 2008, pp. 183–84.

198 Brashler, Anne
Getting Jesus in the Mood

1992 MD Challenged at the Carroll County Public Library in Westminster because the widely praised short story collection is "smutty" and contains pornography aimed at Jesus Christ.

Source: 11, Sept. 1992, pp. 137–38.

199 Brautigan, Richard
The Abortion: An Historical Romance

1978 CA Removed from high school library in Redding due to "unsuitable obscene and sexual references." A California state appeals court ruled in 1989 in *Wexner v. Anderson Union High School District Board of Trustees* that the school board acted improperly when it banned this book.

Source: 11, Jan. 1979, p. 11; Mar. 1989, p. 52.

200 Brautigan, Richard
A Confederate General from Big Sur

1978 CA Removed from high school library in Redding due to "unsuitable obscene and sexual references." A California state appeals court ruled in 1989 in *Wexner v. Anderson Union High School District Board of Trustees* that the school board acted improperly when it banned this book.

Source: 11, Jan. 1979, p. 11; Mar. 1989, p. 52.

201   Brautigan, Richard
The Pill vs. the Springhill
Mine Disaster

1978 CA   Removed from high school library in Redding
due to "unsuitable obscene and sexual
references." A California state appeals court
ruled in 1989 in _Wexner v. Anderson Union_
High School District Board of Trustees that
the school board acted improperly when it
banned this book.

1988 GA   Removed from the shelves of the Southeast
Whitfield High School library because it
includes four poems that use "inappropriate"
language or have sexual connotations.
Source: 11, Jan. 1979, p. 11; Jan. 1989, p. 7; Mar. 1989, p. 52.

202   Brautigan, Richard
The Revenge of the Lawn

1978 CA   Removed from high school library in Redding
due to "unsuitable obscene and sexual
references." A California state appeals court
ruled in 1989 in _Wexner v. Anderson Union_
High School District Board of Trustees that
the school board acted improperly when it
banned this book.
Source: 11, Jan. 1979, p. 11; Mar. 1989, p. 52.

203   Brautigan, Richard
Rommel Drives on Deep into Egypt

1978 CA   Removed from high school library in Redding
due to "unsuitable obscene and sexual
references." A California state appeals court
ruled in 1989 in _Wexner v. Anderson Union_
High School District Board of Trustees that
the school board acted improperly when it
banned this book.
Source: 11, Jan. 1979, p. 11; Mar. 1989, p. 52.

204   Brautigan, Richard
Trout Fishing in America

1978 CA   Removed from high school library in Redding
due to "unsuitable obscene and sexual
references." A California state appeals court
ruled in 1989 in _Wexner v. Anderson Union_
High School District Board of Trustees that the
school board acted improperly when it
banned this book.
Source: 11, Jan. 1979, p. 11; Mar. 1989, p. 52.

205   Bredes, Don
Hard Feelings

1981 WI   Removed from the Montello High School library.

1982 MI   Challenged in Flat Rock because of
"objectionable" language.
Source: 11, Sept. 1981, p. 126; Sept. 1982, p. 156.

206   Briggs, Raymond
Father Christmas

1979 MI   Removed from all elementary classrooms in
Holland after several parents complained that
the work portrays Santa Claus as having a
negative attitude toward Christmas.

1988 OR   Challenged at the Albany Public Library
because it contains cursing, drinking, and a
negative image of Santa Claus.
Source: 9; 11, Jan. 1980, p. 7; Jan. 1989, p. 3.

207   Brink, Andre
A Dry White Season

1979   Banned in South Africa in Sept. 1979. The ban
was lifted in Nov. 1979, but Brink was branded
a "malicious writer."
Source: 5, Feb. 1980, p. 73.

208   Bronstein, Leo
El Greco

1994 AZ   Retained at Maldonado Elementary School in
Tucson after being challenged by parents
who objected to nudity and "pornographic,"
"perverted," and "morbid" themes.
Source: 11, July 1994, p. 112.

209   Brooks, Bruce
The Moves Make the Man

1992 CA   Removed from a San Lorenzo High School
reading list after a parent complained that
racist terms in the dialogue were offensive to
black students.
Source: 11, Sept. 1992, pp. 140–41.

210   Brown, Claude
Manchild in the Promised Land

1974 WI   Removed from high school libraries in
Waukesha.

1976 FL   Removed from high school libraries in
Plant City.

1977 LA   Removed from classroom use and placed on
the restricted shelf in the Baton Rouge school
library after Concerned Citizens and Taxpayers
for Decent Books listed the book along with
64 other "offensive" works.

1980 OH   Removed from high school libraries in North
Jackson due to "filth and obscenity."

1987 OR   Challenged at the Parkrose High School
because the content is "violent, the language

offensive, and women are degraded." The protestors also questioned its relevance, claiming that Parkrose students have no need to understand life in a black ghetto.

Source: 8, pp. 469–70; 9; 11, May 1980, p. 51; Sept. 1987, p. 176; Nov. 1987, p. 240.

211 Brown, Dan
The Da Vinci Code

2006 Banned in Egypt. The culture minister told parliament, "We ban any book that insults any religion. We will confiscate this book." Parliament was debating the book at the request of several Coptic Christian members who demanded a ban because, "It's based on Zionist myth, and it contains insults towards Christ, and it insults the Christian religion and Islam."

2006 Banned in Iran.

Source: 11, Sept. 2006, p. 232; Jan. 2007, p. 35.

212 Brown, Dee
Bury My Heart at Wounded Knee

1974 WI Removed in Wild Rose by a district administrator because the book was "slanted" and "if there's a possibility that something might be controversial, then why not eliminate it."

Source: 11, Nov. 1974, p. 145.

213 Brown, Laurene Krasny, and Marc Brown
Dinosaurs Divorce

1995 GA Challenged at the Rebecca Minor Elementary School in Gwinnett County because the book could offend children whose parents are going through a divorce and create fears and anxiety in children from stable families.

Source: 11, Sept. 1995, p. 157.

214 Brown, Marc Tolon
Buster's Sugartime

2009 OK Challenged, but retained at the Union district New elementary school libraries despite a parent's complaint that the book features two same-sex couples and their children.

Source: 11, Mar. 2010, pp. 53–54.

215 Browne, Sir Thomas
Religio Medici

1645 The Catholic Church placed it on the *Index Librorum Prohibitorum* (Index of Prohibited Books) in Rome, Italy for its skeptical, rationalist perspective, and its allegiance to the Anglican Church. The book remained listed until 1966.

Source: 1, pp. 282–83.

216 Browning, Elizabeth Barrett
Aurora Leigh

1857 MA Condemned in Boston as "the hysterical indecencies of an erotic mind."

Source: 4, p. 42.

217 Bruno, Giordano
On the Infinite Universe and Worlds

1592 Author imprisoned, tried on charges of blasphemy, immoral conduct, and heresy, and executed in Rome, Italy on February 17, 1600. Placed on the *Index Librorum Prohibitorum* (Index of Prohibited Books) in 1603, where it remained through the last edition of the Index, in effect until 1966.

Source: 8, pp. 273–75.

218 Bryant, Sara Cone
Epaminondas and His Auntie

1989 SC Retained, but moved from the children's section to the folk life section at the Spartanburg County Library because "the book's drawings were stereotypical and demeaning to black people."

Source: 11, Nov. 1989, pp. 236–37.

219 Budbill, David
Bones on Black Spruce Mountain

1988 VT Challenged at the Bennington School District because of inappropriate language.

1993 PA Challenged in the Gettysburg public schools because of offensive language.

Source: 11, Mar. 1989, p. 61; Mar. 1994, p. 55.

220 Bunch, Robert
Invisible Marijuana and Psychedelic Mushroom Gardens

2000 IL Challenged at the Warrenville Public Library because "it provides a step-by-step manual for circumventing the law."

Source: 11, Mar. 2000, p. 48.

221 Bunn, Scott
Just Hold On

1988 WA Banned at the Covington Junior High School in Vancouver because the book is devoid of hope and positive role models.

Source: 11, Mar. 1989, p. 61; May 1989, p. 79.

222   Bunting, Eve
Karen Kepplewhite Is the World's Best Kisser

1989 OR Challenged at the Little Butte Intermediate School in Eagle Point because the book was too mature for the elementary class students.
Source: 11, Jan. 1990, pp. 4–5.

223   Burgess, Anthony
A Clockwork Orange

1973 UT A book seller in Orem was arrested for selling the novel. Charges were later dropped, but the book seller was forced to close the store and relocate to another city.
1976 CO Removed from Aurora high school due to "objectionable" language.
1977 MA Removed from high school classrooms in Westport because of "objectionable" language.
1982 AL Removed from two Anniston high school libraries, but later reinstated on a restricted basis.
Source: 8, pp. 440–41; 11, May 1976, p. 70; Jan. 1977, p. 8; Mar. 1983, p. 37.

224   Burgess, Melvin
Doing It

2005 AR Challenged in the Fayetteville High School library. The complainant also submitted a list of more than fifty books, citing the books as too sexually explicit and promoting homosexuality.
Source: 11, Sept. 2005, p. 215.

225   Burroughs, Augusten
Running with Scissors

2007 MI Challenged in the Howell High School because of the book's strong sexual content. In response to a request from the president of the Livingston Organization for Values in Education, or LOVE, the county's top law enforcement official reviewed the books to see whether laws against distribution of sexually explicit materials to minors had been broken. "After reading the books in question, it is clear that the explicit passages illustrated a larger literary, artistic or political message and were not included solely to appeal to the prurient interests of minors," the Livingston County prosecutor wrote. "Whether these materials are appropriate for minors is a decision to be made by the school board, but I find that they are not in violation of the criminal laws."

2010 FL Challenged as a suggested reading in a class where juniors and seniors earn college credit
New   in Hillsborough County. Four high schools—Plant, Middleton, Hillsborough, and Bloomingdale—voted to keep the book and place a "Mature Reader" label on the front cover. Three high schools—Sickles, Robinson, and Lennard—will require parental consent. Gaither High School and Riverview High School voted to ban the book. The book was banned at Riverview because, "This book has extremely inappropriate content for a high school media center collection. The book contained explicit homosexual and heterosexual situations, profanity, underage drinking and smoking, extreme moral shortcomings, child molesters, graphic pedophile situations and total lack of negative consequences throughout the book."
Source: 11, May 2007, p. 116; May 2010, pp. 103–4.

226   Burroughs, Edgar Rice
Tarzan

1929 CA Removed from the Los Angeles Public Library because Tarzan was allegedly living in sin with Jane.
Source: 10, p. 130.

227   Burroughs, William, and Allen Ginsberg
The Yage Letters

1976 CO Banned from use in Aurora High School English classes on the grounds of "immorality."
Source: 11, May 1976, p. 70; May 1977, p. 79.

228   Burroughs, William
Naked Lunch

1965 MA Found obscene in Boston Superior Court. The finding was reversed by the State Supreme Court the following year.
Source: 4, p. 89; 6, pp. 388–89; 8, p. 472.

229   Buss, Fran Leeper
Journey of the Sparrows

1994 IN Challenged at the Carmel Junior High School because a parent objected to profanity and language dealing with urination, rape, violence, and sex. The parent also objected to the depiction of illegal immigration. The book was retained.
Source: 11, Mar. 1995, p. 43; July 1995, p. 111.

230 Butler, William
The Butterfly Revolution

1987 KS Challenged as a supplemental reading list at the Fort Scott High School library because the book "suggested dislike of the Bible, belief in atheism, vile social habits, obscene language, and plots against adult authority."
Source: 11, May 1987, p. 90.

231 Butz, Arthur R.
The Hoax of the Twentieth Century

1984 Removed from the shelves of the University of Calgary library by the Royal Canadian Mounted Police. Import of the book was banned, after the university bought its copy, under a Canadian law barring import of materials considered seditious, treasonable, immoral, or indecent.

1995 Seized from the Didsbury, Alberta, Canada Public Library and shredded.
Source: 8, pp. 82–85; 11, Jan. 1985, p. 15.

232 Cabell, James Branch
Jurgen: A Comedy of Justice

1920 NY The New York Society for the Suppression of Vice seized all plates and copies of the book and editor was charged with violating the anti-obscenity provisions of the New York State Penal Code.

1953 Banned in Ireland.
Source: 4, p. 64; 13, pp. 126–27; 15, Vol. III, pp. 412–13.

233 Cain, James M.
Serenade

1949 MA After receiving complaints from patrons of the Free Public Library in Worcester, the state attorney general ordered that copies of the novel be removed from library shelves. The case appeared before the Superior Court of Suffolk County, Massachusetts, which judged the book "not obscene." The attorney general filed an appeal with the Supreme Judicial Court where, in September 1950, the novel was cleared again in a 4-3 decision in *Attorney General v. Books Named "Serenade,"* 326 Mass. 324, 94 N.E.2d 259 (1950). In presenting the majority decision, Judge Spalding write that the sexual episodes were "not portrayed in a manner that would have a 'substantial tendency to deprave or corrupt readers by inciting lascivious thoughts or arousing lustful desires.'"
Source: 13, p. 210.

234 Calderone, Mary S., and James W. Ramey
Talking with Your Child about Sex: Questions and Answers for Children from Birth to Puberty

1986 GA The Gainesville Public Library prohibits young readers from checking out this book along with forty other books. The books, on subjects ranging from hypnosis to drug abuse to breast-feeding and sexual dysfunction, are kept in a locked room.
Source: 11, July 1986, p. 117; Sept. 1986, pp. 151–52; Nov. 1986, p. 207.

235 Caldwell, Erskine
God's Little Acre

1933 MA Sued for obscenity but acquitted.
1948 Banned in Ireland.
1950 MA Banned as indecent, obscene, and impure.
1960 Banned in Australia.
Source: 2, p. 148; 4, p. 83; 15, Vol. III, p. 643, Vol. IV, p. 701.

236 Caldwell, Erskine
Tobacco Road

1953 Banned in Ireland.
Source: 4, pp. 83–84.

237 Caldwell, Erskine
Tragic Ground

1944 MA Boston Watch and Ward Society lodged a complaint with the police, claiming the novel was "obscene" and dealt with "low life matters." Miss. E. Margaret Anderson of the Dartmouth Book Stall in Boston was arrested for her "distributing obscene material." In delivering a ruling, Judge Adlow observed to the police, "It's not for me or for you to try to establish literary tastes of the community." He stated that he found the novel to be "dull," but concluded that "the judges of the Municipal Court and the members of the Police Department were not qualified to pass on the literary value of books."
Source: 13, pp. 252–53.

238 Califia, Pat
Sapphistry: The Book of Lesbian Sexuality

1982 CA Challenged as an "inappropriate" recommended text for college students at Long Beach State University.

1984   Seized and shredded by the British customs office.

Source: 11, Sept. 1982, p. 158; Jan. 1985, p. 16.

---

239   **Callen, Larry**
Just-Right Family: Cabbage Patch Kids series

1987   NC   Challenged at the Rutherford County Elementary School library because the book used ungrammatical writing.

Source: 11, Nov. 1987, p. 239.

---

240   **Calvin, John**
Civil and Canonical Law

1542   Forbidden by the Sorbonne in Paris, France.
1555   Banned in England.
1559   Listed as heresy in the *Index Librorum Prohibitorum* (List of Prohibited Books) in Rome, Italy.

Source: 4, p. 14.

---

241   **Cameron, Paul**
Exposing the AIDS Scandal

1990   IL   Challenged at the Downers Grove Public Library because it is factually inaccurate and promotes common fallacies related to the disease.

Source: 11, Mar. 1991, p. 61.

---

242   **Canaday, John**
The Artist as Visionary

1994   AZ   Retained at Maldonado Elementary School in Tucson after being challenged by parents who objected to nudity and "pornographic," "perverted," and "morbid" themes.

Source: 11, July 1994, p. 112.

---

243   **Canaday, John**
Painting in Transition: Precursors of Modern Art

1994   AZ   Retained at Maldonado Elementary School in Tucson after being challenged by parents who objected to nudity and "pornographic," "perverted," and "morbid" themes.

Source: 11, July 1994, p. 112.

---

244   **Capote, Truman**
In Cold Blood: A True Account of a Multiple Murder and Its Consequences

2000   GA   Banned, but later reinstated after community protests at the Windsor Forest High School in Savannah. The controversy began in early 1999 when a parent complained about sex, violence, and profanity in the book that was part of an Advanced Placement English class.

Source: 11, Mar. 2001, p. 76.

---

245   **Carle, Eric**
Draw Me a Star

1996   WA   This children's book dealing with the creation story was challenged in the elementary school libraries in the Edmonds School District because the book is illustrated with highly stylized representations of a naked woman and man.
1999   NY   Challenged, but retained in the Dorothy B. Bunce Elementary School library in Pavilion despite a parent's objection to a collage picture of a naked man and woman representing Adam and Eve.

Source: 11, Nov. 1996, pp. 211–12; May 1999, pp. 83–84.

---

246   **Carpenter, Edward**
Iolaus: An Anthology of Friendship

1984   Seized by the British Customs Office as "indecent and obscene." When first published in London, England in 1902, the book was not suppressed.

Source: 11, Jan. 1985, p. 16.

---

247   **Carroll, Jim**
The Basketball Diaries

1998   GA   Challenged, but retained at the Gwinnett County Library after the county solicitor declined to give a legal opinion on whether the book is harmful to minors. The library board had voted 2-1 to ban the book if the solicitor found the book meets the state's legal definition of harmful to minors.

Source: 11, Sept. 1998, pp. 139–40; Nov. 1998, p. 191; Jan. 1999, p. 19.

---

248   **Carroll, Lewis**
Alice's Adventures in Wonderland

1931   Banned in China on the ground that "Animals should not use human language, and that it was disastrous to put animals and human beings on the same level."

Source: 4, p. 49.

---

249   **Cart, Michael**
My Father's Scar

2004   TX   Challenged at the Montgomery County Memorial Library System along with fifteen other young adult books with gay-positive themes. The objections were posted at the Library Patrons of Texas Web site. The language describing the books is similar to that posted at the Web site of the Fairfax County, Virginia-based Parents Against Bad Books in Schools, to which Library Patrons of Texas links.

Source: 11, Nov. 2004, pp. 231–32.

250   Carter, Alden R.
Sheila's Dying

1992 NJ Restricted to those in the eighth grade or above at the Pitman Middle School library be cause the book promotes teenage stealing, drinking, profanity, and premarital sex.

Source: 11, July 1992, p. 106; Jan. 1993, p. 27.

251   Carter, Forrest
The Education of Little Tree

1995 OR Challenged, but retained at the Astoria Elementary School. The complainants wanted the book removed because it includes profanity, mentions sex, and portrays Christians as "liars, cheats and child molesters."

Source: 11, Jan. 1996, p. 17; Mar. 1996, p. 64.

252   Carter, Jimmy
Keeping Faith: Memories of a President

1983 Banned from the 1983 Moscow, Russia International Book Fair along with more than fifty other books because it is "anti-Soviet."

Source: 11, Nov. 1983, p. 201.

253   Carter, Judy
The Homo Handbook: Getting in Touch with Your Inner Homo

2005 AR Challenged in the Fayetteville High School library. The complainant also submitted a list of more than fifty books, citing the books as too sexually explicit and promoting homosexuality.

Source: 11, Sept. 2005, p. 215.

254   Carus, Marianne
What Joy Awaits You

1988 UT The Utah State Textbook Commission declined to remove this elementary school book from its list of approved texts. The book contains essays by Plymouth settler John Smith and early American writer Washington

Irving which refer to Indians as "savages" and "bloodthirsty" and was branded as racist and demeaning to contemporary Indian people.

Source: 11, May 1988, p. 104.

255   Casanova de Seingalt
Memoires (History of My Life)

1820 Original manuscript confined to the German publisher's safe and never published in unexpurgated form until the twentieth century.

1834 Placed on the *Index Librorum Prohibitorum* (Index of Prohibited Books) in Rome, Italy.

1863 Condemned in France.

1933 Banned in Ireland.

1935 Banned by Mussolini.

1943 MI Seized by police in Detroit.

Source: 4, p. 31.

256   Casey, Bernie
Look at the People

1980 NC Removed from the Southport school libraries due to inappropriate words and ideas.

Source: 11, Sept. 1980, p. 100.

257   Cashdan, Linda
It's Only Love

1994 OR Expurgated by an apparent self-appointed censor at the Coquille Public Library along with several other books. Most were mysteries and romances in which single words and sexually explicit passages were whited out by a vandal who left either dots or solid ink pen lines where the words had been.

Source: 11, Sept. 1994, p. 148.

258   Cast, P. C. and Kristin Cast
***House of Night* series**

2009 TX Banned at Henderson Junior High School in
New the Stephenville Independent School District. The entire teen vampire series was banned for sexual content and nudity. Since the series has not been completed, "Stephenville ISD actually banned books that have not yet been published and perhaps even books that have yet to be written. There is no way the district could know the content of these books, and yet they have been banned."

Source: 11, Nov. 2009, pp. 197–98, 225.

259 **Cavendish, Richard, ed.**
Man, Myth and Magic: Illustrated Encyclopedia of Mythology, Religion and the Unknown

1986 CA Challenged by the "God Squad," a group of three students and their parents, at the El Camino High School in Oceanside because the book "glorified the devil and the occult." The debate evoked interest in witchcraft books in other Oceanside school libraries.
Source: 11, Sept. 1986, p. 151; Nov. 1986, p. 224; Jan. 1987, p. 9.

260 **Cervantes Saavedra, Miguel de**
Don Quixote

1640 Placed on the Index in Madrid, Spain for one sentence: "Works of charity negligently performed are of no worth."

1981 The Chilean military junta banned the novel for supporting individual freedom and attacking authority.
Source: 1, pp. 83–84; 4, p. 16.

261 **Chamberlain, Wilt**
Wilt

1975 MI Banned from the Gaylord Middle School library because pupils "are more interested in learning how to dribble and shoot" than in his off-court activities.
Source: 9; 11, Sept. 1975, p. 138.

262 **Chambers, Aidan**
Dance on My Grave: A Life and Death in Four Parts

1993 OR Challenged at the Deschutes County Library in Bend because it "encourages and condones" homosexuality.

2004 TX Challenged at the Montgomery County Memorial Library System along with fifteen other young adult books with gay-positive themes. The objections were posted at the Library Patrons of Texas Web site. The language describing the books is similar to that posted at the Web site of the Fairfax County, Virginia-based Parents Against Bad Books in Schools, to which Library Patrons of Texas links.
Source: 11, Sept. 1993, pp. 158–59; Nov. 2004, pp. 231–32.

263 **Chapman, Robert L.**
New Dictionary of American Slang

1994 MI Labeled and restricted at the Walled Lake School District in Commerce Township because "This book contains words which might be offensive to the reader."
Source: 11, Sept. 1994, pp. 146–47.

264 **Charyn, Jerome**
Billy Budd, KGB

1992 AK Challenged at the Noel Wien Library in Fairbanks because it was too sexually explicit and violent.
Source: 11, Sept. 1992, p. 161; Nov. 1992, p. 196.

265 **Chaucer, Geoffrey**
Canterbury Tales

1908 "Expurgated almost from its first appearance in America, and was still being subjected to revisions as late as 1928. Even editions available today and considered otherwise acceptable avoid some four-letter words."

1995 IL Removed from a senior college preparatory literature course at the Eureka High School because some parents thought the sexual content of some of the tales was not appropriate for the students.
Source: 8, pp. 426–28; 11, Nov. 1995, p. 185; Jan. 1996 p. 14; 15, Vol. II, p. 617.

266 **Chbosky, Stephen**
The Perks of Being a Wallflower

2002 VA Challenged, along with seventeen other titles in the Fairfax County elementary and secondary libraries, by a group called Parents Against Bad Books in Schools. The group contends the books "contain profanity and descriptions of drug abuse, sexually explicit conduct, and torture."

2003 NY Removed as a reading assignment in an elective sociology course at the Massapequa High School because of its "offensive" content.

2004 TX Challenged at the Montgomery County Memorial Library System along with fifteen other young adult books with gay-positive themes. The objections were posted at the Library Patrons of Texas Web site. The language describing the books is similar to that posted at the Web site of the Fairfax County, Virginia-based Parents Against Bad Books in Schools, to which Library Patrons of Texas links.

2005 AZ Arizona Superintendent of Public Instruction sent a letter to charter schools and public school principals and district superintendents asking them to make sure that the book is no longer available to minors or any other students. The book contains numerous sexual references, including a scene where a girl is forced to have oral sex with a boy during a party.

2005 WI Retained in the Arrowhead High School curriculum in Merton. Reading the book was optional and parents could choose to have their children read something else.

2006 IL Retained on the Northwest Suburban High School District 214 reading list in Arlington Heights, along with eight other challenged titles. A board member, elected amid promises to bring her Christian beliefs into all board decision-making, raised the controversy based on excerpts from the books she'd found on the Internet. Chbosky's novel, which contains references to masturbation, homosexuality, and bestiality, got the bulk of the criticism.

2007 NY Challenged on the Commack High School summer reading list because the novel contains a two-page date rape scene. Educators in Commack revamped their reading list after finding students weren't interested in the choices and Chbosky's novel was added to attract "reluctant readers."

2008 IN New Removed from Portage High School classrooms for topics such as homosexuality, drug use, and sexual behavior. The novel chronicles the freshman year of high school of a young man struggling with awkwardness and the changing world around him.

2009 OH New Challenged on Wyoming high school district's suggested reading list. The book contains frank and sometimes explicit descriptions of sex, drugs, suicide, and masturbation.

2009 VA New Restricted at the William Byrd and Hidden Valley high schools in Roanoke to juniors and seniors. Freshmen and sophomores, however, will need parental permission to check out the book.

2009 WI New Challenged at the West Bend Community Memorial Library as being "obscene or child pornography" in a section designated "Young Adults." The library board unanimously voted 9–0 to maintain, "without removing, relocating, labeling, or otherwise restricting access," the book in the young adult section at the West Bend Community Memorial Library. The vote was a rejection of a four-month campaign conducted by the citizen's group West Bend Citizens for Safe Libraries to move fiction and nonfiction books with sexually explicit passages from the young adult section to the adult section and label them as containing sexual material.

Source: 11, Jan. 2003, p. 10; Jan. 2004, pp. 12–13; Nov. 2004, pp. 231–32; Jan. 2005, p. 11; May 2005, pp. 111–12; Jan. 2006, p. 9; July 2006, pp. 210–11; Sept. 2007, pp. 184–85; Jan. 2009, pp. 8–9; May 2009, pp. 80–81; Sept. 2009, pp. 169–70; Nov. 2009, pp. 202–3; Jan. 2010, pp. 13–14.

267 Chelminski, Rudolph
Paris

1981 FL Nine pages, depicting Parisian nightlife and showing pictures of nude dancers, were removed by the Indian River County school superintendent.

Source: 9; 11, Mar. 1982, p. 43.

268 Chevalier, Tracy
Girl with a Pearl Earring

2006 Banned in Iran. "The new government intends to take positive steps for reviving neglected values and considering religious teachings in the cultural field."

Source: 11, Jan. 2007, p. 35.

269 Chick, Jack T.
The Big Betrayal

1981 Banned in Canada.
1981 NJ Challenged in New Jersey as immoral and indecent anti-Catholic literature.

Source: 11, Jan. 1982, pp. 24–25.

270 Childress, Alice
A Hero Ain't Nothin' but a Sandwich

1976 NY Removed from Island Trees School Union Free District High School library in 1976 along with nine other titles because they were considered "immoral, anti-American, anti-Christian, or just plain filthy." Returned to the library after the U.S. Supreme Court ruling on June 25, 1982 in *Board of Education, Island Trees Union Free School District No. 26 et al. v. Pico et al.*, 457 U.S. 853 (1982).

1978 GA Removed from the Savannah school libraries due to "objectionable" language.

1978 TX Removed from the San Antonio high school libraries due to "objectionable" passages, but later reinstated after teachers filed a grievance in protest.

1994 MD Challenged at the Aberdeen High School in Bel Air because the novel is "racist and vulgar."

1994 SC Challenged at the Lamar Elementary School library in Darlington by a parent who stated that "offensive language in the book makes it unsuitable for any children."

Source: 11, Sept. 1978, p. 123; Nov. 1982, p. 197; July 1978, p. 87; May 1994, p. 85; Jan. 1995, p. 12.

271 Childress, Alice
Rainbow Jordan

1986 GA Challenged at the Gwinnett County public schools because of "foul language and sexual references."

1986 WA Banned from Spokane middle schools because the book's storyline about a prostitute's daughter was "too mature."
Source: 11, Mar. 1987, p. 65; July 1998, p. 110.

272 Chomsky, Noam, and Edward S. Herman
Manufacturing Consent: The Political Economy of the Mass Media

2006 The Turkish Chief Public Prosecution Office in Ankara decided to prosecute two publishers that released the book because it "degrades the Turkish identity and the Turkish Republic, and fuels hatred and discrimination among the people." The publishers could face up to six years in prison if found guilty.
Source: 11, Sept. 2006, p. 234.

273 Chopin, Kate
The Awakening

2006 IL Retained on the Northwest Suburban High School District 214 reading list in Arlington Heights, along with eight other challenged titles. A board member, elected amid promises to bring her Christian beliefs into all board decision-making, raised the controversy based on excerpts from the books she'd found on the Internet. First published in 1899, this novel so disturbed critics and the public that it was banished for decades afterward.
Source: 11, July 2006, pp. 210–11.

274 Christelow, Eileen
Jerome and the Witchcraft Kids

1991 KS Challenged, but retained in the Wichita public schools because it promotes witchcraft.
Source: 11, Jan. 1992, p. 26.

275 Christensen, James C., Renwick St. James and Alan Dean Foster
Voyage of the Basset

2006 UT Retained in the Davis County Library. The complainant objected to the book after her five-year-old son borrowed it from the children's section and showed her the illustrations it contains of topless mermaids and other partially clothed mythical creatures. The author is a retired Brigham Young University art professor and co-chair of the Mormon Arts Foundation.
Source: 11, Nov. 2006, p. 319.

276 Christopher, John
The Prince in Waiting

1988 OR Challenged at the Canby junior high school library because it promotes "positive attitudes toward the occult and ridicule toward Christianity."
Source: 11, May 1989, p. 78.

277 Christopher, Matt
The Kid Who Only Hit Homers

1989 OR Challenged at the Beaverton School District because the book mentions the occult, witchcraft, and astrology.
Source: 11, Jan. 1990, pp. 4–5.

278 Chute, Carolyn
The Beans of Egypt

1996 ME Challenged at the Oxford Hills High School in Paris. A parent stated that "teachers are not qualified to explore the issues of rape, incest, suicide and mental illness contained in Chute's novel."
Source: 11, Nov. 1996, p. 212.

279 Clancy, Tom
The Hunt for Red October

1997 WV Removed from the Jackson County school libraries along with sixteen other titles.
Source: 11, Jan. 1998, p. 13.

280 Clapp, Patricia C.
Witches' Children

1990 MD Challenged at Cannon Road Elementary School library in Silver Spring because students who read it will be encouraged "to dabble with the occult."
1991 MD Challenged at the Howard County schools because the book was "not appropriate positive pleasurable reading for the young age group."
Source: 11, Mar. 1991, p. 43; Mar. 1992, p. 40.

281 Clark, Mary Higgins
I'll Be Seeing You

1994 PA Challenged at the Big Spring School in Carlisle.
Source: 11, Mar. 1995, p. 56.

282   **Chick, Jack T.**
Double Cross

1981   Banned in Canada.
1981 NJ Challenged in New Jersey as immoral and indecent anti-Catholic literature.
Source: 11, Jan. 1982, pp. 24–25.

283   **Clark, Walter Van Tilburg**
The Ox-Bow Incident

1980 IL Challenged in Johnston City "because of the profanity and the use of God's name in vain."
Source: 11, Sept. 1980, p. 107.

284   **Clauser, Suzanne**
A Girl Named Sooner

1988 CO Removed from the Stott Elementary School library in Arvada after a parent complained that its graphic sex scenes make it inappropriate for children.
1991 OR Removed by decision of the school board from the library at the Jefferson Middle School because of its explicit sexual content.
Source: 11, July 1988, p. 119; July 1992, p. 103.

285   **Clavell, James**
Shogun

2002 VA Challenged, along with seventeen other titles in the Fairfax County elementary and secondary libraries, by a group called Parents Against Bad Books in Schools. The group contends the books "contain profanity and descriptions of drug abuse, sexually explicit conduct, and torture."
Source: 11, Jan. 2003, p. 10.

286   **Cleaver, Eldridge**
Soul on Ice

1969 CA Barred from elective courses on black studies by California Superintendent of Instruction.
1973 CT Challenged, but retained in the Ridgefiled senior high school ethnic studies class.
1975 CT Challenged at the Greenwich High School library because the book is "crime provoking and anti-American as well as obscene and pornographic.
1976 NY Removed from Island Trees Union Free School District High School library in 1976 along with nine other titles because they were considered "immoral, anti-American, anti-Christian, or just plain filthy." Returned to the library after the U.S. Supreme Court ruling on June 25, 1982, in *Board of Education, Island Trees Union Free School District No. 26 et al. v. Pico et al.*, 457 U.S. 853 (1982).

1979 WA Challenged at Omak due to "profane language."
Source: 4, p. 100; 11, May 1975, p. 87; July 1979, p. 75; Nov. 1982, p. 197; 14, pp. 260–61.

287   **Cleland, John**
Fanny Hill

1749   Author imprisoned on the orders of the British secretary of state on a charge of "corrupting the King's subjects."
1821 MA Banned in Massachusetts in the first known U.S. obscenity case.
1963 NJ The highest court in New Jersey declared it obscene.
1965   Seized and burned in Japan.
1965   Seized in Berlin, Germany.
1965   Burned in Manchester.
Source: 4, p. 29; 6, pp. 533–34; 8, pp. 330-32; 15, Vol. I, pp. 561–62, Vol. II, p. 610.

288   **Clerc, Charles, and Louis Leiter, ed.**
Seven Contemporary Short Novels

1999 OR Removed from the Baker City High School language arts program because of two selections in the book. *The Bluest Eye*, by Toni Morrison, includes a description of a father raping his eleven-year-old daughter. *Being There*, by Jerzy Kosinski, includes descriptions of sexual relations.
Source: 11, May 1999, p. 70.

289   **Clinton, Cathryn**
A Stone in My Hand

2003 FL Challenged, but retained in the Marion County Public Library System in Ocala de spite a complaint that the subject matter was too mature and the book "was written one-sidedly, specifically showing one party to be fully wrong." Reviewers noted that the book is told from a Muslim perspective and that it can be taken to be anti-Israel. An Ocala resident noted that "this book will help further hatred of Jews, anti-Semitism, and hatred of Israel, on the part of children, that target audience."
Source: 11, Nov. 2003, pp. 227–28; Jan. 2004, pp. 7–8; Mar. 2004, pp. 47–48.

290   **Close, Robert S.**
Love Me Sailor

1945   Politicians, churchmen, and civic leaders denounced the book as likely to corrupt the morals of young, and librarians publicly burned copies.
Source: 6, p. 535.

291 Clutton-Brock, Juliet
Horse

2004 MT Challenged, but retained at the Smith Elementary School in Helena despite a parent's concern that it "promotes evolution."
Source: 11, May 2004, p. 97; July 2004, p. 157.

292 Cody, Robin
Ricochet River

2000 OR Retained by the West Linn-Wilsonville School Board in Wilsonville despite objections that the book contains explicit depictions of teenage sexual encounters without explanation of the consequences.
Source: 11, Jan. 2001, p. 36.

293 Cohen, Barbara
Unicorns in the Rain

1986 CO Challenged at the Jefferson County school library because the book "puts too much emphasis on drugs and sex."
Source: 11, Jan. 1987, p. 10; Mar. 1987, p. 49.

294 Cohen, Daniel
Curses, Hexes and Spells

1986 TN Placed on restricted status at the Claxton Elementary School library because the book "contains satanic themes."
1989 OK Removed from the Cleveland middle school libraries because witchcraft is a "religion" and the First Amendment bars the teaching of religion in schools.
1990 MD Removed from elementary school libraries in Howard County because it is virtual "how-to" manual on demon worship.
1997 TX Removed from the Kirby Junior High School in Wichita Falls because of "Satanic" themes.
Source: 11, Mar. 1987, p. 50; July 1989, p. 128; Jan. 1991, pp. 11–12; July 1997, p. 95.

295 Cohen, Daniel
Ghostly Warnings

1999 NE Challenged, but retained at the Hastings Public Library along with forty other books on the topics of witches, magic, the zodiac, fortune telling, and ghost stories (most of the Dewey Decimal category 133.47). The books were called "demonic" and unsuitable for young children.
Source: 11, May 1999, p. 66; July 1999, p. 104.

296 Cohen, Daniel
The Headless Roommate and Other Tales of Terror

1993 NJ Restricted from fourth and fifth graders at the Old Turnpike School in Tewksbury Township because of its violence.
Source: 11, July 1993, p. 100.

297 Cohen, Daniel
Phantom Animals

1999 NE Challenged, but retained at the Hastings Public Library along with forty other books on the topics of witches, magic, the zodiac, fortune telling, and ghost stories (most of the Dewey Decimal category 133.47). The books were called "demonic" and unsuitable for young children.
Source: 11, May 1999, p. 66; July 1999, p. 104.

298 Cohen, Daniel
The Restless Dead: Ghostly Tales from Around the World

1989 OR Challenged at the Ochoco Elementary School in Prineville because the book is "totally preoccupied with the macabre, occult, and demonic activity."
Source: 11, Jan. 1990, pp. 4–5.

299 Cohen, Daniel
Southern Fried Rat and Other Gruesome Tales

1991 MD Challenged at the Matthew Henson Middle School in Waldorf because the collection of folktales contains stories involving unusual violence, relate humorous anecdotes of drug use in school and of ways for students to cheat on exams.
Source: 11, July 1991, p. 129.

300 Cohen, Daniel
The World's Most Famous Ghosts

2002 KY Proposed for removal, along with more than fifty other books, from the high school library in Russell Springs by a teachers' prayer group.
Source: 11, May 2002, p. 116.

301 Cohen, Susan, and Daniel Cohen
When Someone You Know Is Gay

1998 WI Removed from the Barron School District because the 1992 data is outdated. The ACLU of Wisconsin filed suit against the school district on Feb. 16, 1999. The books were then returned to the library while a federal court considered the lawsuit. On October 8, 1999, it was agreed that the book will remain available to students as part of the school district's settlement of the federal lawsuit.

Source: 11, Jan. 1999, p. 9; Mar. 1999, p. 37; May 1999, p. 68; Jan. 2000, p. 28.

302   Cole, Babette
Mommy Laid An Egg

1998 MO Moved from the children's section to the adult section of the Camden County Library because the book explains the birth process from conception to delivery.

Source: 11, Mar. 1998, p. 40.

303   Cole, Brock
The Goats

1992 WA Removed from the Housel Middle School library in Prosser because it contains a passage describing the rescue of a naked girl.

1994 NH Challenged at the Timberland Regional Middle School in Plaistow because parents said it contained "offensive and inappropriate" language for seventh graders.

1997 IN Challenged in the Vigo County School District classrooms and libraries because the book is "morally offensive and inappropriate for middle school students." In November 1997, the Vigo County School Corporation committee affirmed that the novel is appropriate for use by middle and high school students in classrooms and libraries.

2000 NH Challenged in the Londonderry schools because "its sexuality that drive the book." The book was eventually returned to the library and curriculum.

Source: 8, pp. 340–41; 11, Mar. 1993, p. 43; Jan. 1995, p. 25; Jan. 1998, p. 11; Mar. 1998, p. 55.

304   Cole, Joanna
Asking about Sex and Growing Up

1994 AK Challenged, but retained in Anchorage School District elementary school libraries after the school board voted to "retain the book despite complaints that it is inappropriate for elementary school children and teaches values opposed to those of the majority of parents."

Source: 11, May 1994, p. 97.

305   Cole, Joanna
Bony-Legs

1986 CO Challenged at the Jefferson County school library because the book deals with subjects such as "witchcraft, cannibalism, and white magic."

Source: 11, Mar. 1987, p. 49.

306   Cole, Joanna
How You Were Born

1987 WA Placed on restricted shelves at the Evergreen School District elementary school libraries in Vancouver in accordance with the school board policy to restrict student access to sex education books in elementary school libraries.

Source: 11, May 1987, p. 87.

307   Cole, Joanna
I'm Mad at You

1988 MO Placed on "restricted access" at the North Kansas City elementary schools because "some children might not understand the book's use of humor and sarcasm."

Source: 11, July 1988, p. 121; Sept. 1988, pp. 151–52.

308   Cole, Joanna
A Snake's Body

1988 OR Challenged at the Multnomah County Library in Portland because the photographs of a python crushing and eating a chick would upset and sadden children.

Source: 11, Jan. 1990, pp. 4–5.

309   Cole, William
Oh, That's Ridiculous!

1990 OH Challenged as inappropriate for children and kept off the Mansfield school library shelves for over a year after a complaint against it got lost in the shuffle of a school system reorganization. It was returned to open access in January when the Board of Education voted to retain the title.

Source: 11, May 1990, p. 106.

310   Colfer, Eoin
The Supernaturalist

2008 NY
New   Restored by the Lackawanna School Board along with several other books following accusations of censorship by some parents and teachers. The books were pulled from the middle school library recommended list because of concerns that the books deal with the occult.

Source: 11, May 2008, pp. 115–16.

311 Collen, Lindsey
The Rape of Sita

1993   Banned by the Mauritian government and temporarily withdrawn by its publisher after protests by Hindu fundamentalists. Won a
1994   Commonwealth Writers Prize for the best book from Africa.

Source: 1, pp. 277–78.

312 Collier, James Lincoln, and Christopher Collier
Jump Ship to Freedom

1993 VA   Removed from the Fairfax County elementary school libraries because its young black hero, a slave, questions his own intelligence, refers to himself as a "nigger," and is called that by other characters.

1996 IL   Challenged at the Nathan Hale Middle School in Crestwood because it "was damaging to the self-esteem of young black students."

Source: 11, July 1993, pp. 102–3; Sept. 1993, p. 146; Jan. 1994, p. 13; Mar. 1997, p. 39.

313 Collier, James Lincoln, and Christopher Collier
My Brother Sam Is Dead

1984 GA   Challenged at the Gwinnett County school libraries because some of its characters use profanity. An abridged version with the profanity deleted has been substituted in the elementary school libraries.

1989 OH   Removed from the curriculum of fifth grade classes in New Richmond because the 1974 Newbery Honor Book contained the words "bastard," "goddamn," and "hell" and did not represent "acceptable ethical standards for fifth graders."

1991 SC   Challenged in the Greenville County Schools because the book uses the name of God and Jesus in a "vain and profane manner along with inappropriate sexual references."

1993 KS   Challenged at the Walnut Elementary School in Emporia by parents who said that it contained profanity and graphic violence.

1994 CA   Removed from fifth grade classes at Bryant Ranch Elementary School in the Placentia-Yorba Linda Unified School District because "the book is not G-rated. Offensive language is offensive language. Graphic violence is graphic violence, no matter what the context."

1994 PA   Challenged, but retained at the Palmyra area schools due to profanity and violence.

1996 CA   Retained in the Antioch elementary school libraries after a parent complained about the novel's profanity and violence.

1996 CO   Challenged in the Jefferson County Public Schools in Lakewood because of "the persistent usage of profanity" in the book, as well as references to rape, drinking, and battlefield violence.

1998 VA   Challenged at the McSwain Elementary School in Staunton because of "bad language."

1998 VA   Challenged as a gifted fifth-grade student assignment in Tucker-Capps Elementary School in Hampton because the book uses vulgar and profane language and contains scenes of graphic violence.

2000 IL   Challenged in the fifth-grade Oak Brook Butler District 53 curriculum because of violence and inappropriate language.

2009 GA   Retained in all Muscogee County elementary
New   school libraries, despite a parent's concerns about profanity in the book.

Source: 8, pp. 136–37; 11, Sept. 1983, p. 139; Mar. 1990, p. 48; July 1991, p. 129; July 1993, pp. 126–27; Sept. 1994, p. 149; Nov. 1994, p. 190; Jan. 1995, p. 26; July 1996, p. 121; Jan. 1997, p. 25; July 1998, p. 110; Mar. 1999, p. 40; Mar. 2000, p. 49; May 2009, p. 93.

314 Collier, James Lincoln, and Christopher Collier
War Comes to Willy Freeman

1994 MN   Removed from the Nettleton Math and Science Magnet School in Duluth because of objections to the book's portrayal of African American characters as demeaning, and claims that use of the word "nigger" in the text led students to use it outside the classroom.

1996 IL   Pulled from two classes at Western Avenue School in Flossmoor after a parent complained that the book "represents totally poor judgment, a complete lack of racial sensitivity and is totally inappropriate for fifth-graders. This book is an education in racism, a primer for developing prejudice."

Source: 11, Sept. 1994, pp. 150–51; Jan. 1997, p. 9.

315 Collier, James Lincoln, and Christopher Collier
With Every Drop of Blood

1997 SC   Challenged at the Lonnie B. Nelson Elementary School in Columbia because passages considered racist were "inappropriate for fifth grade."

2000 IL   Challenged in the fifth-grade Oak Brook Butler District 53 curriculum because the book contains racial slurs.

Source: 11, July 1997, p. 94; Mar. 2000, p. 49.

316 Collignon, Jeff
Her Monster

1997 SC Removed from the Lakeview Middle School library in Greenville by the school district administrator because the book's sexual content "is inappropriate for middle school students."
Source: 11, May 1997, pp. 61–62.

317 Collins, Jackie
Lovers and Gamblers

1988 Destroyed in Beijing, China and legal authorities threatened to bring criminal charges against the publishers.
Source: 11, Jan. 1989, p. 15.

318 Collins, Jim
Unidentified Flying Objects

1984 FL Challenged at the Escambia County School District because the complainant claimed the book indicated that "Ezekiel had seen a UFO when he spoke in the Bible about seeing something that looked like a wheel in the sky."
Source: 11, Sept. 1984, p. 156.

319 Colman, Hila
Diary of a Frantic Kid Sister

1982 TX Removed from the Hurst-Euless-Bedford School District libraries because the book uses the word "intercourse."
Source: 9; 11, May 1982, p. 84.

320 Comfort, Alex, and Jane Comfort
The Facts of Love

1981 KS Challenged in Great Bend Public Library.
1982 ID Challenged at the Boise Public Library.
Source: 11, May 1982, p. 84.

321 Comfort, Alex
The Joy of Sex: The Cordon Bleu Guide to Lovemaking

1996 NJ Removed from the Clifton Public Library and replaced with a dummy book made of styrofoam. The library's new policy restricts to adults any material containing "patently offensive graphic illustrations or photographs of sexual or excretory activities or contact as measured by contemporary community standards for minors."
Source: 11, July 1996, pp. 118–19.

322 Comfort, Alex
Joy of Sex

1978 KY Confiscated from three bookstores by police in Lexington.
1979 AL Removed from the Fairhope Public Library.
1987 Banned in Ireland to protect the young.
1994 CT Challenged at the Guilford Free Library, but the Board of Directors voted to reaffirm the library's circulation and book selection policies, which allow all patrons access to all library materials.
2009 KS New Restricted minors' access in the Topeka and Shawnee County Public Library because Kansans for Common Sense Policy contended that the material is "harmful to minors under state law." Later the board voted 6-3 in favor of adopting a staff recommendation to keep the books where they are currently located on the shelves in the library's Health Information Neighborhood section.
Source: 4, p. 93; 11, July 1979, p. 93; May 1987, p. 110; Sept. 1994, p. 165; May 2009, pp. 77–78; July 2009, p. 139.

323 Comfort, Alex
More Joy of Sex

1978 KY Confiscated from three bookstores by police in Lexington.
1979 AL Removed from the Fairhope Public Library.
1996 NJ Restricted to patrons over eighteen years of age at the Main Memorial Library in Clifton. The book is hidden behind the checkout counter and on the shelves is a dummy book jacket. The book was described as hard-core pornography by the complainant.
Source: 4, p. 93; 11, July 1979, p. 93; Mar. 1996, p. 63; May 1996, p. 83.

324 Comfort, Alex
The New Joy of Sex

2005 ID Challenged at the Nampa Public Library along with seven other books because "they are very pornographic in nature and they have very explicit and detailed illustrations and photographs which we feel don't belong in a library." The library board approved policy changes that restrict children's access to any holdings that may fall under the state's harmful to minors statute and barred the library from buying movies rated NC-17 or X. The book was relocated to the director's office in 2008 and it was eventually restored to the collection in 2008.
Source: 11, May 2008, pp. 96–97; July 2008, pp. 140–41; Nov. 2008, pp. 254–55.

325 Comte, Auguste
The Course of Positive Philosophy

1869 The Catholic Church placed the third edition on the *Index Librorum Prohibitorum* (Index of Prohibited Books) in Rome, Italy. It was still prohibited when the last Index was compiled in 1948.
Source: 1, pp. 60–61.

326 Confucius
Analects

250 B.C. The first ruler of the Chin Dynasty, wishing to abolish the feudal system, consigned to the flames all books relating to the teaching of Confucius; he also buried alive hundreds of his disciples.

191 B.C. In 191 B.C., the rulers of the Han Dynasty rescinded the book-burning edict. Because the teachings of Confucius were handed down orally from master to disciple, scholars were able to reconstruct the texts from memory and from hidden manuscripts that escaped destruction.

1966 In the twentieth century, the Analects and the Confucian canon were again attacked. During the Great Proletarian Cultural Revolution of 1966-74, Mao Zedong and the leaders of the Communist Party called for a comprehensive attack on the "four old" elements within Chinese society—culture, thinking, habits and customs. During 1973–74, the Communist Party criticized Confucian thinking as promoting an ideology of exploitation, elitism, social hierarchy, and preservation of the status quo.
Source: 4, p. 1; 8, pp. 205–6.

327 Conly, Jane Leslie
Crazy Lady

1996 IL Challenged at the Prospect Heights school libraries because of "swear words."

1997 CA Parental notification is required at the San Jose Unified School District for the use of the book as a supplemental reading assignment because of objectionable language. The Newbery Honor Book uses the words "damn," "hell," and "bitch" five times.
Source: 11, Mar. 1996, p. 46; Mar. 1998, p. 55.

328 Connell, Vivian
The Chinese Room

1950 MA Removed from sale, along with thirteen other books, in Fall River as "indecent, obscene or impure, or manifestly tend to corrupt the morals of youth."

1950 NJ Middlesex County prosecutor Matthew Melko collaborated with the local Committee on Objectionable Literature to produce a list of objectionable publications. Bantam Books then sued Melko in *Bantam Books v. Melko, Prosecutor of Middlesex County*, 25 N.J. Super. 292, 96 A.2d 47 (1953) for banning the book. Ultimately, the New Jersey Supreme Court granted county prosecutors the right to ban the distribution and sale of publications they found objectionable or obscene, and the court further condoned the creation of censorship committees to aid prosecutors in such actions. The decision of the high court agreed that Connell's novel was not obscene.
Source: 13, pp. 45–46.

329 Connell, Vivian
September in Quinze

1952 Banned in Ireland after the Irish Board of Censors found the novel "obscene" and "indecent."

1954 The novel became the subject of litigation after the British Treasury Counsel examined the novel and determined it was "obscene." Hutchinson Publishing and its director, Katherine Webb, were each fined 500 pounds.
Source: 13, pp. 208–09.

330 Conner, Macet Al, and Gerry Contreras
You and Your Family

1982 PA Challenged and nearly banned from the Allentown schools because the book asked questions about the students' families, e.g., "Every family has rules. Who makes rules in your family?"
Source: 11, Mar. 1983, p. 52.

331 Conniff, Richard
The Devil's Book of Verse

1983 TN Publication canceled by Dodd, Mead & Company because of language in the book considered "objectionable" by Thomas Nelson, Inc. of Nashville—Dodd, Mead's parent company.
Source: 11, Nov. 1983, p. 188.

332 Conrad, Joseph
The Nigger of the Narcissus

1984 IL Challenged in the Waukegan School District because Conrad's work uses the word "nigger."
Source: 11, July 1984, p. 105.

333   Conrad, Pam
Holding Me Here

1991   VA   Challenged at the Lynchburg school libraries because the book contains "cursing and profane language and uses God's name" in a slanderous manner.
Source: 11, Sept. 1991, p. 178.

334   Conran, Shirley
Lace

1984   LA   Challenged at the Covington Public Library as "pornographic." The complainant checked the book out after watching the TV series and found that while the TV program had been tastefully done, in the book "pornographic styling [was] unnecessary."
Source: 11, July 1984, p. 103.

335   Conroy, Pat
Beach Music

2007   WV
New   Suspended from the Nitro High, Kanawha County honors English and Advanced Placement literature classes after parents complained about the book's scenes of violence, sexual assault, child rape, suicide, and more. A Kanawha County Board of Education member suggested the institution of a book rating system. Eventually, the book was approved for return to the classroom, as long as students are offered alternative texts.
Source: 11, Jan. 2008, p. 42; Mar. 2008, p. 80.

336   Conroy, Pat
The Great Santini

1992   MN   Removed from the Eagan High School classroom in Burnsville.
1993   CA   Challenged as "obscene and pornographic," but retained in the Anaheim Union High School District.
1993   NY   Challenged, but retained on the Guilderland High School's list of approved reading materials. A student filed the complaint stating that it was offensive and inappropriate for students his age.
Source: 11, Mar. 1993, p. 56; Sept. 1993, p. 160; Nov. 1993, pp. 192–93; Jan. 1994, p. 14.

337   Conroy, Pat
The Lords of Discipline

1992   GA   Challenged in the Cobb County schools because of passages that include profane language and describe sadomasochistic acts.
1992   MN   Removed from an elective English course by the Westonka School Board after parents complained about bad language and sex in the story.
1999   GA   Banned, but later reinstated after community protests at the Windsor Forest High School in Savannah. The controversy began when a parent complained about sex, violence, and profanity in the book that was part of an Advanced Placement English class.
Source: 11, July 1992, p. 110; Mar. 1993, p. 44; Mar. 2000, p. 63; Mar. 2001, p. 76.

338   Conroy, Pat
The Prince of Tides

1988   SC   Removed as a reading assignment for an advanced English class at the St. Andres Parish Public School because it is "trashy pulp pornography." Following the challenge, the school board passed a resolution urging teachers to "use professional judgement and discretion in selecting works. . which. . . contain passages which most people would find abhorrent."
2007   WV
New   Suspended from the Nitro High School honors English and Advanced Placement literature classes after parents complained about the book's scenes of violence, sexual assault, child rape, suicide, and more. A Kanawha County Board of Education member suggested the institution of a book rating system. Eventually, the book was approved for return to the classroom, as long as students are offered alternative texts.
Source: 11, May 1988, p. 89; Jan. 2008, p. 42; Mar. 2008, p. 80.

339   Conroy, Pat
The Water Is Wide

1991   SC   Challenged in the Greenville County schools because the book uses the name of God and Jesus in a "vain and profane manner along with inappropriate sexual references."
Source: 11, July 1991, p. 130.

340   Cook, Robin
Coma

1992   PA   Removed from Big Spring High School English classes in Newville, but retained in the library. The decision came in response to complaints that the book is obscene and encourages the maltreatment of women and "radical feminism."
Source: 11, Jan. 1993, p. 13; Mar. 1993, p. 44.

341   Cooke, John Peyton
The Lake

1991   OR   Challenged for having too much violence, but retained at the Multnomah County Library.
Source: 11, Jan. 1992, p. 6.

342 Cooney, Caroline
The Terrorist

2000 IA   Challenged, but retained at the Franklin Middle School in Cedar Rapids despite objections that the book negatively portrays the Islamic religion and Arabs. The book is on the Iowa Teen Award list.

2000 MD   Retained in Rockville on Montgomery County middle school reading lists, over objections that the book is anti-Arab.
> Source: 11, May 2000, p. 77; Jan. 2001, p. 35.

343 Cooney, Nancy H.
Sex, Sexuality and You: A Handbook for Growing Christians

1985 MA   Because of its approach to abortion, the book was removed from the library shelves of the Roman Catholic chancery of Worcester, dropped from their sex education program, and is no longer used as a reference source.
> Source: 11, Mar. 1986, pp. 38–39.

344 Copernicus, Nicolaus
On the Revolution of Heavenly Spheres

1616   Copernicus was the first person to propose the theory that the earth moves around the sun, and the Catholic Church viewed the Copernican theory as a challenge to orthodoxy. In 1616, the book was placed on the *Index Librorum Prohibitorum* (Index of Prohibited Books) in Rome, Italy. The general prohibition against Copernicus's theories remained in effect until 1753, and his name was not removed from the Index until 1835.
> Source: 1, p. 248.

345 Corman, Carolyn
Tell Me Everything

1997 WV   Removed from the Jackson County school libraries along with sixteen other titles.
> Source: 11, Jan. 1998, p. 13.

346 Cormier, Robert
After the First Death

1989 OR   Challenged as an assigned ninth-grade reading in the Troutdale schools because of the book's portrayal of teen suicide as well as the way the U.S. Army and the Palestine Liberation Organization were depicted.

2000 CT   Challenged, but retained in the Manchester curriculum despite charges that the book is "offensively graphic in its descriptions of violence, terrorism, and suicidal thoughts."

2000 VA   Challenged, but retained on the Liberty High School ninth-grade gifted and talented reading list in Fauquier. Opponents of the book charged that it was too violent and treated suicide in a cavalier manner. Other parents cited inappropriate sexual content or gender stereotyping.
> Source: 11, Mar. 1990, p. 63; May 2000, p. 92; Sept. 2000, p. 145.

347 Cormier, Robert
Beyond the Chocolate War

2000 PA   Retained as optional reading for eighth graders at Rice Avenue Middle School in Girard. A grandmother found the book offensive and didn't want her granddaughters reading it.
> Source: 11, May 2000, p. 92.

348 Cormier, Robert
The Chocolate War

1981 MI   Challenged and temporarily removed from the English curriculum in two Lapeer high schools because of "offensive language and explicit descriptions of sexual situations in the book."

1982 MD   Removed from the Liberty High School in Westminster due to the book's "foul language," portrayal of violence and degradation of schools and teachers.

1983 RI   Challenged at the Richmond High School because the book was deemed "pornographic" and "repulsive."

1984 AZ   Removed from the Lake Havasu High School freshman reading list. The school district board charged the Havasu teachers with failing to set good examples for students, fostering disrespect in the classroom, and failing to support the board.

1984 SC   Banned from the Richland Two School District middle school libraries in Columbia due to "language problems," but later reinstated for eighth graders only.

1985 NY   Challenged at the Cornwall High School because the novel is "humanistic and destructive of religious and moral beliefs and of national spirit."

1985 PA   Banned from the Stroudsburg High School library because it was "blatantly graphic, pornographic and wholly unacceptable for a high school library."

1986 FL   Removed from the Panama City school classrooms and libraries because of "offensive" language.

1986 MA Challenged at Barnstable High School in Hyannis because of the novel's profanity, "obscene references to masturbation and sexual fantasies," and "ultimately because of its pessimistic ending." The novel, complainants said, fostered negative impressions of authority, of school systems, and of religious schools.

1987 CA Challenged at the Moreno Valley Unified School District libraries because it "contains profanity, sexual situations, and themes that allegedly encourage disrespectful behavior."

1988 FL West Hernando Middle School principal recommended that Cormier's novel be removed from the school library shelves because it is "inappropriate."

1990 CT Challenged as suitable curriculum material in the Harwinton schools because it contained profanity and subject matter that set bad examples and gave students negative views of life.

1990 CT Challenged as suitable curriculum material in the Burlington schools because it contained profanity and subject matter that set bad examples and gave students negative views of life.

1990 NH Suspended from classroom use, pending review, at the Woodsville High School in Haverhill because the novel contains expletives, references to masturbation and sexual fantasies, and derogatory characterizations of a teacher and of religious ceremonies.

1992 CT Challenged at the New Milford schools because the novel contains language, sexual references, violence, subjectivity, and negativism that are harmful to students.

1993 AZ Challenged in the Kyrene elementary schools because of a masturbation scene.

1994 GA Returned to the Hephzibah High School tenth-grade reading list in Augusta after the complainant said, "I don't see anything educational about that book. If they ever send a book like that home with one of my daughters again I will personally burn it and throw the ashes on the principal's desk."

1994 NY Challenged as required reading in the Hudson Falls schools because the book has recurring themes of rape, masturbation, violence, and degrading treatment of women.

1995 MA Challenged at the Nauset Regional Middle School in Orleans due to profanity and sexually explicit language.

1995 PA Challenged in the Stroudsburg school system on the grounds that the will "foster more disobedience."

1996 CA Removed from the middle school libraries in the Riverside Unified School District as inappropriate for seventh- and eighth-graders to read without class discussion due to mature themes, sexual situations, and smoking.

1996 PA Removed from the East Stroudsburg ninth-grade curriculum after complaints about the novel's language and content.

1998 OK Banned from the Broken Arrow schools because it is the "antithesis of the district's character development curriculum." The board of education is considering forming a parent committee to review all books listed on the district's electronic bookshelf and to design a ratings system for more than four hundred titles found there.

1998 TX Removed from the Greenville Intermediate School library because "it contained blasphemy, profanity, and graphic sexual passages."

1999 NY Challenged on the required reading list for ninth graders at Colton schools due to references to masturbation, profanity, disrespect of women, and sexual innuendo.

2000 CO Challenged as part of the Silverheels Middle School's supplemental reading material in South Park because parents objected to sexually suggestive language in the book.

2000 MA Challenged on the eighth-grade reading list of the Lancaster School District, due to the book's language and content.

2000 OH Challenged at the Maple Heights School because "the book teaches immorality."

2000 PA Retained as optional reading for eighth-graders at Rice Avenue Middle School in Girard. A grandmother found the book offensive and didn't want her granddaughters reading it.

2000 VA Challenged in York County due to sexually explicit language.

2001 FL Challenged, but retained at the Dunedin Highland Middle School in St. Petersburg despite objections to profanity, scenes about masturbation and sexual fantasy, and segments of the book that were considered denigrating to girls.

2001 OH Challenged at a Beaver Local Board of Education meeting in Lisbon as a "pornographic" book that should be removed from high school English classes.

2002 VA Challenged, along with seventeen other titles in the Fairfax County elementary and secondary libraries, by a group called Parents Against Bad Books in Schools. The group contends the books "contain profanity and descriptions of drug abuse, sexually explicit conduct, and torture."

2006 CT Challenged, but retained in the West Hartford schools. Parents of a King Philip Middle School eighth-grader thought the language, sexual content, and violence make the book PG-13.

2006 NC Challenged in the Wake County schools because the book has "vulgar and sexually explicit language." Parents are getting help from Called2Action, a Christian group that says its mission is to "promote and defend our shared family and social values."

2007 ID New Challenged in the Coeur d'Alene School District. Some parents say the book, along with five others, should require parental permission for students to read them.

2007 IL New Challenged as required reading for seventh-grade students at the John H. Kinzie Elementary School in Chicago.

2007 MD New Removed from the Harford County High School curriculum because its message on the dangers of bullying is overshadowed by instances of vulgar language, including homophobic slurs. In November 2007, the Harford County's school superintendent reversed her decision to bar Cormier's novel and returned it to the classroom. Teachers now have the option of using the novel in a course that deals with harassment and decision making, but must get permission from all parents of students in the class.

2007 OH New Challenged at the Northridge School District in Johnstown because, "if these books were a movie, they would be rated R, why should we be encouraging them to read these books?"

2007 OR New Challenged as an optional reading in a bullying unit at the Lake Oswego Junior High School because the novel is "peppered with profanities, ranging from derogatory slang terms to sexual encounters and violence." Students are given a list of book summaries and a letter to take to their parents. Four of the eight optional books offered are labeled as having "mature content/language."

Source: 9; 11, Mar. 1981, p. 48; Sept. 1982, p. 156; Sept. 1983, p. 152; Sept. 1984, p. 138; Jan. 1985, p. 10; Mar. 1985, p. 45; May 1985, p. 79; May 1986, p. 79; Nov. 1986, p. 209; July 1987, pp. 125, 126–28; Sept. 1987, pp. 168–69, Mar. 1988, p. 45; May 1990, p. 87; Mar. 1991, p. 44; May 1991, p. 90; May 1992, pp. 96–97; Jan. 1994, p. 34; July 1994, p. 130; Nov. 1994, p. 190; Jan. 1995, p. 13; Mar. 1995, p. 55; May 1995, p. 70; July 1995, p. 94; Nov. 1995, p. 184; May 1996, p. 99; July 1996, p. 82; Nov. 1996, p. 198; July 1998, p. 106; Sept. 1998, pp. 140–41; Sept. 1999, p. 122; Jan. 2000, p. 16; Mar. 2000, pp. 49, 51–52; May 2000, pp. 78, 92; Sept. 2000, pp. 144–45; Mar. 2001, pp. 43, 57; Jan. 2002, pp. 49–50; Jan. 2003, p. 10; July 2006, pp. 184–85, 187; Sept. 2006, p. 231; July 2007, pp. 147–49; Sept. 2007, p. 181; Nov. 2007, pp. 242–43; Jan. 2008, pp. 28–29.

349 Cormier, Robert
Fade

1990 WY Challenged in the Campbell County junior

high schools because of sexual and violent themes.

Source: 11, Jan. 1991, p. 13; Mar. 1991, p. 62.

350 Cormier, Robert
Heroes

2002 VA Challenged, along with seventeen other titles in the Fairfax County elementary and secondary libraries, by a group called Parents Against Bad Books in Schools. The group contends the books "contain profanity and descriptions of drug abuse, sexually explicit conduct, and torture."

Source: 11, Jan. 2003, p. 10.

351 Cormier, Robert
I Am the Cheese

1985 NY Challenged at the Cornwall High School because the novel is "humanistic and destructive of religious and moral beliefs and of national spirit."

1986 FL Banned from the Bay County's four middle schools and three high schools in Panama City because of "offensive" language. The controversy snowballed further on May 7, 1987, when 64 works of literature were banned from classroom teaching at Bay and Mosley High Schools by the Bay County school superintendent. After 44 parents filed a suit against the district claiming that its instructional aids policy denies constitutional rights, the Bay County School Board reinstated the books. "Banned" from Bay High School: *A Farewell to Arms*, by Ernest Hemingway; *The Great Gatsby*, by F. Scott Fitzgerald; *Intruder in the Dust*, by William Faulkner; *Lost Horizon*, by James Hilton; *Oedipus Rex* by Sophocles; *The Red Badge of Courage*, by Stephen Crane; *A Separate Peace*, by John Knowles; *Shane*, by Jack Shaefer; *Three Comedies of American Life*, edited by Joseph Mersand. "Banned" from Mosley High School: *Adventures in English Literature*, by Patrick Murray; *After the First Death*, by Robert Cormier; *Alas, Babylon*, by Pat Frank; *Animal Farm*, by George Orwell; *Arrangement in Literature*, by Edmund J. Farrell; *The Autobiography of Benjamin Franklin*; *Best Short Stories*, edited by Raymond Harris; *Brave New World*, by Aldous Huxley; *The Call of the Wild*, by Jack London; *The Canterbury Tales*, by Geoffrey Chaucer; *The Crucible*, by Arthur Miller; *Death Be Not Proud*, by John Gunther; *Deathwatch*, by Robb White; *Desire under the Elms, The Emperor Jones,* and *Long Day's*

Journey into Night, by Eugene O'Neill; *Exploring Life through Literature*, by Edmund J. Farrell; *Fahrenheit 451*, by Ray Bradbury; *The Fixer*, by Bernard Malamud; *Miss Julie*, by August Strindberg; *The Glass Menagerie*, by Tennessee Williams; *Great Expectations*, by Charles Dickens; *The Great Gatsby*, by F. Scott Fitzgerald; *Growing Up by Russell Baker; Hamlet, King Lear, The Merchant of Venice,* and *Twelfth Night*, by William Shakespeare; *Hippolytus*, by Euripides; *In Cold Blood*, by Truman Capote; *The Inferno*, by Dante; *The Little Foxes*, by Lillian Hellman; *Lord of the Flies*, by William Golding; *Major British Writers*, by G. B. Harrison; *The Man Who Came to Dinner*, by George S. Kaufman and Moss Hart; *The Mayor of Casterbridge*, by Thomas Hardy; *McTeague*, by Frank Norris; *Mister Roberts*, by Thomas O. Heggen; *The Oedipus Plays of Sophocles; Of Mice and Men* and *The Pearl*, by John Steinbeck; *The Old Man and the Sea*, by Ernest Hemingway; *On Baile's Strand*, by W. B. Yeats; *The Outsiders*, by S. E. Hinton; *Player Piano*, by Kurt Vonnegut; *The Prince and the Pauper*, by Mark Twain; *Prometheus Unbound*, by Percy Bysshe Shelley; *Tale Blazer Library* and *A Raisin in the Sun*, by Lorraine Hansberry; *To Kill a Mockingbird*, by Harper Lee; *Watership Down*, by Richard Adams; *Winterset*, by Maxwell Anderson; *Wuthering Heights*, by Charlotte Bronte; *The Red Badge of Courage*, by Stephen Crane; *A Separate Peace*, by John Knowles.

2004 NV   Challenged on the seventh-grade honors English reading list at Elko Junior High School because of the book's sexual content.

Source: 8, pp. 88–93; 11, Mar. 1985, p. 45; Nov. 1986, p. 209; Mar. 1987, p. 52; July 1987, pp. 126–28; Sept. 1987, pp. 168–69; Nov. 1987, p. 224; Jan. 2005, pp. 9–10.

352   Cormier, Robert
Tenderness

2002 VA   Challenged, along with seventeen other titles in the Fairfax County elementary and secondary libraries, by a group called Parents Against Bad Books in Schools. The group contends the books "contain profanity and descriptions of drug abuse, sexually explicit conduct, and torture."

Source: 11, Jan. 2003, p. 10.

353   Cormier, Robert
We All Fall Down

1984 CA   Pulled from elementary and junior high school libraries in Stockton after parents complained that it glorifies alcoholism and

violence, contains a violent rape scene, and its characters use too much profanity.

2000 FL   Removed from the Carver Middle School library in Leesburg after parents complained about the book's content and language.

2000 TX   Restricted in Arlington middle and high schools to students who have written parental permission, due to concerns over violent content.

2001 PA   Challenged in the Tamaqua Area School District because the book "might not be appropriate for younger schoolmates." The school board is considering the establishment of a restricted materials section in the district's middle-school library for books deemed objectionable. Students would need parental permission to access any title placed there.

2003 KS   Pulled from a Baldwin ninth grade class by the school district superintendent because "it was clear to him it wasn-t fit for his own daughter or granddaughter." The original complaint objected to fifty passages that contained profanity and sexual content.

2005 NJ   Challenged at the Cherry Hill Public Library's young adult section by a parent claiming its "deplorable" content was unfit for young minds. The book was retained.

Source: 11, Mar. 1995, p. 39; May 2000, p. 75; July 2000, p. 103; Mar. 2001, p. 54; July 2001, p. 145; Nov. 2003, p. 229; Jan. 2004, p. 12; Nov. 2005, p. 296.

354   Corsaro, Maria, and Carole Korzeniowsky
Woman's Guide to a Safe Abortion

1984 MA   Challenged at the Walpole Public Library because the book is "inaccurate factually, because it is deliberately misleading and deceitful, and because its avowed purpose is to promote a behavior—killing unborn babies. . . By maintaining and displaying this material at public expense, to the public, and in particular to pregnant women who are vulnerable and may be in need of real guidance, the Walpole Public Library is promoting and abetting abortion."

Source: 11, Nov. 1984, p. 184.

355   Cory, Donald Webster
Homosexuality in America

1989 SC   Returned to shelves of the Horry County School District middle school libraries in Conway after an attorney advised that the 1988 state health education law did not prohibit books on homosexuality and abortion. Other titles temporarily removed include: *The Abortion Controversy in America*, by Carol Emmens; *Kids Having Kids*, by Janet Bode; and *Who They Are: The Right-to-Lifers*, by C. Paige.

Source: 11, July 1989, p. 143.

356 **Cottrell, Randall**
Wellness: Stress Management

1992 OR Rejected as a supplemental health book in the Eagle Point schools because three women complained that the book cited yoga and Transcendental Meditation as ways to reduce stress, but failed to mention Christian prayer.

Source: 11, Jan. 1993, p. 12.

357 **Coupe, Peter**
The Beginner's Guide to Drawing Cartoons

1999 WA Removed from the Meadow Ridge Elementary School library in Spokane after a mother complained that nude cartoon characters of Adam and Eve were a bad influence on children.

Source: 11, May 1999, p. 68.

358 **Courtenay, Bryce**
The Power of One

1996 TX Retained on the Round Rock Independent High School reading list after a challenge that the book was too violent.

Source: 11, May 1996, p. 99.

359 **Coville, Bruce**
Am I Blue?

2004 IA Challenged in the Solon eighth-grade language arts class because the short fictional story explores a boy's confusion with his sexual identity and the gay fairy godfather who helps him overcome homophobia at school. The short story, published in *Am I Blue?: Coming out from Silence* by Marion Dane Bauer, ed., was eventually retained.

Source: 11, Jan. 2005, p. 8.

360 **Coville, Bruce**
The Dragonslayers

1995 SC Challenged in the Berkeley County School District because of the "witchcraft" and "deception" and because a "main character openly disobeys his parents."

Source: 11, Mar. 1996, p. 63.

361 **Coville, Bruce**
Jeremy Thatcher, Dragon Hatcher

1993 IA Returned to the shelves of the Carroll Middle School library after an "avalanche" of appeals overturned a Reconsideration of Instructional Materials Committee decision that the book be removed because it "was not forthright with the message it intended to present."

1993 IA Returned to the shelves of the Fairview Elementary library after an "avalanche" of appeals overturned a Reconsideration of Instructional Materials Committee decision that the book be removed because it "was not forthright with the message it intended to present."

Source: 11, Nov. 1993, p. 191.

362 **Coville, Bruce**
My Teacher Glows in the Dark

1995 CA Contested in the classrooms and school libraries in Palmdale because the book includes the words "armpit farts" and "farting."

Source: 11, Mar. 1996, p. 45.

363 **Coville, Bruce**
My Teacher Is an Alien

1994 PA Challenged in the Elizabethtown schools because it demeans teachers and parents as dumb and portrays the main character as handling a problem on her own, rather than relying on the help of others.

Source: 11, Mar. 1995, p. 44.

364 **Coward, Noel**
Blithe Spirit

1989 OR Challenged in the Springfield schools because the play encourages occult activities.

Source: 11, Mar. 1990, p. 63.

365 **Cox, Elizabeth**
Night Talk

2008 GA New Challenged at the South Gwinnett High School's library because the story, which portrays the friendship of a white girl and a black girl during the Civil Rights era, contains "graphic sex scenes that read like a how to guide." A school committee, comprised of three teachers and four parents, denied the request to restrict the book's use or have it removed from the media center.

Source: 11, Mar. 2009, pp. 37–38.

366 Cox, R. David
Student Critic

1979 IN   Expurgated in Warsaw to remove four pages of a story entitled "A Chip off the Old Block" because the story contains the words "damn" and "hell."
Source: 11, May 1979, p. 64.

367 Cranmer, Thomas and Others
The Book of Common Prayer

1553   Cranmer was responsible for the writing of most of the first Book of Common Prayer in 1549, brought into compulsory use in the Church of England by act of Parliament, and for the 1552 revision of the book. In 1553, the Catholic Queen Mary banned the use of the Prayer Book. Crammer was convicted of treason and heresy and executed.
Source: 1, p. 31.

368 Crichton, Michael
Congo

1995 CA   Challenged as an optional text in an Yerba Buena High School interdisciplinary course by the father of two black students who said it is part of racially discriminatory practices. The parent has filed an $8 million civil rights suit against the school district.
Source: 11, Jan. 1996, p. 13.

369 Crowley, Aleister
Magick in Theory and Practice

1988 OR   Challenged at the Dalles-Wasco County Public Library because the book promotes criminal activity in its depiction of human and animal sacrifice.
Source: 11, Jan. 1989, p. 15.

370 Crumb, R.
The R. Crumb Coffee Table Art Book

1999 IN   Challenged at the Alexandrian Public Library in Mount Vernon.
Source: 11, Nov. 1999, p. 171.

371 Cruse, Howard
Stuck Rubber Baby

2004 TX   Challenged at the Montgomery County Memorial Library System along with fifteen other titles. The objections to the books, which contain young-adult fiction with gay-positive themes, were posted at the Library Patrons of Texas Web site. The language describing the books is similar to that posted at the Web site of the Fairfax County, Virginia-based Parents Against Bad Books in Schools, to which Library Patrons of Texas links.
Source: 11, Nov. 2004, pp. 231–32.

372 Crutcher, Chris
Athletic Shorts

1995 SC   Challenged at the Charleston County School library because the books deals with divorce, violence, AIDS, and homosexuality.
1999 AK   Pulled from the elementary school collections, but retained at the middle school libraries in Anchorage. A parent challenged the book of short stories because of the book's lack of respect for parents and God, its treatment of homosexuality, and its bad language.
Source: 11, July 1995, p. 94; May 1999, p. 65.

373 Crutcher, Chris
Chinese Handcuffs

1998 WI   Challenged, but retained at the Lincoln High School in Wisconsin Rapids. A parent complained about "the book's depiction of incest, rape, animal torture, teen drug use, breaking and entering, illegal use of a video camera, profanity directed to a school principal, and graphic sexual references."
2009 IN New   Retained in Delphi Community High School's curriculum despite claims of inappropriate sexual content and graphic language.
Source: 11, May 1998, p. 89; May 2009, p. 94.

374 Crutcher, Chris
Deadline

2009 KY New   Withdrawn from classroom use and the approved curriculum at the Montgomery County, High School, but available at the high school library and student book club. Some parents have complained about five novels containing foul language and covering topics—including sex, child abuse, suicide, and drug abuse—unsuited for discussion in coed high school classes. They also contend that the books don't provide the intellectual challenge and rigor that students need in college preparatory classes. The titles appeared on suggested book lists compiled by the Young Adult Library Services Association, a division of the American Library Association, for twelve- to eighteen-year-olds who are "reluctant readers." The

superintendent removed the book because it wasn't on the pre-approved curriculum list and couldn't be added by teachers in the middle of a school year without permission.
Source: 11, Jan. 2010, pp. 16–17; Mar. 2010, p. 56.

375 Crutcher, Chris
In the Time I Get

2004 IA Challenged in the Solon eighth-grade language arts class because the short story is about a man who befriends a young man dying of AIDS. The short story, published in *Athletic Shorts,* by Chris Crutcher, was eventually retained.
Source: 11, Jan. 2005, p. 8.

376 Crutcher, Chris
Running Loose

1986 GA Challenged at the Gwinnett County public schools because of its discussion of sex.
Source: 11, Mar. 1987, p. 65.

377 Crutcher, Chris
Stotan!

1997 WV Removed from the Jackson County school libraries along with sixteen other titles.
Source: 11, Jan. 1998, p. 13.

378 Crutcher, Chris
Whale Talk

2005 AL Removed from all five Limestone County high school libraries because of the book's use of profanity.
2005 MI Challenged at the Grand Ledge High School.
2005 SC Removed from the suggested reading list for a pilot English-literature curriculum by the superintendent of the South Carolina Board of Education.
2007 IA Challenged at the Missouri Valley High School because the book uses racial slurs and profanity.
Source: 11, May 2005, p. 107; July 2005, pp. 153–54; May 2007, p. 98; July 2007, p. 149; 14, pp. 295–97.

379 Cunningham, Antonia, ed.
Guinness Book of World Records

2002 WI Retained in the Waukesha elementary schools despite a challenge that the book was sexually explicit.
Source: 11, May 2002, p. 136.

380 Currie, Ian
You Cannot Die: The Incredible Findings of a Century of Research on Death

1987 MI Challenged at the Plymouth-Canton school system in Canton because the book is "not only offensive to our faith, but it is a dangerous teaching to children today when the suicide rate is so high."
Source: 11, May 1987, p. 110.

381 Curry, Hayden, and Denis Clifford
A Legal Guide for Lesbian and Gay Couples

1993 OR Challenged at the Deschutes County Library in Bend because it "encourages and condones" homosexuality.
Source: 11, Sept. 1993, pp. 158–59.

382 Curtis, Christopher Paul
The Watsons Go to Birmingham—1963

2002 VA Challenged in the Stafford County middle schools because a parent was offended. The book is a 1996 Newbery Honor winner and the same year was named a Coretta Scott King Honor Book.
Source: 11, July 2002, pp. 154–55.

383 Curtis, Helena
Biology

1982 CA San Diego school system was threatened with a lawsuit unless the book was removed because "it treats the topic of evolution in a dogmatic manner."
Source: 11, Mar. 1983, p. 40.

384 Cusack, Isabel
Mr. Wheatfield's Loft

1988 OR Challenged at the Springfield Public Library because of profanity and the appearance of the subject of prostitution.
Source: 11, Jan. 1990, pp. 4–5.

385 Cushman, Karen
The Midwife's Apprentice

1998 KS Challenged in the Newton schools and public library because a parent thought the 1996 Newbery Award-winning book was "not appropriate for middle school students."
Source: 11, July 1998, pp. 108–9.

386   Dacey, John S.
Adolescents Today

1985 PA   The Norwin School Board decided to retain the textbook used in the district's tenth-grade health classes despite accusations that it is amoral, anti-family, and has a Marxist bent. A group of nineteen parents filed a federal lawsuit in March 1987. The suit charged that in the book abstaining from sex until marriage is portrayed unfavorably, birth control techniques are evaluated, and homosexuality is taught as a natural stage of sexual development.

Source: 11, July 1985, p. 135; July 1987, p. 131.

387   Dahl, Roald
The BFG

1987 IA   Challenged at the Amana first-grade curriculum because the book was "too sophisticated and did not teach moral values."

Source: 11, Sept. 1987, pp. 194–95.

388   Dahl, Roald
Charlie and the Chocolate Factory

1988 CO   Removed from a locked reference collection at the Boulder Public Library. The book was originally locked away because the librarian thought the book espouses a poor philosophy of life.

Source: 11, Jan. 1989, p. 27.

389   Dahl, Roald
The Enormous Crocodile

1988 OR   Challenged at the Multnomah County Library in Portland because of the book's sinister nature and the negative action of animals.

Source: 11, Jan. 1989, p. 3.

390   Dahl, Roald
George's Marvelous Medicine

1995 VA   Challenged at the Stafford County Schools because the book "posed a safety threat because the boy in the story warms household items, such as paint thinner and soap, to make a potion."

Source: 11, Sept. 1995, pp. 159–60.

391   Dahl, Roald
James and the Giant Peach

1991 FL   Challenged at the Deep Creek Elementary School in Charlotte Harbor because it is "not appropriate reading material for young children."

1991 WI   Challenged at the Pederson Elementary School in Altoona because the book uses the word "ass" and parts of the book deal with wine, tobacco, and snuff.

1992 FL   Challenged at the Morton Elementary School library in Brooksville because the book contains a foul word and promotes drugs and whiskey.

1995 VA   Challenged at the Stafford County Schools because the tale contains crude language and encourages children to disobey their parents and other adults. The book was removed from the classrooms and placed in the library, where access was restricted.

1999 TX   Banned from an elementary school in Lufkin because it contains the word "ass."

Source: 11, July 1991, p. 108; Mar. 1992, p. 65; Jan. 1993, p. 27; Sept. 1995, p. 160; Jan. 2000, p. 8.

392   Dahl, Roald
Matilda

1993 MI   Retained on the shelves in the Grand Rapids school libraries, but not allowed to be read in the elementary classrooms. Ten parents complained about the book, calling it offensive and "appalling in its disrespect for adult figures and children."

1994 ME   Challenged, but retained in the Margaret Chase Smith School library in Skowhegan after the complainant came to understand that attaching a warning label also would amount to censorship.

1995 VA   Challenged at the Stafford County Schools because the tale contains crude language and encourages children to disobey their parents and other adults. The book was removed from the classrooms and placed in the library, where access was restricted.

Source: 11, Nov. 1993, p. 179; May 1994, p. 98; Sept. 1995, p. 160.

393   Dahl, Roald
The Minipins

1995 VA   Challenged at the Stafford County Schools because the tale contains crude language and encourages children to disobey their parents and other adults. The book was removed from the classrooms and placed in the library, where access was restricted.

Source: 11, Sept. 1995, p. 160.

394   Dahl, Roald
Revolting Rhymes

1990 IA   Challenged at the Northeast High School in

Goose Lake because of its alleged violence, the use of the word "slut," and the subject of witches.

1992 MA Banned in the Rockland elementary schools after a parent complained that the book of fractured fairy tales was offensive and inappropriate for children.

1995 VA Challenged at the Stafford County Schools because the book spoofs nursery rhymes.

Source: 11, May 1990, p. 105; Jan. 1993, p. 8; Sept. 1995, pp. 159–60.

---

395 Dahl, Roald
Rhyme Stew

1990 DE Moved from the children's section to the adult section at the Dover Public Library. The complainant called for the establishment of a national rating system similar to that of the motion picture industry that would classify books according to local community standards.

Source: 11, Mar. 1991, p. 42.

---

396 Dahl, Roald
The Witches

1987 IA Challenged at the Amana first-grade curriculum because the book was "too sophisticated and did not teach moral values."

1990 IA Challenged at the Goose Lake Elementary School because of its alleged violence, the use of the word "slut," the subject of witches, and the fact that "the boy who is turned into a mouse by the witches will have to stay a mouse for the rest of his life."

1991 OR Challenged at the Dallas Elementary School library because the book entices impressionable or emotionally disturbed children into becoming involved in witchcraft or the occult.

1992 CA Placed on a library restricted list by the Escondido Union Elementary School District after four parents filed complaints that it promoted the occult and was too frightening. Returned to the shelves of the Escondido Union School District school libraries after the school board lifted a partial ban. A complaint was filed by four parents who stated the book promoted satanism. The district still retains bans on four books, including *Halloween ABC*, which some parents charged with promoting the occult.

1992 CA Challenged at the La Mesa-Spring Valley School District because it includes horrifying depictions of witches as ordinary-looking women, against whom there is no defense. Other opponents added that it promotes the religion of Wicca, or witchcraft.

1993 PA Challenged at Pine Forge Elementary School in the Boyertown area.

1993 WI Challenged in the Spencer schools because it desensitizes children to crimes related to witchcraft.

1994 MI Challenged, but retained at the Battle Creek Elementary School library despite the protests from a parent who said the book is satanic.

1995 VA Challenged at the Stafford County Schools because the tale contains crude language and encourages children to disobey their parents and other adults. The book was to be removed from the classrooms and placed in the library, where access could be restricted.

1998 OH Challenged, but retained at the Dublin school district despite objections that the book is "derogatory toward children and conflicts with family religious and moral beliefs."

Source: 11, Sept. 1987, pp. 194–95; May 1990, p. 105; Jan. 1992, p. 26; May 1992, pp. 78–79; Nov. 1992, pp. 196–97; July 1993, p. 127; Sept. 1993, p. 157; May 1994, p. 85; Nov. 1994, p. 200; Sept. 1995, p. 160; Sept. 1998, p. 156.

---

397 Dahrendorf, Ralf
Class and Class Conflict in Industrial Society

1985 Banned in South Korea.

Source: 5, Apr. 1986, pp. 30–33.

---

398 Dakin, Edwin
Mrs. Eddy

1929 The Christian Science Church attempted to suppress this biography of Mary Baker Eddy, the Church's founder, by demanding its withdrawal from sale.

Source: 15, Vol. III, p. 418.

---

399 Daldry, Jeremy
The Teenage Guy's Survival Guide

2005 AR Restricted, but later returned to general circulation shelves with some limits on student access, based on a review committee's recommendations, at the Holt Middle School parent library in Fayetteville despite a parent's complaint that it was sexually explicit.

Source: 11, May 2005, p. 135; Sept. 2005, p. 215; Nov. 2005, pp. 295–96.

---

400 Dalrymple, Douglas J., and Leonard J. Parsons
Marketing Management: Text and Cases

1981 NE Seven pages of this book were expurgated at

the University of Nebraska-Omaha because they contain a case study dealing with a firm that sells contraceptive devices.

Source: 11, Jan. 1982, p. 19.

---

401   Dalrymple, Willard
Sex Is for Real

1977   MI   Banned from the Brighton High School library along with all the other sex education materials.

Source: 11, Sept. 1977, p. 133.

---

402   Dandicat, Edwidge
Krik! Krak!

2004   WI   Challenged by a parent at the Arrowhead High School in Merton as an elective reading list assignment because the book contains "sexually explicit and inappropriate material."

Source: 11, Jan. 2005, p. 11.

---

403   Dante Alighieri
The Divine Comedy

1497   Burned in Florence, Italy.
1581   Prohibited by Church authorities in Lisbon, Portugal, until all copies were delivered to the Inquisition for correction.
1978   Banned in Ethiopia.

Source: 4, p. 6; 5, Sept./Oct. 1978, p. 66.

---

404   Dante Alighieri
On Monarchy

1329   Dante argued against papal control over secular authority and the Pope condemned the book in Rome, Italy.
1329   Publicly burned in the marketplace of Bologna, Italy.
1500   In the sixteenth century, the Spanish Inquisition banned it, and it was listed on the Catholic Church's first *Index Librorum Prohibitorum* (Index of Prohibited Books), where it remained until the nineteenth century.

Source: 1, p. 234.

---

405   Darwin, Charles B.
On the Origin of Species

1859   Banned from Trinity College in Cambridge, England.
1925   TN   Tennessee passed a law prohibiting teachers from teaching the theory of evolution in state supported schools. John T. Scopes, a science teacher in Dayton, volunteered to be the test case for Tennessee's anti-evolution law. The Scopes "monkey trial," eventually, was

thrown out on a technicality.

1935   Banned in Yugoslavia.
1937   Banned in Greece.
1968   AR   The U.S. Supreme Court considered a case similar to Scopes. Susan Epperson, a high school biology teacher, challenged the constitutionality of the Arkansas Anti-Evolution Statute of 1928, which provided that teachers who used a textbook that included Darwin's theory of evolution could lose their jobs. The Supreme Court ruled that the law was unconstitutional and conflicted with the First and Fourteenth Amendments. Government power could not be used to advance religious beliefs. In the early 1980s, Arkansas state board of education required the teaching of both creationism and evolution in public schools. This law were ruled unconstitutional in 1987 by the U.S. Supreme Court in *Edwards v. Aguillard* as advocating a religious doctrine and violating the establishment clause of the First Amendment.
1980   LA   In the early 1980s, Arkansas and Louisiana state boards of education required the teaching of both creationism and evolution in public schools. These laws were ruled unconstitutional in 1987 by the U.S. Supreme Court in *Edwards v. Aguillard* as advocating a religious doctrine and violating the establishment clause of the First Amendment. Battles about the teaching of evolution, however, still rage on, especially at the local school board level.

Source: 4, p. 42; 8, pp. 276–79.

---

406   Darwin, Erasmus
Zoonomia

1817   Sixty-five years before his grandson Charles Darwin revolutionized biological science, Darwin formulated an evolutionary system in this treatise on animal life. Placed on the Catholic Church's *Index Librorum Prohibitorum* (Index of Prohibited Books) in Rome, Italy, where it remained listed until 1966.

Source: 1, pp. 359–60.

---

407   Davis, Deborah
My Brother Has AIDS

2004   TX   Challenged at the Montgomery County Memorial Library System along with fifteen other young adult books with gay-positive themes. The objections were posted at the Library Patrons of Texas Web site. The language describing the books is similar to that posted at the Web site of the Fairfax County, Virginia-based Parents Against Bad

Books in Schools, to which Library Patrons of Texas links.

Source: 11, Nov. 2004, pp. 231–32.

408   Davis, Jenny
Sex Education

1993   ND   Challenged at Hughes Junior High School in Bismarck because it is "offensive."

Source: 11, Sept. 1993, p. 145.

409   Davis, Jim
Garfield: His Nine Lives

1989   MI   Moved to the adult section of the Public Libraries of Saginaw after patrons requested that children be denied access.

Source: 11, May 1989, p. 77.

410   Davis, Kathryn
The Dakotas: At the Wind's Edge

1983   ND   Banned from sale in all Medora bookstores because some Medora residents did not approve of some of Davis's fictional embellishments to the history of their town.

Source: 11, July 1983, p. 123.

411   Davis, Lindsey
Silver Pigs

2002   VA   Challenged, along with seventeen other titles in the Fairfax County elementary and secondary libraries, by a group called Parents Against Bad Books in Schools. The group contends the books "contain profanity and descriptions of drug abuse, sexually explicit conduct, and torture."

Source: 11, Jan. 2003, p. 10.

412   Davis, Terry
Vision Quest

1984   WA   Challenged at the Mead School District.
1984   WI   Placed on a restricted reading list by the New Berlin School Board because it is "vulgar and not educational."
1984   WI   Challenged at the West Milwaukee High School library because it is "obscene."
1986   WI   Banned from the West Allis-West Milwaukee school libraries because of its profanities.
1993   ND   Moved from the Hughes Junior High School in Bismarck to the high school because a parent considered some passages obscene, pornographic, or inappropriate for junior high students.

Source: 11, July 1984, p. 101; Sept. 1984, pp. 139–40; Nov. 1984, pp. 186, 196; Jan. 1985, p. 10; Mar. 1986, p. 39; Mar. 1987, p. 51; Sept. 1993, p. 145; Nov. 1993, pp. 178–79; Jan. 1994, p. 38.

413   Day, Doris
Doris Day: Her Own Story

1982   AL   Removed from two Anniston high school libraries due to the book's "shocking" contents particularly "in light of Miss Day's All-American image," but later reinstated on a restricted basis.

Source: 11, Mar. 1983, p. 37.

414   Day, Susan, and Elizabeth McMahan
The Writer's Resource: Readings for Composition

1991   MO   Banned from the Jasper schools because a character in a story used profanity and slang.

Source: 11, Jan. 1992, p. 8.

415   De Clements, Barthes
No Place for Me

1991   CO   Challenged in the Douglas County school libraries in Castle Rock because it introduces children to witchcraft.

Source: 11, May 1991, p. 89.

416   de Haan, Linda, and Stern Nijland
King & King

2004   IN   Moved from the children's section to the adult section at the Shelbyville-Shelby County Public Library because the book's homosexual story was considered inappropriate by a parent.
2004   NC   Restricted to adults at the Freeman Elementary School in Wilmington the children's book is about a prince whose true love turns out to be another prince.
2005   OK   Challenged by seventy Oklahoma state legislators calling for the book to be removed from the children's section and placed in the adult section of the Metropolitan Library System in Oklahoma City.
2006   MA   Parents of a Lexington second-grader protested that their son's teacher read the fairy tale about gay marriage to the class without warning parents first. The book was used as part of a lesson about different types of weddings. "By presenting this kind of issue at such a young age, they're trying to indoctrinate our children," stated the parent. The incident renewed the efforts of Waltham-based Parents' Rights Coalition to rid the state's schools of books and lessons that advance the "homosexual agenda" in public schools. U.S. District Court Judge Mark Wol ruled February 23, 2007, that public schools

are "entitled to teach anything that is reasonably related to the goals of preparing students to become engaged and productive citizens in our democracy." Wolf said the courts had decided in other cases that parents' rights to exercise their religious beliefs were not violated when their children were exposed to contrary ideas in school. The parents appealed to the U.S. Court of Appeals for the First Circuit, which dismissed the case on January 31, 2008. The courts said, "There is no evidence of systemic indoctrination. There is no allegation that the student was asked to affirm gay marriage. Requiring a student to read a particular book is generally not coercive of free exercise rights. Public schools are not obligated to shield individual students from ideas which potentially are religiously offensive, particularly when the school imposes no requirement that the student agree with or affirm those ideas, or even participate in discussions about them." The parents plan to appeal to the U.S. Supreme Court claiming the curriculum violated their right to religious freedom.

2007 PA Retained at the Lower Macungie Library. The donated book was challenged because, "let them be kids . . . and not worry about homosexuality, race, religion. Just let them live freely as kids."

2008 New Withdrawn from two Bristol, England primary schools following objections from parents who claimed the book was unsuitable for children and that they had not been consulted on their opinions.

Source: 11, May 2004, p. 97; July 2004, pp. 137–38; May 2005, pp. 108–9; July 2006, pp. 186–87; May 2007, pp. 105–6; Jan. 2008, pp. 25–26; Mar. 2008, p. 79; July 2008, pp. 146, 166; Sept. 2008, pp. 194–95.

---

417 de Jenkins, Lyll Becerra
The Honorable Prison

1992 WA Challenged at the Commodore Middle School in Bainbridge Island as inappropriate by three parents because of violence, sexual scenes, and "lack of family values."

Source: 11, May 1992, p. 84.

---

418 de Schweinitz, Karl
Growing Up: How We Become Alive, Are Born and Grow

1987 WA Placed on restricted shelves at the Evergreen School District elementary school libraries in Vancouver in accordance with the school board policy to restrict student access to sex education books in elementary school libraries.

Source: 11, May 1987, p. 87.

---

419 De Veaux, Alexis
Na-ni

1988 VA Removed from open shelves to students in grades K-2 at South Accomack Elementary Schools after the county school board agreed that it contains vulgar words ("dog turd") and improper punctuation.

Source: 11, May 1988, p. 87.

---

420 Dean, Roger
Album Cover Album

1987 WA Challenged at the Evergreen School District Junior High School library in Vancouver because "of the way some of the covers represented women" citing one album cover depicting the "Statue of Liberty with bare breasts as exemplary of several photos that were pretty raw toward women."

Source: 11, May 1987, p. 102.

---

421 Defoe, Daniel
Adventures of Robinson Crusoe

1720 Placed on the Spanish Index.

Source: 4, p. 25.

---

422 Defoe, Daniel
Moll Flanders

1930 U.S. Customs raised its ban.

Source: 4, p. 25; 8, pp. 367–68.

---

423 Defoe, Daniel
Political History of the Devil

1743 Listed on the *Index Librorum Prohibitorum* (List of Prohibited Books) in Rome, Italy.

Source: 4, p. 25.

---

424 Defoe, Daniel
Roxana

1930 U.S. Customs raised its ban.

Source: 4, p. 25.

---

425 Defoe, Daniel
The Shortest Way with the Dissenters

1703 Burned and the author fined, imprisoned, and pilloried in London, England.

Source: 4, p. 25.

426 Del Vecchio, John M.
The Thirteenth Valley:
A Novel

1993 IL Banned from the Amundsen High School classrooms in Chicago because of "explicit sexual content."
Source: 11, Sept. 1993, pp. 147–48.

427 DeLillo, Don
Americana

1980 UT Removed from the Davis County Library.
Source: 11, Nov. 1980, p. 127.

428 Dell, Floyd
Janet March

1923 MA Banned in Boston.
1923 NY New York Society for the Suppression of Vice lodged a formal complaint with the New York City district attorney, charging the book was "obscene." Instead of fighting the threat, the publisher, Alfred A. Knopf, promised to cease printing future copies of the book and withdrew the book.
Source: 13, pp. 122–23.

429 DeMille, Nelson
The Charm School

1999 MA Removed from the Waltham High School summer reading list because of two sexually graphic passages.
Source: 11, Jan. 2000, p. 14.

430 Dengler, Marianna
A Pebble in Newcomb's Pond

1984 CA Judged unacceptable at the Thompson Junior High School in Bakersfield.
Source: 11, July 1984, p. 105.

431 Denneny, Michelle; Charles Ortlieb; and Thomas Steele
First Love/Last Love: New Fiction from Christopher Street

1993 OR Challenged at the Deschutes County Library in Bend because it "encourages and condones" homosexuality.
Source: 11, Sept. 1993, pp. 158–59.

432 DeSaint, Niki
AIDS: You Can't Catch It Holding Hands

1993 KS Challenged at the Derby Library because "the book didn't say abstinence is the answer and just teach it."
Source: 11, July 1993, p. 124.

433 Descartes, Rene
Discourse on Method

1640 Prohibited at the University of Leiden in Netherlands because it was considered anti-Protestant. Calvinists persuaded the University of Leiden to ban Cartesian doctrine from all lectures and writings.
1640 Prohibited at the University of Utrecht in Netherlands because it was considered anti-Protestant.
1663 Placed on the *Index Librorum Prohibitorum* (Index of Prohibited Books) in Rome, Italy, fourteen years after his death.
Source: 6, pp. 665–66.

434 Dessen, Sarah
Just Listen

2007 FL Challenged in the Hillsborough County
New   school system because it was considered too intense for teens.
Source: 11, Mar. 2008, p. 59.

435 Deuker, Carl
On the Devil's Court

1999 VA Challenged, but retained at the Virginia Run Elementary School in Centreville despite a parent's claim that the book espouses "pro-Satanism."
Source: 11, Nov. 1999, pp. 172–73.

436 Deveraux, Jude
A Knight in Shining Armor

1993 CA Retained at the Lassen Union High School in Quincy. The book was checked out from a recreational reading library provided by the English instructor. Parents called the romance novel "obscene."
Source: 11, Nov. 1993, p. 193.

437 Diagram Group
Man's Body: An Owner's Manual

1979 OR Banned from the Monroe High School when parents complained that the reference book's portrayals of male and female anatomies were too explicit.
Source: 9; 11, May 1979, p. 51.

438 Diagram Group
Woman's Body: An Owner's Manual

1979 OR Banned from the Monroe High School when parents complained that the reference book's portrayals of male and female anatomies were too explicit.

1987 WI Challenged at the Evansville High School library because the book is "filth" and it is "sick," even though it is on a restricted shelf behind the librarian's desk.
Source: 9; 11, May 1979, p. 51; May 1987, p. 102.

439 Dickens, Charles
Oliver Twist

1949 NY A group of Jewish parents in Brooklyn went to court claiming that the assignment of Dickens's novel to senior high school literature classes violated the rights of their children to receive an education free of religious bias in *Rosenberg v. Board of Education of the City of New York*, 196 Misc. 542, 92 N.Y. Supp. 2d 344.
Source: 8, pp. 271–73; 12, pp. 23, 230.

440 Dickens, Frank
Albert Herbert Hawkins—the Naughtiest Boy in the World

1985 CO Relegated to an adult shelf at the Castle Rock elementary school libraries because it "advocates defiance of adult authority by showing misbehavior for which the protagonist goes unpunished." The Douglas County Board of Education reversed its ruling seven months later and decided the book could go back into general circulation.
Source: 11, May 1985, p. 76; Sept. 1985, p. 151; Nov. 1985, p. 203.

441 Dickens, Frank
Albert Herbert Hawkins and the Space Rocket

1985 CO Relegated to an adult shelf at the Castle Rock elementary school libraries because it "advocates defiance of adult authority by showing misbehavior for which the protagonist goes unpunished," the Douglas County Board of Education reversed its ruling seven months later and decided the book could go back into general circulation.
Source: 11, May 1985, p. 76; Sept. 1985, p. 151; Nov. 1985, p. 203.

442 Dickey, Eric Jerome
The Other Woman

2005 AR Challenged in the Fayetteville High School library. The complainant also submitted a list of more than fifty books, citing the books as too sexually explicit and promoting homosexuality.
Source: 11, Sept. 2005, p. 215.

443 Dickey, James
Deliverance

1973 ND Burned in Drake, but U.S. District Court ruled that teachers should be allowed to use this title in eleventh- and twelfth-grade English classes.

1974 MD Challenged in Montgomery County on the grounds that it employs "gutter language" and depicts "perverted acts."

1993 ND Moved from the Hughes Junior High School in Bismarck to the High School because a parent considered some passages obscene, pornographic, or inappropriate for junior high students.

1998 CT Challenged, but retained in the Sheehan High School English curriculum in Wallingford because the book was too "graphic and contained explicit language." After two hundred people attended a special board meeting and after listening to the teachers and "articulate" students, the board denied that request for removal.
Source: 11, July 1975, p. 118; Nov. 1975, p. 174; Sept. 1993, p. 145; Nov. 1993, pp. 178–79; Jan. 1994, p. 38; July 1998, p. 120.

444 Diderot, Denis, and Jean Le Rond d'Alembert
Encyclopedie

1759 Censored repeatedly during the twenty-one years of its publication. In 1759, the Catholic Church placed the first seven volume and in 1804, the entire work on the *Index Librorum Prohibitorum* (Index of Prohibited Books) in Rome, Italy where it remained until 1966.
Source: 1, pp. 91–94.

445 Dieckman, Ed, Jr.
The Secret of Jonestown: The Reason Why

1990 IL Challenged at the La Grange Public Library because it promotes "hate" for the Jewish people. "It is a Nazi book and it doesn't belong in La Grange."
Source: 11, May 1990, p. 84.

446   Diehl, William
Sharky's Machine

1982   LA   Challenged at the Northside High School Library in Lafayette due to "the book's treatment of drugs, prostitution, and race."
Source: 11, May 1982, p. 83.

447   Doig, Ivan
Dancing at the Rascal Fair

2007   ID   Challenged in the Coeur d'Alene School District
New   because sexual descriptions in the book were not appropriate. Some parents say the book, along with five others, should require parental permission for students to read them.
Source: 11, Sept. 2007, p. 181.

448   Donleavy, John P.
The Ginger Man

1955   Originally published by Girodias in Paris. Author expurgated that text himself to permit publication in England.
Source: 4, p. 97.

449   Dorner, Marjorie
Nightmare

1995   MN   Pulled from the Winona Middle School media center and classroom libraries because of language and violence in the book.
Source: 11, Jan. 1996, p. 11.

450   Dorris, Michael
A Yellow Raft in Blue Water

1997   TX   Challenged as required reading for freshmen in the Advanced Placement Honors English Class at Clear Lake High School in Houston. A parent described the contents as "not suggestive, not explicit, but pornographic, and in the guise of multi-cultural reading."

1999   GA   Challenged at the Pebblebrook High School in Marietta because of the book's profanity and explicit sexual language.
Source: 11, Mar. 1998, p. 42; May 1999, p. 66.

451   Dorson, Richard M.
America in Legend: Folklore from the Colonial Period to the Present

1977   GA   Removed from a library in Cobb County because the book "condones draft dodging" and contains the song "Casey Jones," which includes several stanzas describing the fabled railroad engineer's sexual prowess.
Source: 11, Sept. 1977, p. 133.

452   Doyle, Robert P.
Banned Books

1999   VA   Banned from a display at Spotswood High School in Harrisonburg after a parent determined that some materials listed in the publication were inappropriate for students. Students were not required to read or even look at the publication, nor were they required to read any of the books listed in the publication.
Source: 11, Jan. 2000, p. 16; Mar. 2000, pp. 39, 45.

453   Doyle, Sir Arthur Conan
The Adventures of Sherlock Holmes

1929   Banned in the USSR because of its references to occultism and spiritualism.
Source: 4, p. 56.

454   Dozois, Gardner, ed.
Isaac Asimov's Skin Deep

1995   OH   Challenged in the Fairfield County District Library because it includes profanity and explicit sex scenes.
Source: 11, Nov. 1995, p. 184; Jan. 1996, p. 29.

455   Dragnich, Alex N.
Serbs and Croats: The Struggle in Yugoslavia

1994   IL   Challenged at the Lincolnwood Public Library because the book is "pro-Serbian and anti-Croatian.
Source: 11, Mar. 1995, p. 53.

456   Dragonwagon, Crescent, and Paul Zindel
To Take a Dare

1989   OR   Challenged at the Crook County Middle School library because of "excessive use of profanity."
Source: 11, May 1989, p. 93.

457   Dramer, Dan
Monsters

1986   CO   Challenged at the Jefferson County school libraries in Lakewood. The book is a junior high text of monster stories including several Greek myths on the Cyclops, the Minotaur, and Medusa, as well as stories of several modern monsters such as King Kong, Dracula, and Frankenstein's monster. The Jefferson County School Board refused to ban the book.
Source: 11, May 1986, p. 82; Sept. 1986, p. 173; Nov. 1986, p. 224.

458 **Draper, John William**
History of the Conflict between Religion and Science

1876   First American book to be listed on the *Index Librorum Prohibitorum* (Index of Prohibited Books) in Rome, Italy. In the last twenty years of his life, Draper sought to apply Charles Darwin's theories of biological evolution to human history and politics.
Source: 1, pp. 137–38.

459 **Draper, Sharon M., and Adam Lowenbein**
Romiette and Julio

2006 VA Challenged in the Albemarle County schools, spurring a debate over the age-appropriate-ness of material with sexual innuendo and fictional online chat room chatter. The school board determined to move the book from the supplemental summer reading list after fifth grade to the sixth-grade second semester curriculum.
Source: 11, Jan. 2007, pp. 15–16.

460 **Dreiser, Theodore**
An American Tragedy

1927 MA Banned in Boston.
1933   Burned by the Nazis in Germany because it "deals with low love affairs."
Source: 2, p. 133; 4, p. 61; 6, p. 690; 8, p. 315; 15, Vol. III, pp. 404, 407.

461 **Dreiser, Theodore**
Dawn

1932   Banned in Ireland.
Source: 4, p. 61.

462 **Dreiser, Theodore**
Genius

1916 NY Suppressed by the New York Society for the Suppression of Vice.
1933   Burned by the Nazis in Germany because it "deals with low love affairs."
Source: 2, p. 100; 4, p. 61; 6, p. 690; 13, pp. 84–85; 15, Vol. II, pp. 631–32.

463 **Dreiser, Theodore**
Sister Carrie

1900 NY Suppressed in New York City.
1958 VT Banned in Vermont.
Source: 4, p. 61; 9, p. 141.

464 **Driggs, John, and Stephen Finn**
Intimacy between Men

1991 AR Challenged, but retained at the Rogers-Hough Memorial Library, because "we're headed down the road to another San Francisco community."
Source: 11, Sept. 1991, pp. 151, 177.

465 **Drill, Esther**
Deal with It! A Whole New Approach to Your Body, Brain, and Life as a gURL

2001 FL Challenged, but retained at the Marion-Levy Public Library System in Ocala.
2004 TX Challenged at the Montgomery County Memorial Library System along with fifteen other young adult books with gay-positive themes. The objections were posted at the Library Patrons of Texas Web site. The language describing the books is similar to that posted at the Web site of the Fairfax County, Virginia-based Parents Against Bad Books in Schools, to which Library Patrons of Texas links.
2005 AR Challenged, but retained in the Fayetteville Public school libraries. The complainant also submitted a list of more than fifty books, citing the books as too sexually explicit and promoting homosexuality.
2009 WI New Challenged at the West Bend Community Memorial Library as being "pornographic and worse than an R-rated movie." The library board unanimously voted 9–0 to maintain, "without removing, relocating, labeling, or otherwise restricting access," the books in the young adult category at the West Bend Community Memorial Library. The vote was a rejection of a four-month campaign conducted by the citizen's group West Bend Citizens for Safe Libraries to move fiction and nonfiction books with sexually explicit passages from the young adult section to the adult section and label them as containing sexual material.
Source: 11, Nov. 2001, p. 246; Nov. 2004, pp. 231–32; Jan. 2005, pp. 5–6; May 2005, p. 135; Sept. 2005, p. 215; Nov. 2005, pp. 295–96; May 2009, pp. 80–81; Sept. 2009, pp. 169–70.

466 **Dubberley, Emily**
Sex for Busy People: The Art of the Quickie for Lovers on the Go

2009 KS New Restricted minors' access in the Topeka and Shawnee County Public Library because Kansans for Common Sense contended that the material is "harmful to minors under state law." Later the board organization voted 6-3 in favor of adopting a staff recommendation to keep the books where they are currently located on the shelves in the library's Health Information Neighborhood section.

Source: 11, May 2009, pp. 77-78; July 2009, p. 139.

467   Dumas, Alexandre
Camille

1850	Banned in England.
1852	Banned in France.
1863	Banned in Italy.
1958	Ban lifted in USSR.

Source: 4, p. 48; 14, p. 74.

468   Duncan, Lois
Daughters of Eve

1997 WV Removed from the Jackson County school libraries along with sixteen other titles.

2000 VA Removed from the Fairfax County middle school libraries and classrooms because "it promotes risky behavior and violence and also seeks to prejudice young vulnerable minds on several issues."

2005 IN Challenged at the Lowell Middle School because of the book's profanity and sexual content.

Source: 11, Jan. 1998, p. 13; July 2000, p. 105; May 2005, pp. 109–10.

469   Duncan, Lois
Don't Look Behind You

1993 IN Challenged at the Charlestown Middle School library because of graphic passages, sexual references, and alleged immorality in the book.

Source: 11, July 1993, p. 124.

470   Duncan, Lois
Killing Mr. Griffin

1988 CA Challenged at the Sinnott Elementary School in Milpitas because the book contained "needlessly foul" language and had no "redeeming qualities."

1992 CA Pulled from a Bonsall Middle School eighth-grade reading list because of disgusting violence and profanity.

1995 PA Challenged in the Shenandoah Valley Junior-Senior High School curriculum because of violence, strong language and unflattering references to God.

2000 PA Challenged in a Bristol Borough middle school for violence and language.

Source: 11, July 1988, pp. 122–23; Sept. 1988, p. 179; Mar. 1993, p. 43; July 1995, p. 99; May 2000, p. 78.

471   Duong, Thu Huong
Novel without a Name

1991 Forbidden in Vietnam. Duong was arrested and imprisoned without trail. She was charged with having contacts with "reactionary" foreign organizations and with having smuggled "secret documents" out of the country.

Source: 6, p. 702; 8, pp. 146–47.

472   Duong, Thu Huong
Paradise of the Blind

1988 Banned in Vietnam. The novel outraged Vietnamese leaders, particularly the sections describing the 1953–56 land reform campaign—ts excesses and its management, its destructive effects. Party Secretary Nguyen Van Linh publicly denounced Duong as "a whore;" he issued a second banning order. The depictions of these situations and their repercussions established her leadership of the dissident movement, leading to her arrest and the banning of her works.

Source: 8, pp. 151–52.

473   Durack, Mary, and Elizabeth Durack
Kookanoo and the Kangaroo

1978 MD Removed from Howard County because, "it would be hard for primary youngsters to make the distinction between the aborigines in Australia and black children in the U.S."

Source: 11, Mar. 1978, p. 30.

474   Durang, Christopher
Laughing Wild

1998 FL Challenged at the Manatee County School District in Bradenton Beach because the play contains references to Dr. Ruth Westheimer and uses several slang words for sexual acts.

Source: 11, May 1998, p. 71.

475   Durant, Penny
When Heroes Die

1993 OR Challenged at the Seaside Public Library for promoting homosexuality.

Source: 11, Jan. 1994, p. 36.

476   Durrell, Lawrence
The Black Book

1961 Seized by the U.S. Customs Bureau.

Source: 4, p. 88.

477 **_Earth Science_**

1987 MI Challenged at the Plymouth-Canton school system in Canton because this book "teaches the theory of evolution exclusively. It completely avoids any mention of Creationism. . . The evolutionary propaganda also underminds [sic] the parental guidance and teaching the children are receiving at home and from the pulpits."

Source: 11, Nov. 1981, pp. 162–63; May 1987, p. 109.

478 Eban, Abba
My People: The History of the Jews

1983 Banned from the 1983 Moscow, Russia International Book Fair along with more than fifty other books because it is "anti-Soviet."

Source: 11, Nov. 1983, p. 201.

479 Ebert, Alan
The Homosexual

1982 MI Challenged at the Niles Community Library because, "it belongs on the shelves of a porno-shop."

Source: 11, Jan. 1983, p. 8.

480 Edgerton, Clyde
The Floatplane Notebooks

1992 VA Challenged at the Carroll County High School in Hillsville because "it was wishy-washy" and "could warp a child's mind." The complainants circulated a petition demanding the firing of an English teacher and the dismissal of all school officials connected with the decision to use the novel.

Source: 11, May 1992, p. 84; Sept. 1992, p. 143.

481 Edgerton, Clyde
Walking across Egypt

1997 VA Removed from a Clover Hill High School class in Richmond because the book refers to African-Americans as "niggers," is punctuated with profanity, and is "unacceptable and unnecessary."

Source: 11, May 1997, p. 67.

482 Ehrenreich, Barbara
Nickel and Dimed: On (Not) Getting By in America

2003 NC Criticized as the book chosen for the University of North Carolina at Chapel Hill summer reading program by Republican state lawmakers, citing a "pattern" of the university being anti-Christian. In 2002, three freshmen sued the university over its choice of _Approaching the Qur' an: The Early Revelations,_ by Michael A. Sells. The federal lawsuit was filed on the students' behalf by the Family Policy Network, a Christian group based in Virginia. Court later rejected the argument that the reading requirement violated the U.S. Constitution.

2010 PA New Challenged at the Easton Area School District (2010), but retained despite a parent's claim the book promotes "economic fallacies" and socialist ideas, as well as advocating the use of illegal drugs and belittling Christians.

Source: 11, Sept. 2003, p. 182; May 2010, p. 107.

483 Ehrlich, Max
The Reincarnation of Peter Proud

1976 CO Banned from use in Aurora High School English classes on the grounds of "immorality."

Source: 11, May 1976, p. 70; May 1977, p. 79.

484 Ehrlich, May
Where It Stops, Nobody Knows

1998 SC Removed from the Cayce-West Columbia School District's Congaree Elementary School library because of a blasphemy and slang term for sex.

Source: 11, Mar. 1999, p. 36.

485 El Saadawi, Nawal
The Hidden Face of Eve: Women in the Arab World

1980 Prohibited from entry to many Arab countries including Egypt, where Egyptian customs and excise authorities barred it under the Importing of Foreign Goods Act. The author was imprisoned in 1981 under the Sadat regime, blacklisted from Egyptian television and radio, and the target of numerous death threats by Muslim fundamentalists. In 1993, she left Egypt, fearing for her life, and moved to the United States.

1980 Burned in Tehran, Iran along with the publishing house.

Source: 8, pp. 245–47.

486 Eleveld, Mark, ed.
The Spoken Word Revolution: Slam, Hip Hop & the Poetry of a New Generation

2006 WA Challenged, but retained in the Sequim School District despite complaints that the book contains "profanity and references to sex, drugs, and mistreatment of women that are inappropriate for young teens."

Source: 11, Sept. 2006, p. 257.

---

487 Eliot, George
Adam Bede

1859   Attacked as "the vile outpourings of a lewd woman's mind" and withdrawn from the British circulating libraries.

Source: 4, p. 45.

---

488 Eliot, George
Silas Marner

1978 CA Banned from the Anaheim Union High School District English classrooms according to the Anaheim Secondary Teachers Association.

Source: 11, Jan. 1979, p. 6.

---

489 Eliot, John
The Christian Commonwealth

1661 MA Banned in Massachusetts for stating that even royal authorities owed their power to higher source. Any Massachusetts citizen who owned copies of the banned work had to "cancel or deface" them and bring them to local judges, who would then dispose of them.

Source: 1, pp. 37–38.

---

490 Elish, Dan
Born Too Short: The Confessions of an Eighth-Grade Basket Case

2005 MD Banned in Carroll County schools. No reason stated.

Source: 11, Mar. 2006, pp. 70–71.

---

491 Elliot, David
An Alphabet for Rotten Kids

1999 WA Pulled from the Spokane School District libraries after a parent complained its depictions of children hitting animals and destroying property gave her second-grader the wrong message.

Source: 11, May 1999, p. 68.

---

492 Ellis, Bret Easton
American Psycho

1991 MO The Carthage public librarian was directed first "to take the book off the shelf and keep it under the circulation desk" and then "lose it." The incident involving the novel "snowballed" and was one of the reasons why, under protest, the librarian submitted her resignation.

Source: 11, Nov. 1991, p. 195.

---

493 Ellis, Havelock
Studies in the Psychology of Sex

1898   Condemned and burned in England.
1941   Banned from the mail by the U.S. Post Office Department unless addressed to a doctor.
1953   Banned in Ireland.

Source: 4, pp. 56–57; 6, pp. 732–33.

---

494 Ellison, Ralph
Invisible Man

1975 PA Excerpts banned in Butler.
1975 WI Removed from the high school English reading list in St. Francis.
1994 WA Retained in the Yakima schools after a five-month dispute over what advanced high school students should read in the classroom. Two parents raised concerns about profanity and images of violence and sexuality in the book and requested that it be removed from the reading list.

Source: 11, July 1975, p. 105; Nov. 1994, pp. 202–3.

---

495 Elson, Robert T.
Prelude to World War II

1989 OR Challenged at the Douglas County Library in Roseburg because the book contains nudity and violent photos harmful to children researching the war.

Source: 11, Jan. 1990, pp. 4–5.

---

496 Elwell, Walter A., ed.
Evangelical Commentary on the Bible

1991 OR Challenged, but retained at the Multnomah County Library by a patron who believed public funds should not be expended on religious books.

Source: 11, Jan. 1992, p. 6.

---

497 Emerson, Zack
Echo Company

1993 AZ Restricted access at the Marana Unified School District because of complaints about profanity.

Source: 11, Sept. 1993, p. 143.

498 ***Encyclopaedia Britannica***

1986 Banned and then pulped in Turkey because it was a "means of separatist propaganda."
Source: 3, p. 319.

499 ***The Endless Quest***

1985 IA Challenged in Newton because the books in the series contain excessive violence, destruction, witchcraft, and the occult. The titles in the series include: *The Hero of Washington Square, The King's Quest, Light on Quest Mountain, Spell of the Winter Wizard,* and *Under the Dragon's Wing.*
Source: 11, Mar. 1986, p. 38.

500 Enger, Eldon D., et al.
Concepts in Biology

1980 MA Two pages removed from the Waltham High School text due to their explicit nature.
Source: 11, Jan. 1981, p. 10.

501 Erasmus, Desiderus
Colloquies

1526 Condemned, along with The Praise of Folly, by the Sorbonne and the Parlement of Paris, France for allegedly heretical sympathies with Lutheranism. All of Erasmus's works were listed in the first *Index Librorum Prohibitorum* (Index of Prohibited Books) established in 1559, a ban that remained until the 1930s.
Source: 1, pp. 48–49.

502 Erdoes, Richard, and Alfonso Ortiz
American Indian Myths and Legends

1997 AK Removed from the Anchorage school library shelves that are accessible to students. The anthology, which contains some sexually explicit tales, was placed in special resource collections available only to teachers.
Source: 11, Mar. 1998, p. 39; May 1998, pp. 70–71.

503 Escher, M. C.
The Graphic Work of M. C. Escher

1994 AZ Retained at Maldonado Elementary School in Tucson after being challenged by parents who objected to nudity and "pornographic," "perverted," and "morbid" themes.
Source: 11, July 1994, p. 112.

504 Escoffier, Jeffrey
John Maynard Keynes

2000 CA Removed from the Anaheim school district because school officials said the book is too difficult for middle school students and that it could cause harassment against students seen with it. The American Civil Liberties Union (ACLU) of Southern California filed suit in *Doe v. Anaheim Union High School District* alleging that the removal is "a pretext for viewpoint-based censorship." The ACLU claims no other books have been removed from the junior high library for similar reasons, even though several, such as works by Shakespeare and Dickens, are more difficult reading. The ACLU contends that the school officials engaged in unconstitutional viewpoint discrimination by removing the book because it contains gay and lesbian material. In March 2001, the school board approved a settlement that restored the book to the high school shelves and amended the district's policy to prohibit the removal of books for subject matter involving sexual orientation, but the book will not be returned to the middle school.
Source: 11, Mar. 2001, p. 53; May 2001, p. 95; July 2001, p. 173.

505 Esquivel, Laura
Like Water for Chocolate: A Novel in Monthly Installments, with Recipes, Romances, and Home Remedies

2004 WI Challenged at the Arrowhead High School in Merton as an elective reading list assignment by a parent because the book contains "sexually explicit and inappropriate material."
Source: 11, Jan. 2005, p. 11.

506 Etchison, Dennis
Cutting Edge

1988 OR Challenged at the Eugene Public Library for its language, sexual nature, and "perversity."
Source: 11, Jan. 1989, p. 3.

507 Evans, Tabor
Longarm in Virginia City

1985 IN Challenged at the Allen County Public Library in Fort Wayne as "pornographic and objectionable."

1988 OR Removed from the Jordan Valley Union High School because it was "too sexually graphic."

2001 AR Challenged, but retained at the Springdale Public Library along with all other "western" novels because the writings include "pornographic, sexual encounters."

Source: 11, July 1985, pp. 111–12; Jan. 1989, p. 3; Nov. 2001, p. 277.

---

508 Everetts, E.
Holt Basic Readings

1983 TN Challenged at the Hawkins County school system in Church Hill by the Citizens Organized for Better Schools because they claim the reading series indoctrinates students in "secular humanist" beliefs. Over 400 specific objections were filed against the reading series including specific complaints against the following works included in the series: *Rumpelstiltskin; Cinderella; The Wizard of Oz*, by L. Frank Baum; Shakespeare's *Macbeth; Anne Frank: The Diary of a Young Girl*; readings from anthropologist Margaret Mead; science fiction writer Isaac Asimov; and fairy tale creator Hans Christian Andersen. On October 24, 1986, U.S. District Court Judge Thomas G. Hull ruled in favor of the citizens' group and that the school's use of the textbook series "burdened" the plaintiffs' First Amendment rights to exercise freedom of religion. He ordered the Hawkins County public schools to excuse fundamentalist children from reading class. On August 24, 1987, a three-judge panel of the U.S. Court of Appeals for the Sixth Circuit reversed Judge Hull's decision by ruling unanimously that public school students can be required to read and discuss the disputed books, even though parts of those books might conflict with their beliefs. The court further ruled that there was no evidence that "the conduct required of the students was forbidden by their religion." On February 22, 1988, the U.S. Supreme Court declined to consider the appeal. The denial of *certiorari* in the case of *Mozert v. Hawkins County* left standing the August decision by the U.S. Court of Appeals for the Sixth Circuit.

Source: 11, Jan. 1984, p. 11; Mar. 1984, p. 40; May 1984, p. 79; July 1984, pp. 112–13; Jan. 1987, pp. 1, 36–38; May 1987, pp. 75, 104–7; Sept. 1987, pp. 166–67; Nov. 1987, pp. 217–18; Mar. 1988, pp. 40–41, 58; May 1988, pp. 94–95.

---

509 Evslin, Bernard
Cerberus

1990 MO Removed from the elementary school library shelves, but retained in the junior and senior high school libraries in the Francis Howell School District in St. Peters. Allegedly, the book's story line is too graphic, its titles too gruesome, and its illustrations "pornographic." (The illustrations are drawings by Michelangelo and other Masters.) The book was said to "encourage satanism."

Source: 11, May 1990, p. 84; July 1990, pp. 126–27; Sept. 1990, p. 159.

---

510 Eyerly, Jeannette
Someone to Love Me

1997 WV Removed from the Jackson County school libraries along with sixteen other titles.

Source: 11, Jan. 1998, p. 13.

---

511 Fanon, Frantz
The Wretched of the Earth

1985 Banned in South Korea.

Source: 5, Apr. 1986, pp. 30–33.

---

512 Farmer, Philip J.
Image of the Beast

1981 WV Challenged at the Chapmanville Public Library because the book puts "mental pictures in the mind [that] have no place in the library."

Source: 11, Mar. 1981, p. 41.

---

513 Farrell, James
Studs Lonigan: A Trilogy

1942 *Young Lonigan* was published in 1932 with the notice that it was "limited to physicians, social workers, teachers, and other persons having a professional interest in the psychology of adolescence." Banned in Canada.
1948 PA Seized in Philadelphia.
1953 Banned in Ireland.
1953 Banned in overseas libraries controlled by the U.S. Information Agency.
1953 MN Banned in St. Cloud.

Source: 2, p. 148; 4, p. 85.

---

514 Farrell, James
A World I Never Made

1935 Tried for obscenity in the U.S. and acquitted.
1957 The U.S. Information Agency banned all of Farrell's novels from overseas libraries under its control.
1957 MN Banned in St. Cloud. In 1957, the U.S. Information Agency banned all of Farrell's novels from overseas libraries under its control.
1957 WI Banned in Milwaukee.

Source: 2, p. 159; 14, pp. 301–2; 15, Vol. III, pp. 648, 650.

515 Fassbender, William
You and Your Health

1987 WA Challenged in the Seattle school system because of its views on substance abuse and morality, as well as promiscuity.
Source: 11, July 1987, p. 131.

516 Fast, Howard
Citizen Tom Paine

1947 NY Banned from high school libraries in New York City because it was allegedly written by a spokesman of a totalitarian movement and because it contains incidents and expressions not desirable for children, and was improper and indecent.

1953 Withdrawn from U.S. Information Agency libraries overseas.
Source: 4, p. 89; 7, pp. 111–12; 15, Vol. IV, p. 700.

517 Fast, Howard
The Immigrants

1982 NC Restricted to high school students with parental permission at the Governor Morehead School in Raleigh due to the explicit sexual scenes and vulgarities.
Source: 11, Nov. 1982, p. 205.

518 Fast, Howard
Second Generation

1982 NC Restricted to high school students with parental permission at the Governor Morehead School in Raleigh due to the explicit sexual scenes and vulgarities.
Source: 11, Nov. 1982, p. 205.

519 Faulkner, William
As I Lay Dying

1986 KY Banned in the Graves County School District in Mayfield because it contained "offensive and obscene passages referring to abortion and used God's name in vain." The decision was reversed a week later after intense pressure from the ACLU and considerable negative publicity.

1987 KY Challenged as a required reading assignment in an advanced English class of Pulaski County High School in Somerset because the book contains "profanity and a segment about masturbation."

1991 MD Challenged, but retained in the Carroll County schools. Two school board members were concerned about the book's coarse language and dialect.

1994 KY Banned at Central High School in Louisville temporarily because the book uses profanity and questions the existence of God.
Source: 11, Nov. 1986, p. 208; May 1987, p. 90; Mar. 1992, p. 64; Nov. 1994, p. 189.

520 Faulkner, William
The Hamlet

1954 Banned in Ireland.
Source: 4, p. 77.

521 Faulkner, William
Mosquitoes

1948 PA Seized in raid in Philadelphia.
1954 Banned in Ireland.
Source: 4, p. 78.

522 Faulkner, William
Pylon

1954 Blacklisted by the National Organization of Decent Literature; condemned by local censorship groups; banned in Ireland.
Source: 4, p. 78.

523 Faulkner, William
A Rose for Emily

1996 AZ Challenged as required reading in an honors English class at the McClintock High School in Tempe by a teacher on behalf of her daughter and other African-American students at the school. In May 1996, a class-action lawsuit was filed in U.S. District Court in Phoenix, alleging that the district deprived minority students of educational opportunities by requiring racially offensive literature as part of class assignments. In January 1997, a federal judge dismissed the lawsuit stating he realized that "language in the novel was offensive and hurtful to the plaintiff," but that the suit failed to prove the district violated students' civil rights or that the works were assigned with discriminatory intent. The U.S. Court of Appeals for the Ninth Circuit in San Francisco ruled that requiring public school students to read literary works that some find racially offensive is not discrimination prohibited by the equal protection clause or Title VI of the 1964 Civil Rights Act. The ruling came in the case *Monteiro v. Tempe Union High School District*.
Source: 11, May 1997, p. 72; Jan. 1999, pp. 13–15.

524   Faulkner, William
Sanctuary

1948 PA   The novel along with eight other novels were identified as obscene in criminal proceedings in the Court of Quarter sessions in Philadelphia County. Indictments were brought by the state district attorney against five booksellers who were charged with possessing and intending to sell the books. In *Commonwealth v. Gordon*, 66 D. & C. 101 (1949), the court determined that the novel is not obscene. Faulkner was awarded the Nobel Prize for literature in 1950. Although the novel did not go to court again, by 1954, it was again condemned as obscene by numerous local censorship groups throughout the U.S., and the National Organization of Decent Literature placed it on the disapproval list. Also in 1954, Ireland banned the novel, along with most of the author's other works, because of the language such as "son of a bitch," "whore," "slut," and "bastard" combined with the brutal violence of the story. Irish and U.S. Censors also objected to the character Ruby, who prostituted herself to obtain money to free her common-law husband from jail, to obtain legal fees and to pay their expenses.

1954   Ireland banned the novel, along with most of the author's other works, because of the language such as "son of a bitch," "whore," "slut," and "bastard" combined with the brutal violence of the story. Irish and U.S. Censors also objected to the character Ruby, who prostituted herself to obtain money to free her common-law husband from jail, to obtain legal fees and to pay their expenses.

Source: 4, p. 78; 8, pp. 378–79.

525   Faulkner, William
Soldier's Pay

1954   Banned in Ireland.
1954   Blacklisted by the National Organization of Decent Literature; condemned by local censorship groups.

Source: 4, p. 78.

526   Faulkner, William
Wild Palms

1948 PA   Seized in raid in Philadelphia.
1954   Banned in Ireland.

Source: 4, p. 77.

527   Federico, Ronald
Sociology

1982 FL   Removed from the Florida list of approved textbooks because, as the Pro-Family Forum argued, the textbook attacks religion and promotes nudity and profanity.

Source: 11, July 1982, p. 125.

528   Feelings, Muriel
Jambo Means Hello: The Swahili Alphabet

1994 NY   Challenged by a school board member in the Queens school libraries because it "denigrate[s] white American culture, 'promotes racial separation, and discourages assimilation.'" The rest of the school board voted to retain the book.

Source: 11, July 1994, pp. 110–11; Sept. 1994, p. 166.

529   Ferguson, Alane
Show Me the Evidence

1993 IN   Challenged at the Charlestown Middle School library because of graphic passages, sexual references, and alleged immorality in the book.

Source: 11, July 1993, p. 124.

530   Ferlinghetti, Lawrence
Coney Island of the Mind

1976 CO   Banned for use in Aurora High School English classes on the grounds of "immorality."

Source: 11, May 1976, p. 70; May 1977, p. 79; 12, pp. 128–32, 238.

531   Ferlinghetti, Lawrence
Starting from San Francisco

1976 CO   Banned for use in Aurora High School English classes on the grounds of "immorality."

Source: 11, May 1976, p. 70; May 1977, p. 79; 12, pp. 128–32, 238.

532   Ferris, Jean
Eight Seconds

2004 TX   Challenged at the Montgomery County Memorial Library System along with fifteen other young adult books with gay-positive themes. The objections were posted at the Library Patrons of Texas Web site. The language describing the books is similar to that posted at the Web site of the Fairfax County, Virginia-based Parents Against Bad Books in Schools, to which Library Patrons of Texas links.

Source: 11, Nov. 2004, pp. 231–32.

533 Fielding, Henry
Tom Jones

1749   Banned in France.
        Source: 4, p. 29.

534 Fierstein, Harvey
The Sissy Duckling

2004 TX Challenged at the Montgomery County
          Memorial Library System along with fifteen
          other young adult books with gay-positive
          themes. The objections were posted at the
          Library Patrons of Texas Web site. The
          language describing the books is similar to
          that posted at the Web site of the Fairfax
          County, Virginia-based Parents Against Bad
          Books in Schools, to which Library
          Patrons of Texas links.
          Source: 11, Nov. 2004, pp. 231–32.

535 Fitzgerald, F. Scott
The Great Gatsby

1987 SC Challenged at the Baptist College in
          Charleston because of "language and sexual
          references in the book."
          Source: 11, July 1987, p. 133.

536 Fitzgerald, Frances
***Cities on a Hill: A Journey through
Contemporary American Cultures***

1993 OR Challenged at the Deschutes County Library
          in Bend because it "encourages and
          condones" homosexuality.
          Source: 11, Sept. 1993, pp. 158–59.

537 Fitzgerald, John D.
The Great Brain

1992 NY Removed from a list of supplemental reading
          material for fourth graders at the Port Jervis
          schools because the novel contains a
          discussion of suicide.
          Source: 11, Nov. 1992, pp. 186–87.

538 Fitzhugh, Louise
Harriet the Spy

1983 OH Challenged in the Xenia school libraries
          because the book "teaches children to lie,
          spy, back-talk, and curse."
          Source: 6, pp. 832–33; 9; 11, Sept. 1983, p. 139;
          Nov. 1983, p. 197.

539 Fitzhugh, Louise
The Long Secret

1993 MT Challenged in the Eagle Cliffs Elementary
          School library in Billings because the book is
          "demented" and pokes fun at religion.
          Source: 11, Jan. 1994, p. 36.

540 Fitzhugh, Louise
Sport

1998 IA Challenged at the Madison Elementary
          School in Cedar Rapids due to "cuss words"
          and other harsh language.
          Source: 11, May 1998, pp. 87–88.

541 Flaubert, Gustave
Madame Bovary

1857   Flaubert was brought to trail in 1857 for the
        novel under a French law, first passed in May
        1819, which aimed to suppress the exhibition,
        distribution, or sale of any printed matter
        constituting and "outrage to public and
        religious morality and to public decency."
1864   Placed on the *Index Librorum Prohibitorum*
        (List of Prohibited Books) in Rome, Italy.
1954   Banned by the National Organization of
        Decent Literature.
        Source: 4, p. 47; 6, pp. 834–35; 8, pp. 362–63; 10, p. 142.

542 Flaubert, Gustave
Novembre

1935 NY The New York Society for the Suppression of
          Vice charged a bookseller with selling an
          obscene book. The City Magistrates Court of
          New York City, Fourth District, Borough of
          Manhattan dismissed the complaint and
          discharged the defendant, after noting that
          there was not sufficient cause to hold the
          defendant for trail.
          Source: 13, pp. 174–75.

543 Flora, James
Grandpa's Ghost Stories

1994 MT Challenged as inappropriate at the
          Broadwater Elementary School Library in
          Billings because "[children] don't need to be
          allowed to read anything they want."
          Source: 11, May 1994, p. 84.

544 Fogelin, Adrian
My Brother's Hero

2006 FL Removed from the Hillsborough County fourth-grade reading list, although the book is on the Sunshine State Young Reader's Award list of books for third, fourth, and fifth-graders.
Source: 11, Nov. 2006, pp. 290–91.

545 Follett, Ken
Eye of the Needle

1993 KS Banned from the Marysville high school and junior high school libraries along with five other Follett novels—*The Key to Rebecca, Lie Down with Lions, Night Over Water, The Pillars of the Earth,* and *Triple*—because the books were "pornographic." Later, however, the board decided to reconsider its vote, follow an established review procedure, and retain the six books.
Source: 11, May 1993, pp. 70–71; Nov. 1993, p. 177; Jan. 1994, p. 35.

546 Follett, Ken
The Hammer of Eden

2000 MT Challenged at the Great Falls High School library. Parents called for the review of all library books and the adoption of stricter rules to keep "obscenity" off library shelves.
Source: 11, Mar. 2001, p. 54.

547 Follett, Ken
Night over Water

1993 OH Returned to the open shelves at the Medina High School library despite some sexually explicit passages. The complainant then filed a police complaint against the Medina city schools, claiming the district is pandering obscenity to its students.
Source: 11, May 1993, p. 86; July 1993, p. 101.

548 Follett, Ken
Pillars of the Earth

1994 KS Moved to a new "reserve" section of the Chanute school library. The book came under fire because of some use of obscenity and graphic violence.

2009 TX Removed from a Cleburne summer reading
New   list for a dual credit, high school English class because the novel contains a rape scene and passages of explicit sex.
Source: 11, Sept. 1994, p. 146; Mar. 1995, p. 40; May 2009, pp. 107–8.

549 Ford, Michael Thomas
One Hundred Questions and Answers about AIDS

1993 WI Challenged because it encourages sexual activity, but retained in the Eau Claire public school libraries.

1997 WV Removed from the Jackson County school libraries along with sixteen other titles.
Source: 11, July 1993, p. 104; Sept. 1993, p. 159; Jan. 1998, p. 13.

550 Forrest, Katherine
Beverly Malibu

1991 IL Challenged, but retained at the Oak Lawn Public Library because the sleuth in the mystery is a lesbian.
Source: 11, Nov. 1991, p. 209.

551 Forster, E. M.
Maurice

1995 NH Banned from the Mascenic Regional High School in New Ipswich because it is about gays and lesbians. An English teacher was fired for refusing to remove the book. An arbitrator ruled in April 1996 that she can return to work in September without a year's back pay. The Mascenic Regional School Board is appealing the ruling. The teacher was eventually reinstated after a decision by the state's Public Employee Labor Relations Board.
Source: 11, Sept. 1995, p. 166; Jan. 1996, p. 15; July 1996, pp. 130–31; Jan. 1997, p. 27.

552 Forsyth, Frederick
The Devil's Alternative

1983 WA Removed from the Evergreen School District of Vancouver along with twenty-nine other titles. The American Civil Liberties Union of Washington filed suit contending that the removals constitute censorship, a violation of plaintiff's rights to free speech and due process, and the acts are a violation of the state Open Meetings Act because the removal decisions were made behind closed doors.
Source: 11, Nov. 1983, pp. 185–86.

553 Fossey, Dian
Gorillas in the Mist

1993 PA Teachers at the Westlake Middle School in Erie using felt-tip pens, blacked out passages pertaining to masturbation and mating.
Source: 11, July 1993, p. 109.

554   Fox, Mem
Guess What?

1991 IL   Challenged at the Cook Memorial Library in Libertyville because it features witches, boiling cauldrons, names of punk rockers, and a reference that could be interpreted as meaning "God is dead."
Source: 11, Sept. 1991, p. 153.

555   Fox, Paula
The Slave Dancer

1996 GA   Challenged, but retained by the Fayette County school system. The 1974 Newbery Medal winner about a thirteen-year-old boy who is snatched from the docks of New Orleans and put on a slave ship bound for Africa. The book was considered objectionable because of language that is "insensitive and degrading."

1998 PA   Challenged as part of the curriculum at the North Bedford County School District in Loysburg because of the book's graphic detail and derogatory racial references.

2005 KY   Challenged at the Shelbyville East Middle School because the book is a too-graphic depiction of the slave trade.
Source: 11, May 1996, p. 99; Mar. 1999, p. 40; May 2005, pp. 110–11.

556   France, Anatole
(Jacques-Anatole Thibault)
Penguin Island

1922   Placed on the Catholic Church's *Index Librorum Prohibitorum* (Index of Prohibited Books) in Rome, Italy, along with all of his works. They remained on the Index until 1966. Anatole France received Nobel Prize in literature in 1921.
Source: 1, p. 252.

557   Franco, Betsy, ed.
You Hear Me?: Poems and Writings by Teenage Boys

2002 GA   Challenged in the Houston County public schools by a parent concerned about the book's language and topics.
Source: 11, Sept. 2002, pp. 195–96.

558   Frank, Anne
Anne Frank: The Diary of a Young Girl

1982 VA   Challenged in Wise County due to protests of several parents who complained the book

contains sexually offensive passages.

1983 AL   Four members of the Alabama State Textbook Committee called for the rejection of this title because it is a "real downer."

1998 TX   Removed for two months from the Baker Middle School in Corpus Christi after two parents charged that the book was pornographic. The book was returned after students waged a letterwriting campaign to keep it, and a review committee recommended the book's retention.

2010 VA
New   Challenged at the Culpeper County public school by a parent requesting that her daughter not be required to read the book aloud. Initially, it was reported that officials have decided to stop assigning a version of Anne Frank's diary, one of the most enduring symbols of the atrocities of the Nazi regime, due to the complaint that the book includes sexual material and homosexual themes. The director of instruction announced the edition, published on the fiftieth anniversary of Frank's death in a concentration camp, will not be used in the future despite the fact the school system did not follow its own policy for handling complaints. The remarks set off a hailstorm of criticism online and brought international attention to the 7,600-student school system in rural Virginia. The superintendent said, however, that the book will remain a part of the English classes, although it may be taught at a different grade level.
Source: 8, pp. 402–3; 11, Mar. 1983, p. 39; July 1998, pp. 119–20; Mar. 2010, pp. 57–58; May 2010, p. 107.

559   Frank, E. R.
America

2007 OH   Challenged in the Ravenna schools because, "What we kept finding and going over was sexual content and profanity," said the complainant. The novel has received several awards including the *New York Times* Notable Book Award. It also was a Garden State Teen Book Award nominee.
Source: 11, May 2007, p. 93.

560   Frank, E. R.
Life is Funny

2005 CA   Pulled from the shelves of two Merced middle-school libraries because of an "X-rated" passage describing two teens' first experience with sexual intercourse.
Source: 11, May 2005, p. 107.

561 Frank, Mel, and Ed Rosenthal
Marijuana Grower's Guide

2004 WY Challenged at the Teton County Public Library in Jackson because "tax dollars are being used to purchase a how-to crime manual."
Source: 11, May 2004, p. 98.

562 Frank, Pat
Alas, Babylon

1987 IL Challenged at the Taylorville Junior High School because it "contains profane language."
Source: 11, Sept. 1987, p. 194.

563 Franklin, Benjamin
The Autobiography of Benjamin Franklin

1789 "The expurgation of Benjamin Franklin seems to have increased over the years until he became in the early twentieth century one of the most censored and yet at the same time one of the most widely reprinted writers in American history. Two essays, in particular, are frequently expurgated, 'Advice on the Choice of a Mistress' and the 'Letters to the Royal Academy of Brussels.'"

1957 As Chief Judge Clarke noted in *Roth v. United States*, 345 U.S. 476, the discussed works by Franklin "which a jury could reasonably find 'obscene,' according to the judge's instructions in the case at bar" would also have subjected a person to prosecution if sent through the mails in 1957 and "to punishment under the federal obscenity statute."
Source: 8, pp. 411–12; 10, p. 134; 15, Vol. II, p. 616.

564 Freedom Writers
The Freedom Writers Diary: How a Teacher and 150 Teens Used Writing to Change Themselves and the World around Them

2007 MI Challenged in the Howell High School along with several other books because of strong sexual content. In response to a request from the president of the Livingston Organization for Values in Education, or LOVE, the county's top law enforcement official reviewed the books to see whether laws against distribution of sexually explicit materials to minors had been broken. "After reading the books in question, it is clear that the explicit passages illustrated a larger literary, artistic, or political message and were not included solely to appeal to the prurient interests of minors," the Livingston County prosecutor wrote. "Whether these materials are appropriate for minors is a decision to be made by the school board, but I find that they are not in violation of the criminal laws." The best-selling book has achieved national acclaim and was made into a recent hit movie.
Source: 11, Mar. 2007, pp. 51–52; May 2007, p. 118.

565 Freud, Sigmund
Introductory Lectures on Psychoanalysis

1930 Censored in the Soviet Union.
1934 Pope Pius XI published a statement in Rome, Italy criticizing psychoanalysis and Freud's ideas on religious belief. Freud's writings were considered off-limits to Catholics as dangerous to faith and morals according to canon law.
1939 Burned by the Nazis.
Source: 1, pp. 169–70.

566 Freymann-Weyr, Garret
My Heartbeat

2004 TX Challenged at the Montgomery County Memorial Library System along with fifteen other young adult books with gay-positive themes. The objections were posted at the Library Patrons of Texas Web site. The language describing the books is similar to that posted at the Web site of the Fairfax County, Virginia-based Parents Against Bad Books in Schools, to which Library Patrons of Texas links.
Source: 11, Nov. 2004, pp. 231–32.

567 Friday, Nancy
Men in Love

1981 IL Temporarily placed in storage on the second floor of the Alpha Park Library and restricted to patrons over eighteen years old unless they have written parental consent because several area residents objected to its "vulgarity."
Source: 11, Jan. 1982, p. 9; May 1982, p. 100.

568 Friday, Nancy
Women on Top: How Real Life Has Changed Women's Fantasies

1994 GA Removed from the Chestatee Regional Library System in Gainesville because the book on women's sexual fantasies is "pornographic and obscene" and lacks "literary merit." After months of protest and maneuvering, the library's only copy was destroyed when the child of a patron accidentally dropped it into a dishpan full of water. The book is out of print and the library does not plan to replace it.

1996 PA Challenged at the Chester County Library at Charlestown because of graphic details about sex acts and fantasies.

1997 Winnipeg, Manitoba, Canada police seized the novel from the public library.

1997 GA Pulled from the Gwinnett County Public Library shelves after two residents complained about its sexually explicit content. Following four years of controversy over keeping adult-themed books from children, the board approved two new policies. One policy creates a "parental advisory" shelf of non-fiction sex and health books that extensively and explicitly depict human sex acts, either visually or verbally, or books the library staff deems are appropriate only for adults. The other policy allows parents to decide—with electronic designations on new library cards—whether their child can check out books on the parental advisory shelf. Parents also can restrict further what types of books the child can get from the library.

Source: 6, p. 415; 11, Nov. 1994, p. 187; Mar. 1995, p. 39; May 1995, p. 65; Nov. 1996, p. 194; Jan. 1997, p. 8; Mar. 1997, p. 49; May 1997, p. 60; Nov. 1997, p. 165.

---

569 Fritz, Jean
Around the World in a Hundred Years: Henry the Navigator—Magellan

1995 MD Removed from the Carroll County schools because a passage on the burning of the library in Alexandria during the fourth century said that "Christians did not believe in scholarship" and mentioned intellectual suppression by Christians. "It's a sweeping generalization and it's definitely anti-Christian."

Source: 11, Nov. 1995, p. 186.

---

570 Fuentes, Carlos
Aura

2009 PR New Banned from the curriculum in Puerto Rican public high schools along with four other books because of coarse language. Written by one of Latin America's most prominent contemporary writers, the novel contains a brief romantic encounter beneath a crucifix. It is a scene that prompted Mexico's former interior secretary to try to have the book dropped from a reading list at his daughter's private school, without success. Fuentes said that the attempt boosted sales. The other titles banned were: *Antologia Personal*, by Jose Luis Gonzalez; *Mejor te lo Cuento: Antologia Personal, 1978-2005*, by Juan Antonio Ramos; *Reunion de Espejos*, by Jose Luis Vega; and *El Entierro de Cortijo: 6 de Octubre de 1982*, by Edgardo Rodriguez Julia.

Source: 11, Nov. 2009, p. 204.

---

571 Fuentes, Carlos
The Death of Artemio Cruz

1994 WA Retained in the Yakima schools after a five-month dispute over what advanced high school students should read in the classroom. Two parents had raised concerns about profanity and images of violence and sexuality in the book and requested that it be removed from the reading list.

Source: 11, Nov. 1994, pp. 202–3.

---

572 Fuentes, Carlos
The Old Gringo

1996 NC Retained in the Guilford County school media centers after a parent wanted the book removed because of its explicit language.

Source: 11, Jan. 1997, p. 25.

---

573 Fugard, Athol
Master Harold and the Boys

1982 A South African order banning printed copies of the play was imposed in Dec. 1982, but was lifted temporarily a week later.

Source: 5, Mar. 1983, p. 47.

---

574 Gaines, Ernest J.
The Autobiography of Miss Jane Pittman

1995 TX Pulled from a seventh-grade class in Conroe after complaints about racial slurs in the book. School officials later reinstated it.

2006 WA Challenged as an eighth-grade district-wide reading assignment in the Puyallup schools because "racial slurs and stereotyping are used throughout the book, as well as scenes of sex, rape, and implied incest." The Puyallup School Board voted to uphold an earlier decision by a district committee requiring eighth-graders to read the novel. In explaining their vote, each board member recounted the difficulty of balancing valid concerns on each side of the debate. "It wasn't a sole issue of dealing with racism or the "n-word." "But it is our hope by giving them an explanation of the word and where it came from they'll understand it's inappropriate to use it in the future."

Source: 11, Mar. 1995, p. 46; May 1995, p. 84; Jan. 2007, pp. 11–12; Mar. 2007, pp. 74–75.

575 Gaines, Ernest
A Lesson before Dying

1999 GA Banned, but later reinstated after community protests at the Windsor Forest High School in Savannah. The controversy began in early 1999 when a parent complained about sex, violence, and profanity in the book that was part of an Advanced Placement English class.

2004 LA Removed from the college book store at Louisiana College, Pineville by the college president because a love scene described in the book clashes with the school's Christian values.

Source: 11, Mar. 2000, p. 63; Mar. 2001, p. 76; Mar. 2004, pp. 53–54.

576 Galbraith, John Kenneth
The Affluent Society

1972 NJ Removed from the Roselle high school library list along with *The Age of Keynes*, by Robert Lekachman, *The Struggle for Peace*, by *Leonard Beaton*, and *Today's Isms: Communism, Fascism, Capitalism, Socialism*, by William Ebenstein. The president of the board said, "The books were too liberal and I disagree with their points of view." Months later, after considerable public protest, the superintendent of schools placed a rush order for the books and said that they would be on the library bookshelves.

Source: 7, pp. 5–7.

577 Galdone, Joanna
The Tailypo: A Ghost Tale

1988 LA Challenged at the Jefferson Terrace Elementary School library in East Baton Rouge because "it is too scary" and gave the complainant's "child a nightmare."

Source: 11, May 1988, p. 87.

578 Gale, Jay
A Young Man's Guide to Sex

1993 AK Removed from the Kenai Peninsula Borough School District libraries in Homer because it was thought to have "outdated material that could be harmful to student health."

1993 TN Challenged, but retained at the Cleveland Public Library along with seventeen other

books, most of which are on sex education, AIDS awareness, and some titles on the supernatural.

Source: 11, Sept. 1993, p. 146; Jan. 1994, p. 33.

579 Galileo, Galilei
Dialogue Concerning the Two Chief World Systems

1633 Banned by Pope Urban VIII in Rome, Italy for heresy and breach of good faith and sentenced to prison for an indefinite period. It was not until 1824, when Canon Settele, a Roman astronomy professor, published a work on modern scientific theories, that the Roman Catholic Church finally announced its acceptance of "general opinion of modern astronomers." In the papal Index of 1835, the names of Galileo, Copernicus, and Kepler were removed. On October 31, 1992, Pope John Paul II formally rehabilitated Galileo — 359 years, four months, and nine days after Galileo had been forced to recant his heresy that the earth moved around the sun.

Source: 4, p. 17; 8, pp. 231–33.

580 Gallagher, I. J.
The Case of the Ancient Astronauts

1984 FL Challenged at the Escambia County school district because the complainant claimed the book indicated that "Ezekiel had seen a UFO when he spoke in the Bible about seeing something that looked like a wheel in the sky."

Source: 11, Sept. 1984, p. 156.

581 Gao Xingjian
Fugitives

1989 All works by Gao Xingjian banned in China. The Chinese government denounced the awarding of the 2000 Nobel Prize in Literature to Gao, accusing the Nobel committee of being politically motivated.

Source: 7, p. 184.

582 Garcia-Marquez, Gabriel
Love in the Time of Cholera

1998 MD Challenged, but retained on the Montgomery County reading lists and school library shelves. A parent had complained that the book should be removed from all county schools because it contained "perverse sexual acts, adults having sex with children, and rape."

Source: 11, May 1998, p. 70; July 1998, p. 119.

583 Garcia-Marquez, Gabriel
One Hundred Years of Solitude

1986 CA Purged from the book list for use at the Wasco Union High School because the book, whose author won the 1982 Nobel Prize for literature, was "garbage being passed off as literature."

1990 SC Removed from the Advanced Placement English reading list at St. Johns High School in Darlington because of profane language.

1997 VA Challenged for sexual explicitness, but retained on the Stonewall Jackson High School's academically advanced reading list in Brentsville.

1998 MD Challenged on the Montgomery County reading lists and school library shelves.

Source: 11, July 1986, p. 119; May 1989, p. 78; Jan. 1991, p. 18; Nov. 1997, pp. 169–70; Jan. 1998, p. 29; May 1998, p. 70.

584 Garden, Nancy
Annie on My Mind

1988 OR Challenged at the Cedar Mill Community Library in Portland because the book portrays lesbian love and sex as normal.

1990 ME Challenged in Sedgwick by a parent when she learned that the novel was included in the seventh- and eighth-grade library. The parent objected to the lesbian relationship portrayed. The book was retained.

1992 TX Challenged in the Colony Public Library because "it promotes and encourages the gay lifestyle."

1993 KS Removed at the Olathe East High School.

1993 KS The Kansas City school district donated the book to the city's public library.

1993 MI Challenged, but retained at the Lapeer West High School library.

1993 MO Challenged at several Kansas City area schools after the books were donated by a national group that seeks to give young adults "fair, accurate, and inclusive images of lesbians and gay men." Protesters burned copies of the book but the Kansas City School District kept Garden's novel on the high school shelves.

1993 MO The book was returned to general circulation at the Shawnee Mission School District.

1993 MO Removed by the Lee's Summit superintendent from the schools. The federal district court in Kansas, later found the removal of the book unconstitutional and ordered it restored to the school district's libraries.

1993 OR Challenged because it "encourages and condones" homosexuality, but retained at the Bend High School.

1994 KS Removed from shelves of the Chanute High School Library and access to them limited to only those students with written parental permission because of concerns about its content.

1994 MO Challenged, but retained at the Liberty High School library.

Source: 8, pp. 404–6; 11, Jan. 1990, pp. 4–5; July 1992, pp. 125–26; Sept. 1993, pp. 158–59; Nov. 1993, pp. 191–92; Jan. 1994, p. 13; Mar. 1994, pp. 51–52; May 1994 p. 84; July 1994, p. 129; Sept. 1994, pp. 140–41; Mar. 1995, p. 40; Mar. 1996, p. 54.

585 Garden, Nancy
Good Moon Rising

2004 TX Challenged at the Montgomery County Memorial Library System along with fifteen other young adult books with gay-positive themes. The objections were posted at the Library Patrons of Texas Web site. The language describing the books is similar to that posted at the Web site of the Fairfax County, Virginia-based Parents Against Bad Books in Schools, to which Library Patrons of Texas links.

Source: 11, Nov. 2004, pp. 231–32.

586 Garden, Nancy
Holly's Secret

2004 TX Challenged at the Montgomery County Memorial Library System along with fifteen other young adult books with gay-positive themes. The objections were posted at the Library Patrons of Texas Web site. The language describing the books is similar to that posted at the Web site of the Fairfax County, Virginia-based Parents Against Bad Books in Schools, to which Library Patrons of Texas links.

Source: 11, Nov. 2004, pp. 231–32.

587 Garden, Nancy
Witches

1986 CA Challenged by the "God Squad," a group of three students and their parents, at the El Camino High School in Oceanside because the book "contains a lot of information on witch covens. This information can be easily used to form a coven."

1997 KS Removed from the Kirby Junior High School in Wichita Falls because of "Satanic" themes.

Source: 11, Sept. 1986, p. 151; Nov. 1986, p. 224; Jan. 1987, p. 9; July 1997, p. 95.

588 Gardner, Benjamin Franklin
Black

1976 OH Removed from the Dayton schools after complaints that the work contained "hard-core pornography."
Source: 11, Jan. 1977, p. 7.

589 Gardner, John C.
Grendel

1978 MD Challenged at the Frederick County school system because the novel is "anti-Christian, antimoral, full of vulgarity."

1986 CA Placed on a restricted list at the Wasco High School which prohibits the novel's use in the classroom until every student in the class receives parental permission. The novel is the only book on the restricted list, and an objection by the high school principal to the "profane" nature of the novel was the catalyst that generated the restricted list policy.

1986 IN Challenged in the Indianapolis schools as an accelerated English class assignment.

1991 UT Challenged at the Viewmont High School in Farmington because the book "was obscene and should not be required reading."

1992 NJ Challenged, but retained as part of the Pinelands Regional High School's English curriculum in Bass River Township because of obscenities.

1993 GA Challenged in the Clayton County School District's supplemental reading list for advanced English students in Jonesboro because the book was too violent and graphic.

1997 CO Challenged, but retained on the Douglas County high school reading list. Parents complained that the novel was too obscene and violent for high school students. The school board also declined to create a rating system for books.

2008 OR Retained in the Sherwood School District
New sophomore honors English reading list after concerns were expressed about some of the novel's scenes describing torture and mutilation.
Source: 11, Mar. 1978, p. 39; May 1978, p. 58; May 1986, pp. 81–82; July 1986, p. 119; Jan. 1987, p. 32; May 1989, p. 87; May 1991, p. 92; Jan. 1993, p. 11; Mar. 1993, p. 56; May 1993, p. 87; May 1997, p. 78; Jan. 2009, p. 23.

590 Garrigue, Sheila
Between Friends

1983 IA Challenged in the Des Moines schools due to the use of the word "damn."
Source: 11, May 1983, p. 73.

591 Garrison, Eric Marlowe
Mastering Multiple Position Sex

2009 OH Challenged, but retained at the Pataskala
New Public Library. The library decided to implement a new juvenile library card. A parent or guardian will be able to sign off on the card, thereby restricting his or her child's borrowing rights to juvenile materials.
Source: 11, Jan. 2010, pp. 12–13; Mar. 2010, p. 53.

592 Gassner, John, and Clive Barnes, eds.
Best American Plays: Sixth Series, 1963–1967

1984 OK Challenged at the Miami High School library because the anthology contains "The Toilet," by Leroi Jones [Imamu Amiri Baraka].
Source: 11, May 1984, p. 87.

593 Gates, Doris
Two Queens of Heaven

1979 AZ Placed on restricted shelves in the libraries of Prescott elementary schools because it contains two illustrations of a bare-breasted goddess.
Source: 11, Jan. 1980, p. 6.

594 Gautier, Theophile
Mademoiselle de Maupin

1831 Banned until 1853 by Nicholas I in Russia.

1917 NY Challenged in New York City and finally cleared in 1921 after a long court fight.
Source: 4, p. 43; 15, Vol. III, p. 413.

595 Genet, Jean
Our Lady of the Flowers

1957 Seized from the Birmingham, England Public Library.

1958 Banned in France.
Source: 4, p. 88; 13, pp. 178–79.

596 Genet, Jean
The Thief's Journal

1961 Banned in Ireland. The Irish Board of Censors found the novel "obscene" and "indecent," objecting particularly to the author's handling of the theme of homosexuality and the poetic treatment of crime.
Source: 13, p. 246.

597   George, Jean Craighead
Julie of the Wolves

1982 MO   Challenged in Mexico because of the book's "socialist, communist, evolutionary, and anti-family themes."

1989 CO   Challenged in Littleton school libraries because "the subject matter was better suited to older students, not sixth graders."

1994 AZ   Challenged at the Erie Elementary School in Chandler because the book includes a passage that some parents found inappropriate in which a man forcibly kisses his wife. The Newbery Award-winning book, depicting the experiences of an Eskimo girl, was chosen by the teacher of a third-, fourth-, and fifth-grade class for the Antarctic unit she was teaching.

1995 CA   Challenged in the classrooms and school libraries in Palmdale because the book describes a rape.

1996 CA   Challenged at the Hanson Lane Elementary School in Ramona because the award-winning book includes an attempted rape of a thirteen-year-old girl.

1996 PA   Removed from the sixth-grade curriculum of the New Brighton Area School District in Pulaski Township because of a graphic marital rape scene.

Source: 11, Nov. 1982, p. 215; Sept. 1989, p. 186; Jan. 1995, p. 9; Mar. 1996, p. 45; May 1996, p. 88; Jan. 1997, p. 9.

598   Gettings, Fred
Dictionary of Demons

2000 OH   Moved out of the circulating collection of the Norwood High School library because of concerns that the book promotes the occult.

Source: 11, May 2000, p. 75.

599   Gibbon, Edward
History of the Decline and Fall of the Roman Empire

1783   Placed on the *Index Librorum Prohibitorum* (List of Prohibited Books) in Rome, Italy because it contradicted official church history.

Source: 4, p. 33.

600   Gibran, Kahlil
Spirits Rebellious

1908   The collection of short stories protesting religious and political tyranny, was publicly burned in the Beirut, Lebanon marketplace. Gibran was exiled from Lebanon and excommunicated from the Maronite Church.

1908   Suppressed by the Syrian government.

Source: 1, pp. 320–21.

601   Gibson, Walter Brown
Complete Illustrated Book of Divination and Prophecy

1987 MI   Challenged at the Plymouth-Canton school system in Canton because the book deals with witchcraft.

Source: 11, May 1987, p. 110; Jan. 1988, p. 11.

602   Gide, Andre
If It Die

1938   Banned in Soviet Union.

1952   Placed on the *Index Librorum Prohibitorum* (List of Prohibited Books) in Rome, Italy.

1953   Banned in Ireland.

Source: 4, p. 59; 13, p. 114; 15, Vol. III, p. 648.

603   Giles, Gail
Shattering Glass

2007 OR New   Challenged as an optional reading in a bullying unit at the Lake Oswego Junior High School because the novel is "peppered with profanities, ranging from derogatory slang terms to sexual encounters and violence." Students are given a list of book summaries and a letter to take to their parents. Four of the eight optional books offered are labeled as having "mature content/language."

Source: 11, July 2007, p. 149.

604   Gilstrap, John
Nathan's Run

1998 PA   Removed from the Annville-Cleona Middle-High School library because "the obscene/profane language and violence in this book are of a degree that it [was] concluded to be inappropriate for a middle/ high school library collection."

2000 WA   Challenged in the Everett School District due to sexual explicitness and violence.

Source: 11, Sept. 1998, p. 141; Mar. 1999, p. 40; Sept. 2000, p. 144.

605   Ginsberg, Allen
Collected Poetry, 1947–1980

1989 GA   Removed from the Murray County High School library in Chatsworth because "it was really gutter stuff."

1989 IN   Challenged at the North Central High School library in Indianapolis because explicit descriptions of homosexual acts were deemed inappropriate subject matter for high school students.

Source: 11, July 1989, p. 128; Jan. 1990, p. 9; Mar. 1990, pp. 61–62.

606   Ginsberg, Allen
Howl and Other Poems

1957 CA   Seized by U.S. Customs officials in San Francisco.

2000 FL   Prohibited in the Jacksonville Forrest High School Advanced Placement English class because of descriptions of homosexual acts. The class syllabus warns students and parents that some people might find the reading objectionable and offers an alternative assignment. The prohibition led to the review of all materials taught in the class.
Source: 4, p. 97; 6, pp. 955–56; 7, pp. 459–60; 11, Jan. 2001, p. 12.

607   Ginsberg, Allen
Kaddish and Other Poems

1976 CO   Banned for use in Aurora High School English classes on the grounds of "immorality."
Source: 11, May 1976, p. 70; May 1977, p. 79; 12, pp. 128–32, 238.

608   Giovanni, Nikki
My House

1975 WI   Banned from the Waukesha public school libraries.

1990 NY   Challenged at the West Gennessee High School in Syracuse because the book contains obscenities.

1992 FL   Challenged at the Duval County public school libraries because it contains the word "nigger" and was accused of vulgarity, racism, and sex.
Source: 11, July 1975, p. 104; July 1990, p. 127; July 1992, p. 105.

609   Glasser, Ronald J.
365 Days

1982 ME   Banned, but later reinstated by a U.S. District Court ruling in Baileyville. The class-action suit, filed by the Maine Civil Liberties Union on behalf of Michael Sheck, a former Woodland High School student, and four current students and their parents. The book was hailed by literary critics at the time of its publication for its honest portrayal of the soldiers and the war. The book was ordered removed from the high-school library by the school committee after the parents of one student complained about the expletives and four-letter words it contained.
Source: 11, Mar. 1982, p. 33.

610   Glenn, Mel
Who Killed Mr. Chippendale?:
A Mystery in Poems

1999 AL   Removed from the Central School library in Hunstville as inappropriate for fourth graders. After the book's removal, the complainant called for the formation of a group of parents to go through all the library's books, as well as monitor new books. The school's principal stated, "If a book is sexual, if it is racial, if it's violent, we'll pull it off the shelves."
Source: 11, July 1999, p. 93.

611   Godchaux, Elma
Stubborn Roots

1937 LA   Seized and destroyed by New Orleans police.
Source: 15, Vol. III, p. 650.

612   Goethe, Johann Wolfgang von
Faust

1808   Production suppressed in Berlin, Germany until certain dangerous passages concerning freedom were deleted.

1939   Franco purged Spanish libraries of all of Goethe's writings.
Source: 4, p. 35.

613   Goethe, Johann Wolfgang von
The Sorows of Werther

1776   Prohibited in Denmark.

1939   Purged from Spanish libraries by Spanish dictator Francisco Franco.
Source: 4, p. 35; 8, pp. 298–99.

614   Going, K. L.
Fat Kid Rules the World

2007 IL   Challenged as a suggested summer reading at the Alsip Prairie Junior High because the book is "laced with profanity and other mature content." The District 126 superintendent plans to retain the award-winning selection as one of the many titles offered to students to read, preferably from the recommended summer reading list, before school begins.

2007 SC
New   Removed from the Pickens County middle- and high-school library shelves because "the language, the sexual references, and drug use are not appropriate for middle-school students." In 2004, the book was named a Michael Printz honor book for excellence in young-adult literature by the Young Adult Library Services Association.
Source: 11, May 2007, pp. 93–94; Nov. 2007, pp. 242–43.

615   Gold, Robert S., ed.
Point of Departure

1983   WA   Removed from the required reading list at the North Thurston High School because of the book's "alleged strong language and allusions to sexual conduct." The decision was later reversed.

Source: 11, July 1983, p. 109; Nov. 1983, p. 187.

616   Goldfarb, Mace
Fighters, Refugees, Immigrants: A Tale of the Hmong

1988   IA   Restricted to teachers only at the Des Moines elementary schools because the book "could lead students to form a derogatory image of Southeast Asians if they are not mature enough."

Source: 11, Mar. 1988, p. 46.

617   Golding, William
Lord of the Flies

1974   TX   Challenged at the Dallas Independent School District High School libraries.
1981   NC   Challenged at Owen High School because the book is "demoralizing inasmuch as it implies that man is little more than an animal."
1981   SD   Challenged at the Sully Buttes High school.
1983   AZ   Challenged at the Marana High School as an inappropriate reading assignment.
1984   TX   Challenged at the Olney Independent School District because of "excessive violence and bad language."
1988   A committee of the Toronto, Ontario, Canada Board of Education ruled on June 23, 1988, that the novel is "racist and recommended that it be removed from all schools." Parents and members of the black community complained about a reference to "niggers" in the book and said it denigrates blacks.
1992   IA   Challenged in the Waterloo schools because of profanity, lurid passages about sex, and statements defamatory to minorities, God, women, and the disabled.
2000   NY   Challenged, but retained on the ninth-grade accelerated English reading list in Bloomfield. The board was still set to review *Catcher in the Rye*, by J. D. Salinger, and *A Death in the Family*, by James Agee.

Source: 11, Jan. 1975, p. 6; July 1981, p. 103; Jan. 1982 p. 17; Jan. 1984, pp. 25–26; July 1984, p. 122; Sept. 1988, p. 152; July 1992, p. 126; Mar. 2000, p. 64.

618   Goode, Erich, and Richard Troiden, eds.
Sexual Deviance and Sexual Deviants

1977   PA   Destroyed by the St. Mary's Public Library Board.

Source: 11, Sept. 1977, p. 100.

619   Goodwin, June
Cry Amandla!: South African Women and the Question of Power

1984   Banned by the Directorate of Publications in Cape Town, South Africa. Without giving a reason, the Directorate declared "it will be an offense to import or distribute" the work.

Source: 11, Nov. 1984, p. 197.

620   Gordimer, Nadine
Burger's Daughter

1979   Banned on July 5, 1979, in South Africa. The decision was lifted in Oct. 1979 when the government's Publication Appeal Board overruled the earlier decision of a censorship committee. Two previous novels by Gordimer also were banned but later reinstated. In 1980, Gordimer was awarded the CNA Prize, one of South Africa's highest literary awards, for the novel. She also was awarded the Nobel Prize in literature in 1991.

Source: 5, Nov./Dec. 1979, p. 69; Apr. 1980, p. 73; 8, pp. 31–32.

621   Gordimer, Nadine
July's People

1993   PA   Challenged in the honors and academic English classes in the Carlisle schools. Teachers must send parents a letter warning about the work's content and explaining that their children may read alternate selections.
1994   WA   Retained in the Yakima schools after a five-month dispute over what advanced high school students should read in the classroom. Two parents raised concerns about profanity and images of violence and sexuality in the book and requested that it be removed from the reading list.

Source: 11, July 1993, p. 127; Nov. 1994, pp. 202–3.

622   Gordon, Sharon
Cuba

2006   FL   Removed from all Miami-Dade County school libraries because of a parent's complaint that the book does not depict an accurate life in

Cuba. The American Civil Liberties Union (ACLU) of Florida filed a lawsuit challenging the decision to remove this book and the twenty-three other titles in the same series from the district school libraries. In granting a preliminary injunction in July 2006 against the removal, Judge Alan S. Gold of U.S. District Court in Miami characterized the matter as a "First Amendment issue" and ruled in favor of the ACLU of Florida, which argued that the books were generally factual and that the board should add to its collection, rather than remove books it disagreed with. When the district court entered a preliminary injunction ordering the school district immediately to replace the entire series on library shelves, the Miami-Dade School Board appealed the decision to the Eleventh Circuit Court in Atlanta. In a February 5, 2009, two to one decision, the U.S. Court of Appeals for the Eleventh Circuit said the board did not breach the First Amendment, and ordered a Miami federal judge to lift a preliminary injunction that had allowed the book to be checked out from school libraries. But the three judge panel's opinion—not unlike the School Board's initial vote—was so fraught with political rhetoric such as "book banning" that further appeals seem inevitable. On November 13, 2010, the U.S, Supreme Court declined to take up the case. The action let stand a 2-1 ruling by the U.S. Court of Appeals for the Eleventh Circuit that the school board's decision to remove the book was not censorship in violation of the First Amendment.

Source: 11, May 2007, pp. 91–92.

---

623   Gordon, Sol
Facts about Sex: A Basic Guide

1984   AR   Challenged and recommended for a "parents only" section at the Concord school library because the book "has in it terms that would be considered vulgar by any thoughtful person."

Source: 11, Jan. 1985, p. 7; May 1985, p. 75; Jan. 1986, pp. 7–8.

---

624   Gordon, Sol
You: The Teenage Survival Book

1982   TX   Removed from the Hurst-Euless-Bedford School District libraries.

Source: 9; 11, May 1982, p. 84.

---

625   Gould, Lois
Necessary Objects

1976   KS   Removed from the Hutchinson High School library due to its explicit sexual content.

Source: 11, Jan. 1977, p. 7.

---

626   Gould, Lois
Such Good Friends

1976   KS   Removed from the Hutchinson High School library due to its explicit sexual content.

Source: 11, Jan. 1977, p. 7.

---

627   Gould, Steven C.
Jumper

1995   NY   Challenged at the Plattsburgh schools because of vulgarity, sex, and excessive violence.

1995   OR   Challenged at the West Linn-Wilsonville School District because according to the complainant "it was inappropriate for school children to read" because of a violent scene when the book's main character escapes from a sexual attack by a group of male truck drivers.

Source: 11, July 1995, p. 110; Jan. 1996, p. 16.

---

628   Gramick, Jeannine, and Pat Furey
The Vatican and Homosexuality: Reactions to the "Letter to the Bishops of the Catholic Church on the Pastoral Care of Homosexual Persons"

1993   OR   Challenged at the Deschutes County Library in Bend because it "encourages and condones" homosexuality.

Source: 11, Sept. 1993, pp. 158–59.

---

629   Graves, Robert
I, Claudius

1955   Banned in South Africa under the Customs Act of 1955.

Source: 4, p. 76.

---

630   Gravett, Paul
Manga: 60 Years of Japanese Comics

2006   CA   Removed from all branches of the San Bernardino County Library because "there are a couple of pretty graphic scenes, especially one showing sex with a big hamster, that are not especially endearing to our community standards."

Source: 11, July 2006, pp. 181–82.

631   Grawunder, Ralph, and Marion Steinmann
Life and Health

1980 CO   Banned from the Boulder Valley Board of Education's health and sex education classes attended only by students with parental permission.

1985 OH   Challenged in the Parma classrooms because "it preaches a religion of moral indifference."
Source: 11, Jan. 1981, p. 9; Mar. 1986, p. 42.

632   Gray, Heather M., and Samantha Phillips
Real Girl/Real World: Tools for Finding Your True Self

2006 NJ   Challenged, but retained at the Cape May County Library. The book explores issues such as body image, emerging sexuality, and feminism.
Source: 11, Jan. 2007, p. 29.

633   Green, G. Dorsey, and D. Merilee Clunis
Lesbian Couple

1990 IA   Challenged at the Muscatine Public Library because it is "wrong to promote immorality."
Source: 11, Nov. 1990, p. 225.

634   Green, John
Looking for Alaska

2008 NY New   Challenged, but retained for the eleventh-grade Regents English classes in Depew despite concerns about graphic language and sexual content. The school sent parents a letter requesting permission to use the Michael L. Printz Award for Excellence in Young Adult Literature novel and only three students were denied permission to read the book.
Source: 11, May 2008, p. 117.

635   Green, Jonathon, comp.
Cassell Dictionary of Slang

2006 NC   Banned in the Wake County schools under pressure from one of a growing number of conservative Christian groups using the Internet to encourage schoolbook bans.
Source: 11, Sept. 2006, p. 231.

636   Greenberg, Jerrold S., and Robert Gold
Holt Health

1993 OH   Challenged in the Garrettsville school system because it "condones" homosexuality.
Source: 11, Nov. 1993, pp. 179–80.

637   Greenburg, David
Slugs

1984 WA   Challenged at the Evergreen School District libraries because of its graphic descriptions of "slugs being dissected with scissors" and its verses describing the roasting, toasting, stewing, and chewing of the creatures were potentially frightening to young children.

1985 CA   Banned from the Escondido Elementary School District libraries as "unsuitable and should not have been allowed in the libraries in the first place."
Source: 11, Sept. 1984, p. 155; July 1985, p. 111.

638   Greene, Bette
The Drowning of Stephan Jones

1993 TX   Removed from the curriculum and school library shelves in Boling because the book "teaches anti-Christian beliefs and condones illegal activity." The story is about two gay men who are the objects of prejudice and violence, resulting in the drowning death of one of them.

1995 NH   Banned from the Mascenic Regional High School in New Ipswich because it is about gays and lesbians. An English teacher was fired for refusing to remove the book.

1998 WI   Removed from the Barron School District because of the book's homosexual theme. The ACLU of Wisconsin filed suit against the school district on Feb. 16, 1999. The books were then returned to the library while a federal court considered the lawsuit. On October 8, 1999, it was agreed that the book will remain available to students as part of the school district's settlement of the federal lawsuit.

2002 SC   Banned in the Horry County School District Board middle school libraries because the book is "educationally unsuitable and contains unacceptable language."

2004 TX   Challenged at the Montgomery County Memorial Library System along with fifteen other young adult books with gay-positive themes. The objections were posted at the Library Patrons of Texas Web site. The language describing the books is similar to that posted at the Web site of the Fairfax

County, Virginia-based Parents Against Bad Books in Schools, to which Library Patrons of Texas links.

Source: 8, pp. 445–46; 11, Mar. 1994, p. 53; Sept. 1996, p. 166; Jan. 1996, p. 15; Jan. 1999, p. 9; Mar. 1999, p. 37; May 1999, p. 68; Jan. 2000, p. 28; Nov. 2004, pp. 231–32.

639 Greene, Bette
Summer of My German Soldier

1990 CT Challenged as suitable curriculum material in the Burlington schools because it contains profanity and subject matter that set bad examples and gives students negative views of life.

1996 CT Challenged as suitable curriculum material in the Hawinton schools because it contains profanity and subject matter that set bad examples and gives students negative views of life.

1996 NJ Temporarily removed from an eighth-grade supplemental reading list in Cinnaminson because it contains offensive racial stereotypes.

Source: 11, Mar. 1991, p. 44; May 1991, p. 90; Jan. 1997, p. 10.

640 Greene, Constance
Al(Exandra) the Great

1984 NJ Restricted at the Lindenwold elementary school libraries because of "a problem with language."

Source: 11, Nov. 1984, p. 185.

641 Greene, Constance
Beat the Turtle Drum

1985 MN Challenged at the Orchard Lake Elementary School library in Burnsville.

Source: 11, Nov. 1985, p. 203.

642 Greene, Constance
I Know You, Al

1984 WA Removed from the Hockinson Middle School library because the book did not uphold the principles of the United States, which were "established on the moral principles of the Bible."

1989 OR Challenged at the Multnomah County Library in Portland because of sexual references, the presentation of divorce as a fact of life, and derogatory remarks about friends.

Source: 11, Sept. 1984, p. 139; Jan. 1990, pp. 4–5.

643 Greene, Gael
Dr. Love

1983 AR Challenged at the White County Public Library in Searcy because, "it's the filthiest thing I've ever seen."

Source: 11, Nov. 1983, p. 185; Jan. 1984, p. 25.

644 Greene, Graham
J'Accuse: Nice, the Dark Side

1982 A French court ordered the seizure of all copies of this expose of alleged corruption in Nice, France. The author was also ordered to pay 100 francs for each copy seized to a building developer, Daniel Guy, who is the main figure in the book. Greene told the press that the court had made no attempt to give him or his publishers advance warning about the seizure.

Source: 5, Oct. 1982, p. 34.

645 Greene, Sheppard M.
The Boy Who Drank Too Much

1991 MN Removed from an eighth-grade literature class in the Underwood schools because of the book's alleged sexism, and its seeming toleration of alcohol consumption by minors.

Source: 11, Mar. 1992, p. 44.

646 Griffin, John Howard
Black Like Me

1966 WI A Wisconsin man sued the local school board, claiming that the book contained obscene language for any age level. He further charged that his child was damaged by having read the book as an assignment in English class. The court dismissed the case.

1967 AZ The parent of an Arizona high school student challenged the use of the book in the classroom because of its obscene and vulgar language and the situations depicted. The school board removed the book from the classroom.

1977 PA Language, particularly "four-letter words," was the charge leveled by a Pennsylvania parent and a clergyman, but the challenge was denied.

1982 IL An objection to the subject matter was similarly denied in a challenge in Illinois.

1982 MO The book was placed on a closed shelf when a parent challenged the book on the grounds that it was obscene and vulgar and "because of black people being in the book."

Source: 8, pp. 421–22.

647   Griffin, John Howard
The Devil Rides Outside

1954 MI Bookseller Alfred E. Butler was found guilty and fined for selling the novel to an undercover police officer in Detroit. Butler appealed to the U.S. Supreme Court, which reversed the lower court's decision. In *Butler v. Michigan*, 352 U.S. 380 (1957), the court ruled unconstitutional the standards for defining obscenity that had been used for more than seventy years by U.S. federal and state censors. It declared the view that whatever corrupted the morals of youth was obscene to be an undue restriction on the freedom of speech.
Source: 13, pp. 57–59.

648   Grimm, Jacob, and Wilhelm K. Grimm, Translated by Jack Zipes
The Complete Fairy Tales of the Brothers Grimm

1994 AZ Restricted to sixth- through eighth-grade classrooms at the Kyrene elementary schools due to its excessive violence, negative portrayals of female characters, and anti-Semitic references.
Source: 11, Jan. 1994, p. 34; Sept. 1994, p. 149.

649   Grimm, Jacob
Hansel and Gretel

1992 CA Challenged at the Mount Diablo School District because it teaches children that it is acceptable to kill witches and paints witches as child-eating monsters.
Source: 11, July 1992, p. 108.

650   Grimm, Jacob
Little Red Riding Hood

1990 CA Banned by two California school districts—Culver City and Empire—because an illustration shows Little Red Riding Hood's basket with a bottle of wine as well as fresh bread and butter. The wine could be seen as condoning the use of alcohol.
1990 FL The presence of the wine bottle in the book's illustration motivated challenges by parents of students in the fifth and sixth grades in Clay County Elementary School.
1991 FL A Bradford County teacher initiated a complaint that the book was violent because of the actions of the wolf. The teacher questioned the appropriateness of the little girl taking wine to her grandmother and her grandmother later drinking the wine.

1991 FL Two teachers in Levy County challenged the storybook.
Source: 11, July 1990, p. 128; 14, pp. 217–18.

651   Grimm, Jacob
Snow White

1992 FL Restricted to students with parental permission at the Duval County public school libraries because of its graphic violence: a hunter kills a wild boar, and a wicked witch orders Snow White's heart torn out.
Source: 11, July 1992, pp. 105–6.

652   Grisham, John
The Client

1996 NJ Challenged in a sixth-grade high-level reading class in Hillsborough because of its violence and use of "curse words."
1997 WV Removed from the Jackson County school libraries along with sixteen other titles.
Source: 11, July 1996, p. 122; Sept. 1996, p. 155; Jan. 1998, p. 13.

653   Grisham, John
The Firm

1997 WV Removed from the Jackson County school libraries along with sixteen other titles.
Source: 11, Jan. 1998, p. 13.

654   Grisham, John
The Pelican Brief

1997 WV Removed from the Jackson County school libraries along with sixteen other titles.
Source: 11, Jan. 1998, p. 13.

655   Grisham, John
A Time to Kill

2005 ND Challenged, but retained in the Fargo North High School advanced English classes despite complaints about the novel's graphic rape and murder scenes.
Source: 11, July 2005, p. 161; Sept. 2005, p. 239; Jan. 2006, pp. 14–15.

656   Groening, Matt
The Big Book of Hell

1995 PA Challenged at the Hershey Public Library because "the entire book teaches conduct contrary to wishes of parents" and is "trash" with "no morals." A request was made to "destroy all books of a similar nature."
Source: 11, Sept. 1995, p. 158.

657   Groom, Winston
Forrest Gump

1999 FL   Challenged at the Bay Point School in South Dade County because the novel "pokes fun at blacks, makes numerous references to sex, and uses foul language inappropriate for tenth graders." First-year teacher Michael Weiss was fired over the incident because the book was not on the district's approved list and another instructor was placed on probation.
Source: 11, July 1999, p. 95.

658   Grotius, Hugo
On the Law of War and Peace

1490   The Spanish Inquisition condemned all of his books.

1662   The States-General of Netherlands banned the book.

1700   In the eighteenth century his complete works were placed on the *Index Librorum Prohibitorum* (Index of Prohibited Books) in Rome, Italy, where they remained until 1966.
Source: 1, pp. 239–40.

659   Grove, Vicki
The Starplace

2008 FL   Challenged at the Turner Elementary School
New   in New Tampa because the novel contains a racial epithet. The book about an interracial middle-school friendship in 1960s Oklahoma was highly recommended by Children's Literature Review.
Source: 11, May 2008, p. 96.

660   Gruenberg, Sidonie M.
The Wonderful Story of How You Were Born

1982 FL   Moved from the children's room of the Tampa-Hillsborough County Public Library to the adult section.
Source: 11, Jan. 1982, pp. 4–5.

661   Grumbach, Jane, and Robert Emerson, eds.
Monologues: Women II

1990 CO   Removed from a suggested reading list at Adams City High School after a parent complained about obscene language in the book.
Source: 11, Jan. 1991, p. 15.

662   Guammen, David
To Walk the Line

1974 OK   Banned from all libraries in the Enid public school system libraries.
Source: 11, Mar. 1975, p. 41.

663   Guare, John
Landscape of the Body

1998 FL   Challenged at the Manatee County School District in Bradenton Beach because the play includes a paragraph in which a woman describes being in a pornographic movie.
Source: 11, May 1998, p. 71.

664   Guest, Judith
Ordinary People

1981 OH   Temporarily banned in Enon from junior and senior English classrooms.

1982 NH   Challenged at the Merrimack High School after a parent found the novel obscene and depressing.

1985 NY   Challenged in North Salem as an optional summer reading book because of profanity and graphic sex scenes and because its topic—teenage suicide—was too intense for tenth graders.

1993 CA   Challenged because it is "degrading to Christians," but retained at the Anaheim Union High School District.

1994 IN   No longer required reading at Delta High School in Delaware due to profanity and descriptions of sexual situations in the novel.

1994 SD   Removed from the Faulkton district classrooms.

1996 NY   Temporarily pulled from the Lancaster High School curriculum because two parents contended it contains foul language, graphic references to sex, and inappropriate handling of the subject of suicide.
A Lancaster student took the matter to the New York Civil Liberties Union, which sent a letter to the school board saying that it was "greatly dismayed" with the board's action.

1999 OH   Removed, but later returned to the English classrooms and library shelves at the Fostoria High School despite complaints about the novel's obscene language and sexual innuendos.
Source: 11, Jan. 1982, p. 77; Sept. 1982, p. 170; Sept. 1985, p. 168; May 1993, pp. 86–87; Nov. 1993, pp. 192–93; Jan. 1994, p. 14; Sept. 1994, pp. 150, 152; Sept. 1996, pp. 155–56; Nov. 1996, p. 197; July 1999, p. 104.

665 Guest, Judith
Second Heaven

1991 SC   Challenged in the Greenville County schools because the book uses the name of God and Jesus in a "vain and profane manner along with inappropriate sexual references."
Source: 11, July 1991, p. 130.

666 Gunther, John
Death Be Not Proud

1995 NC   Retained by the Edgecombe County Board of Education in Tarboro after complaints that the "book has words in it that even unsaved people would have spanked their children for saying."
Source: 11, May 1995, p. 84.

667 Gunther, John
Inside Russia Today

1970 IA   Removed from the Glenwood school library shelves along with eight other titles—*The Catcher in the Rye*, by J. D. Salinger; *Who's Afraid of Virginia Woolf*, by Edward Albee; *Looking Backward*, by Edward Bellamy; *The Liberal Hour*, by John Kenneth Galbraith; *Black Like Me*, by John H. Griffin; *Black Power*, by Stokley Carmichael; and an unknown title. After considerable controversy, the banned books were returned to the library shelves.
Source: 7, pp. 234–35.

668 Guterson, David
Snow Falling on Cedars

1997 WA   Challenged in the Snohomish School District by parents who acknowledged the book's literary value, but complained that its descriptions of sexual intercourse, masturbation, and use of obscene language make it inappropriate for high school students. The book won the prestigious PEN/Faulkner award and was named 1995 book of the year by the American Booksellers Association.

1999 TX   Pulled from the Boerne Independent High School library and barred from the curriculum after several parents and students complained about its racial epithets and sexually graphic passages. The book was later returned to the library.

2000 WA   Restricted by the South Kitsap School District board after critics complained about the book's sexual content and profanity. After being approved by committees at the high school and district levels, the book was being considered for the district's approved reading list for high school students. Students are not required to read listed books of which they or their parents disapprove.

2003 CA   Challenged, but retained in the advanced English classes in Modesto. The seven-member Modesto City School Board said administrators should instead give parents more information about the books their children read, including annotations of each text. Parents can opt their children out of any assignment they find objectionable.

2007 ID
New   Challenged in the Coeur d'Alene School District. Some parents say the book, along with five others, should require parental permission for students to read them.
Source: 8, pp. 381–85; 11, Sept. 1997, p. 129; Nov. 1999, p. 163; Jan. 1999, pp. 8, 12; July 2000, p. 106; Jan. 2004, pp. 27–28; Sept. 2007, p. 181.

669 Guthrie, Alfred B., Jr.
The Big Sky

1962 TX   Banned in Amarillo.
1991 MT   Challenged in the Big Timber schools because the book is filled with explicit, vulgar language.
Source: 4, p. 82; 11, Mar. 1992, p. 44.

670 Guthrie, Alfred B., Jr.
The Way West

1962 TX   Banned in Amarillo.
Source: 4, p. 82.

671 Guy, Rosa
Edith Jackson

1984 LA   Removed from all school libraries collections in St. Tammany Parish because its "treatment of immorality and voyeurism does not provide for the growth of desirable attitudes," but later reinstated.
Source: 11, May 1984, p. 69; July 1984, p. 121.

672 Guy, Rosa
The Music of Summer

1994 GA   Removed from Adamson Middle School shelves, and Clayton public libraries and placed in the young adult section for eighth graders and up because of a "really gross" sex scene.
Source: 11, July 1994, p. 109.

673 Haas, Ben
Daisy Canfield

1984 LA Challenged at the Covington Public Library because it "had objectionable language throughout."
Source: 11, July 1984, p. 103.

674 Haddix, Margaret Peterson
Don't You Dare Read This, Mrs. Dunphrey

2003 CA Banned from the Galt Joint Union Elementary School District classrooms in Sacramento and restricted to students with parental permission in the middle school libraries. The novel discusses parental neglect, sexual harassment at an after-school job, and other stresses experienced by the young-adult fictional character. The novel is on the ALA Best Books for Young Adults list.
Source: 11, Mar. 2004, p. 52; May 2004, p. 98.

675 Haddon, Mark
The Curious Incident of the Dog in the Night-Time

2006 TX Challenged at the Galveston County Reads Day because the book could "pollute" young minds.
Source: 11, Mar. 2006, pp. 71–72.

676 Hahn, Mary Downing
The Dead Man in Indian Creek

2010 OR Challenged at the Salem-Keizer School
New   District elementary schools because of the drugs and drug smuggling activities in the book. The book was previously challenged in 1994 in the same school district because of graphic violence, examples of inappropriate parenting and because it was too frightening for elementary students. The book has won awards from the International Reading Association, the Children's Book Council, and the American Library Association.
Source: 11, May 2010, pp. 105–6.

677 Hahn, Mary Downing
Wait Till Helen Comes

1996 KS Challenged in the Lawrence School District curriculum because the book presents suicide as a viable, "even attractive way of dealing with family problems. Ghosts, poltergeists and other supernatural phenomena are presented as documented

reality and these are capable of deadly harm to children."
Source: 11, May 1996, pp. 87–88.

678 Haislip, Barbara
Stars, Spells, Secrets and Sorcery

1993 WI Challenged at Nashotah school library because the book "promotes satanism."
Source: 11, May 1993, p. 86.

679 Haldeman, Joe
War Year

1981 AK Removed from the Soldotna Junior High School library because of its raw language and graphic descriptions of battlefield violence.
Source: 11, July 1981, p. 91.

680 Haley, Gail E.
Go Away, Stay Away

1994 MN Challenged, but retained in the Echo Park Elementary School media center in Apple Valley. A parent filed the complaint because the story "was frightening subject matter and [I] didn't see a good lesson in [it]."
Source: 11, July 1994, p. 129.

681 Hall, Elizabeth
Possible Impossibilities

1985 FL Challenged at the Sikes Elementary School media center in Lakeland because the book "would lead children to believe ideas contrary to the teachings of the Bible."
Source: 11, July 1985, p. 133.

682 Hall, Radclyffe
The Well of Loneliness

1928   Suppressed in England as obscene. The *London Sunday Express* denounced it as "a challenge to every instinct of social sanity and moral decency which distinguishes Christian civilization from the corruptions of paganism."

1929 NY Publisher arrested in New York City.
Source: 4, p. 71; 6, pp. 1,019–21; 15, Vol. III, pp. 416–17.

683 Halle, Louis J.
Men and Nations

1982 KY Challenged in the Jefferson County School District because the book is a "soft sell of communism."
Source: 11, Mar. 1983, p. 41.

684 Hamilton, David
Age of Innocence

1998 GA Despite pressure from protestors demanding that Barnes & Noble face child pornography charges, a prosecutor in Cobb County declined to take the nation's largest bookstore chain to court for carrying Hamilton's book. Activists from Operation Rescue claimed the book contains children in sexually suggestive positions and should be deemed illegal. Barnes & Noble officials noted that the decision follows similar rulings by prosecutors in Texas, Maryland, Kansas, and Wisconsin.

1998 KS Barnes & Noble officials noted that the decision follows similar rulings by prosecutors in Kansas.

1998 MD Barnes & Noble officials noted that the decision follows similar rulings by prosecutors in Maryland.

1998 TX Barnes & Noble officials noted that the decision follows similar rulings by prosecutors in Texas.

1998 WI Barnes & Noble officials noted that the decision follows similar rulings by prosecutors in Wisconsin.

Source: 11, Jan. 1999, p. 20.

685 Hamlin, Liz
I Remember Valentine

1990 TX Challenged at the Commerce High School library because of "pornographic" material in the book. The complainant asked that all "romance" books be removed.

Source: 11, Mar. 1991, p. 43.

686 Hanckel, Frances, and John Cunningham
A Way of Love, A Way of Life: A Young Person's Introduction to What It Means to Be Gay

1982 AL Removed from two Anniston high school libraries, but later reinstated on a restrictive basis.

1982 IA Challenged in Atlantic because it is a "morally corrupting force."

1984 AK Challenged at the Fairbanks North Star Borough School District libraries because schools should teach the basics, "not how to become queer dope users."

1998 WI Challenged at the Barron School District because the book is about homosexuality.

Source: 11, May 1982, p. 82; Mar. 1983, p. 37; Sept. 1984, pp. 137, 149–50; Jan. 1999, p. 9; Mar. 1999, p. 37.

687 Handford, Martin
Where's Waldo?

1989 MI Challenged at the Public Libraries of Saginaw because "on some of the pages there are dirty things."

1993 NY Removed from the Springs Public School library in East Hampton because there is a tiny drawing of a woman lying on the beach wearing a bikini bottom but no top.

Source: 11, May 1989, p. 78; July 1993, p. 100.

688 Hanigan, James P.
Homosexuality: The Test Case for Christian Sexual Ethics

1993 OR Challenged at the Deschutes County Library in Bend because it "encourages and condones" homosexuality.

Source: 11, Sept. 1993, pp. 158–59.

689 Haning, Peter
The Satanists

1986 CA Challenged by the "God Squad," a group of three students and their parents, at the El Camino High School in Oceanside because the book "glorified the devil and the occult."

Source: 11, Sept. 1986, p. 151; Nov. 1986, p. 224; Jan. 1987, p. 9.

690 Hanley, James
Boy

1934 Police seized the book from a lending library in Manchester and charged the librarian with distributing an "obscene publication." Impounded under British obscenity law for its graphic violence and brutal sexuality.

Source: 13, pp. 29–30.

691 Hansberry, Lorraine
A Raisin in the Sun

1979 UT Responding to criticisms from an anti-pornography organization, the Ogden School District restricted circulation of Hansberry's play.

2004 IL Challenged, but retained in the Normal Community High School sophomore literature class despite objections that the play is degrading to African Americans.

Source: 11, May 1979, p. 49; Sept. 2004, pp. 177–78.

692 Harcourt, J. M.
Upsurge

1934 Banned throughout Australia on 20 November 1934 when the Trade and Custom Department released its report, concluding: "This book is not without merit, though somewhat crude. But it is disfigured by some grossly indecent passages, without any excuse of being necessary."
Source: 6, pp. 1,028–29.

693 Hardin, Garrett
Population, Evolution and Birth Control

1977 MI The Brighton School Board voted to remove all sex education books from the high school library.
Source: 11, Sept. 1977, p. 133.

694 Harding, Kat
Lesbian Kama Sutra

2009 KS Restricted minors' access in the Topeka and
New Shawnee County Public Library because the organization Kansans for Common Sense contended that the material is "harmful to minors under state law." Later the board voted 6-3 in favor of adopting a staff recommendation to keep the books where they are currently located on the shelves in the library's Health Information Neighborhood section.
Source: 11, May 2009, pp. 77–78; July 2009, p. 139.

695 Hardy, Thomas
Jude the Obscure

1896 Banned by Bristol, England circulating libraries.
Source: 4, p. 51; 8, pp. 349–51.

696 Hardy, Thomas
Tess of the D'Urbervilles

1891 MA Banned by Mudie's and Smith's circulating libraries and the novel was also the object of banning by the Watch and Ward Society in Boston, which charged that the novel contained illicit sexuality and immorality. The society forced Boston booksellers to agree that they would not advertise or sell the novel, and most adhered to the request.
1896 Banned by Bristol, England circulating libraries.
Source: 4, p. 51; 13, pp. 242–43.

697 Harington, Donald
Lightning Bug

1991 AR Challenged at the Rogers-Hough Memorial Library because the book uses language "very descriptive of. . . perverted sex."
Source: 11, Sept. 1991, p. 151.

698 Harkness, John, and David Helgren, eds.
Populations

1994 NJ Removed from the Palmyra School District's science curriculum after nearly three hours of passionate debate between parents who believed the book presented only one side of how world overpopulation should be addressed and teachers who found it an integral part of the class curriculum.
Source: 11, Mar. 1995, p. 45.

699 Harlan, Elizabeth
Footfalls

1988 OR Challenged at the Obsidian Junior High School in Redmond for its profanity and sexual content.
Source: 11, Jan. 1989, p. 3.

700 Harris, E. Lynn
And This Too Shall Pass

1998 KY Challenged, but retained at the Central High School in Louisville despite claims the book describes homosexual acts in a positive light.
Source: 11, Mar. 1998, p. 55; May 1998, p. 71.

701 Harris, E. Lynn
Invisible Life

1998 KY Challenged, but retained at the Central High School in Louisville despite claims the book is pornographic and a recruitment tool for the gay community.
Source: 11, Mar. 1998, p. 55; May 1998, p. 71.

702 Harris, E. Lynn
Just As I Am

1998 KY Challenged, but retained at the Central High School in Louisville despite claims the book describes homosexual acts in a positive light.
Source: 11, Mar. 1998, p. 55; May 1998, p. 71.

703   Harris, Frank
My Life and Loves

1922   Banned in England.
1922 AL   Imports banned in the U.S. and frequently destroyed by U.S. Customs from 1922 to 1956.

Source: 4, p. 54; 13, pp. 170–71; 15, Vol. III, p. 415.

704   Harris, Raymond, ed.
Best Selling Chapters

1993 NE   Challenged, but retained in a sixth-grade literature class at Hichborn Middle School in Howland. The challenge was directed at the Ray Bradbury story, "A Sound of Thunder," which contains "offensive" language.
1993 NH   Challenged in the Keene Middle School because of some of the language and subject matter in the textbook, specifically in passages from John Steinbeck's *Of Mice and Men; To Kill a Mockingbird*, by Harper Lee; and *A Day No Pigs Would Die*, by Robert Newton Peck. The complainant objected to expressions such as "crazy bastard," "hell" and "damn," "Jesus Christ," and "God Almighty."

Source: 11, Sept. 1993, p. 160; Jan. 1994, p. 15.

705   Harris, Raymond, ed.
Best Short Stories, Middle Level

1993 NE   Challenged, but retained in a sixth-grade literature class at Hichborn Middle School in Howland. The challenge was directed at the Ray Bradbury story, "A Sound of Thunder," which contains "offensive" language.

Source: 11, Sept. 1993, p. 160.

706   Harris, Robie H.
It's Perfectly Normal: A Book about Changing Bodies, Growing Up, Sex, and Sexual Health

1996 PA   Challenged at the Chester County Library because the "book is an act of encouragement for children to begin desiring sexual gratification . . . and is a clear example of child pornography."
1996 UT   Challenged at the Provo Library because it contains discussions of intercourse, masturbation, and homosexuality.
1996 WA   Removed from the Clover Park School District library shelves because parents charged that it was too graphic and could foster more questions than it answers.
1997 MO   Challenged, but retained in the children's section of the Mexico-Audrain County Library. A Baptist minister complained not only about this title, but also about other "material concerning family sensitive issues, such as sexuality, the death of a loved one, or the birth process."
1997 ND   Challenged, but retained at the Fargo Public Library. The statement requesting the book's removal cited the book as "too explicit, pornographic, and too easily accessible to children."
1999 CA   Challenged, but retained at the Auburn-Placer County Library because of sexually explicit material.
2000 MA   Challenged in the Holland Public Library due to its sexually explicit content. The book was moved from the children's to the adult section of the library.
2001 AK   Restricted to elementary school pupils with parental permission at the Anchorage due to objections to the book's "value statements" and because "marriage is mentioned once in the whole book, while homosexual relationships are allocated an entire section."
2001 FL   Challenged at the Marion County Public Library. Critics called the book pornographic and demanded it be permanently removed from the library or placed in a special restricted-access area.
2002 TX   Challenged, but retained in the Montgomery County library system after a conservative Christian group, the Republican Leadership Council, characterized the book as "vulgar" and trying "to minimize or even negate that homosexuality is a problem."
2003 TX   Relocated from the young adult to the adult section of the Fort Bend County Libraries in Richmond. The same title was recently moved to the restricted section of the Fort Bend School District's media centers after a resident sent an e-mail message to the superintendent expressing concern about the book's content. The Spirit of Freedom Republican Women's Club petitioned the superintendent to have it, along with *It's So Amazing*, moved because they contain "frontal nudity and discussion of homosexual relationships and abortion."
2005 AR   Challenged, but retained at the Holt Middle School parent library in Fayetteville despite a parent's complaint that it was sexually explicit.
2007 ME   A Lewiston patron refused to return the
New   acclaimed sex education book from the Auburn public library because she was "sufficiently horrified by the illustrations and sexually graphic, amoral, abnormal contents." A police investigation found the library did not violate the town ordinance against obscenity and the patron who removed the book from the library will stand trial for theft. The book was retained and other patrons donated

four copies of the book, which remains in circulation at the library.

Source: 8, pp. 346–48; 11, Sept. 1996, p. 152; Jan. 1997, p. 8; Mar. 1997, p. 49; Nov. 1997, p. 181; Jan. 1998, p. 27; Nov. 1999, p. 171; Sept. 2000, p. 143; Mar. 2001, p. 54; Nov. 2001, pp. 247, 278; Jan. 2002, p. 13; Nov. 2002, pp. 256–57; Jan. 2003, p. 33; Jan. 2004, p. 9; May 2005, p. 135; Sept. 2005, p. 215; Nov. 2005, pp. 295–96; Nov. 2007, p. 240; Jan. 2008, p. 13; Mar. 2008, p. 78; Nov. 2008, p. 255.

---

707   Harris, Robie H.
It's So Amazing

2003 FL   Relocated from the young adult to the adult section of the Fort Bend County Libraries in Richmond. The same title was recently moved to the restricted section of the Fort Bend School District's media centers after a resident sent an e-mail message to the superintendent expressing concern about the book's content. The Spirit of Freedom Republican Women's Club petitioned the superintendent to have it, along with *It' s Perfectly Normal: A Book about Changing Bodies, Growing Up, Sex, and Sexual Health*, moved because they contain "frontal nudity and discussion of homosexual relationships and abortion."

2005 WI   Relocated to the reference section of the Northern Hills Elementary school media center in Onalaska because a parent complained about its frank yet kid-friendly discussion of reproduction topics, including sexual intercourse, masturbation, abortion, and homosexuality.

Source: 11, Jan. 2004, p. 9; May 2005, p. 135; Sept. 2005, p. 215; Nov. 2005, pp. 281–82, 295–96.

---

708   Hart, Jack
Gay Sex: Manual for Men Who Love Men

1993 WA   Challenged at the Fort Vancouver Regional Library when a group of citizens asked the Goldendale City Council to establish more restrictive criteria for sexually explicit material.

Source: 11, July 1993, p. 103.

---

709   Hartinger, Brent
Geography Club

2005 WA   Withdrawn from Curtis Junior High and Curtis Senior High school libraries after a University Place couple with children in both schools filed a written complaint. They wrote that the book could result in a "casual and loose approach to sex," encourage use of Internet porn, and the physical meeting of people through chat rooms.

2009 WI
New   Challenged at the West Bend Community Memorial Library as being "obscene or child pornography" in a section designated "Young Adults." The library board unanimously voted 9–0 to maintain, "without removing, relocating, labeling, or otherwise restricting access," the books in the young adult category at the West Bend Community Memorial Library. The vote was a rejection of a four-month campaign conducted by the citizen's group West Bend Citizens for Safe Libraries to move fiction and nonfiction books with sexually explicit passages from the young adult section to the adult section and label them as containing sexual material.

Source: 11, Jan. 2006, pp. 12–13; Mar. 2006, p. 73; May 2009, pp. 80–81; Sept. 2009, pp. 169–70.

---

710   Hartley, William H., and William S. Vincent
American Civics

1976 NJ   Challenged in Mahwah by several local residents and a school trustee who argued that it "promotes socialized medicine and considers government a big machine with the people having no voice." The deciding vote on the issue was split, 4-4, in effect denying the use of the textbook for ninth grade.

Source: 7, p. 30.

---

711   Harwood, Richard
Did Six Million Really Die?

1985   In Toronto, Ontario, Canadian law bars the import of materials considered seditious, treasonable, immoral, or indecent; so-called hate crime is included in these categories. Ernest Zundel, the publisher, was charged under S.181 of Canada's Criminal Code with "publishing false news" and was tried in 1985 for publishing a booklet that denies the official accounts of Nazis exterminating Jews in wartime prison camps. The case worked its way in the Canadian courts and ruling in 1992 (*R. v. Zundel*), the Supreme Court in a 4-3 decision held that section 181 of the Criminal Code was indeed unconstitutional as a violation of the right of freedom of expression guarantees.
The code requires the expression to be nonviolent; the court found the novel to be nonviolent. Thus, Zundel was acquitted.

1991   Publishing or distributing neo-Nazi or Holocaust-denial literature is illegal in Germany. Zundel was convicted during the 1991 visit to Germany for inciting racial hatred.

Source: 7, pp. 149–50.

712 Hashak, Israel
Jewish History, Jewish Religion

1995 MA Challenged at the Milford Library because it is anti-Semitic.

Source: 11, May 1995, p. 66.

713 Haskins, Jim
Voodoo and Hoodoo

1992 LA Banned at the Clearwood Junior High School library in Slidell because the book included "recipes" for spells. U.S. District Court Judge Patrick Carr ruled on October 6, 1994, that the St. Tammany Parish School Board cannot ban the book solely because members do not approve of its content. A week later, the board voted 8-5 to appeal the judgment. The school board appealed the decision to the U.S. Court of Appeals for the Fifth Circuit. On April 1, 1996, the St. Tammany Parish School Board, however, ended the four-year attempt to ban the book by returning it to the library. Under the agreement, it will be available only with written parental permission to students in eighth grade or above. Momentum for a settlement occurred after two board members who fought to ban the book left the board in 1994. Additionally, the board's insurer indicated that it might not foot the bill if the board continued to fight the suit.

Source: 11, July 1992, p. 106; Sept. 1992, p. 137; Jan. 1993, p. 23; Mar. 1993, p. 41; Jan. 1995, pp. 19–20; Sept. 1995, p. 153; July 1996, p. 134.

714 Hastings, Selina
Sir Gawain and the Loathly Lady

1989 MI Challenged at the public libraries of Saginaw. The complainant requested the library to "white out the swearing" which appears on page 16 of the book. The objectionable words were "God Damn You."

1992 WI Challenged at the elementary school libraries in Antigo because a parent objected to a reference to the Loathly Lady as a "hell-hag" and to another passage in which the Black Knight suggests that King Arthur "roast in hell."

Source: 11, May 1989, p. 77; Jan. 1993, p. 28.

715 Haugaard, Erick C.
The Samurai's Tale

1995 CA Challenged at the Wilsona School District in Lake Los Angeles because of violence and references to Buddha and ritual suicide.

Source: 11, Jan. 1996, p. 13.

716 Hautzig, Deborah
Hey Dollface

1993 OR Challenged at the Bend High School because it "encourages and condones" homosexuality.

2004 TX Challenged at the Montgomery County Memorial Library System along with fifteen other young adult books with gay-positive themes. The objections were posted at the Library Patrons of Texas Web site. The language describing the books is similar to that posted at the Web site of the Fairfax County, Virginia-based Parents Against Bad Books in Schools, to which Library Patrons of Texas links.

Source: 11, Sept. 1993, pp. 158–59; Nov. 2004, pp. 231–32.

717 Hawes, Hampton
Raise Up Off Me

1989 TX Challenged at the King High School in Corpus Christi because the book contains "vulgar language and descriptions of abnormal sexual activity."

Source: 11, Jan. 1990, p. 32.

718 Hawthorne, Nathaniel
The Scarlet Letter

1852 Banned in Russia by Czar Nicholas I. The ban was lifted four years later when Czar Alexander II came into power.

1852 MA Subject of savage attacks by moralists in 1852. The main complaint of those who wanted to ban the novel was that Hawthorne sided with Hester and condemned her husband's revenge. Strict morality required that Hester suffer in more painful and obvious ways than Hawthorne provided. The citizens of Salem were so incensed by Hawthorne's novel that he moved his family out of the city to a farmhouse in the Bershires.

1925 The National Board of Censorship forced the producers of the film version to change a few things; for one, Hester had to get married.

1961 MI Challenged in Michigan high school English classes by parents claiming that it was "pornographic and obscene." They demanded that the book be taken out of the curriculum, but the request was denied. Challenged again in 1977 a Michigan parent and principal objecting to the inclusion of the novel in the high school curriculum because it dealt with a clergyman's "involvement in fornication." The book was removed from the classroom use and from the recommended reading list.

1977 MI Challenged again by a Michigan parent and principal objecting to the inclusion of the novel in the high school curriculum because it dealt with a clergyman's "involvement in fornication." The book was removed from the classroom use and from the recommended reading list.

1977 MO That same year, a parent in Missouri condemned the book for its use of "4-letter words" and "other undesirable content" and demanded its removal from the high school library. The school librarian recognized that the parent had not read the book because no obscenities appeared in the novel, and she convinced the parent of his error. The book was retained.

1996 TX Banned from the Lindale Advanced Placement English reading list because the book "conflicted with the values of the community."

1999 PA Challenged, but retained in the sophomore curriculum at West Middlesex High School.
Source: 8, pp. 480–81; 9, p. 142; 11, Nov. 1996, p. 199; July 1999, p. 105; 15, Vol. I, p. 562.

719 Hawthorne, Nathaniel
Young Goodman Brown and Other Short Stories

1992 NY Challenged at the Copenhagen Central School because the story may give children the wrong message about witchcraft.
Source: 11, Jan. 1993, p. 12.

720 Hayden, Penny
Confidence

1994 OR Expurgated by an apparent self-appointed censor at the Coquille Public Library along with several other books. Most were mysteries and romances in which single words and sexually explicit passages were whited out by a vandal who left either dots or solid ink pen lines where the words had been.
Source: 11, Sept. 1994, p. 148.

721 Hedayat, Sadegh
The Blind Owl

2006 The widely acclaimed Iranian classic, written in the 1930s, was banned in Iran. "The new government intends to take positive steps for reviving neglected values and considering religious teachings in the cultural field."
Source: 11, Jan. 2007, p. 35.

722 Hedderwick, Mairi
Katie Morag and the Tiresome Ted

1989 MI Challenged at the public libraries of Saginaw because on the last page of the story "the mother's sweater is open to fully expose her breast." The library was asked to cover the drawing with a marker.
Source: 11, May 1989, p. 77.

723 Hedges, Peter
What's Eating Gilbert Grape

2006 IA Banned by the superintendent at the Carroll High School because of parental concerns about an oral sex scene. In response, students started an Internet protest on the social network Facebook. Hundreds joined the group —"Un-ban Gilbert Grape! Censorship is Wrong"— and organizers say they plan to collect signatures calling for a formal review. "Parents were already notified of its content, and had to sign a permission slip for their child to read it." Later, the Carroll school board voted to overturn Superintendent Rob Cordes' decision to ban the book from the high school's literature-to-film class. The author said, "The district shouldn't let those larger themes be obscured by the relatively few pages with sexual content that he intended to drive plot."
Source: 11, Jan. 2007, pp. 12–13; Mar. 2007, p. 73.

724 Hegi, Ursula
Stones from the River

2000 GA Banned, but later reinstated after community protests at the Windsor Forest High School in Savannah. The controversy began in early 1999 when a parent complained about sex, violence, and profanity in the book that was part of an Advanced Placement English class.
Source: 11, Mar. 2000, p. 63; Mar. 2001, p. 76.

725 Heidish, Marcy
Woman Called Moses

1992 NC Removed by a patron at the Wilmington school library because of strong language.
Source: 11, July 1992, p. 107.

726 Heinlein, Robert A.
The Day After Tomorrow

2008 IL New Removed from the Beardstown High School library. A parent requested its removal and a committee determined the novel "rather very adult in nature" and, because the library already had a large selection of other valuable science fiction and spy literature, the committee elected to remove the book from the high school's circulation and donated it to the public library.

Source: 11, Nov. 2008, pp. 229–30.

---

727 Heinlein, Robert
Stranger in a Strange Land

2003 TX Challenged, but retained in the South Texas Independent School District in Mercedes. Parents objected to the adult themes—sexuality, drugs, and suicide—found in the 1962 Hugo Award-winning novel. Heinlein's book was part of the summer Science Academy curriculum. The board voted to give parents more control over their childrens' choices by requiring principals to automatically offer an alternative to a challenged book.

Source: 11, Nov. 2003, pp. 249–50.

---

728 Heller, Joseph
Catch-22

1972 OH Banned in Strongsville, but school board's action was overturned in 1976 by a U.S. District Court in *Minarcini v. Strongsville City School District*, 541 F 2d 577 (6th Cir. 1976).

1974 TX Challenged at the Dallas Independent School District high school libraries.

1979 WA Challenged in Snoqualmie because of its several references to women as "whores."

Source: 4, p. 96; 8, pp. 433–34; 11, Jan. 1975, p. 6; July 1979, p. 85; 12, pp. 145–48.

---

729 Heller, Joseph
Good as Gold

1979 Banned on June 28, 1979, in South Africa. The government's censorship authorities gave no reason.

Source: 5, Nov. /Dec. 1979, p. 69.

---

730 Heller, Joseph
Something Happened

1974 Banned in South Africa. The government's censorship authorities gave no reason.

Source: 5, Nov./Dec. 1979, p. 69.

---

731 Helms, Tom
Against All Odds

1983 WA Removed from the Evergreen School District of Vancouver along with twenty-nine other titles. The American Civil Liberties Union of Washington filed suit contending that the removals constitute censorship, a violation of plaintiff's rights to free speech and due process, and the acts are a violation of the state Open Meetings Act because the removal decisions were made behind closed doors.

Source: 11, Nov. 1983, pp. 185–86.

---

732 Helper, Hinton Rowan
The Impending Crisis of the South: How to Meet It

1857 NC Published in 1857, the author suggested the elimination of slavery and the book was banned in most Southern states. In North Carolina, the Reverend Daniel Worth had to stand trial for owning the text, and in Arkansas three men were hanged for owning the book.

Source: 9, p. 131.

---

733 Helvetius, Claude-Adrien
De L'Esprit

1758 Condemned in Paris, France as atheistic, materialistic, sacrilegious, immoral, and subversive, the epitome of all the dangerous philosophical trends of the age. Banned by the archbishop of Paris in 1758, the Parlement of Paris in 1759, and the Sorbonne in 1759, the book became an underground best seller.

1759 Banned by the Pope in Rome, Italy.

Source: 1, pp. 71–72.

---

734 Hemingway, Ernest
Across the River and into the Trees

1953 Banned in Ireland.
1956 Banned in South Africa as "objectionable and obscene."

Source: 4, p. 80.

---

735 Hemingway, Ernest
A Farewell to Arms

1929 Banned in Italy because of its painfully accurate account of the Italian retreat from Caporetto, Italy.

1929 MA The June 1929 issue of *Scribner's Magazine*, which ran Hemingway's novel, was banned in Boston.

1933 Burned by the Nazis in Germany.
1939 Banned in Ireland.
1974 TX Challenged at the Dallas Independent School District high school libraries.
1980 NY Challenged at the Vernon-Verona-Sherill School District as a "sex novel."

Source: 2, p. 137; 4, pp. 79–80; 11, Jan. 1975, pp. 6–7; May 1980, p. 62.

736 Hemingway, Ernest
For Whom the Bell Tolls

1940   Declared nonmailable by the U.S. Post Office. 1973 On Feb. 21, 1973, eleven Turkish book publishers went on trial before an Istanbul martial law tribunal on charges of publishing, possessing, and selling books in violation of an order of the Istanbul martial law command. They faced possible sentences of between one month's and six month's imprisonment "for spreading propaganda unfavorable to the state" and the confiscation of their books. Eight booksellers also were on trial with the publishers on the same charge involving *For Whom the Bell Tolls.*
Source: 4, p. 80; 5, Summer 1973, xii.

737 Hemingway, Ernest
Hills Like White Elephants:
A Short Story: The Complete Short
Stories of Ernest Hemingway

2009 NH
New   Pulled from a Litchfield Campbell High School elective course classroom after parents voiced their concerns about a short-stories unit called "Love/Gender/Family Unit" that dealt with subject matters including abortion, cannibalism, homosexuality, and drug use. The parents said the stories promoted bad behavior and a "political agenda" and they shouldn't be incorporated into classroom teachings. The Campbell High School English curriculum adviser eventually resigned.
Source: 11, Sept. 2009, p. 154.

738 Hemingway, Ernest
The Killers

1995 CT   Challenged, but retained in the Bridgeport public schools. The short story, published in 1927, repeatedly uses the word "nigger." It was not part of the curriculum, but was chosen by a teacher as part of a unit on violence in literature.
Source: 11, Jan. 1996, p. 30.

739 Hemingway, Ernest
The Sun Also Rises

1930 MA   Banned in Boston.
1933   Burned in Nazi bonfires in Germany.
1953   Banned in Ireland.
1960 CA   Banned in Riverside.
1960 CA   Banned in San Jose.
Source: 4, pp. 79–80; 14, pp. 272–73.

740 Hemingway, Ernest
To Have and Have Not

1938 MI   Banned in Detroit.
1938 NY   Distribution forbidden in Queens.
Source: 4, pp. 79–80; 14, pp. 274–75; 15, Vol. III, p. 652.

741 Hendrix, Harville
Keeping the Love You Find:
A Guide for Singles

1995 MN   Pulled from the Staples-Motley High School health classes because its sexual subject matter was deemed inappropriate for freshmen and sophomores. The book was not a textbook or required reading, but a resource.
Source: 11, May 1995, p. 70.

742 Henege, Thomas
Skim

1983 TN   Publication canceled by Dodd, Mead & Company because of language in the book considered "objectionable" by Thomas Nelson, Inc. of Nashville–Dodd, Mead's parent company.
Source: 11, Nov. 1983, p. 188.

743 Hentoff, Nat
The Day They Came to Arrest
the Book

1990 VA   Challenged in the Albemarle County schools in Charlottesville because it offers an inflammatory challenge to authoritarian roles.
Source: 11, Jan. 1991, p. 18.

744 Herbert, Frank
Soul Catcher

1993 WA   Challenged, but retained at the Lake Washington School District in Kirkland despite objections there is "a very explicit sex scene," it is "a mockery of Christianity," and "very much anti-God."
Source: 11, Jan. 1994, p. 16; Mar. 1994, p. 71.

745 Herge
Tintin in America

1995 WA   Removed from the Spokane School District libraries as racially demeaning and insulting.
Source: 11, Jan. 1996, p. 12.

746 Herman, Victor
Coming Out of the Ice

1998 WA Restricted to seniors at the Mount Baker High School in Bellingham. In addition, before the book is assigned, parents will get a summary of its plot, along with a description of the graphic passages that led one parent to ask that the book be pulled from the high school's curriculum.
Source: 11, July 1998, p. 110.

747 Hermes, Patricia
Solitary Secret

1988 CO Moved from the library at Parker Junior High School to the senior high school because of its graphic detail of sex.
Source: 11, Mar. 1988, p. 45.

748 Heron, Ann
How Would You Feel If Your Dad Was Gay?

1993 AZ Challenged at the Mesa Public Library because it "is vile, sick and goes against every law and constitution."
1993 OH Retained at the Dayton and Montgomery County Public Library.
1994 MA Challenged, but retained in the Oak Bluffs school library. Though the parent leading the protest stated that, "The subject matter . . . is obscene and vulgar and the message is that homosexuality is okay," the selection review committee voted unanimously to keep the book.
Source: 11, Jan. 1994, p. 34; Mar. 1994, p. 69; May 1994, p. 98.

749 Heron, Ann
One Teenager in Ten: Testimony by Gay and Lesbian Youth

1993 OR Challenged at the Deschutes County Library in Bend because it "encourages and condones" homosexuality.
1994 CO Retained at the Estes Park Public Library after challenges to the book for its graphic content.
Source: 11, Sept. 1993, pp. 158–59; Sept. 1994, p. 165.

750 Heron, Ann
Two Teenagers in Twenty

1998 WI Removed from the Barron School District because of the book's homosexual theme and because it contains outdated information about AIDS. The ACLU of Wisconsin filed suit against the school district on Feb. 16, 1999.

The book was then returned to the library while a federal court considered the lawsuit. On October 8, 1999, it was agreed that the book will remain available to students as part of the school district's settlement of the federal lawsuit.
Source: 11, Jan. 1999, p. 9; Mar. 1999, p. 37; May 1999, p. 68; Jan. 2000, p. 28.

751 Herron, Carolivia
Nappy Hair

1998 NY Challenged in Brooklyn because it was considered racially insensitive.
Source: 11, Jan. 1999, p. 10; Mar. 1999, p. 25.

752 Herzberg, Max J.
Myths and Their Meanings

1992 CO Challenged in the Woodland Park High School because the stories about mythological figures like Zeus and Apollo threaten Western civilization's foundations.
Source: 11, May 1992, p. 82.

753 Hesse, Hermann
Steppenwolf

1943 Forbidden by Hitler in Germany for its "lewd lustfulness."
1982 CO Challenged at the Glenwood Springs High School library due to book's references to lesbianism, hermaphroditism, sexual perversion, drug use, murder, and insanity.
Source: 9; 11, Sept. 1982, p. 169; 14, pp. 263–64.

754 Hewitt, Kathryn
Two by Two: The Untold Story

1991 OH Challenged at the Hubbard Public Library because the book alters the story of Noah's Ark, making it secular and confusing to children.
Source: 11, Sept. 1991, p. 153.

755 Hill, Douglas Arthur
Witches and Magic-Makers

1999 NE Challenged, but retained at the Hastings Public Library along with forty other books on the topics of witches, magic, the zodiac, fortune telling, and ghost stories (most of the Dewey Decimal category 133.47). The books were called "demonic" and unsuitable for young children.
Source: 11, May 1999, p. 66; July 1999, p. 104.

756 Hinton, S. E.
The Outsiders

1986 WI   Challenged on an eighth-grade reading list in the South Milwaukee schools because "drug and alcohol abuse was common" in the novel and "virtually all the characters were from broken homes."

1992 IA   Challenged at the Boone School District because the book glamorizes smoking and drinking and uses excessive violence and obscenities.

2000 WV   Challenged at the George Washington Middle School in Eleanor due to objections to the focus on gangs and gang fights.
Source: 11, Jan. 1987, p. 13; Nov. 1992, p. 199; July 2000, p. 106.

757 Hinton, S. E.
Rumble Fish

1991 WV   Challenged at the Poca Middle School in Charleston because the book is "too frank."
Source: 11, Jan. 1992, p. 9.

758 Hinton, S. E.
Tex

1995 FL   Challenged due to foul language and violence, but retained at Campbell Middle School in Daytona Beach.

2000 PA   Restricted by the Central Dauphin school board in Harrisburg due to graphic language.
Source: 11, May 1995, pp. 69–70; July 1995, pp. 110–11; Sept. 2000, p. 144.

759 Hinton, S. E.
That Was Then, This Is Now

1983 CO   Challenged at the Pagosa Springs schools because a parent objected to the "graphic language, subject matter, 'immoral tone,' and lack of literary quality."

1986 WI   Challenged on an eighth-grade reading list in the South Milwaukee schools because "drug and alcohol abuse was common" and "virtually all the characters were from broken homes."

1991 WV   Challenged at the Poca Middle School in Charleston because the book is "too frank."
Source: 9; 11, Mar. 1984, p. 53; Jan. 1987, p. 13; Jan. 1992, p. 9.

760 Hitchcock, Alfred
Alfred Hitchcock's Witches Brew

1982 WI   Challenged at the Fond du Lac school system because the anthology contains stories about magic, witchcraft, and the supernatural.
Source: 11, Mar. 1983, p. 39.

761 Hite, Shere
The Hite Report on Male Sexuality

1983 NC   Challenged at the Southern Pine Public Library because it is inappropriate "for the development of moral character in children or anyone for that matter."
Source: 11, May 1983, p. 85.

762 Hitler, Adolf
Mein Kampf

1932   Banned in Czechoslovakia for its fierce militaristic doctrines.

1933   Banned by a court in Warsaw, Poland for being "insulting."

1933 NY   The American Hebrew and Jewish Tribune, along with other Jewish organizations and individuals, attempted to prevent the first U.S. publication of the book

1937   Banned in Palestine.

1945   Banned in occupied Germany, ban continued by the Federal Republic of Germany. Today, it is only available to the public in excerpted, commented versions.

1989   Banned from the 158 Stars and Stripes bookstores in West Germany. Since all Nazi literature has been banned in West Germany for decades, the circulation manager for the U.S. government chain stated, "we're guests in Germany, and I think we should show certain respect to our hosts."

1992   The ban was removed, then re-applied after public protests in Poland.

1993   Romanian president Ion Iliescu called for a ban, but the government's chief attorney would not comply.

1995   Seized by police.

1996   In Hungary sales were suspended in 1996, and a full ban followed in 1997.

1997   Sales were blocked in Sweden, ostensibly because of copyright issues. The Bavarian state government is the copyright holder, and does not allow any copying or printing in German. It opposes copying or printing in other countries, as well.

1998   In Portugal sales were blocked for a similar reason as Sweden.

2001   The publisher of the first unabridged Czech edition received a three-year suspended sentence for promoting Nazism. Czech police seized some 300 copies of the book.

2009 New   Plans by German scholars to reprint as an academic treatise were rejected by the state copyright holders, who said a new edition of the book could fuel support for far-right groups. The Bavarian authorities reaffirmed a sixty-four-year-old ban on the book after the

Munich-based Institute of Contemporary History, or IFZ, applied for permission to reprint the work.

Source: 4, p. 72; 8, pp. 130–34; 11, Jan. 1989, p. 14; Mar. 2001, p. 62; Sept. 2009, pp. 155–56.

763 Hobbes, Thomas
Leviathan

1661   The House of Commons discussed the revival of the fifteenth-century writ that sentenced heretics to burnings. The bill failed. Hobbes was forbidden thereafter by the English government from publishing his philosophic opinion and turned to the writing of history.

1703   Banned in Holland because of its frank materialism.

1703   Placed on the Catholic Church's *Index Librorum Prohibitorum* (Index of Prohibited Books) in Rome, Italy and remained listed through the last edition of the Index published until 1966.

Source: 1, pp. 187–88.

764 Hobson, Laura Z.
Gentleman's Agreement

1948 NY   Banned from reading lists at DeWitt Clinton High School, Bronx by the high school principal "on the grounds that it makes light of extramarital relations." After considerable protest, the board of superintendents reversed the ban eight months later.

Source: 14, pp. 154–55.

765 Hodges, Hollis
Don't Tell Me Your Name

1985 WA   Relegated to the restricted shelf at the Covington Junior High School library in Vancouver, the Evergreen School Board reversed its earlier ruling and decided to keep the novel despite parents' contention it is sexually explicit and inappropriate for junior high readers.

Source: 11, July 1985, p. 133; Nov. 1985, pp. 203–4; July 1986, p. 118.

766 Hogan, William
The Quartzsite Trip

1985 WA   Challenged at Vancouver Pacific Junior High School library because "the subject matter was too adult for junior high school students."

1987 NE   Placed in a collection for teacher use only in the Lincoln East High School library after a complaint was filed by a teacher.

Source: 11, May 1985, p. 91; July 1985, p. 134; Nov. 1987, p. 225.

767 Hoke, Helen
Witches, Witches, Witches

1988 NV   Challenged at the Smith Valley school libraries because the book "is replete with scenes of intrusion, oppression, cannibalism, abduction, transformation, incantations, deceptions, threats, and sexism."

Source: 11, July 1988, pp. 121–22; Sept. 1988, p. 178.

768 Holland, Margaret, and Craig McKee
The Unicorn Who Had No Horn

1991 WI   Challenged at the Cornell Elementary School library because it allegedly promotes "New Age religion" and includes content related to witchcraft and the occult.

Source: 11, Jan. 1992, p. 6; Mar. 1992, p. 63.

769 Holliday, Laurel
Children in the Holocaust and World War II: Their Secret Diaries

1999 OH   Limited to students in the seventh grade or higher at the Canal Winchester Middle School in Columbus because of references to sex, a self-induced abortion, and drug use.

Source: 11, July 1999, p. 94; Nov. 1999, pp. 171–72.

770 Holmes, Melisa, and Trish Hutchison
Hang-ups, Hook-ups, and Holding Out: Stuff You Need to Know about Your Body, Sex, and Dating

2008 NY New   Retained in the Galway Public Library after complaints about the book's "factual errors, philosophy, and perceived bias." A review of the book by the library determined that the book received excellent reviews and contained no factual errors.

Source: 11, Jan. 2009, p. 22.

771 Homer
The Odyssey

387 B.C.   Plato suggested expurgating Homer for immature readers and Caligula tried to suppress it because it expressed Greek ideals of freedom (35 A.D.).

Source: 4, p. 1.

772 Homes, A.M.
Jack

1996 NC   Placed on the Spindale school library's reserve shelf. This meant parental permission was required for a student to check it out. A parent did not find the novel "proper to be in the library due to the language."

1998 WI Challenged in the Barron School District.

Source: 11, Nov. 1996, pp. 193–94; Jan. 1999, p. 9.

---

773 Hoobler, Dorothy, and Thomas Hoobler
Nelson and Winnie Mandela

1988 OR Challenged at the Hillsboro Public Library by a patron who charged that the Mandelas and the African National Congress are Communist-backed and advocate violence. After being reviewed, the book was retained in the library's collection.

Source: 7, p. 361; 11, Jan. 1989, p. 3.

---

774 Hosseini, Khaled
The Kite Runner

2008 FL New Retained in the Jackson County School District in Marianna after being removed from the required reading list for one class. The school board voted to retain the book in the library by a vote of five to two.

2008 IL New Removed from the reading list at Centennial High School in Champaign due to objections from a parent whose child was assigned the book for summer reading.

2008 NC New Challenged as appropriate study in tenth-grade honors English class at Freedom High School in Morganton because the novel depicts a sodomy rape in graphic detail and uses vulgar language.

2008 NC New Challenged in Burke County schools in Morgantown by parents concerned about the violence and sexual situations portrayed in the book.

Source: 11, May 2008, pp. 97–98; Nov. 2008, pp. 256–57; Jan. 2009, pp. 8, 10.

---

775 Hotze, Sollace
A Circle Unbroken

1994 IL Challenged at Cary Junior High School because references in the book to sex are too explicit for seventh and eighth graders; retained by school board vote.

Source: 11, May 1994, p. 83; July 1994, pp. 128–29.

---

776 Howe, James
Totally Joe

2007 VA New Removed from the Jefferson Elementary School in Bedford County because of "inappropriate content." Administrators pulled the book from the shelf after a parental complaint. While the school system's general policy on content challenges calls for a formal committee's review of the book, that policy was not followed. Rather, officials decided the book was not appropriate for elementary-school students, but did not decide whether to allow the book in middle or high schools.

Source: 11, Jan. 2008, pp. 14, 35.

---

777 Howe, Norma
God, the Universe and Hot Fudge Sundaes

1988 OR Challenged at the Canby Junior High School library because the book "pushes several items of the humanist agenda: death education, anti-God, pro-evolution, anti-Bible, anti-Christian, and logic over faith."

Source: 11, May 1989, p. 78.

---

778 Hoyt, Olga
Demons, Devils and Djinn

1990 KY Challenged at Elkhorn Middle School in Frankfort because "it describes devil worship."

Source: 11, May 1990, p. 84; July 1990, p. 145.

---

779 Hubbard, L. Ron
Mission Earth

1990 GA Challenged at the Dalton Regional Library System because of "repeated passages involving chronic masochism, child abuse, homosexuality, necromancy, bloody murder, and other things that are anti-social, perverted, and anti-everything."

Source: 11, July 1990, p. 125.

---

780 Huegel, Kelly
GLBTQ: The Survival Guide for Queer and Questioning Teens

2005 AR Challenged in the Fayetteville High School library. The complainant also submitted a list of more than fifty books, citing the books as too sexually explicit and promoting homosexuality.

Source: 11, Sept. 2005, p. 215.

---

781 Hughes, Langston
The Best Short Stories by Negro Writers

1976 NY Removed from the Island Trees Union Free District High School library in 1976 along with nine other titles because they were considered "immoral, anti-American, anti-Christian, or just plain filthy"; returned to the library after the U.S. Supreme Court ruling on June 25, 1982, in *Board of Education, Island Trees Union Free School District No. 26 et al. v. Pico et al.*, 457 U.S. 853 (1982).

Source: 11, Nov. 1982, p. 197.

---

782   Hughes, Tracy, ed.
Everything You Need to Know about Teen Pregnancy

1993 TN Challenged, but retained at the Cleveland Public Library along with seventeen other books, most of which are on sex education, AIDS awareness, and some titles on the supernatural.

Source: 11, Sept. 1993, p. 146.

---

783   Hugo, Victor
Hernani

1850   Banned by Nicholas I in Russia.

Source: 4, p. 41.

---

784   Hugo, Victor
Les Miserables

1864   Listed in the *Index Librorum Prohibitorum* (List of Prohibited Books) in Rome, Italy from 1864–1959.

1904 PA Voted out of a library by a Philadelphia school committee because it mentioned a grisette, a young woman combining part-time prostitution with some other occupation.

Source: 2, p. 92; 4, p. 41.

---

785   Hugo, Victor
Notre Dame de Paris

1850   Banned by Nicholas I in Russia.
1864   Listed in the *Index Librorum Prohibitorum* (List of Prohibited Books) in Rome, Italy from 1864–1959.

Source: 4, p. 41.

---

786   Hull, Eleanor
Alice with the Golden Hair

1990 PA Removed, but later reinstated at the Pine Middle School library in Gibsonia because of its adult language.

Source: 11, Nov. 1990, pp. 209–10; Jan. 1991, pp. 28–29.

---

787   Hume, David
On Religion

1827   All of his historical and philosophical works were placed on the *Index Librorum Prohibitorum* (Index of Prohibited Books) in Rome, Italy where they remained until 1966.
1986   Banned in Turkey.

Source: 1, pp. 77–78; 5, July/Aug. 1986, p. 46.

---

788   Humphrey, Derek
Final Exit

1991 IL Challenged at the Cook Memorial Library in Libertyville because the book "diminishes the value of the elderly and encourages breaking the law by assisting homicide and drug abuse."

1992   Banned in Australia. After an appeal by the book distributors, in June 1992, the Australian Film and Literature Board of Review reversed the decision of the censors and classified the Book as Category 1—Restricted. Under this designation, the book must be sealed in plastic and cannot be sold to anyone under the age of eighteen.

1992   Publishers will not publish the work because assisted suicide is against the law in England.

1992   New Zealand custom officials were ordered to seize all copies of the book coming into the country and to hold them until the Office of Indecent Publications could review the suitability of the work. After careful review, the censors determined that the book would be permitted unrestricted entry.

Source: 8, p. 454; 11, Jan. 1992, p. 25.

---

789   Hunter, Evan
The Chisholms

1981 CA A Livermore Valley Unified School District book selection committee voted to remove this title from the Granada High School library due to poor literary quality, gratuitous violence, as well as explicitly sexual passages.

Source: 11, Jan. 1982, p. 8.

---

790   Hurston, Zora Neale
Their Eyes Were Watching God

1997 VA Challenged for sexual explicitness, but retained on the Stonewall Jackson High School's academically advanced reading list in Brentsville. A parent objected to the novel's language and sexual explicitness.

Source: 11, Nov. 1997, pp. 169–70; Jan. 1998, p. 29.

---

791   Hurwin, Davida
Time for Dancing

2002 VA Challenged, along with seventeen other titles in the Fairfax County elementary and secondary libraries, by a group called Parents Against Bad Books in Schools. The group contends the books "contain profanity and descriptions of drug abuse, sexually explicit conduct, and torture."

Source: 11, Jan. 2003, p. 10.

792 Hus, Jan
De Ecclesia

1415   His work denied the pope's infallibility and proposed that the state should supervise the church. Put on trail at the church Council of Constance, Germany, he was convicted of heresy. His books were destroyed, and he was burned at the stake.
Source: 1, pp. 66–67.

793 Hutchins, Maude
A Diary of Love

1950 IL   Banned by the Chicago Police Bureau of Censorship because the book was "so candidly filthy in spots as to constitute a menace to public morals."
Source: 15, Vol. IV, p. 710.

794 Huxley, Aldous
Antic Hay

1930 MA   Banned on grounds of obscenity in Boston.
1952 MD   A Baltimore teacher was dismissed for assigning Huxley's novel to his senior literature class. The teacher's unsuccessful quest for vindication is reported in *Parker v. Board of Education*, 237 F. Supp. 222 (D. Md.).
Source: 4, p. 75; 12, pp. 23, 230.

795 Huxley, Aldous
Brave New World

1932   Banned in Ireland.
1980 MO   Removed from classroom in Miller and challenged frequently throughout the U.S.
1988 OK   Challenged as required reading at the Yukon High School because of "the book's language and moral content."
1993 CA   Challenged as required reading in the Corona Unified School District because it is "centered around negative activity." The book was retained, and teachers selected alternatives if students object to Huxley's novel.
1993 CA   Challenged as required reading in the Norco Unified School District because it is "centered around negative activity." The book was retained, and teachers selected alternatives if students object to Huxley's novel.
2000 AL   Removed from the Foley High School library pending review, because a parent complained that its characters showed contempt for religion, marriage and the family. The parent complained to the school and to Alabama Governor Don Siegelman.

2003 TX   Challenged, but retained in the South Texas Independent School District in Mercedes. Parents objected to the adult themes—sexuality, drugs, and suicide—found in the novel. Huxley's book was part of the summer Science Academy curriculum. The board voted to give parents more control over their childrens' choices by requiring principals to automatically offer an alternative to a challenged book.
2008 ID   Retained in the Coeur D'Alene School District
New   despite objections that the book has too many references to sex and drug use.

Source: 4, p. 75; 5; 8, pp. 424–25; 11, May 1980, p. 52; July 1988, p. 140; Jan. 1994, p. 14; Mar. 1994, p. 70; Nov. 2000, p. 193; Jan. 2001, p. 11; Nov. 2003, pp. 249–50; Jan. 2009, pp. 7–8.

796 Huxley, Aldous
The Doors of Perception

1980 WI   Challenged at the Oconto Unified School District because it "glorifies the use of drugs."
Source: 11, Mar. 1981, p. 41.

797 Huxley, Aldous
Eyeless in Gaza

1926   Banned in Ireland until 1953.
Source: 4, p. 75.

798 Huxley, Aldous
Point Counter Point

1930   Banned in Ireland on the grounds of offending public morals. The banned was not revoked until 1970
Source: 4, p. 75; 13, p. 194.

799 Hyde, Margaret O., and Elizabeth Forsyth
Know about AIDS

1993 TN   Challenged, but retained at the Cleveland Public Library along with seventeen other books, most of which are on sex education, AIDS awareness, and some titles on the supernatural.
Source: 11, Sept. 1993, p. 146.

800 Ibsen, Henrik
A Doll's House

1983 AL   Four members of the Alabama State Textbook Committee called for the rejection of Ibsen's work because it propagates feminist views.
Source: 11, Mar. 1983, p. 39.

801 Ibsen, Henrik
An Enemy of the People

1939   Works purged by Franco government in Spain.
1958   Works formerly banned reported to be extremely popular in USSR.
Source: 4, p. 48.

802 Ibsen, Henrik
Four Great Plays by Ibsen

1991 MD   Challenged, but retained in the Carroll County schools. Two school board members were concerned about the play, *Ghosts*, which deals with venereal disease, incest, and suicide.
Source: 11, Mar. 1992, p. 64.

803 Ibsen, Henrik
Ghosts

1892   Banned in England.
1939   Purged by the Franco government in Spain.
1958   Ban lifted in USSR.
Source: 4, p. 48.

804 *Illustrated Encyclopedia of Family Health*

1986 WY   Removed from the library at Sage Valley Junior High School in Gillettt after a resident said the book contained photographs that were "very nude and very explicit."
1991 OR   Challenged in an intermediate school library in Beaverton because of explicit line drawings of sexual intercourse positions and removed from the library, but maintained for staff use only.
Source: 11, July 1986, p. 118; July 1992, p. 103.

805 Irving, John
A Prayer for Owen Meany

1992 PA   Pulled from the Boiling Springs High School senior literature class in Carlisle after several complaints from parents about its content and language.
2000 WV   Challenged in the Kanawha County high schools as "pornographic, offensive and vulgar." The novel is on the county book list for suggested reading material for the eleventh and twelfth grades.
2009 MA   Removed from the Pelham school district
New   recommended summer reading list after a parent complained about the novel's objectionable language and sexuality.
Source: 11, July 1992, p. 112; Sept. 1992, p. 142; July 2000, p. 10; Sept. 2009, pp. 153–54.

806 Isay, Richard
Being Homosexual: Gay Men and Their Development

1993 OR   Challenged at the Deschutes County Library in Bend because it "encourages and condones" homosexuality.
Source: 11, Sept. 1993, pp. 158–59.

807 Isensee, Rick
Love Between Men

1996 PA   Challenged at the Chester County Library at Charlestown because it was "pornographic and smutty."
Source: 11, Nov. 1996, p. 194.

808 Ives, Vernon
Russia

1955 NY   Removed from library shelves at Proctor high schools on the advice of a textbook commission of the New York Education Department. According to the commission, the book, while not seditious or disloyal, contained passages "that are either untrue or almost certain to evoke untrue inferences."
1955 NY   Removed from library shelves at New Hartford high schools on the advice of a textbook commission of the New York Education Department. According to the commission, the book, while not seditious or disloyal, contained passages "that are either untrue or almost certain to evoke untrue inferences."
1966 LA   Banned by the Avoyelles Parish school board in Marksville because the book was "pro-Russian in comparing Russia to the United States."
Source: 7, pp. 435–36.

809 Izzi, John
Metrication, American Style

1985 RI   Banned at the Toll Gate High School in Warwick because it is "discriminatory toward women."
Source: 11, July 1985, p. 114.

810 Jackson, Jesse
Call Me Charley

1979 MI   Parents of a black fourth-grade student filed suit against Grand Blanc school officials after a teacher read this title to their son's class. The work includes a white character who calls a black youth "Sambo," "nigger," and "coon."
Source: 11, Mar. 1979, p. 38.

811 Jackson, Jon A.
Dead Folks

2009 MT
New

Challenged in the Big Sky High School in Missoula because the local author's work was viewed as too graphic in its discussion of sex.

Source: 11, May 2009, pp. 82–84.

812 Jackson, Shirley
The Lottery

1981 MN

The film version of Jackson's short story was banned in Forest Lake but reinstated by U.S. District Court judge.

Source: 9; 11, July 1981, p. 88.

813 Jacobs, Anita
Where Has Deedie Wooster Been All These Years?

1984 WA

Removed from the Hockinson Middle School library because it is "garbage" and the novel's discussion of a young girl's first menstrual cycle is particularly objectionable.

Source: 11, Sept. 1984, p. 138.

814 Jagendorf, Moritz A.
Tales of Mystery: Folk Tales from Around the World

1992 NE

Removed to a locked closet in the superintendent's office in Banner County because the book "has to do with a lot of negative things and might not be good for someone with low self-esteem or suicide tendencies."

Source: 11, May 1992, p. 80.

815 Jahn-Clough, Lisa
Me, Penelope

2008 FL
New

Challenged in the middle school library in Tavares. The book is part of a collection that requires permission from the school librarian to check out. Objections centered on the book's depiction of a sixteen-year-old who is dealing with the death of her brother and reference to sexual experimentation.

Source: 11, Jan. 2009, pp. 5–6.

816 Jaivin, Linda
Eat Me

2003 FL

Removed from the Marion County Public Library in Ocala. The library director noted that the Australian best-seller was removed because the library lacks a designated erotica collection, and the novel met only three of seventeen criteria used to evaluate books for acquisition. The Marion County Public Library Advisory Board recommended that the library director retain the novel. The board's vote was only a suggestion and the final decision went back to the library director. In Feb. 2004, the director reversed her earlier decision, reinstated the novel, and stated that her personal dislike for the book overshadowed her objectivity and adherence to policy.

Source: 11, Jan. 2004, pp. 7–8; Mar. 2004, pp. 47–48; May 2004, pp. 115–16; Sept. 2004, pp. 175–76.

817 Jakes, John
Bastard

1976 PA

Removed from the Montour High School library.

Source: 11, Nov. 1976, pp. 143–44.

818 James, Henry
Turn of the Screw

1995 FL

Challenged at the St. Johns County Schools in St. Augustine.

Source: 11, Jan. 1996, p. 14.

819 James, Norah C.
Sleeveless Errand

1929

Police in England seized copies at the premises of Scholaris Press and the director of public prosecution cited the "obscene" language used by the characters as evidence of its "shocking depravity." The magistrate ruled in favor of the prosecution and granted the destruction order, stating that the novel suggested "thoughts of the most impure character" to readers of all ages.

Source: 13, p. 223.

820 Jameson, Jenna and Neil Strauss
How to Make Love Like A Porn Star: A Cautionary Tale

2005 TX

Houston mayor ordered city librarians to keep the book behind the counter. After committee review, the best seller was returned to the open shelves.

Source: 11, Mar. 2005, pp. 55–56; May 2005, pp. 131–32.

821 **Jay, Carla, and Allen Young**
The Gay Report

1982 MI Challenged at the Niles Community Library.
Source: 11, Jan. 1983, p. 8.

822 **Jefferson, Thomas**
A Summary View of the Rights of British America

1833 Banned for political reasons in Russia under Czar Nicholas I.
Source: 7, p. 476.

823 **Jenness, Aylette**
Families: A Celebration of Diversity, Commitment and Love

1990 IL Temporarily removed, but later reinstated at the Winfield Public Library because of objections to two of the stories. One involves a gay couple who adopted a baby at birth and the other involves a lesbian couple who raise one of the couple's children.
Source: 11, Mar. 1991, p. 61.

824 **Jennings, Gary**
Black Magic, White Magic

1989 TX Retained at the Ector County school library after being challenged because the book might lure children into the occult.
Source: 11, Jan. 1990, p. 9; May 1990, p. 107.

825 **Jennings, Kevin, ed.**
Becoming Visible: A Reader in Gay and Lesbian History for High School and College Students

1996 MO Banned from the two high school libraries in Mehlville by order of the superintendent. The donated book was removed because it "does not meet the needs of the curriculum."
Source: 11, May 1996, pp. 82–83.

826 **Jeschke, Susan**
The Devil Did It

1990 MD Challenged at the elementary school libraries in Howard County because it shows the devil as "a benign or friendly force."
Source: 11, Jan. 1991, p. 12.

827 **Jewkes, Wilfred Thomas**
The Perilous Journey

1989 MD Pulled from the curriculum of the Baltimore County school system because a three-page retelling of an African-American folk legend was considered racially insensitive. The offensive story was "All God's Chillen Had Wings."
Source: 11, Jan. 1990, p. 11.

828 **Jimenez, Carlos M.**
The Mexican-American Heritage

1996 CA Challenged in the Santa Barbara schools because the book promotes "Mexican nationalism."
Source: 11, May 1996, p. 98.

829 **Johnson, Earvin (Magic)**
What You Can Do to Avoid AIDS

1996 NY Removed from the Horace Greeley High School in Chappaqua because a group of parents complained that the basketball player's written description of oral and anal sex were inappropriate for fourteen- and fifteen-year-olds. Johnson's book is endorsed by the American Medical Association and the Children's Defense Fund.
Source: 11, May 1996, p. 88; July 1996, p. 119.

830 **Johnson, Eric W.**
Love and Sex and Growing Up

1993 TN Challenged, but retained at the Cleveland Public Library along with seventeen other books, most of which are on sex education, AIDS awareness, and some titles on the supernatural.
Source: 11, Sept. 1993, p. 146.

831 **Johnson, Eric W.**
Love and Sex in Plain Language

1982 FL Moved from the children's room of the Tampa-Hillsborough County Public Library.
1988 PA Challenged in the Williamsport schools because of allegedly inaccurate and misleading information in the book.
Source: 11, Jan. 1982, pp. 4–5; May 1988, p. 104.

832 **Johnson, Eric W.**
Sex: Telling It Straight

1987 WA Placed on restricted shelves at the Evergreen School District elementary school libraries in

Vancouver in accordance with the school board policy to restrict student access to sex education books in elementary school libraries.
Source: 11, May 1987, p. 87.

833 Johnson, Julie
Adam & Eve & Pinch Me

1997 SC Challenged at the Greenville middle school libraries because the book uses objectionable language like "damn" and "jerk-ass."
Source: 11, Sept. 1997, p. 126.

834 Johnson, Maureen
The Bermudez Triangle

2009 PA New Challenged at the Leesburg Public Library because of sexual innuendo, drug references, and other adult topics.
Source: 11, July 2009, p. 131.

835 Johnson, Sam, et al.
Beavis and Butt-Head Ensucklopedia

1995 UT Challenged at the Salt Lake County Public Library by a parent because it has "no literary value whatsoever. It was totally perverse garbage, trash. I consider it pornography." The complainant requested the removal of all Beavis and Butt-Head materials, including seven cassettes, seven CDs, and two copies of *MTV's Beavis and Butt-Head Experience.*
Source: 11, May 1995, pp. 67–68.

836 Jonas, Ann
Aardvarks Disembark

1991 OH Challenged at the Hubbard Public Library because the book alters the story of Noah's Ark, making it secular and confusing to children.
Source: 11, Sept. 1991, p. 153.

837 Jones, Clinton R.
Understanding Gay Relatives and Friends

1982 IN Challenged at the Elkhart Public Library because it attempts to "get people to accept the homosexual lifestyle, like there is nothing wrong with it."
Source: 11, Mar. 1983, p. 56.

838 Jones, James
From Here to Eternity

1951 CO Banned in Denver.
1951 MA Banned in Springfield.
1951 MA Banned in Holyoke.
1955 NY Banned from the mails by the New York City post office.
1956 MI The prosecuting attorney in Port Huron, St. Clair County, ordered booksellers and distributors to cease displaying and selling all books that appeared on the disapproved list of the National Organization for Decent Literature, a Catholic censorship group founded in 1938.
Source: 4, p. 94; 13, pp. 82–83.

839 Jong, Erica
Fear of Flying

1982 IN Challenged in Terre Haute as optional reading in an elective course for junior and senior high school students.
Source: 11, May 1982, p. 86.

840 Jordan, June
Living Room

1990 MI Banned from the Baldwin High School library because it contains profanity and racial slurs.
Source: 11, Jan. 1991, p. 12.

841 Josephs, Rebecca
Early Disorders

1988 WI Challenged at the Mukwonago High School because the book's "portrayal of anorexia nervosa was not factual and the account of a girl's life, thoughts, and emotions used pornographic language and made fun of religion."
Source: 11, May 1988, p. 104.

842 Joyce, James
Dubliners

1912 Destroyed by printer because he found passages objectionable.
Source: 4, p. 65.

843 Joyce, James
Exiles

1986 Banned in Turkey.
Source: 5, July/Aug. 1986, p. 46.

844 Joyce, James
Ulysses

1918 Burned in U.S.
1922 Burned in Ireland.
1922 Burned in Canada.
1929 Banned and burned in England.
Source: 4, pp. 65–66; 6, p. 412; 8, pp. 391–92; 15, Vol. III, pp. 411–12, 557–58, 645.

845   Jukes, Mavis
The Guy Book: An Owner's Manual

2006 MT   Challenged in the Lockwood Middle School library by parents who objected to what they believe to be misleading, sexually explicit material in the book. The book was retained. The challenge came on the heels of a December decision by the board to pull three books from the middleschool library. Those books were *The Vanishing Hitchhiker: American Urban Legends*, by Jan Brunvand, and *Urban Legends* and *Alligators in the Sewer*, both by Thomas Craughwell. The same parent brought those titles—and their content—to the attention of the librarian and superintendent.
Source: 11, May 2006, pp. 129–30.

846   Jukes, Mavis
It's a Girl Thing: How to Stay Healthy, Safe and in Charge

1999 FL   Written parental permission is required to see the book at the Palm Beach elementary and middle schools because of concerns that the book—written for preteen girls—is more explicit than some parents would find acceptable.
Source: 11, May 1999, p. 66.

847   Julian, Cloyd J., and Nancy S. Simon
Family Life and Human Sexuality

1987 NE   Challenged as a supplemental text in an elective course in the Omaha School District because the book promotes "Planned Parenthood, abortion, and artificial methods of birth control." The book was adopted after the course's previous text, *Finding My Way*, by Andrew Riker, was replaced because it was considered too controversial.
Source: 11, Nov. 1987, p. 225.

848   Juster, Norton
The Phantom Tollbooth

1988 CO   Removed from a locked reference collection at the Boulder Public Library. The book was originally locked away because the librarian considered it a poor fantasy.
Source: 11, Jan. 1989, p. 27.

849   Kallen, Stuart A.
Ghastly Ghost Stories

1992 IL   Challenged, but retained in the Warrensburg-Latham school library because the series of seven books are "possibly harmful to a child's psychological development."
Source: 11, Jan. 1993, p. 7; Mar. 1993, p. 41.

850   Kallen, Stuart A.
Vampires, Werewolves and Zombies

1993 TN   Challenged, but retained at the Cleveland Public Library along with seventeen other books, most of which are on sex education, AIDS awareness, and some titles on the supernatural.
Source: 11, Sept. 1993, p. 146.

851   Kane, William M., and Mary Bronson Merki
Human Sexuality: Relationships and Responsibilities

1992 WA   Challenged at the Bremerton schools because it allegedly is "based on fraudulent research, stresses homosexuality, and is inappropriate for teenagers."
Source: 11, July 1992, p. 112.

852   Kane, William; Peggy Blake; and Robert Frye
Understanding Health

1983 KY   Challenged in Jefferson County because it contains a chapter on sex education, which includes slang sexual terminology.

1983 OH   Banned from the curriculum at the Oak Hills High School because the book discusses abortion, premarital sex, and euthanasia.
Source: 11, Sept. 1983, p. 142; Nov. 1983, p. 186; July 1984, p. 107; Sept. 1984, p. 157.

853   Kant, Immanuel
The Critique of Pure Reason

1827   Placed on the *Index Librorum Prohibitorum* (List of Prohibited Books) in Rome, Italy until the 20th century.

1928   Purged from Soviet Union libraries.

1939   Purged from Spain's libraries.
Source: 3, p. 163; 4, p. 31; 8, p. 288.

854   Kant, Immanuel
Religion within the Boundaries of Pure Reason

1794   Banned by the Lutheran church because, "Our sacred person you have with your so-called philosophy attempted to bring into contempt. . . and you have at the same time assailed the truth of the Scriptures and the foundations of Creed beliefs. . . We order that henceforth you shall employ your talents to better purpose and that you shall keep silence on matters which are outside of your proper functions."

1928   Prohibited in the Soviet Union along with all of Kant's writings, presumably because the metaphysical and transcendental themes of Kant's works were thought to conflict with Marxist-Leninist ideology.

1939   All of Kant's works were purged from libraries of Spain under the Franco dictatorship.

Source: 3, p. 163; 8, pp. 286–88.

855   Kantor, MacKinlay
Andersonville

1962   TX   Banned from the four Amarillo High schools and at Amarillo College because its political ideas and that its author was cited by the House Un-American Activities Committee.

1963   MI   Withdrawn from the eleventh grade reading list at the Whitehall High School because the book "wasn't fit for high school students."

1967   OH   Challenged, but retained in Amherst high school despite claims the book is "filth."

1969   WI   Challenged in Rock County.

1973   NC   Challenged, but retained in the Buncombe County schools despite claims the book was unsuitable for school libraries because it contains objectionable language.

Source: 4, pp. 11–12; 8, pp. 10–12.

856   Kauffmann, Stanley
The Philanderer

1953   Condemned by legal authorities on the Isle of Man after police received a complaint that a person could obtain the book at Boots' Library. The novel's trial was influential in changing the obscenity law in England, a change motivated largely by the summation of Mr. Justice Sable, who presided over the trial in the Queen's Bench Division in the Old Bailey. Sable warned that if criminal law were to be driven too far in the desire to stamp out the "bawdy muck," there existed a risk of a revolt, "a demand for a change in the law, so that the pendulum may swing to far the other way and allow to creep in things that at the moment we can keep out." The decision was not binding on future cases because it was not a court of appeal judgment, and Customs and postal authorities continued to seize books in transit, but this case set the stage for change in English obscenity laws.

Source: 13, pp. 190–91.

857   Kaufman, Joe
How We Are Born, How We Grow, How Our Bodies Work, and How We Learn

1991   FL   Removed from circulation collection, and now available only as a reference book, at the Old Kings Elementary School in Bunnell because two pages on the reproductive process were found objectionable.

Source: 11, Mar. 1992, p. 40.

858   Kaufman, Sue
Falling Bodies

1982   IN   Challenged in Terre Haute as optional reading in an elective course for junior and senior high school students.

Source: 11, May 1982, p. 86.

859   Kaysen, Susanna
Girl, Interrupted

2006   ME   Removed temporarily from the curriculum, pending its review, from the Orono High School after a parent complained about strong language and vivid descriptions. Movie stars Angelina Jolie and Winona Ryder brought the book into the limelight when they starred in the 2000 film version.

2008   NY New   The New Rochelle Board of Education announced that it would replace all fifty copies of Susanna Kaysen's memoir after school officials tore pages from the book deemed "inappropriate" due to sexual content and strong language. Removed was a scene where the rebellious Lisa encourages Susanna to circumvent hospital rules against sexual intercourse by engaging in oral sex instead. The incident was a hot topic across the blogosphere, transcending political ideology. It was featured on the left leaning Boing Boing, the most widely read blog in the world, as well as the top conservative site, Hot Air, which is owned by Michelle Malkin of Fox News. *The New Yorker* magazine and *The Atlantic Monthly* also picked up the story as well as dozens of blog sites focused on literary and free speech issues.

Source: 11, Mar. 2006, pp. 73–74; Mar. 2009, pp. 56–57.

860   Kazan, Elia
Acts of Love

1980   UT   Removed from the Utah State Library bookmobile.

Source: 11, Nov. 1980, p. 128.

861 Kazantzakis, Nikos
The Last Temptation of Christ

1954 The novel was placed on the Roman Catholic Church's *Index Librorum Prohibitorum* (List of Prohibited Books) in Rome, Italy.

1954 The author was excommunicated in 1954 from the Eastern Orthodox Church in Constantinople, Turkey.

1962 CA Challenged in Long Beach from 1962 to 1965.

1988 Banned in Singapore as a result of pressure from fundamentalist Christians.

1998 NJ Challenged, but retained at the Sussex County Community College in Newton despite an employee's charges that the book is "totally offensive" and "an outrage and insult to every Christian in the world."

Source: 4, p. 68; 8, pp. 260–61; 11, Mar. 1999, p. 47.

862 Keable, Robert
Simon Called Peter

1922 MA The Boston Watch and Ward Society brought charges against Edith Law of Arlington, Massachusetts, the owner of a Boston rental library, who was convicted in the Cambridge District Court in October 1922 and fined $100 for stocking the novel in her rental library. In an appeal, Judge Stone suspended the fine but warned Law that she faced a jail sentence if she were ever again convicted in an obscenity case. The case drew particular attention because the novel had been a best seller for more than a year.

1922 NY The New York Society for the Suppression of Vice tried without success to have the book banned, but the courts refused to hear the complaint.

Source: 13, pp. 219–20.

863 Keefer, Edward C., ed.
Foreign Relations of the United States 1964-68, Volume XXVI, Indonesia, Malaysia-Singapore, Philippines

2001 The U.S. government recalled all copies of this U.S. State Department history book from hundreds of libraries in the U.S. and abroad because it details the U.S. role in Indonesia's deadly purge of communists in the 1960s. The prestigious series, which began in 1861, is often embattled. For example, the history dealing with Greece, Cyprus, and Turkey was printed in February 2000, but is locked up at the Government Printing Office under the label: "Embargo: This publication cannot be released." Officials declined to say why.

Source: 11, Nov. 2001, pp. 245–46.

864 Keehn, Sally
I Am Regina

1996 IL Challenged as optional fifth-grade reading at the Orland Park School District 135 because the book uses unflattering stereotypes to depict Native Americans and uses the word "squaw," which was offensive.

Source: 11, Jan. 1997, p. 10.

865 Keeping, Charles
Through the Window

1985 IA Challenged at the Cedar Rapids Public Library because "the harsh realities of life it depicts are not suitable for young readers."

Source: 11, Sept. 1985, p. 167.

866 Kehret, Peg
Abduction!

2006 MN Challenged, but retained at the two Apple Valley middle- and eight elementary-school libraries despite the complaint that the book was too violent.

Source: 11, July 2006, p. 208.

867 Kellerman, Faye
Milk and Honey

1991 AR Challenged at the Rogers-Hough Memorial Library because of "sacrilegious language."

Source: 11, Sept. 1991, p. 151.

868 Kelley, Leo P.
Night of Fire and Blood

1984 CO Found unsuitable for younger children in Aurora because it deals with "violence and self-mutilation."

Source: 11, May 1984, p. 69.

869 Kellogg, Marjorie
Tell Me That You Love Me, Junie Moon

1978 MD Challenged at the Frederick County school system because it teaches that "it's all right to do things against society's rules."

Source: 11, Mar. 1978, p. 39; May 1978, p. 58.

870 Kellogg, Steven
Pinkerton, Behave!

2000 AR Challenged, but retained at the Elm Tree Elementary School library in Benton despite the objections to a character in the book holding a gun.

2004 IL Challenged, but retained at the Evanston Public Library despite complaints that the image of a masked burglar pointing a gun at woman is too violent for young readers.

Source: 11, Jan. 2001, p. 35; July 2004, p. 157; Nov. 2004, pp. 255–56.

---

871   Kenan, Randall
James Baldwin

2000 CA Removed from the Anaheim school district because school officials said the book is too difficult for middle school students and that it could cause harassment against students seen with it. The American Civil Liberties Union (ACLU) of Southern California filed suit in *Doe v. Anaheim Union High School District* alleging that the removal is "a pretext for viewpoint-based censorship." The ACLU claims no other books have been removed from the junior high library for similar reasons, even though several, such as works by Shakespeare and Dickens, are more difficult reading. The ACLU contends that the school officials engaged in unconstitutional viewpoint discrimination by removing the book because it contains gay and lesbian material. In March 2001, the school board approved a settlement that restored the book to the high school shelves and amended the district's policy to prohibit the removal of books for subject matter involving sexual orientation, but the book will not be returned to the middle school.

Source: 11, Mar. 2001, p. 53; May 2001, p. 95; July 2001, p. 173.

---

872   Kennedy, X. J.
Literature: Introduction to Fiction, Poetry and Drama

1993 CA Challenged in the Ojai schools because selections contained foul language and blasphemy, and they glamorize sexual misconduct.

Source: 11, Jan. 1994, p. 37.

---

873   Kepler, Johannes
The New Astronomy

1619 Banned by the Vatican in Rome, Italy under a general prohibition on reading or teaching heliocentric theory. The ban on his theories remained in effect until 1753.

Source: 1, pp. 212–13.

---

874   Kerr, M. E.
Dinky Hocker Shoots Smack

1977 WA Removed from Kent elementary school libraries because of complaints about "vulgarity" and "defamation of the word of God in the work."

1998 FL Challenged, but retained at the Merritt Brown Middle School library in Panama City despite a parent's concern that passages are "sacrilegious and morally subversive."

Source: 9; 11, Mar. 1977, p. 36; Sept. 1998, p. 139.

---

875   Kerr, M. E.
Gentle Hands

1983 VA Challenged at the Lake Braddock Secondary School because the book is "anti-Semitic" and "glamorizes drug abuse and makes drugs 'tempting' to teenagers."

Source: 11, July 1983, p. 109; Nov. 1983, p. 187; Mar. 1984, p. 53.

---

876   Kesey, Ken
One Flew over the Cuckoo's Nest

1971 CO Challenged in the Greeley Public school district as a non-required American Culture reading.

1974 OH Five residents of Strongsville sued the board of education to remove the novel. Labeling it "pornographic," they charged the the novel "glorifies criminal activity, has a tendency to corrupt juveniles and contains descriptions of bestiality, bizarre violence, and torture, dismemberment, death, and human elimination."

1975 NY Removed from public school libraries in Randolph.

1975 OK Removed from public school libraries in Alton.

1977 MA Removed from the required reading list in Westport.

1978 ID Banned from the St. Anthony Freemont High School classrooms and the instructor fired— *Fogarty v. Atchley*.

1982 NH Challenged at the Merrimack High School.

1986 WA Challenged as part of the curriculum in an Aberdeen High School honors English class because the book promotes "secular humanism." The school board voted to retain the title.

2000 CA Challenged in the Placentia-Yorba Linda Unified School District after complaints by parents stated that teachers "can choose the best books, but they keep choosing this garbage over and over again."

Source: 8, pp. 478–79; 11, Jan. 1977, p. 8; May 1978, p. 57; July 1978, pp. 96, 100; Sept. 1982, p. 170; 12, pp. 104–11, 229; Nov. 1986, p. 225; Mar. 2001, p. 55; 15, Vol. IV, p. 714.

877 Kesey, Ken
Sometimes a Great Notion

1998 WA Challenged for use in Richland high school
English classes along with six other titles
because the "books are poor-quality
literature and stress suicide, illicit sex,
violence, and hopelessness."
Source: 11, Mar. 1999, p. 40.

878 Kessel, Joyce K.
Halloween

1992 AZ Challenged at the Neely Elementary School in
Gilbert because the book shows the dark side
of religion through the occult, the devil, and
satanism.
Source: 11, May 1992, p. 78; July 1992, p. 124.

879 Keyes, Daniel
Flowers for Algernon

1976 FL Banned from the Plant City public schools
because of references to sex.
1977 PA Banned from the Emporium public schools
because of references to sex.
1981 AR Banned from the Glen Rose High School library.
1983 OH Challenged at the Oberlin High School
because several pages of the novel detail a
sexual encounter of the protagonist.
1984 WY Challenged as a required reading at the
Glenrock High School because several
"explicit love scenes were distasteful."
1986 NC Challenged at the Charlotte-Mecklenburg
schools as a tenth-grade supplemental reading
because it is "pornographic."
1996 VA Challenged, but retained in the Yorktown
schools. A parent complained about the
profanity and references to sex and drinking
in the novel.
1997 GA Removed from the ninth-grade curriculum by
the Rabun County Board of Education
because it was "inappropriate" for the
ninth grade.
Source: 11, July 1976, p. 85; May 1977, p. 73; July 1981,
p. 91; Jan. 1984, p. 26; July 1984, p. 122; Jan. 1987, p. 12;
Mar. 1987, p. 54; May 1987, p. 103; July 1987, p. 150;
May 1996, p. 100; July 1997, p. 97.

880 Kidd, Flora
Between Pride and Passion

1984 OR More than fifty Harlequin romances donated
by Glide residents were threatened with
removal from the high school library because
"teenagers already have trouble with their
emotions without being stimulated by poorly
written books."
Source: 11, July 1984, p. 104.

881 Kilgore, Kathleen
The Wolfman of Beacon Hill

1989 OR Challenged at the Pilot Butte Junior High
School in Bend because the material does
not enlighten, uplift, or encourage
character-building traits.
Source: 11, Jan. 1990, pp. 4–5.

882 Killingsworth, Monte
Eli's Songs

1992 OR Challenged in the Rural Dell School District in
Molalla because the book is "anti-local," has
"logger-bashing" sentiments and an
"ecological slant."
Source: 11, July 1992, pp. 124–25.

883 Kincaid, Jamaica
Lucy

1994 PA Challenged at the West Chester schools as
"most pornographic." The book was changed
from required to optional reading.
Source: 11, Jan. 1995, p. 25; Mar. 1995, p. 45; May 1995, p. 71.

884 Kincaid, James Russell
***Erotic Innocence: The Culture of
Child Molesting***

2002 TX Challenged, but retained in the Montgomery
County library system after a conservative
Christian group, the Republican Leadership
Council, characterized the book as "helping
to lay the groundwork for a culture of child
molesters and homosexuals."
Source: 11, Jan. 2003, p. 33.

**885 King, Frederick; Herbert Rudman;
and Doris Leavell**
Understanding the Social Sciences

1987 AL Removed from Alabama's list of approved
texts—and from the state's classrooms—
because the book promotes the "religion of
secular humanism." U.S. District Court Judge
W. Brevard Hand ruled on March 4, 1987, that
thirty-nine history and social studies texts
used in Alabama's 129 school systems
"discriminate against the very concept of
religion and theistic religions in particular, by
omissions so serious that a student learning
history from them would not be apprised of
relevant facts about America's history. . . .
References to religion are isolated and the
integration of religion in the history of
American society is ignored." The series
includes: *Understanding People;*

Understanding Families; Understanding Communities; Understanding Religions of the World; Understanding Our Country; and *Understanding the World.* On August 26, 1987, the U.S. Court of Appeals for the Eleventh Circuit unanimously overturned Judge Hand's decision by ruling that the information in the book was "essentially neutral in its religious content." The fact that the texts omitted references to religion was not "an advancement of secular humanism or an active hostility toward theistic religion."

Source: 11, Jan. 1987, p. 6; May 1987, pp. 75, 104–7; Sept. 1987, pp. 166–67; Nov. 1987, pp. 217–18; Jan. 1988, p. 17; Mar. 1988, p. 40.

886 King, Larry
Tell It to the King

1989 MI Challenged at the Public Libraries of Saginaw because it is "an insult to one's intelligence" and contains foul language.
Source: 11, May 1989, p. 77.

887 King, Stephen
The Bachman Books

1987 IA Removed from the West Lyon Community School library in Larchwood because "it does not meet the standards of the community."
Source: 11, May 1987, p. 86; July 1987, p. 125.

888 King, Stephen
Carrie

1975 NV Challenged at the Clark High School library in Las Vegas because it is "trash."
1978 VT Placed in special closed shelf at the Vergennes Union High School library because it could "harm" students, particularly "younger girls."
1987 IA Removed from the West Lyon Community School library in Larchwood because "it does not meet the standards of the community."
1991 NY Banned from the Altmar-Parish-Williamstown district libraries.
1994 ND Challenged, along with eight other Stephen King novels, in Bismarck by a local minister and a school board member, because of "age appropriateness."
1994 PA Challenged by a parent at the Boyertown Junior High East library. The parent "objected to the book's language, its violence, and its sexual descriptions, as well as what she described as a 'Satanic killing' sequence."
Source: 11, Jan. 1979, p. 6; May 1987, p. 86; July 1987, p. 125; Mar. 1992, p. 40; May 1994, pp. 84–85.

889 King, Stephen
Christine

1985 AL The Washington County Board of Education voted unanimously to ban the novel from all county school libraries because the book contains "unacceptable language" and is "pornographic."
1987 IA Removed from the West Lyon Community School library in Larchwood because "it does not meet the standards of the community."
1989 CT Removed from the Washington Middle School library in Meriden after a parent complained about offensive passages.
1990 MT Removed from the Livingston Middle School library because it was deemed not "suitable for intended audience," owing to violence, explicit sex, and inappropriate language.
1993 IL Challenged at the Webber Township High School library in Bluford along with all other King novels.
1994 ND Challenged, along with eight other Stephen King novels, in Bismarck by a local minister and a school board member, because of "age appropriateness."
Source: 11, Jan. 1986, p. 7; May 1987, p. 86; July 1987, p. 125; May 1989, p. 75; Jan. 1991, p. 12; July 1993, p. 124; May 1994, pp. 84–85.

890 King, Stephen
Cujo

1984 MS Challenged at the Rankin County School District because it is "profane and sexually objectionable."
1985 AL The Washington County Board of Education voted unanimously to ban the novel from all county school libraries because the book contains "unacceptable language" and is "pornographic."
1985 CA Rejected for purchase by the Hayward school trustees because of "rough language" and "explicit sex scenes."
1985 NY Removed from the shelves of the Bradford school library "because it was a bunch of garbage."
1987 WI Removed from a high school library in Durand pending review by a nine-member panel of school personnel and community members.
1992 IL Challenged from Sparta schools. The school board honored the parents' request to bar their children from using the book, but refused to ban the book.
1992 ME Challenged, but retained at a South Portland middle school despite complaints of "profanity" and sexual references.
1994 ND Challenged, along with eight other Stephen King novels, in Bismarck by a local minister

and a school board member, because of "age appropriateness."

1998 FL Challenged at the West Hernando Middle School in Brooksville because of the book's sexually explicit scenes and language.

1998 OR Removed at the Crook County High School in Prineville because it contains "profanity, sexual content, and other factors." The parent also requested that all books by Stephen King be removed from the school because, "I object to any book written by Stephen King as he writes horror fiction, which has no value." Three other King books are under review: *The Running Man*, *Bachman Books*, and *The Green Mile, Part 1*.

Source: 8, pp. 442–44; 11, May 1984, p. 69; Jan. 1985, p. 8; May 1985, pp. 75, 77; July 1985, p. 111; Jan. 1986, p. 7; Nov. 1987, p. 226; May 1994, pp. 84–85; July 1998, p. 110; Jan. 1999, p. 7.

891 King, Stephen
The Dark Half

1994 OR Retained in the Roseburg High School library despite a parent's complaint that the book contains "extreme, bloodthirsty violence."

1998 WI Banned, but later reinstated in the Stanley-Boyd School District high school library despite a parent's objection to the "profane" language in the first chapter. The school board enacted a new policy that allows parents to call the school librarian and restrict their children's access to certain books or authors.

Source: 11, Sept. 1994, pp. 166–67; Jan. 1999, p. 9; Mar. 1999, p. 37.

892 King, Stephen
The Dead Zone

1987 IA Removed from the West Lyon Community School library in Larchwood because "it does not meet the standards of the community."

1992 FL Restricted to high school students with parental permission at the Duval County school system because of "filthy language" in the book.

1992 IN Banned in the Peru school system along with *Cujo* and *Christine* because the books are "filthy."

1994 ND Challenged, along with eight other Stephen King novels, in Bismarck by a local minister and a school board member, because of "age appropriateness."

Source: 11, May 1987, p. 86; July 1987, p. 125; May 1992, pp. 79, 80; July 1992, pp. 105, 106; May 1994, pp. 84–85.

893 King, Stephen
Different Seasons

1987 IA Removed from the West Lyon Community School library in Larchwood because "it does not meet the standards of the community."

1989 CT Removed from the Washington Middle School library in Meriden after a parent complained about offensive passages.

1992 MN Challenged at the Eagan High School in Burnsville.

2001 FL Accessible to West Hernando Middle School library students in Brooksville only if they have a signed and verified permission slip from their parents. A student was offended by references to oral sex and prison rape scenes in the short story "Rita Hayworth and Shawshank Redemption," the basis for the 1994 movie *The Shawshank Redemption*.

Source: 11, May 1987, p. 86; July 1987, p. 125; May 1989, p. 75; Mar. 1993, p. 56; Jan. 2002, p. 15.

894 King, Stephen
The Drawing of the Three

1994 ND Challenged, along with eight other Stephen King novels, in Bismarck by a local minister and a school board member, because of "age appropriateness."

Source: 11, May 1994, pp. 84–85.

895 King, Stephen
The Eyes of the Dragon

1994 ND Challenged, along with eight other Stephen King novels, in Bismarck by a local minister and a school board member, because of "age appropriateness."

Source: 11, May 1994, pp. 84–85.

896 King, Stephen
Firestarter

1983 WY Challenged at the Campbell County School System because of its alleged "graphic descriptions of sexual acts, vulgar language, and violence."

1989 CT Removed from the Washington Middle School library in Meriden after a parent complained about offensive passages.

Source: 11, Mar. 1984, p. 39; May 1989, p. 75.

897 King, Stephen
Four Past Midnight

1992 IL Challenged at the Sparta High School library, along with all other King novels, due to violence, sex, and explicit language.

Source: 11, July 1992, p. 106.

898   King, Stephen
Gerald's Game

1998 FL   Removed from Columbia High School in Lake City because of the book's portrayal of graphic violence and lewd sexual conduct. A parent threatened to take legal action against the school system if the school did not decide to remove all "offensive" library books.
Source: 11, Jan. 1999, pp. 7–8.

899   King, Stephen
It

1987 NE   Challenged in the Lincoln school libraries because of the novel's "corruptive, obscene nature."

1992 NY   Placed on a "closed shelf" at the Franklinville Central High School library because of explicit sexual acts, violence, and profane language. Students will need parental permission to check it out.
Source: 11, Nov. 1987, p. 225; Mar. 1993, p. 41.

900   King, Stephen
Night Shift

1987 IA   Removed from the West Lyon Community School library in Larchwood because "it does not meet the standards of the community."

1988 WI   Removed from the Green Bay School District classrooms because the book contains a short story entitled "Children of the Corn," which "teaches about the occult and rebellion by children and makes a mockery of Christianity." The book was returned, however, after questions were raised by school board members about the administrative decision to ban the book.
Source: 11, May 1987, p. 86; July 1987, p. 125; Jan. 1989, p. 11; Mar. 1989, p. 44.

901   King, Stephen
Pet Sematary

1994 ND   Challenged, along with eight other Stephen King novels, in Bismarck by a local minister and a school board member, because of "age appropriateness."
Source: 11, May 1994, pp. 84–85.

902   King, Stephen
Salem's Lot

1986 TX   Banned from the Cleveland Independent High School English classes overruling a review committee's recommendation, even after teachers already had inked out objectionable words with a felt-tip marker. A single copy is available in the restricted section of the high school library to students who have a permission slip signed by their parents.

1988 VT   Banned from the Goochard High School library because of sexually explicit language.
Source: 11, Jan. 1987, p. 12; Mar. 1987, pp. 54–55; Sept. 1988, p. 152.

903   King, Stephen
The Shining

1983 WY   Challenged at the Campbell County School System because "the story contains violence, demonic possession and ridicules the Christian religion." The novel is now available to all students in grades seven through twelve, at the discretion of district librarians.

1986 WA   Removed from the Evergreen School District's four junior high school libraries in Vancouver because the book's "descriptive foul language" made it unsuitable for teenagers.

1990 MT   Removed from the Livingston Middle School library because it was deemed not "suitable for intended audience," owing to violence, explicit sex, and inappropriate language.

1994 ND   Challenged, along with eight other Stephen King novels, in Bismarck by a local minister and a school board member, because of "age appropriateness."
Source: 11, Jan. 1984, p. 10; Mar. 1984, p. 39; May 1986, p. 81; July 1987, p. 125; Jan. 1991, p. 12; May 1994, pp. 84–85.

904   King, Stephen
The Skeleton Crew

1993 ID   Challenged at the Salmon High School library because of graphic street language about homosexuality, among other reasons.
Source: 11, July 1993, p. 124.

905   King, Stephen
The Stand

1989 OR   Restricted to ninth grade students with parental consent at the Whitford Intermediate School in Beaverton because of "sexual language, casual sex, and violence."
Source: 11, Jan. 1990, pp. 4–5.

906   King, Stephen
Survivor Type: A Short Story from Skeleton Crew

2009 NH   Pulled from a Litchfield Campbell High School elective course classroom after
New   parents voiced their concerns about a short-stories unit called "Love/Gender/Family Unit" that dealt with subject matters

including abortion, cannibalism, homosexuality, and drug use. The parents said the stories promoted bad behavior and a "political agenda" and they shouldn't be incorporated into classroom teachings. The Campbell High School English curriculum adviser eventually resigned.

Source: 11, Sept. 2009, p. 154.

907 King, Stephen
The Talisman

1993 ID Challenged at the Salmon High School library because of graphic street language about homosexuality, among other reasons.

Source: 11, July 1993, p. 124.

908 King, Stephen
Thinner

1994 ND Challenged, along with eight other Stephen King novels, in Bismarck by a local minister and a school board member, because of "age appropriateness."

Source: 11, May 1994, pp. 84–85.

909 King, Stephen
The Tommyknockers

1992 FL Restricted to high school students with parental permission at the Duval County school system because of "filthy language" in the book and "it's extremely graphic."

Source: 11, May 1992, p. 79; July 1992, p. 105.

910 Kingsolver, Barbara
Animal Dreams

2007 PA Challenged in the Manheim Township schools
New due to sexual references. The book was moved from the ninth-grade English curriculum to the eleventh-grade curriculum.

Source: 11, July 2007, pp. 149–50.

911 Kingsolver, Barbara
The Bean Trees

1998 IL Temporarily restricted in the Yorkville schools because it is "obscene, coarse, disgusting, and irreverent."

2009 CA Challenged at the William S. Hart Union High
New School District in Saugus as required summer reading for the honors English program because the novel includes sexual scenes and vulgar language. Students have the option of alternative assignments that still meet objectives and teaching goals.

Source: 11, July 1998, p. 108; Sept. 1998, p. 156; Jan. 2010, pp. 15–16.

912 Kingston, Jeremy
Witches and Witchcraft

1987 KY Removed from the Duerson-Oldham County Public Library in LaGrange because "young or immature minds may become intrigued by Satan as a result of reading the book."

Source: 11, Sept. 1987, p. 174.

913 Kinsey, Alfred
Sexual Behavior in the Human Female

1953 Banned in South Africa.
1953 Banned in Ireland.
1953 Banned in U.S. Army post exchanges in Europe as having "no worthwhile interest for soldiers."

Source: 4, p. 75.

914 Kinsey, Alfred
Sexual Behavior in the Human Male

1953 Banned in South Africa.
1953 Banned in Ireland.
1953 Banned in U.S. Army post exchanges in Europe as having "no worthwhile interest for soldiers."

Source: 4, p. 75.

915 Kipling, Rudyard
Drums of the Fore and Aft

1899 IN Removed from the Sunday school library of the Crawfordsville First Methodist Episcopal Church because a parishioner complained that it was "fairly reeking with profanity, and the most outrageous slang."

Source: 15, Vol. II, p. 624.

916 Kipling, Rudyard
The Elephant's Child

1993 IA Challenged in the Davenport Community School District because the book is "99 percent" violent. Throughout the book, when the main character, an elephant child, asks a question, he receives a spanking instead of answers.

Source: 11, July 1993, p. 99.

917 Kipling, Rudyard
Just So Stories

1990 NC Challenged at the Hardin Park Elementary School library in Watauga County because the word "nigger" appears in the story "How the Leopard Got Its Spots."

Source: 11, July 1990, p. 145.

918 Kirk, Marshall, and Hunter Madison
After the Ball: How America Will Conquer Its Hatred and Fear of Homosexuals in the '90s

1993 OR Challenged at the Deschutes County Library in Bend because it "encourages and condones" homosexuality.
Source: 11, Sept. 1993, pp. 158–59.

919 Kirkwood, James
There Must Be a Pony! A Novel

1984 Seized by the British customs office as "indecent and obscene."
Source: 11, Jan. 1985, p. 16.

920 Kittredge, Mary
Teens with AIDS Speak Out

1993 TN Challenged, but retained at the Cleveland Public Library along with seventeen other books, most of which are on sex education, AIDS awareness, and some titles on the supernatural.
Source: 11, Sept. 1993, p.146.

921 Kitzinger, Sheila
Being Born

1991 OR Challenged at the Lakeview school libraries because the complainant's son asked "rather pointed questions" about childbirth.
1993 NV Challenged, but retained at the Washoe County Library System in Reno because, "Nobody in their right mind would give a book like that to children on their own, except the library."
Source: 11, Nov. 1991, p. 209; Sept. 1994, p. 147; Nov. 1994, pp. 200–01.

922 Klause, Annette Curtis
Blood and Chocolate

2001 TX Temporarily pulled from the LaPorte Independent School District school library shelves until the district can review and possibly amend its selection policies.
Source: 11, Nov. 2001, p. 247.

923 Klausen, Jytte
The Cartoons That Shook the World

2009 CT
New Yale University Press in New Haven removed twelve cartoons of the Prophet Muhammad from an upcoming book about how they caused outrage across the Muslim world, citing fears of violence. A Danish newspaper originally published the cartoons—including one depicting Muhammad wearing a bomb-shaped turban—in 2005. Other Western publications reprinted them. The following year, the cartoons triggered massive protests from Morocco to Indonesia. Rioters torched Danish and other Western diplomatic missions. Some Muslim countries boycotted Danish products. Islamic law generally opposes any depiction of the prophet, even favorable, for fear it could lead to idolatry.
Source: 11, Nov. 2009, pp. 204–7.

924 Klein, Aaron
Science and the Supernatural

1993 TN Challenged, but retained at the Cleveland Public Library along with seventeen other books, most of which are on sex education, AIDS awareness, and some titles on the supernatural.
Source: 11, Sept. 1993, p. 146.

925 Klein, Norma
Angel Face

1990 TX Challenged at the Commerce High School library because of "pornographic" material in the book. The complainant asked that all "romance" books be removed.
Source: 11, Mar. 1991, p. 43.

926 Klein, Norma
Beginners' Love

1999 SC Challenged, but retained in the Chester High School library with the provision that parents can instruct the school not to let their own children borrow it. The book's graphic description of sex, discussions of abortion, and the character's use of marijuana were considered objectionable by some parents. South Carolina Attorney General Charlie Condon ruled that the school board could reasonably conclude that the novel was "pervasively vulgar" and "educationally unsuitable" and, thus, removal by the board would not violate the First Amendment.
Source: 11, Mar. 1999, p. 36; Nov. 1999, p. 163.

927 Klein, Norma
Confessions of an Only Child

1985 GA Challenged, but retained in a Gwinnett County Elementary School library because "the use of a profanity by the lead character's father during a single episode destroyed the entire book."
Source: 11, Mar. 1986, p. 57; Mar. 1986, p. 57; July 1986, p. 135.

928 Klein, Norma
Family Secrets

1991 MD Removed from the Howard County middle school media centers because the book's "constant reference to the sex act" and "inappropriate foul language."
Source: 11, Mar. 1992, p. 40.

929 Klein, Norma
Give Me One Good Reason

1984 CO Challenged at the Widefield School District because the book is "filled with promiscuity, homosexuality, abortion, and profanity."
Source: 11, May 1984, p. 69.

930 Klein, Norma
Honey of a Chimp

1984 PA Removed from the Hanover School District's elementary and secondary libraries, but later placed on a "restricted shelf" at middle school libraries, because the book contained "strong sexual content, bias to liberal values and morals, and indecent language. The material condones certain values, attitudes, and behaviors."
Source: 11, Jan. 1985, p. 9.

931 Klein, Norma
It's Not What You Expect

1980 MD Removed from all the Montgomery County elementary school libraries.
Source: 11, May 1980, p. 51.

932 Klein, Norma
It's OK If You Don't Love Me

1981 CA Banned in Hayward County because of the book's sexually explicit passages and "rough language."
1983 CO Removed from the shelves of the Widefield High School library because it portrays "sex as the only thing on young people's minds."
1984 WA Removed from the Vancouver School District due to its sexual passages, but later reinstated at the high school level libraries.
Source: 11, Mar. 1982, p. 44; May 1983, p. 71; July 1984, p. 104.

933 Klein, Norma
Just Friends

1994 CT Challenged at the Hamden Middle School because it is "nothing more than pornographic smut."

1998 MO Banned at, but later returned to, the Cameron High School library after student complaints. The book was initially challenged because it was "too explicit and did not link actions to consequences."
2000 CA Removed from the mandatory reading program at the Norman L. Sullivan Middle School in Bonsall due to sexually explicit language.
Source: 11, Nov. 1994, p. 189; July 1998, p. 119; May 2000, p. 76.

934 Klein, Norma
Love Is One of the Choices

1983 WA Removed from the Evergreen School District of Vancouver along with twenty-nine other titles. The American Civil Liberties Union of Washington filed suit contending that the removals constitute censorship, a violation of plaintiff's rights to free speech and due process, and the acts are a violation of the state Open Meetings Act because the removal decisions were made behind closed doors.
Source: 11, Nov. 1983, pp. 185–86.

935 Klein, Norma
Mom, the Wolf Man and Me

1980 FL Challenged at the Orlando due to its "objectionable" subject matter.
Source: 11, Mar. 1981, p. 47.

936 Klein, Norma
My Life as a Body

1989 OR Challenged at the Douglas County Library in Roseburg because the book condones homosexuality and premarital sex.
1991 OR Challenged for being too explicit, but retained at the Multnomah County Library.
Source: 11, Jan. 1990, pp. 4–5; Jan. 1992, p. 6.

937 Klein, Norma
Naomi in the Middle

1977 NY Restricted in Brockport to students with parental permission.
1980 FL Challenged at the Orlando Public Library.
1980 LA Banned in Monroe because "it is certainly not our intention to have objectionable materials on library shelves."
1986 NC Challenged at the Charlotte public library system because the book "is a perfect picture of secular humanism."
1992 CA Challenged at the Napa City-County Library because of sexually explicit language.

1995 AZ Challenged at the Mesa Public Libraries because of four pages of inappropriate material describing human sexual anatomy and how babies are conceived.
Source: 11, Nov. 1977, p. 155; July 1980, p. 76; Mar. 1981, p. 47; Jan. 1987, p. 31; July 1992, p. 105; July 1995, p. 109.

---

938 Klein, Norma
The Queen of the What Ifs

1989 CA Pulled from the Monte Vista Middle School library in Tracy after two parents complained that its sexual content made the book inappropriate for middle school students. About a half dozen other titles also were removed and the parents have indicated a desire to review all books ordered for the library.
Source: 11, May 1989, p. 75.

---

939 Klein, Norma
Sunshine

1975 LA Removed from the East Baton Rouge Parish after the parents of a student said they found the language and content of the book offensive.
Source: 11, July 1975, p. 104.

---

940 Klein, Norma
That's My Baby

1998 MO Banned at, but later returned to, the Cameron High School library after student complaints. The book was initially challenged because it was "too explicit and did not link actions to consequences."
Source: 11, July 1998, p. 119.

---

941 Klein, Norma
What It's All About

1984 IA Challenged at the Dubuque Community School District because, "it condones and even endorses immoral behavior because it contains profanity, nudity, sexual relationships outside of marriage and an excessive number of people who are divorced."
Source: 11, Sept. 1984, p. 155.

---

942 Klein, Stanley
Steck-Vaughn Social Studies

1987 AL Removed from Alabama's list of approved texts—and from the state's classrooms—because the book promotes the "religion of secular humanism." U.S. District Court Judge W. Brevard Hand ruled on March 4, 1987, that thirty-nine history and social studies texts used in Alabama's 129 school systems "discriminate against the very concept of religion and theistic religions in particular, by omissions so serious that a student learning history from them would not be apprised of relevant facts about America's history. . . . References to religion are isolated and the integration of religion in the history of American society is ignored." The series includes: *Our Family; Our Neighbors; Our Communities; Our Country Today; Our Country' s History;* and *Our World Today.* On August 26, 1987, the U.S. Court of Appeals for the Eleventh Circuit unanimously overturned Judge Hand's decision by ruling that the information in the book was "essentially neutral in its religious content." The fact that the texts omitted references to religion was not "an advancement of secular humanism or an active hostility toward theistic religion."
Source: 11, Jan. 1987, p. 6; May 1987, pp. 75, 104–7; Sept. 1987, pp. 166–67; Nov. 1987, pp. 217–18; Jan. 1988, p. 17; Mar. 1988, p. 40.

---

943 Knott, Blanche
Truly Tasteless Jokes

1988 AZ Removed from open display at the Casa Grande Public Library and restricted to adult use only with proof of age before checking the book out or even looking at it.
Source: 11, Jan. 1989, p. 7.

---

944 Knowles, Jo (Johanna Beth)
Lessons from a Dead Girl

2009 KY Withdrawn from classroom use and the
New approved curriculum at the Montgomery County High School, but available at the high school library and student book club. Some parents have complained about five novels containing foul language and cover topics— including sex, child abuse, suicide, and drug abuse—unsuited for discussion in coed high school classes. They also contend that the books don't provide the intellectual challenge and rigor that students need in college preparatory classes. The titles appeared on suggested book lists compiled by the Young Adult Library Services Association, a division of the American Library Association, for twelve- to eighteen-year-olds who are "reluctant readers." The superintendent removed the book because it wasn't on the pre-approved curriculum list and couldn't be

added by teachers in the middle of a school year without permission.

Source: 11, Jan. 2010, pp. 16–17; Mar. 2010, p. 56.

Christian Andersen contains the phrase "go to hell."

Source: 11, Nov. 1992, p. 197.

945 Knowles, John
A Separate Peace

1980 NY Challenged in Vernon-Verona-Sherill School District as a "filthy, trashy sex novel."

1985 PA Challenged at the Fannett-Metal High School in Shippensburg because of its allegedly offensive language.

1989 TN Challenged as appropriate for high school reading lists in the Shelby County school system because the novel contained "offensive language."

1991 IL Challenged, but retained in the Champaign high school English classes despite claims that "unsuitable language" made it inappropriate.

1991 IL Challenged by the parent of a high school student in Troy citing profanity and negative attitudes. Students were offered alternative assignments while the school board took the matter under advisement, but no further action was taken on the complaint.

1996 NC Challenged at the McDowell County schools because of "graphic language."

Source: 11, May 1980, p. 62; Nov. 1985, p. 204; Jan. 1990, pp. 11–12; Jan. 1997, p. 11; 14, pp. 256–57.

946 Knowlton, Charles
Fruits of Philosophy: The Private Companion of Married Couples

1832 MA The author was brought to trail in Taunton, Massachusetts, and charged with distributing "obscene material," then filed $50 and court costs.

1832 MA In December 1832, Knowlton was found guilty of distributing his book and sentenced to three months of hard labor in the Cambridge House of Corrections.

1834 MA Knowlton appeared in court of Greenfield three different times, but the case was finally dismissed because the jury in all three trials could not come to a decision.

1877 The book was also challenged in British courts and eventually the defendants recovered their stock of books, stamped in red "Recovered from Police" and sold them.

Source: 14, pp. 148–50.

947 Knudsen, Eric
Teller of Tales

1992 GA Challenged in the Columbia County school libraries because the biography of Hans

948 Koertge, Ronald
The Arizona Kid

1993 OR Challenged because it "encourages and condones" homosexuality, but retained at the Bend High School.

1994 MN Pulled from and later restored to the seventh-grade English classroom at Minnetonka Middle School West after a parent found the content inappropriate for twelve- and thirteen-year-olds.

Source: 11, Sept. 1993, pp. 158–59; Nov. 1993, p. 192; July 1994, p. 114; Sept. 1994, p. 166.

949 Koertge, Ronald
The Brimstone Journals

2007 MO Challenged, but retained at the William Chrisman High School library in Independence. A parent was concerned about profanity as well as some of the subjects discussed in the book.

Source: 11, Sept. 2007, p. 205.

950 Koertge, Ronald
Where the Kissing Never Stops

2000 PA Retained as optional reading for eighth graders at Rice Avenue Middle School in Girard. A grandmother found the book offensive and didn't want her granddaughters reading it.

Source: 11, May 2000, p. 92.

951 Koontz, Dean R.
Funhouse

1995 NC Removed from the South Brunswick Middle School Library in Boiling Spring Lakes by a patron because the book "contains material on orgies, rape, and lesbianism. There is also blasphemy and the book promotes domestic violence and alcohol abuse." The book was donated by the Lions Club in a book drive.

Source: 11, Nov. 1995, pp. 183–84; Jan. 1996, p. 11.

952 Koontz, Dean R.
Night Chills

1992 OR Challenged at the Mountain View High School in Bend because it contains "explicit" sexual incidents.

Source: 11, Jan. 1993, p. 9.

953 Koontz, Dean R.
The Voice of the Night

2000 ME Challenged as extra reading material at Westcott Junior High School in Westbrook because the novel describes people having sex and the mutilation of animals and people.
Source: 11, Mar. 2000, p. 50.

954 Koontz, Dean R.
Watchers

1996 PA Removed from the Hickory High School curriculum in Sharon by the superintendent because the language was offensive.
Source: 11, Mar. 1997, p. 50.

955 Kopay, David, and Perry D. Young
*The David Kopay Story:
An Extraordinary Self-Revelation*

1993 OR Challenged because it "encourages and condones" homosexuality, but retained at the Bend High School.
Source: 11, Sept. 1993, pp. 158–59; Nov. 1993, p. 192.

956 *The Koran*

1530 First Arabic edition published in Europe (Venice) ordered to be burned by the Pope in Rome, Italy.
1790 Ban lifted by the Spanish Index.
1926 Restricted to students of history in USSR.
1960 During the Chinese Cultural Revolution of the 1960s and 1970s, study of the *Koran* was forbidden and its reading in mosques prohibited.
1986 Under the socialist military government in Ethiopia, it was reported that copies of the *Koran* were destroyed or confiscated by the army, Koranic schools and mosques were closed or razed, Muslims were prohibited from praying and some were ordered to Christianity and burn the *Koran*.
1995 A Malay translation was banned by the government of Malaysia. The banning was part of an official policy aimed at outlawing "deviant" Islamic sects.
Source: 4, p. 5; 8, pp. 251–53.

957 Korman, Gordon
Jake Reinvented

2007 AZ Challenged in the Higley Unified School
New District in Gilbert because the novel contains themes of teen drinking, sex, and violence.
Source: 11, Jan. 2008, p. 36.

958 Kornblum, William, and Joseph Julian
Social Problems

1993 OK Reinstated at the Anadarko Public Schools after a textbook review committee recommendation. The text was challenged by a minister who complained about the book's references to homosexuality, lesbians, and child molesters.
Source: 11, Sept. 1993, p. 160.

959 Kosinski, Jerzy
Being There

1989 NE Challenged as a reading assignment for an eleventh-grade English class at Crete High School.
1989 PA Reinstated after being removed from the Mifflinburg High School because the book's main character has a homosexual experience.
1993 IA Challenged as required reading in a senior advanced English course in Davenport because of a description of masturbation.
1995 CT Challenged on the curricular reading list at Pomperaug High School in Southbury because sexually explicit passages are not appropriate high school reading.
Source: 11, May 1989, pp. 79, 93; July 1993, p. 105; July 1995, p. 98.

960 Kotzwinkle, William, and Glenn Murray
Walter the Farting Dog

2004 WI Challenged, but retained on the library shelves of the West Salem Elementary School despite the book's use of the word "fart" and "farting" twenty-four times.
Source: 11, May 2004, p. 118; July 2004, p. 138.

961 Kotzwinkle, William
Nightbook

1980 SD Challenged at the Huron Public Library because "there's not a page in [the book] fit to be read by anyone."
Source: 11, July 1980, p. 84.

962 Kovic, Ron
Born on the Fourth of July

1982 MD Placed on a closed shelf in Maryland after a parent objected to the book as un-American, finding fault also with its language and its display of sex.
Source: 7, 64.

963 **Krantz, Judith**
Mistral's Daughter

1985 PA Banned from the Stroudsburg High School library because it was "blatantly graphic, pornographic, and wholly unacceptable for a high school library."
Source: 11, May 1985, p. 79.

964 **Kroeker, Gary**
The Magi

1998 CA Banned at the Los Altos High School in Hacienda Heights because the novel was "too racy." The author is an English teacher at the school.
Source: 11, July 1998, p. 104; Mar. 1999, p. 35.

965 **Kroll, Ken**
Enabling Romance: A Guide to Love, Sex and Relationships for the Disabled

1996 NJ Removed from the Clifton Public Library and replaced with a dummy book made of styrofoam. The library's new policy restricts to adults any material containing "patently offensive graphic illustrations or photographs of sexual or excretory activities or contact as measured by contemporary community standards for minors."
Source: 11, July 1996, pp. 118–19.

966 **Kropp, Paul**
Wilted

1983 WA Banned from the Evergreen School District libraries in Vancouver because the "sexual scenes were a bit much for elementary schools."
Source: 11, Sept. 1983, p. 139.

967 **Kung, Hans**
Infallible? An Inquiry

1979 The Vatican in Rome, Italy withdrew the Swiss priest and prominent Catholic theologian's permission to teach in the name of the church and prohibited Catholic institutions from employing him.
Source: 8, pp. 249–50.

968 **Kushner, Ellen**
Mystery of the Secret Room

1992 SC Challenged at the Berkeley County school libraries because the book teaches witchcraft.
Source: 11, July 1992, p. 108.

969 **Kuskin, Karla**
The Dallas Titans Get Ready for Bed

1989 OR Challenged at the Douglas County Library in Roseburg because children are not ready for illustrations and conversation about jockstraps.
Source: 11, Jan. 1990, pp. 4–5.

970 **Lader, Lawrence**
Foolproof Birth Control

1977 MI Banned from the Brighton High School library along with all other sex education materials.
Source: 11, Sept. 1977, p. 133.

971 **Laine, James W.**
Shivaji: Hindu King in Islamic India

2003 Hindu fundamentalists, contending that he had insulted the reputation of Shivaji, the seventeenth century century Hindu king and warrior, ransacked the institute in Pune, India, where he had conducted research for his book. The book was banned in Maharashtra State in India, which brought criminal charges against Laine and his publisher and threatened to extradite him to India. A high court in Bombay stayed the criminal charges against him.
Source: 1, pp. 303–5.

972 **Laing, Frederick**
Tales from Scandinavia

1992 NE Removed to a locked closet in the superintendent's office in Banner County because the book "has to do with a lot of negative things and might not be good for someone with low self-esteem or suicide tendencies."
Source: 11, May 1992, p. 80.

973 **Landis, James David**
The Sisters Impossible

1985 OK Removed from the Sallisaw school libraries due to offensive language. Later, returned to the shelves of the Eastside Elementary School library in Sallisaw after the school board agreed to an out-of-court settlement with a group of parents who filed a suit to reverse the board's 1985 decision to ban the book. The book was originally banned because it uses "hell" seven times and the words "fart" and "bullshit" once each in its 169 pages.

1988 AK Challenged in the Fairbanks school libraries because of "the language in the book and to a scene in which aspiring young ballerinas danced naked in a dressing room before class."

1997 GA Challenged because of objectionable language, but retained at the J. G. Dyer Elementary School library in Gwinnett County.

Source: 11, July 1985, p. 112; Mar. 1986, pp. 60, 65–66; July 1986, p. 136; Mar. 1988, p. 71; July 1997, p. 109; Sept. 1997, p. 148.

974 Langley, Andrew
100 Greatest Tyrants

2006 Challenged at the Mount Isa, Queensland, Australia, high school by a legislator who described the book as offensive and inappropriate for history studies in any Australian school. The school principal refused to remove the book from the library, describing it as a useful resource for generating debate and critical-thinking skills among students.

Source: 11, Jan. 2007, pp. 33–34.

975 Langton, Jane
The Fragile Flag

1986 CO Challenged at the Jefferson County school library because the book portrays the U.S. government as "shallow" and "manipulative," and "lacking in intelligence and responsibility."

Source: 11, Jan. 1987, p. 29; Mar. 1987, p. 49.

976 LaPlace, John
Health

1981 NY Banned from senior high school classrooms in the Diocese of Buffalo.

1984 NJ Challenged at the Randolph High School by a group of parents and clergy who say "the textbook is too liberal and should be replaced or supplemented by a more traditional book."

Source: 11, Jan. 1981, p. 10; July 1984, p. 106.

977 Larrick, Nancy, and Eve Merriam
Male and Female under 18

1977 MA Banned by the Chelsea School Board from the high school library because of objections to one poem by a teenage girl. The banning was reversed by a U.S. District Court ruling in *Right to Read Defense Committee v. School Committee of the City of Chelsea*, 454 F. Supp. 703 (D. Mass. 1978).

Source: 4, p. 104; 12, pp. 12–14, 148–53, 229, 239.

978 Larson, Rodger
What I Know Now

2004 TX Challenged at the Montgomery County Memorial Library System along with fifteen other young adult books with gay-positive themes. The objections were posted at the Library Patrons of Texas Web site. The language describing the books is similar to that posted at the Web site of the Fairfax County, Virginia-based Parents Against Bad Books in Schools, to which Library Patrons of Texas links.

Source: 11, Nov. 2004, pp. 231–32.

979 Laurence, Margaret
Christmas Birthday Story

1982 ME Challenged at the York school system.

Source: 11, July 1982, p. 124.

980 Laurence, Margaret
A Jest of God

1984 Challenged at the Peterborough, Ontario, Canada County schools after a resolution from the nearby Burleigh-Anstruther municipal council asked that the books be reviewed for their moral content.

Source: 11, Mar. 1985, p. 45.

981 Laurence, Margaret
The Stone Angel

1984 Challenged at the Peterborough, Ontario, Canada County schools after a resolution from the nearby Burleigh-Anstruther municipal council asked that the books be reviewed for their moral content.

Source: 11, Mar. 1985, p. 45.

982 Lawrence, D. H.
Collected Paintings

1929 Banned by U.S. Customs.

Source: 10, p. 142; 15, Vol. III, p. 414.

983 Lawrence, D. H.
Lady Chatterley's Lover

1929 Banned by U.S. Customs.
1932 Banned in Ireland.
1932 Banned in Poland.
1959 Banned in Australia.
1959 Banned in Japan.
1959 Banned in India.
1960 Banned in Canada until 1962.

1987 Dissemination of Lawrence's novel has been stopped in China because the book "will corrupt the minds of young people and is also against the Chinese tradition."
Source: 2, p. 137; 4, pp. 69–70; 6, pp. 1,382–86; 8, pp. 354–57; 11, July 1987, pp. 135–36; 15, Vol. III, pp. 407, 414.

984 Lawrence, D. H.
Paintings of D. H. Lawrence

1929 Barred by U.S. Customs.
Source: 4, p. 69.

985 Lawrence, D. H.
Pansies

1928 Seized by postal authorities in England and was substantially altered prior to its republication in 1929.
Source: 3, p. 170; 13, pp. 184–85.

986 Lawrence, D. H.
The Rainbow

1915 Ordered destroyed by the British magistrate's court.
Source: 2, p. 100; 4, p. 69; 13, pp. 198–99.

987 Lawrence, D. H.
Sons and Lovers

1961 OK An Oklahoma City group called Mothers United for Decency hired a trailer, dubbed it "smutmobile," and displayed books deemed objectionable, including Lawrence's novel.
Source: 4, p. 119.

988 Lawrence, D. H.
Women in Love

1922 NY Seized by John Summers of the New York Society for the Suppression of Vice and declared obscene.
Source: 8, p. 394; 11, p. 142; 15, Vol. III, p. 415.

989 Lawrence, Jerome, and Robert E. Lee
Inherit the Wind

1997 OH Challenged, but retained at the Lakewood High School. The book was challenged by parents who objected to what they called the play's allegedly anti-religious nature.
Source: 11, May 1997, p. 79.

990 Lawrence, Margaret
The Diviners

1984 Challenged at the Peterborough, Ontario, Canada County schools after a resolution from the nearby Burleigh-Anstruther municipal council asked that the books be reviewed for their moral content.

1997 NJ Removed from the summer reading list for the Clark School District's seventh graders because of detailed descriptions of sexual intercourse. A group called Parents Against Pornographic Adult Literature was formed to ensure reading lists are correctly oriented and reviewed for Clark students.
Source: 11, Mar. 1985, p. 45; Nov. 1997, p. 169.

991 Lawson, Robert
They Were Strong and Good

1991 OR Challenged because the novel "glorifies slavery and racism," but retained at the Multnomah County Library.
Source: 11, Jan. 1992, p. 6.

992 Leach, Maria
Whistle in the Graveyard: Folktales to Chill Your Bones

1992 AZ Challenged at the Neely Elementary School in Gilbert because the book shows the dark side of religion through the occult, the devil, and satanism.
Source: 11, May 1992, p. 78; July 1992, p. 124.

993 Lebert, Benjamin
Crazy

2003 TX Removed from the Canyon Vista Middle School in Round Rock by the principal who decided a parent was correct in being concerned about the book's availability. The parent called the book "vulgar; it talked about parts of the body." There was free use of the 'F-word' and several 'Cwords.' The book was taken off the shelf at the district's other junior high school library.
Source: 11, Nov. 2003, p. 229.

994 Lederer, William J., and Eugene Burdick
The Ugly American

1953 Senator Joe McCarthy led an investigation of the Overseas Library Program. In response to the investigation, "no material by any controversial persons, Communists, fellow travelers, etc. will be used' by the U.S. overseas libraries. The novel was temporarily censored in 1958 by George A. Allen, director of the U.S. Information Agency, the federal agency responsible for U.S. overseas libraries, because the book "would not be in the interest of the United States." In December 1958, Allen changed his mind. Senator J. W. Fullbright criticized the novel from the Senate floor in 1959. He was upset by the portrayal of American overseas as "boobs or worse," while Russian diplomats were portrayed as "talented, dedicated servants of communism." In 1963 survey by the Wisconsin English Department chairpersons and school administrators, a Wisconsin teacher and a group of parents objected to the novel because of its critical pictures of Americans abroad. Other have been critical of the novel based on its "filthy language and reference to sex" and its profane and vile language.

Source: 8, pp. 180–81.

---

995 Lee, Harper
To Kill a Mockingbird

1977 MN Challenged in Eden Valley and temporarily banned due to words "damn" and "whore lady" used in the novel.

1980 NY Challenged in the Vernon-Verona-Sherill School District as a "filthy, trashy novel."

1981 IN Challenged at the Warren Township schools because the book does "psychological damage to the positive integration process " and "represents institutionalized racism under the guise of 'good literature.'" After unsuccessfully banning Lee's novel, three black parents resigned from the township human relations advisory council.

1984 IL Challenged in the Waukegan School District because the novel uses the word "nigger."

1985 AZ Retained on a supplemental eighth-grade reading list in the Casa Grande Elementary School District, despite the protests by black parents and the National Association for the Advancement of Colored People who charged the book was unfit for junior high use.

1985 MO Challenged in the Kansas City junior high schools.

1985 MO Challenged at the Park Hill Junior High School because the novel "contains profanity and racial slurs."

1995 CA Challenged at the Santa Cruz Schools because of its racial themes.

1995 LA Removed from the Southwood High School Library in Caddo Parish because the book's language and content were objectionable.

1996 MS Challenged at the Moss Point School District because the novel contains a racial epithet.

1996 TX Banned from the Lindale Advanced Placement English reading list because the book "conflicted with the values of the community."

2001 GA Challenged by a Glynn County School Board member because of profanity. The novel was retained.

2001 OK Returned to the freshmen reading list at Muskogee High School despite complaints over the years from black students and parents about racial slurs in the text.

2004 IL Challenged, but retained in the Normal Community High School sophomore literature class despite concerns the novel is degrading to African Americans.

2004 NC Challenged at the Stanford Middle School in Durham because the 1961 Pulitzer Prize-winning novel uses the word "nigger."

2006 TN Challenged at the Brentwood Middle School because the book contains "profanity" and "contains adult themes such as sexual intercourse, rape, and incest." The complainants also contend that the book's use of racial slurs promotes "racial hatred, racial division, racial separation, and promotes white supremacy."

2007 NJ New — Retained in the English curriculum by the Cherry Hill Board of Education. A resident had objected to the novel's depiction of how blacks are treated by members of a racist white community in an Alabama town during the Depression. The resident feared the book would upset black children reading it.

2009 New — Removed from the St. Edmund Campion Secondary School classrooms in Brampton, Ontario, Canada because a parent objected to language used in the novel, including the word "nigger."

Source: 8, p. 483; 11, Mar. 1978, p. 31; May 1980, p. 62; Mar. 1982, p. 47; July 1984, p. 105; May 1985, p. 80; July 1985, p. 134; Mar. 1986, pp. 57–58; May 1995, p. 68; Nov. 1995, p. 183; Nov. 1996, pp. 196–97, 199; Nov. 2001, pp. 277–78; Jan. 2002, p. 50; Jan. 2004, p. 11; May 2004, pp. 98–99; Mar. 2006, p. 74; Mar. 2008, p. 80; May 2008, pp. 117–18; Nov. 2009, pp. 203–4.

---

996 Lee, Joanna
I Want to Keep My Baby

1994 NC Removed from the Morehead High School library in Rockingham County because of "antireligious sentiments—the girl's comment that her boyfriend was 'her God'—and sexual situations." After a three-hour public debate, the Rockingham County School Board later reversed its previous ban against the book.

Source: 11, Sept. 1994, p. 148; Nov. 1994, p. 201.

997 Legman, Gershon, ed.
***The Limerick: 1,700 Examples
with Notes, Variants and Index***

1991 IL Challenged at the Oak Lawn Public Library
because the book contains bawdy limericks
with explicit sexual references.
Source: 11, Nov. 1991, p. 209; Jan. 1992, p. 26.

998 LeGuin, Ursula K.
A Fisherman of the Inland Sea

2006 TX Removed from the West Brazoria Junior High
School library because of inappropriate
language. Books on "sensitive topics such as
death, suicide, physical or sexual abuse, and
teenage dating relationships" were moved to
a restricted "young-adult" section from which
students can borrow only with written
parental permission.
Source: 11, Nov. 2006, pp. 289–90.

999 LeGuin, Ursula K.
Lathe of Heaven

1984 WA Challenged on a Washougal High School
reading list because it contained "profuse
profanity."
Source: 11, Sept. 1984, p. 157.

1000 Lehrman, Robert
Juggling

1990 MN Challenged at Woodbury Library. The book is
about the life and sexual encounters of a
teenage soccer player.
Source: 11, July 1990, p. 145.

1001 L'Engle, Madeleine C.
Many Waters

1991 OH Challenged at the Hubbard Library because
the book alters the story of Noah's Ark,
making it secular and confusing to children.
Source: 11, Sept. 1991, p. 153.

1002 L'Engle, Madeleine C.
A Wrinkle in Time

1985 FL Challenged, but retained on the media center
shelves of the Polk City Elementary School. A
student's parent filed the complaint,
contending the story promoted witchcraft,
crystal balls, and demons.

1990 AL Challenged in the Anniston schools because
the book sends a mixed signal to children
about good and evil. The complainant also
objected to listing the name of Jesus Christ
together with the names of great artists,
philosophers, scientists, and religious
leaders when referring to defenders of Earth
against evil.

1996 NC Challenged, but retained by the Catawba
County School Board in Newton. A parent
requested the book be pulled from the school
libraries because it allegedly undermines
religious beliefs.
Source: 11, July 1985, p. 133; Mar. 1991, p. 62; May 1996,
pp. 97–98.

1003 Lenin, Vladimir I.
The State and Revolution

1927 Seized as subversive in Hungary.

1927 MA Seized as obscene in Boston.

1933 Burned In Munich, Germany by the
Nazi government.

1940 OK In Oklahoma City a vigilante group raided a
bookstore owned by Robert Wood, who was
also the state secretary of the Communist
Party. They seized copies of the book along
with other Communist literature, various
works of fictions and books on economics,
and copies of the U.S. Constitution and the
Declaration of Independence. Mr. and Mrs.
Wood, along with several other people who
happened to be in the store, were arrested on
charges of "criminal syndicalism" and
held incommunicado. Six people including
the Woods were sentenced to ten years in
prison. A court of appeals overturned the
convictions in 1943.

1954 RI Seized by Providence postal authorities
attempting to withhold from delivery to
Brown University 75 copies of this
"subversive" title.

1989 Banned in Grenada along with eighty-five
other titles.
Source: 4, p. 60; 7, pp. 461–63.

1004 Letts, Billie
Where the Heart Is

2001 PA Challenged in the Tamaqua Area School
District because the book "might not be
appropriate for younger schoolmates." The
school board is considering the establishment
of a restricted materials section in the district's
middle-school library for books deemed
objectionable. Students would need parental
permission to access any title placed there.

2002 WY Retained in the Natrona County School
District after being challenged for graphic
violence, obscene language, and drug use.
Source: 11, Mar. 2001, p. 54; July 2001, p. 145; Sept. 2002,
p. 223.

1005 Levenkron, Steven
The Best Little Girl in the World

2000 PA Retained as optional reading for eighth graders at Rice Avenue Middle School in Girard. A grandmother found the book offensive and didn't want her granddaughters reading it.
Source: 11, May 2000, p. 92.

1006 Levin, Ira
Rosemary's Baby

1976 CO Banned from use in Aurora High School English classes on the grounds of "immorality."
1977 MA Removed from the required reading list in Westport.
Source: 11, Jan. 1977, p. 8; May 1977, p. 79.

1007 Levin, Ira
Stepford Wives

1979 IN Prohibited for use in the Warsaw schools because of its "questionable nature" and because it might offend someone in the community.
Source: 11, Mar. 1980, p. 40.

1008 Levine, Ellen
I Hate English

1994 NY Challenged by a school board member in the Queens school libraries because, "The book says what a burden it is they have to learn English. They should just learn English and don't complain about it." The rest of the school board voted to retain the book.
Source: 11, July 1994, pp. 110–11; Sept. 1994, p. 166.

1009 Levitt, Steven D., and Stephen J. Dubner
Freakonomics: A Rogue Economist Explores the Hidden Side of Everything

2006 IL Retained on the Northwest Suburban High School District 214 reading list in Arlington Heights, along with eight other challenged titles. A board member, elected amid promises to bring her Christian beliefs into all board decision-making, raised the controversy based on excerpts from the books she'd found on the Internet.
Source: 11, July 2006, pp. 210–11.

1010 Levoy, Myron
Alan and Naomi

1981 GA Challenged in Gwinnett County because of objections to the book's language ("hell" and "damn") and mature subject matter.
1991 MD Challenged, but retained in the Carroll County schools. Two school board members were concerned about the "sad ending" and "poor" portrayal of Jews.
Source: 11, Nov. 1981, p. 168; Mar. 1992, p. 64.

1011 Levy, Edward
Came a Spider

1986 WA Removed and later returned to the shelves of the Freeman High School library in Spokane because it contained a two-page description of teenagers engaged in sexual intercourse.
Source: 11, May 1986, pp. 80–81.

1012 Lewin, Esther
Random House Thesaurus of Slang

1992 OR Placed on a limited access shelf at the Floyd Light Middle School library in Portland.
Source: 11, May 1992, p. 81.

1013 Lewis, C. S.
The Lion, the Witch and the Wardrobe

1990 MD Challenged in the Howard County school system because it depicts "graphic violence, mysticism, and gore."
Source: 11, Jan. 1991, p. 28.

1014 Lewis, Richard, comp.
There Are Two Lives: Poems by Children of Japan

1999 PA Despite being on the library's open shelves for twenty-five years, this book is now restricted to students with parental permission at the Annville-Cleona Elementary School library because an anonymous parent "objected to the entire book."
Source: 11, May 1999, pp. 66–67.

1015 Lewis, Sinclair
Cass Timberlane

1953 Banned in Ireland.
1954 Banned in East Berlin, Germany.
Source: 4, p. 70.

1016   Lewis, Sinclair
Elmer Gantry

1927   Banned in Glasgow, Scotland.
1927   MA Banned in Boston.
1927 NJ   Banned in Camden.
1931   U.S. Post Office banned any catalog listing of this title.
1931   Banned in Ireland.
> Source: 2, p. 133; 4, pp. 70–71; 14, pp. 126–27; 15, Vol. III, pp. 404–5.

1017   Lewis, Sinclair
It Can't Happen Here

1937   Banned in Germany. In 1954, all of Sinclair Lewis's books were banned in East Berlin.
> Source: 7, pp. 266–67.

1018   Lewis, Sinclair
Kingsblood Royal

1947 NY   In New York City, the Society for the Suppression of Vice sought to prevent sales of the book after complaints arose about the suggested sexual content of the novel. The society's efforts to bring charges against the book were fruitless, and only a few booksellers agreed to remove the novel from their stock.
1953   Banned in Ireland for the use of the term nigger and the "suggestive sexuality."
1953 IL   Removed from Illinois libraries on a mother's complaint that her daughter had borrowed a book that was offensive.
> Source: 4, p. 71; 14, pp. 203–204.

1019   Leyland, Winston, ed.
My Deep Dark Pain Is Love: A Collection of Latin American Gay Fiction

1984   Seized and shredded by the British Customs Office.
> Source: 11, Jan. 1985, p. 16.

1020   Leyland, Winston, ed.
Now the Volcano: An Anthology of Latin American Gay Literature

1984   Seized and shredded by the British Customs Office.
> Source: 11, Jan. 1985, p. 16.

1021   Li, Hongzhi
Zhuan Falun: The Complete Teachings of Falun Gong

1996   The Chinese government's Press and Publications Administration issued a notice banning five Falun Gong publications for propagating ignorance and superstition. On July 22, 1999, the government declared that Falun Gong, as an "evil cult" that advocated superstition and jeopardized social stability, was now an illegal organization. It was prohibited "to distribute books, video/audio tapes or any other materials that propagate Falun Dafa (Falun Gong)" and thousands of people were sent to labor camps, psychiatric wards, or prisons.
> Source: 8, pp. 308–10.

1022   Lieberman, Gail
Sex and Birth Control: A Guide for the Young

1993 TN   Challenged at the Cleveland Public Library along with seventeen other books, most of which are on sex education, AIDS awareness, and some titles on the supernatural.
> Source: 11, Sept. 1993, p. 146.

1023   Lightner, A. M.
Gods or Demons?

1988 OR   Challenged at the Canby Junior High School library because the book "promotes a secular humanistic belief in evolution and portrays the 'Bible as myth.'"
> Source: 11, May 1989, p. 78.

1024   Lindgren, Astrid
The Children on Troublemaker Street

1992 WY   Challenged at the Sweetwater County Library in Green River because of concerns about how it depicts the "almost swearing of a four-year-old-child."
> Source: 11, July 1992, p. 126.

1025   Lindgren, Astrid
The Runaway Sleigh Ride

1995 IN   Challenged in the Kokomo-Howard County Public Library because it makes "light of a drinking situation." The book is by the author of the Pippi Longstocking series.

1999 CT Removed, but later returned to the Enfield elementary school libraries despite a parent's objection to passages in which characters sing songs praising drinking.
Source: 11, Mar. 1996, p. 46; May 1999, pp. 65–66; July 1999, p. 104.

1026 Lingeman, Richard R.
Drugs from A to Z: A Dictionary

1986 IA Challenged, but retained in the Des Moines school libraries because the book "not only gives definitions of drugs but also tells how and what to use to get a cheap high—which could be lethal."
Source: 11, July 1986, p. 135.

1027 Lion, Elizabeth M.
Human Sexuality in Nursing Process

1982 President of the National Black Nurses Association called on nursing schools to boycott this text because it contains material that is "offensive and insensitive" to blacks.
Source: 11, Jan. 1983, p. 23.

1028 Lionni, Leo
In the Rabbit's Garden

1986 OR Challenged at the Naas Elementary School library in Boring because the story about two rabbits living in a lush garden paradise made a mockery of the Bible's tale of Adam and Eve. Unlike the story of Adam and Eve, Lionni rewards his bunnies for eating the forbidden fruit by allowing them to live happily ever after.
Source: 11, Mar. 1987, p. 66.

1029 Lipke, Jean C.
Conception and Contraception

1977 MI The Brighton School Board voted to remove all sex education books from the high school library.
Source: 11, Sept. 1977, p. 133.

1030 Lippman, Laura
The Crack Cocaine Diet: A Short Story from Hardly Knew Her

2009 NH
New Pulled from a Litchfield Campbell High School elective course classroom after parents voiced their concerns about a short-stories unit called "Love/Gender/Family Unit" that dealt with subject matters including abortion, cannibalism, homosexuality, and drug use. The parents said the stories promoted bad behavior and a "political agenda" and they shouldn't be incorporated into classroom teachings. The Campbell High School English curriculum said the short story was not intended to glorify bad behavior, rather, it was chosen for its tone and point of view and to show the often devastating consequences of drug use. The English curriculum adviser eventually resigned.
Source: 11, Sept. 2009, p. 154.

1031 Lipsyte, Robert
The Contender

1989 TN Challenged as a summer youth program reading assignment in Chattanooga because "it sounds like pretty explicit stuff."
Source: 11, Nov. 1989, p. 162.

1032 Lipsyte, Robert
One Fat Summer

1997 NY Removed from the required reading list at the Jonas E. Salk Middle School in Levittown because it was "sexually explicit and full of violence." The book was a *New York Times* Outstanding Children's Book of 1977.

1997 SC Challenged at the Greenville middle school libraries because the book includes a passage on masturbation.

1999 FL Pulled from Rock Crusher Elementary School in Crystal River after a parent complained that it contains derogatory terms for African-Americans, Jews, and Italians and describes a male character masturbating.

2004 CT Pulled from the Ansonia Public Library local schools' display following a parental complaint about a paragraph describing the masturbation fantasy of a teenage boy.
Source: 11, Sept. 1997, pp. 126–28; Jan. 2000, p. 11; Nov. 2004, p. 229.

1033 Llywelyn, Morgan
Druids

2001 VA Removed from middle school libraries in Fairfax County due to its depictions of oral sex and rape.
Source: 11, Sept. 2000, pp. 145–46; May 2001, p. 96.

1034 Locke, John
An Essay Concerning Human Understanding

1700 Placed on the *Index Librorum Prohibitorum* (List of Prohibited Books) in Rome, Italy.

1701 Prohibited reading at Oxford in London, England. A Latin version was permitted only on the proviso that "no tutors were to read with their students this essential investigation into the basis of knowledge."

Source: 1, pp. 96–97; 3, p. 174; 4, p. 24.

1035 Locker, Sari
Sari Says: The Real Dirt on Everything from Sex to School

2002 IA Removed from the shelves at the James Kennedy Public Library in Dyersville because it deals with sexual issues.

Source: 11, Sept. 2002, p. 196; Nov. 2002, pp. 255–56.

1036 Lockhart, E.
The Boy Book: A Study of Habits and Behaviors, Plus Techniques for Taming Them

2009 TX New — Challenged in the Keller Independent School District because some say it is "too adult for young eyes."

Source: 11, May 2009, pp. 79–80.

1037 Lockridge, Ross, Jr.
Raintree Country

1953 NY Attacked in New York City as "1066 pages of rank obscenity, blasphemy and sacrilege . . . inimical to faith and morals [and] within the prohibition of the Catholic Index."

Source: 15, Vol. IV, p. 709.

1038 Loewen, James W., and Charles Sallis, eds.
Mississippi: Conflict and Change

1980 MS Rejected from use in the Mississippi public schools because the textbook stressed black history too much. A U.S. District Court ruled that the criteria used for rejecting this text were not justifiable in Loewen v. Turnipsend, 488 F. Supp. 1138 (N. D. Miss. 1980).

Source: 11, July 1980, p. 86; 12, pp. 167–71, 239.

1039 Lofting, Hugh John
Doctor Dolittle

1988 — Expurgated in the 1960s by J. B. Lippincott Company in the effort to make the books conform to the changing sensibilities of a world that was beginning "to coalesce into one international, multiracial society." The 1988 version of the Dr. Dolittle books, published by Dell Publishing, was the result of radical censoring by two editors at Dell and by Christopher Lofting, the author's son.

Source: 14, pp. 111–12.

1040 Logan, Daniel
America Bewitched: The Rise of Black Magic and Spiritism

1986 CA Challenged by the "God Squad," a group of three students and their parents, at the El Camino High School in Oceanside because the book "glorified the devil and the occult."

Source: 11, Sept. 1986, p. 151; Nov. 1986, p. 224; Jan. 1987, p. 9.

1041 Logan, Jake
Slocum series

2001 AR Challenged, but retained at the Springdale Public Library along with all other "western" novels because the writings include "pornographic, sexual encounters."

Source: 11, Nov. 2001, p. 277.

1042 London, Jack
The Call of the Wild

1929 — Banned in Italy.
1929 — Banned in Yugoslavia.
1933 — Burned in Nazi bonfires in Germany.

Source: 4, p. 63.

1043 Longstreet, Stephen, ed.
The Drawings of Renoir

1994 AZ Retained at Maldonado Elementary School in Tucson after being challenged by parents who objected to nudity and "pornographic," "perverted," and "morbid" themes.

Source: 11, July 1994, p. 112.

1044 Lopez, Tiffany Ana
Growing Up Chicana/o: An Anthology

2002 VA Challenged, along with seventeen other titles in the Fairfax County elementary and secondary libraries, by a group called Parents Against Bad Books in Schools. The group contends the books "contain profanity and descriptions of drug abuse, sexually explicit conduct, and torture."

Source: 11, Jan. 2003, p. 10.

1045 Louys, Pierre
Aphrodite

1929 — Banned by U.S. Customs Department as lascivious, corrupting, and obscene. In 1930 a New York book dealer, E. B. Marks, was fined $250 for possessing a copy of Aphrodite in contravention of the state laws on obscene publications. In 1935, an attempt was made to import the publication into America. This was banned, although the authorities overlooked a 49-cent edition, openly advertised in the *New York Times Book Review* and apparently, despite postal regulations, available through the mail.

Source: 3, p. 176; 4, p. 60.

1046 Louys, Pierre
The Songs of Bilitis

1929   Banned by U.S. Customs Department as lascivious, corrupting, and obscene.

Source: 4, p. 60.

1047 Louys, Pierre
The Twilight of the Nymphs

1929   Banned by U.S. Customs Department as lascivious, corrupting, and obscene.

Source: 4, p. 60.

1048 Lowen, Paul
Butterfly

1988 OR Challenged at the Tigard Public Library because of explicit sex and extreme physical and psychological cruelty.

Source: 11, Jan. 1990, pp. 4–5.

1049 Lowry, Lois
Anastasia Again!

2005 FL Removed from the Lake Wales elementary school library because of a complaint that the book's references to beer, *Playboy* magazine, and Anastasia making light of wanting to kill herself were inappropriate for children.

Source: 11, May 2005, p. 107.

1050 Lowry, Lois
Anastasia at Your Service

1984 WY Challenged at the Casper school libraries.

Source: 11, Mar. 1985, p. 42.

1051 Lowry, Lois
Anastasia Krupnik

1986 CA Removed by the school's principal, and later returned to the Roosevelt Elementary School library in Tulare with the word "shit" whited out.

1991 KS Challenged, but retained in the Wichita public schools because it was offensive.

1992 WI Removed from, but later returned to the Stevens Point Area School elementary recommended reading list due to the book's

profanity and occasional references to underage drinking.

1998 SC Removed from the Cayce-West Columbia School District's Congaree Elementary School library because of Lowry's use of a vulgarity for human waste, as well as the use of a slang term for sex.

Source: 11, Mar. 1987, p. 49; Jan. 1992, p. 26; Mar. 1993, p. 45; May 1993, p. 87; Mar. 1999, p. 36.

1052 Lowry, Lois
Autumn Street

1984 WY Challenged at the Casper school libraries.

Source: 11, Mar. 1985, p. 42.

1053 Lowry, Lois
Find a Stranger, Say Good-bye

1984 WY Challenged at the Casper school libraries.

Source: 11, Mar. 1985, p. 42.

1054 Lowry, Lois
The Giver

1994 CA Temporarily banned from classes by the Bonita Unified School District in La Verne and San Dimas after four parents complained that violent and sexual passages were inappropriate for children.

1995 MT Restricted to students with parental permission at the Columbia Falls school system because of the book's treatment of themes of infanticide and euthanasia.

1996 OH Challenged at the Lakota High School in Cincinnati.

1999 FL Challenged, but retained at a Lake Butler public middle school. A parent complained because the issues of infanticide and sexual awakening are discussed in the book.

1999 OH Challenged at the Troy Intermediate School in Avon Lake as an "optional" reading choice for sixth-grade students. A pastor objected to the books "mature themes"—suicide, sexuality, and euthanasia.

2003 MO Challenged as a suggested reading for eighth-grade students in Blue Springs. Parents called the book "lewd" and "twisted" and pleaded for it to be tossed out of the district. The book was reviewed by two committees and recommended for retention, but the controversy continues in 2005.

2006 KS Challenged, but retained at the Seaman Unified School District 345 elementary school library.

2007 CA Appalled by descriptions of adolescent
New   pill-popping, suicide, and lethal injections

given to babies and the elderly, two parents demanded that the Mt. Diablo School District, headquartered in Concord eliminate the controversial but award-winning book from the school reading lists and libraries.

Source: 11, Mar. 1995, p. 42; Jan. 1996, p. 11; Nov. 1996, p. 198; May 1999, p. 70; Jan. 2000, p. 13; Mar. 2005, pp. 57–58; May 2006, p. 153; Jan. 2008, p. 8.

1055 Lowry, Lois
The One Hundredth Thing about Caroline

1984 WY Challenged at the Casper school libraries.

Source: 11, Mar. 1985, p. 42.

1056 Lowry, Lois
A Summer to Die

1984 WY Challenged at the Casper school libraries.

Source: 11, Mar. 1985, p. 42.

1057 Lowry, Lois
Taking Care of Terrific

1984 WY Challenged at the Casper school libraries.

Source: 11, Mar. 1985, p. 42.

1058 Ludlum, Robert
The Matarese Circle

1983 NE Restricted at the Pierce High School to students with parental consent because the book contains unnecessarily rough language and sexual descriptions.

Source: 11, May 1983, p. 72.

1059 Ludwig, Coy L.
Maxfield Parrish

1994 AZ Retained at Maldonado Elementary School in Tucson after being challenged by parents who objected to nudity and "pornographic," "perverted," and "morbid" themes.

Source: 11, July 1994, p. 112.

1060 Lund, Doris
Eric

1994 NC Pulled from Lexington Middle School classrooms because of the intense way in which it addresses death.

Source: 11, July 1994, p. 115.

1061 Luther, Martin
Address to the German Nobility

1520 Luther's books were burned in Liege in October 1520.

1520 Luther's books were burned in Louvain in October 1520.

1520 Luther's books were burned in Cologne in late 1520.

1520 Luther's books were burned in Mainz in late 1520.

1521 Luther was excommunicated by Pope Leo X in Rome, Italy in 1521. Luther's works remained on the Vatican's *Index Librorum Prohibitorum* (Index of Prohibited Books) until 1930. They were still prohibited, however, according to the church's canon law barring Catholics under penalty of mortal sin from reading books "which propound or defend heresy or schism."

1521 Charles V issued an edict in Germany against Luther and ordered his books seized. At the same time he sent him a safe conduct to appear before the Diet of Worms. The Diet issued an edict against him, and threatened to exterminate his followers.

1522 Following the Diet of Worms Luther's works and those of his disciples were destroyed and banned in England.

1522 Following the Diet of Worms Luther's works and those of his disciples were destroyed and banned in France.

1522 Following the Diet of Worms Luther's works and those of his disciples were destroyed and banned in the Netherlands.

1522 Following the Diet of Worms Luther's works and those of his disciples were destroyed and banned in Spain.

Source: 4, pp. 11–12; 8, pp. 267–69.

1062 Luther, Martin
Works

1520 Luther's books were burned in Liege, Belgium in October 1520.

1520 Luther's books were burned in Louvain, Belgium in October 1520.

1520 Luther's books were burned in Cologne, Germany in late 1520.

1520 Luther's books were burned in Mainz, Germany in late 1520.

1521 Luther was excommunicated by Pope Leo X in Rome, Italy in 1521. Luther's works remained on the Vatican's *Index Librorum Prohibitorum* (Index of Prohibited Books) until 1930. They were still prohibited, however, according to the church's canon law barring Catholics under penalty of mortal sin from reading books "which propound or defend heresy or schism."

1521   Charles V issued an edict in Germany against Luther and ordered his books seized. At the same time he sent him a safe conduct to appear before the Diet of Worms. The Diet issued an edict against him, and threatened to exterminate his followers.

1522   Following the Diet of Worms Luther's works and those of his disciples were destroyed and banned in England.

1522   Following the Diet of Worms Luther's works and those of his disciples were destroyed and banned in France.

1522   Following the Diet of Worms Luther's works and those of his disciples were destroyed and banned in Spain.

1522   Following the Diet of Worms Luther's works and those of his disciples were destroyed and banned in the Netherlands.

Source: 4, pp. 11–12; 8, pp. 267–69.

1063   **Lynch, Chris**
Extreme Elvin

2003 GA   Removed from the Crawford County Middle School library because the book deals with complex issues teenagers confront.

Source: 11, Jan. 2004, p. 9.

1064   **Lynch, Chris**
The Iceman

1995 TX   Removed from the Carroll Middle School Library in Southlake because of "profanity" and it "was not highly recommended for its literary value."

1996 KS   Challenged at the Haysville Middle School library when a parent counted thirty-six places where profanity was used in the book.

1998 CT   Challenged on the summer reading list at the Windsor Locks Middle School because of the book's language and the main character's violent behavior. The superintendent proposed a plan to segregate "controversial" materials in the library and require parental permission to read them.

1999 WI   Removed from the Medford Middle School library because of foul language and the opinion that it was not "inspiring."

Source: 11, May 1995, p. 67; Mar. 1997, p. 49; Jan. 1999, p. 7; May 1999, p. 69.

1065   **Maas, Peter**
Serpico

1982 MN   Challenged in the Zimmerman School District

high school libraries. Maas's book was available to students under eighteen only with parental permission.

Source: 11, Sept. 1982, p. 156.

1066   **Maas, Peter**
The Valachi Papers

1966   U.S. Department of Justice sued author to restrain the book's publication.

Source: 4, p. 99.

1067   **Machiavelli, Niccolo**
Discourses

1555   Placed in the *Index Librorum Prohibitorum* (List of Prohibited Books) in Rome, Italy.

Source: 4, p. 9.

1068   **Machiavelli, Niccolo**
The Prince

1555   Placed in the *Index Librorum Prohibitorum* (List of Prohibited Books) in Rome, Italy.

Source: 4, pp. 9–10; 10, pp. 156–57.

1069   **Mackler, Carolyn**
The Earth, My Butt, and Other Big Round Things

2006 MD   Banned by the Carroll County Superintendent in Westminster, but after protests from students, librarians, national organizations, and the publisher, the book was returned to the high school libraries, but not middle schools. The superintendent objected to the book's use of profanity and its sexual references. The book was named the 2004 Michael L. Printz Honor Book, the American Library Association Best Book for Young Adults, and the International Reading Association's 2005 Young Adults' Choice, among other accolades.

Source: 11, Mar. 2006, pp. 70–71.

1070   **Mackler, Carolyn**
Love and Other Four Letter Words

2001 IL   Removed from the Lincoln Junior High School in Naperville because in addition to swear words and discussions about "getting wasted," the book contains graphic passages about masturbation and sexual intercourse.

Source: 11, Jan. 2002, pp. 15–16.

1071   Mackler, Carolyn
Vegan Virgin Valentine

2007 FL   Challenged in the Mandarin High School library in Jacksonville because of inappropriate language.

Source: 11, May 2007, p. 91.

1072   Madaras, Lynda, and Dane Saavedra
What's Happening to My Body? Book for Boys: A Growing-up Guide for Parents & Sons

1986 IL   Challenged at the Mt. Morris School District seventh grade class because it is written from a "permissive point of view."

1993 AK   Challenged in the Kenai Peninsula Borough schools in Homer because of objections to the way masturbation and homosexuality were presented and to slang words used to describe sexual methods as well as the male anatomy.

1993 TN   Challenged, but retained at the Cleveland Public Library along with seventeen other books, most of which are on sex education, AIDS awareness, and some titles on the supernatural.

1994 NV   Challenged, but retained at the Washoe County Library System in Reno because "nobody in their right mind would give a book like that to children on their own, except the library."

1994 WI   Missing from the Northside Intermediate School library in Milton after a parent complained "I don't think my ten-year-old son, or anyone's, needs to know that stuff."

1997 FL   Removed from the media center at Denn John Junior Middle School in Kissimmee because it describes inappropriate subjects like group masturbation. The book is accessible to parents only through the guidance office.

Source: 11, Mar. 1987, p. 53; July 1987, pp. 149–50; Sept. 1993, p. 146; Jan. 1994, p. 33; July 1994, pp. 111–12; Sept. 1994, p. 147; Nov. 1994, pp. 200–201; Nov. 1997, p. 167.

1073   Madaras, Lynda, and Area Madaras
What's Happening to My Body? Book for Girls: A Growing-up Guide for Parents & Daughters

1986 IL   Challenged at the Mt. Morris School District seventh grade class because it is written from a "permissive point of view."

1993 TN   Challenged, but retained at the Cleveland Public Library along with seventeen other books, most of which are on sex education, AIDS awareness, and some titles on the supernatural.

1997 FL   Removed from the media center at the Denn Junior Middle School in Kissimmee because it describes inappropriate subjects like group masturbation. The book is accessible to parents only through the guidance office.

1998 WA   Challenged at the Crescent Harbor Elementary School library in Oak Harbor because of the book's frankness and use of slang terminology for body parts and sexual acts. H. W. Wilson's *Children's Catalogue* recommends the book for children from nine to fifteen and the book is also featured on Disney's "Parent Express" Web site.

Source: 11, Mar. 1987, p. 53; July 1987, pp. 149–50; Sept. 1993, p. 146; Nov. 1997, p. 167; Sept. 1998, pp. 141–42.

1074   Madaras, Lynda
Lynda Madaras Talks to Teens about AIDS: An Essential Guide for Parents, Teachers & Young People

1993 TN   Challenged, but retained at the Cleveland Public Library along with seventeen other books, most of which are on sex education, AIDS awareness, and some titles on the supernatural.

Source: 11, Sept. 1993, p. 146.

1075   Madden, David
The Suicide's Wife

1984 LA   Challenged at the Covington Public Library because it was "just too immorally written all the way through."

Source: 11, July 1984, p. 103.

1076   Madonna
Sex

1992   Banned in Ireland.
1992 AZ   In Mesa, the mayor ordered the library not to shelve the book.
1992 CO   The Pikes Peak Library in Colorado Springs cancelled the library's order after citizen protest.
1992 CT   Challenged at the Manchester Public Library.
1992 IA   Challenged at the Des Moines Public Library.
1992 IL   Challenged at the Champaign Public Library.
1992 IN   Challenged at South Bend Public Library.
1992 KS   Challenged at Topeka and Shawnee County Public Library.
1992 MI   Ingham County the library board declined to ban the controversial book.
1992 MO   The St. Louis Public Library cancelled the library's order after citizen protest.

1992 NE The Omaha Public Library did not plan to buy the book, but six of seven City Council members asked the library to remove it from any potential acquisitions list.

1992 TX The mylar-wrapped, spiral-bound book of photographs of the exhibitionist pop star Madonna in revealing and erotic poses raised challenges across the country soon after its release in Oct. 1992. In several cities political leaders exerted pressure on libraries not to acquire or to restrict circulation of the book. In Houston, a group called Citizens Against Pornography (CAP) mobilized efforts to have the book removed. The public library agreed to keep the book, but not allow it to circulate and to restrict in-library access to adults only.

1992 TX In Austin, the county attorney told the library that to make the book available to minors in any way was illegal.

1993 IL Retained at the Downers Grove Public Library.

1993 IL Excluded at the Naperville Public Library.

1993 MI Challenged, but retained at the Monroe County Library System following a three-and-half meeting that at times degenerated into a screaming match.

1993 WA Challenged at Spokane Public Library.

1993 WI Challenged at the Beloit Public Library, along with other adult literature, after complaints that minors were perusing the book's photographs of erotic poses and skimpy outfits.

Source: 6, p. 1,211; 11, Jan. 1993, pp. 1, 31–33; Mar. 1993, pp. 37–38; May 1993, pp. 65–66; July 1993, p. 104; Nov. 1993, p. 179.

1077 Magnus, Erica
The Boy and the Devil

1987 KY Challenged at the Science Hill Elementary School library because the book "hints of a satanic cult" since "there's no way a person can outwit the devil without God's help and nowhere is God mentioned in the book."

Source: 11, May 1987, p. 86; July 1987, pp. 147–48.

1078 Maguire, Gregory
Wicked: The Life and Times of the Wicked Witch of the West

2008 NY
New Retained in the tenth-grade honors program of the Canandaigua Academy in Ontario County despite concerns about the sexual content on a few pages of the book. The district will offer alternative reading for anyone who objects to the book.

Source: 11, Jan. 2009, p. 23.

1079 Mah, Adeline Yen
A Thousand Pieces of Gold: My Discovery of China's Character in the History and Meaning of Its Proverbs

2002 VA Challenged, along with seventeen other titles in the Fairfax County elementary and secondary libraries, by a group called Parents Against Bad Books in Schools. The group contends the books contain profanity and descriptions of drug abuse, sexually explicit conduct, and torture.

Source: 11, Jan. 2003, p. 10.

1080 Mahfouz, Naguib
Children of the Alley

1959 Banned by Cairo, Egypt's Al-Azhar University condemning it as "blasphemous," and calling the author a heretic for causing offense to the prophets of Islam and for misrepresenting the character of Muhammad. In 1988, Mahfouz won the Nobel Prize and fundamentalist renewed their attacks, fearing that the prize would be used as a pretext to remove the book from the proscribed list. In October 1994, Mahfouz was stabbed several times in the neck as he sat in a car outside his Cairo home. A few weeks after the attack, the novel was published in the Egyptian press for the first time in thirty-five years. As of mid-1997, however, the novel has not been published in book form in Egypt.

Source: 8, pp. 219–20.

1081 Mailer, Norman
Ancient Evenings

1985 CA Rejected for purchase by the Hayward school trustees because of "rough language" and "explicit sex scenes."

Source: 11, July 1985, p. 111.

1082 Mailer, Norman
The Naked and the Dead

1949 Banned in Canada.
1949 Banned in Australia.

Source: 4, p. 96; 6, p. 412.

1083 Mailer, Norman
Why Are We in Vietnam?

1987 AL The Huntsville assistant city attorney requested that the novel be removed from the public library shelves. After considerable controversy, the book was eventually returned to the public library shelves.

Source: 7, pp. 529–30.

1084   Maimonides
The Guide of the Perplexed

1200   Condemned by his orthodox opponents as heresy. Copies of the publication were burned when discovered, it was barred from Jewish homes, and anyone reading it was excommunicated; the work was still facing bans in the 19th century. Orthodox Jewish opponents objected to Maimonides's sympathy for Aristotelian thought, which was considered fundamentally incompatible with Hebrew tradition. Maimonides was probably the first Jewish author to have his works burned.
Source: 3, p. 29; 8, pp. 237–38.

1085   Malamud, Bernard
The Fixer

1976   CO   Banned from use in Aurora High School English classes.
1976   NY   Removed from the Island Trees Union Free School District High School library in 1976 along with nine other titles because they were considered "immoral, anti-American, anti-Christian, or just plain filthy." Returned to the library after the U.S. Supreme Court ruling on June 25, 1982, in *Board of Education, Island Trees Union Free School District No. 26 et al. v. Pico et al.*, 457 U.S. 853 (1982).
Source: 11, May 1977, p. 79; Nov. 1982, p. 197.

1086   Malcolm X, and Alex Haley
The Autobiography of Malcolm X

1993   FL   Challenged in the Duval County public schools because the slain Black Muslim leader advocated anti-white racism and violence.
1994   FL   Restricted at the Jacksonville middle school libraries because it presents a racist view of white people and is a "how-to manual" for crime.
Source: 11, Sept. 1993, p. 147; May 1994, p. 83.

1087   Maloney, Ray
The Impact Zone

1989   OR   Challenged at the Multnomah County Library in Portland because of profanity and sexual references.
Source: 11, Jan. 1990, pp. 4–5.

1088   Malory, Sir Thomas
Le Morte D'Arthur

1987   KY   Challenged as a required reading assignment at the Pulaski County High School in Somerset because it is "junk."
Source: 11, May 1987, p. 90.

1089   Manchester, William Raymond
The Glory and the Dream

1989   AR   Challenged at the Conway High School as having inappropriate sexual and racial content.
Source: 11, July 1989, p. 129; Sept. 1989, p. 186.

1090   Mandela, Nelson
The Struggle Is My Life

1988   Confiscated in Grenada.
1990   Banned in South Africa. The ban was lifted after Mandela was released from prison in 1990.
Source: 7, pp. 471–72.

1091   Mandeville, Bernard
The Fable of the Bees

1723   Presented twice by an Middlesex, England grand jury for blasphemy.
1740   Burned in France.
1966   The Vatican listed it on the *Index Librorum Prohibitorum* (Index of Prohibited Books) in Rome, Italy, where it remained until 1966.
Source: 1, pp. 104–6.

1092   Manes, Stephen
Slim Down Camp

1992   IL   Challenged at the Des Plaines Public Library because it contains "repeated profanity and immoral situations."
Source: 11, May 1992, p. 79.

1093   Manet, Edouard
Manet

1994   AZ   Retained at Maldonado Elementary School in Tucson after being challenged by parents who objected to nudity and "pornographic," "perverted," and "morbid" themes.
Source: 11, July 1994, p. 112.

1094   Mann, Patrick
Dog Day Afternoon

1978   VT   Placed in a special closed shelf at the Vergennes Union High School library. Decision upheld in *Bicknell v. Vergennes Union High School Board*, 475 F. Supp. 615 (D. Vt. 1979), 638 F. 2d 438 (2d Cir. 1980).
Source: 11, Jan. 1979, p. 6; 12, pp. 151, 239; 14, pp. 113–15; 15, Vol IV, p. 715.

1095 Manson, Marilyn
The Long, Hard Road out of Hell

1998 IL Challenged because of explicit references to sex, violence, and the occult, but retained at the West Chicago Public Library.
Source: 11, Jan. 1999, p. 19.

1096 Maple, Eric
Devils and Demons

1988 FL Challenged at the Essrig Elementary School in Carrollwood because the book contains a pledge to Satan.
Source: 11, Jan. 1989, p. 7.

1097 Mapplethorpe, Robert
Mapplethorpe

1998 Seized by police from the University of Central England library in Birmingham, England. Lawyers acting for the Crown Prosecution Service decided parts of it were likely to "deprave or corrupt" under the 1959 Obscene Publications Act, and advised the police that they had grounds to ask the university to destroy it. The university and publisher have refused to destroy the book. The Crown Prosecution Service concluded that there was insufficient evidence to expect a conviction.
Source: 11, May 1998, p. 75; Mar. 1999, p. 48.

1098 Maraini, Fosco
Tokyo

1983 WV Challenged at the Cherry River Elementary School library in Richwood because the book includes a photograph of the backsides of nude Japanese men in a public bath.
Source: 11, July 1983, p. 122.

1099 Marchetti, Victor, and John D. Marks
The CIA and the Cult of Intelligence

1972 The Central Intelligence Agency obtained a U.S. Court injunction against its publication. Towards the close of its 1974-1975 term the U.S. Supreme Court declined for the second time to review an appeal by the authors, thus upholding the CIA's right to enforce its secrecy agreement with Marchetti, a former employee, and required him to submit material before publication.
Source: 4, p. 100; 5, Spring 1976, pp. 88–89.

1100 Marcus, Eric
Is It a Choice? Answers to Three Hundred of the Most Frequently Asked Questions about Gays and Lesbians

1993 IA Challenged at the Indianola Public Library because it was not "of much concern to the Christian believing people of this community." The book is about homosexuality.
Source: 11, Jan. 1994, p. 35.

1101 Marcus, Eric
The Male Couple's Guide to Living Together: What Gay Men Should Know about Living with Each Other and Coping in a Straight World

1990 IA Challenged at the Muscatine Public Library because it is "wrong to promote immorality."
Source: 11, Nov. 1990, p. 225.

1102 Marianna
Miss Flora McFlimsey's Easter Bonnet

1991 MI Challenged at the Troy Public Library because it contained an offensive and unflattering illustration of a black doll.
Source: 11, Jan. 1992, p. 26.

1103 Mariels, Elaine Nicpon
Human Anatomy and Physiology

1998 FL Challenged, but retained in the Escambia County schools because of pictures showing a vaginal birth, vaginal warts caused by herpes, and a self-examination for breast cancer.
Source: 11, July 1998, p. 107.

1104 Marsden, John
Letters from the Inside

1997 OH Challenged, but retained as required reading for the Youngstown, Ohio State University English Festival because the book contains the "F-word."
Source: 11, May 1997, p. 66.

1105 Martin, Michael
Kurt Cobain

2009 MN Removed from all elementary and middle Farmington school library because the book was "very dark and violent and made references to the use of Ritalin as being a precursor to the use of illicit drugs. It also covered topics such as mental illness and suicide."
New
Source: 11, Jan. 2010, p. 11.

1106   Martin, Tony
The Jewish Onslaught: Despatches from the Wellesley Battlefront

1994   MD   Criticized at the Enoch Pratt Free Library in Baltimore because the book accuses Jews of masterminding the slave trade and blocking the advance of African Americans. "There's no reason for our public library to spend shrinking public funds to promote the circulation of such hatred."
Source: 11, Sept. 1994, p. 146.

1107   Martin, W. K.
Marlene Dietrich

2000   CA   Removed from the Anaheim school district because school officials said the book is too difficult for middle school students and that it could cause harassment against students seen with it. The American Civil Liberties Union (ACLU) of Southern California filed suit in *Doe v. Anaheim Union High School District* alleging that the removal is "a pretext for viewpoint-based censorship." The ACLU claims no other books have been removed from the junior high library for similar reasons, even though several, such as works by Shakespeare and Dickens, are more difficult reading. The ACLU contends that the school officials engaged in unconstitutional viewpoint discrimination by removing the book because it contains gay and lesbian material. In March 2001, the school board approved a settlement that restored the book to the high school shelves and amended the district's policy to prohibit the removal of books for subject matter involving sexual orientation, but the book will not be returned to the middle school.
Source: 11, Mar. 2001, p. 53; May 2001, p. 95; July 2001, p. 173.

1108   Martinac, Paula
k. d. lang

2000   CA   Removed from the Anaheim school district because school officials said the book is too difficult for middle school students and that it could cause harassment against students seen with it. The American Civil Liberties Union (ACLU) of Southern California filed suit in *Doe v. Anaheim Union High School District* alleging that the removal is "a pretext for viewpoint-based censorship." The ACLU claims no other books have been removed from the junior high library for similar reasons, even though several, such as works by Shakespeare and Dickens, are more difficult reading. The ACLU contends that the school officials engaged in unconstitutional viewpoint discrimination by removing the book because it contains gay and lesbian material. In March 2001, the school board approved a settlement that restored the book to the high school shelves and amended the district's policy to prohibit the removal of books for subject matter involving sexual orientation, but the book will not be returned to the middle school.
Source: 11, Mar. 2001, p. 53; May 2001, p. 95; July 2001, p. 173.

1109   Marx, Karl, and Friedrich Engels
German Ideology

1953   East Germany rewrote or expurgated all of Marx's writing.

1974   Marx's texts were included on the South African Index of Objectionable Literature. Marx's works were removed from the list in 1991.

1985   Banned in South Korea.
Source: 5, Apr. 1986, pp. 30–33; 7, pp. 127–29.

1110   Marx, Karl
Capital

1894   Reprinting was forbidden in Russia. Ban lifted in 1897.

1929   Prohibited reading in China.

1939   Banned by the Nazi government from 1939 to 1945 in Germany and German-occupied countries.

1940   OK   Banned in Oklahoma City. Bookstore owners were sentenced to ten years in prison and fined $5,000,000 for selling Marx's work.

1950   MA   Challenged at the Boston Public Library from 1950 to 1953 because of the book's communistic message.

1953   East Germany rewrote or expurgated all of Marx's writing.

1953   FL   Removed from the Brooksfield Public library because they were "communist propaganda."

1953   WI   Restricted at Marquette University in Milwaukee. Instructors submitted the names of students who borrowed the book; the list was subsequently turned over to the archbishop.

1974   Marx's texts were included on the South African Index of Objectionable Literature. Marx's works were removed from the list in 1991.

1987   In South Korea, where communism is illegal, the government sued the publisher in court, charging a violation of South Korea's National Security Law.
Source: 4, pp. 44–45; 7, pp. 127–29.

1111 Marx, Karl
The Communist Manifesto

1878		Prohibited in Germany.
1929		Prohibited in China.
1950	MA	Challenged at the Boston Public Library until 1953 because of the book's communistic message.
1974		Marx's texts were included on the South African Index of Objectionable Literature. Marx's works were removed from the list in 1991.
1987		In South Korea, where communism is illegal, the government sued the publisher in court, charging a violation of South Korea's National Security Law.

Source: 4, pp. 44–45; 7, pp. 127–29; 8, pp. 122–25.

1112 Masland, Robert P. Jr., ed., and David Estridge, ex. ed.
What Teenagers Want to Know about Sex: Questions and Answers

1993	AK	Challenged in the Kenai Peninsula Borough schools in Homer because it presents "sexual relations in an amoral light."

Source: 11, Jan. 1994, pp. 33–34.

1113 Mason, Bobbie Ann
In Country

1994	GA	Recalled as supplemental reading in two college preparatory English classes at the Charlton County High School in Folkston. All of the parents of the forty-eight students in the classes had given permission for their children to read the book. But it was removed from their hands in May after one of those parents complained it included profanity.
1994	PA	Challenged at the West Chester schools as "most pornographic."
2009 New	IN	Retained in Delphi Community High School's curriculum despite claims of inappropriate sexual content and graphic language.

Source: 11, Sept. 1994, p. 150; Jan. 1995, p. 25; Mar. 1995, p. 45; July 1995, p. 99; May 2009, p. 94.

1114 Masters, Edgar Lee
Spoon River Anthology

1974	OH	Several students brought suit against the Scioto-Darby School District in Willard for removing two pages because the poems were "inappropriate" and their language might be offensive to some. The case was dismissed in *Kramer v. Scioto-Darby City School District*, Civil Action 72-406, Southern District of Ohio, Mar. 8, 1974.

Source: 12, pp. 133–34, 238.

1115 Mathabane, Mark
Kaffir Boy

1993	CA	Challenged at the Amador High School in Sutter Creek.
1993	NJ	Challenged at the Manasquan schools because of a brief but graphic passage involving homosexuality.
1996	CT	Challenged as part of the sophomore curriculum at the Lewis S. Mills High School in Burlington because of brutal and graphic language.
1996	NC	Temporarily pulled from the Greensboro high school libraries after a resident sent letters to school board members and some administrators charging that the book could encourage young people to sexually assault children.
1997	CA	Challenged, but retained on a core reading list for high school sophomores, at the Lincoln Unified School District in Stockton. Some parents referred to the book as "pornographic and racially insensitive."
1999	OH	Removed from a Federal Hocking High School English class in Athens because it contains a sexually graphic passage that some have deemed offensive.
2000	CA	Removed from sophomore reading list at Armijo High School in Fairfield due to its sexual content.
2000	MI	Kearsley school officials deleted six sentences describing a homosexual molestation scene in the book after some parents found it offensive.
2006	CA	Retained at the East Union High School in Manteca senior English class. The controversial autobiography was challenged as inappropriate because a passage uses the words "penis" and "anus" to describe a scene in which a group of young boys are about to prostitute themselves to a group of men for food.
2007 New	CA	Banned from the Burlingame Intermediate School. The book has been challenged frequently since its publication in 1986 because of two graphic paragraphs describing men preparing to engage in anal sex with young boys. It earned the 1987 Christopher Award for literature, "affirming the highest values of the human spirit." It was also a finalist for the Robert F. Kennedy Award for books representing "concern for the poor and the powerless."

Source: 11, Jan. 1994, pp. 15, 38; July 1996, p. 119; Mar. 1997, p. 38; May 1997, p. 62; July 1997, pp. 109–10; May 1999, p. 70; Mar. 2000, p. 50; Nov. 2000, p. 195; July 2006, pp. 209–10; July 2007, pp. 145–46.

1116 Matthiessen, Peter
In the Spirit of Crazy Horse

1983 SD South Dakota Governor William J. Janklow named three South Dakota bookstores in a $20-million libel suit because the bookstores refused to stop selling Matthiessen's book. A Sioux Falls judge ruled on June 18, 1984 that Matthiessen's work is not defamatory and threw out the case.

Source: 6, pp. 1,555–56; 8, pp. 100–105; 11, July 1983, p. 112; Jan. 1984, p. 18; May 1984, p. 75; July 1984, p. 116; Sept. 1984, p. 148.

1117 May, Julian
A New Baby Comes

1987 WA Placed on restricted shelves at the Evergreen School District elementary school libraries in Vancouver in accordance with the school board policy to restrict student access to sex education books in elementary school libraries.

Source: 11, May 1987, p. 87.

1118 Mayer, Mercer
Liza Lou & the Yellow Belly Swamp

1988 OR Challenged at the Douglas County Library in Roseburg because of scary pictures and references to boiling children.

Source: 11, Jan. 1990, pp. 4–5.

1119 Mayer, Mercer
A Special Trick

1992 OR Challenged at the Coburg Elementary School in Eugene for allegedly satanic art. The book was retained, but an accompanying audiotape that encourages children to look closely at the art work was removed by the school principal.

Source: 11, July 1992, p. 103.

1120 Mayle, Peter
What's Happening to Me? The Answers to Some of the World's Most Embarrassing Questions

1983 NV Challenged and eventually moved from the Henderson Public Library children's section to the adult shelves because the book is "too sexually explicit and unsuitable for children."

1993 TN Challenged, but retained at the Cleveland Public Library along with seventeen other books, most of which are on sex education, AIDS awareness, and some titles on the supernatural.

Source: 11, Mar. 1984, p. 39; May 1984, p. 71; Sept. 1993, p. 146.

1121 Mayle, Peter
Where Did I Come From?

1980 CT Banned from elementary classrooms in Hamden because it was judged not appropriate.

1994 NV Challenged at the Washoe County Library System in Reno because, "Nobody in their right mind would give a book like that to children on their own, except a library."

Source: 11, Mar. 1980, p. 32; Sept. 1994, p. 147.

1122 Mazer, Harry
I Love You, Stupid

1982 IA Banned from Des Moines junior high school libraries after a parent's complaint that the book was "morally inappropriate."

1983 WA Removed from the Evergreen School District of Vancouver along with twenty-nine other titles. The American Civil Liberties Union of Washington has filed suit contending that the removals constitute censorship, a violation of plaintiff's rights to free speech and due process, and the acts are a violation of the state Open Meetings Act because the removal decisions were made behind closed doors.

Source: 11, Sept. 1982, p. 155; Nov. 1983, pp. 185–86.

1123 Mazer, Harry
The Last Mission

1984 NJ Challenged at the Pequannock Valley Middle School in Pompton Plains because of its "language."

1986 WI Moved from the Alexander Middle School library to the Nekoosa High School library because of "profanity" in the book.

1995 TX Banned, but later reinstated in the Carroll Middle School Library in Southlake. In the original complaint, a parent requested its removal because of excessive profanity.

1999 CA Challenged, but retained at the Auburn-Placer County Library because of sexually explicit material.

Source: 11, Nov. 1984, p. 185; Mar. 1985, p. 59; Jan. 1987, p. 10; May 1995, p. 67; July 1995, p. 95; Sept. 1995, p. 159; Nov. 1999, p. 171.

1124 Mazer, Harry
Snow Bound

1987 WI Challenged at the Stoughton Middle School reading program because the book includes "several profane oaths invoking the deity, two four-letter words for bodily wastes, and the term 'crazy bitch' and 'stupid female.'"

Source: 11, May 1987, p. 103.

1125   Mazer, Norma Fox
Out of Control

1995 OK   Banned at the Cooper Middle School Library in Putnam City because of language "inappropriate for that age level."

1995 OK   Challenged at the Oklahoma City Metropolitan Library System, but retained.
Source: 11, July 1995, p. 94.

1126   Mazer, Norma Fox
Saturday, the Twelfth of October

1977 VT   Removed from the seventh-grade classroom in Chester after a parent described the book as "filthy."
Source: 11, Mar. 1978, p. 31.

1127   Mazer, Norma Fox
Up in Seth's Room

1982 WY   Removed from the Campbell County School District libraries and classrooms. After complaints of three district media specialists about the "illegitimately constituted" review committee, however, the book was reinstated.
Source: 11, Mar. 1983, p. 51.

1128   McAlpine, Helen, and William McAlpine
Japanese Tales and Legends

1995 CA   Challenged at the Wilsona School District in Lake Los Angeles because of depictions of violence and references to Buddha and ritual suicide.
Source: 11, Jan. 1996, p. 13.

1129   McBain, Ed
Alice in Jeopardy

2006 WA   Challenged at the Sno-Isle Libraries in Arlington because of "curse words and graphic sex scenes."
Source: 11, Jan. 2007, p. 11.

1130   McBride, Will, and Helga Fleischhauer-Hardt
Show Me!

1975 MA   Publisher prosecuted on obscenity charges in Massachusetts. The judge ruled as a matter of law that the title was not obscene.

1976   Publisher prosecuted on obscenity charges in Toronto, Ontario, Canada. The judge ruled as a matter of law that the title was not obscene.

1976 NH   Publisher prosecuted on obscenity charges in New Hampshire. The judge ruled as a matter of law that the title was not obscene.

1976 OK   Publisher prosecuted on obscenity charges in Oklahoma. The judge ruled as a matter of law that the title was not obscene.

1984 CA   Frequently challenged in libraries across the country, e.g., at the Stanislaus County library.

1984 CA   Challenged at the San Jose library because the book "condones child molestation or child pornography." Less than two weeks later, the copy of the book was reported lost by the borrower, a member of the Turlock Action Committee, which organized the movement to ban the book.

1985 WA   Challenged at the Seattle Public Library because "it is inappropriate for the library collection."

1986 CA   Challenged at the Alameda County Library because "we are giving the pedophile a platform on which to stand" and placed on restrictive shelves in three branches.

1986 NY   Challenged at the Steele Memorial Library in Elmira because it "promotes masturbation, sex between young people, and incest."
Source: 11, Nov. 1984, pp. 183, 195; Jan. 1985, pp. 7, 27; May 1985, p. 79; July 1985, pp. 112–13; Mar. 1986, p. 37; May 1986, p. 97; Jan. 1987, pp. 29–31.

1131   McCall, Don
Jack the Bear

1978 IA   Removed from the Monticello school library due to "objectionable" language.
Source: 11, May 1978, p. 56.

1132   McCammon, Robert
Boy's Life

1994 NY   Challenged as required reading in the Hudson Falls schools because the book has recurring themes of rape, masturbation, violence, and degrading treatment of women.
Source: 11, Nov. 1994, p. 190; Jan. 1995, p. 13; Mar. 1995, p. 55.

1133   McCammon, Robert
Mystery Walk

1992 OR   Challenged in the Salem-Keizer school libraries because, "it is full of violence and profanity."
Source: 11, July 1992, p. 125.

1134   McCarthy, Cormac
Child of God

2007 TX   Removed as an appropriate pre-Advanced
New   English Placement reading at the Jim Ned High School in Tuscola.
Source: 11, Jan. 2008, pp. 41–42.

1135 McCarthy, Mary
The Group

1964 Placed on its "Publication Restricted or Prohibited" list by New Zealand Customs. Faced with public disapproval, the comptroller of Customs lifting the prohibition.

1964 Banned in Ireland on January 21, 1964. The Irish Board of Censors found the work "obscene" and "indecent," objecting particularly to the author's handling of the characters' sexuality, suggestions of homosexuality and "promiscuity." The work was officially banned from sale in Ireland until 1967.

1982 IN Challenged in Terre Haute as an optional reading in an elective English course for junior and senior high school students.

Source: 8, pp. 343–44; 11, May 1982, p. 86.

**1136 McCoy, Kathy, and
Charles Wibbelsman**
The New Teenage Body Book

1990 MA Withdrawn as a textbook, but retained as a "classroom resource," in the ninth-grade health classes in Pembroke because it is "obscene." Parents have asked that the abstinence-based sex education program *Sex Respect* be substituted. Complainant wants school officials indicted for distributing obscene materials to children.

Source: 11, Jan. 1991, p. 17; Mar. 1991, p. 44; Jan. 1992, p. 8.

**1137 McCuen, Gary E., and
David L. Bender**
The Sexual Revolution

1977 MI Banned from the Brighton High School library along with all other sex education materials.

Source: 11, Sept. 1977, p. 133.

1138 McCullers, Carson
Member of the Wedding

2001 PA Challenged in the Tamaqua Area School District because the book "might not be appropriate for younger schoolmates." The school board is considering the establishment of a restricted materials section in the district's middle-school library for books deemed objectionable. Students would need parental permission to access any title placed there.

Source: 11, Mar. 2001, p. 54; July 2001, p. 145.

1139 McCunn, Ruthanne Lum
Thousand Pieces of Gold

1984 CA Removed from elementary school library shelves in Sonoma County because certain passages were too "sexually explicit."

1992 WA Challenged at the Commodore Middle School in Bainbridge Island as inappropriate by three parents because of violence, sexual scenes, and "lack of family values."

1994 CA Rejected as an addition to a core literature list by the Amador County Unified School District because "it makes America look bad."

Source: 11, Sept. 1984, p. 137; May 1992, p. 84; July 1994, p. 109.

1140 McDermott, Beverly Brodsky
The Golem: A Jewish Legend

1993 NY A first grade teacher asked the Newburgh school officials to ban this Caldecott Award-winning children's book about the persecution of Jews in sixteenth-century Prague. The teacher objected to the strong language and threatening artwork that children might not understand.

Source: 11, Nov. 1993, p. 178.

1141 McDonald, Brian
***In the Middle of the Night: The
Shocking True Story of a Family
Killed in Cold Blood***

2009 CT
New Challenged at the Cheshire Public Library. McDonald's book revisits 2007, when Joshua Komisarjevsky and Steven Hayes allegedly invaded the Cheshire home of Dr. William Petit, beating him with a baseball bat and raping, torturing, and murdering his wife and two daughters. Complainants want the book kept off the library shelves until the men accused of the crime have been tried.

Source: 11, Jan. 2010, pp. 7–8; Mar. 2010, p. 51.

1142 McFarland, Philip J., et al.
Themes in World Literature

1995 AZ Challenged at the Tempe Union High School District in Mesa. The story, "A Rose for Emily," by William Faulkner was objectionable because it uses the word "nigger" six times as well as other demeaning phrases.

Source: 11, Jan. 1996, p. 13; May 1996, p. 98.

1143   McGahern, John
The Dark

1965   Banned in Ireland. No detailed official statement was required to be made available for the historical record, but it was assumed the novel was banned on the basis of several passages that dealt with the central character's discovery of his sexuality.
Source: 6, pp. 1,480–81.

1144   McHargue, Georgess
Meet the Werewolf

1983   WA   Challenged at the Evergreen School District in Vancouver because the book was "full of comments about becoming a werewolf, use of opium, and pacts with the devil."

1985   FL   Challenged because the book would lead children to believe ideas contrary to the teachings of the Bible, but retained by the Sikes Elementary School media center in Lakeland.

1992   NY   Challenged at the Barringer Road Elementary School in Ilion because the book's passages on the occult were objectionable.
Source: 11, Sept. 1983, p. 139; July 1985, p. 133; Jan. 1993, p. 9.

1145   McHugh, Vincent
The Blue Hen's Chicken

1947   NY   Confiscated in New York City because the poetry book contained a part titled "Suite from Catullus," eight short poems that were variations on a theme of the Roman poet.
Source: 15, Vol. IV, p. 699.

1146   McKay, Susan
Living Law

1981   MS   Removed from the Mississippi state-approved textbook list because of complaints that the book "undermines" the values parents teach at home.
Source: 11, May 1981, p. 67; July 1981, p. 93.

1147   McKissack, Patricia
Mirandy and Brother Wind

1991   FL   Challenged at the Glen Springs Elementary School in Gainesville because of the book's use of black dialect.
Source: 11, July 1991, p. 129.

1148   McMillan, Rosalyn
Knowing

1999   NC   Challenged, but retained at the Cumberland County Library in Fayetteville despite a complaint that the book contains profanity. In addition, the complainant suggested that the library move sexually explicit materials, as well as ones about homosexuality, into an adult section and establish a review committee to screen materials.
Source: 11, July 1999, p. 94; Jan. 2000, pp. 27–28.

1149   McNally, John, ed.
When I Was a Loser: True Stories of (Barely) Surviving High School by Today's Top Writers

2007   RI   Challenged as a Cumberland high school reading
New   assignment because the entire compilation is filled with essays that are "lewd, contain profanity, and references to bestiality."
Source: 11, Jan. 2008, pp. 38–39.

1150   Mead, Richelle
Vampire Academy series

2009   TX   Banned at Henderson Junior High School in
New   the Stephenville, Tex. Independent School District (ISD). The entire teen vampire series was banned for sexual content or nudity. Since the series has not been completed, "Stephenville ISD actually banned books that have not yet been published and perhaps even books that have yet to be written. There is no way the district could know the content of these books, and yet they have been banned."
Source: 11, Nov. 2009, pp. 197–98, 225.

1151   Medved, Michael
Hollywood vs. America: Popular Culture and the War against Traditional Values

1997   IN   Withdrawn from the freshman curriculum at Greencastle High School because of the graphic language in Medved's work, especially the chapter devoted to popular music.
Source: 11, July 1997, p. 98.

1152   Meeks, Linda, and Philip Heit
Your Relationship

1990   IL   Challenged in the Barrington School District because the book has a chapter on incest that creates "ugly imagery for innocent minds."
Source: 11, Jan. 1991, p. 29.

1153 Melville, Herman
Moby Dick

1996 TX Banned from the Advanced Placement English reading list at the Lindale schools because it "conflicts with the values of the community."
Source: 11, Nov. 1996, p. 199.

1154 Mercado, Nancy E., ed.
Tripping over the Lunch Lady and Other Short Stories

2007 VA
New After a challenge and three appeals, the York County School Board chose to keep the collection of short stories in the Magruder Elementary School library in Williamsburg despite claims that it is offensive to children with loved ones serving in the military and inappropriate for elementary school students. A parent wanted the book removed because one of the short stories contained references to war, bombs, and soldier casualties.
Source: 11, Jan. 2008, p. 27.

1155 Meretzky, Eric
Zork: The Malifestro Quest

1990 MI Challenged at the Jeffers Elementary School in Spring Lake because it "is a disgrace to the Lord and to the Spring Lake school system."
Source: 11, May 1990, p. 84; July 1990, p. 145.

1156 Meriwether, Louise
Daddy Was a Numbers Runner

1977 CA Removed from all Oakland junior high school libraries and its use restricted in senior high schools, following a complaint about the book's explicit depiction of ghetto life.
Source: 11, May 1977, p. 71.

1157 Mernissi, Fatima
The Veil and the Male Elite: A Feminist Interpretation of Women's Rights in Islam

1991 Banned in Morocco. Authorities regarded as particularly threatening Mernissi's contention that the sacred texts were manipulated as political weapons and that commonly accepted hadith are based on falsehood. Saudia Arabia is ruled by Muslim religious law, or sharia, which encompasses the hadith. Moroccan legal family codes at the time were also based on sharia.

1991 Banned in Saudia Arabia.
1991 Banned in Syria.

2003 The book was translated for the first time into Farsi and published in Tehran, Iran by Ney Publications. In August 2003, its translator, publisher, and the Iranian official who authorized the book's publication were convicted by the Criminal Court of Tehran, Iran of "insulting and undermining the holy tenets of Islam," "sullying the person of the Prophet Muhammad," and "distorting Islamic history" by "publishing false, slanderous, and fabricated texts." The court also ordered that copies of Mernissi's book be shredded.
Source: 8, pp. 305–6.

1158 Merriam-Webster Editorial Staff
Merriam-Webster Collegiate Dictionary

1982 NM Removed from classrooms in Carlsbad schools because the dictionary defines "obscene" words.
1989 NJ Challenged in the Upper Pittsgrove Township schools because the definition of sexual intercourse was objectionable.
1993 NV Challenged, but the 1,100 copies of the dictionary were returned to the Sparks Elementary School classrooms. A sixth-grade teacher objected to the book because it includes obscene words.
2010 CA
New Pulled from the Menifee Union School District because a parent complained when a child came across the term "oral sex." Officials said the district is forming a committee to consider a permanent classroom ban of the dictionary.
Source: 11, Nov. 1982, p. 206; Jan. 1990, p. 11; Jan. 1994, p. 37; Mar. 2010, p. 55.

1159 Merriam, Eve
Halloween ABC

1989 OR Challenged at the Douglas County Library in Roseburg because the book encourages devil worshipping.
1991 KS Challenged in the Wichita public schools because it is "satanic and disgusting."
1991 MD Challenged at the Howard County school libraries because "there should be an effort to tone down Halloween and there should not be books about it in the schools."
1992 CO Challenged at the Acres Green Elementary School in Douglas County.
1992 WA Challenged and retained, but will be shelved with other works generally available only to older students and won't be used in future Halloween displays at the Federal Way School District in Seattle. The compromise was for a group of parents who objected to the book's satanic references.

1993 TX Challenged, but retained at the Ennis Public Library.

1993 WA Challenged, but retained in the Othello elementary school libraries because the book "promotes violent criminal and deviant behavior."

1993 WI Challenged in the Cameron Elementary School library in Rice Lake because the "poems promote satanism, murder, and suicide." The book was retained.

1994 WA Challenged in the Spokane School District library by a father who found the poems morbid and satanic. In particular, the parent disapproved of one poem which "appears to be a chant calling forth the Devil."

1995 MA Challenged in the Sandwich Public Library because it is "too violent for young children."

2000 NY Challenged, but retained in the Wellsville elementary school library despite complaints the book promotes violence.

Source: 11, Jan. 1990, pp. 4–5; Sept. 1991, p. 178; Jan. 1992, p. 26; May 1992, p. 94; Mar. 1993, p. 43; July 1993, pp. 103–4; Sept. 1993, p. 159; Jan. 1994, pp. 13–14; Mar. 1994, pp. 69–70; Jan. 1995, p. 9; Mar. 1995, p. 41; Sept. 1995, p. 158; Mar. 2001, p. 75.

1160 Merriam, Eve
The Inner City Mother Goose

1972 CA Challenged in San Francisco.

1972 MD Challenged in Baltimore.

1972 MN Challenged in Minneapolis.

1972 NY An Erie County judge called for a grand jury investigation of this satirical book of adult nursery rhymes, alleging it taught crime.

2000 NY Removed from the Whitney Point middle school library after a parent complained about its language and content.

Source: 4, p. 91; 11, July 2000, p. 104.

1161 Merrick, Gordon
One for the Gods

1984 Seized by the British Customs Office.

Source: 11, Jan. 1985, p. 26.

1162 Metalious, Grace
Peyton Place

1957 TN The city of Knoxville activated a city ordinance that permitted the Knoxville City Board of Review to suppress any publication that it considered to be obscene. The target was Metalious novel; local dealers were forbidden to sell it. When one indignant newsstand owner tested the ordinance, it was ruled unconstitutional.

1958 Banned in Ireland from 1958 until the introduction of the Censorship of Publications Bill in 1967.

1958 Temporary ban lifted in Canada.

1959 RI The Rhode Island Commission to Encourage Morality in Youth brought action against Bantam and three other New York paperback publishers. The Rhode Island Superior Court upheld the decision, which was later reversed by the U.S. Supreme Court in *Bantam Books, Inc. et al., v. Joseph A. Sullivan, et al.*

Source: 4, p. 97; 8, pp. 373–74.

1163 Meyer, Michael, ed.
Bedford Introduction to Literature

2000 FL The Paxon School for Advanced Studies in Jacksonville principal authorized teachers to cut out the play Angels in America from the textbook. The Duval County School Board first banned the play three years ago after learning that it was being used in a class at Douglas Anderson School of the Arts. The play is the first half of Tony Kushner's work depicting the United States in the 1980s as the AIDS epidemic began to spread. It won the 1993 Pulitzer Prize for drama and several Tony awards, including best play.

Source: 11, Mar. 2001, p. 56.

1164 Meyer, Stephenie H.
Twilight series

2008 CA New Removed from and later reinstated in the middle school libraries of the Capistrano Unified School District. The books were initially ordered removed by the district's instructional materials specialist, who ordered that the books be moved from middle school to high school collections. That order was rescinded and the books remain in the middle school libraries.

2009 New Banned in Australia for primary school students because the series is too racy. Librarians have stripped the books from shelves in some junior schools because they believe the content is too sexual and goes against religious beliefs. They even have asked parents not to let kids bring their own copies of Stephenie Meyer's smash hit novels—which explore the stormy love affair between a teenage girl and a vampire—to school.

2009 UT New Challenged at the Brockbank Junior High in Magna by a parent over the sexual content in the Mormon author's fourth novel, *Breaking Dawn*.

Source: 11, Nov. 2008, p. 253; Jan. 2009, p. 5; May 2009, p. 80; Nov. 2009, pp. 207–8.

1165 Mezrich, Ben
Bringing Down the House: The Inside Story of Six M.I.T. Students Who Took Vegas for Millions

2004 OR Challenged in the Beaverton schools as supplemental reading because it contains profanity and abundant references to prostitution and gambling. In 2004, the book was number eighteen on *The New York Times's* paperback nonfiction best-seller list.
Source: 11, Mar. 2005, pp. 58–59.

1166 Mill, John Stuart
Social Philosophy

1856 Listed on the *Index Librorum Prohibitorum* (List of Prohibited Books) in Rome, Italy.
Source: 4, p. 42.

1167 Mill, John Stuart
System of Logic

1856 Listed on the *Index Librorum Prohibitorum* (List of Prohibited Books) in Rome, Italy.
Source: 4, p. 42.

1168 Millard, Anne, and Patricia Vanags
The Usborne Book of World History

1998 GA Restricted to teachers only in the Gwinnett County schools after objections to nude drawings depicting life in ancient civilizations. Complainants also objected to *The Usborne Time Traveler Books (Pharaohs and Pyramids)*, by Tony Allan.
Source: 11, Sept. 1998, pp. 143–44.

1169 Miller, Arthur
The Crucible

1982 PA Challenged at the Cumberland Valley High School, Harrisburg because the play contains "sick words from the mouths of demon-possessed people. It should be wiped out of the schools or the school board should use them to fuel the fire of hell."
1987 KY Challenged as a required reading assignment at the Pulaski County High School in Somerset because it is "junk."
1999 PA Challenged, but retained in the sophomore curriculum at West Middlesex High School.
Source: 11, Mar. 1983, pp. 52–53; May 1987, p. 90; July 1999, p. 105.

1170 Miller, Arthur
Death of a Salesman

1974 TX Challenged at the Dallas Independent School District high school libraries.
1981 IN Banned from English classes at Spring Valley Community High School in French Lick because the play contains the words "goddamn," "son of a bitch," and "bastard."
1987 KY Challenged as a required reading assignment at the Pulaski County High School in Sinking Valley because it is "junk."
1997 IL Challenged, but retained at Egyptian High School in Tamms. The play was considered offensive by some because of "profanity."
Source: 11, July 1975, pp. 6–7; May 1981, p. 68; May 1987, p. 90; May 1997, p. 78.

1171 Miller, Deborah A., and Alex Waigandt
Coping with Your Sexual Orientation

1994 NJ Moved from the Chestnut Ridge Middle School library in Washington Township because school administrators have been accused of "indoctrinating children in the gay lifestyle."
Source: 11, Sept. 1994, p. 148.

1172 Miller, Henry
Opus Pistorum

1993 NC Removed from the Cumberland County library system because it lacks "serious literary or artistic merit for this library's collection."
Source: 11, Mar. 1993, p. 42.

1173 Miller, Henry
Sexus

1950 Banned in France.
1956 Banned in Norway.
Source: 4, p. 74.

1174 Miller, Henry
Tropic of Cancer

1934 Banned from U.S. Customs. In 1964, the U.S. Supreme Court found the novel not obscene.
1986 Banned in Turkey.
Source: 4, p. 74; 5, July/Aug. 1986, p. 46; 6, pp. 1,597–98; 8, pp. 387–89.

1175 Miller, Henry
Tropic of Cancer

1953 CA   Ban upheld by U.S. Court of Appeals in San Francisco.

1989   An appeals court in Istanbul, Turkey, authorized a public burning of Miller's 1939 novel as sexually exploitative.

Source: 4, p. 74; 6, pp. 1,597–98; 8, pp. 387–89; 11, May 1989, p. 90.

1176 Miller, Jim, ed.
The Rolling Stone Illustrated History of Rock and Roll

1982 KY   Challenged in Jefferson County because it "will cause our children to become immoral and indecent."

Source: 11, Mar. 1983, p. 41.

1177 Milton, John
Paradise Lost

1758   Listed on the *Index Librorum Prohibitorum* (List of Prohibited Books) in Rome, Italy.

Source: 4, p. 22.

1178 Mishima, Yukio
The Sound of Waves

1993 WA   Challenged, but retained at the Lake Washington School District in Kirkland despite objections that it is "crude, vulgar, degrading to women, seductive, enticing, and suggestive."

2001 CA   Challenged in the Newark Unified School District because the book is sexually explicit.

Source: 11, Jan. 1994, p. 16; Mar. 1994, p. 71; Mar. 2001, p. 55.

1179 Mitchell, Margaret
Gone with the Wind

1978 CA   Banned from the Anaheim Union High School District English classrooms according to the Anaheim Secondary Teachers Association.

1984 IL   Challenged in the Waukegan School District because the novel uses the word "nigger."

Source: 11, Jan. 1979, p. 6; July 1984, p. 105.

1180 Mitchell, Stephen
Gilgamesh: A New English Version

2006 NJ   Challenged in the Clearview Regional High School in Harrison Township because the modern translation of one of the oldest known pieces of literature was considered sexually descriptive and unnecessarily explicit. The work itself dates back to about 1700 B.C., some one thousand years before the writings of Homer.

Source: 11, Jan. 2007, p. 10.

1181 Mochizuki, Ken
Baseball Saved Us

2006 CT   Challenged, but retained on the second-grade reading list in the New Milford schools despite the fact the word "Jap" is used to taunt the main character in the book. The children's story is about the World War II Japanese-American internment.

Source: 11, July 2006, pp. 183–84.

1182 Moe, Barbara A.
Everything You Need to Know about Sexual Abstinence

1996 LA   Pulled from the Ouachita Parish School library in Monroe because of sexual content. The Louisiana chapter of the ACLU filed a lawsuit in the federal courts on October 3, 1996, claiming that the principal and the school superintendent violated First Amendment free speech rights and also failed to follow established procedure when they removed the book. The three-year-old school library censorship case headed to court after the Ouachita Parish School Board made no decision to seek a settlement at a special meeting April 12, 1999. On August 17, 1999, the Ouachita Parish School Board agreed to return the book to the library and to develop a new book-selection policy that follows state guidelines for school media programs.

Source: 11, Sept. 1996, pp. 151–52; Jan. 1997, p. 7; July 1999, p. 93; Jan. 2000, p. 27.

1183 Mohr, Richard D.
A More Perfect Union: Why Straight America Must Stand Up for Gay Rights

1996 ME   Challenged, but retained at the Belfast Free Library because "homosexuality destroys marriages and families; it destroys the good health of the individual and the innocent are infected by it."

Source: 11, May 1996, p. 97.

1184 Momaday, N. Scott
House Made of Dawn

1989 OR   Challenged at the Reynolds High School in Troutdale because two pages of the 1969 Pulitzer Prize winner were sexually explicit.

1996 TX Retained on the Round Rock Independent High School reading list after a challenge that the book was too violent.

Source: 11, Jan. 1990, p. 32; May 1996, p. 99.

1185 Montaigne, Michel de
Essays

1595 Sections banned in France.
1676 Listed on the *Index Librorum Prohibitorum* (List of Prohibited Books) in Rome, Italy.

Source: 1, pp. 98–100; 4, p. 15; 8, pp. 234–36.

1186 Moore, Alan
The League of Extraordinary Gentlemen: Black Dossier

2009 KY New

Challenged at the Jessamine County Public Library in Nicolasville. A petition with 950 signatures was presented to the board to overturn its collection policy. The petition specifically asked for the removal of four works on the grounds that they "offended me in that they depict sexual acts and/or describe such acts in a way that in my opinion are contrary to the Jessamine County public opinion" of what should be in a public, taxpayer-supported collection. The petition concluded the works constituted a public safety issue in that they encourage sexual predators. In addition to Moore's graphic novel, the other works challenged were *Snuff*, by Chuck Palahniuk, *Choke*, a DVD based on a novel by Palahniuk; and the DVD *Ron White: You Can't Fix Stupid*. The graphic novel eventually got two employees fired for breaching library policies, the library director was threatened with physical harm, and the book was recataloged, along with other graphic novels with mature trends, to a separate but unrestricted graphic novels section of the library.

Source: 11, Jan. 2010, pp. 8–9; Mar. 2010, p. 52.

1187 Moore, George
Esther Waters

1894 Excluded from British circulating libraries, as both Mudie's Library and Smith's Library refused to stock it, viewing it as too risqué because the main character suffers as the result of her one sexual indiscretion, but she does not die, and because of the candid manner in which her situation is presented.

Source: 14, pp. 132–33.

1188 Morris, Desmond
The Naked Ape

1976 NY Removed from the Island Trees Union Free School District High School library in 1976 along with nine other titles because they were considered "immoral, anti-American, anti-Christian, or just plain filthy." Returned to the library after the U.S. Supreme Court ruling on June 25, 1982, in *Board of Education, Island Trees Union Free School District No. 26 et al. v. Pico et al.*, 457 U.S. 853 (1982).

1989 PA Reinstated after being removed from the Mifflinburg High School because the book includes material on human sexuality that is "explicit, almost manual description of what some would refer to as deviant sexual relations."

Source: 11, Nov. 1982, p. 197; May 1989, p. 93.

1189 Morrison, Lillian
Remember Me When This You See

1986 GA Challenged at the Gwinnett County Elementary School library because a line from the poetry book— "Don't make love in a potato field/Potatoes have eyes"— was objectionable.

Source: 11, Mar. 1987, p. 65.

1190 Morrison, Toni
Beloved

1995 FL Challenged at the St. Johns County Schools in St. Augustine.

1996 TX Retained on the Round Rock Independent High School reading list after a challenge that the book was too violent.

1997 ME Challenged by a member of the Madawaska School Committee because of the book's language. The 1987 Pulitzer Prize winning novel has been required reading for the Advanced Placement English class for six years.

1998 FL Challenged in the Sarasota County schools because of sexual material.

2006 IL Retained on the Northwest Suburban High School District 214 reading list in Arlington Heights, along with eight other challenged titles. A board member, elected amid promises to bring her Christian beliefs into all board decision-making, raised the controversy based on excerpts from the books she'd found on the Internet.

2007 ID Challenged in the Coeur d'Alene School District. Some parents say the book, along with five others, should require parental permission for students to read them.

2007 KY
New
Pulled from the senior Advanced Placement (AP) English class at Eastern High School in Louisville because two parents complained that the Pulitzer Prize-winning novel about antebellum slavery depicted the inappropriate topics of bestiality, racism, and sex. The principal ordered teachers to start over with the *The Scarlet Letter* by Nathaniel Hawthorne in preparation for upcoming AP exams.

Source: 11, Jan. 1996, p. 14; May 1996, p. 99; Jan. 1998, p. 14; July 1998, p. 120; July 2006, pp. 210–11; May 2007, pp. 98–99; July 2007, p. 147; Sept. 2007, p. 181.

1191   Morrison, Toni
The Bluest Eye

1994 AK
Pulled from an eleventh grade classroom at Lathrop High School in Fairbanks by school administrators because "It was a very controversial book; it contains lots of very graphic descriptions and lots of disturbing language."

1994 PA
Challenged at the West Chester schools as "most pornographic."

1994 PA
Banned from the Morrisville Borough High School English curriculum after complaints about its sexual content and objectionable language.

1995 FL
Challenged at the St. Johns County Schools in St. Augustine.

1995 MA
Challenged on the optional summer reading list at the Lynn schools because of the book's sexual content.

1998 MD
Challenged on Montgomery County reading lists and school library shelves.

1999 NH
Removed from the reading list for ninth- and tenth-graders at Stevens High School in Claremont because of a parent's complaint about the book's sexual content.

2003 CA
Challenged, but retained at the Kern High School District in Bakersfield despite complaints of the book's sexually explicit material.

2005 CO
Banned from the Littleton curriculum and library shelves after complaints about its explicit sex, including the rape of an eleven-year-old girl by her father.

2007 MI
New
Challenged in the Howell High School along with several other books because of strong sexual content. In response to a request from the president of the Livingston Organization for Values in Education, or LOVE, the county's top law enforcement official reviewed the books to see whether laws against distribution of sexually explicit materials to minors had been broken. "After reading the books in question, it is clear that the explicit passages illustrated a larger literary, artistic, or political message and were not included solely to appeal to the prurient interests of minors," the Livingston County prosecutor wrote. "Whether these materials are appropriate for minors is a decision to be made by the school board, but I find that they are not in violation of the criminal laws."

2009 IN
New
Retained in Delphi Community High School's curriculum despite claims of inappropriate sexual content and graphic language.

Source: 8, p. 321; 11, May 1994, p. 86; Jan. 1995, p. 25; Mar. 1995, pp. 44–45; May 1995, p. 71; July 1995, p. 98; Jan. 1996, p. 14; May 1998, p. 70; Sept. 1999, pp. 121–22; Mar. 2004, pp. 50–51; May 2004, pp. 118–19; Jan. 2006, p. 13; Mar. 2007, pp. 51–52; May 2007, pp. 117–18; May 2009, p. 24.

1192   Morrison, Toni
Song of Solomon

1993 OH
Challenged, but retained in the Columbus schools. The complainant believed that the book contains language degrading to blacks, and is sexually explicit.

1994 GA
Removed from required reading lists and library shelves in the Richmond County School District after a parent complained that passages from the book were "filthy and inappropriate."

1995 FL
Challenged at the St. Johns County Schools in St. Augustine.

1998 MD
Removed from the St. Mary's County schools' approved text list by the school superintendent overruling a faculty committee recommendation. Complainants referred to the novel as "filth," "trash," and "repulsive."

2009 MI
New
Reinstated in the Shelby school Advanced Placement English curriculum, but parents are to be informed in writing and at a meeting about the book's content. Students not wanting to read the book can choose an alternative without academic penalty. The superintendent had suspended the book from the curriculum.

Source: 11, July 1993, p. 108; Sept. 1993, p. 160; May 1994, p. 86; Jan. 1996, p. 14; Mar. 1998, p. 42; July 2009, pp. 140–41.

1193   Morrison, Toni
Sula

2000 MD
Challenged on the Poolesville High School reading list because of the book's sexual content and language. On Oct. 5, 2000, Montgomery County Circuit Court Judge Paul McGuckian dismissed the bid to ban the work from the curriculum. The school, however, decided to remove the book from the summer reading list.

Source: 11, Nov. 2000, p. 196; Jan. 2001, pp. 36–37.

1194 Mosca, Frank
All-American Boy

1993 KS Challenged in the Kansas City school district, which donated the book to the city's public library.

1993 MO Challenged at several Kansas City area schools after the books were donated by a national group that seeks to give young adults "fair, accurate and inclusive images of lesbians and gay men." At the Shawnee Mission School District the book was returned to general circulation; at the Olathe East High School the book was removed; protesters burned copies of the book but the Kansas City School District kept Mosca's novel on the high school shelves.

1993 MO The school superintendent removed the book in Lee's Summit.

Source: 11, Mar. 1994, pp. 51–52; May 1994, p. 84.

1195 *Mother Goose: Old Nursery Rhymes*

1983 FL Challenged at the Dade County Public Library by a Miami Metro Commissioner because the anthology of nursery rhymes contains the following anti-Semitic verse: "Jack sold his gold egg/to a rogue of a Jew/who cheated him out of/half of his due."

Source: 11, July 1983, p. 107; Jan. 1984, p. 25.

1196 Mowat, Farley
And No Birds Sang

1994 OH Challenged in the Northwestern Middle School library, Springfield because of "improper language."

Source: 11, July 1994, p. 111.

1197 Mowat, Farley
Never Cry Wolf

1987 FL Removed from the Panama City school classrooms and libraries because of "offensive" language.

Source: 11, July 1987, pp. 126–28; Sept. 1987, pp. 168–69.

1198 Mowat, Farley
Woman in the Mists: The Story of Dian Fossey & the Mountain Gorillas of Africa

1991 NE Removed from a required reading list in the Omaha public schools because the book has racial slurs, passages degrading to women, profanity, and a long discussion of the aftermath of Fossey's abortion.

Source: 11, Mar. 1992, p. 44.

1199 Muller, Gilbert H., and Harvey S. Wiener, comps.
The Short Prose Reader

1994 MD Challenged at the Cecil County Board of Education in Elkton. Many deemed the text controversial because it included essays dealing with issues of abortion, gay rights, alcohol, and sex education.

Source: 11, Mar. 1995, p. 55.

1200 Mungo, Raymond
Liberace

2000 CA Removed from the Anaheim school district because school officials said the book is too difficult for middle school students and that it could cause harassment against students seen with it. The American Civil Liberties Union (ACLU) of Southern California filed suit in *Doe v. Anaheim Union High School District* alleging that the removal is "a pretext for viewpoint-based censorship." The ACLU claims no other books have been removed from the junior high library for similar reasons, even though several, such as works by Shakespeare and Dickens, are more difficult reading. The ACLU contends that the school officials engaged in unconstitutional viewpoint discrimination by removing the book because it contains gay and lesbian material. In March 2001, the school board approved a settlement that restored the book to the high school shelves and amended the district's policy to prohibit the removal of books for subject matter involving sexual orientation, but the book will not be returned to the middle school.

Source: 11, Mar. 2001, p. 53; May 2001, p. 95; July 2001, p. 173.

1201 Murdoch, Iris
The Nice and the Good

1977 Banned in South Africa.

Source: 5, Nov./Dec. 1977, p. 68.

1202 Murphy, Barbara Beasley
Home Free

1988 NJ Retained at the Hillcrest School library in East Ramapo, but the book will not be lent to a fourth or fifth grader who is not deemed an "advanced reader or critical thinker" by a parent, teacher, or librarian. The book contains the word "nigger."

Source: 11, May 1988, p. 86.

1203   Murphy, Barbara Beasley
No Place to Run

1982 AL   Removed from two Anniston high school libraries due to "the curse words and using the Lord's name in vain," but later reinstated on a restricted basis.
Source: 11, Mar. 1983, p. 37.

1204   Murray, William
Tip on a Dead Crab

1983 TN   Publication canceled by Dodd, Mead & Company because of language in the book considered "objectionable" by Thomas Nelson, Inc. of Nashville—Dodd, Mead's parent company.
Source: 11, Nov. 1983, p. 188.

1205   Myers, Lawrence W.
Improvised Radio Jamming Techniques

1991 OR   Challenged for promoting illegal actions, but retained at the Multnomah County Library.
Source: 11, Jan. 1992, p. 6.

1206   Myers, Walter Dean
Fallen Angels

1990 OH   Challenged in the Bluffton schools because of its use of profane language.
1992 GA   Restricted as supplemental classroom reading material at the Jackson County High School because of undesirable language and sensitive material.
1994 PA   Challenged at the West Chester schools.
1995 OH   Removed from a twelfth-grade English class in Middleburg Heights after a parent complained of its sexually explicit language. The novel won the Coretta Scott King Award and was named Best Book of 1988 by *School Library Journal*.
1997 OH   Challenged, but retained at the Lakewood High School. The book was challenged by parents who objected to the novel's violence and vulgar language.
1999 CA   Removed from the Laton Unified School District because the novel about the Vietnam War contains violence and profanity.
1999 MI   Removed as required reading in the Livonia public schools because it contains "too many swear words."
2000 TX   Challenged, but retained in the Arlington school district's junior high school libraries despite a parent's complaint that the book's content was too strong for younger students.

2002 MS   Banned from the George County schools because of profanity.
2002 VA   Challenged, along with seventeen other titles in the Fairfax County elementary and secondary libraries, by a group called Parents Against Bad Books in Schools. The group contends the books "contain profanity and descriptions of drug abuse, sexually explicit conduct, and torture."
2003 IN   Banned at the Franklin Central High School in Indianapolis because of concerns about the book's profanity. The book was assigned in English classes for sophomores.
2005 KS   The book was assigned in English classes for sophomores. Removed from the Blue Valley School District's high school curriculum in Overland Park.
2006 IL   The book was challenged by parents and community members along with thirteen other titles. Retained on the Northwest Suburban High School District 214 reading list in Arlington Heights, along with eight other challenged titles. A board member, elected amid promises to bring her Christian beliefs into all board decision-making, raised the controversy based on excerpts from the books she'd found on the Internet.
2007 ID   Challenged in the Coeur d'Alene School
New   District. Some parents say the book, along with five others, should require parental permission for students to read them.
2008 NC   Challenged on the accelerated reading list at
New   Chinquapin Elementary School in Duplin County because the book is littered with hundreds of expletives, including racial epithets and slang terms for homosexuals.
Source: 8, pp. 451–53; 11, Nov. 1990, p. 211; Sept. 1992, p. 142; Jan. 1995, p. 25; Mar. 1996, p. 49; May 1996, p. 79; Nov. 1999, pp. 164–65; Jan. 2001, p. 36; Jan. 2003, p. 10; Mar. 2003, p. 55; Jan. 2004, pp. 11–12; Nov. 2005, pp. 282–83; July 2006, pp. 210–11; Sept. 2007, p. 181; May 2008, p. 97.

1207   Myers, Walter Dean
Fast Sam, Cool Clyde and Stuff

1983 OH   Challenged by an elementary school administrator in Akron.
Source: 9; 11, May 1983, p. 86.

1208   Myers, Walter Dean
Hoops

1989 CO   Challenged in Littleton school libraries because the book "endorses" drinking, stealing, and homosexuality, uses offensive words, and contains a sex scene.

2000 OH Challenged but retained in Vanlue High School English classes despite objections that the book is evil and depicts drugs, alcohol, and sex.

2009 IA New Challenged in the Council Bluffs schools because it contains "derogatory remarks, racial slurs, and sexual content."

Source: 11, Sept. 1989, p. 186; July 2000, p. 125; May 2009, p. 77.

1209 Myers, Walter Dean
Young Martin's Promise

1994 NY Challenged by a school board member in the Queens school libraries because King "was a leftist hoodlum with significant Communist ties. King was a hypocritical adulterer." The rest of the school board voted to retain the book.

Source: 11, July 1994, pp. 110–11; Sept. 1994, p. 166.

1210 Myracle, Lauren
ttfn

2008 OK New Removed from the Marietta Middle School library due to descriptions of sex and drug use. The book, which is recommended for older students, depicts online conversations between three eleventh-grade girls.

Source: 11, Nov. 2008, p. 232

1211 Myracle, Lauren
ttyl

2007 NY New Challenged at the William Floyd Middle School library in Mastic because the book includes "curse words, crude references to the male and female anatomy, sex acts and adult situations like drinking alcohol and flirtation with a teacher that almost goes too far." A spokesman for the William Floyd School District said the book will remain in the library, and that the book is very popular with students across the country. The spokesperson also said unlike many books that young people read, the book deals with controversial subjects without glorifying negative behaviors. It is the first book written entirely in the format of instant messaging—the title itself is a shorthand reference to "talk to you later."

2008 TX New Challenged in the Round Rock Independent School District middle school library due to the book's descriptions of sex, porn, alcohol, and inappropriate teacher-student relationships. The school offers parents the ability to tell the school if they do not want their children to check out particular books at the library.

2009 WI New Challenged, but retained at the John Muir Middle School library in Wausau despite a parent's request that the book be removed because of sexually explicit content. The author said, "The book's dialogue about sex and alcohol is frank but the characters criticize those who engage in those behaviors."

2010 CT New Retained in the Ponus Ridge Middle School library in Norwalk. While many critics decry its style as "grammatically incorrect," most who take exception point to its foul language, sexual content, and questionable sexual behavior.

Source: 11, May 2007, p. 92; Nov. 2008, pp. 232–33; Jan. 2009, pp. 6–7; July 2009, p. 140; May 2010, p.127.

1212 Myrer, Anton
A Green Desire

1985 PA Banned from the Stroudsburg High School library because it was "blatantly graphic, pornographic and wholly unacceptable for a high school library."

Source: 11, May 1985, p. 79.

1213 Nabokov, Vladimir
Lolita

1955 Banned as obscene in England from 1955 to 1959.

1956 Banned as obscene in France from 1956 to 1959.

1959 Banned as obscene in Argentina.

1960 Banned as obscene in New Zealand.

1982 The South African Directorate of Publications announced on Nov. 27, 1982, that *Lolita* had been taken off the banned list, eight years after a request for permission to market the novel in paperback had been refused.

2006 FL Challenged at the Marion-Levy Public Library System in Ocala. The Marion County commissioners voted to have the county attorney review the novel that addresses the themes of pedophilia and incest, to determine if it meets the state law's definition of "unsuitable for minors."

Source: 4, p. 81; 5, Apr. 1983, p. 47; 8, pp. 359–60; 11, Mar. 2006, pp. 69–70; Nov. 2006, p. 317.

1214 Nasrin, Taslima
Lajja (Shame)

1993 Banned in Bangladesh on the grounds that it had "created misunderstanding among communities." A fatwa, or death decree, was issued by a mullah, or Muslim cleric, of the Council of Soldiers of Islam, a militant group based in Sylhet, Bangladesh. The author fled to Stockholm, Sweden, and remained in exile in Europe and the United States.

Source: 8, pp. 255–58.

1215   National Register Publishing Co. Staff
Official Catholic Directory

1991 OR   Challenged by a patron who believed public funds should not be expended on religious books, but retained at the Multnomah County Library.
Source: 11, Jan. 1992, p. 6.

1216   Naylor, Phyllis Reynolds
Achingly Alice

2002 MO   Banned from the Webb City school library because the book promotes homosexuality and discusses issues "best left to parents."
Source: 11, Nov. 2002, p. 256.

1217   Naylor, Phyllis Reynolds
The Agony of Alice

2000 VA   Challenged, but retained at the Franklin Sherman Elementary School library and on the Fairfax County approved reading list. The book, however, is limited in its classroom use to small discussion groups for girls only.
Source: 11, Mar. 2000, p. 62.

1218   Naylor, Phyllis Reynolds
Alice in Lace

2002 MO   Banned from the Webb City school library because the book promotes homosexuality and discusses issues "best left to parents."
Source: 11, Nov. 2002, p. 256.

1219   Naylor, Phyllis Reynolds
Alice on Her Way

2008 WA   Restricted to students who have parental
New   consent at the Icicle River Middle School library in Leavenworth due to its depiction of sexuality. One other book, Gary Paulsen's *Harris and Me*, has been similarly restricted at the school for almost a decade. Parents challenged the book's use during classroom reading because of "two cuss words."
Source: 11, May 2008, p. 97.

1220   Naylor, Phyllis Reynolds
Alice on the Outside

2005 KY   Available with parental permission in the librarian's office at Shelbyville East Middle School because the book is "too sexually explicit" for middle-school students.
Source: 11, May 2005, p. 108; July 2005, pp. 185–86.

1221   Naylor, Phyllis Reynolds
Alice the Brave

2004 TX   Challenged in the Mesquite Pirrung Elementary School library due to sexual references.
Source: 11, Nov. 2004, p. 231.

1222   Naylor, Phyllis Reynolds
Alice, In Between

1998 CT   Removed from the Monroe sixth-grade required reading list after some parents called attention to the book's sexual content. The series of books by the Newbery Award-winning children's author includes *The Agony of Alice* and *Outrageously Alice*.
Source: 11, Nov. 1998, p. 182.

1223   Naylor, Phyllis Reynolds
All But Alice

1997 ME   Restricted to students with parental permission at the Monroe Elementary School library in Thorndike.
1997 MN   Removed from the elementary school libraries in the Rosemount-Apple Valley-Eagan Independent School District # 196 because of a brief passage in which the seventh-grade heroine discusses sexually oriented rock lyrics with her father and older brother; the school board considered the book inappropriate for the ages of the students.
Source: 11, Sept. 1997, pp. 126, 148; Nov. 1997, p. 166.

1224   Naylor, Phyllis Reynolds
The Fear Place

1998 IA   Challenged at the Madison Elementary School in Cedar Rapids. A review committee asked that the book carry a warning about objectionable language and that teachers consider notifying parents if they are going to use the book in class.
Source: 11, May 1998, pp. 87–88.

1225   Naylor, Phyllis Reynolds
The Grooming of Alice

2002 MO   Banned from the Webb City school library because the book promotes homosexuality and discusses issues "best left to parents."
Source: 11, Nov. 2002, p. 256.

1226   Naylor, Phyllis Reynolds
Reluctantly Alice

2006 NC   Challenged in the Wake County schools. Parents are getting help from Called2Action, a Christian group that says its mission is to "promote and defend our shared family and social values."

Source: 11, Sept. 2006, p. 231.

1227   Naylor, Phyllis Reynolds
Send No Blessings

1993 WA Challenged at the Cedar Valley Elementary School in Kent because parents claimed the book condones child molestation and promiscuity.

Source: 11, Mar. 1993, p. 55.

1228   Naylor, Phyllis Reynolds
Witch Herself

1989 TX Retained at the Ector County school library after being challenged because the book might lure children into the occult.

Source: 11, Jan. 1990, p. 9; May 1990, p. 107.

1229   Naylor, Phyllis Reynolds
Witch Water

1989 TX Retained at the Ector County school library after being challenged because the book might lure children into the occult.

Source: 11, Jan. 1990, p. 9; May 1990, p. 107.

1230   Naylor, Phyllis Reynolds
Witch's Sister

1988 OR Challenged at the Multnomah County Library in Portland because the occult topic could be frightening and traumatic for children.

1989 TX Retained at the Ector County school library after being challenged because the book might lure children into the occult.

Source: 11, Jan. 1989, p. 3; Jan. 1990, p. 9; May 1990, p. 107.

1231   Nehring, James
Why Do We Gotta Do This Stuff, Mr. Nehring?

1994 ID Challenged, but retained by the Pocatello Library Board which refused to remove or label books that contain obscene language.

Source: 11, May 1994, pp. 97–98.

1232   Nelson, O. T.
The Girl Who Owned a City

2000 ME Challenged in the Fort Fairfield schools because the book promotes violence, including explaining how to make a Molotov cocktail.

Source: 11, July 2000, p. 104.

1233   Nelson, Theresa
Earthshine

1997 AK Challenged, but retained in the Anchorage school libraries. Parents of a student wanted the book removed from all public school libraries because "it contains profanity and deals with subjects like homosexuality, abortion, and children running away from home."

Source: 11, May 1997, p. 77.

1234   Neufeld, John
Freddy's Book

1977 IL Removed from the elementary school library in Spring Valley after a parent complained about the book's theme.

1989 MI Challenged, but retained at the Lake Fenton Elementary School library because of the book's descriptions of male and female genitalia, menstruation, erections, sexual intercourse, and wet dreams. The book was, however, placed on a restricted shelf and requires parents to check the book out. Partly as a result of the controversy, all of the district's library books were slated to be reviewed by a four-member committee consisting of a parent, teacher, librarian, and district administrator.

Source: 11, Jan. 1978, p. 6; Jan. 1990, p. 9.

1235   Neville, Henry
Isle of Pines

1668 MA Banned the year of its publication after authorities in the Massachusetts colony discovered it while searching for unlicensed material on the premise of the only two printers in the colony.

Source: 13, p. 116.

1236   Newman, Felice
The Whole Lesbian Sex Book

2007 AR
New   The father of two teenage boys asked city officials to fine the Bentonville Public Library for keeping the book on open shelves. He wanted the city to pay him $10,000 per child, the maximum allowed under Arkansas obscenity law. After receiving the original complaint, the library advisory committee board voted to remove the book from circulation and look for a similar, less graphic resource for the open stacks. The library director said she disagreed with the complainant's conclusion that having Newman's book in the library follows an "immoral social agenda."

Source: 11, July 2007, p. 143.

1237 Newman, Leslea
Gloria Goes to Gay Pride

1992 NY Removed from the Brooklyn School District's curriculum because the school board objected to words that were "age inappropriate."

1993 OH Retained at the Dayton and Montgomery County Public Library.

1994 AZ Challenged at the Chandler Public Library because the book is a "skillful presentation to the young child about lesbianism/homosexuality."

Source: 11, May 1992, p. 83; Mar. 1994, p. 69; July 1994, p. 128; Nov. 1994, p. 187.

1238 Newman, Leslea
Heather Has Two Mommies

1992 NC Challenged, but retained at the Cumberland County Library. Opponents argued the book promoted a dangerous and ungodly lifestyle from which children must be protected.

1992 NY Removed from the Brooklyn School District's curriculum because the school board objected to words that were "age inappropriate."

1993 AZ Challenged at the Mesa Public Library because it "is vile, sick, and goes against every law and constitution."

1993 GA Moved from the children's section to the young adult section at the Chestatee Regional Library System in Gainesville. Three area legislators wanted the book removed and said, "We could put together a resolution to amend the Georgia state constitution to say that tax dollars cannot be used to promote homosexuality, pedophilia, or sado-masochism."

1993 MD Challenged at the Wicomico County Free Library in Salisbury.

1993 NC Moved from the children's section to the adult section in Elizabethtown library because it "promotes a dangerous and ungodly lifestyle from which children must be protected."

1993 NJ Moved from the children's section to the adult section at the Mercer County Library System in Lawrence.

1993 NJ Challenged at the North Brunswick Public Library.

1993 OH Retained at the Dayton and Montgomery County Public Library.

1994 AZ Challenged at the Chandler Public Library because the book is a "skillful presentation to the young child about lesbianism/homosexuality."

1994 MA Challenged, but retained in the Oak Bluffs school library. Though the parent leading the protest stated "The subject matter . . . is obscene and vulgar and the message is that homosexuality is okay," the selection review committee voted unanimously to keep the book.

1994 OR Removed by officials at the Cottage Grove Lane County Head Start Center.

1998 TX Challenged at the Wichita Falls Public Library. The deacon body of the First Baptist Church requested that any literature that promotes or sanctions a homosexual lifestyle be removed. The Wichita Falls City Council established a policy that allows library card holders who collect 300 signatures to have children's books moved to an adult portion of the library. U.S. District Court Judge Jerry Buchmeyer struck down the library resolution as unconstitutional and the books were returned.

1999 ID Challenged, but retained in the juvenile non-fiction section of the Nampa Public Library.

Source: 11, May 1992, p. 83; Jan. 1993, pp. 9, 28; May 1993, p. 71; July 1993, pp. 100–101, 126; Sept. 1993, pp. 143–44; Nov. 1993, pp. 177–78; Jan. 1994, pp. 13, 34–35; Mar. 1994, p. 69; May 1994, p. 98; July 1994, pp. 110, 115; Sept. 1994, pp. 147–48, 166; Nov. 1994, p. 187; July 1998, pp. 106–7; Jan. 1999, pp. 8–9; Mar. 1999, p. 36: May 1999, p. 67; Sept. 1999, p. 131; Nov. 1999, p. 172; Nov. 2000, pp. 201–2.

1239 Newton, Michael
The Encyclopedia of Serial Killers

2002 FL Challenged and retained in the Hillsborough County School District over a parent's objections to the book's "gruesome details."

Source: 11, July 2002, p. 179.

1240 Nichols, John
The Milagro Beanfield War

1999 OH Pulled from a junior English class at the Shawnee High School in Lima because it contained offensive material, including sex and violence.

Source: 11, July 1999, p. 97.

1241 Nix, Garth
Shade's Children

2001 NY Challenged, but retained at the Transit Middle School library in Williamsville after objections that the book "is vulgar, obscene, and educationally unsuitable."

Source: 11, May 2001, p. 124.

1242 Nixon, Joan Lowery
Whispers from the Dead

2008 NY Restored by the Lackawanna School Board
New   along with several other books following accusations of censorship by some parents

and teachers. The books were pulled from the middle school library recommended list because of concerns that the books deal with the occult.

Source: 11, May 2008, p. 116.

1243 Noel, Janet
The Human Body

1982 ME The York Middle School review committee voted unanimously to remove the book from the library "because of the inappropriateness of written and pictorial material." After a backlash from anti-censorship parents, the book was moved from the middle school library to the junior high library for use by seventh and eighth graders.

Source: 11, July 1982, pp. 123–24.

1244 Norstog, Knut J., and
Andrew J. Meyerriecks
Biology

1986 OK A Sallisaw Senior High School biology teacher removed pages 467–76 from the textbook because they were "irrelevant" to the school's curriculum requirements. The pages contained information on reproduction and birth control. The teacher said he was "trying to circumvent a problem, rather than create one, when students were forced to take the books parents might find objectionable into their homes."

Source: 11, July 1986, p. 121.

1245 Norton, Jim
Happy Endings: The Tales of a
Meaty-Breasted Zilch

2007 MS New Available upon request, but not placed in general circulation at the Jackson-George Regional Library System in Pascagoula after complaints that the comedian's best-selling book is "garbage that doesn't belong in a library."

Source: 11, Nov. 2007, p. 263.

1246 Nunokawa, Jeff
Oscar Wilde

2000 CA Removed from the Anaheim school district because school officials said the book is too difficult for middle school students and that it could cause harassment against students seen with it. The American Civil Liberties Union (ACLU) of Southern California filed suit in *Doe v. Anaheim Union High School District* alleging that the removal is "a pretext for viewpoint-based censorship." The ACLU claims no other books have been removed from the junior high library for similar reasons, even though several, such as works by Shakespeare and Dickens, are more difficult reading. The ACLU contends that the school officials engaged in unconstitutional viewpoint discrimination by removing the book because it contains gay and lesbian material. In March 2001, the school board approved a settlement that restored the book to the high school shelves and amended the district's policy to prohibit the removal of books for subject matter involving sexual orientation, but the book will not be returned to the middle school.

Source: 11, Mar. 2001, p. 53; May 2001, p. 95; July 2001, p. 173.

1247 Nye, Robert
Beowulf, a New Telling

1998 OR Challenged, but retained in the Hood River County schools. A parent complained that the book was "inappropriate for middle school students because of the evil intentions of its characters, graphic descriptions of gore and mutilations, and descriptions of monstrous characters."

Source: 11, July 1998, p. 121.

1248 Oates, Joyce Carol
Sexy

2007 MT Retained at Jefferson High School in Boulder despite objections to "inappropriate" language and sexually explicit passages in the novel.

Source: 11, Jan. 2008, p. 25.

1249 Oates, Joyce Carol
Where Are You Going, Where Have
You Been?

1990 PA Challenged in the Tyrone schools because of its use of profane language.

Source: 11, Mar. 1991, pp. 61–62.

1250 Oates, Stephen
Portrait of America, Vol. II

1984 WI Returned to the Racine Unified School District curriculum just one week after the school board voted to ban it. Opponents of the books on the board charged that the social studies volumes contained "judgmental writing" and, in the words of one board member, "a lot more funny pictures of Republicans and nicer pictures of Democrats." Opponents also said that one text did not present an adequate analysis of the Vietnam War.

Source: 11, Sept. 1984, p. 158.

1251   O'Brien, Edna
August Is a Wicked Month

1960   All novels published by Edna O'Brien during the 1960s were banned in Ireland by the Censorship of Publications Board: *The Country Girls* (1960); *The Lonely Girl* (1962) and its reprint *Girl with Green Eyes* (1964); *Girls in Their Married Bliss* (1964); and *August Is a Wicked Month* (1965). O'Brien's work gained notoriety in Ireland in the 1960s because of its detailed exploration of female sexuality.
1965   Banned in Australia.
1965   Banned in Rhodesia.
1965   Banned in South Africa.
Source: 6, pp. 1,749–50.

1252   O'Brien, Kate
The Land of the Spices

1941   Banned in Ireland by the Censorship of Publications Board. The impact of the banning was considerable. In the short term, it drew attention to the extremes to which the Censorship Board went in recommending books to be banned, particularly those by Irish authors. In the long term, the 1942 Irish Senate debate initiated the discussions that led to the creation of a Censorship of Publications Appeal Board in 1946.
Source: 6, pp. 1,750–51.

1253   O'Brien, Sharon
Willa Cather

2000 CA   Removed from the Anaheim school district because school officials said the book is too difficult for middle school students and that it could cause harassment against students seen with it. The American Civil Liberties Union (ACLU) of Southern California filed suit in *Doe v. Anaheim Union High School District* alleging that the removal is "a pretext for viewpoint-based censorship." The ACLU claims no other books have been removed from the junior high library for similar reasons, even though several, such as works by Shakespeare and Dickens, are more difficult reading. The ACLU contends that the school officials engaged in unconstitutional viewpoint discrimination by removing the book because it contains gay and lesbian material. In March 2001, the school board approved a settlement that restored the book to the high school shelves and amended the district's policy to prohibit the removal of books for subject matter involving sexual orientation, but the book will not be returned to the middle school.
Source: 11, Mar. 2001, p. 53; May 2001, p. 95; July 2001, p. 173.

1254   O'Brien, Tim
In the Lake of the Woods

1998 WA   Challenged for use in the Richland high school English classes along with six other titles because the "books are poor-quality literature and stress suicide, illicit sex, violence, and hopelessness."
Source: 11, Mar. 1999, p. 40.

1255   O'Brien, Tim
The Things They Carried

1992 WI   Determined unsuitable for classroom reading in Waukesha because of "anti-American attitudes, offensive language, political bias, and disturbing fiction."
2000 PA   Challenged, but retained at the Pennridge high school despite a protest of the book's strong language. O'Brien was a finalist for the 1990 Pulitzer Prize and the National Book Critics Circle Award.
2002 MS   Banned from the George County schools because of profanity.
2006 IL   Retained on the Northwest Suburban High School District 214 reading list in Arlington Heights, along with eight other challenged titles. A board member, elected amid promises to bring her Christian beliefs into all board decision-making, raised the controversy based on excerpts from the books she'd found on the Internet.
Source: 11, Jan. 2001, p. 37; Mar. 2003, p. 55; July 2006, pp. 210–11.

1256   O'Connor, Flannery
The Complete Stories

2000 LA   Prohibited at the Opelousas Catholic High School by Bishop Edward J. O'Donnell of Lafayette along with any "similar book." Some parents protested when they saw the word "nigger" in the collection of short stories assigned for the summer reading of students after their junior year.
Source: 11, Jan. 2001, p. 13.

1257   O'Connor, Frank
Dutch Interior

1940   Banned in Ireland. The Irish Republic's Censorship Board was not required to state publicly why it banned individual books as

"indecent or obscene," but it was widely believed that O'Connor's novel and short stories were so treated primarily because of their critique of the Irish Catholic middle class.
Source: 6, pp. 1,757–58.

1258   O'Connor, Jane
Just Good Friends

1988   OR   Removed from the Jefferson Magnet Arts Library, and transferred to a middle school in Eugene because of the book's sexual references.
Source: 11, Jan. 1989, p. 3.

1259   O'Connor, Jane
Lu Lu and the Witch Baby

1991   IL   Challenged at the Dakota Primary School because it "promotes lying and witchcraft."
Source: 11, May 1991, p. 89.

1260   O'Donnell, E. P.
Green Margins

1937   LA   Seized and destroyed by New Orleans police.
Source: 15, Vol. III, p. 650.

1261   O'Faolain, Sean
Midsummer Night Madness and Other Stories

1932   Banned in Ireland.
Source: 6, pp. 1,761–62.

1262   Oh, Minya
Bling Bling: Hip Hop's Crown Jewels

2008   WI   Retained with limited access at the
New   Maplewood Middle School Library in Menasha. The book for reluctant readers contains photographs and interviews with rap artists and focuses on how hip-hop taste for flashy jewelry typifies their musical and cultural evolution of the last twenty-five years. In addition to retaining the book, board members voted unanimously to adopt procedures intended to secure and record parental consent before limited access books are released to students.
Source: 11, July 2008, p. 164.

1263   O'Hara, Frank
Lunch Poems

1976   CO   Banned for use in Aurora High School English classes on the grounds of "immorality."
Source: 11, May 1977, p. 79.

1264   O'Hara, John
Appointment in Samarra

1941   Declared not mailable by the U.S. Department of Post Office because of "obscene Language." The novel remained on the U.S. Post Office's index of banned books through the mid-1950s. The novel also attracted the attention of the National Organization for Decent Literature (NODL), a Roman Catholic organization that identified "objectionable" literature and advised members against reading "offensive" and "objectionable" novels. In 1953, NODL found the novel to be "objectionable" and placed in on their list of blacklisted books. The list was then sent to cooperating book dealers who agreed to remove the book from their racks.
1941   MI   Banned from sale in Port Huron.
1941   MI   Banned from sale in Detroit.
1950   MN   Banned from sale in St. Cloud during the 1950s. Sales were limited in numerous other cities, through the efforts of local chapters of the NODL, until the demise of the organization in the late 1950s.
Source: 4, p. 86; 8, pp. 409–10.

1265   O'Hara, John
Ten North Frederick

1957   MI   Banned by Police Commissioner in Detroit, a series of local bans and seizures spread over a two-year period from 1957 to 1958.
Source: 4, pp. 86–87.

1266   O'Hara, Mary
My Friend Flicka

1990   FL   Pulled from fifth- and sixth-grade optional reading lists in Clay County schools because the book uses the word "bitch" to refer to a female dog, as well as the word "damn."
Source: 11, Jan. 1991, p. 16.

1267   O'Huigin, Sean
Scary Poems for Rotten Kids

1990   MI   Challenged in the Livonia schools because the poems frightened first-grade children.
Source: 11, Mar. 1991, p. 62.

1268   O'Keeffe, Georgia
Georgia O'Keeffe

1994   AZ   Retained at Maldonado Elementary School in Tucson after being challenged by parents who objected to nudity and "pornographic," "perverted," and "morbid" themes.
Source: 11, July 1994, p. 112.

1269   ***The Old Farmer's Almanac***

1941   During World War II, according to Robb Sagendorph, the U.S. Army temporarily banned the publication on the grounds that its weather forecasts aided the enemy.
Source: 6, p. 45.

1270   **O'Malley, Kevin, illus.**
Froggy Went A-Courtin'

1996 MD   Restricted at the Baltimore County school libraries because of Froggy's nefarious activities including burning money, and speeding away from the cat police, as well as robbery and smoking. The book is to be kept in restricted areas of the libraries where only parents and teachers will be allowed to check it out and read it to children.
Source: 11, Jan. 1997, p. 7; Mar. 1997, p. 35.

1271   **Opie, Iona Archibald, and Peter Opie, eds.**
I Saw Esau: The Schoolchild's Pocket Book

2007 TN   Challenged at the Cedar Grove Elementary School in Murfreesboro. The complainant stated, "I understand that it is a book of poetry, but there is a fine line between poetry art and porn and this book's illustrations are absolutely offensive in every way." The book is a collection of schoolyard jokes, riddles, insults, and jump-rope rhymes and is illustrated by Maurice Sendak.
Source: 11, May 2007, p. 94.

1272   **Oppenheim, Irene**
Living Today

1984 WI   Returned to the Racine Unified School District curriculum just one week after the school board voted to ban it. The home economics text was criticized for encouraging premarital sex and advocating that unmarried couples live together.
Source: 11, Sept. 1984, p. 158.

1273   **Orenstein, Peggy**
Schoolgirls: Young Women, Self-esteem and the Confidence Gap

1996 OH   Challenged in Courtland High School because of its "rotten, filthy language." The teacher offered the parents a black marker with which to delete offending passages, but the parents wanted it banned. The school board voted to continue the book.
Source: 11, Mar. 1997, p. 50.

1274   **Orgel, Doris**
The Devil in Vienna

2000 IA   Challenged, but retained at the Grant Wood Elementary School media center in Cedar Rapids despite objections to the book's inclusion of a brief incident of an old man exposing himself to a six-year-old girl.
Source: 11, Mar. 2000, p. 61.

1275   **Ortiz, Victoria**
The Land and People of Cuba

1974 FL   Removed from the Rockaway Junior High School school library in Miami by the principal because the book "was anti-American propaganda favoring the pro-Castro viewpoint."

1974 FL   Rejected by Dade County's public libraries.
Source: 7, pp. 294–95.

1276   **Orwell, George**
1984

1981 FL   Challenged in the Jackson County School Board because Orwell's novel is "pro-communist and contained explicit sexual matter."
Source: 8, pp. 141–42; 9; 11, May 1981, p. 73.

1277   **Orwell, George**
Animal Farm

1963 WI   A Wisconsin survey revealed that the John Birch Society had challenged the novel's use; it objected to the words "masses will revolt."

1968 NY   The New York State English Council's Committee on Defenses Against Censorship conducted a comparable study in New York State English classrooms. Its findings identified the novel on its list of "problem books"; the reason cited was that "Orwell was a communist."

1977   Suppressed from being displayed at the 1977 Moscow, Russia International Book Fair.

1982 GA   A survey of censorship challenges in the schools, conducted in DeKalb County for the period 1979 to 1982, revealed that the novel had been objected to for its political theories.

1987 FL   Banned from Bay County's four middle schools and three high schools in Panama City by the Bay County school superintendent. After 44 parents filed a suit against the district claiming that its instructional aids policy denies constitutional rights, the Bay County School Board reinstated the book, along with sixty-four others banned.

2002   Banned from schools in the United Arab Emirates, along with 125 others. The Ministry of Education banned it on the grounds that it contained written or illustrated material that contradicts Islamic and Arab values—in this text, pictures of alcoholic drinks, pigs, and other "indecent images."

Source: 8, pp. 15–16.

1278 Ostrovsky, Victor, and Claire Hoy
By Way of Deception: The Making and Unmaking of a Mossad Officer

1990   The government of Israel initiated the challenges through lawsuits seeking to block publication.

1990   The Israelis won a court order in Toronto, Ontario, Canada, that blocked publication. Israel's request was based on its claim that the book "would disseminate confidential information and that this information could endanger the lives of various people in the employ of the State of Israel and would be detrimental to the State of Israel."

1990 NY   The New York Supreme Court found the Israeli claims of endangered lives "groundless" and that the "heavy presumption against a prior restraint on publication" had not been overcome. Following this ruling, the Israeli government withdrew its lawsuit in Canada.

Source: 7, p. 84.

1279 Ovid
The Art of Love

8 A.D.   Emperor Augustus banished the author.

1497   Burned in Florence, Italy.

1599   Proscribed in the Tridentine Index of 1564, and in England in 1599 a translation by the poet Christopher Marlowe was burned at Stationer's Hall on the orders of the archbishop of Canterbury, on account of its immorality.

1929   Barred by U.S. Customs.

Source: 3, p. 224; 4, p. 2; 6, pp. 1,787–88; 8, p. 320.

1280 Ovid
Elegies

1497   Burned in Florence, Italy.

1599   Burned in England.

Source: 4, p. 2.

1281 Oxenbury, Helen
Tiny Tim: Verses for Children

1987 NJ   Challenged at the Cherry Hill Elementary School because the book is too violent. One rhyme reads: "I had a little brother, his name is Tiny Tim. I put him in the bathtub to teach him how to swim. He drank up all the water. He ate up all the soap. He died last night with a bubble in his throat." In another rhyme, a man "who had a face made out of cake" was baked in an oven and exploded.

Source: 11, July 1987, p. 149.

1282 Packer, Kenneth L., and Jeannine Bower
Let's Talk about Health

1986 OR   Challenged at the Salem-Keizer School District because of the book's handling of issues such as dating, premarital sex, homosexuality, and masturbation.

Source: 11, May 1986, p. 84.

1283 Paine, Thomas
The Age of Reason

1792   Author and publisher imprisoned in France.

1797   Prosecuted in England, and Richard Carlile was prosecuted for publishing the works of Paine, was fined 1,000 pounds and imprisoned for two years in 1819. But because Paine never hesitated to speak his mind, by the end of his life he had become an outcast in America, England, and France. Although he spent his final years in America, he was ostracized and shunned as an atheist and as a traitor to the cause of freedom. He survived a murder attempt, was stripped of his right to vote, and labeled a blasphemer.

Source: 2, p. 7; 4, pp. 33–34; 8, pp. 202–3.

1284 Paine, Thomas
The Rights of Man

1792   Author and publisher imprisoned in France.

1797   Prosecuted in England, and Richard Carlile was prosecuted for publishing the works of Paine, was fined 1,000 pounds and imprisoned for two years in England (1819). But because Paine never hesitated to speak his mind, by the end of his life he had become an outcast in America, England, and France. Although he spent his final years in America, he was ostracized and shunned as an atheist and as a traitor to the cause of freedom. He survived a murder attempt, was stripped of his right to vote, and labeled a blasphemer.

Source: 4, pp. 33–34; 8, pp. 160–62.

1285 Palahniuk, Chuck
Choke: A Novel

2005 AR   Challenged in the Fayetteville High School

library. The complainant also submitted a list of more than fifty books, citing the books as too sexually explicit and promoting homosexuality.

Source: 11, Sept. 2005, p. 215.

1286   Parish, James Robert
Whoopi Goldberg:
Her Journey from Poverty to
Mega-Stardom

2000 WI   Challenged in the Muskego-Norway School District because it contains vulgar language.

Source: 11, July 2000, p. 105; Nov. 2000, p. 216.

1287   Park, Barbara
Junie B. Jones and Some Sneaky,
Peeky Spying

2006 NC   Challenged in the Wake County schools. Parents are getting help from Called2Action, a Christian group that says its mission is to "promote and defend our shared family and social values."

Source: 11, Sept. 2006, p. 231.

1288   Park, Barbara
Junie B. Jones and the Stupid
Smelly Bus

1998 NJ   Challenged, but retained in the second-grade reading curriculum at the Harmony Township school. A parent complained that the book sends a message to children that extreme emotions such as hate are fine, and that the book never resolves any of the issues it raises or points out that there are ways to handle negative emotions constructively.

Source: 11, Nov. 1998, pp. 191–92.

1289   Park, Barbara
Mick Harte Was Here

1998 SC   Challenged, but retained at the Liberty Middle School Library in Seneca after a seventh grader's grandmother complained to school officials.

2004 ND   Challenged, but retained at the Centennial Elementary School library in Fargo after parents complained to school officials that the book contains themes and language inappropriate for elementary students.

Source: 11, May 1998, p. 70; Nov. 2004, pp. 229–30; Jan. 2005, p. 27; May 2005, p. 131.

1290   Parker, Stephen
Life before Birth: The Story of the
First Nine Months

1987 WA   Placed on restricted shelves at the Evergreen School District elementary school libraries in Vancouver in accordance with the school board policy to restrict student access to sex education books in elementary school libraries.

Source: 11, May 1987, p. 87.

1291   Parks, Gordon
The Learning Tree

1976 WY   Temporarily banned from the junior high school in Cheyenne.

1978 MD   Citizens United for Responsible Education demanded that Park's novel be removed from the Montgomery County school system.

1979 RI   Challenged at the Westerly High School.

1982 WA   Subject of a court challenge by the Moral Majority of Washington State in Mead because it includes "objectionable material, swearing, obscene language, explicit detail of premarital sexual intercourse, other lewd behavior, specific blasphemies against Jesus Christ and excessive violence and murder." The case was dismissed by U.S. District Court Judge Robert McNichols.

1991 FL   Removed from, and then restored to, a Suwannee High School library because the book is "indecent."

1992 MN   Challenged at the Eagan High School in Burnsville on the grounds that it contains vulgar and sexually explicit language, and descriptions of violent acts.

2006 AL   Challenged on the summer reading list at LeFlore High School in Mobile because the author frequently used inappropriate words, such as "nigga," "bitch," "bastard," and "ass."

Source: 9; 11, July 1976, p. 68; Sept. 1978, p. 123; May 1979, p. 59; Nov. 1982, p. 212; Jan. 1992, p. 25; Mar. 1993, p. 56; Nov. 2006, p. 290.

1292   Parsipur, Shahrnush
Touba and the Meaning of Night

1989   Banned in Iran because of the novel's controversial depiction of women. The main character's exploration of orthodox religion, Sufism, nationalism, and other forms of thoughts did not sit comfortably with the Islamic Republic. In addition to the novel's content, Parsipur's writing style blurs the boundaries between reality and fiction. Imprisoned both by the shah's security agency and later the Islamic Republic, the author sought political refugee status and

moved to the United States in 1994.
A critically acclaimed bestseller in Iran, the novel, like all of the author's books of fiction and memoir remains banned.

Source: 1, pp. 353–54.

1293 Parsipur, Shahrnush
Women without Men: A Novel of Modern Iran

1989 Banned in Iran as "un-Islamic" because of its treatment of the themes of virginity, rape, prostitution, failed marriage, and references to Western culture. The novella proved to be far too radical in its critique of male patriarchy, and while it brought Parsipur success, it also prompted the government to arrest her. Mohammad Reza Aslani, the publisher and owner of Noghreh Publishing, was also arrested, and his publishing house was immediately closed down. In 1994, Parsipur sought political refugee status and moved to the United States.

Source: 1, pp. 353–54.

1294 Parsons, Alexander
Leaving Disneyland

2005 MD Banned in Carroll County schools. No reason stated.

Source: 11, Mar. 2006, pp. 70–71.

1295 Partridge, Eric
Dictionary of Slang and Unconventional English

1973 FL Challenged in Pinellas County due to profanity.

Source: 11, Mar. 1974, p. 32.

1296 Pascal, Blaise
Pensees

1789 Placed on the *Index Librorum Prohibitorum* (List of Prohibited Books) in Rome, Italy.

Source: 4, p. 24.

1297 Pascal, Blaise
The Provincial Letters

1657 Burned in France for its alleged anti-religiosity. Louis XIV ordered in 1660 that it "be torn up and burned. . . at the hands of the High Executioner, fulfillment of which is to be certified to His Majesty within the week; and that meanwhile all printers, booksellers, vendors and others, of whatever rank and station, are explicitly prohibited from printing selling, and distributing, and even from

having in their possession the said book. . . under the pain of public, exemplary punishment."

1664 First placed on the *Index Librorum Prohibitorum* (List of Prohibited Books) in Rome, Italy. Pascal's works remained there until the 20th century.

Source: 3, p. 229.

1298 Pascal, Francine
Hanging Out with Cici

1986 CO Challenged at the Greeley-Evans School District in Greeley because the book contained "obscenities, allusions to sexual references, and promoted contempt for parents and acceptance of drug use."

Source: 11, Sept. 1986, p. 171.

1299 Pasternak, Boris Leonidovich
Doctor Zhivago

1958 Moscow, Russia condemned the book, refused to publish it, and vilified the author.

Source: 4, p. 73; 6, pp. 1,823–24; 8, pp. 44–45.

1300 Paterson, Katherine
Bridge to Terabithia

1986 NE The Newbery Award-winning book was challenged as sixth-grade recommended reading in the Lincoln schools because it contains "profanity" including the phrase "Oh, Lord" and "Lord" used as an expletive.

1990 CT Challenged as suitable curriculum material in the Harwinton and Burlington schools because it contains language and subject matter that set bad examples and give students negative views of life.

1992 CA Challenged at the Apple Valley Unified School District because of vulgar language.

1992 PA Challenged at the Mechanicsburg Area School District because of profanity and references to witchcraft.

1992 TX Challenged and retained in the libraries, but will not be required reading, at the Cleburne Independent School district because of profane language.

1993 KS A challenge to this Newbery Award-winning book in Oskaloosa led to the enactment of a new policy that requires teachers to examine their required material for profanities. Teachers will list each profanity and the number of times it was used in the book, and forward the list to parents, who will be asked to give written permission for their children to read the material.

1993 PA Challenged in the Gettysburg public schools because of offensive language.

1995 ME Challenged at the Medway schools because the book uses "swear words."

1996 PA Removed from the fifth-grade classrooms of the New Brighton Area School District in Pulaski Township due to "profanity, disrespect of adults, and an elaborate fantasy world they felt might lead to confusion."

2002 CT Challenged in the middle school curriculum in Cromwell due to concern that it promotes witchcraft and violence.

Source: 11, Mar. 1987, p. 67; Mar. 1991, p. 44; May 1992, p. 95; Sept. 1992, pp. 162–63; Nov. 1992, p. 198; Mar. 1993, p. 45; July 1993, pp. 105–6; Mar. 1994, p. 55; July 1995, p. 97; May 1996, p. 88; Sept. 2002, p. 197; Nov. 2002, pp. 257–58.

1301 Paterson, Katherine
The Great Gilly Hopkins

1983 KS Challenged at the Lowell Elementary School in Salina because the book used the words "God," "damn" and "hell" offensively.

1985 MN Challenged at the Orchard Lake Elementary School library in Burnsville because "the book took the Lord's name in vain" and had "over forty instances of profanity."

1988 CO Challenged at the Jefferson County elementary schools because "Gilly's friends lie and steal, and there are no repercussions. Christians are portrayed as being dumb and stupid."

1991 CT Pulled from, but later restored to, the language arts curriculum at four Cheshire elementary schools because the book is "filled with profanity, blasphemy and obscenities, and gutter language."

1992 TX Challenged at the Alamo Heights School District elementary schools because it contains the words "hell" and "damn."

1993 KS Challenged at the Walnut Elementary School in Emporia by parents who said that it contains profanity and graphic violence.

1997 NV Challenged due to explicit language, but retained in the Lander County School District.

Source: 11, July 1983, p. 121; Nov. 1985, p. 203; Mar. 1988, p. 45; Mar. 1992, p. 42; May 1992, p. 96; July 1992, pp. 109–10; Jan. 1993, p. 13; July 1993, pp. 126–27; Mar. 1998, p. 56.

1302 Paterson, Katherine
Jacob Have I Loved

1989 NJ Challenged at the Bernardsville schools as unsuitable for a sixth-grade reading class. The Newbery award-winning book was offensive to several parents on moral and religious grounds.

1993 PA Challenged in the Gettysburg public schools because of offensive language.

Source: 11, Jan. 1990, p. 33; Mar. 1994, p. 55.

1303 Paterson, Thomas
American Foreign Policy, Vol. II

1984 WI Returned to the Racine Unified School District curriculum just one week after the school board voted to ban it. Opponents of the books on the board charged that the social studies volumes contained "judgmental writing" and, in the words of one board member, "a lot more funny pictures of Republicans and nicer pictures of Democrats." Opponents also said that one text did not present an adequate analysis of the Vietnam War.

Source: 11, Sept. 1984, p. 158.

1304 Patrick, John, and Carol Berkin
The History of the American Nation

1987 MA Challenged at the Amherst-Pelham Regional Junior High School by a group of parents who charge that, among other things, it is sexist and distorts the history of minorities.

Source: 11, Jan. 1988, p. 11.

1305 Patterson, James
Cradle and All: A Novel

2007 NY New — Removed from the Westhampton Beach High School's ninth-grade reading list because of "inappropriate sexual content." The reading list contains more than three hundred books from which ninth-graders must choose to read for course credit.

Source: 11, Jan. 2008, pp. 37–38; Mar. 2008, p. 63.

1306 Patterson, Lillie
Halloween

1992 AZ Challenged at the Neely Elementary School in Gilbert because the book shows the dark side of religion through the occult, the devil, and satanism.

Source: 11, May 1992, p. 78; July 1992, p. 124.

1307 Paulsen, Gary
The Foxman

1994 IL Challenged at Cary Junior High School because references in the book to sex are too explicit for seventh and eighth graders; retained by a school board vote.

Source: 11, May 1994, p. 83; July 1994, pp. 128–29.

1308 Paulsen, Gary
Harris and Me

1997 NV Challenged due to explicit language, but retained in the Lander County School District.
Source: 11, Mar. 1998, p. 56.

1309 Paulsen, Gary
Nightjohn

1998 VA Challenged as a seventh-grade summer reading option in Prince William County because the book "was rife with profanity and explicit sex."
Source: 11, Nov. 1998, p. 183.

1310 Paulsen, Gary
Zero to Sixty: The Motorcycle Journey of a Lifetime

2006 TX Removed from the West Brazoria Junior High School library because of depictions of sex acts and profanity. Books on "sensitive topics such as death, suicide, physical or sexual abuse, and teenage dating relationships" were moved to a restricted "young-adult" section from which students can borrow only with written parental permission.
Source: 11, Nov. 2006, pp. 289–90.

1311 Peck, M. Scott
The Road Less Traveled

2003 LA Removed from the college bookstore at Louisiana College, Pineville, by the college president because "profane language in the book clashes with the school's Christian values."
Source: 11, Mar. 2004, pp. 53–54.

1312 Peck, Robert Newton
A Day No Pigs Would Die

1988 CO Challenged in Jefferson County school libraries because "it is bigoted against Baptists and women and depicts violence, hatred, animal cruelty, and murder."

1990 CT Challenged as suitable curriculum material in the Burlington schools because it contains language and subject matter that set bad examples and give students negative views of life.

1990 CT Challenged as suitable curriculum material in the Harwinton schools because it contains language and subject matter that set bad examples and give students negative views of life.

1993 FL Challenged at the Sherwood Elementary School in Melbourne because the book could give the "impression that rape and violence are acceptable." The comment was made in reference to a descriptive passage about a boar mating a sow in the barnyard.

1994 UT Removed from seventh-grade classes at Payson Middle School after several parents "had problems with language, with animal breeding, and with a scene that involves an infant grave exhumation."

1994 WI Challenged, but retained on the shelves at Waupaca school libraries after a parent "objected to graphic passages dealing with sexuality in the book."

1995 OK Challenged at the Pawhuska Middle School because the book uses bad language, gives "gory" details of mating, and lacks religious values.

1995 SC Pulled from an Anderson middle school library because of the "gory" descriptions of two pigs mating, a pig being slaughtered, and a cow giving birth.

1996 MO Challenged at the Anderson Junior High School because of its content.

1997 MI Banned from the St. Lawrence School in Utica because of a passage involving pig breeding. The teacher quit her job over the banning of the novel.
Source: 11, May 1988, p. 85; July 1988, pp. 119–20, 139; Sept. 1988, pp. 151, 177; Mar. 1991, p. 44; May 1991, p. 90; July 1993, pp. 97–98; May 1994, pp. 98–99; July 1994, pp. 117, 129; July 1995, p. 98; Mar. 1996, p. 46; Jan. 1997, p. 10; May 1997, p. 64.

1313 Peck, Robert Newton
Soup

1992 NJ Challenged as a fourth-grade reading assignment at the Woodbridge schools because of objectionable language and because "it teaches children how to lie, manipulate, steal, and cheat."
Source: 11, Jan. 1993, p. 12.

1314 Peck, Robert Newton
Trig

1985 WI Challenged at the Cunningham Elementary School in Beloit because the book "encourages disrespectful language."
Source: 11, July 1985, p. 134.

1315 Pell, Derek
Doktor Bey's Suicide Guidebook

1986 IA Placed "on reserve" at the Prairie High School library in Cedar Rapids because the book "could push a classmate contemplating suicide over the edge."
Source: 11, Sept. 1986, p. 152.

1316 Pelzer, Dave
A Child Called It

2000 DE Removed from the Sussex Central Middle School until the committee completes its review because of the book's profanity and violence.
Source: 11, July 2000, p. 105.

1317 Penney, Alexandra
How to Make Love to a Man...Safely

1995 TX Former Weslaco librarian filed a federal lawsuit charging that she was fired for publicly discussing that city's efforts to ban Penney's work from the library.
Source: 11, Sept. 1995, p. 155.

1318 Perkins, Al
Don and Donna Go to Bat

1987 VT Returned to Shaftsbury Elementary School library. The complainant stated that children should not be exposed to "sexist attitudes in the story."
Source: 11, Sept. 1987, p. 194.

1319 Perry, Shawn, ed.
Words of Conscience: Religious Statements of Conscientious Objectors

1982 WI Access restricted in Coleman due to the book's alleged political overtones.
Source: 11, July 1982, p. 126.

1320 Perry, Troy
The Lord Is My Shepherd and He Knows I'm Gay

1982 MI Challenged at the Niles Community Library because of the book's "pornographic" nature.
Source: 11, Jan. 1983, p. 8.

1321 Peters, Lisa Westberg
Our Family Tree: An Evolution Story

2006 KS Retained in the Seaman Unified School District 345 elementary school library. Objections were raised because the book is about the scientific theory of evolution.
Source: 11, May 2006, p. 153.

1322 Petronius, Gaius
Satyricon

1934 Ordered destroyed by the police court of the City of Westminster in London, England.
Source: 4, p. 3; 13, pp. 206–7.

1323 Pettit, Mark
A Need to Kill

1998 NE Challenged in the Lincoln middle school libraries. The book is about an executed child-killer and contains passages concerning murder, masturbation, and perverse sex, considered inappropriate for junior high.
Source: 11, July 1998, p. 106.

1324 Pfeiffer, Susan
About David

1986 FL Challenged at the Bay County's four middle schools and three high schools in Panama City because it contains "profanity and sexual explicit passages."
Source: 11, Nov. 1986, p. 209.

1325 Picoult, Jodi
My Sister's Keeper

2008 MI New Pulled from classrooms in Clawson as too racy for middle school students. The novel is the story of a young girl who sues her parents because they want her to donate a kidney to her sister.
Source: 11, Mar. 2009, p. 40.

1326 Picoult, Jodi
Nineteen Minutes

2008 IL New Restricted to high school students with parental permission at the Beardstown High School library because the novel "describes sex, uses foul language, and contains other 'R-rated' content."
Source: 11, Sept. 2008, pp. 229–30.

1327 Picoult, Jodi
The Tenth Circle

2007 NY New Removed from the Westhampton Beach High School's ninth-grade reading list because of "inappropriate sexual content." The reading list contains more than three hundred books from which ninth-graders must choose to read for course credit.
Source: 11, Jan. 2008, pp. 37–38; Mar. 2008, p. 63.

1328 Pierce, Ruth I.
Single and Pregnant

1984 AR Challenged and recommended for a "parents only" section at the Concord school library because the author had "little to say that would discourage premarital sex."
Source: 11, Jan. 1985, p. 7; May 1985, p. 75; Jan. 1986, pp. 7–8.

1329 Pierce, Tamara
Alanna: Song of the Lioness, Book One

1989 OR Removed by a library staff member, but later returned to the shelves of the David Hill Elementary School in Hillsboro because of sexual references and the use of an amulet to prevent pregnancy.
Source: 11, Jan. 1990, pp. 4–5.

1330 Pierce, Tamara
In the Hand of the Goddess: Song of the Lioness, Book Two

1989 OR Removed by a library staff member, but later returned to the shelves of the David Hill Elementary School in Hillsboro because of sexual references and use of an amulet to prevent pregnancy.
Source: 11, Jan. 1990, pp. 4–5.

1331 Pierce, Tamara
The Woman Who Rides Like a Man: Song of the Lioness, Book Three

1989 OR Removed by a library staff member, but later returned to the shelves of the David Hill Elementary School in Hillsboro because of sexual references and the use of an amulet to prevent pregnancy.
Source: 11, Jan. 1990, pp. 4–5.

1332 Pike, Christopher
Bury Me Deep

2000 ID Removed from the Nampa West Middle School due to its violence and sexual content.
Source: 11, May 2000, p. 74.

1333 Pike, Christopher
Chain Letter 2

2000 ID Removed from the Nampa West Middle School due to its violence and sexual content.
Source: 11, May 2000, p. 74.

1334 Pike, Christopher
Die Softly

1999 CA Removed from Escondido middle school libraries along with 24 other novels by the best-selling author. Passages deemed offensive made references to whiskey drinking, bribery, sex, and a nightmare about dismemberment.
Source: 11, July 1998, p. 104; Nov. 1999, p. 161.

1335 Pike, Christopher
Final Friends: The Party

1998 CA Recommended for removal from Escondido middle school libraries because the book is "vulgar and unsuitable."
Source: 11, July 1998, p. 104.

1336 Pike, Christopher
The Graduation: Final Friends Book 3

1992 PA Challenged at the Weatherly Area Middle School library because parents were upset by passages in the book dealing with depression, suicide, and contraception.
Source: 11, May 1992, p. 81; July 1992, p. 125.

1337 Pike, Christopher
Last Act

2000 ID Removed from the Nampa South Middle School due to its violence and sexual content.
Source: 11, May 2000, p. 74.

1338 Pike, Christopher
The Listeners

2000 ID Removed from the Nampa West Middle School due to its violence and sexual content.
Source: 11, May 2000, p. 74.

1339 Pike, Christopher
The Lost Mind

2000 ID Removed from the Nampa West Middle School due to its violence and sexual content.
Source: 11, May 2000, p. 74.

1340 Pike, Christopher
The Midnight Club

2000 ID Removed from the Nampa West Middle School due to its violence and sexual content.
Source: 11, May 2000, p. 74.

1341 Pike, Christopher
Remember Me 3

2000 ID Removed from the Nampa West Middle School due to its violence and sexual content.
Source: 11, May 2000, p. 74.

1342 Pike, Christopher
Remember Me

1998 SC Removed from the Liberty Middle School library in Seneca after a seventh-grader's grandmother complained to school officials.
Source: 11, May 1998, p. 70.

1343 Pike, Christopher
Road to Nowhere

1998 CA Recommended for removal from Escondido middle school libraries because the book is "vulgar and unsuitable."
Source: 11, July 1998, p. 104.

1344 Pike, Christopher
The Star Group

2000 ID Removed from the Nampa West Middle School due to its violence and sexual content.
Source: 11, May 2000, p. 74.

1345 Pike, Christopher
Witch

2000 ID Removed from the Nampa West Middle School due to its violence and sexual content.
Source: 11, May 2000, p. 74.

1346 Pilkey, Dav
Adventures of Captain Underpants

2000 CT Removed from the Maple Hill School in Naugatuck due to concerns that it caused unruly behavior among children.
Source: 8, p. 430; 11, May 2000, p. 73.

1347 Pilkey, Dav
The Adventures of Super Diaper Baby

2003 CA Challenged, but retained in the Riverside Unified School District classrooms and libraries, despite a complaint of the book's "inappropriate" scatological storyline.
Source: 8, p. 431; 11, Sept. 2003, p. 201.

1348 Pilkey, Dav
Captain Underpants and the Invasion of the Incredibly Naughty Cafeteria Ladies from Outer Space (and the Subsequent Assault of Equally Evil Lunchroom Zombie Nerds)

2000 WI Challenged, but retained at the Orfordville Elementary School library. A parent charged that the book taught students to be disrespectful, not to obey authority, not to obey the law, including God's law, improper spelling, to make excuses and lie to escape responsibility, to make fun of what people wear, and poor nutrition.
Source: 11, Mar. 2000, p. 62.

1349 Pilkey, Dav
Captain Underpants and the Perilous Plot of Professor Poopypants

2002 TX Removed from the Page Consolidated School District because a parent "didn't care for the language. I didn't care for the innuendo." The board approved a policy requiring that the consolidated school board approve all library purchases and allowing them to reject materials "that label or characterize undeserving individuals in a derogatory manner."
Source: 8, p. 430.

1350 Pinkwater, Daniel
The Devil in the Drain

1987 WI Challenged in the Galesville-Ettrick School District.
Source: 11, Nov. 1987, p. 226.

1351 Pipher, Mary
Reviving Ophelia

1998 WA Challenged for use in the Richland high school English classes along with six other titles because the "books are poor-quality literature and stress suicide, illicit sex, violence, and hopelessness."
Source: 11, Mar. 1999, p. 40.

1352 Plante, David
The Catholic

1986 Banned in South Africa.
Source: 5, June 1986, p. 41.

1353 Plath, Sylvia
The Bell Jar

1979 IN Prohibited for use in the Warsaw schools.
1981 IL Challenged in Edwardsville when three hundred residents signed a petition against Plath's novel because it contains sexual material and advocates an "objectionable" philosophy of life.
1998 WA Challenged for use in the Richland high school English classes along with six other titles because the "books are poor-quality literature and stress suicide, illicit sex, violence, and hopelessness."
Source: 8, pp. 418–19; 11, Mar. 1980, p. 40; July 1981, p. 102; Mar. 1999, p. 40.

1354 Platt, Kin
Head Man

1982 MO The Anaconda School Board handed school

principal Patrick Meloy a list of thirty-four restricted titles including Platt's book and gave him authority to censor or destroy any book he believes is "pornographic."

1983 IA Challenged at the Elkader Central High School library because the book's description of the Los Angeles ghetto by a youth gang leader contains "street talk and four-letter words offensive to Elkader residents."

1984 MS Challenged at the Rankin County School District because it is "profane and sexually objectionable."

Source: 11, Mar. 1983, p. 41; July 1983, p. 121; May 1984, p. 70; Jan. 1985, p. 8.

1355 Pollan, Michael
The Botany of Desire: A Plant's-Eye View of the World

2006 IL Retained on the Buffalo Grove High School, along with eight other challenged titles. A board member, elected amid promises to bring her Christian beliefs into all board decision-making, raised the controversy based on excerpts from the books she'd found on the Internet.

Source: 11, July 2006, pp. 210–11.

1356 Pomeroy, Wardell B.
Boys and Sex

1983 NM Challenged at the Santa Fe High School library by a school librarian because of its "sordid, suggestive, permissive type of approach."

1988 NY Removed from two Greece middle school libraries because the book "promotes prostitution, promiscuity, homosexuality, and bestiality."

1990 WI Pulled from the Black River Falls Middle School library because the book "dealt with bestiality, masturbation and homosexuality, and endorsed pre-adolescent and premarital sex."

1994 CO Pulled from the Rangely Middle School library shelves.

2000 NC Challenged in the Charlotte Public Library because of its sexual content.

Source: 11, May 1983, p. 85; July 1988, p. 121; Sept. 1988, p. 178; May 1991, p. 75; May 1994, p. 83; Sept. 2000, p. 143.

1357 Pomeroy, Wardell B.
Girls and Sex

1983 NM Challenged at the Santa Fe High School library by a school librarian because of its "sordid, suggestive, permissive type of approach."

1990 W Pulled from the Black River Falls Middle School library because the book "dealt with bestiality, masturbation and homosexuality, and endorsed pre-adolescent and premarital sex."

1994 CO Pulled from the Rangely Middle School library shelves.

2000 NC Challenged in the Charlotte Public Library because of its sexual content.

Source: 11, May 1983, p. 85; May 1991, p. 75; May 1994, p. 83; Sept. 2000, p. 143.

1358 Ponce, Charles
The Game of Wizards

1986 CA Challenged by the "God Squad," a group of three students and their parents, at the El Camino High School in Oceanside because the Chinese yin and yang symbol is drawn on page 95. The complainant wrote, "This is the symbol of Confucianism and represents reincarnation. This book also deals with transcendental meditation."

Source: 11, Sept. 1986, p. 151; Nov. 1986, p. 224; Jan. 1987, p. 9.

1359 Portal, Colette
The Beauty of Birth

1982 FL Moved from the children's room of the Tampa-Hillsborough County Public Library to the adult section.

Source: 11, Jan. 1982, pp. 4–5.

1360 Porter, Jean Stratton
Her Father's Daughter

1991 OR Removed from the Clatskanie Library District because of alleged bigotry against the Japanese.

Source: 11, July 1992, p. 103.

1361 Potok, Chaim
My Name Is Asher Lev

1983 Banned from the 1983 Moscow, Russia International Book Fair along with more than fifty other books because it is "anti-Soviet."

Source: 11, Nov. 1983, p. 201.

1362 Prelutsky, Jack
The Headless Horseman Rides Tonight and Other Poems to Trouble Your Sleep

1982 NY Challenged at the Victor Elementary School media center in Rochester because it "was too frightening for young children to read."

Source: 11, July 1982, p. 142.

1363 Prelutsky, Jack
Nightmares: Poems to Trouble Your Sleep

1979 WA Placed in the professional reading section of the Kirkland district libraries where it would be unavailable to students without a teacher's permission.

1987 NV Challenged at the Paul E. Culley Elementary School in Las Vegas because the poems were too frightening for small children.

1988 OR Placed in a "reserved" section at Little Butte Intermediate School in Eagle Point because the book could "disturb a child's sleep and offered no learning experience."

1993 SC Removed from the Berkeley County schools that include fourth graders and younger children due to violent passages.

1993 WI Removed from the Eau Claire elementary school libraries because the poems "graphically describe violent acts against children that would be criminal activity if acted out."

Source: 11, Sept. 1979, p. 104; Jan. 1988, p. 32; Jan. 1989, p. 3; Sept. 1993, pp. 148–49; Mar. 1994, p. 53.

1364 Prelutsky, Jack
Rolling Harvey down the Hill

1989 CT Challenged at the Consolidated School library in New Fairfield because the book of children's verses is "repulsive" and against the country's "moral fiber."

Source: 11, July 1989, p. 127.

1365 Pressfield, Steven
Gates of Fire

2002 VA Retained in the Fairfax County Public Schools

Source: 11, July 2002, p. 179.

1366 Preston, Richard
The Hot Zone

1998 WA Challenged for use in the Richland high school English classes along with six other titles because the "books are poor-quality literature and stress suicide, illicit sex, violence, and hopelessness."

Source: 11, Mar. 1999, p. 40.

1367 Price, Richard
Bloodbrothers

1985 PA Banned from the Stroudsburg High School library because it was "blatantly graphic, pornographic, and wholly unacceptable for a high school library."

Source: 11, May 1985, p. 79.

1368 Price, Richard
Wanderers

1978 VT Banned from the Vergennes Union High School library. Decision upheld in *Bicknell v. Vergennes Union High School Board*, 475 F. Supp. 615 (D. Vt. 1979), 638 F. 2d 438 (2d Cir. 1980).

Source: 11, Jan. 1979, p. 6; 12, pp. 151, 239; 15, Vol. IV, p. 715.

1369 Price, Susan
The Devil's Piper

1988 OR Challenged at the Canby Junior High School library because it "could encourage young minds to pursue occult, suicide, or adopt ill attitudes."

Source: 11, May 1989, p. 78.

1370 Proulx, Annie
Brokeback Mountain

2005 TX Retained at St. Andrew's Episcopal School in Austin. The private school returned a three million dollar donation rather than submit to the donor's request that the short story be removed from the school's list of optional reading for twelfth graders.

Source: 11, Jan. 2006, p. 37.

1371 Pullman, Philip
The Broken Bridge

1997 WV Removed from the Jackson County school libraries along with sixteen other titles.

Source: 11, Jan. 1998, p. 13.

1372 Pullman, Philip
The Golden Compass

2007 New Removed, but later returned to the library shelves at dozens of schools in the publicly funded Halton, Ontario, Canada, Catholic School District despite a challenge that the books were "written by an atheist where the characters and text are anti-God, anti-Catholic, and anti-religion." The book and two other Pullman titles from the Dark Materials trilogy were pulled from public display for review, but are available to students upon request.

2007 New The publicly funded Calgary, Alberta, Canada, Catholic School District returned the book to its library shelves two months after ordering its removal. Detractors accused the book of having antireligious content. Similar concerns prompted the Catholic League, a Roman-Catholic antidefamation organization in the

U.S., to urge parents to boycott a movie version of the book that was released in December 2007.

2007 CO New Pulled from the library shelves at Ortega Middle School in Alamosa for what critics regard as the book's anti-religious views. District officials later returned the book to circulation.

2007 KY New Challenged at the Conkwright Middle School in Winchester because the main character drinks wine and ingests poppy with her meals, and the book presents an anti-Christian doctrine.

2007 TX New Challenged at the Shallowater Middle School in Lubbock because of the book's "anti-religious messages."

2007 WI New Pulled from the St. John Neumann Middle School and Lourdes High School in Oshkosh because of concerns about what critics call its "anti-Christian message."

2008 New Retained by the publicly funded Dufferin-Peel Catholic School District in Mississauga, Ontario, Canada with a sticker on the inside cover telling readers "representations of the church in this novel are purely fictional," and are not reflective of the real Roman Catholic Church or the Gospel of Jesus Christ.

Source: 11, Jan. 2008, pp. 13–14, 36; Mar. 2008, pp. 61, 63, 77–78; May 2008, p. 116.

1373 Purdy, Candace, and Stan Kendziorski
Understanding Your Sexuality

1982 ME Challenged at the York school system.

1984 PA Challenged at the Chambersburg Area Senior High School health class because "the Christian child must go to school and be subjected to the immoral teachings of this book."

Source: 11, July 1982, p. 124; Jan. 1985, pp. 11–12.

1374 Puzo, Mario
The Godfather

1975 IA Challenged at the Grinnell-Newburg school system because the book is "vulgar and obscene by most religious standards."

Source: 9; 11, Mar. 1975, p. 41; May 1975, p. 87.

1375 Pyle, Howard
King Stork

1989 MI Challenged at the public libraries of Saginaw because it "would encourage boys beating girls when the drummer beats the enchantress with a switch until she becomes a 'good' princess."

1993 MT Unavailable to children unless they have written permission from their parents to check out the book or to read it in the library at the Sandstone Elementary School library in Billings. The objections to the near hundred-year-old book included a scene in which a husband beat his witchy wife into submission and illustrations from the 1973 edition of a princess in revealing clothing.

Source: 11, May 1989, p. 77; July 1993, p. 99.

1376 Pynchon, William
The Meritorius Price of Our Redemption

1650 MA First publicly burned in the United States, where it was destroyed by the Massachusetts Colony authorities. Although Pynchon was one of the founders of the colony, and a signatory to its charter, his book proved so contentious in its criticism of the puritan orthodoxy that dominated the theological attitudes of the colony, that after it had been read by the General Council, it was condemned to be burned by the common executioner in the Market Place. Pynchon himself was publicly censured and escaped further punishment only by sailing back to England.

Source: 3, pp. 247–48.

1377 Quinlan, Patricia
Tiger Flowers

1999 TX Challenged, but retained on the library shelves of a Dallas-Fort Worth-area elementary school. The children's book is about a boy whose uncle dies from AIDS.

Source: 11, Nov. 1999, p. 172.

1378 Rabelais, Francois
Gargantua & Pantagruel

1533 Blacklisted in Paris, France by French Parliament; censored by the Sorbonne in 1552.

1554 Banned by Henry II in England.

1664 Listed on the *Index Librorum Prohibitorum* (List of Prohibited Books) in Rome, Italy.

1930 U.S. Customs Department lifted ban.

1938 Banned in South Africa.

1951 IA City and county law enforcement officers obtained a warrant and raided the Dubuque Public Library, where they seized the novel as obscene. The book was later returned to library shelves, as "restricted" material.

Source: 4, p. 14; 6, pp. 2,003–4; 14, pp. 151–52.

1379 Radishchev, Alkeksandr Nikolaevich
A Journey from St. Petersburg to Moscow

1790 Catherine II the Great issued orders for the book to be confiscated and the whole edition destroyed because the book "is trying in every possible way to break down respect for authority and for the authorities, to stir up in the people indignation against their superiors and against the government." Radishchev was quickly arrested and condemned to death; his sentence was later commuted to an exile in Siberia. After almost six years in exile, Catherine having died, her successor Paul I issued orders for many in disfavor during his mother's resign, including Radishchev to be released. Alexander I, the next czar, granted him full pardon in 1801.
Source: 7, pp. 275–77.

1380 Radlauer, Ruth, and Ed Radlauer
Chopper Cycle

1982 MI Challenged at the Morrish Elementary School in Swartz Creek because of its negative approach to law enforcement.
Source: 11, Nov. 1982, p. 215.

1381 Rampling, Anne
Belinda

1988 OR Challenged at the Multnomah County Library in Portland because of its sexual nature.
Source: 11, Jan. 1989, p. 3.

1382 Randal, Jonathan C.
After Such Knowledge, What Forgiveness?—My Encounters with Kurdistan

2002 Confiscated by order of a Turkish state security court. The Istanbul State Security Court sentenced the publisher to six months in jail but converted the sentence to a fine of $500. The book remained banned after the trail. The International Freedom to Publish Committee selected the publisher as the 2005 recipient of the Jeri Laber International Freedom to Publish Award. He was recognized for his long commitment to Kurdish writings in the face of great political obstacles—and personal peril—over the past decades.
Source: 7, pp. 13–14.

1383 Randall, Dudley
Black Poets

1982 IL Banned for use in English classrooms at the Tinley Park High School because the book "extols murder, rape, theft, incest, sodomy, and other acts."
Source: 11, Mar. 1983, p. 40.

1384 Randolph, Vance, comp.
Pissing in the Snow and Other Ozark Folktales

1988 AR Challenged at the Rogers-Hough Memorial Library because the book is "vulgar and obscene."
Source: 11, July 1988, p. 119.

1385 Rapp, Adam
The Buffalo Tree

2005 PA Banned from the Muhlenberg High School. Several months later the board reversed that decision and determined that a reading list be made available to parents including a rating system, plot summaries of all assigned books, and the identification of any potentially objectionable content.
Source: 11, July 2005, pp. 161–62; 13, pp. 32–34.

1386 Raucher, Herman
Summer of '42

1975 IA Challenged at the Grinnell-Newburg school system as "vulgar and obscene by most religious standards."

1978 KY Removed from the reading list of an elective English course at Pulaski County High School after a parent complained about "four-letter language" in the work.
Source: 9; 11, Mar. 1975, p. 41; May 1975, p. 87; Mar. 1979, p. 27.

1387 Ray, Ron
Gays in or out of the Military

1996 LA Pulled from the Ouachita Parish School library in Monroe because of sexual content. The Louisiana chapter of the ACLU filed a lawsuit in the federal courts on October 3, 1996, claiming that the principal and the school superintendent violated First Amendment free speech rights and also failed to follow established procedure when they removed the book. The three-year-old school library censorship case headed to court after the Ouachita Parish School Board made no decision to seek a settlement at a special meeting April 12, 1999. On August 17, 1999, the Ouachita Parish School Board agreed to return the book to the library and to develop a new book-selection policy that follows state guidelines for school media programs.

Source: 11, Sept. 1996, pp. 151–52; Jan. 1997, p. 7; July 1999, p. 93; Jan. 2000, p. 27.

1388 Reavin, Sam
The Hunters Are Coming

1999 ME Challenged at the Cousens Memorial School library in Lyman because the book portrays hunters in a negative light.

Source: 11, May 1999, p. 83.

1389 Reddin, Keith
Life and Limb

1998 FL Challenged at the Manatee County school district in Bradenton Beach because the play contains references to pornographic magazines, most of them fictional.

Source: 11, May 1998, p. 71.

1390 Reed, Rick
Obsessed

1996 GA Permanently removed from the East Coweta County High School library because of several sexually and violently graphic passages.

Source: 11, Jan. 1997, p. 7; Mar. 1997, p. 35.

1391 Reiss, Johanna
The Upstairs Room

1993 IN Removed from the required reading list for fourth graders at Liberty Elementary School. The Newbery Honor Book about a girl in Holland hiding from the Nazis during World War II was investigated because of profanity.

1996 ME Challenged as assigned reading for sixth-grade students in Sanford because of profanity.

Source: 11, July 1993, p. 105; July 1996, p. 118.

1392 Remarque, Erich Maria
All Quiet on the Western Front

1929 Austrian soldiers forbidden to read it.

1929 Barred from Czech military libraries by the war department.

1929 IL Seized by U.S. Customs in Chicago.

1929 MA Banned in Boston on grounds of obscenity.

1930 Banned in Thuringia, Germany and consigned to the Nazi bonfires.

1933 Banned in Italy because of the book's anti-war propaganda.

Source: 2, pp. 137, 139; 4, pp. 6–7; 15, Vol. III, pp. 417–18.

1393 Remarque, Erich Maria
The Road Back

1931 Banned in Ireland.

Source: 4, p. 81.

1394 Renan, Ernest
Life of Jesus

1897 Condemned by the Catholic Church and placed on the *Index Librorum Prohibitorum* (Index of Prohibited Books) in Rome, Italy, along with nineteen other works by Renan, and remained listed until 1966. The biography was the first to use modern historical methods to recount the life of Jesus.

Source: 1, pp. 190–92.

1395 Rench, Janice E.
Understanding Sexual Identity: A Book for Gay Teens & Their Friends

1994 CO Pulled from the Rangely Middle School library shelves.

1994 NJ Moved from the Chestnut Ridge Middle School library to the guidance center in Washington Township because school administrators have been accused of "indoctrinating children in the gay lifestyle."

1997 PA Restricted to students with parental permission at the Brownsville Area High School District library because a parent complained the book contains references to gays and lesbians. The controversy prompted the Greater Pittsburgh chapter of the ACLU to write to the school district saying it would challenge in court any effort to ban the book from the high school library because of its references to homosexuality. The book's author offered to donate three copies to the high school, since the library's copy was never returned.

Source: 11, May 1994, p. 83; Sept. 1994, p. 148; Sept. 1997, p. 126; Nov. 1997, p. 181; Jan. 1998, p. 11.

1396 Rennison, Louise
Angus, Thongs and Full-Frontal Snogging: Confessions of Georgia Nicolson

2008 WI New Retained with limited access at the Maplewood Middle School Library in Menasha. The coming-of-age novel, which has sexual content, was found offensive by a parent. In addition to retaining the book, board members voted unanimously to adopt procedures intended to secure and record parental consent before limited access books are released to students.

Source: 11, July 2008, p. 164.

1397 Rennison, Louise
Knocked Out by My Nunga-Nungas: Further, Further Confessions of Georgia Nicolson

2002 WI Challenged at the Oregon Middle School by a parent who was particularly offended by a passage in which a boy touches a girl's breast.
Source: 11, Jan. 2003, p. 10.

1398 Rennison, Louise
On the Bright Side, I'm Now the Girlfriend of a Sex God: Further Confessions of Georgia Nicolson

2005 MT Retained in the Bozeman School District's middle-school libraries despite a complaint that an unstable person seeing a girl reading the book might think from the title that the girl is promiscuous and stalk her.
Source: 11, Mar. 2005, p. 74.

1399 Reuben, David
Everything You Always Wanted to Know about Sex, but Were Afraid to Ask

1984 MO Challenged at the William Chrisman High School in Independence because the book is "filthy." The Reuben's work was on a bookshelf in the classroom and was the personal property of the teacher.
Source: 11, July 1984, p. 106.

1400 Revesz, Therese Ruth
Witches

1992 VA Pulled, but later placed on reserve to children with parental permission at the Forrest Elementary School library in Hampton.
Source: 11, July 1992, p. 108; Sept. 1992, p. 139.

1401 Reynolds, Marilyn
Detour for Emmy

2000 AZ Removed from Dysart Unified School District libraries, Dysart for its portrayal of teenage pregnancy.

2005 TX Challenged in the Action Middle School library in Granbury because it "talks very vividly about sexual encounters of a fifteen-year-old." The book was cited as one of the American Library Association's Best Books for Young Adults in 1993.
Source: 11, May 2000, p. 73; Nov. 2005, pp. 280–81; Jan. 2006, pp. 10–11.

1402 Rhyne, Nancy
Murder in the Carolinas

1992 SC Removed from the Berkeley County elementary and middle school libraries because the book—real-life stories of South Carolina murders based on newspaper accounts contained descriptions of actual murders that were too graphic for young readers.
Source: 11, July 1992, pp. 107–8.

1403 Richards, Arlene K., and Irene Willis
What to Do If You or Someone You Know Is under 18 and Pregnant

1991 WI Challenged at the Racine Unified School District libraries because the book uses street language to describe sexual intercourse and contraceptives, contains "sexually suggestive and provocative" language, and "promotes teenage sexual promiscuity."
Source: 11, Jan. 1992, p. 27.

1404 Richardson, Justin, and Peter Parnell
And Tango Makes Three

2006 IL Challenged at the Shiloh Elementary School library. A committee of school employees and a parent suggested the book be moved to a separate shelf, requiring parent permission before checkout. The school's superintendent, however, rejected the proposal and the book remained on the library shelf.

2006 MO Moved from the children's fiction section to children's nonfiction at two Rolling Hill's Consolidated Library's branches in Savannah and St. Joseph after parents complained it had homosexual undertones. The illustrated book is based on a true story of two male penguins that adopted an abandoned egg at New York City's Central Park in the late 1990s.

2007 CA Challenged at the Lodi Public Library by a resident deriding what she called its "homosexual story line that has been sugarcoated with cute penguins."

2007 NC Pulled from four elementary-school libraries in the Charlotte-Mecklenburg after a few parents and Mecklenburg County Commissioner Bill James questioned the controversial but true story. The books were returned after the local paper questioned the ban. It should be noted that there was no formal request for the book's removal.

2008 New Withdrawn from two Bristol, England primary schools following objections from parents who claimed the book was unsuitable for children and that they had not been consulted on their opinions.

2008 CA Retained in the Chico Unified School District,
New over complaints that the book is inappropriate for elementary school students. The district review committee determined that the book meets library selection standards and district policy.

2008 IA Challenged in the elementary school library
New in Ankeny by parents who do not want their children to read the story of two male penguin parents in the Central Park Zoo due to concerns that it promotes homosexuality. On Dec. 15, 2008, the Ankeny school board members voted six to one to keep the book.

2008 MD Retained by the Calvert County Library in
New Prince Frederick after requests that the book be removed from the children's section and shelved in a labeled alternative section.

2008 OH Challenged, but retained at the Eli Pinney
New Elementary School in Dublin despite a parent's concerns that the book "is based on one of those subjects that is best left to be discovered by students at another time or in another place."

2008 VA Returned to the general circulation shelves in
New the sixteen elementary school libraries in Loudoun County despite a complaint about its subject matter.

2009 MN Retained in the Meadowview Elementary
New School in Farmington despite a parent's concern that "a topic such as sexual preference does not belong in a library where it can be obtained by young elementary students."

2009 MO Challenged, but retained in the North Kansas
New City schools despite a parent's concern that the book wasn't age-appropriate, didn't follow the district's policy on human sexuality education, and tries to indoctrinate children about homosexuality. In subsequent discussions, the schools appear to be headed towards segregating elementary school libraries according to "age appropriateness." Students might be restricted to view or check out materials in their own age class or younger.

Source: 11, May 2006, p. 129; Jan. 2007, p. 9; Mar. 2007, pp. 71–72; July 2007, p. 163; May 2008, pp. 116–17; July 2008, pp. 146, 164, 166; Jan. 2009, pp. 6, 21–22; Mar. 2009, p. 55; May 2009, p. 94; Mar. 2010, pp. 52–53, 73.

1405 Richardson, Samuel
Pamela

1744 Condemned by the Roman Catholic Church in Rome, Italy and was prohibited reading for Catholics. It appeared on the *Index Librorum Prohibitorum* (List of Prohibited Books) mainly because it was a novel that related a suggestively romantic relationship. The work appears on the Index of Benedict XIV, issued

in 1758, and the Indexes of Pope Leo XIII, issued in 1881 and 1900 and still in force in 1906.

Source: 3, p. 135; 6, pp. 2,039–40; 8, pp. 371–72.

1406 Rigaud, Milo
Secrets of Voodoo

1998 IA Challenged, but retained at the Madison Elementary School in Cedar Rapids.

Source: 11, May 1998, pp. 87–88.

1407 Riker, Andrew, et al.
Married Life

1981 IL Challenged in Collinsville.
1982 KY Challenged in Jefferson County because it "pushes women's lib which is very degrading to women and will destroy the traditional family."

Source: 11, May 1981, p. 68; Mar. 1983, p. 41.

1408 Riker, Andrew, et al.
Finding My Way

1982 GA Challenged in Walker County by the Eagle Forum because its "treatment of sexual matters was too explicit and its method of presentation faulty."
1982 IN Challenged in Tell City.
1987 WY Challenged at the Laramie Junior High School because the book "doesn't stress saying 'No.'"
1991 OK Challenged at the Grove High School because it was "too graphic for presentation in the classroom."

Source: 11, May 1982, p. 85; July 1982, p. 142; Sept. 1987, p. 177; Sept. 1991, p. 179.

1409 Riker, Audrey Palm, and
Holly Brisbane
Married and Single Life

1984 WI Returned to the Racine Unified School District curriculum just one week after the school board voted to ban it. The home economics text was criticized for encouraging premarital sex and advocating that unmarried couples live together.

Source: 11, Sept. 1984, p. 158; Jan. 1985, p. 10.

1410 Riley, Andy
The Book of Bunny Suicides: Little Fluffy Rabbits Who Just Don't Want to Live Anymore

2008 OR Retained at the Central Linn High School
New library in Halsey. The 2003 book depicts cartoon rabbits killing themselves in various

ways, from sitting in front of a bobsled run to impaling themselves on Darth Vader's light saber. A parent complained about the book, saying initially she would burn it rather than return it. The story drew national attention and prompted readers to send the school district about twenty-four copies of the book.

Source: 11, Jan. 2009, p. 22; Mar. 2009, p. 56.

1411 Ringgold, Faith
Tar Beach

1994 WA Challenged in the Spokane elementary school libraries because it stereotypes African Americans as eating fried chicken and watermelon and drinking beer at family picnics. The book is based on memories of its author's family rooftop picnics in 1930s Harlem. The book won the 1992 Coretta Scott King Illustrator Award for its portrayal of minorities.

Source: 11, Jan. 1995, p. 9; Mar. 1995, p. 54.

1412 Robbins, Harold
The Carpetbaggers

1961 CT Sales restricted in Waterbury on the grounds of obscenity.
1961 CT Sales restricted in Bridgeport.
1961 NY Sales restricted in Rochester.
1961 RI Sales restricted in Warwick.
1961 TX Sales restricted in Mesquite.
1965 Banned in South Africa.
1982 Malaysian police confiscated the works of Robbins because they were considered "prejudicial to the public interest."

Source: 4, p. 88; 5, Jan. 1983, p. 45; 13, p. 40.

1413 Robbins, Harold
The Lonely Lady

1980 VA Challenged in Abingdon because of the book's "pornographic" nature.

Source: 11, Jan. 1981, p. 5.

1414 Robbins, Harold
Never Love a Stranger

1949 PA Identified, along with eight other novels, as obscene in criminal proceedings in the Court of Quarter sessions in Philadelphia County, Pennsylvania. The court refused to declare the novel "obscene" and in Robbin's novel, references to sexual activity are brief and general, and the main character's language is important to developing that character.

Source: 14, pp. 236–37.

1415 Robbins, Russell H.
Encyclopedia of Witchcraft and Demonology

1994 MI Removed from the Detroit public school libraries after a complaint that the book was "obscene, perverse, and immoral."

Source: 11, Mar. 1994, p. 51.

1416 Roberts, J. R.
Ambush Moon: Gunsmith Series 148

1995 OH Challenged, but retained in the Fairfield County District Library in Lancaster because it includes profanity and explicit sex scenes.

Source: 11, Nov. 1995, p. 184; Jan. 1996, p. 29.

1417 Roberts, J. R.
The Gunsmith: Hands of the Strangler

1994 SD Challenged, but retained at the Selby Library because of an inappropriate sex scene.

Source: 11, July 1994, p. 129.

1418 Roberts, Willo Davis
The View from the Cherry Tree

1995 NV Retained in Elko County classrooms despite the complaint of the elementary school student. School officials said parents complained that the book contains language inappropriate for sixth graders, including a cat named S.O.B.

Source: 11, Sept. 1995, p. 160.

1419 Robinson, David
Herbert Armstrong's Tangled Web

1981 OK A suit was filed in Tulsa alleging that the book was based on privileged communications, whose secrecy is protected by law. A restraining order temporarily stopped the release of this book.

Source: 11, Jan. 1982, p. 23.

1420 Rock, Gail
The House without a Christmas Tree

1983 IA Challenged in the Des Moines schools due to the use of the word "damn."

Source: 11, May 1983, p. 73.

1421 Rockwell, Thomas
How to Eat Fried Worms

1988 NJ Retained in the Middletown elementary school libraries despite a parent's objection that the book contains violence and vulgar language.

1991 IN Removed from the LaVille Elementary School library in LaPaz by a library user because the book contains the word "bastard."

Source: 11, May 1988, p. 103; Sept. 1991, p. 153.

1422 Rodgers, Mary
Freaky Friday

2001 FL Pulled, but later returned to the library shelves of Hernando County schools after a parent's complaint about the book's references to drinking and smoking, characters who take God's name in vain, and the claim it advocates violence.

Source: 11, Mar. 2001, p. 53; May 2001, p. 123.

1423 Rodriguez, Abraham, Jr.
The Boy without a Flag: Tales of the South Bronx

1994 MN Retained in the Rosemount High School after a complaint about "profane language and promiscuity in the stories."

Source: 11, July 1994, p. 130.

1424 Rodriguez, Luis J.
Always Running

1996 IL Challenged as an optional reading at the Guilford High School in Rockford because it is "blatant pornography."

1998 CA Challenged, but retained on the San Jose Unified School District optional reading list at district high schools despite complaints that the book is "pornographic and offensive in its stereotyping of Latinos." The book will be kept in libraries, but students must have parental consent to check it out.

1998 CA Removed from the Santa Rosa high school reading lists.

1998 CA Removed, pending review, at the Fremont schools.

2003 CA Challenged, but retained in three Beyer High School classrooms in Modesto despite complaints that the book is "pornographic." The decision reversed the actions of district administrators who had removed the book in early November 2003. The book won the *Chicago Sun Times* Carl Sandburg Literary Award and was designated as a *New York Times* notable book.

2004 CA Pulled from the Santa Barbara schools after a parent complained about graphic passages depicting violence and sex.

Source: 11, July 1996, p. 118; Sept. 1998, pp. 142–43; Jan. 2003, pp. 27–28; Mar. 2004, pp. 51–52; Jan. 2005, p. 7; 13, pp. 8–11.

1425 Rojas, Don
One People, One Destiny: The Caribbean and Central America Today

1989 Confiscated by custom officials in Grenada along with *Maurice Bishop Speaks; Thomas Sankara Speaks: The Burkina Faso Revolution, 1983–87*, and other books by Nelson Mandela, Karl Marx, Che Guevara, Fidel Castro, and Malcom X. The books were labeled as "subversive to the peace and security of the country."

Source: 11, Mar. 1989, pp. 49–50; July 1989, pp. 141–42.

1426 Roman, Jo
Exit House

1994 AR Challenged at the Springdale Public Library because it presented suicide as "a rational and sane alternative."

Source: 11, July 1994, p. 128.

1427 Ronan, Margaret, and Eve Ronan
Astrology and Other Occult Games

1982 OH Challenged in the Akron school system because the book promotes Satan.

Source: 11, Mar. 1983, p. 38.

1428 Roquelaire, A. E. [Anne Rice]
Beauty's Punishment

1992 GA Removed from the shelves of the Lake Lanier Regional Library system in Gwinnett County following complaints that centered around sexuality.

1996 OH Removed from the Columbus Metropolitan Library as hard-core pornography.

Source: 11, Jan. 1993, p. 7; July 1996, pp. 119–20.

1429 Roquelaire, A. E.
Beauty's Release

1992 GA Removed from the shelves of the Lake Lanier Regional Library system in Gwinnett County following complaints that centered around sexuality.

1996 OH Removed from the Columbus Metropolitan Library as hard-core pornography.

Source: 11, Jan. 1993, p. 7; July 1996, pp. 119–20.

1430 Roquelaire, A. E.
The Claiming of Sleeping Beauty

1992 GA Removed from the shelves of the Lake Lanier Regional Library system in Gwinnett County following complaints that centered around sexuality.

1996 OH Removed from the Columbus Metropolitan Library as hard-core pornography.
Source: 11, Jan. 1993, p. 7; July 1996, pp. 119–20.

1431 Roth, Philip
Goodbye, Columbus

1980 VA Challenged in Abingdon because of the book's "pornographic" nature.
Source: 11, Jan. 1981, p. 5.

1432 Roth, Philip
Portnoy's Complaint

1969 Many libraries were attacked for carrying this novel, and some librarians' jobs were threatened.
Source: 4, p. 99.

1433 Rounds, Glen
Wash Day on Noah's Ark

1991 OH Challenged at the Hubbard Public Library because the book alters the story of Noah's Ark, making it secular and confusing to children.
Source: 11, Sept. 1991, p. 153.

1434 Rousseau, Jean-Jacques
Confessions

1806 Placed on I*ndex Librorum Prohibitorum* (Index of Prohibited Books) in Rome, Italy in 1806 by Pope Pius VII and later renewed the prohibition because of the sexual adventures that Rousseau recounted.

1929 Banned by the U.S. Customs Department for being injurious to public morals.

1935 Banned in the USSR.
Source: 4, p. 30; 8, pp. 325–26.

1435 Rousseau, Jean-Jacques
Emile

1762 Condemned in Paris, France by the archbishop and Parlement of Paris, the Sorbonne, and the Inquisition. Rousseau fled France to avoid arrest in 1762.

1763 Banned in Geneva.

1766 Placed on the Spanish and Roman in 1766 *Index Librorum Prohibitorum* (Index of Prohibited Books) and remained forbidden to Catholics until 1966.
Source: 1, pp. 88–90.

1436 Rowling, J. K.
Harry Potter and the Chamber of Secrets

1999 CA Parents objected to the book's use in two Moorpark elementary schools.

1999 CO Parents objected to the book's use in the Douglas County schools.

1999 NY Parents objected to the book's use in suburban Buffalo, among other districts.

1999 SC Challenged in South Carolina schools because "the book has a serious tone of death, hate, lack of respect, and sheer evil."

2000 Retained in the Durham School District, Ontario, Canada after a challenge of the series because of concerns about witchcraft.

2000 Banned from the Christian Outreach College library in Brisbane, Australia because the book was considered violent and dangerous.

2000 AL Challenged, but retained in Arab school libraries and accelerated reader programs over objections that the author "is a member of the occult and the book encourages children to practice witchcraft."

2000 CA Retained at Orange Grove Elementary School in Whittier; it was challenged for dealing with magic and bad experiences.

2000 CA Challenged in the Fresno Unified School District classrooms by a religious group voicing concerns about sorcery and witchcraft.

2000 FL Challenged in six Santa Rosa County schools in Pace for its presentation of witchcraft.

2000 IL Challenged, but retained in Frankfort School District 157-C. Parents were concerned that the book contains lying and smart-aleck retorts to adults.

2000 MI Restricted to fifth- through eighth-graders who have written parental permission in the Zeeland schools. No future installments can be purchased and teachers are prohibited from reading the books aloud in class. The book was considered objectionable because of the intense story line, the violence, the wizardry, and the sucking of animal blood.

2000 MI Removed from the Bridgeport Township public school because it promotes witchcraft.

2000 NH Challenged, but retained in the Newfound Area School District in Bristol despite an objection the book "is scary."

2000 NY Challenged in the Salamanca elementary school libraries because a family complained about the book's dark themes.

2000 OR Challenged in Bend at the Three Rivers Elementary School due to references to witchcraft and concerns the book will lead children to hatred and rebellion.

2000 TX — Restricted to students with parental permission in the Santa Fe School District because critics say the book promotes witchcraft.

2001 FL — Challenged, but retained in the Duval County school libraries despite a complaint about witchcraft depicted in the book.

2001 NM — Burned in Alamagordo outside Christ Community Church because the Potter series is "a masterpiece of satanic deception."

2001 PA — Challenged in the Owen J. Roberts School District classrooms in Bucktown because the "books are telling children over and over again that lying, cheating, and stealing are not only acceptable, but that they're cool and cute."

2002 — Challenged in Moscow, Russia by a Slavic cultural organization that alleged the stories about magic and wizards could draw students into Satanism.

2002 AR — A federal judge overturned restricted access to the Harry Potter book after parents of a Cedarville fourth-grader filed a federal lawsuit challenging the restrictions, which required students to present written permission from a parent to borrow the book. The novel was originally challenged because it characterized authority as "stupid" and portrays "good witches and good magic."

2002 KY — Proposed for removal, along with more than fifty other titles, by a teachers' prayer group at the high school in Russell Springs because the book deals with ghosts, cults, and witchcraft.

2003 CT — Challenged, but retained in the New Haven schools despite claims the series "makes witchcraft and wizardry alluring to children."

2006 GA — The Gwinnett County school board rejected a parent's pleas to take Harry Potter books out of school libraries, based on the claim they promote witchcraft. The Georgia Board of Education ruled December 14 that the parent had failed to prove her contention that the series "promote[s] the Wicca religion," and therefore that the book's availability in public schools does not constitute advocacy of a religion. On May 29, 2007, Superior Court judge Ronnie Batchelor upheld the Georgia Board of Education's decision to support local school officials. County school board members have said the books are good tools to encourage children to read and to spark creativity and imagination.

2007 MA New — Removed from the St. Joseph School in Wakefield because the themes of witchcraft and sorcery were inappropriate for a Catholic school.

Source: 11, Jan. 2000, pp. 1, 26; Mar. 2000, pp. 46, 48, 50, 63; May 2000, p. 77; July 2000, p. 124; Sept. 2000, pp. 165–66; Nov. 2000, pp. 193–94, 216; Jan. 2001, pp. 11, 12, 13, 15; Mar. 2001, pp. 43, 62, 75; July 2001, p. 146; Jan. 2002, p. 49; Mar. 2002, p. 61; May 2002, p. 116; Sept. 2002, p. 197; Mar. 2003, p. 77; May 2003, p. 95; July 2003, pp. 137, 159; July 2006, pp. 207–8; Sept. 2006, p. 231; Nov. 2006, p. 289; Mar. 2007, pp. 72–73; July 2007, p. 151; Sept. 2007, pp. 205–6; Jan. 2008, pp. 36–37.

1437 — Rowling, J. K.
Harry Potter and the Goblet of Fire

2000 — Retained in the Durham School District, Ontario, Canada after a challenge of the series because of concerns about witchcraft.

2000 — Banned from the Christian Outreach College library in Queensland, Australia because the book was considered violent and dangerous.

2000 AL — Challenged, but retained in Arab school libraries and accelerated reader programs over objections that the author "is a member of the occult and the book encourages children to practice witchcraft."

2000 CA — Challenged in the Fresno Unified School District classrooms by a religious group voicing concerns about sorcery and witchcraft.

2000 FL — Challenged in six Santa Rosa County schools in Pace for its presentation of witchcraft.

2000 NH — Challenged, but retained in the Newfound Area School District in Bristol despite an objection the book "is scary."

2000 TX — Restricted to students with parental permission in the Santa Fe school district because critics say the book promotes witchcraft.

2001 FL — Challenged, but retained in the Duval County school libraries despite a complaint about witchcraft depicted in the book.

2001 NM — Burned in Alamagordo outside Christ Community Church because the Potter series is "a masterpiece of satanic deception."

2001 PA — Challenged in the Owen J. Roberts School District classrooms in Bucktown because the "books are telling children over and over again that lying, cheating, and stealing are not only acceptable, but that they're cool and cute."

2002 — Challenged in Moscow, Russia by a Slavic cultural organization that alleged the stories about magic and wizards could draw students into Satanism.

2002 AR — A federal judge overturned restricted access to the Harry Potter book after parents of a Cedarville fourth-grader filed a federal lawsuit challenging the restrictions, which required students to present written permission from a parent to borrow the book. The novel was originally challenged because it characterized authority as "stupid" and portrays "good witches and good magic."

2002 KY Proposed for removal, along with more than fifty other titles, by a teachers' prayer group at the high school in Russell Springs because the book deals with ghosts, cults, and witchcraft.

2003 CT Challenged, but retained in the New Haven schools despite claims the series "makes witchcraft and wizardry alluring to children."

2006 GA The Gwinnett County school board rejected a parent's pleas to take Harry Potter books out of school libraries, based on the claim they promote witchcraft. The Georgia Board of Education ruled December 14 that the parent had failed to prove her contention that the series "promote[s] the Wicca religion," and therefore that the book's availability in public schools does not constitute advocacy of a religion. On May 29, 2007, Superior Court judge Ronnie Batchelor upheld the Georgia Board of Education's decision to support local school officials. County school board members have said the books are good tools to encourage children to read and to spark creativity and imagination.

2007 MA New Removed from the St. Joseph School in Wakefield because the themes of witchcraft and sorcery were inappropriate for a Catholic school.

Source: 11, Nov. 2000, pp. 193–94, 216; Jan. 2001, pp. 11, 12, 13, 15; Mar. 2001, pp. 43, 62, 75; July 2001, p. 146; Jan. 2002, p. 49; Mar. 2002, p. 61; May 2002, p. 116; Sept. 2002, p. 197; Mar. 2003, p. 77; May 2003, p. 95; July 2003, pp. 137, 159; July 2006, pp. 207–8; Sept. 2006, p. 231; Nov. 2006, p. 289; Mar. 2007, pp. 72–73; July 2007, p. 151; Sept. 2007, pp. 205–6; Jan. 2008, pp. 36–37.

1438 Rowling, J. K.
Harry Potter and the Half-Blood Prince

2006 CA Removed by the Wilsona School District trustees from a list recommended by a parent-teacher committee for the Vista San Gabriel Elementary School library in Palmdale along with twenty three other books. Trustees said one rejected book contained an unsavory hero who made a bad role model for children; another was about a warlock, which they said was inappropriate; and others were books with which they were unfamiliar and didn't know whether they promoted good character or conflicted with textbooks. Rejected titles included three bilingual *Clifford the Big Red Dog* books, *Disney's Christmas Storybook*, two books from the Artemis Fowl series, *Beauty is a Beast*, *California (Welcome to the USA)*, and *The Eye of the Warlock*. The Wilsona School District board approved new library book-selection guidelines in wake of

the trustees' controversial decision. Books now cannot depict drinking alcohol, smoking, drugs, sex, including "negative sexuality, implied or explicit nudity, cursing, violent crime or weapons, gambling, foul humor, and dark content."

2006 GA The Gwinnett County school board rejected a parent's pleas to take Harry Potter books out of school libraries, based on the claim they promote witchcraft. The Georgia Board of Education ruled December 14 that the parent had failed to prove her contention that the series "promote[s] the Wicca religion," and therefore that the book's availability in public schools does not constitute advocacy of a religion. On May 29, 2007, Superior Court judge Ronnie Batchelor upheld the Georgia Board of Education's decision to support local school officials. County school board members have said the books are good tools to encourage children to read and to spark creativity and imagination.

2007 MA New Removed from the St. Joseph School in Wakefield because the themes of witchcraft and sorcery were inappropriate for a Catholic school.

Source: 11, May 2006, p. 127; July 2006, pp. 207–8; Sept. 2006, pp. 229–31; Nov. 2006, pp. 287–88; Mar. 2007, pp. 72–73; July 2007, p. 151; Sept. 2007, pp. 205–6; Jan. 2008, pp. 36–37.

1439 Rowling, J. K.
Harry Potter and the Prisoner of Azkaban

1999 CA Parents objected to the book's use in two Moorpark elementary schools.

1999 CO Parents objected to the book's use in the Douglas County schools.

1999 NY Parents objected to the book's use in suburban Buffalo, among other districts.

1999 SC Challenged in South Carolina schools because "the book has a serious tone of death, hate, lack of respect, and sheer evil."

2000 Retained in the Durham School District, Ontario, Canada after a challenge of the series because of concerns about witchcraft.

2000 Banned from the Christian Outreach College library in Brisbane, Australia because the book was considered violent and dangerous.

2000 AL Challenged, but retained in Arab school libraries and accelerated reader programs over objections that the author "is a member of the occult and the book encourages children to practice witchcraft."

2000 CA Retained at Orange Grove Elementary School in Whittier; it was challenged for dealing with magic and bad experiences.

2000 CA   Challenged in the Fresno Unified School District classrooms by a religious group voicing concerns about sorcery and witchcraft.

2000 FL   Challenged in six Santa Rosa County schools in Pace for its presentation of witchcraft.

2000 IL   Challenged, but retained in Frankfort School District 157-C. Parents were concerned that the book contains lying and smart-aleck retorts to adults.

2000 MI   Restricted to fifth- through eighth-graders who have written parental permission in the Zeeland schools. No future installments can be purchased and teachers are prohibited from reading the books aloud in class. The book was considered objectionable because of the intense story line, the violence, the wizardry, and the sucking of animal blood.

2000 MI   Removed from the Bridgeport Township public school because it promotes witchcraft.

2000 NH   Challenged, but retained in the Newfound Area School District in Bristol despite an objection the book "is scary."

2000 NY   Challenged in the Salamanca elementary school libraries because a family complained about the book's dark themes.

2000 OR   Challenged in Bend at the Three Rivers Elementary School due to references to witchcraft and concerns the book will lead children to hatred and rebellion.

2000 TX   Restricted to students with parental permission in the Santa Fe School District because critics say the book promotes witchcraft.

2001 FL   Challenged, but retained in the Duval County school libraries despite a complaint about witchcraft depicted in the book.

2001 NM   Burned in Alamagordo outside Christ Community Church because the Potter series is "a masterpiece of satanic deception."

2001 PA   Challenged in the Owen J. Roberts School District classrooms in Bucktown because the "books are telling children over and over again that lying, cheating, and stealing are not only acceptable, but that they're cool and cute."

2002   Challenged in Moscow, Russia by a Slavic cultural organization that alleged the stories about magic and wizards could draw students into Satanism.

2002 AR   A federal judge overturned restricted access to the Harry Potter book after parents of a Cedarville fourth-grader filed a federal lawsuit challenging the restrictions, which required students to present written permission from a parent to borrow the book. The novel was originally challenged because it characterized authority as "stupid" and portrays "good witches and good magic."

2002 KY   Proposed for removal, along with more than fifty other titles, by a teachers' prayer group at the high school in Russell Springs because the book deals with ghosts, cults, and witchcraft.

2003 CT   Challenged, but retained in the New Haven schools despite claims the series "makes witchcraft and wizardry alluring to children."

2006 GA   The Gwinnett County school board rejected a parent's pleas to take Harry Potter books out of school libraries, based on the claim they promote witchcraft. The Georgia Board of Education ruled December 14 that the parent had failed to prove her contention that the series "promote[s] the Wicca religion," and therefore that the book's availability in public schools does not constitute advocacy of a religion. On May 29, 2007, Superior Court judge Ronnie Batchelor upheld the Georgia Board of Education's decision to support local school officials. County school board members have said the books are good tools to encourage children to read and to spark creativity and imagination.

2007 MA New   Removed from the St. Joseph School in Wakefield because the themes of witchcraft and sorcery were inappropriate for a Catholic school.

Source: 11, Jan. 2000, pp. 1, 26; Mar. 2000, pp. 46, 48, 50, 63; May 2000, p. 77; July 2000, p. 124; Sept. 2000, pp. 165–66; Nov. 2000, pp. 193–94, 216; Jan. 2001, pp. 11, 12, 13, 15; Mar. 2001, pp. 43, 62, 75; July 2001, p. 146; Jan. 2002, p. 49; Mar. 2002, p. 61; May 2002, p. 116; Sept. 2002, p. 197; Mar. 2003, p. 77; May 2003, p. 95; July 2003, pp. 137, 159; July 2006, pp. 207–8; Mar. 2007, pp. 72–73; July 2007, p. 151; Sept. 2007, pp. 205–6; Jan. 2008, pp. 36–37.

1440   **Rowling, J. K.**
Harry Potter and the Sorcerer's Stone

1999 CA   Parents objected to the book's use in two Moorpark elementary schools.

1999 CO   Parents objected to the book's use in the Douglas County schools.

1999 NY   Parents objected to the book's use in suburban Buffalo, among other districts.

1999 SC   Challenged in South Carolina schools because "the book has a serious tone of death, hate, lack of respect, and sheer evil."

2000   Retained in the Durham School District, Ontario, Canada after a challenge of the series because of concerns about witchcraft.

2000   Banned from the Christian Outreach College library in Brisbane, Australia because the book was considered violent and dangerous.

2000 AL   Challenged, but retained in Arab school libraries and accelerated reader programs over the objections the author "is a member of the occult and the book encourages children to practice witchcraft."

2000 CA Challenged, but retained in the Simi Valley School District. A parent complained that the book was violent, anti-family, had a religious theme, and lacked educational value.

2000 CA Retained at Orange Grove Elementary School in Whittier. It was challenged for dealing with magic and bad experiences.

2000 CA Challenged in the Fresno Unified School District classrooms by a religious group voicing concerns about sorcery and witchcraft.

2000 FL Challenged in six Santa Rosa County schools in Pace for its presentation of witchcraft.

2000 IA Challenged in the Cedar Rapids school libraries because the book romantically portrays witches, warlocks, wizards, goblins, and sorcerers.

2000 IL Challenged, but retained in Frankfort School District 157-C. Parents were concerned that the book contains lying and smart-aleck retorts to adults.

2000 MI Temporarily restricted to fifth- through eighth-graders who have written parental permission in the Zeeland schools. The Zeeland school superintendent overturned most of the restriction including that no future installments could be purchased. One restriction remains is that teachers are prohibited from reading the books aloud in kindergarten through fifth grade classes. The book was considered objectionable because of the intense story line, the violence, the wizardry, and the sucking of animal blood.

2000 MI Removed from the Bridgeport Township public school because it promotes witchcraft.

2000 NH Challenged, but retained in the Newfound Area School District in Bristol despite an objection that the book "is scary."

2000 NY Challenged in the Salamanca elementary school libraries because a family complained about the book's dark themes.

2000 OR Challenged in Bend at the Three Rivers Elementary School due to references to witchcraft and concerns the book will lead children to hatred and rebellion.

2000 TX Restricted to students with parental permission in the Santa Fe School District because critics say the book promotes witchcraft.

2001 FL Challenged, but retained in the Duval County school libraries despite a complaint about witchcraft depicted in the book.

2001 NM Burned in Alamagordo outside Christ Community Church because the Potter series is "a masterpiece of satanic deception."

2001 PA Challenged in the Owen J. Roberts School District classrooms in Bucktown because the "books are telling children over and over again that lying, cheating, and stealing are not only acceptable, but that they're cool and cute."

2002 Challenged in Moscow, Russia by a Slavic cultural organization that alleged the stories about magic and wizards could draw students into Satanism.

2002 In February 2002, board of education officials in the United Arab Emirates banned twenty-six books from the schools, including Rowling's novels because "they have written or illustrated material that contradicts Islamic and Arab values."

2002 AR A federal judge overturned restricted access to the Harry Potter book after parents of a Cedarville fourth-grader filed a federal lawsuit challenging the restrictions, which required students to present written permission from a parent to borrow the book. The novel was originally challenged because it characterized authority as "stupid" and portrays "good witches and good magic."

2002 KY Proposed for removal, along with more than fifty other titles, by a teachers' prayer group at the high school in Russell Springs because the book deals with ghosts, cults, and witchcraft.

2003 CT Challenged, but retained in the New Haven schools despite claims the series "makes witchcraft and wizardry alluring to children."

2006 GA The Gwinnett County school board rejected a parent's pleas to take Harry Potter books out of school libraries, based on the claim they promote witchcraft. The Georgia Board of Education ruled December 14 that the parent had failed to prove her contention that the series "promote[s] the Wicca religion," and therefore that the book's availability in public schools does not constitute advocacy of a religion. On May 29, 2007, Superior Court judge Ronnie Batchelor upheld the Georgia Board of Education's decision to support local school officials. County school board members have said the books are good tools to encourage children to read and to spark creativity and imagination.

2007 MA New Removed from the St. Joseph School in Wakefield because the themes of witchcraft and sorcery were inappropriate for a Catholic school.

Source: 8, pp. 240–43; 11, Jan. 2000, pp. 1, 26; Mar. 2000, pp. 46, 48, 50, 63; May 2000, p. 77; July 2000, pp. 104, 124; Sept. 2000, pp. 165–66; Nov. 2000, pp. 193–94, 216; Jan. 2001, pp. 11, 12, 13, 15; Mar. 2001, pp. 43, 62, 75; July 2001, p. 146; Jan. 2002, p. 49; Mar. 2002, p. 61; May 2002, p. 116; Sept. 2002, p. 197; Mar. 2003, p. 77; May 2003, p. 95; July 2003, pp. 137, 159; July 2006, pp. 207–8; Nov. 2006, p. 289; Mar. 2007, pp. 72–73; July 2007, p. 151; Sept. 2007, pp. 205–6; Jan. 2008, pp. 36–37.

1441 **Royko, Mike**
Boss: Richard J. Daley of Chicago

1972 CT Barred from the Ridgefield High School reading

list because it "downgrades police departments."

1983 NY Challenged in the Hannibal High School because the book is "detrimental to students and contributed to social decay because it contains rough language."

Source: 4, p. 99; 5; 11, May 1983, p. 74; July 1983, p. 123.

1442 Ruby, Laura
Lily's Ghosts

2006 FL Removed from the Hillsborough County fourth-grade reading list, although the book is on the Sunshine State Young Reader's Award list of books for third- through fifth-graders.

2006 FL Removed from the Pinellas school district fourth-grade reading list, although the book is on the Sunshine State Young Reader's Award list of books for third- through fifth-graders.

Source: 11, Nov. 2006, pp. 290–91.

1443 Ruddell, Robert B., et al.
Person to Person

1982 KY Challenged in the Jefferson County School District because the book "confuses sex roles."

1985 WA The Evergreen School Board in Vancouver banned the textbook because some members said it is too favorable to alternative lifestyles. The controversy centered on a chapter titled "Changing Life Styles," in which the book describes relationships other than the traditional family.

Source: 11, Mar. 1983, p. 41; May 1985, p. 79; July 1985, p. 115.

1444 Rushdie, Salman
The Satanic Verses

1988 Banned in Pakistan. In Pakistan five people died in riots against the book. Another man died a day later in Kashmir. Ayatollah Khomeini issued a fatwa or religious edict, stating, "I inform the proud Muslim people of the world that the author of the *Satanic Verses*, which is against Islam, the prophet, and the Koran, and all those involved in its publication who were aware of its content, have been sentenced to death."

1989 Banned in Saudi Arabia.
1989 Banned in Egypt.
1989 Banned in Somalia.
1989 Banned in Sudan.
1989 Burned in West Yorkshire, England and temporarily withdrawn from two bookstores on the advice of police who took threats to staff and property seriously.

1989 Banned in Malaysia.
1989 Banned in Qatar.
1989 Banned in Indonesia.
1989 Banned in South Africa.
1989 Banned in India because of its criticism of Islam.
1989 Banned in Bangladesh.
1989 Owning or reading it was declared a crime under penalty of fifteen months' imprisonment in Venezuela.
1989 The government of Bulgaria restricted its distribution.
1989 The government of Poland restricted its distribution.
1989 Banned under the threat of fines in Japan. In 1991, Hitoshi Igarashi, the Japanese translator was stabbed to death.
1989 KS Challenged at the Wichita Public Library because the book is "blasphemous to the prophet Mohammed."
1991 The Italian translator, Ettore Capriolo, was seriously wounded.
1993 William Nygaard, the book's Norwegian publisher, was shot and seriously injured.

Source: 3, pp. 269–70; 6, pp. 2,071–75; 8, pp. 291–96; 11, Mar. 1989, p. 47; July 1989, p. 125; Sept. 1989, p. 185.

1445 Russell, Bertrand
What I Believe

1929 MA Banned in Boston.

Source: 4, p. 62.

1446 Russo, Vito
The Celluloid Closet: Homosexuality in the Movies

1993 OR Challenged at the Deschutes County Library in Bend because it "encourages and condones" homosexuality.

Source: 11, Sept. 1993, pp. 158–59.

1447 Sachar, Louis
The Boy Who Lost His Face

1991 CA Challenged at the Thousand Oaks Library because of inappropriate language.

1993 CA Challenged at the Golden View Elementary school in San Ramon because of its profanity, frequent use of obscene gestures, and other inappropriate subject matter.

1993 IN Removed from the Jackson Township Elementary School in Clay City due to "unsuitable words."

1993 NY Removed from the Cuyler Elementary School library in Red Creek because "the age level and use of some swear words may make it inappropriate to younger children."

Source: 11, Mar. 1992, p. 39; May 1993, p. 71; July 1993, p. 97; Sept. 1993, p. 157; Mar. 1994, p. 51.

1448 Sachar, Louis
Marvin Redpost: Is He a Girl?

2000 AL Challenged in Chapman Elementary School libraries in Huntsville because it contains a fantasy about kissing your elbow and changing sexes.

2000 IL Challenged in the New Lenox elementary school because its young hero plays with girls and dreams that he wears a dress to baseball practice.
Source: 11, Mar. 2000, p. 47; July 2000, p. 104.

1449 Sachar, Louis
Sideways Stories from Wayside Schools

1992 AZ Challenged at the Neely Elementary School in Gilbert because the book shows the dark side of religion through the occult, the devil, and satanism.
Source: 11, May 1992, p. 78; July 1992, p. 124.

1450 Sachar, Louis
There's a Boy in the Girls' Bathroom

1998 AR Challenged, but retained in the fifth-grade Pea Ridge curriculum after objections to "inappropriate language."
Source: 11, May 1998, p. 89.

1451 Sachar, Louis
Wayside School Is Falling Down

1995 WI Removed from the list of suggested readings from the Antigo elementary reading program because the book included passages condoning destruction of school property, disgraceful manners, disrespectful representation of professionals, improper English, and promotion of peer pressure.
Source: 11, July 1995, p. 100.

1452 Sade, Marquis de
Juliette

1791 Author imprisoned much of his life in France.
1948 Still on the *Index Librorum Prohibitorum* (List of Prohibited Books) in Rome, Italy.
1962 Seized by British Customs.
1982 Greek police confiscated thousands of books by Marquis de Sade. The publisher, Themis Banousis, was sentenced to two years' imprisonment for violating the laws on indecent literature by translating and publishing the works of de Sade. Forty-seven other publishers were reported arrested in mid-Sept. 1982 for defying the ban.
1982 Malaysian police confiscated the works of de Sade because they were considered "prejudicial to the public interest."
Source: 4, p. 34; 5, Jan. 1983, pp. 44–45.

1453 Sade, Marquis de
Justine or the Misfortunes of Virtue

1791 Author imprisoned much of his life in France.
1948 Still on the *Index Librorum Prohibitorum* (List of Prohibited Books) in Rome, Italy.
1962 Seized by British Customs.
Source: 4, p. 34.

1454 Said, Edward W.
The Politics of Dispossession: The Struggle for Palestinian Self-Determination

1996 Removed from West Bank and Gaza bookstores, the confiscation reportedly having been ordered by the Ministry of Information. The first raid occurred on a small bookstore in central Ramallah. Sales of the book were banned.
Source: 7, p. 411.

1455 Salinger, J. D.
Catcher in the Rye

1960 OK Since its publication, this title has been a favorite target of censors. A teacher in Tulsa was fired for assigning the book to an eleventh grade English class. The teacher appealed and was reinstated by the school board, but the book was removed from use in the school.

1963 OH A delegation of parents of high school students in Columbus asked the school board to ban the novel for being "anti-white" and "obscene." The school board refused the request.

1975 PA Removed from the Selinsgrove suggested reading list. Based on parents' objections to the language and content of the book, the school board voted 5-4 to ban the book. The book was later reinstated in the curriculum when the board learned that the vote was illegal because they needed a two-thirds vote for removal of the text.

1977 NJ Challenged as an assignment in an American literature class in Pittsgrove. After months of controversy, the board ruled that the novel could be read in the Advanced Placement class, but they gave parents the right to decide whether or not their children would read it.

1978 WA Removed from the Issaquah Optional High School reading list.

1979 MI Removed from the required reading list in Middleville.

1980 OH Removed from the Jackson-Milton school libraries in North Jackson.

1982 Removed from the school libraries in Morris, Manitoba, Canada along with two other books because they violate the committee's guidelines covering "excess vulgar language, sexual scenes, things concerning moral issues, excessive violence, and anything dealing with the occult."

1982 AL Removed from two Anniston high school libraries, but later reinstated on a restrictive basis.

1983 MT Challenged at the Libby High School due to the "book's contents."

1985 FL Banned from English classes at the Freeport High School in De Funiak Springs because it is "unacceptable" and "obscene."

1986 WY Removed from the required reading list of a Medicine Bow Senior High School English class because of sexual references and profanity in the book.

1987 ND Banned from a required sophomore English reading list at the Napoleon High School after parents and the local Knights of Columbus chapter complained about its profanity and sexual references.

1988 IN Challenged at the Linton-Stockton High School because the book is "blasphemous and undermines morality."

1989 CA Banned from the classrooms in Boron High School because the book contains profanity.

1991 IL Challenged at the Grayslake Community High School.

1992 FL Challenged in the Duval County public school libraries because of profanity, lurid passages about sex, and statements defamatory to minorities, God, women, and the disabled.

1992 IA Challenged in the Waterloo schools.

1992 IL Challenged at the Jamaica High School in Sidell because the book contains profanities and depicted premarital sex, alcohol abuse, and prostitution.

1992 PA Challenged at the Cumberland Valley High School in Carlisle because of a parent's objections that it contains profanity and is immoral.

1993 CA Challenged as required reading in the Corona-Norco Unified School District because it is "centered around negative activity." The book was retained and teachers selected alternatives if students object to Salinger's novel.

1994 NH Challenged as mandatory reading in the Goffstown schools because of the vulgar words used and the sexual exploits experienced in the book.

1994 WI Challenged, but retained at the New Richmond High School for use in some English classes.

1995 FL Challenged at the St. Johns County Schools in St. Augustine.

1996 ME Challenged at the Oxford Hills High School in Paris. A parent objected to the use of "the 'F' word."

1997 CA Removed because of profanity and sexual situations from the required reading curriculum of the Marysville Joint Unified School District. The school superintendent removed it to get it "out of the way so that we didn't have that polarization over a book."

1997 GA Challenged, but retained at the Glynn Academy High School in Brunswick. A student objected to the novel's profanity and sexual references.

2000 AL Challenged, but retained on the shelves of Limestone County school district despite objections about the book's foul language.

2000 GA Banned, but later reinstated after community protests at the Windsor Forest High School in Savannah. The controversy began in early 1999 when a parent complained about sex, violence, and profanity in the book that was part of an Advanced Placement English class.

2001 GA Challenged by a Glynn County school board member because of profanity. The novel was retained.

2001 SC Removed by a Dorchester District 2 school board member in Summerville because it "is a filthy, filthy book."

2004 ME Challenged, but retained as an assigned reading in the Noble High School in North Berwick. Teachers will provide more information to parents about why certain books are studied.

2009 MT Challenged in the Big Sky High School in
New Missoula.

Source: 8, pp. 436–38; 9; 11, Nov. 1978, p. 138; Jan. 1980, pp. 6–7; May 1980, p. 51; Mar. 1983, pp. 37–38; July 1983, p. 122; July 1985, p. 113; Mar. 1987, p. 55; July 1988, p. 123; Jan. 1988, p. 10; Sept. 1988, p. 177; Nov. 1989, pp. 218–19; July 1991, pp. 129–30; May 1992, p. 83; July 1992, pp. 105, 126; Jan. 1993, p. 29; Jan. 1994, p. 14, Mar. 1994, pp. 56, 70; May 1994, p. 100; Jan. 1995, p. 12; Jan. 1996, p. 14; Nov. 1996, p. 212; May 1997, p. 78; July 1997, p. 96; May 2000, p. 91; July 2000, p. 123; Mar. 2001, p. 76; Nov. 2001, pp. 246–47; 277–78; Jan. 2005, pp. 8–9; Mar. 2005, pp. 73–74; May 2009, pp. 82–84.

1456 **Salinger, J. D.**
Nine Stories

1987 VA Removed from the reading list of a writing class at Franklin High School after a parent of one student was offended by some of the language in a story.

Source: 11, July 1987, p. 131.

1457 Salinger, Margaretta M.
Great Paintings of Children

1994 AZ Retained at Maldonado Elementary School in Tucson after being challenged by parents who objected to nudity and "pornographic," "perverted," and "morbid" themes.
Source: 11, July 1994, p. 112.

1458 Salomon, George, and Feitelson, Rose
The Many Faces of Anti-Semitism

1983 Banned from the 1983 Moscow, Russia International Book Fair along with more than fifty other books because it is "anti-Soviet."
Source: 11, Nov. 1983, p. 201.

1459 Sams, Ferrol
Run with the Horsemen

1995 VA Challenged in the Rockingham County schools because of sexual content.
Source: 11, Nov. 1995, p. 188; Jan. 1996, p. 18.

1460 Samuels, Gertrude
Run, Shelley, Run

1977 AR Removed and destroyed from the Hot Springs Central Junior High School library because of objectionable language.
1979 UT Challenged at the Ogden School District and placed in a restricted circulation category.
1981 SD Removed from the Onida High School due to "objectionable" language.
1981 SD Removed from the Blunt High School due to "objectionable" language.
1982 NC Removed from the Troutman Middle School library.
1987 NC Challenged at Alexander Central High School and East Junior High School libraries in Taylorsville because of "foul language."
1995 PA Removed from the Palmyra middle school classroom because of its language and the portrayal of incidents involving nudity, lesbianism, and prostitution.
Source: 9; 11, Mar. 1977, p. 36; May 1979, p. 49; May 1981, pp. 65–66; Mar. 1982, p. 45; May 1987, p. 87; July 1987, p. 149; July 1995, pp. 98–99; Jan. 1996, p. 17.

1461 Sanchez, Alex
Rainbow Boys

2004 TX Challenged at the Montgomery County Memorial Library System along with fifteen other young adult books with gay-positive themes. The objections were posted at the Library Patrons of Texas Web site. The language describing the books is similar to that posted at the Web site of the Fairfax County, Virginia-based Parents Against Bad Books in Schools, to which Library Patrons of Texas links.
2005 AR Challenged in the Fayetteville High School library. The complainant also submitted a list of more than fifty books, citing the books as too sexually explicit and promoting homosexuality.
2006 NY Removed from the Webster Central School District summer reading list for high-school students after receiving complaints from parents about explicit sexual content. The book won the International Reading Association's 2003 Young Adults' Choice Award, and the American Library Association selected it as a Best Book for Young Adults. A year later the book returned to the list after district officials reviewed the process used to select books on the list.
Source: 11, Nov. 2004, pp. 231–32; Nov. 2006, pp. 291–92; July 2007, p. 165.

1462 Sanders, Lawrence
The Seduction of Peter S.

1985 PA Banned from the Stroudsburg High School library because it was "blatantly graphic, pornographic, and wholly unacceptable for a high school library."
Source: 11, May 1985, p. 78.

1463 Sanford, John
Winter Prey

1994 OR Expurgated by an apparent self-appointed censor at the Coquille Public Library along with several other books. Most were mysteries and romances in which single words and sexually explicit passages were whited out by a vandal who left either dots or solid ink pen lines where the words had been.
Source: 11, Sept. 1994, p. 148.

1464 Santiago, Esmeralda
When I Was Puerto Rican

2001 CA Challenged in the Newark Unified School District because the book is sexually explicit.
2002 VA Challenged, along with seventeen other titles by the Fairfax County elementary and secondary libraries, in a group called Parents Against Bad Books in Schools. The group contends the books "contain profanity and descriptions of drug abuse, sexually explicit conduct, and torture."
Source: 11, Mar. 2001, p. 55; Jan. 2003, p. 10.

1465 Sapphire
Push

2005 AL Challenged, but retained at Fayetteville High School in Fayetteville despite a parent's complaint that it was sexually explicit. The complainant also submitted a list of more than fifty books, citing the books as too sexually explicit and promoting homosexuality.
Source: 11, May 2005, p. 135; Sept. 2005, p. 215; Nov. 2005, pp. 295–96.

1466 Sarton, May
The Education of Harriet Hatfield

1995 NH Removed from the Mascenic Regional High School in New Ipswich because it is about gays and lesbians. An English teacher was fired for refusing to remove the book.
Source: 11, Sept. 1995, p. 166; Jan. 1996, p. 15.

1467 Sartre, Jean-Paul
Age of Reason

1973 On Feb. 21, 1973, eleven Turkish book publishers went on trial before an Istanbul martial law tribunal on charges of publishing, possessing, and selling books in violation of an order of the Istanbul martial law command. They faced possible sentences of between one month's and six months' imprisonment "for spreading propaganda unfavorable to the state" and the confiscation of their books. Eight booksellers also were on trial with the publishers on the same charge involving the *Age of Reason*.
Source: 5, Summer 1973, xii.

1468 Sartre, Jean-Paul
Saint Genet

1984 Seized by the British Customs Office as "in decent and obscene."
Source: 11, Jan. 1985, p. 26.

1469 Saunders, Richard, and Brian Macne
Horrorgami

1993 OR Removed from the Glendale school libraries in Grants Pass for its alleged "satanic" content. The book is a craft book on origami, but incorporates stories about werewolves and vampires, and is allegedly illustrated with satanic symbols.
Source: 11, July 1993, p. 101.

1470 Savonarola, Girolamo
Writings

1498 After a ceremony of degradation, the author was hung on a cross and burned with all his writings, sermons, essays, and pamphlets in Italy.
Source: 1, pp. 53–55; 4, p. 8.

1471 Schechter, Harold, and David Everitt
The A-Z Encyclopedia of Serial Killers

2002 FL Challenged and retained in the Hillsborough County School District because of a parent's objection to the book's "gruesome details."
Source: 11, July 2002, p. 179.

1472 Schniedewind, Nancy
Open Minds to Equality: a Sourcebook of Learning Activities to Affirm Diversity and Promote Equity

2007 Challenged at the publicly funded Waterloo, Kitchener, Ontario, Canada, Catholic School District because it presents homosexuality as "morally neutral." The book is used as an optional resource for teachers, and students never see the book. A citizens' organization in Kitchener, Defend Traditional Marriage and Family, objected because the book could lead people "to reject scriptural teaching on homosexual acts."
Source: 11, Nov. 2007, p. 240.

1473 Schnitzler, Arthur
Casanova's Homecoming

1930 Simon & Schuster was brought to court for publishing this work.
1939 Banned by Mussolini in Rome, Italy.
Source: 4, p. 57; 13, pp. 42–43; 15, Vol. III, p. 636.

1474 Schnitzler, Arthur
Reigen

1929 NY A bookseller was convicted by the Court of Special Sessions for selling the book. The Appellate Division upheld the conviction, basing their decision more on the "exquisite handling of the licentious" described in the introduction rather than the text. Since the book had been pirated and privately printed, the author was in complete ignorance of the introduction. The conviction was sustained by the highest state court. Shortly afterwards the book, which had been studied widely in college and university courses in German literature, was published by Modern Library, and no further attempt was made to suppress it.
Source: 4, p. 57; 15, Vol. III, p. 420.

1475 Schouweiler, Thomas
The Devil: Opposing Viewpoints

2004 PA Challenged at the Chestnut Ridge Middle School in Washington Township. The complainants want the school district to seek parental approval before elementary and middle school students can check out books related to the occult.
Source: 11, May 2004, pp. 117–18.

1476 Schrag, Ariel, ed.
Stuck in the Middle: Seventeen Comics from an Unpleasant Age

2009 SD New Pulled from the school library collections at two Sioux Falls public middle schools. The book is the work of sixteen cartoonists who recreated true tales from their middle-school years. The book's major themes are bullying and boy-girl awkwardness. Masturbation and marijuana show up in passing, and several of the vignettes include words most parents wouldn't want to hear from their children.
Source: 11, Jan. 2010, p. 13.

1477 Schreier, Alta
Vamos a Cuba (A Visit to Cuba)

2006 FL New Removed from all Miami-Dade County school libraries because of a parent's complaint that the book does not depict an accurate life in Cuba. The American Civil Liberties Union (ACLU) of Florida filed a lawsuit challenging the decision to remove this book and the twenty-three other titles in the same series from the district school libraries. In granting a preliminary injunction in July 2006 against the removal, Judge Alan S. Gold of U.S. District Court in Miami characterized the matter as a "First Amendment issue" and ruled in favor of the ACLU of Florida, which argued that the books were generally factual and that the board should add to its collection, rather than remove books it disagreed with. When the district court entered a preliminary injunction ordering the school district immediately to replace the entire series on library shelves, the Miami-Dade School Board appealed the decision to the Eleventh Circuit Court in Atlanta. In a February 5, 2009, two to one decision, the U.S. Court of Appeals for the Eleventh Circuit said the board did not breach the First Amendment, and ordered a Miami federal judge to lift a preliminary injunction that had allowed Vamos a Cuba to be checked out from school libraries. But the three judge panel's opinion—not unlike the School Board's initial vote—was so fraught with political rhetoric such as "book banning" that further appeals seem inevitable. On November 13, 2010, the U.S, Supreme Court declined to take up the case. The action let stand a 2-1 ruling by the U.S. Court of Appeals for the Eleventh Circuit that the school board's decision to remove the book was not censorship in violation of the First Amendment.
Source: 11, July 2006, p. 207; Sept. 2006, pp. 230–31; Nov. 2006, p. 288; Jan. 2007, p. 8; May 2007, pp. 91–92; Mar. 2009, pp. 43–45; Jan. 2010, pp. 25–27

1478 Schusky, Ernest L.
Introduction to Social Science

1985 OR Challenged in the South Umpqua School District because the book presents a variety of concepts that are "controversial and inappropriate for seventh graders. The book's sections on death education, extrasensory perception, genetic planning, group therapy, and religious values had little to do with the teaching of basic social studies."
Source: 11, Mar. 1986, p. 42.

1479 Schwartz, Alvin
And the Green Grass Grew All Around

2000 PA Removed from elementary and middle school library shelves by the Central Dauphin school board in Harrisburg due to its explicit language.
Source: 11, Sept. 2000, p. 144.

1480 Schwartz, Alvin
Cross Your Fingers, Spit in Your Eye

1992 AZ Challenged at the Neely Elementary School in Gilbert because the book shows the dark side of religion through the occult, the devil, and satanism.
Source: 11, May 1992, p. 78; July 1992, p. 124.

1481 Schwartz, Alvin
Ghosts! Ghost Stories in Folklore

1998 WY Challenged, but retained in the Campbell County School District despite the claims that "the book misleads the reader—that ghosts are actually possible. . . This book blurs the line between fantasy and reality for younger children."
Source: 11, Mar. 1999, p. 38; May 1999, p. 84.

1482   Schwartz, Alvin
In a Dark, Dark Room and Other Scary Stories

1986 CO   Challenged at the Jefferson County school libraries in Lakewood because the book is "too morbid for children." The Jefferson County School Board refused to ban the book.
Source: 11, Sept. 1986, p. 173; Nov. 1986, p. 224.

1483   Schwartz, Alvin
More Scary Stories to Tell in the Dark

1988 OR   Challenged at the Dry Hollow Elementary School in The Dalles because it is too scary and violent.
1992 AZ   Challenged at the Neely Elementary School in Gilbert because the book shows the dark side of religion through the occult, the devil, and satanism.
1992 WA   Challenged at the Lake Washington School District in Kirkland as unacceptably violent for children.
1993 AZ   Restricted access at the Marana Unified School District because of complaints about violence and cannibalism.
1994 MT   Challenged, but retained at the Whittier Elementary School library in Bozeman. The book was challenged because it would cause children to fear the dark, have nightmares, and give them an unrealistic view of death.
1994 WA   Removed from Vancouver School District elementary school libraries after surviving two previous attempts (1991, 1993). Also challenged at neighboring Evergreen School District libraries in 1994 because "This book. . . is far beyond other scary books."
1995 CA   Challenged in the Tracy school libraries because of the book's violent content and graphic nature.
1995 MI   Challenged as "objectionable" and "disgusting," but retained on Harper Woods school district reading lists.
2006 KY   Retained in the Greater Clark County elementary-school libraries despite a grandmother's request to ban the Scary Stories books written by Alvin Schwartz. She wanted all four or five volumes in the series banned because, she said, they depict cannibalism, murder, witchcraft and ghosts, and include a story about somebody being skinned.
Source: 11, Jan. 1989, p. 3; May 1992, pp. 78, 94–95; July 1992, p. 124; Sept. 1993, p. 143; July 1994, p. 111; Sept. 1994, pp. 148–49, 166; May 1995, p. 65; July 1995, p. 111; Nov. 2006, pp. 317–18.

1484   Schwartz, Alvin
More Tales to Chill Your Bones

1992 CT   Challenged at the West Hartford elementary and middle school libraries because of violence and the subject matter.
1992 WA   Challenged at the Lake Washington School District in Kirkland as unacceptably violent for children.
1994 WA   Removed from Vancouver School District elementary school libraries after surviving two previous attempts (1991, 1993). Challenged at neighboring Evergreen School District libraries in 1994 because "This book. . . is far beyond other scary books."
Source: 11, May 1992, pp. 94–95; Sept. 1992, p. 137; July 1994, p. 111; Sept. 1994, pp. 148–49.

1485   Schwartz, Alvin
Scary Stories to Tell in the Dark

1990 MI   Challenged in the Livonia schools because the poems frightened first grade children.
1992 AZ   Challenged at the Neely Elementary School in Gilbert because the book shows the dark side of religion through the occult, the devil and satanism.
1992 CT   Challenged at the West Hartford elementary and middle school libraries because of violence and the subject matter.
1992 IN   Challenged at the elementary school library in Union County.
1992 WA   Challenged at the Lake Washington School District in Kirkland as unacceptably violent for children.
1993 AZ   Restricted access at the Marana Unified School District because of complaints about violence and cannibalism.
1993 KY   Challenged by a parent of a student at Happy Valley Elementary School in Glasgow who thought it was too scary.
1994 WA   Removed from Vancouver School District elementary school libraries after surviving two previous attempts (1991, 1993). Also challenged at neighboring Evergreen School District libraries in Vancouver because, "This book. . . is far beyond other scary books."
Source: 11, Mar. 1991, p. 62; May 1992, pp. 78, 94–95; July 1992, p. 124; Sept. 1992, p. 137; Jan. 1993, p. 27; Sept. 1993, pp. 143, 158; July 1994, p. 111; Sept. 1994, pp. 148–49.

1486   Schwartz, Alvin
Scary Stories

1993 OH   Challenged in Columbus because children shouldn't be "scared by materials that they read in schools."
1995 CT   Restricted to students in fourth grade or

higher in the Enfield elementary schools. The school board was petitioned to remove all "horror" stories from the elementary schools.

Source: 11, May 1993, pp. 85–86; May 1995, p. 69.

1487 Schwartz, Alvin
Telling Fortunes: Love Magic, Dream Signs, and Other Ways to Learn the Future

1998 GA Challenged at Hightower Elementary School in Rockdale because the "book involves instructions and teaches young kids how to tell the future by reading tea leaves, tarot cards, palms, crystal balls, by interpreting dreams, and by looking at an egg."

Source: 11, Mar. 1999, p. 35.

1488 Schwartz, Joel L.
Upchuck Summer

1988 NJ Removed from the Winslow Elementary School No. 4 because of "age inappropriateness." The specific problem was the explicitness of scenes in the protagonist recounts a fantasy about two "older kids" kissing while nude.

Source: 11, Jan. 1989, p. 8.

1489 Schwartz, Joel L., Aidan Macfarlane, and Ann McPherson.
Will the Nurse Make Me Take My Underwear Off?

1994 GA Challenged at the Chestatee Regional Library in Gainesville.

Source: 11, Nov. 1994, p. 187.

1490 Scoppettone, Sandra
Happy Endings Are All Alike

1983 WA Removed from the Evergreen School District of Vancouver along with twenty-nine other titles. The American Civil Liberties Union of Washington filed suit contending that the removals constitute censorship, a violation of plaintiff's rights to free speech and due process, and the acts are a violation of the state Open Meetings Act because the removal decisions were made behind closed doors.

Source: 11, Nov. 1983, pp. 185–86.

1491 Scott, Elizabeth
Living Dead Girl

2009 IL
New Challenged, but retained at the Effingham Helen Matthes Library despite concerns

about its graphic content and the unsatisfactory ending. The book is about a fifteen-year-old's perspective of living with her captor after being forcibly kidnapped and imprisoned at the age of ten. The book has received several accolades from book critics.

Source: 11, Nov. 2009, pp. 219–20.

1492 Sebold, Alice
The Lovely Bones

2007 CT Challenged at the Coleytown Middle School library in Westport. The school superintendent acknowledged that the book is "for mature readers" and also acknowledged "the book is appropriate to be part of a middle school library collection serving students from ages eleven to fourteen, many of whom possess the maturity level to read this book."

2008 MA Moved to the faculty section of the John W.
New McDevitt Middle School library in Waltham because its content was too frightening for middle school students.

Source: 11, Mar. 2007, p. 71; May 2008, p. 97.

1493 Sedaris, David
I Like Guys: A Short Story from Naked

2009 NH Pulled from a Litchfield Campbell High School
New elective course classroom after parents voiced their concerns about a short-stories unit called "Love/Gender/Family Unit" that dealt with subject matters including abortion, cannibalism, homosexuality, and drug use. The parents said the stories promoted bad behavior and a "political agenda" and they shouldn't be incorporated into classroom teachings. The Campbell High School English curriculum adviser said the short story was selected not only for its tone and style, but also its message of respect and acceptance, not for advocating homosexuality. The English curriculum adviser eventually resigned.

Source: 11, Sept. 2009, p. 154.

1494 Seeley, Robert A.
A Handbook for Conscientious Objectors

1982 WI Access restricted in Coleman due to the book's alleged political overtones.

Source: 11, July 1982, p. 126.

1495 Segel, Elizabeth
Short Takes

1994 MD Challenged at the Cecil County Board of Education in Elkton. Many deemed the text controversial because it included essays dealing with issues of abortion, gay rights, alcohol, and sex education.

Source: 11, Mar. 1995, p. 55.

1496 Seierstad, Åsne
The Bookseller of Kabul

2008 MI
New
Removed from Roosevelt High School's library and classrooms in Wyandotte because it "is too sexually explicit." The book is a nonfiction account of what life is like inside an Afghan household. The school said the book went through several reviews and was approved for high school students before being placed on the assigned reading list for the class.

2009 OH
New
Challenged, but retained on Wyoming high school district's reading list despite concerns about its sexual content. After a second challenge to a different title, the district reviewed all books on reading lists. Staff members rated each book on its relationship to the course, its uniqueness, its appropriateness, and the extent to which it "could create controversy among students, parents, and community groups."

Source: 11, Mar. 2009, pp. 40–41; Nov. 2009, pp. 202–3.

1497 Selby, Hubert, Jr.
Last Exit to Brooklyn

1965 MA
A local city attorney sought an injunction against the book, but state attorney (later U.S. Senator) Brooke directed dismissal of the complaint.

1966
Banned in Italy.

1966
Placed on a restricted list in Russia.

1966
Banned in Ireland.

1966 CT
A circuit court in Connecticut issued a temporary injunction against the book, "as obscene and pornographic." The injunction was overturned and sales were permitted again.

1967
Judged obscene by jury in England.

Source: 4, p. 98; 6, pp. 2,187–88; 8, pp. 462–63.

1498 Selzer, Adam
How to Get Suspended and Influence People

2009 ID
New
Challenged at the Nampa Public Library by a parent appalled that the cover included an abstract drawing of a nude woman and the back cover contains some profanity. The book explores the theme of censorship through the eyes of a gifted eighth-grader who is suspended after making an avant-garde sex-education video for a class project.

Source: 11, Jan. 2010, p. 8.

1499 Sendak, Maurice
In the Night Kitchen

1977 IL
Removed from the Norridge school library due to "nudity for no purpose."

1977 MO
Expurgated in Springfield by drawing shorts on the nude boy.

1985 WI
Challenged at the Cunningham Elementary School in Beloit because the book desensitizes "children to nudity."

1988 IL
Challenged at the Robeson Elementary School in Champaign because of "gratuitous" nudity.

1989 NJ
Challenged at the Camden elementary school libraries because of nudity.

1992 MN
Challenged at the Elk River schools because reading the book "could lay the foundation for future use of pornography."

1994 TX
Challenged at the El Paso Public Library because "the little boy pictured did not have any clothes on and it pictured his private area."

2006 NC
Challenged in the Wake County schools. Parents are getting help from Called2Action, a Christian group that says its mission is to "promote and defend our shared family and social values."

Source: 9; 11, May 1977, p. 71; Sept. 1977, p. 134; July 1985, p. 134; Mar. 1989, p. 43; Nov. 1989, p. 217; Mar. 1993, p. 41; Sept. 1994, p. 148; Sept. 2006, p. 231.

1500 Sendak, Maurice
Some Swell Pup

1988 OR
Challenged at the Multnomah County Library in Portland because in it a dog urinates on people, and children abuse animals.

Source: 11, Jan. 1989, p. 3.

1501 Servetus, Michael
Christianity Restored

1531
The publication in 1531 of *On the Errors of the Trinity* made Servetus notorious and a hunted man, threatened by both the French and Spanish Inquisitions and the Protestants, who banned his book and closed cities to him. In 1532, the Inquisition in Toulouse issued a decree ordering his arrest. He went underground in Paris and assumed a new identity. On October 27, 1553, Servetus was burned at the stake.

1723
Almost two centuries after its first publication, Richard Mead, the physician to the king of England, tried to publish Servetus's work. In 1723, the government seized and burned the whole printing and imprisoned Mead and his printer.

Source: 8, pp. 221–23.

1502   Seth, Roland
Witches and Their Craft

1987 MI Challenged at the Plymouth-Canton school system in Canton because the book contains information about witches and the devil.
Source: 11, May 1987, p. 110; Jan. 1988, p. 11.

1503   Seuss, Dr.
The Lorax

1989 CA Challenged in the Laytonville Unified School District because the book "criminalizes the foresting industry."
Source: 11, Nov. 1989, p. 237; Jan. 1990, pp. 32–33.

1504   Shafak, Elif
The Bastard of Istanbul

2006   Prize-winning novelist went on trial in Istanbul, Turkey, accused of belittling Turkishness. The novel had been at the top of Turkish bestsellers lists since its publication, but its treatment of the mass murder of Ottoman Armenians in 1915 angered government officials.
Source: 11, Jan. 2007, pp. 35–36.

1505   Shakespeare, William
Hamlet

1978   Banned in Ethiopia.
Source: 5, Sept./Oct. 1978, p. 66.

1506   Shakespeare, William
King Lear

1788   Prohibited on the English stage until 1820.
Source: 4, p. 18.

1507   Shakespeare, William
The Merchant of Venice

1931 NY Eliminated from the high school curricula of Manchester.
1931 NY Eliminated from the high school curricula of Buffalo.
1949 NY A group of Jewish parents in Brooklyn went to court claiming that the assignment of Shakespeare's play to senior high school literature classes violated the rights of their children to receive an education free of religious bias in *Rosenberg v. Board of Education of the City of New York*, 196 Misc. 542, 92 N.Y. Supp. 2d 344.
1980 MI Banned from classrooms in Midland.
1986   Banned from the ninth-grade classrooms in Kitchener, Ontario, Canada until the Ontario Education Ministry or Human Rights Commission rules whether the play is anti-Semitic.

1986   Banned from the ninth-grade classrooms in Waterloo, Ontario, Canada until the Ontario Education Ministry or Human Rights Commission rules whether the play is anti-Semitic.
Source: 4, p. 19; 11, July 1980, p. 76; Sept. 1986, p. 154; 12, pp. 23, 230.

1508   Shakespeare, William
Tragedy of King Richard II

1597   Contains a scene in which the King was deposed, and it so infuriated Queen Elizabeth in London, England that she ordered the scene eliminated from all copies.
Source: 4, p. 18.

1509   Shakespeare, William
Twelfth Night

1996 NH Removed from a Merrimack high school English class because of a policy that bans any instruction that has "the effect of encouraging or supporting homosexuality as a positive lifestyle alternative."
Source: 11, May 1996, p. 96.

1510   Shannon, George
Unlived Affections

1993 IL Removed from the library at the Lundahl Junior High School in Crystal Lake because the book is unfit for sixth grade.
Source: 11, July 1993, p. 98; 14, pp. 281–82.

1511   Sharpe, Jon
***Trailsman* series**

2001 AR Challenged, but retained at the Springdale Public Library along with all other "western" novels because the writings include "pornographic, sexual encounters."
Source: 11, Nov. 2001, p. 277.

1512   Sharpio, Amy
Sun Signs: The Stars in Your Life

1992 VA Pulled, but later placed on reserve to children with parental permission, at the Forrest Elementary School library in Hampton.
Source: 11, July 1992, p. 108; Sept. 1992, p. 139.

1513   Shaw, George Bernard
Man and Superman

1905 NY The New York Public Library withdrew it from public shelves because books "calculated to make light of dishonesty and criminality were worse than books merely indecent in statement."

1929   Banned from all public libraries in Yugoslavia.
Source: 2, p. 87; 4, p. 55; 15, Vol. II, p. 625.

1514   Shaw, George Bernard
Mrs. Warren's Profession

1905   Suppressed in London, England.
1929   Banned from all public libraries in Yugoslavia.
Source: 4, p. 55.

1515   Shaw, Irwin
Beggarman Thief

1985 PA Banned from the Stroudsburg High School library because it was "blatantly graphic, pornographic, and wholly unacceptable for a high school library."
Source: 11, May 1985, p. 79.

1516   Shaw, Irwin
Nightwork

1985 PA Banned from the Stroudsburg High School library because it was "blatantly graphic, pornographic and wholly unacceptable for a high school library."
Source: 11, May 1985, p. 79.

1517   Sheehan, Kathryn, and Mary Waidner
Earth Child

1992 OK Challenged at the Tulsa County schools because the book promotes the Hindu religion and other religious rituals. Opponents also claimed the book is a manual for altering children's minds through psychological games and hypnotic techniques.
Source: 11, Nov. 1992, p. 187.

1518   Sheffield, Margaret, and Sheila Bewley
Where Do Babies Come From?

1981 FL Moved from the children's section to the adult section of the Tampa-Hillsborough County Public Library by order of the Tampa City Council.
1987 WA Placed on restricted shelves at the Evergreen School District elementary school libraries in Vancouver in accordance with the school board policy to restrict student access to sex education books in elementary school libraries.
Source: 11, Jan. 1982, p. 4; July 1986, p. 118; Sept. 1986, p. 172; May 1987, p. 87.

1519   Sheldon, Sidney
Bloodline

1980 VA Challenged in Abingdon.
1981 TN Challenged in Elizabethton.
Source: 11, Jan. 1981, p. 5; May 1981, p. 66.

1520   Shengold, Nina, ed.
The Actor's Book of Contemporary Stage Monologues

1988 VA Challenged at the Salem Junior High School in Virginia Beach because it contains racial slurs, profanity, and lewd descriptions.
Source: 11, Mar. 1989, p. 43.

1521   Sherman, Josepha, and T. K. F. Weisskopf
Greasy Grimy Gopher Guts

2000   Retained in the collection of the Kingston Frontenac Public Library in Kingston, Ontario, Canada. It had been challenged as unsuitable for children.
Source: 11, Sept. 2000, p. 165.

1522   Shoup, Barbara
Wish You Were Here

1997 WV Removed from the Jackson County school libraries along with sixteen other titles.
Source: 11, Jan. 1998, p. 13.

1523   Showers, Paul, and Kay Sperry Showers
Before You Were a Baby

1987 WA Placed on restricted shelves at the Evergreen School District elementary school libraries in Vancouver in accordance with the school board policy to restrict student access to sex education books in elementary school libraries.
Source: 11, May 1987, p. 87.

1524   Showers, Paul
A Baby Starts to Grow

1987 WA Placed on restricted shelves at the Evergreen School District elementary school libraries in Vancouver in accordance with the school board policy to restrict student access to sex education books in elementary school libraries.
Source: 11, May 1987, p. 87.

1525 **Shreve, Susan**
Masquerade

1982 OR Removed from the Grants Pass middle school libraries because of the profanity, violence, and sexual innuendos in the book.
Source: 11, Mar. 1983, p. 39.

1526 **Shulman, Irving**
The Amboy Dukes

1949 Cleared of obscenity charges in Brantford, Ontario, Canada.
1949 MI Book under fire by local authorities in Detroit.
1949 NJ Book under fire by local authorities in Newark.
1949 WI Book under fire by local authorities in Milwaukee.
Source: 4, p. 89.

1527 **Shusterman, Neal**
Unwind

2009 KY New Withdrawn from classroom use and the approved curriculum at the Montgomery County High School, but available at the high school library and student book club. Some parents have complained about five novels containing foul language and covering topics—including sex, child abuse, suicide, and drug abuse—unsuited for discussion in coed high school classes. They also contend that the books don't provide the intellectual challenge and rigor that students need in college preparatory classes. The titles appeared on suggested book lists compiled by the Young Adult Library Services Association, a division of the American Library Association, for twelve- to eighteen-year-olds who are "reluctant readers." The superintendent removed the book because it wasn't on the pre-approved curriculum list and couldn't be added by teachers in the middle of a school year without permission.
Source: 11, Jan. 2010, pp. 16–17; Mar. 2010, p. 56.

1528 **Shyer, Marlene Fanta**
Welcome Home, Jellybean

1991 MD Challenged, but retained in the Carroll County schools. Two school board members considered the book depressing.
Source: 11, Mar. 1992, p. 64.

1529 **Sidhwa, Bapsi**
Cracking India

2005 FL Challenged at Deland High School, near Daytona Beach as part of the school's International Baccalaureate Program, whose curriculum is college-level. In a letter sent home, parents were offered the option of having their children assigned an alternate book. A parent objected to a two-page scene in which the narrator brushes off an older cousin's attempt to trick her into performing oral sex.
Source: 11, Jan. 2006, pp. 13–14.

1530 **Sijie, Dai**
Balzac and the Little Chinese Seamstress

2004 WA Pulled from the Federal Way's Todd Beamer High School English classes and library by the superintendent, who overruled a committee of educators and parents that unanimously recommended keeping the book. The novel about censorship was considered sexually explicit and inappropriate for high-school students.
Source: 11, July 2004, p. 139.

1531 **Silko, Leslie Marmon**
Ceremony

1995 FL Removed at the Nease High School in St. Augustine as a required summer reading book for honors English students because of its language, sexual descriptions, and subject matter. The book was recommended for honor students by the National Council of Teachers of English.
1996 TX Retained on the Round Rock Independent High School reading list after a challenge that the book was too violent.
Source: 11, Nov. 1995, p. 184; Jan. 1996, p. 14; May 1996, p. 99.

1532 **Silverstein, Alvin, and Virginia B. Silverstein**
The Reproductive System: How Living Creatures Multiply

1987 WA Placed on restricted shelves at the Evergreen School District elementary school libraries in Vancouver in accordance with the school board policy to restrict student access to sex education books in elementary school libraries.
Source: 11, May 1987, p. 87.

1533 **Silverstein, Charles, and Edmund White**
The Joy of Gay Sex

1977 KY Confiscated from three Lexington bookstores by the local police.
1981 CA Challenged at the San Jose Public Library.

1984   Seized and shredded by the British Customs Office.

1997 CA   Challenged at the Belmont Public Library because it is "pornographic."

2004 PA   Challenged, but retained in the Marple Public Library in Broomall along with several sexual instruction manuals including: *Sex Toys 101: A Playfully Uninhibited Guide*, by Rachel Venning; *Great Sex Tips*, by Anne Hooper; *Ultimate Guide to Fellatio*, by Violet Blue; and *The Illustrated Guide to Extended Massive Orgasm*, by Steve Bodansky because the books are "seriously objectionable in text and pictures due to the sexually explicit material."

2005 ID   Challenged at the Nampa Public Library along with seven other books because "they are very pornographic in nature and they have very explicit and detailed illustrations and photographs which we feel don't belong in a library." The library board approved policy changes that restrict children's access to any holdings that may fall under the state's harmful to minors statute and barred the library from buying movies rated NC-17 or X. The book was relocated to the director's office in 2008 and it was eventually restored to the collection in 2008.

2008 MT New   Challenged in the Lewis and Clark Library in Helena due to objections over its content. The book has been in the library's collection since 1993. The library director accepted the recommendation of the library's collection review committee that the book be retained in the collection.

2009 KS New   Restricted minors' access in the Topeka and Shawnee County Public Library because Kansans for Common Sense contended that the material is "harmful to minors under state law." Later the board organization voted 6-3 in favor of adopting a staff recommendation to keep the books where they are currently located on the shelves in the library's Health Information Neighborhood section.

Source: 11, Mar. 1978, p. 40; Jan. 1982, p. 9; Jan. 1985, p. 26; Sept. 1997, p. 125; Mar. 2004, p. 50; May 2004, p. 117; July 2006, p. 183; May 2008, pp. 96–97; July 2008, pp. 140–41; Nov. 2008, pp. 231–32, 254–55; May 2009, pp. 77–78; July 2009, p. 139.

1534   **Silverstein, Charles, and Felice Picano**
The New Joy of Gay Sex

1993 MT   Challenged, but retained at the Lewis and Clark Library in Helena.

1994 MO   Challenged at the River Bluffs Regional Library in St. Joseph as "pornography." The controversy began after a patron removed a copy of the book from the library and refused to return it, submitting instead a petition with 700 signatures calling for its permanent removal.

1995 MO   Challenged at the Kansas City Public Library. The complainants asked the Jackson County prosecutor's office to ban the book under state's obscenity and sodomy laws.

1996 NJ   Restricted to patrons over eighteen years of age at the Main Memorial Library in Clifton. The book is hidden behind the checkout counter and on the shelves is a dummy book jacket. The book was described as hard-core pornography by the complainant.

Source: 11, July 1993, p. 100; Sept. 1993, p. 158; Nov. 1994, p. 188; Jan. 1995, p. 7; July 1995, p. 94; Mar. 1996, p. 63; May 1996, p. 83.

1535   **Silverstein, Charles**
Man to Man

1986   Seized in London, England as "indecent or obscene" and "contrary to the prohibition contained in Section 42 of the Customs Consolidation Act, 1876."

Source: 5, May 1986, p. 38.

1536   **Silverstein, Shel**
The Giving Tree

1988 CO   Removed from a locked reference collection at the Boulder Public Library. The book was locked away originally because the librarian considered it sexist.

Source: 11, Jan. 1989, p. 27.

1537   **Silverstein, Shel**
A Light in the Attic

1985 WI   Challenged at the Cunningham Elementary School in Beloit because the book "encourages children to break dishes so they won't have to dry them."

1986 ND   Removed from the shelves of the Minot Public School libraries by the assistant superintendent "in anticipation of a parent's complaint." The superintendent found "suggestive illustrations" on several pages of Silverstein's work. Upon the recommendation of a review committee, the book was returned to the shelves.

1986 NE   Challenged at the elementary schools in the Papillion-LaVista School District in Omaha because the book promotes "behavior abusive to women and children, suicide as a way to manipulate parents, mockery of God, and selfish and disrespectful behavior."

1986 WI   Challenged at the Big Bend Elementary School library in Mukwonago because some of Silverstein's poems "glorified Satan, suicide and cannibalism, and also encouraged children to be disobedient."

1986 WI Challenged at the West Allis-West Milwaukee school libraries because the book "suggests drug use, the occult, suicide, death, violence, disrespect for truth, disrespect for legitimate authority, rebellion against parents," and because it inspires young people to commit "acts of violence, disbelief, and disrespect."

1987 CA Challenged at the Moreno Valley Unified School District libraries because it "contains profanity, sexual situations, and themes that allegedly encourage disrespectful behavior."

1987 DE Challenged at the Appoquinimink schools in Middletown because the book "contains violence, idealizes death, and makes light of manipulative behavior."

1989 IN Challenged at the South Adams school libraries because the book is "very vile" and "contains subliminal or underlying messages and anti-parent material."

1989 SD Challenged at the Hot Springs Elementary School as suitable classroom material because of its "objectionable" nature.

1989 TX The poem "Little Abigail and the Beautiful Pony" from this award-winning children's book was banned from second grade classes in Huffman because a mother protested that it "exposes children to the horrors of suicide."

1992 FL Restricted to students with parental permission at the Duval County public school libraries because the book features a caricature of a person whose nude behind has been stung by a bee.

1992 PA Challenged at the West Mifflin schools because the poem "Little Abigail and the Beautiful Pony" is morbid.

1993 FL Challenged at the Fruitland Park Elementary School library in Lake County because the book "promotes disrespect, horror, and violence."

1996 MO Challenged, but retained on the Webb City school library shelves. A parent had protested that the book imparts a "dreary" and "negative" message.

Source: 11, July 1985, p. 134; May 1986, p. 80; Sept. 1986, p. 172; Nov. 1986, p. 224; Jan. 1987, p. 12; Mar. 1987, pp. 51, 67–68; May 1987, p. 101; July 1987, p. 125; May 1989, p. 80; July 1989, p. 129; Jan. 1990, p. 32; July 1992, p. 105; Mar. 1993, p. 45; July 1993, p. 97; Sept. 1993, p. 157; May 1996, p. 97.

1538 Silverstein, Shel
Where the Sidewalk Ends

1983 OH Challenged at the Xenia school libraries because the book is "anti-Christian, against parental and school authorities, and

emphasized the use of drugs and sexual activity."

1986 ND Removed from the shelves of the Minot public school libraries by the assistant superintendent "in anticipation of a parent's complaint." Upon the recommendation of a review committee, the book was returned to the shelves.

1986 WI Challenged at the Big Bend Elementary School library in Mukwonago because some of Silverstein's poems "glorified Satan, suicide and cannibalism, and also encouraged children to be disobedient."

1986 WI Challenged at the West Allis-West Milwaukee school libraries because the book "suggests drug use, the occult, suicide, death, violence, disrespect for truth, disrespect for legitimate authority, rebellion against parents," and because it inspires young people to commit "acts of violence, disbelief, and disrespect."

1987 CA Challenged at the Moreno Valley Unified School District libraries because it "contains profanity, sexual situations, and themes that allegedly encourage disrespectful behavior."

1989 IL Reversing an earlier decision to remove the poem "Dreadful" from the library's copy of this book in a Riverdale elementary school, the school board retained the book and poem, which was challenged for bad taste.

1990 CA Retained in the Modesto district libraries and classrooms after being challenged as inappropriate for young readers.

1993 FL Challenged at the Fruitland Park Elementary School library in Lake County because the book "promotes disrespect, horror, and violence."

1993 PA Challenged at the Central Columbia School District in Bloomsburg because a poem titled "Dreadful" talks about how "someone ate the baby."

Source: 11, Sept. 1983, p. 139; Nov. 1983, p. 197; May 1986, p. 80; Sept. 1986, p. 172; Nov. 1986, p. 224; Mar. 1987, p. 51; May 1987, p. 101; July 1987, p. 125; Mar. 1990, p. 61; May 1990, p. 105; May 1993, p. 86; July 1993, p. 97; Sept. 1993, p. 157.

1539 Simon, Neil
Brighton Beach Memoirs

1991 IL Challenged at the Grayslake Community High School.

1996 TX Removed from the required reading and optional reading lists from the Dallas schools because of passages containing profanity and sexually explicit language.

Source: 11, July 1991, pp. 129–30; May 1996, p. 88.

1540 Simon, Sidney
Values Clarification

1979 IN Burned in Warsaw.
Source: 9; 11, Mar. 1980, p. 40.

1541 Sinclair, April
Coffee Will Make You Black

1996 IL Removed from the curriculum at the Julian High School in Chicago because the book was not appropriate for freshman as required reading because of sexually explicit language.
Source: 11, May 1996, p. 87.

1542 Sinclair, Upton
The Jungle

1929 Banned from public libraries in Yugoslavia.
1933 Burned in the Nazi bonfires because of Sinclair's socialist views.
1956 Banned in East Germany in 1956 as inimical to Communism.
1985 Banned in South Korea.
Source: 4, p. 63; 5, Apr. 1986, pp. 30–33.

1543 Sinclair, Upton
Oil!

1919 Banned from public libraries in Yugoslavia.
1927 MA Forbidden in Boston because of its comments on the Harding Administration—although Harding had died in 1923 and his cronies were long dispersed. Sinclair defended the case himself, at a cost of $2,000, and addressed a crowd of some 2,000 people on Boston Commons, explaining at length the character and intent of his book. The court suppressed nine pages of the book, including a substantial portion of the Biblical "Song of Solomon." The bookseller from whose store the book had been seized was fined $100 and the offending pages were blacked out.
1933 Burned by the Nazi bonfires because of Sinclair's socialist views.
1956 Banned in East Germany in 1956 as inimical to Communism.
Source: 2, p. 133; 3, pp. 282–83; 4, p. 63.

1544 Sinclair, Upton
Wide Is the Gate

1929 Banned from public libraries in Yugoslavia.
1933 Burned in the Nazi bonfires in Germany because of Sinclair's socialist views.

1953 Banned in Ireland.
1956 Banned in East Germany as inimical to Communism.
Source: 4, p. 63.

1545 Sioux City Community School District
Sioux City, Past and Present

1984 IA Banned from the Sioux City schools because the textbook is "racist and offensive."
Source: 11, Mar. 1985, p. 43.

1546 Sissley, Emily L., and Bertha Harris
The Joy of Lesbian Sex

1984 Seized by the British Customs Office.
Source: 11, Jan. 1985, p. 26.

1547 Sittenfeld, Curtis
Prep: A Novel

2008 CA New Pulled from the accelerated reading program in the Heritage Oak Private School in Yorba Linda. A parent complained that the book was "pornographic."
Source: 11, May 2008, p. 95.

1548 Sizer, Frances Sienkiewicz, et al.
Making Life Choices: Health Skills and Concepts

1997 NC The Franklin County school board ordered three chapters cut out of the ninth-grade health textbooks. Those chapters dealt with AIDS, HIV, and other sexually transmitted diseases; pairing, marriage, and parenting; and sexual behavior and contraception.
Source: 11, Nov. 1997, p. 169.

1549 Skarmeta, Antonio
Burning Patience

1995 ME Challenged as required reading in a freshman English class Orono High School because of the book's sexual content. The book was made into the successful film *The Postman*.
Source: 11, Nov. 1995, p. 186.

1550 Slepian, Jan
The Alfred Summer

1983 VA Challenged in Charlotte County due to "objectionable" words in the text.
1991 CT Pulled, but later restored to the language arts curriculum at four Cheshire elementary schools because the book is "filled with profanity, blasphemy and obscenities, and gutter language."
Source: 11, Nov. 1983, p. 197; Mar. 1992, p. 42; May 1992, p. 96; July 1992, pp. 109–10.

1551 Slier, Deborah, ed.
Make a Joyful Sound

1992 WA Challenged at the Deer Park elementary schools because the poetry collection contains the poem, "The Mask," by Dakari Kamaru Hru. A Deer Park parent complained that, "This is religious indoctrination. We in the Western World would refer to it as devil worship. It also smacks of New Age religion."
Source: 11, May 1992, pp. 84–85.

1552 Small, Beatrice
To Love Again: A Historical Romance

1993 ID Challenged at the Pocatello Public Library because a patron considered the romance novel "pornographic."
Source: 11, Mar. 1994, p. 69.

1553 Smiley, Jane
A Thousand Acres

1994 WA Banned at the Lynden High School. Winner of the Pulitzer Prize for fiction in 1991, it was described as having "no literary value in our community right now." School officials note that the protestors have tried to block an anti-drug program, a multicultural program, and a Valentine's Day dance, saying that they did not reflect the values parents want taught.
1996 TX Retained on the Round Rock Independent High School reading list after a challenge that the book was too violent.
Source: 11, May 1994, p. 88; May 1996, p. 99.

1554 Smith, Betty
Joy in the Morning

1997 WV Removed from the Jackson County school libraries along with sixteen other titles.
Source: 11, Jan. 1998, p. 13.

1555 Smith, Lee
Fair and Tender Ladies

2007 VA New Challenged in the Washington County schools because of a few "crude" words deemed too graphic for teenage honor students. The author claimed the book provides teens with a safe forum to address issues such as unwanted pregnancy. The novel demonstrates the necessity of a good education and highlights the importance of southwestern Virginia's heritage.
Source: 11, Jan. 2008, pp. 35–36.

1556 Smith, Lillian
Strange Fruit

1944 MA Majority of bookstores in Boston removed the book from sale. The book's distributor was charged in 1945 under the Massachusetts laws governing obscene material, in that he had distributed a publication that was "obscene, indecent, impure, or manifestly tends to corrupt the morals of youth." The court found the bookseller guilty and fined him $200, later reduced to $25. The fact that the novel might promote "lascivious thoughts and . . . . arouse lustful desire" outweighed any artistic merit that the novel might possess.
1944 MI Majority of bookstores in Detroit removed the book from sale.
1953 Banned in Ireland.
Source: 3, p. 305; 4, pp. 78–79; 15, Vol. IV, p. 698.

1557 Smith, Patrick
A Land Remembered

2003 FL Challenged, but retained in the Indian River County Schools in Vero Beach despite two parents' complaints about racially offensive language. One of the parents said the book's use of the 'Nword' created a hostile learning environment for his children.
Source: 11, Jan. 2004, p. 28.

1558 Smith, Rebecca M.
Family Matters: Concepts in Marriage and Personal Relationships

1986 NY Challenged as proposed ninth-grade curriculum textbook in the Buffalo schools because it promotes "secular humanism." In particular, the complainant objected to references to the psychological theories of Erik Erikson, Sigmund Freud, Abraham Maslow, and Jean Piaget.
Source: 11, Mar. 1987, p. 68.

1559 Smith, Robert Kimmell
Chocolate Fever

1992 OH Challenged at the Gahanna-Jefferson Public Schools because it contains the words "damn" and "sucks."
Source: 11, Jan. 1993, p. 12.

1560 Smith, Robert Kimmell
Jelly Belly

1992 OH Challenged at the Gahanna-Jefferson Public Schools because it contains the words "damn" and "sucks."
Source: 11, Jan. 1993, p. 12.

1561   Smith, Robert Kimmell
Mostly Michael

1992   OH   Challenged at the Gahanna-Jefferson Public Schools because it contains the words "damn" and "sucks."
Source: 11, Jan. 1993, p. 12.

1562   Smith, Wallace
Bessie Cotter

1935   Charged with selling an "obscene book" and "intent to corrupt" and was ordered to appear before the Bow Street magistrate in London, England. The court fined Heinemann "for publishing an allegedly indecent American book" and ordered the book to be removed from distribution.
Source: 13, pp. 25–26.

1563   Smucker, Barbara
Runaway to Freedom

1991   MD   Challenged, but retained in the Carroll County schools. Two school board members were offended by its allegedly coarse language.

1993   DE   Challenged at the West Dover Elementary School because it is offensive to African Americans. The objectionable passage reads, "Massa lay on the feather bed and nigger lay on the floor."
Source: 11, Mar. 1992, p. 64; Jan. 1994, p. 15.

1564   Snepp, Frank
A Decent Interval

1978   The U.S. Justice Department filed a civil complaint against the author demanding a lifetime ban on his writing or speaking about the CIA.
Source: 4, p. 100; 8, pp. 36–39; 15, Vol. IV, p. 717.

1565   Snow, Edgar
Red Star over China

1985   Banned in South Korea.
Source: 5, Apr. 1986, pp. 30–33.

1566   Snyder, Jane McIntosh
Sappho

2000   CA   Removed from the Anaheim school district because school officials said the book is too difficult for middle school students and that it could cause harassment against students seen with it. The American Civil Liberties Union (ACLU) of Southern California filed suit in *Doe v. Anaheim Union High School District* alleging that the removal is "a pretext for viewpoint-based censorship." The ACLU claims no other books have been removed from the junior high library for similar reasons, even though several, such as works by Shakespeare and Dickens, are more difficult reading. The ACLU contends that the school officials engaged in unconstitutional viewpoint discrimination by removing the book because it contains gay and lesbian material. In March 2001, the school board approved a settlement that restored the book to the high school shelves and amended the district's policy to prohibit the removal of books for subject matter involving sexual orientation, but the book will not be returned to the middle school.
Source: 11, Mar. 2001, p. 53; May 2001, p. 95; July 2001, p. 173.

1567   Snyder, Zilpha Keatley
The Egypt Game

1995   TX   Challenged in the Richardson schools because it shows children in dangerous situations, condones trespassing and lying to parents, and teaches children about the occult. The school board declined to ban the award-winning novel but did decide that parents should be notified when it is used in class.

2009   TX   Challenged as part of a reading list in a
New   fourth-grade class at Southern Hills Elementary School in Wichita Falls because the book includes scenes depicting Egyptian worship rituals. The Newbery Award-winning book has been an optional part of the school district's curriculum for years. "I'm not going to stop until it's banned from the school district. I will not quiet down. I will not back down. I don't believe any student should be subjected to anything that has to do with evil gods or black magic," said the student's father.
Source: 11, Mar. 1995, p. 56; Jan. 2010, p. 17.

1568   Snyder, Zilpha Keatley
The Headless Cupid

1989   KS   Challenged at the Hays Public Library because the book "could lead young readers to embrace satanism."

1990   MI   Retained in the Grand Haven school libraries after a parent objected to the book because it "introduces children to the occult and fantasy about immoral acts."

1991   MD   The Newbery Award-winning book was retained on the approved reading list at Matthew Henson Middle School in Waldorf despite objections to its references to witchcraft.

1992 CA Challenged in the Escondido school because it contains references to the occult.
Source: 11, July 1989, p. 143; May 1990, p. 106; Sept. 1991, pp. 155–56; Sept. 1992, p. 161.

1569 Snyder, Zilpha Keatley
The Witches of Worm

1982 FL Restricted in Escambia County to sixth graders and above because "it contains 183 pages of rejection, fear, hatred, occult ritual, cruel pranks, lies and even an attempted murder by arson all perpetrated by a twelve-year-old girl."

1988 OR Challenged at the Kennedy High School in Mt. Angel for its witchcraft theme and scary illustrations.

1990 MI Retained in the Grand Haven school libraries after a parent objected to the book because it "introduces children to the occult and fantasy about immoral acts."
Source: 11, July 1982, p. 123; Jan. 1989, p. 3; May 1990, p. 106.

1570 Solotareff, Gregoire
Don't Call Me Little Bunny

1989 OR Challenged at the Douglas County Library in Roseburg because the character gets away with bad behavior.

1995 IL Challenged in the Cook Memorial Library in Libertyville because the actions taken by the bunny character in the book were anti-social and inappropriate for children's reading.
Source: 11, Jan. 1990, pp. 4–5; Jan. 1996, p. 29.

1571 Solzhenitsyn, Aleksandr Isayevich
August 1914

1974 Barred from publication in the USSR; the author was stripped of Soviet citizenship and deported.
Source: 4, p. 9.

1572 Solzhenitsyn, Aleksandr Isayevich
Cancer Ward

1974 Barred from publication in the USSR; the author was stripped of Soviet citizenship and deported.
Source: 4, p. 91.

1573 Solzhenitsyn, Aleksandr Isayevich
Candle in the Wind

1974 Barred from publication in the USSR; the author was stripped of Soviet citizenship and deported.
Source: 4, p. 91.

1574 Solzhenitsyn, Aleksandr Isayevich
The First Circle

1974 Barred from publication in the USSR; the author was stripped of Soviet citizenship and deported.
Source: 4, p. 91.

1575 Solzhenitsyn, Aleksandr Isayevich
The Gulag Archipelago

1974 Barred from publication in the USSR; the author was stripped of Soviet citizenship and deported.
Source: 4, p. 91; 8, pp. 76–77.

1576 Solzhenitsyn, Aleksandr Isayevich
The Love Girl and the Innocent

1974 Barred from publication in the USSR; the author was stripped of Soviet citizenship and deported.
Source: 4, p. 91.

1577 Solzhenitsyn, Aleksandr Isayevich
One Day in the Life of Ivan Denisovich

1974 Barred from publication in the USSR; the author was stripped of Soviet citizenship and deported.

1976 NH Removed from the Milton High School library due to objectionable language.

1976 NJ Challenged in Mahwah.

1979 WA Challenged in Omak.

1981 MA Challenged in the Mohawk Trail Regional High School in Buckland because of profanity in the book.

1995 WY Removed from the Lincoln Count high school curriculum because of "considerable obscenities."

1999 IA Retained at the Storm Lake High School despite objections to the novel's profanity.
Source: 4, p. 91; 11, May 1976, p. 61; Jan. 1977, p. 8; July 1979, pp. 10–11; July 1995, p. 100; July 1999, p. 105.

1578 Solzhenitsyn, Aleksandr Isayevich
Stories and Prose Poems

1974 Barred from publication in the USSR; the author was stripped of Soviet citizenship and deported.
Source: 4, p. 91.

1579 Sones, Sonya
One of Those Hideous Books Where the Mother Dies

2010 WI
New Challenged at the Theisen Middle School in Fond du Lac because a parent's belief that

the book's "sexual content was too mature for eleven- to fourteen-year-olds." The book has won several awards, including being named a 2005 Best Book for Young Adults by the American Library Association. The same parent plans to request removal of six other books from the library, including the *Sisterhood of the Traveling Pants* series, another set of books by Sones,and *Get Well Soon*, by Julie Halpern.

Source: 11, Mar. 2010, p. 54; May 2010, pp. 127-28.

1580   Sones, Sonya
What My Mother Doesn't Know

2003 CA   Removed from the library shelves of the Rosedale Union School District in Bakersfield because of discomfort with Sones's poem, "Ice Capades"—a teenage girl's description of how her breasts react to cold.

2004 TX   Challenged at the Bonnette Junior High School library in Deer Park because the book includes foul language and references to masturbation. The book was selected as a "Best Book for Young Adults," by ALA in 2002; "Young Adults Choice," by the International Reading Association in 2003; and included on the Texas Lone Star State Reading List.

2007 WI
New   Available only to seventh- and eighth-graders at the Spring Hill School library after a parent wanted the book, which deals with masturbation, groping, and sexual fantasy, among other themes, to be removed from the library and the accelerated reading program.

Source: 11, Nov. 2003, p. 227; Jan. 2005, p. 7; July 2007, pp. 144–45.

1581   Soyinka, Wole
The Man Died: Prison Notes of Wole Soyinka

1984   Banned in Nigeria. The 1984 Public Officers Decree—Protection Against False Accusation—"made it a criminal offence to publish any article that brought the government or any public official into disrepute." Thus, any published statement, true or false, that could embarrass any government official was forbidden. Soyinka received the 1986 Nobel Prize in literature.

Source: 7, p. 321.

1582   Spargo, Edward
Topics for the Restless

1986 CO   Challenged at the Jefferson County school libraries in Lakewood. The textbook is a collection of stories and essays designed to promote critical thought among high school students. Parents found "most objectionable" selections from the *Feminine Mystique*, which they said was too favorable to the Equal Rights Amendment; a story on Marilyn Monroe; "Death with Dignity," which addresses what children should be taught about death; and "Hiroshima – Death and Rebirth I and II," stories they claimed "make Americans feel guilty about bombing Hiroshima." The Jefferson County School Board refused to ban the book.

Source: 11, May 1986, p. 82; Sept. 1986, p. 173; Nov. 1986, p. 224.

1583   Sparks, Beatrice
Jay's Journal

1998 WA   Challenged for use in the Richland high school English classes along with six other titles because the "books are poor-quality literature and stress suicide, illicit sex, violence, and hopelessness."

Source: 11, Mar. 1999, p. 40.

1584   Speare, Elizabeth George
The Sign of the Beaver

2000 FL   Challenged in a Pinellas County elementary school for use of the word "squaw" to refer to Native American women.

Source: 11, May 2000, p. 76.

1585   Speare, Elizabeth George
Witch of Blackbird Pond

2002 CT   Challenged in the middle school curriculum in Cromwell based on concern that it promotes witchcraft and violence. The book is the recipient of the 1959 Newbery Medal for children's literature.

Source: 11, Sept. 2002, p. 197; Nov. 2002, pp. 257–58.

1586   Spencer, Scott
Endless Love

1991 SC   Banned from the Berkeley County High School media center because of "explicit pornographic passages and adult material for teenage readers."

Source: 11, Mar. 1992, p. 41.

1587 Spiegelman, Art, and
Francoise Mouly
Raw

1992 OR Challenged at the Douglas County Library in
Roseburg because "it's full of cartoon
pornography."
Source: 11, Jan. 1993, p. 9.

1588 Spies, Karen Bornemann
*Everything You Need to Know
about Incest*

1996 LA Pulled from the Ouachita Parish School
library in Monroe because of sexual content.
The Louisiana chapter of the ACLU filed a
lawsuit in the federal courts on October 3,
1996, claiming that the principal and the
school superintendent violated First
Amendment free speech rights and also
failed to follow established procedure when
they removed the book. The three-year-old
school library censorship case headed to
court after the Ouachita Parish School Board
made no decision to seek a settlement at a
special meeting April 12, 1999. On August 17,
1999, the Ouachita Parish School Board
agreed to return the book to the library and
to develop a new book-selection policy that
follows state guidelines for school
media programs.
Source: 11, Sept. 1996, pp. 151–52; Jan. 1997, p. 7; July
1999, p. 93; Jan. 2000, p. 27.

1589 Spinelli, Jerry
Jason and Marceline

1992 NJ Challenged at the Pitman Middle School
library because the book promotes stealing,
drinking, profanity, and premarital sex.
1993 ND Challenged, but retained as part of the
curriculum at Hughes Junior High School in
Bismarck. The controversy centered around
the use of profanity and sexually explicit
language.
Source: 11, July 1992, p. 106; Jan. 1993, p. 27; Sept. 1993,
p. 145; Jan. 1994, p. 38.

1590 Spinelli, Jerry
Space Station, Seventh Grade

1988 OR Challenged at the La Grande Middle School
library because "profanity, sexual obscenity,
immoral values are throughout the book."
Source: 11, May 1989, p. 93.

1591 Spinoza, Baruch
Ethics

1679 His writings were widely banned in Holland
as atheistic and subversive.
1679 The Catholic Church placed all of his work on
the *Index Librorum Prohibitorum* (Index of
Prohibited Books) in Rome, Italy. His works
remained listed until 1966.
Source: 1, pp. 101–3.

1592 Spraggett, Allen
*Arthur Ford: The Man Who Talked
with the Dead*

1987 M Challenged at the Plymouth-Canton school
system in Canton because the book deals
with witchcraft.
Source: 11, May 1987, p. 110.

1593 Stadtmauer, Saul
Visions of the Future: Magic Boards

1984 OR Removed from the Philomath Middle School
library because it was "badly written."
1991 OR Challenged at the Dallas school library
because the book entices impressionable or
emotionally disturbed children into becoming
involved in witchcraft or the occult.
1992 VA Pulled, but later placed on reserve to children
with parental permission at the Forrest
Elementary School library in Hampton.
Source: 11, Sept. 1984, p. 138; Jan. 1992, p. 26; July 1992,
p. 108; Sept. 1992, p. 139.

1594 Stamper, J. P.
More Tales for the Midnight Hour

1992 AZ Challenged at the Neely Elementary School in
Gilbert because the book shows the dark side
of religion through the occult, the devil, and
satanism.
Source: 11, May 1992, p. 78; July 1992, p. 124.

1595 Stanislawski, Michael
*Tsar Nicholas I and the Jews:
The Transformation of Jewish Society
in Russia, 1825–1855*

1983 Banned from the 1983 Moscow International
Book Fair along with more than fifty other
books because it is "anti-Soviet."
Source: 11, Nov. 1983, p. 201.

1596 Stanley, Lawrence A., ed.
Rap, The Lyrics

1993 WA Parent requested that all offensive materials be labeled at the Sno-Isle Regional Library in Marysville.
Source: 11, July 1993, p. 103.

1597 Stanway, Andrew
The Lovers' Guide

1996 NJ Removed from the Clifton Public Library and replaced with a dummy book made of styrofoam. The library's new policy restricts to adults any material containing "patently offensive graphic illustrations or photographs of sexual or excretory activities or contact as measured by contemporary community standards for minors."
Source: 11, July 1996, pp. 118–19.

1598 Starhawk, and Hilary Valentine
The Twelve Wild Swans: A Journey to the Realm of Magic, Healing, and Action: Rituals, Exercises and Magical Training in the Reclaiming Tradition

2001 AR Challenged, but retained at the Springdale Public Library despite a complaint that the book is a "witchcraft manual" and "turns people away from God and Bible scriptures."
Source: 11, Nov. 2001, p. 277.

1599 Stark, Evan, ed.
Everything You Need to Know about Sexual Abuse

1991 WI Challenged at the Arcadia schools because the book presents sexual abuse situations too descriptively.
Source: 11, Sept. 1991, p. 154.

1600 Starkey, Marion Lena
The Tall Man from Boston

1985 FL Challenged at the Sikes Elementary School media center in Lakeland because the book "would lead children to believe ideas contrary to the teachings of the Bible."
Source: 11, July 1985, p. 133.

1601 Steel, Danielle
Changes

1985 PA Banned from the Stroudsburg High School library because it was "blatantly graphic, pornographic and wholly unacceptable for a high school library."
Source: 11, May 1985, p. 79.

1602 Steel, Danielle
Crossings

1985 PA Banned from the Stroudsburg High School library because it was "blatantly graphic, pornographic and wholly unacceptable for a high school library."
Source: 11, May 1985, p. 79.

1603 Steel, Danielle
The Gift

1996 OH Challenged at a Coventry school because "the schools had no business teaching his children about sex, that it was the job of the parents."
Source: 11, Jan. 1997, p. 11.

1604 Steer, Dugald
Wizardology: The Book of the Secrets of Merlin

2007 CT Challenged at the West Haven's Molloy Elementary School library because the book exposes children to the occult.
Source: 11, May 2007, p. 91.

1605 Steig, William
Abel's Island

1990 FL Pulled from the fifth- and sixth-grade optional reading lists in Clay County schools because of references to drinking wine which administrators determined violated the district's substance abuse policy. The objectionable passage reads: "At home he had to drink some wine to dispel the chill in his bones. He drank large draughts of his wine and ran about everywhere like a wild animal, shouting and yodeling."
Source: 11, Jan. 1991, p. 16.

1606 Steig, William
The Amazing Bone

1986 NJ Challenged at the West Amwell school libraries in Lambertville because a parent objected to "the use of tobacco by the animals."
1993 WA Challenged at the Discovery Elementary School library in Issaquah because of the graphic and detailed violence.
Source: 11, Mar. 1987, p. 65; Mar. 1994, p. 70.

1607 Steig, William
Caleb and Kate

1992 PA Pulled from the Boyertown elementary school library shelves because the book "depicts a dismal outlook on marriage and life." The book was eventually returned.

Source: 11, Mar. 1993, p. 42; May 1993, p. 86.

1608 Steig, William
Sylvester and the Magic Pebble

1970 CA Book receives the Randolph J. Caldecott Medal for the best-illustrated book of 1969. In 1970, a nationwide campaign began to remove the book from schools and public libraries across the United States. Challenged in Palto Alto.
1970 IL   Challenged in Woodriver.
1970 IL   Removed "for reevaluation" in East Alton.
1970 KS Challenged in Kansas.
1970 MD Challenged in Maryland.
1970 MD The library in Wicomico County answered the challenge by retaining the book.
1970 MD The library in Prince George County answered the challenge by retaining the book.
1970 NE Challenged in Lincoln.
1970 NY Challenged in Queens.
1970 OH Removed "for reevaluation" in Toledo.
1970 OH Challenged in Ohio.
1970 PA Challenged in Pennsylvania.
1970 SC Challenged in South Carolina.
1970 WY Challenged in Wyoming.
1971 IL   The Illinois Police Association wrote to librarians asking them to remove the book because its characters, all shown as animals, present police as pigs—although in favorable portrayals. Similar problems reported in eleven other states.

Source: 4, p. 87; 7, pp. 477–80.

1609 Steiger, Brad
Beyond Belief: True Mysteries of the Unknown

1995 CA Challenged at the Hemet Elementary School. The teacher was placed on paid administrative leave after a parent complained that the book deals with the supernatural and the occult.

Source: 11, May 1995, p. 65.

1610 Stein, Sol
The Magician

1981 WI Challenged in Montello.

Source: 11, May 1981, p. 73.

1611 Steinbeck, John
East of Eden

1982   Removed from school libraries in Morris, Manitoba, Canada.
1982 AL Removed from two Anniston high school libraries because it is "ungodly and obscene," but later reinstated on a restrictive basis.
1991 SC Challenged in the Greenville schools because the book uses the name of God and Jesus in a "vain and profane manner along with inappropriate sexual references."

Source: 11, Mar. 1983, p. 37; July 1991, p. 130.

1612 Steinbeck, John
Grapes of Wrath

1939 CA Banned in Kern County, the scene of Steinbeck's novel.
1939 IL   Burned by the East St. Louis Public Library.
1939 MO Banned in Kansas City.
1939 NY Barred from the Buffalo Public Library on the grounds that "vulgar words" were used.
1953   Banned in Ireland.
1973   On Feb. 21, 1973, eleven Turkish book publishers went on trial before an Istanbul martial law tribunal on charges of publishing, possessing and selling books in violation of an order of the Istanbul martial law command. They faced possible sentences of between one month's and six months' imprisonment "for spreading propaganda un favorable to the state" and the confiscation of their books. Eight booksellers were also on trial with the publishers on the same charge involving the *Grapes of Wrath*.
1980 IA   Banned in Kanawha High School classes.
1980 NY Challenged in Vernon-Verona-Sherill School District.
1981 VT Challenged as required reading for Richford High School English students due to the book's language and portrayal of a former minister who recounts how he took advantage of a young woman.
1982   Banned in Morris, Manitoba, Canada.
1982 AL Removed from two Anniston high school libraries, but later reinstated on a restrictive basis.
1986 NC Challenged at the Moore County school system in Carthage because the book contains the phase "God damn."
1986 NC Challenged at the Cummings High School in Burlington as an optional reading assignment because the "book is full of filth. My son is being raised in a Christian home and this book takes the Lord's name in vain and has all kinds of profanity in it." Although the parent spoke to the press, a formal complaint with the school demanding the book's removal was not filed.
1991 SC Challenged in the Greenville schools because the book uses the name of God and Jesus in a "vain and profane manner along with inappropriate sexual references."

1993 TN Challenged in the Union City High School classes.
Source: 4, p. 82; 5, Summer 1973, p. xii; 8, pp. 61–70; 9, p. 142; 11, May 1980, pp. 52, 62; Jan. 1982, p. 18; Mar. 1983, p. 37; July 1986, p. 120; Nov. 1986, p. 210; Jan. 1987, p. 32; July 1991, p. 130; Mar. 1994, p. 55; 15, Vol. III, pp. 651–52.

1613 Steinbeck, John
In Dubious Battle

1953 Banned in Ireland.
Source: 4, p. 83.

1614 Steinbeck, John
Of Mice and Men

1953 Banned in Ireland.
1974 IN Banned in Syracuse.
1977 PA Banned in Oil City.
1977 SC Challenged in Greenville by the Fourth Province of the Knights of the Ku Klux Klan.
1979 MI Banned in Grand Blanc.
1980 NY Challenged in Vernon-Verona-Sherill School District.
1980 OH Challenged in Continental.
1981 AZ Challenged in Saint David.
1982 IN Challenged in Tell City due to "profanity and using God's name in vain."
1983 AL Banned from classroom use at the Scottsboro Skyline High School due to "profanity."
1984 TN The Knoxville School Board chairman vowed to have "filthy books" removed from Knoxville's public schools and picked Steinbeck's novel as the first target due to "its vulgar language."
1987 KY Reinstated at the Christian County school libraries and English classes after being challenged as vulgar and offensive.
1988 IL Challenged at the Wheaton-Warrenville Middle School.
1988 MI Challenged at the Berrien Springs High School because the book contains profanity.
1988 WV Challenged in the Marion County schools.
1989 AL Removed from the Northside High School in Tuscaloosa because the book "has profane use of God's name."
1989 AR Removed from the White Chapel High School in Pine Bluff because of objections to language.
1989 TN Challenged as a summer youth program reading assignment in Chattanooga because "Steinbeck is known to have had an anti-business attitude." In addition, "he was very questionable as to his patriotism."
1989 TN Challenged as appropriate for high school reading lists in the Shelby County school system because the novel contained "offensive language."
1990 KS Challenged, but retained in a Salina tenth-grade English class despite concerns that it

contained "profanity" and "takes the Lord's name in vain."
1990 TX Challenged in the Riveria schools because it contains profanity.
1991 CA Challenged by a Fresno parent as a tenth-grade English college preparatory curriculum assignment, citing "profanity" and "racial slurs." The book was retained, and the child of the objecting parent was provided with an alternative reading assignment.
1991 FL Removed and later returned to the Suwannee High School library because the book is "indecent."
1991 PA Challenged as curriculum material at the Ringgold High School in Carroll Township because the novel contains terminology offensive to blacks.
1991 TN Challenged at the Jacksboro High School because the novel contains "blasphemous" language, excessive cursing, and sexual overtones.
1991 VA Challenged as required reading in the Buckingham County schools because of profanity.
1992 AL A coalition of community members and clergy in Mobile requested that local school officials form a special textbook screening committee to "weed out objectionable things." Steinbeck's novel was the first target because it contained "profanity" and "morbid and depressing themes."
1992 CA Challenged at the Modesto High School as recommended reading because of "offensive and racist language." The word "nigger" appears in the book.
1992 FL Challenged in the Duval County public school libraries because of profanity, lurid passages about sex, and statements defamatory to minorities, God, women, and the disabled.
1992 IA Challenged in the Waterloo schools.
1992 LA Challenged at the Oak Hill High School in Alexandria because of profanity.
1992 OH Temporarily removed from the Hamilton High School reading list after a parent complained about its vulgarity and racial slurs.
1993 AZ Challenged as an appropriate English curriculum assignment at the Mingus Union High School because of "profane language, moral statement, treatment of the retarded, and the violent ending."
1994 GA Challenged at the Loganville High School because of its "vulgar language throughout."
1994 TN Pulled from a classroom by Putnam County school superintendent "due to the language." Later, after discussions with the school district counsel, it was reinstated.
1995 GA Challenged at the Stephens County High School library in Toccoa Falls because of

"curse words. The book was retained.

1995 KS Challenged in the Galena school library because of the book's language and social implications.

1995 MN Retained in the Bemidji schools after challenges to the book's "objectionable" language.

1995 VA Challenged, but retained in a Warm Springs High School English class.

1997 FL Removed, restored, restricted, and eventually retained at the Bay County schools in Panama City. A citizen group, the 100 Black United, Inc., requested the novel's removal and "any other inadmissible literary books that have racial slurs in them, such as the using of the word 'nigger.'"

1997 IL Banned from the Washington Junior High School curriculum in Peru because it was deemed "age inappropriate."

1997 MN Challenged as a reading list assignment for a ninth-grade literature class, but retained at the Sauk Rapids-Rice High School in St. Cloud. A parent complained that the book's use of racist language led to racist behavior and racial harassment.

1997 OH Challenged, but retained in the Louisville high school English classes because of profanity.

1998 AR Challenged, but retained in the Bryant school library because of a parent's complaint that the book "takes God's name in vain fifteen times and uses Jesus's name lightly."

1998 CA Challenged in O'Hara Park Middle School classrooms in Oakley because it contains racial epithets.

1998 WI Challenged at the Barron School District.

1999 PA Challenged, but retained in the sophomore curriculum at West Middlesex High School despite objections to the novel's profanity.

1999 WI Challenged in the Tomah School District because the novel is violent and contains obscenities.

2002 MI Challenged as required reading at the high school in Grandville because the book "is full of racism, profanity, and foul language."

2002 MS Banned from the George County schools because of profanity.

2003 IL Challenged in the Normal Community High School because the book contains "racial slurs, profanity, violence, and does not represent traditional values." An alternative book, Steinbeck's *The Pearl*, was offered but rejected by the family challenging the novel. The committee then recommended *The House on Mango Street* and *The Way to Rainy Mountain* as alternatives.

2006 PA Retained in the Greencastle-Antrim tenth-grade English classes. A complaint was filed

because of "racial slurs" and profanity used throughout the novel. The book has been used in the high school for more than thirty years, and those who object to its content have the option of readingan alternative reading.

2007 IA New Challenged at the Newton High School because of concerns about profanity and the portrayal of Jesus Christ. Newton High School has required students to read the book since at least the early 1980s. In neighboring Des Moines, it is on the recommended reading list for ninth-grade English, and it is used for some special education students in the eleventh and twelfth grades.

2007 KS New Retained in the Olathe ninth-grade curriculum despite a parent calling the novel a "worthless, profanity-riddled book" which is "derogatory towards African Americans, women, and the developmentally disabled."

Source: 8, pp. 474–76; 9; 11, Mar. 1975, p. 41; Nov. 1977, p. 155; Jan. 1978, p. 7; Mar. 1979, p. 27; May 1980, p. 62; July 1980, p. 77; May 1982, pp. 84–85; July 1983, p. 198; July 1984, p. 104; May 1988, p. 90; July 1988, p. 140; Sept. 1988, pp. 154, 179; Nov. 1988, p. 201; Jan. 1989, p. 28; Nov. 1989, p. 162; Jan. 1990, pp. 10–12; Mar. 1990, p. 45; Mar. 1991, p. 62; July 1991, p. 110; Jan. 1992, p. 25; Mar. 1992, p. 64; July 1992, pp. 111–12, 126; Sept. 1992, pp. 140, 163 64; Jan. 1993, p. 29; Mar. 1994, p. 53; Mar. 1995, pp. 46, 53; May 1995, p. 84; July 1995, pp. 93, 111–12; Sept. 1995, pp. 157–58; Jan. 1996, p. 29; Mar. 1996, pp. 50, 63; May 1997, pp. 63, 79; Nov. 1997, pp. 167–69; Jan. 1998, pp. 28–29; July 1998, pp. 107, 120; Jan. 1999, p. 9; July 1999, p. 105; Jan. 2000, p. 16; Mar. 2000, p. 52; Nov. 2002, p. 280; Mar. 2003, p. 55; Jan. 2004, p. 11; Sept. 2004, pp. 177–78; Jan. 2007, pp. 29–30; July 2007, pp. 146–47; Jan. 2008, pp. 27–28.

1615 Steinbeck, John
The Red Pony

1980 NY Challenged at the Vernon-Verona-Sherill School District as a "filthy, trashy, sex novel."

1994 GA Challenged in the Oconee County school libraries because a parent complained the book contained profanity. The Oconee School Board voted to evaluate all 40,000 volumes in the system's library and remove any books and teaching materials from the public school that contain "explicit sex and pornography."

1996 NC Challenged, but retained on a recommended reading list, at Holmes Middle School in Eden. A parent complained that there were curse words on ten different pages of the book.

1997 AL Challenged in the Attalla school system because the book contains "profanity and violence."

Source: 11, May 1980, p. 62; Sept. 1994, p. 145; Sept. 1996, p. 170; May 1997, p. 62.

1616 **Steinbeck, John**
The Wayward Bus

1953 Placed on list of books disapproved by the Gathings Committee (a House of Representatives select committee on indecent literature).

1953 Banned in Ireland.

Source: 4, p. 83.

1617 **Stendhal (Marie-Henri Beyle)**
The Red and the Black

1850 Banned in Russia by Czar Nicholas I, whose motto in a campaign to suppress liberal thought was "autocracy, orthodoxy, and nationality."

1864 Placed on the *Index Librorum Prohibitorum* (Index of Prohibited Books) in Rome, Italy and confirmed by the Index of Pope Leo XIII in 1897. The novel and all of Stendhal's "love stories" remained on the list through the last edition compiled in 1948 and in effect until 1966.

1939 Purged from Spanish libraries by the dictatorship of Francisco Franco.

Source: 8, pp. 284–85.

1618 **Stern, Howard**
Miss America

1996 VA Challenged at the Prince William County Library. Two newly appointed members of the library board want to limit young people's access to books by removing them from the collection or by creating an "adults-only" section of the library.

1997 CO Challenged in the Pikes Peak Library District in Colorado Springs because the book is considered "obscene."

Source: 11, Nov. 1996, p. 194; July 1997, p. 93.

1619 **Stern, Howard**
Private Parts

1994 AL Challenged, but retained at the Scott Public Library in Alabaster. The Shelby County District Attorney called the book "obscene" and threatened to prosecute the library for circulating it, although no action was taken.

1994 TX Challenged at the Weslaco Public Library. A petition, with more than 300 signatures, was presented to city officials asking them to more closely monitor what books the library purchases. The librarian labeled as "too liberal" subsequently resigned. Former Weslaco librarian filed a federal lawsuit in 1995 charging that she was fired for publicly discussing that city's efforts to ban Stern's work from the library.

Source: 11, Nov. 1994, p. 189; Mar. 1995, p. 53; Sept. 1995, p. 153.

1620 **Stewart, Jon, Ben Karlin, and David Javerbaum**
America (The Book): A Citizen's Guide to Democracy Inaction

2004 MS Returned to circulation at the Jackson-George Regional Library System in Pascagoula. The library board had banned the best-selling satirical book because the book contained an image of Supreme Court judges' faces superimposed on naked bodies. The book was named a Book of the Year by *Publishers Weekly*, the industry trade magazine.

Source: 11, Mar. 2005, p. 73; 13, pp. 15–17.

1621 **Stillman, Peter R.**
Introduction to Myth

1982 WA Challenged as a text for an elective course for junior and senior high school students in Renton because it was considered anti-Christian by some parents.

Source: 11, Sept. 1982, p. 171.

1622 **Stine, R. L.**
Beach House

1996 AR Challenged at the Pulaski Heights Elementary School library in Little Rock along with similar Stine titles. The book, part of the "Fear Street" series, includes graphic descriptions of boys intimidating and killing girls.

Source: 11, Nov. 1996, p. 211.

1623 **Stine, R. L.**
Double Date

2003 GA Removed from the Crawford County Middle School library because the book deals with complex issues teenagers confront.

Source: 11, Jan. 2004, p. 9.

1624 **Stine, R. L.**
Ghost Camp

1997 GA Challenged, but retained at the Jackson Elementary School library in Gwinnett County. A concerned parent complained because of graphic content and references to the occult.

Source: 11, Sept. 1997, p. 148.

1625 **Stine, R. L.**
Goosebumps

1996 FL Challenged at the Bay County elementary schools because of "satanic symbolism, disturbing scenes and dialogue." *The Barking Ghost*, for satanic symbolism and gestures, possession and descriptions of dogs as menacing and attacking; *Night of the Living Dummy II*, for spells or chants, violence and vandalism; *The Haunted Mask*, for graphic description of the ugly mask, demonic possession, violence, disturbing scenes and dialogue; *The Scarecrow Walks at Midnight*, for satanic acts and symbolism, and disturbing scenes; and *Say Cheese and Die!*, for promoting mischief, demonic possession, a reference to Satan and his goals, a disturbing scene describing a death, and a scene that tells of a child disappearing from a birthday party.

1997 MN Challenged, but retained in the Anoka-Hennepin school system because "children under the age of twelve may not be able to handle the frightening content of the books."

Source: 11, July 1996, p. 134; Mar. 1997, p. 35; May 1997, p. 77.

1626 Stine, R. L.
The Haunted Mask

1994 MI Challenged, but retained at the Battle Creek Elementary School library despite protests from a parent who said the book is satanic.

Source: 11, Nov. 1994, p. 200.

1627 Stirling, Nora
You Would If You Loved Me

1980 UT Removed from the Utah State Library bookmobile.

Source: 11, Nov. 1980, p. 128.

1628 Stock, Gregory
The Kid's Book of Questions

1990 VA Challenged in the Albemarle County schools in Charlottesville because it is "inappropriate in an academic class." One parent cited a question from the book, which asked whether a child had ever farted and blamed someone else.

Source: 11, Jan. 1991, p. 18.

1629 Stoker, Bram
Dracula

1994 TX Eliminated from required reading lists for juniors and seniors in advanced English classes at the Colony High School in Lewisville because, "the book contains unacceptable descriptions in the introduction, such as 'Dracula is the symptom of a wish, largely sexual, that we wish we did not have.'"

Source: 11, July 1994, p. 116.

1630 Stopes, Marie
Married Love

1930 PA Declared "not obscene or immortal" in Philadelphia after two social workers imported copies of the book to use in their work. The case went before Judge Kirkpatrick, U.S. District Judge for the Eastern District of Pennsylvania. Despite the judge's decision, the book was again seized later that year and again went to court, where it was determined was not obscene.

1931 Banned in Ireland by the Irish Censorship Board for its discussion of contraception.

Source: 14, pp. 225–26.

1631 Stoppard, Miriam
The Magic of Sex

1996 NJ Restricted to patrons over eighteen years of age at the Main Memorial Library in Clifton. The book is hidden behind the checkout counter and on the shelves is a dummy book jacket. The book was described as hard-core pornography by the complainant.

1999 CA Challenged, but retained at the Auburn-Placer County Library because of sexually explicit material.

Source: 11, Mar. 1996, p. 63; May 1996, p. 83; Nov. 1999, p. 171.

1632 Stoppard, Miriam
Woman's Body

1995 GA Challenged at the Gwinnett-Forsyth Regional Library because it is "too sexually explicit to be on regular library shelves."

Source: 11, Jan. 1996, p. 29.

1633 Storm, Hyemeyohsts
Seven Arrows

1985 OR Challenged at the Creswell High School because the book contains references to masturbation, rape, and incest.

Source: 11, Mar. 1985, p. 45; May 1985, p. 81.

1634 Stowe, Harriet Beecher
Uncle Tom's Cabin

1852 Banned in Russia.

1855 Prohibited in Italy and all papal states.

1984 IL Challenged in the Waukegan School District because the novel contains the word "nigger."

Source: 8, pp. 185–87; 11, July 1984, p. 105.

1635   Strasser, Todd
Angel Dust Blues

1983 NY Challenged as reading material for the Manhasset Public Library's young adult Popsicle series because of "explicit and graphic sex scenes of a most crude and exploitative nature" and "blasphemy."

1987 NC Challenged at Alexander Central High School and East Junior High School libraries in Taylorsville because of "sexually explicit passages."

1989 OR Challenged at the Crook County Middle School in Prineville because of explicit language.
Source: 11, Nov. 1983, p. 185; May 1987, p. 87; July 1987, p. 149; Jan. 1990, pp. 4–5.

1636   Strasser, Todd
Friends 'til the End

1985 TX Challenged at the Arlington junior high school libraries because of "sexually descriptive words."
Source: 11, Mar. 1985, p. 60.

1637   Strasser, Todd
Give a Boy a Gun

2007 PA Retained at the Bangor Area Middle School
New   despite a student's aunt's concerns about the book's depiction of school violence.
Source: 11, Mar. 2008, p. 79.

1638   Street Law

1983 MD Challenged in Linthicum Heights because it is "biased and pressures teenagers to make moral judgments."
Source: 11, Nov. 1983, p. 186; Mar. 1984, p. 53.

1639   Stroud, Jonathan
The Amulet of Samarkand

2008 NY Restored by the Lackawanna School Board
New   following accusations of censorship by some parents and teachers. The book was pulled from the middle school library recommended list because of concerns that the book deals with the occult.
Source: 11, May 2008, p. 116.

1640   Stroud, Jonathan
The Golem's Eye

2008 NY Restored by the Lackawanna School Board
New   along with several other books following accusations of censorship by some parents and teachers. The book was pulled from the middle school library recommended list because of concerns that the book deals with the occult.
Source: 11, May 2008, p. 116.

1641   Stroud, Jonathan
Ptolemy's Gate

2008 NY Restored by the Lackawanna School Board
New   along with several other books following accusations of censorship by some parents and teachers. The book was pulled from the middle school library recommended list because of concerns that the book deals with the occult.
Source: 11, May 2008, p. 116.

1642   Sturges, Jock
Radiant Identities

1998 GA Despite pressure from protestors demanding that Barnes & Noble face child pornography charges, a prosecutor in Cobb County declined to take the nation's largest bookstore chain to court for carrying Sturges's book. Activists from Operation Rescue claimed the book contains children in sexually suggestive positions and should be deemed illegal.

1998 KS Barnes & Noble officials noted that the decision follows similar rulings by prosecutors in Kansas.

1998 MD Barnes & Noble officials noted that the decision follows similar rulings by prosecutors in Maryland.

1998 TX Barnes & Noble officials noted that the decision follows similar rulings by prosecutors in Texas.

1998 WI Barnes & Noble officials noted that the decision follows similar rulings by prosecutors in Wisconsin.
Source: 11, Jan. 1999, p. 20.

1643   Stwertka, Eve and Albert
Marijuana

1997 PA Challenged at the Stanwood Elementary School in Hempfield because its chapters on purchasing related paraphernalia and marijuana recipes were considered inappropriate.
Source: 11, July 1997, p. 94.

1644   Styron, William
The Confessions of Nat Turner

1987 IA Removed from the Thompson High School library in Mason City after a parent objected to some "sexual materials" in the book.
Source: 11, July 1987, p. 126; Sept. 1987, p. 174.

1645   Styron, William
Sophie's Choice

1979   Banned in South Africa.
2002 CA   Returned to La Mirada High School library after a complaint about its sexual content prompted the school to pull the award-winning novel about a tormented Holocaust survivor.
Source: 5, Apr. 1980, p. 72; 8, pp. 384–85; 11, Mar. 2002, p. 105.

1646   Sullivan, Tim, ed.
Cold Shocks

1993 NJ   Challenged at the Montclair Public Library because the language in the collection of horror stories "was not conducive to a sixth grader." The complainant demanded that books with possibly offensive contents be labeled with warnings and kept in a limited-access section.
Source: 11, July 1993, p. 100.

1647   Sullivan, Tom, and Derek Gill
If You Could See What I Hear

1980 UT   Removed from the Utah State Library bookmobile.
Source: 11, Nov. 1980, p. 128.

1648   Summers, Montague
The Popular History of Witchcraft

1986 CA   Challenged by the "God Squad," a group of three students and their parents, at the El Camino High School in Oceanside because the book "glorified the devil and the occult."
Source: 11, Sept. 1986, p. 151; Nov. 1986, p. 224; Jan. 1987, p. 9.

1649   Suzuki, D. T.
Zen Buddhism: Selected Writings

1987 MI   Challenged at the Plymouth-Canton school system in Canton because "this book details the teachings of the religion of Buddhism in such a way that the reader could very likely embrace its teachings and choose this as his religion."
Source: 11, May 1987, p. 109.

1650   Swarthout, Glendon
Bless the Beasts and the Children

1987 SD   Banned in the Dupree High School English classes because of what the school board called "offensive language and vulgarity."
Source: 11, Jan. 1988, p. 12.

1651   Swedenborg, Emanual
Arcana Coelesta

1721   His most notable scientific volume, *Principia*, which proposed a rational mathematical explanation of the universe, was placed on the Catholic Church's *Index Librorum Prohibitorum* (Index of Prohibited Books) in Rome, Italy and remained listed for more than two centuries.
1747   Banned as heretical for contradicting Lutheran doctrine in Sweden.
Source: 1, pp. 16–18.

1652   Sweedloff, Peter
Men and Women

1977 MI   Banned from the Brighton High School library along with all other sex education materials.
Source: 11, Sept. 1977, p. 133.

1653   Sweeney, Joyce
Shadow

1997 KS   Challenged, but retained on the Anderson County Junior/Senior High School library shelves in Garnett. A parent objected to the book's "graphic language."
Source: 11, July 1997, p. 109.

1654   Swift, Jonathan
Drapier's Letters

1724   All attempts to prosecute the printer or to identify the anonymous writer were frustrated by the aroused Irish nation.
Source: 4, p. 25.

1655   Swift, Jonathan
Gulliver's Travels

1726   Denounced as wicked and obscene in Ireland.
Source: 4, p. 25.

1656   Swift, Jonathan
Tale of a Tub

1704   Placed on the *Index Librorum Prohibitorum* (List of Prohibited Books) in Rome, Italy.
Source: 1, pp. 324–25; 3, p. 135.

1657   Talbert, Marc
Dead Birds Singing

1993 ND   Challenged, but retained as part of the curriculum, at Hughes Junior High School in Bismarck because it is "offensive."
Source: 11, Sept. 1993, p. 145; Jan. 1994, p. 38.

1658 The Talmud

600s	The history of suppression of the *Talmud* is many centuries long. Early attempts to ban it date at least to the seventh and eight centuries.
1144	In Paris, France the Catholic Church ordered the burning of the *Talmud* on charges of blasphemy and immorality.
1190	With his *Guide for the Perplexed,* Maimonides, the Jewish philosopher, aroused the Christians' resentment, which culminated in the first official burning of Hebrew books by orders of Dominicans, Franciscans, and others in Cairo, Egypt.
1239	Pope Gregory IX ordered the burning of all Jewish books in Rome, Italy.
1244	Pope Innocent IV ordered Louis IX of France to burn all copies in France.
1264	Pope Clement IV appointed a committee of censors in Rome, Italy to expunge any anti-Christian material. Jews were only allowed to have expurgated copies.
1415	Pope Benedict XII in Rome, Italy ordered all copies of Talmudic books to be sent to bishops for preservation, but Jews were forbidden to keep copies.
1490	Grand Inquisitor Tomás Torquemada burned thousands of Jewish books by order of Ferdinand and Isabella of Spain.
1492	As Jews were expelled from Spain and Portugal, all Jewish books were confiscated.
1530	At the urging of Martin Luther, German principalities expelled Jews and suppressed their books.
1553	Pope Julius III in Rome, Italy halted its printing.
1555	Jewish houses were searched throughout Europe. The library of the Hebrew school in Cremona, Italy was destroyed by the Roman Inquisition and thousands of books were burned.
1555	Pope Pius IV in Rome, Italy relaxed its prohibition, allowing the distribution of expurgated versions. It was, however, placed on the newly created *Index Librorum Prohibitorum* (Index of Prohibited Books) the same year.
1592	Pope Clement VIII issued a bull in Rome, Italy which ordered reinstatement of the ban on its possession by either Jews or Christians.
1926	Along with other religious works, removed from many libraries in the Soviet Union. Printing was also sharply restricted.
1939	Most Jewish schools in Germany were destroyed by the Nazi government, along with Jewish religious texts.
1965	The Second Vatican Council in Rome, Italy brought about a positive change in attitude with the Catholic Church formally acknowledging the common foundations of Christianity and Judaism and renouncing anti-Semitism.

Source: 3, pp. 55–56; 4, p. 5; 6, p. 844; 8, pp. 300–303.

1659 Tamar, Erika
Fair Game

1995	AR	Challenged at the Springdale Public Library because "ethics take a back seat to graphic sexual material. Perhaps there is a less prurient work that explores the issue of rape vs. consensual sex or date rape."

Source: 11, Sept. 1995, p. 157.

1660 Tan, Amy
The Joy Luck Club

1996	TX	Banned from the Lindale Advanced Placement English reading list because the book "conflicted with the values of the community."
2004	WI	Challenged at the Arrowhead High School in Waukesha as an elective reading list assignment by a parent because the book contains "sexually explicit and inappropriate material."

Source: 11, Nov. 1996, p. 199; Jan. 2005, p. 11.

1661 Tarbox, Katherine
A Girl's Life Online

2008 New	NY	Challenged in the English 11 Regents class at Baker High School in Baldwinsville because of the book's graphic language. The cautionary tale about Internet safety is one of the five books students could select for the contemporary literature class unit on "teenage struggles."

Source: 11, July 2008, p. 143.

1662 Tax, Meredith
Families

1982	WI	Challenged in Mosinee because it teaches family living.
1994	VA	Eliminated from the Fairfax County School's Family Life Education program after "parents complained that it glorifies divorce and shows two women living together."

Source: 9; 11, May 1982, p. 87; May 1994, p. 88; Sept. 1994, p. 153.

1663 Taylor, Mildred D.
The Friendship

1997	MD	Challenged, but retained in the Prince George's County school system after a parent claimed the book has "no redeeming value."

Source: 11, Sept. 1997, p. 149.

1664 Taylor, Mildred D.
The Land

2008 FL
New
Removed from the Turner Elementary School media-center shelves in New Tampa as age inappropriate. A parent challenged the book because the novel contains a racial epithet. The book was a 2002 Coretta Scott King Author Award recipient.

Source: 11, May 2008, p. 96.

1665 Taylor, Mildred D.
Mississippi Bridge

2001 VA Challenged, but retained at the Donahoe Elementary School library in Sandston despite objections of its "negative content and [that] it's riddled with prejudice." The novel by the Newbery Medal-winning author tells the story of a young black man who tries to save white passengers in a bus accident, despite being ordered earlier to give up his seat to "white folks."

Source: 11, May 2001, p. 97; July 2001, p. 174.

1666 Taylor, Mildred D.
Roll of Thunder, Hear My Cry

1993 LA Removed from the ninth-grade reading list at the Arcadia High School. The 1976 Newbery Medal-winning book was charged with racial bias.

1998 CA Challenged in O'Hara Park Middle School classrooms in Oakley because it contains racial epithets.

2000 AL Challenged in Chapman Elementary School libraries in Huntsville because it uses racial slurs in dialogue to make points about racism.

2004 FL Challenged, but retained as a part of the Seminole County school curriculum despite the concerns of a African American couple who found the book inappropriate for their thirteen-year-old son. The award-winning book depicts the life of an African American family in rural Mississippi in the 1930s and uses the word "nigger."

Source: 11, May 1993, p. 72; July 1998, p. 107; Mar. 2000, p. 47; Mar. 2004, pp. 75–76.

1667 Taylor, Theodore
The Cay

1992 CA Challenged as required reading at the Moorpark schools because it allegedly maligns African Americans.

1995 CA Removed from the Oak Grove School District's core reading list for seventh-graders in San Jose because of offensive, racist language.

Placed on an "extended" list for use in the eighth grade.

1997 MD Challenged, but retained at the Prince George's County school system after a parent claimed the book has "no redeeming value."

Source: 11, May 1992, p. 95; July 1995, p. 96; Sept. 1997, p. 149.

1668 Taylor, William
Agnes the Sheep

1995 GA Removed from the Nesbit Elementary School in Gwinnett County because it overused the words "hell, damn, and God." Although other parents wanted the book restored in the elementary school, the County Board of Education refused to reinstate the book.

Source: 11, Jan. 1996, p. 11; Mar. 1996, p. 64.

1669 Tchudi, Stephen
Probing the Unknown: From Myth to Science

1995 MI Challenged in the West Branch-Rose City school district because it discusses occult beliefs.

Source: 11, Jan. 1996, p. 15.

1670 Telander, Rick
Heaven Is a Playground

1983 WA Removed from the Evergreen School District of Vancouver along with twenty-nine other titles. The American Civil Liberties Union of Washington filed suit contending that the removals constitute censorship, a violation of plaintiff's rights to free speech and due process, and the acts are a violation of the state Open Meetings Act because the removal decisions were made behind closed doors.

Source: 11, Nov. 1983, pp. 185–86.

1671 *Teleny: A Novel Attributed to Oscar Wilde*

1984 Seized by the British Customs Office as "indecent and obscene."

Source: 11, Jan. 1985, p. 26.

1672 Terkel, Studs
Working: People Talk about What They Do All Day and How They Feel about What They Do

1978 WI Challenged in Wales due to the book's "obscene language."

1982 PA Challenged in the senior vocational-technical English class in Girard because some parents and students considered the book obscene.

1983 AZ Deleted from the seventh- and eighth-grade curriculum in the Washington School District due to "profane language. When we require idealistic and sensitive youth to be burdened with despair, ugliness and hopelessness, we shall be held accountable by the Almighty God."

1983 WA Removed from an optional reading list at the South Kitsap High School because the chapter "Hooker" demeaned marital status and degraded the sexual act.

Source: 9; 11, July 1978, p. 89; Sept. 1978, p. 123; July 1982, p. 143; Nov. 1983, p. 187; Jan. 1984, pp. 10–11.

1673 Terris, Susan
Stage Brat

1990 PA Removed from, but later reinstated at the Pine Middle School library in Gibsonia because "it talks of adults slithering around in hot tubs, abortions, palm reading and horoscopes as ways of making life decisions, anti-religious language, and four-letter words."

Source: 11, Nov. 1990, pp. 209–10; Jan. 1991, pp. 28–29.

1674 Terry, Wallace
Bloods: An Oral History of the Vietnam War by Black Veterans

1987 FL Banned from the West Hernando Middle School library in Spring Hill because of "harsh language and presents a moral danger to students." The librarian filed a grievance, and the book was returned to the shelves following a ruling by the American Arbitration Association. Forty minutes after the book was returned, the book was removed again, pending a review by an advisory committee.

Source: 7, pp. 60–61; 11, May 1987, p. 85; Sept. 1987, pp. 173–74; Jan. 1988, p. 9.

1675 Thom, James Alexander
Follow the River

2002 IN Removed from the tenth grade curriculum at the high school in Noblesville after a parent objected to passages about an imagined rape; the book remains in the library collection.

Source: 11, May 2002, p. 117.

1676 Thomas, Piri
Down These Mean Streets

1972 NY Removed from the junior high school library Community School Board 1250, Queens. Decision upheld by the court's ruling in *President's Council, District 25 v. Community School Board No. 25*, 457 F. 2d 289 (2d Cir. 1972), 409 U.S. 998 (1972).

1976 NY Removed from the Island Trees Union Free School District High School library along with nine other titles because they were considered "immoral, anti-American, anti-Christian, or just plain filthy." Returned to the library after the U.S. Supreme Court ruling on June 25, 1982 in *Board of Education, Island Trees Union Free School District No. 26 et al. v. Pico et al.*, 457 U.S. 853 (1982).

Source: 11, July 1973, p. 115; Nov. 1982, p. 197; 12, pp. 142–44, 239.

1677 Thompson, Charlotte E.
Single Solutions: An Essential Guide for the Career Woman

1991 OR Challenged for technical errors, but retained at the Multnomah County Library.

Source: 11, Jan. 1992, p. 6.

1678 Thompson, Craig
Blankets

2006 MO Challenged in the Marshall Public Library because some members of the community the book was deemed the book "pornographic." The book was moved to the adult book section, rather than the young-adult area where it had been shelved before.

Source: 11, Nov. 2006, p. 289; Jan. 2007, pp. 9–10; May 2007, p. 115; July 2007, pp. 163–64.

1679 *The Three Billy Goats Gruff*

1984 OR Challenged at the Eagle Point Elementary School library because the story was too violent for children.

Source: 11, Sept. 1984, p. 155.

1680 Tindal, Matthew
Rights of the Christian Church Asserted

1707 An English grand jury made a presentation against the book, and in 1710, it was proscribed by Parliament and burned.

Source: 1, pp. 287–88.

1681 Toer, Pramoedya Ananta
The Fugitive

1949 Banned in Indonesia. The author has spent much of his life imprisoned for political reasons for fourteen years and on house or city (Jakarta) arrest for an additional twenty years, from 1979 to 1999. Toer wrote the novel in 1949 while he was imprisoned by the Dutch from 1947 to 1950 for his role in

Indonesia's anticolonial revolution. With the success of the revolution in 1949, the novel was published in 1950, was acclaimed and then banned because it contained elements of class conflict and was perceived as a potential threat to society. In the following years, his works—thirty novels and books—were burned and banned in Indonesia because they were considered "subversive." Ownership of his books led some to imprisonment and torture. Toer has won many national and international awards for his works.

Source: 8, pp. 55–57.

1682 Toland, John
Christianity Not Mysterious

1697   Burned for heresy by the Irish Parliament.
1896   Presented by an English grand jury. Toland escaped arrest by fleeing to Holland.

Source: 1, pp. 39–40.

1683 Tolkien, J. R. R. (John Ronald Reuel)
Lord of the Rings

2001 NM Burned in Alamagordo outside Christ Community Church along with other Tolkien novels as satanic.

Source: 11, Mar. 2002, p. 61.

1684 Tolstoy, Leo
The Kreutzer Sonata

1880   Forbidden publication in Russia.
1890   Banned by the U.S. Post Office Department.
1890 PA A Philadelphia vendor was indicted for selling a translation of the novel and taken to court. The court declared the novel to possess "very little dramatic interest or literary merit" and acknowledged as bizarre Tolstoy's recommendation of complete celibacy for all people, married or otherwise, but he also stated that "it cannot, on that account, be called an obscene libel."
1926   Banned in Hungary.
1929   Banned in Italy.

Source: 4, p. 49; 10, p. 144; 13, pp. 134–35; 15, Vol. II, pp. 621–22.

1685 Toriyama, Akira
Dragon Ball: The Monkey King

2009 MD Removed from the Wicomico County school
New   media centers because the Japanese graphic novels depict some violence and show nudity.

Source: 11, Jan. 2010, p. 9.

1686 Touchette, Charleen
It Stops with Me: Memoir of a Canuck Girl

2005 RI Removed from the Woonsocket Harris Public Library shelves after the author's father challenged the book. He wrote, "If members of a family wish to harm one another, those actions should be kept private and should not draw in others by involving matters of public policy." The book was later returned to the shelves.

Source: 11, Mar. 2006, p. 91.

1687 *The Treasury of American Poetry*

1981 VA Challenged at the Gretna High School library because it contained eight objectionable words. The review committee recommended to cut out pages or ink over the offending words.

Source: 11, May 1981, p. 66.

1688 Trocchi, Alexander
Cain's Book

1964   Police in Sheffield, England, raided a number of bookstores and confiscated the novel. Eventually, the court ruled that the book was obscene. This marked the first time a judgment of obscenity had been made based not on the vulgar language, depiction of sexual activity, or depravity in a work but on the lifestyle it advocated. Lord Chief justice Parker determined that the narrator's heroin addiction was the reason for censoring the book.

Source: 14, p. 72.

1689 Trotsky, Leon
Report of the Siberian Delegation

1903   Banned by the imperial government in 1903 and by the government of the Soviet Union in 1927.
1930 MA Banned in Boston.
1933   Banned in Germany.
1934   Banned in Italy.

Source: 7, pp. 426–27.

1690 Trueman, Terry
Stuck in Neutral

2003 WI Challenged, but retained on the reading list for eighth-graders at the Evansille High School despite concerns about profanity, sexual imagery, and violence.

Source: 11, Jan. 2004, p. 13.

1691 Trumbo, David
Johnny Got His Gun

1977 CA Challenged and/or censored in California for the language and for several passages describing sexual encounters.

1977 CO Challenged and/or censored in Colorado for the description of the main character after he had been maimed in the war.

1977 MI Challenged and/or censored in schools: in Michigan for too much profanity, too gruesome details of a human being, expressing unpatriotic and anti-American ideas, and sexual passages.

1977 TX Challenged and/or censored in Texas as unpatriotic and anti-American.

1977 WI Challenged and/or censored in Wisconsin in 1977 and 1982 for too much profanity and as antiwar.

1982 IL Challenged and/or censored in llinois as too violent.

1982 VT Challenged and/or censored in Vermont.

Source: 8, pp. 107–9.

1692 Tryon, Thomas
The Other

1982 NH Challenged at the Merrimack High School.

Source: 11, Sept. 1982, p. 170.

1693 Tucker, Todd
Notre Dame vs. the Klan: How the Fighting Irish Defeated the Ku Klux Klan

2008 IN
New Indiana University-Purdue University Indianapolis (IUPUI) administrators have found that a student-employee was guilty of racial harassment merely for reading in a public area an historical account of Notre Dame students' fight with members of the Ku Klux Klan. The student-employee contacted the American Civil Liberties Union of Indiana and six months later received a letter stating that IUPUI "regret[s] this situation took place," is committed to upholding freedom of expression on its campus, and no documents regarding this incident exist in the employee's file.

Source: 11, July 2008, pp. 159–60.

1694 Turkle, Brinton
Do Not Open

1990 CA Challenged at the Jackson Elementary School because of objections to its pictures of supernatural beings.

Source: 11, May 1990, p. 105.

1695 Twain, Mark [Samuel L. Clemens]
The Adventures of Huckleberry Finn

1885 MA Banned in Concord as "trash and suitable only for the slums."

1905 NY Excluded from the children's room of the Brooklyn Public Library on the grounds that "Huck not only itched but scratched, and that he said sweat when he should have said perspiration."

1930 Confiscated at the USSR border.

1957 NY Dropped from the New York City list of approved books for senior and junior high schools, partly because of objections to frequent use of the term "nigger."

1969 FL Removed from the Miami Dade Junior College required reading list because the book "creates an emotional block for black students that inhibits learning."

1976 IL Challenged as a "racist" novel at the New Trier High School in Winnetka.

1981 PA Challenged as a "racist" novel at the Tamamend Junior High in Warrington.

1982 IA Challenged as a "racist" novel in Davenport Public Schools.

1982 TX Challenged as a "racist" novel at the Spring Independent School District in Houston.

1982 VA Challenged as a "racist" novel at the Mark Twain Intermediate School in Fairfax County.

1983 PA Challenged as a "racist" novel in State College Area School District.

1984 IL Challenged as a "racist" novel in Springfield.

1984 IL Challenged as a "racist" novel in Waukegan schools.

1988 IL Removed from the required reading in the Rockford public schools because the book contains the word "nigger."

1988 LA Removed from a required reading list and school libraries in Caddo Parish because of racially offensive passages.

1988 MI Challenged at the Berrien Springs High School.

1989 TN Challenged at the Sevier County High School in Sevierville because of racial slurs and dialect.

1990 PA Challenged on an Erie High School supplemental English reading list because of its derogatory references to African Americans.

1990 TX Challenged in Plano Independent School District because the novel is "racist."

1991 AZ Challenged in the Mesa Unified School District because the book repeatedly uses the word "nigger" and damages the self-esteem of black youth.

1991 LA Removed from the required reading list of the Terrebone Parish public schools in Houma because of the repeated use of the word "nigger."

1991 MI Temporarily pulled from the Portage classrooms after some black parents complained that their children were uncomfortable with the book's portrayal of blacks.

1992 CA Challenged at the Modesto High School as a required reading because of "offensive and racist language." The word "nigger" appears in the book.

1992 NC Challenged in the Kinston Middle School when the superintendent told the novel could not be assigned because the students were too young to read the book because of its use of the word "nigger."

1993 PA Challenged at the Carlisle area schools because the book's racial slurs are offensive to both black and white students.

1994 GA Challenged in English classes at Taylor County High School in Butler because it contains racial slurs and bad grammar and does not reject slavery. The book will be taught in the tenth rather than the ninth grade.

1994 TX Challenged, but retained on high school reading lists, by the Lewisville school board.

1995 CA Removed from the required reading lists in East San Jose high schools in response to objections raised by African-American parents. They said the book's use of racial epithets, including frequent use of the word "nigger," erodes their children's self-esteem and affects their performance in school.

1995 CT Removed from the eighth-grade curriculum at a New Haven middle school because parents complained it undermined the self-esteem of black youth.

1995 DC Removed from the curriculum of the National Cathedral School in Washington, D.C. because of the novel's content and language.

1995 WI Challenged in the Kenosha Unified School District. The complaint was filed by the local NAACP, which cited the book as offensive to African-American students.

1996 AZ Challenged as required reading in an honors English class at the McClintock High School in Tempe by a teacher on behalf of her daughter and other African-American students at the school. In May 1996, a class-action lawsuit was filed in U.S. District Court in Phoenix, alleging that the district deprived minority students of educational opportunities by requiring racially offensive literature as part of class assignments. In January 1997, a federal judge dismissed the lawsuit stating he realized that "language in the novel was offensive and hurtful to the plaintiff," but that the suit failed to prove the district violated students' civil rights or that the works were assigned with discriminatory intent. The U.S. Court of Appeals for the Ninth Circuit in San Francisco ruled that requiring public school students to read literary works that some find racially offensive is not discrimination prohibited by the equal protection clause or Title VI of the 1964 Civil Rights Act. The ruling came in the case *Monteiro v. Tempe Union High School District*.

1996 PA Dropped from the mandatory required reading list at the Upper Dublin schools because of its allegedly insensitive and offensive language.

1996 TX Banned from the Lindale Advanced Placement English reading list because the book "conflicted with the values of the community."

1996 WA Challenged for being on the approved reading list in the Federal Way schools because it "perpetuates hate and racism."

1997 IN Challenged at the Columbus North High School because the book is "degrading, insensitive, and oppressive."

1997 NJ Removed from classrooms in the Cherry Hill schools in January 1997 after concerns were raised about its racial epithets and the depiction of its African-American characters. In December 1997, however, the school board approved a new curriculum that places the book in the context of nineteenth-century racial relations and presents the works of African-American writers, including Frederick Douglass, Maya Angelou, and Langston Hughes.

1997 OH Challenged in the South Euclid-Lyndhurst City Schools because a student complained that some classmates snickered and giggled as the word "nigger" was read aloud by students.

1997 VA Challenged, but retained at McLean High School in Fairfax despite a parent's complaint that the book offends African Americans.

1998 GA Challenged in the Dalton County schools because the book's language is offensive.

1998 GA Challenged in the Whitfield County schools because the book's language is offensive.

1998 PA The Pennsylvania NAACP called for the removal of the book from required reading lists in school districts across the state because of its offensive racial language.

1999 AK Recommended for removal from the Fairbanks North Star Borough School District's required reading lists because of its frequent use of the word "nigger."

2000 OK Challenged, but retained in the Enid schools. The novel was previously removed from the curriculum in Enid in 1977 after similar protests. It was returned to the required reading list in 1991.

2001 IL Challenged in the Kankakee School District because the book uses the word "nigger."

2002 OR Challenged in the Portland schools by an

African-American student who said he was offended by an ethnic slur used in the 1885 novel.

2003 IL Challenged in the Normal Community High School sophomore literature class as being degrading to African Americans. *The Chosen* was offered as an alternative to Twain's novel.

2004 WA Pulled from the reading lists at the three Renton high schools after an African American student said the book degraded her and her culture. The novel, which is not required reading in Renton schools but is on a supplemental list of approved books, was eventually retained for classroom usage.

2006 AZ Challenged as required reading at Cactus High in Peoria. The student and mother have threatened to file a civil-rights complaints because of alleged racial treatment, the segregation of the student, and the use of a racial slur in the classroom.

2006 MI Pulled from classes in Taylor schools because of complaints about its liberal use of common racial slurs.

2007 MN New Challenged, but retained in the Lakeville High School as required reading for sophomores. The district will conduct staff training about race issues and revise the way it weighs requests for curriculum changes. The district will also let its staff offer alternative assignments on racially sensitive issues in ways which "students do not feel ostracized because they have opted out of the assignment."

2007 MN New Challenged, but retained in the St. Louis Park High School in Minneapolis as required reading for sophomores. The district will conduct staff training about race issues and revise the way it weighs requests for curriculum changes. The district will also let its staff offer alternative assignments on racially sensitive issues in ways which "students do not feel ostracized because they have opted out of the assignment."

2007 TX New Challenged at Richland High School in North Richland Hills because of racial epithets.

2008 CT New Retained in the Manchester School District with the requirement that teachers attend seminars on how to deal with issues of race before teaching the book in their classrooms.

Source: 2, pp. 86–87; 4, pp. 49–50; 6, pp. 398–400; 11, May 1969, p. 52; July 1976, p. 87; Sept. 1976, p. 116; Nov. 1981, p. 162; Jan. 1982, pp. 11, 18; May 1982, p. 101; July 1982, p. 126; Sept. 1982, p. 171; Jan. 1984, p. 11; May 1984, p. 72; July 1984, pp. 121–22; Nov. 1984, p. 187; 8, Sept. 1988, pp. 152–53; Nov. 1988, p. 201; Jan. 1989, p. 11; Mar. 1989, p. 43; May 1989, p. 94; Jan. 1991, pp. 17–18; Mar. 1991, pp. 44–45; May 1991, pp. 90–92; Mar. 1992, pp. 43, 64; July 1992, p. 126; Sept. 1992, p. 140; May 1993, p. 73; May 1994, pp. 99–100; Mar. 1995, p. 42; May 1995, pp. 68, 69, 83; July 1995, pp. 96–97; Jan. 1996, p. 13; Mar. 1996, pp. 64–65; May 1996, p. 98; July 1996, p. 120; Sept. 1996, p. 153; Nov. 1996, pp. 198–99; Jan. 1997, p. 12; Mar. 1997, p. 40; May 1997, pp. 65–66, 72; July 1997, pp. 95–96, 97–98; Sept. 1997, p. 149; Nov. 1997, p. 182; Mar. 1998, p. 56; May 1998, pp. 72–73; Nov. 1998, p. 182; Jan. 1999, pp. 13–15; July 1999, pp. 93–94; Mar. 2000, p. 52; July 2000, p. 125; Mar. 2001, p. 57; Jan. 2003, pp. 11–12; Jan. 2004, p. 11; May 2004, p. 91; Jan. 2007, pp. 14–15; Mar. 2007, pp. 50–52; May 2007, p. 99; May 2007, p. 99; July 2007, p. 164; Jan. 2008, pp. 40–41; Mar. 2008, pp. 61–62; Jan. 2009, pp. 22–23; 15, Vol. II, p. 617.

1696 Twain, Mark [Samuel L. Clemens]
The Adventures of Tom Sawyer

1876 CO Excluded from the children's room in the Denver Public Library.

1876 NY Excluded from the children's room in the Brooklyn Public Library.

1930 Confiscated at the USSR border.

1985 Removed from London, England school libraries by education officials who found it "racist" and "sexist."

1990 TX Challenged in the Plano Independent School District because the novel is racist.

1992 IL Retained in the O'Fallon schools, but parents will be able to request that their children not be required to read the book. A parent had sought the book's removal, charging that its use of the word "nigger" is degrading and offensive to black students.

1997 IN Challenged in the Columbus schools because the book is "degrading, insensitive, and oppressive." It was suggested that middle school students in the district might use an edited version that deletes controversial language.

Source: 4, pp. 49–50; 11, Sept. 1985, p. 156; Jan. 1991, p. 18; Mar. 1991, pp. 45–46; May 1991, p. 92; May 1992, p. 97; Sept. 1994, p. 152; July 1997, pp. 97–98.

1697 Twain, Mark [Samuel L. Clemens]
Eve's Diary

1906 MA Removed from circulation at the Charlton Library in Worcester because the "Edenic costumes" worn by Eve in the book's fifty illustrations had created an inordinate demand for it among the library's patrons.

Source: 15, Vol. II, p. 626.

1698 Ungerer, Tomi
Beast of Monsieur Racine

1989 AR Challenged at the Rogers-Hough Memorial Library because the book is violent.

Source: 11, Sept. 1991, p. 151.

1699   Ungerer, Tomi
Zeralda's Ogre

1989 OR   Removed from the Cascades Elementary School in Lebanon because the book had frightening illustrations.
Source: 11, Jan. 1990, pp. 4-5.

1700   Updike, John
Rabbit Is Rich

1996 PA   Removed from the library at Sun Valley High School in Aston because it contains "offensive language and explicit sexual scenes." The novel won the Pulitzer Prize for fiction in 1982.
Source: 11, May 1996, pp. 83-84.

1701   Updike, John
Rabbit Run

1962   Banned in Ireland because the Irish Board of Censors found the work "obscene" and "indecent," objecting particularly to the author's handling of the characters' sexuality, the "explicit sex acts" and "promiscuity." The work was officially banned from sales in Ireland until the introduction of the revised Censorship Publications Bill in 1967.
1976 ME   Restricted to high school students with parental permission in the six Aroostock County community high school libraries because of passages in the book dealing with sex and an extramarital affair.
1986 WY   Removed from the required reading list for English class at the Medicine Bow Junior High School because of sexual references and profanity in the book.
Source: 8, pp. 376–77; 11, Mar. 1977, p. 36; Mar. 1987, p. 55; 13, pp. 196–97.

1702   Valentine, Johnny
The Daddy Machine

1993 MD   Challenged in the Wicomico County Free Library in Salisbury along with three other books on homosexuality intended for juvenile readers.
Source: 11, Jan. 1994, p. 35.

1703   Valentine, Johnny
The Duke Who Outlawed Jelly Beans

1993 MD   Challenged in the Wicomico County Free Library in Salisbury along with three other books on homosexuality intended for juvenile readers.

1993 NC   Moved from the children's section to the adult section at the Elizabethtown library.
1993 OH   Retained at the Dayton and Montgomery County Public Library.
1998 FL   Challenged at the Brevard County Library. When the request failed to have the book banned, the complainant kept the book from other patrons by keeping it checked out for a year.
Source: 11, May 1993, p. 71; July 1993, pp. 100–101; Jan. 1994, p. 35; Mar. 1994, p. 69; July 1998, p. 105.

1704   Van Devanter, Lynda, and Christopher Morgan
Home before Morning

1988 MD   Challenged at the Esperanza Middle School library in Lexington because the book's "liberal use of profanity and explicit portrayals of situations."
Source: 11, Nov. 1988, p. 201.

1705   Van Lustbader, Eric
White Ninja

1995 VA   Challenged at the Prince William County Library because of passages that describe the vicious rape and flaying of a young woman.
Source: 11, Jan. 1996, p. 12; Nov. 1996, pp. 194, 211; Jan. 1997, p. 26.

1706   Van Slyke, Helen
Public Smiles, Private Tears

1989 MI   Challenged at the Public Libraries of Saginaw because the book is "pornographic" with no redeeming value.
Source: 11, May 1989, p. 77.

1707   Van Vooren, Monique
Night Sanctuary

1983 AR   Challenged at the White County Library in Searcy by a local parent, a minister and a group called the Institute for American Ideals.
Source: 11, Nov. 1983, p. 185; Jan. 1984, p. 25.

1708   *Vasilissa the Beautiful: Russian Fairy Tales*

1990 AR   Challenged at the Mena schools because the book contains "violence, voodoo, and cannibalism."
Source: 11, July 1990, p. 147.

1709   **Vergil, Polydore**
De Inventoribus Rerum

1551   Included in a 1551 list of books condemned by the Sorbonne in Paris, France.

1559   Included in the Spanish *Index Librorum Prohibitorum* (Index of Prohibited Books).

1564   Placed on the Roman Catholic Church *Index Librorum Prohibitorum* (Index of Prohibited Books) issued by Pope Paul IV in Rome, Italy.

1569   Included in the Liege Index.

Source: 1, pp. 69–70.

1710   **Vidal, Gore**
Live from Golgotha

1992   TX   Challenged at the Carrollton Public Library because the book is "offensive and pornographic."

Source: 11, Mar. 1993, p. 42.

1711   **Vinge, Joan D.**
Catspaw

1995   IA   Restricted to Mediapolis junior high students with parental consent because it was "unredeeming and destructive" as well as "morally decadent."

Source: 11, May 1994, p. 83; July 1995, p. 109.

1712   **Voigt, Cynthia**
David and Jonathan

1998   TX   Placed on the teacher reserve shelf, available for students to check out after they consult with a teacher, at the Colleyville Middle School in Grapevine-Colleyville. The novel, which chronicles the effects of the Holocaust on a group of adolescent boys in the 1950s, was found "to be disturbing and full of sexual references, crude language and adult themes such as suicide, masturbation, and abortion."

Source: 11, May 1998, p. 88; July 1998, p. 106.

1713   **Voigt, Cynthia**
Homecoming

1992   VA   Challenged at the Lynchburg middle and high school English classes because it presents readers with negative role models and values.

Source: 11, Sept. 1992, p. 164.

1714   **Voigt, Cynthia**
Tell Me If the Lovers Are Losers

1997   WV   Removed from the Jackson County school libraries along with sixteen other titles.

Source: 11, Jan. 1998, p. 13.

1715   **Voigt, Cynthia**
When She Hollers

1997   WV   Removed from the Jackson County school libraries along with sixteen other titles.

Source: 11, Jan. 1998, p. 13.

1716   **Voltaire, Francois M. [Francois-Marie Arouet]**
Candide

1806   Placed the book on the *Index Librorum Prohibitorum* (List of Prohibited Books) of 1806 by Pope Pius VII in Rome, Italy.

1929   MA   Seized by U.S. Customs in Boston and declared as obscene.

1935   Declared as obscene and suppressed in the USSR.

1944   Voltaire's best-known work remained anathema to American authorities as late as 1944 when Concord Books, issuing a sale catalog that included the book, was informed by the Post Office that such a listing violated U.S. postal regulations on sending obscene matter through the mails.

Source: 2, p. 137; 3, p. 354; 4, p. 27; 8, pp. 323–24; 15, Vol. III, pp. 418–19.

1717   **Voltaire, Francois M. [Francois-Marie Arouet]**
Letters Conccering the English Nation

1734   Printed clandestinely, banned by the French Parlement, and burned by the public executioner.

1752   Placed on the Catholic Church's *Index Librorum Prohibitorum* (Index of Prohibited Books) in Rome, Italy, along with thirty-eight other books by Voltaire. The Spanish Index also prohibited all of his writings.

Source: 1, pp. 185–86.

1718   **Von Ziegesar, Cecily**
Only in Your Dreams: A Gossip Girl Novel

2009   FL   New   Challenged at the Leesburg Public Library because of sexual innuendo, drug references, and other adult topics. Responding to a call by parents, church, and community leaders to remove this novel along with twelve other provocative books available to teens at the Leesburg Public Library, city commissioners voted 4-1 to separate all books based on age groups. High-school books will be placed in a separate area in the library stairwell.

Source: 11, July 2009, p. 131; Nov. 2009, p. 201.

1719   Vonnegut, Kurt
Breakfast of Champions

1995 IL   Challenged in the Monmouth School District
            Library because it is "pornographic trash."
            Source: 11, Mar. 1996, p. 45.

1720   Vonnegut, Kurt
Cat's Cradle

1972 OH   The Strongsville School Board voted to
            withdraw this title from the school library;
            this action was overturned in 1976 by a U.S.
            District Court in *Minarcini v. Strongsville City
            School District*, 541 F. 2d 577 (6th Cir. 1976).
1982 NH   Challenged at the Merrimack High School.
            Source: 4, p. 95; 11, Sept. 1982, p. 170; 12, pp. 145–48.

1721   Vonnegut, Kurt
God Bless You, Mr. Rosewater

1972 OH   The Strongsville School Board voted to
            withdraw this title from the school library;
            this action was overturned in 1976 by a U.S.
            District Court.
            Source: 4, p. 95.

1722   Vonnegut, Kurt
Slaughterhouse-Five

1972 MI   Banned in Rochester because the novel
            "contains and makes references to religious
            matters" and thus fell within the ban of the
            establishment clause. An appellate court
            upheld its usage in the school in *Todd v.
            Rochester Community Schools*, 41 Mich. App.
            320, 200 N. W. 2d 90.
1973 ND   Challenged in many communities, but burned
            in Drake.
1975 NY   Banned in Levittown.
1979 OH   Banned in North Jackson.
1982 FL   Banned in Lakeland because of the "book's
            explicit sexual scenes, violence, and obscene
            language."
1984 WI   Barred from purchase at the Washington Park
            High School in Racine by the district
            administrative assistant for instructional
            services. In 1986, restricted to students who
            have parental permission at the four Racine
            Unified District high school libraries because
            of "language used in the book, depictions of
            torture, ethnic slurs, and negative portrayals
            of women."
1985 KY   Challenged at the Owensboro High School
            library because of "foul language, a section
            depicting a picture of an act of bestiality, a
            reference to 'Magic Fingers' attached to the
            protagonist's bed to help him sleep, and the

sentence: 'The gun made a ripping sound like
the opening of the fly of God Almighty.'"
1986 WI   Restricted to students who have parental
            permission at the four Racine Unified District
            high school libraries because of "language
            used in the book, depictions of torture,
            ethnic slurs, and negative portrayals of women."
1987 GA   Banned from the Fitzgerald schools because
            it was filled with profanity and full of explicit
            sexual references."
1987 KY   Challenged at the LaRue County High School
            library because "the book contains foul
            language and promotes deviant sexual
            behavior."
1988 LA   Challenged in the Baton Rouge public high
            school libraries because the book is "vulgar
            and offensive."
1989 MI   Challenged in the Monroe public schools as
            required reading in a modern novel course for
            high school juniors and senior because of the
            book's language and the way women are
            portrayed.
1996 TX   Retained on the Round Rock Independent
            High School reading list after a challenge that
            the book was too violent.
1998 VA   Challenged as an eleventh-grade summer
            reading option in Prince William County
            because the book "was rife with profanity
            and explicit sex."
2000 RI   Removed as required reading for sophomores
            at the Coventry High School after a parent
            complained that it contained vulgar language,
            violent imagery, and sexual content.
2006 IL   Retained on the Northwest Suburban High
            School District 214 reading list in Arlington
            Heights, along with eight other challenged
            titles. A board member, elected amid
            promises to bring her Christian beliefs into all
            board decision-making, raised the controversy
            based on excerpts from the books she'd
            found on the Internet.
2007 MI   Challenged in the Howell High School along
            with several other books because of strong
            sexual content. In response to a request from
            the president of the Livingston Organization
            for Values in Education, or LOVE, the county's
            top law enforcement official reviewed the
            books to see whether laws against
            distribution of sexually explicit materials to
            minors had been broken. "After reading the
            books in question, it is clear that the explicit
            passages illustrated a larger literary, artistic,
            or political message and were not included
            solely to appeal to the prurient interests of
            minors," the Livingston county prosecutor
            wrote. "Whether these materials are
            appropriate for minors is a decision to be
            made by the school board, but I find that they

are not in violation of the criminal laws."

Source: 8, pp. 165–70; 11, Jan. 1974, p. 4; May 1980, p. 51; Sept. 1982, p. 155; Nov. 1982, p. 197; Sept. 1984, p. 158; Jan. 1986, pp. 9–10; Mar. 1986, p. 57; Mar. 1987, p. 51; July 1987, p. 147; Sept. 1987, pp. 174–75; Nov. 1987, p. 224; May 1988, pp. 86–87; July 1988, pp. 139–40; July 1989, p. 144; May 1996, p. 99; Nov. 1998, p. 183; Jan. 2001, p. 14; July 2006, pp. 210–11; May 2007, pp. 117–18; 12, pp. 78–79.

1723   Vonnegut, Kurt
Welcome to the Monkey House

1969 AL   A Montgomery teacher was dismissed for assigning this title to her eleventh-grade English class because the book promoted "the killing off of elderly people and free sex." The teacher brought suit and won in *Parducci v. Rutland*, 316 F.Supp. 352, (M. D. Ala 1970).

1977 MN   Pulled from the high school classes in Bloomington.

Source: 11, Jan. 1970, p. 28; July 1977, p. 101; 12, pp. 126–27, 238.

1724   Wagner, Jane
J. T.

1981 NC   Removed from classroom use in Raleigh due to book's racial stereotyping, but later reinstated by an ad hoc review committee.

Source: 11, Nov. 1981, p. 170.

1725   Walker, Alice
The Color Purple

1984 CA   Challenged as an appropriate reading for Oakland High School honors class due to the work's "sexual and social explicitness" and i its "troubling ideas about race relations, man's relationship to God, African history, and human sexuality." After nine months of haggling and delays, a divided Oakland Board of Education gave formal approval for the book's use.

1985 CA   Rejected for purchase by the Hayward school trustees because of "rough language" and "explicit sex scenes."

1986 VA   Removed from the open shelves of the Newport News school library because of its "profanity and sexual references" and placed in a special section accessible only to students over the age of eighteen or who have written permission from a parent.

1989 MI   Challenged at the public libraries of Saginaw because it was "too sexually graphic for a 12-year-old."

1989 TN   Challenged as a summer youth program reading assignment in Chattanooga because of its language and "explicitness."

1990 WY   Challenged as an optional reading assignment in the Ten Sleep schools.

1992 NC   Challenged as a reading assignment at the New Bern High School because the main character is raped by her stepfather.

1992 PA   Banned in the Souderton Area School District as appropriate reading for tenth graders because it is "smut."

1995 CT   Challenged on the curricular reading list at Pomperaug High School in Southbury because sexually explicit passages aren't appropriate high school reading.

1995 FL   Challenged at the St. Johns County Schools in St. Augustine.

1995 OR   Retained as an English course reading assignment in the Junction City high school after a challenge to Walker's Pulitzer Prize-winning novel caused months of controversy. Although an alternative assignment was available, the book was challenged due to "inappropriate language, graphic sexual scenes, and book's negative image of black men."

1996 NC   Challenged, but retained as part of the reading list for Advanced Placement English classes at Northwest High School in High Point. The book was challenged because it is "sexually graphic and violent."

1996 TX   Retained on the Round Rock Independent High School reading list after a challenge that the book was too violent.

1997 WV   Removed from the Jackson County school libraries along with sixteen other titles.

1999 OH   Challenged, but retained as part of a supplemental reading list at the Shawnee School in Lima. Several parents described its content as vulgar and "X-rated."

1999 VA   Removed from the Ferguson High School library in Newport News. Students may request and borrow the book with parental approval.

2002 VA   Challenged, along with seventeen other titles in the Fairfax County elementary and secondary libraries, by a group called Parents Against Bad Books in Schools. The group contends the books "contain profanity and descriptions of drug abuse, sexually explicit conduct, and torture."

2008 NC   Challenged in Burke County schools in
New   Morgantown by parents concerned about the homosexuality, rape, and incest portrayed in the book.

Source: 11, July 1984, p. 103; Sept. 1984, p. 156; Mar. 1985, p. 42; May 1985, pp. 75, 91; July 1985, p. 111; Nov. 1986, p. 209; May 1989, p. 77; Sept. 1989, p. 162; May 1990, p. 88; Sept. 1992, p. 142; Mar. 1993, p. 44; May 1993, p. 74; July 1995, p. 98; Sept. 1995, pp. 135, 160–61; Jan. 1996, p. 14; May 1996, p. 99; Mar. 1997, p. 50; May 1997, pp. 78–79; Sept. 1997, p. 149; Jan. 1998, p. 13; Sept. 1999, pp. 131–32; Nov. 1999, p. 163; Jan. 2003, p. 10; Jan. 2009, p. 10.

1726   Walker, Alice
The Temple of My Familiar

1997 WV Removed from the Jackson County school libraries along with sixteen other titles.
Source: 11, Jan. 1998, p. 13.

1727   Walker, Alice
Warrior Marks: Female Genital Mutilation and the Sexual Blinding of Women

1995 TX Former Weslaco librarian filed a federal lawsuit charging that she was fired for publicly discussing that city's efforts to ban Walker's work from the library.
Source: 11, Sept. 1995, p. 153.

1728   Walker, Barbara G.
The Woman's Encyclopedia of Myths and Secrets

1988 OR Restricted to non-required assignments at the North Bend High School library because the book "is of no benefit to anyone."
Source: 11, Jan. 1990, pp. 4–5.

1729   Walker, Kate
Peter

1998 WI Challenged at the Barron School District.
2004 TX Challenged at the Montgomery County Memorial Library System along with fifteen other young adult books with gay-positive themes. The objections were posted at the Library Patrons of Texas Web site. The language describing the books is similar to that posted at the Web site of the Fairfax County, Virginia-based Parents Against Bad Books in Schools, to which Library Patrons of Texas links.
Source: 11, Jan. 1999, p. 9; Nov. 2004, pp. 231–32.

1730   Walker, Margaret
Jubilee

1977 SC Challenged in the Greenville County school libraries by the Titan of the Fourth Province of the Knights of the Ku Klux Klan because the novel produces "racial strife and hatred."
2010 IL Challenged at the Jacksonville High School by
New   a pastor who said he found the fictionalized story of the author's grandmother, who was born as a slave in Georgia, "offensive" and "trashy" and a novel about the way of life in the Old South. "We believe it is to promote superiority for white people and to step on black people and make them feel inferior."
Source: 11, May 1977, p. 73; May 2010, pp. 104–5.

1731   Wallace, Daisy, ed.
Witch Poems

1993 MT Challenged at the Bozeman elementary school libraries because it scared a kindergartner.
Source: 11, Sept. 1993, p. 158.

1732   Wallace, Irving
The Fan Club

1974 CA The twenty-six branch librarians of Riverside County were advised that the book was not selected for circulation, and patrons should be told the county selection committee could not in good conscience spend tax money on it; further, that it was not their policy to purchase "formula-written commercial fiction."
1982   Malaysian police confiscated the works of Wallace because the books were considered "prejudicial to the public interest."
1988   Destroyed in Beijing, China and legal authorities threatened to bring criminal charges against the publishers.
Source: 4, p. 91; 5, Jan. 1983, p. 45; 11, Jan. 1989, p. 15.

1733   Walls, Jeannette
The Glass Castle: A Memoir

2009 CA Challenged at the William S. Hart Union High
New   School District in Saugus as required summer reading for the honors English program. The 2005 memoir chronicles the author's harsh childhood and family life and includes profanity, criticisms of Christianity, and accounts of sexual abuse and prostitution. Students have the option of alternative assignments that still meet objectives and teaching goals.
Source: 11, Jan. 2010, pp. 15–16.

1734   Wambaugh, Joseph
The Black Marble

1985 PA Banned from the Stroudsburg High School library because it was "blatantly graphic, pornographic and wholly unacceptable for a high school library."
Source: 11, May 1985, p. 79.

1735   Wambaugh, Joseph
The Delta Star

1985 PA Banned from the Stroudsburg High School library because it was "blatantly graphic, pornographic and wholly unacceptable for a high school library."
Source: 11, May 1985, p. 79.

1736   Wambaugh, Joseph
The Glitter Dome

1985 PA   Banned from the Stroudsburg High School library because it was "blatantly graphic, pornographic and wholly unacceptable for a high school library."
Source: 11, May 1985, 79.

1737   Wambaugh, Joseph
The New Centurions

1985 PA   Banned from the Stroudsburg High School library because it was "blatantly graphic, pornographic and wholly unacceptable for a high school library."
Source: 11, May 1985, p. 79.

1738   Warren, Patricia Nell
The Front Runner

1982 MI   Challenged at the Three Rivers Public Library because it "promotes homosexuality and perversion."
Source: 11, Mar. 1983, p. 29.

1739   Warren, Robert Penn
All the King's Men

1974 TX   Challenged at the Dallas Independent School District high school libraries.
Source: 11, Jan. 1975, pp. 6–7.

1740   Watkins, Yoko Kawashima
So Far from the Bamboo Grove

2006 MA   Removed from the sixth-grade English curriculum at Dover-Sherborn Middle School due to scenes hinting at rape, violence against women by Korean men, and a distorted presentation of history. It is part of the state's recommended reading list for the grade level. The book is based on the real-life experiences of Watkins, whose father was a Japanese government official. In a reversal of its decision, the Dover Regional School committee voted unanimously to keep the book as part of a sixth-grade language arts unit on survival. The school is exploring other texts to bring balance to the unit in response to the criticism leveled against the book by some parents and community members.
Source: 11, Jan. 2007, pp. 13–14; Mar. 2007, pp. 73–74.

1741   Watson, Jane Werner, and Sol Chambers
The Golden Book of the Mysterious

1988 MD   Challenged at the Winchester Elementary School because of the book's reference to witchcraft, sorcery, spells, fortune-telling, reincarnation, werewolves, vampires, and ghosts.
Source: 11, July 1988, p. 120; Sept. 1988, p. 178.

1742   Waugh, Evelyn
Brideshead Revisited

2005 AL   Alabama Representative Gerald Allen (R-Cottondale) proposed legislation that would prohibit the use of public funds for the "purchase of textbooks or library materials that recognize or promote homosexuality as an acceptable lifestyle." The bill also proposed that novels with gay protagonists and college textbooks that suggest homosexuality is natural would have to be removed from library shelves and destroyed. The bill would impact all Alabama school, public, and university libraries. While it would ban books like *Heather Has Two Mommies*, it could also include classic and popular novels with gay characters such as Evelyn Waugh's *Brideshead Revisited*, *The Color Purple* or *The Picture of Dorian Gray*.
Source: 11, Jan. 2005, p. 5.

1743   Waxman, Stephanie
What Is a Girl? What Is a Boy?

1983 MN   After the Minnesota Civil Liberties Union sued the Elk River School Board, the board reversed its decision to restrict this title to students who have written permission from their parents.
1991 VT   Challenged at the Blue Mountain schools in Wells River.
1994 GA   Placed in a special nonfiction section where an adult must request it for a child at the Lake Lanier Regional Library in Lawrenceville after a group of parents complained that the book is not appropriate for young children.
1994 GA   Moved to the nonfiction section of the Gwinnet-Forsyth Regional Library.
Source: 11, Sept. 1982, pp. 155–56; May 1983, p. 71; Sept. 1983, p. 153; Sept. 1991, p. 178; Nov. 1994, p. 187; Jan. 1995, p. 6.

1744   *We the People–History of the U.S.*

1981 MS   Removed from the Mississippi state-approved textbook list.
Source: 11, July 1981, p. 93.

1745   Webb, James
Fields of Fire

1988 SC   Challenged at the Fort Mill High School because the book contains "offensive language and explicit sex scenes." School officials decided to retain the novel, but to explore the possibility of setting up a "restricted" shelf for "controversial" books.
Source: 11, July 1988, p. 122; Sept. 1988, pp. 178–79.

1746   Wei Hui, Zhou
Shanghai Baby

2001   Banned in China because it contains "too much decadence and too much sexual description" and officials believed that it would "give a bad influence to a new generation." Police publicly raided book fairs and confiscated and burned copies of the novel.
Source: 13, p. 217.

1747   Welch, James
Fools Crow

1999 MT   Banned from Laurel High School classrooms because the contents are "objectionable, inappropriate, disgusting, and repulsive." Two copies remain in the library.
2000 MT   Challenged, but retained at the Bozeman High School despite objections to its descriptions of rape, mutilation, sex, and violence.
Source: 11, July 1999, p. 96; Mar. 2000, p. 51; July 2000, p. 125; July 2007, p. 148.

1748   Welch, James
Winter in the Blood

1996 TX   Retained on the Round Rock Independent High School reading list after a challenge that the book was too violent.
Source: 11, May 1996, p. 99.

1749   Wells, Rosemary
Shy Charles

1991 OR   Challenged because the mother allegedly is portrayed too negatively, but retained at the Multnomah County Library.
Source: 11, Jan. 1992, p. 6.

1750   Wentworth, Harold, and Stuart B. Flexner
Dictionary of American Slang

1979 FL   Returned to the publisher after a parent complained to the Stuart Middle School.

1981 CO   Removed from the Westminster elementary and secondary school libraries.
Source: 11, July 1979, p. 75; Mar. 1982, pp. 42–43.

1751   Wersba, Barbara
Whistle Me Home

2005 MD   Banned in Carroll County schools. No reason stated.
Source: 11, Mar. 2006, pp. 70–71.

1752   Wertenbaker, Lael Tucker
The World of Picasso

1994 AZ   Retained at Maldonado Elementary School in Tucson after being challenged by parents who objected to nudity and "pornographic," "perverted," and "morbid" themes.
Source: 11, July 1994, p. 112.

1753   West, Stanley Gordon
Finding Laura Buggs

2007 ND   Challenged in the Fargo School District
New   classrooms because the book includes passages on such topics as sexual bondage, incest, murder, and infanticide. According to district policy, the complainant does not have standing to request either formal or informal reviews because she doesn't have a child in classes using the book. The complainant also contacted the Montana Department of Public Instruction and several state legislators.
Source: 11, July 2007, pp. 148–49.

1754   West, Stanley Gordon
Until They Bring the Streetcars Back

2007 ND   Challenged in the Fargo School District
New   classrooms because the book includes passages on such topics as sexual bondage, incest, murder, and infanticide. According to district policy, the complainant does not have standing to request either formal or informal reviews because she doesn't have a child in classes using the book. The complainant also contacted the Montana Department of Public Instruction and several state legislators.
Source: 11, July 2007, pp. 148–49.

1755   Westheimer, David
Von Ryan's Express

1977 IL   Challenged at the North Suburban District Library in Loves Park because the novel contains "vulgar sexual expressions, profanity, and a discussion of a scene of gross immorality."
Source: 11, July 1977, p. 99.

1756   Wharton, William
Birdy

1988 ME   Banned, but later returned to the shelves of the Mary E. Taylor Middle School in Camden. The book was originally removed because it contained ten phrases and sentences that contain sexual material and "offensive" language.
Source: 11, Jan. 1988, pp. 8, 28.

1757   White, Edmund, and Adam Mars-Jones
The Darker Proof: Stories from a Crisis

1993 OR   Challenged at the Deschutes County Library in Bend because it "encourages and condones" homosexuality.
Source: 11, Sept. 1993, pp. 158–59.

1758   White, Edmund, ed.
Faber Book of Gay Short Fiction

2000 NC   Challenged in the Charlotte Public Library because of its sexual content.
Source: 11, Sept. 2000, p. 143.

1759   White, Ellen Emerson
Long Live the Queen

1991 WA   Challenged in the Mount Vernon school libraries because it contained a word parents found objectionable.
Source: 11, Mar. 1992, p. 41.

1760   White, Ryan, and Ann Marie Cunningham
Ryan White: My Own Story

1996 PA   Removed from the curriculum, but placed on library shelves, with restricted access, at the Stroudsburg middle school because a section "uses a gutter term for sodomy and another approves of teen smoking."
Source: 11, Mar. 1997, p. 37.

1761   Whitlock, Katherine
Bridge of Respect: Creating Support for Lesbian and Gay Youth

1990 IA   Challenged at the Muscatine Public Library because it is "wrong to promote immorality."
Source: 11, Nov. 1990, p. 225.

1762   Whitman, Walt
Leaves of Grass

1870 NY   Banned, informally, in New York bookstores. As per their usual practice, the Watch and Ward Society in the New York Society for the Suppression of Vice placed pressure on booksellers to suppress the sale of the book in their shops. Booksellers agreed not to advertise the book nor to suggest its sale to customers.

1870 PA   Banned, informally, in Philadelphia bookstores in the 1870s.

1880 MA   Banned in Boston in the 1880s. As per their usual practice, the Watch and Ward Society in Boston Society for the Suppression of Vice placed pressure on booksellers to suppress the sale of the book in their shops. Booksellers agreed not to advertise the book nor to suggest its sale to customers.
Source: 2, p. 38; 4, p. 45; 8, pp. 465–67; 15, Vol. I, p. 562, II, p. 610.

1763   Wiebe, Rudy
The Story-Makers: A Selection of Modern Short Stories

1984   Removed from the Halton County, Ontario, Canada School District because the short story anthology contains "The Sins of Jesus," by Isaac Babel. According to the complainants, some Christians consider the story "blasphemous because the Lord Jesus appears as a slightly confused comic character who in the end seems to accept that he has made a mistake."
Source: 11, Nov. 1984, p. 188.

1764   Wieler, Diane
Bad Boy

1996 PA   Challenged at the State College area middle school libraries. Three parents requested the book's removal, charging that it was full of profanity and portrayed underage drinking and other problems. In addition, the portrayal of the homosexual relationship between two secondary characters "conveys a wrong message."
Source: 11, Nov. 1996, p. 211; Jan. 1997, p. 9.

1765   Wilde, Oscar
The Happy Prince and Other Stories

1988 OR   Challenged at the Springfield Public Library because the stories were "distressing and morbid."
Source: 11, Jan. 1989, p. 3.

1766 Wilde, Oscar
Salome

1892   Lord Chamberlain withheld the play license in London, England on the grounds that it introduced biblical characters.

1895   MA   Book banned in Boston.

Source: 4, p. 55.

1767 Wilder, Laura Ingalls
Little House in the Big Woods

1996   CA   Removed from the classrooms, but later reinstated, for third-graders at the Lincoln Unified School District in Stockton. Complainants also want the book removed from the library because it "promotes racial epithets and is fueling the fire of racism."

Source: 11, Jan. 1997, p. 9; Mar. 1997, p. 50.

1768 Wilder, Laura Ingalls
Little House on the Prairie

1993   LA   Challenged at the Lafourche Parish elementary school libraries in Thibodaux because the book is "offensive to Indians."

1993   SD   Banned in the Sturgis elementary school classrooms due to statements considered derogatory to Native Americans.

1998   MN   Temporarily removed at the Yellow Medicine East Elementary School near Granite Falls due to the book's racist statements against Native Americans.

Source: 11, July 1993, pp. 124–25; Mar. 1994, p. 55; Mar. 1999, p. 36.

1769 Willhoite, Michael
Daddy's Roommate

1992   GA   Restricted to adults at the Lake Lanier Regional Library System in Gwinnett County.

1992   NC   Challenged at the Wayne County Public Library in Goldsboro.

1992   NC   Challenged at the Fayetteville Public Library.

1992   NM   Challenged at the Roswell Public Library.

1992   NY   Removed from the Brooklyn School District's curriculum because the school board objected to words that were "age inappropriate."

1992   OR   Challenged at the Tillamook Public Library because it "promotes a dangerous and ungodly lifestyle from which children must be protected."

1992   PA   Challenged at the Dauphin County Library System because the book's intent "is indoctrination into a gay lifestyle."

1992   TX   Challenged at the Grand Prairie Memorial Library.

1992   WA   Challenged at the Timberland Regional Libraries in Olympia because the book promotes homosexuality and is offensive.

1993   AK   Challenged at the Juneau school libraries.

1993   AZ   Challenged at the Mesa Public Library because it "is vile, sick and goes against every law and constitution."

1993   FL   Moved from the children's section to the adult section at the Manatee Public Library.

1993   FL   Challenged at the Alachua County Library in High Springs.

1993   MA   Challenged at the Seekonk library.

1993   MD   Challenged at the Wicomico County Free Library in Salisbury.

1993   MN   Challenged as a reading in the Rosemount-Apple Valley-Eagan Independent School District # 196.

1993   NC   Moved from the children s section to the adult section at the Elizabethtown library.

1993   NC   Challenged at the Cumberland County Public Library.

1993   NJ   Moved from the children's section to the adult section of the Mercer County Library System in Lawrence.

1993   NJ   Challenged at the North Brunswick Public Library.

1993   OH   Retained at the Dayton and Montgomery County Public Library.

1993   TN   Challenged at the Chattanooga-Hamilton County Library Bicentennial Library.

1993   WI   Challenged at the Sussex Public Library.

1994   AZ   Challenged at the Chandler Public Library because the book is a "skillful presentation to the young child about lesbianism/homosexuality."

1994   OR   Removed by Lane County Head Start officials in Cottage Grove from its anti-bias curriculum.

1994   TX   Removed from the children's section of the Fort Worth Public Library because critics say it legitimizes gay relationships.

1998   FL   Challenged at the Brevard County Library. When a request to ban the book failed, the complainant kept the book from other patrons by keeping it checked out for a year.

1998   KS   Challenged, but retained at the Hays Public Library. A resident objected to "the teaching of the homosexual lifestyle as another way to show love."

1998   TX   Challenged at the Wichita Falls Public Library when the request to have the book banned failed, the complainant kept the book from other patrons by keeping it checked out for a year. The deacon body of the First Baptist Church requested that any literature that promotes or sanctions a homosexual lifestyle be removed. The Wichita Falls City Council established a policy that allows library card holders who collect three hundred signatures to have children's books moved to an adult portion of the library. U.S. District Court Judge Jerry Buchmeyer struck down the library resolution as unconstitutional and the books were returned.

1999 ID Challenged, but retained in the juvenile non-fiction section of the Nampa Public Library.

2000 ID Challenged, but retained at the Ada Community Library.

Source: 11, May 1992, pp. 83, 95; Sept. 1992, p. 162; Nov. 1992, pp. 197–99; Jan. 1993, pp. 7, 9, 10, 28; May 1993, pp. 69–71; July 1993, pp. 101, 106–7, 123–26; Sept. 1993, pp. 143–46; Nov. 1993, p. 179; Jan. 1994, pp. 13, 34–36; Mar. 1994, p. 69; July 1994, p. 115; Sept. 1994, pp. 147–48, 166; Nov. 1994, p. 187; Jan. 1995, pp. 4, 6, 8; Sept. 1995, p. 159; May 1998, pp. 69, 88; July 1998, pp. 105–7; Jan. 1999, pp. 8–9; Mar. 1999, p. 36; May 1999, p. 67; Sept. 1999, p. 131; Nov. 1999, p. 172; Mar. 2000, pp. 44, 61; Nov. 2000, pp. 201–202.

1770 Williams-Garcia, Rita
Like Sisters on the Homefront

2000 PA Removed from Central Dauphin school district, Harrisburg elementary and middle school library shelves due to explicit language.

Source: 11, Sept. 2000, p. 144.

1771 Williams, Chancellor
The Destruction of African Civilization and the Origin of African Civilization

1993 MD Challenged at the Prince George County high school libraries because the two volumes promote "racism against white people." In a complaint filed with the state, the works were called "racist pornography" written "to provoke emotions and actions of racial prejudice, bias, hatred and hostility towards citizens and students in Maryland."

Source: 11, Nov. 1993, p. 177.

1772 Williams, Garth
The Rabbit's Wedding

1959 AL Removed from the "open" shelves to the "reserved" shelves at the Montgomery Public Library because an illustration of the lapin couple, the buck was black while the doe was white. Such miscegenation, stated an editor in Orlando, was "brainwashing. . . . as soon as you pick up the book and open its pages you realize these rabbits are integrated." *The Home News* of Montgomery, Ala., added that the book was integrationist propaganda obviously aimed at children in their formative years.

Source: 3, p. 250.

1773 Williams, Jaston; Joe Sears; and Ed Howard
Greater Tuna

1991 IL Challenged at the Grayslake Community High School.

Source: 11, July 1991, pp. 129–30.

1774 Williams, Jay
The Magic Grandfather

1989 OR Challenged at the Little Butte Intermediate School in Eagle Point because the book used swear words, and deals with magic and witches.

Source: 11, Jan. 1990, pp. 4–5.

1775 Williams, Roger
The Bloudy Tenent of Persecution

1644 Burned publicly by order of the British Parliament.

Source: 8, pp. 215–16.

1776 Willingham, Calder
End as a Man

1947 NY New York Society for Suppression of Vice sought a ban.

1948 PA Seized in Philadelphia raid.

Source: 4, p. 96; 14, pp. 129–30.

1777 Wilson, August
Fences

1993 PA Challenged in the honors and academic English classes in Carlisle schools because it is "demeaning to women." Teachers must send parents a letter warning about the work's content and explaining that their children may read alternate selections.

Source: 11, July 1993, p. 127.

1778 Wilson, Colin
The Sex Diary of Gerard Orme

1964 CT A bookseller in New Britain was arrested for selling this title.

Source: 4, p. 99.

1779 Wilson, Colin
Witches

1986 OR Challenged at the Albany Library because the book "is satanic in nature, thereby having tremendous drawing power to the curious and unsuspecting."

Source: 11, July 1986, p. 136.

1780   Wilson, Edmund
Memoirs of Hecate County

1946 CA   Booksellers in San Francisco were arrested for selling the work and taken to trial. A bookseller was charged with selling an "obscene" book, but the first trail was dismissed because it resulted in a hung trail. In the second trial of *People v. Wepplo*, 78 Cal. App. 2D 959, 178 P.2d 853 (1947), the jury acquitted the bookseller. Banned from the U.S. mail in 1956.

1946 MA   Shipment ceased because of its censorship laws.

1946 NY   Confiscated by the New York City police from four Doubleday bookshops after the New York Society for Suppression of Vice charged that it was salacious and lascivious. Booksellers in New York City were arrested for selling the work and taken to trial.

1946 PA   Copies of the book were confiscated in Philadelphia and the publisher ceased shipment to Massachusetts because of its censorship laws.

1956   Banned from the U.S. mail.

Source: 4, pp. 76–77; 8, pp. 365–66; 15, Vol. IV, pp. 697–99.

1781   Winship, Elizabeth; Frank Caparulo, and Vivian K. Harlin
Human Sexuality

1992 GA   Challenged in the Fulton County schools because the "book is a 'how-to' book. It's not only explicit, but it promotes promiscuity in a subtle way that the determined abstainer would have second thoughts about their position." The group alleged that the text "undermines parents' authority, encourages breaking the law, and tears down normal sexual barriers by co-ed, hardcore, adult subject matter covered."

1994 MO   Removed from use in health classes by the Belleville School District School Board after parents had complained that the book "didn't stress abstinence from sex by high school students," and because "it didn't say whether sexual relations before marriage, homosexuality, masturbation, or abortion are right or wrong."

1994 GA   Banned in the Fulton County high schools because the book was too graphic, out-of-date, and did too little to persuade students not to have sex.

Source: 11, May 1992, pp. 82–83; May 1994, p. 87; Sept. 1994, p. 150.

1782   Winship, Elizabeth
Perspectives on Health: Human Sexuality

1994 IN   Retained by unanimous school board vote, two mothers nevertheless protested by removing their daughters from classes at an Argos Community School using this textbook because they felt it is "too explicit and sends mixed messages about abstinence." They also objected to treatment of abortion and homosexuality.

Source: 11, May 1994, p. 99.

1783   Winsor, Kathleen
Forever Amber

1946   Copies burned at British ports and by the public library in Birmingham, England.

1946 MA   Temporary injunction issued against sale of the book in Springfield. Attorney General George Rowell cited as due cause for banning the book some seventy references to sexual intercourse; thirty-nine illegitimate pregnancies; seven abortions; ten descriptions of women undressing, dressing or bathing in the presence of men; five references to incest; thirteen references ridiculing marriage; and forty-nine "miscellaneous objectionable passages." Rowell lost his case, and Judge Donahue of the Massachusetts Supreme Court defined the book as "a soporific rather an aphrodisiac. . . . while the novel was conducive to sleep, it was not conducive to a desire to sleep with a member of the opposite sex."

1952   Banned in New Zealand after the Minister of Customs, reviewed a copy seized by Customs officers.

1953   Banned in Ireland.

Source: 3, p. 95; 4, p. 93; 8, pp. 336–38; 15, Vol. IV, pp. 696–98.

1784   Winthrop, Elizabeth
The Castle in the Attic

1995 ME   Challenged at the Medway schools because the book uses swear words and deals with sorcery.

Source: 11, July 1995, p. 97.

1785   Witt, Mary A., et al.
The Humanities: Cultural Roots and Continuities

1986 FL   Banned from classroom use, but returned to the Columbia High School library in Lake City because of "offensive" language. The school board banned two sections of the text that contained modern adaptation of *The Miller's Tale*, by Chaucer and *Lysistrata*, by Aristophanes. In December 1986, four parents filed a lawsuit charging that their children's rights were violated when the textbook was banned from classroom use. On January 30, 1988, the U.S. District Court for the Middle District of Florida ruled that in *Virgil v. School Board of Columbia County* "the school board acted within its broad range of discretion in determining educational suitability" and thus may constitutionally ban a textbook because of sex and vulgarity. Upholding this ruling, the U.S. Court of Appeals for the Fourth Circuit ruled on January 16, 1989, that the school board did not violate students' constitutional rights when it removed the textbook.

Source: 11, July 1986, p. 119; Nov. 1986, p. 207; Mar. 1987, p. 51; Nov. 1987, p. 223; May 1988, pp. 81, 98; Sept. 1988, p. 150; Mar. 1989, p. 52.

1786   Wittlinger, Ellen
Sandpiper

2007 AL
New

Challenged at the Brookwood High School's library due to a complaint that the book has sexual content and language. The grandmother stated that the school should "teach abstinence and no sex before marriage." Wittlinger, the book's author, said in a letter to the school system that she was very surprised to learn that her book was being called "offensive" and "sick" because she said the purpose of the book is not meant to be a how-to guide for oral sex. Instead, it is a cautionary tale to teach kids that oral sex is "real" sex and not just the "cool thing to do." The board decided eventually to retain the book "on the advice of legal counsel."

Source: 11, Nov. 2007, p. 239; Jan. 2008, p. 7; Mar. 2008, p. 77.

1787   Wolf, Eric
Peasant Wars of the Twentieth Century

1985

Banned in South Korea.

Source: 5, Apr. 1986, pp. 30–33.

1788   Wolfe, Daniel
T. E. Lawrence

2000 CA

Removed from the Anaheim school district because school officials said the book is too difficult for middle school students and that it could cause harassment against students seen with it. The American Civil Liberties Union (ACLU) of Southern California filed suit in *Doe v. Anaheim Union High School District* alleging that the removal is "a pretext for viewpoint-based censorship." The ACLU claims no other books have been removed from the junior high library for similar reasons,

even though several, such as works by Shakespeare and Dickens, are more difficult reading. The ACLU contends that the school officials engaged in unconstitutional viewpoint discrimination by removing the book because it contains gay and lesbian material. In March 2001, the school board approved a settlement that restored the book to the high school shelves and amended the district's policy to prohibit the removal of books for subject matter involving sexual orientation, but the book will not be returned to the middle school.

Source: 11, Mar. 2001, p. 53; May 2001, p. 95; July 2001, p. 173.

1789   Wolfe, Thomas
Of Time and the River

1983 AL

Four members of the Alabama State Textbook Committee called for the rejection of Wolfe's work for use in Alabama public schools.

Source: 11, Mar. 1983, p. 39; 14, pp. 242–43.

1790   Wolff, Tobias
This Boy's Life: A Memoir

2005 KS

Removed from the Blue Valley School District's high school curriculum in Overland Park. The book was challenged by parents and community members because of "foul language, and references to alcohol and sexual activity."

Source: 11, Nov. 2005, pp. 282–83.

1791   Wolk, Robert L., and Arthur Henley
The Right to Lie

1987 MI

Challenged at the Plymouth-Canton school system in Canton because the book is "a psychological guide to everyday deceit."

Source: 11, May 1987, p. 110.

1792   Wood, Audrey
Elbert's Bad Word

1992 GA

Challenged in the Columbia County school libraries because Elbert visits a friendly gardener who is a "practicing wizard."

Source: 11, Nov. 1992, p. 197.

1793   Wood, Bari
Amy Girl

1988 NJ

Removed from the shelves of the Northern Burlington County Regional High School library because of its "descriptions of underage drinking and teenage sex."

Source: 11, Mar. 1988, p. 46.

1794 Wood, Maryrose
Sex Kittens and Horn Dawgs Fall in Love

2006 FL Removed along with nine other titles from a library order at the Hernando County schools. Among the other books culled from Nature Coast Technical High School's order were Barbara Kingsolver's first novel, *The Bean Trees*; *The Clan of the Cave Bear*, by Jean Auel; *Boy's Life*, by Robert McCammon; and the abridged young-adult version of *The Power of One*, by Bryce Courtenay. A board member led the charge against those books, reading profanity-laced passages and castigating the school officials who placed the order. Other books the school system wants to have reviewed are: *Are You in the House Alone?*; *Rainbow Boys*; *Rats Saw God*; and *The King Must Die*.
Source: 11, July 2006, p. 182.

1795 Woodroofe, Patrick
The Second Earth: The Pentateuch Retold

1992 VA Removed from the Warrenton Junior High School library because a single parent complained about its "anti-Christian" ideas and its illustrations.
Source: 11, May 1992, pp. 81–82.

1796 Woolley, Persia
Queen of the Summer Stars

1995 NY Challenged, but retained at the Case Junior High School Library in Watertown because, although the book contains scenes of sex, kidnapping, rape and incest, the themes of love, loyalty, honor and trust are more obvious to the reader.
Source: 11, May 1995, p. 66; July 1995, pp. 109–10.

1797 Worth, Valerie
Imp and Biscuit: The Fortune of Two Pugs

1990 AR Challenged at the Mena schools because the book contains "violence, voodoo and cannibalism."
Source: 9, July 1990, p. 147.

1798 Wright, Peter
Spycatcher

1987 Banned in India.
1987 Banned in England because the author had violated his secrecy oath under the Official Secrets Act. After a two-and-a-half-year battle, the courts determined that three London newspapers could publish excerpts from the former intelligence agent's memoirs.
Source: 8, pp. 173–76; 11, Nov. 1987, p. 229; May 1988, p. 93; Jan. 1989, p. 15.

1799 Wright, Richard
Black Boy

1972 MI Removed from classroom use in Michigan after parents objected to the book's sexual overtones and claimed that it was unsuitable for impressionable sophomores.
1975 LA Challenged, but retained in the East Baton Rouge schools despite claims the book contains obscenity, filth or pornography.
1975 TN Removed from Tennessee schools for being obscene, instigating hatred between the races and encouraging immorality.
1976 NY Restricted to students with parental approval at the Island Trees, N. Y. Union Free School District High School library in 1976; restriction lifted after the U.S. Supreme Court ruling on June 25, 1982, in *Board of Education, Island Trees Union Free School District No. 26 et al. v. Pico et al.*, 457 U.S. 853 (1982).
1987 NE Challenged in the Lincoln school libraries because of the novel's "corruptive, obscene nature."
1987 NE Nebraska Governor Kay Orr's "kitchen cabinet" called for the novel's removal, asserting it had a "corruptive obscene nature" and citing the use of profanity throughout and the incidents of violence. The book was removed from library shelves, then returned after the controversy abated.
1996 TX Retained on the Round Rock Independent High School reading list after a challenge that the book was too violent.
1997 FL Challenged in the Jacksonville public schools by a minister who said the book contains "profanity and may spark hard feelings between students of different races."
2007 MI Challenged in the Howell High School along with several other books because of strong sexual content. In response to a request from the president of the Livingston Organization for Values in Education, or LOVE, the county's top law enforcement official reviewed the books to see whether laws against distribution of sexually explicit materials to minors had been broken. "After reading the books in question, it is clear that the explicit passages illustrated a larger literary, artistic, or political message and were not included solely to appeal to the prurient interests of

minors," the Livingston County prosecutor wrote. "Whether these materials are appropriate for minors is a decision to be made by the school board, but I find that they are not in violation of the criminal laws."

Source: 8, pp. 23–28; 11, May 1978, p. 57; Nov. 1982, p. 197; Nov. 1987, p. 225; May 1996, p. 99; Sept. 1997, p. 127; Mar. 2007, pp. 51–52; May 2007, pp. 117–18

1800   Wright, Richard
Native Son

1978 NH   Challenged in Goffstown.
1978 NJ   Challenged in Elmwood Park due to "objectionable" language.
1981 MA   Challenged in North Adams due to the book's "violence, sex, and profanity."
1988 MI   Challenged at the Berrien Springs High School in classrooms and libraries because the novel is "vulgar, profane, and sexually explicit."
1994 WA   Retained in the Yakima schools after a five-month dispute over what advanced high school students should read in the classroom. Two parents raised concerns about profanity and images of violence and sexuality in the book and requested that it be removed from the reading list.
1996 NC   Challenged as part of the reading list for Advanced Placement English classes at Northwest High School in High Point. The book was challenged because it is "sexually graphic and violent."
1998 CA   Removed from Irvington High School in Fremont after a few parents complained the book was unnecessarily violent and sexually explicit.
1998 IN   Challenged in the Hamilton High School curriculum in Fort Wayne because of the novel's graphic language and sexual content.

Source: 11, May 1978, p. 57; July 1978, p. 98; Sept. 1981, p. 125; Nov. 1981, p. 170; Jan. 1989, p. 28; Nov. 1994, pp. 202–3; Mar. 1997, p. 50; Sept. 1997, p. 149; Sept. 1998, p. 142; Mar. 1999, p. 39.

1801   WritersCorps
Paint Me Like I Am: Teen Poems

2009 NJ   The principal at the Landis Intermediate
New   School in Vineyard removed two pages that included the poem "Diary of an Abusive Step-father" after a thirteen-year-old Landis student's mother questioned its appropriateness. The thirty-one-line poem is peppered with profanity and details a violent relationship between an adult and child. San Francisco-based WritersCorps, an art organization linking writers with teens in urban areas to provide outlets for their experiences, produced the anthology.

2009 WI   Retained in the combined middle and high
New   school library in the North Fond du Lac School District provided it has a label designating it as appropriate for high school students. Younger students could also access the book with prior parental permission. A parent asked the school district to reconsider the book due to mature language.

Source: 11, July 2009, pp. 131–32; May 2010, pp. 128–29.

1802   Wycliffe, John
On Civil Lordship

1377   Condemned by the Pope in Rome, Italy.
1381   A Council at Oxford, England prohibited his work as heretical and forbade him from preaching or lecturing.
1415   A church council in Germany ordered his bones exhumed and burned and his ashes thrown into a running stream.

Source: 1, pp. 228–29.

1803   Wyden, Peter, and Barbara Wyden
Growing Up Straight: What Every Thoughtful Parent Should Know about Homosexuality

1993 OR   Challenged at the Deschutes County Library in Bend because it "encourages and condones" homosexuality.

Source: 11, Sept. 1993, pp. 158–59.

1804   Yashima, Taro
Crow Boy

1994 NY   Challenged by a school board member in the Queens school libraries because it "denigrate[s] white American culture, 'promotes racial separation, and discourages assimilation.'" The rest of the school board voted to retain the book.

Source: 11, July 1994, pp. 110–11; Sept. 1994, p. 166.

1805   Yates, Elizabeth
Amos Fortune, Free Man

1989 MD   Temporarily removed from the classrooms as an optional reading assignment in the Montgomery County schools because the 1950 Newbery Award-winning book contained "racist dialogue, fostered stereotypes, and could be degrading to black children who read it."

Source: 11, Mar. 1990, p. 62.

1806   Yep, Laurence
Dragonwings

1992 PA   Challenged at the Apollo-Ridge schools in Kittanning because of the frequent use of the word "demon" in the book. The Newbery Award-winning book might encourage children to "commit suicide because they think they can be reincarnated as something or someone else." On Sept. 15, 1992, Judge Joseph Nickleach denied a request seeking to ban the book from the district's curriculum. In his opinion, Nickleach wrote: "The fact that religions and religious concepts are mentioned in school does not automatically constitute a violation of the establishment clause."

1999 IN   Challenged at the Henryville schools because of graphic violence, profanity, references to demons and prostitution, and alcohol and drug use depicted in a positive light.
Source: 11, Sept. 1992, pp. 142–43; Jan. 1993, p. 18; Nov. 1999, p. 164.

1807   Young, Lawrence A.
Recreational Drugs

1982 CA   Challenged in the Alameda County Library because it allegedly encourages drug use.
Source: 11, Sept. 1982, p. 169.

1808   Zacks, Richard
History Laid Bare: Love, Sex, and Perversity from the Ancient Etruscans to Warren G. Harding

1999 NC   Challenged, but retained at the Cumberland County Library in Fayetteville despite a complaint that the book deals with sexual history and customs. In addition, the complainant suggested that the library move sexually explicit materials, as well as ones about homosexuality, into an adult section and establish a review committee to screen materials.
Source: 11, July 1999, p. 94; Jan. 2000, pp. 27–28.

1809   Zacks, Richard
An Underground Education: The Unauthorized and Outrageous Supplement to Everything You Thought You Knew about Art, Sex, Business, Crime, Science, Medicine, and Other Fields of Human Knowledge

1999 NC   Challenged, but retained at the Cumberland County Library in Fayetteville despite a complaint that the book deals with sexual history and customs. In addition, the complainant suggested that the library move sexually explicit materials, as well as ones about homosexuality, into an adult section and establish a review committee to screen materials.
Source: 11, July 1999, p. 94; Jan. 2000, pp. 27–28.

1810   Zemach, Margot
Jake and Honeybunch Go to Heaven

1982 CA   The San Francisco Public Library, after surveying librarians employed in their library, refused to acquire the book because it is "racially offensive." *The New York Times* stated, "In this case, librarians are deliberately keeping a widely acclaimed book by a major author-artist off their shelves in the name of morality."

1982 IL   The Chicago Public Library, after surveying librarians employed in their library, refused to acquire the book because it is "racially offensive."

1982 WI   The Milwaukee Public Library, after surveying librarians employed in their library, refused to acquire the book because it is "racially offensive."
Source: 14, pp. 189–90.

1811   Zindel, Paul
Loch

1997 NV   Challenged due to explicit language, but retained at the Lander County School District.
Source: 11, Mar. 1998, p. 56.

1812   Zindel, Paul
My Darling, My Hamburger

1973 MN   Removed from the Frazee School library.
1976 NY   Removed from the Lyons Elementary School library.
1979 IA   Removed from the Hiawatha Public Library.
1980 IL   Challenged in Champaign.
1982 KY   Challenged in Jefferson County.
1987 SD   Banned in the Dupree High School English classes because of what the school board called "offensive language and vulgarity."
Source: 11, Nov. 1973, p. 135; July 1976, p. 86; Mar. 1979, p. 27; May 1980, p. 61; Mar. 1983, p. 41; Jan. 1988, p. 12.

1813   Zindel, Paul
Pigman

1985 MO   Challenged at the Hillsboro School District because the novel features "liars, cheaters and stealers."

1990 CT Challenged as suitable curriculum material in the Burlington schools because it contains profanity and subject matter that set bad examples and give students negative views of life.

1990 CT Challenged as suitable curriculum material in the Harwinton schools because it contains profanity and subject matter that set bad examples and give students negative views of life.

1992 VA Challenged at the Lynchburg middle and high school English classes because the novel contains twenty-nine instances of "destructive, disrespectful, antisocial and illegal behavior . . . placed in a humorous light, making it seem acceptable."

Source: 11, Mar. 1985, p. 44; Mar. 1991, p. 44; May 1991, p. 90; Sept. 1992, p. 164.

1814 Zinn, Howard
A People's History of the United States

2009 VA New Challenged in the North Stafford High School advanced-placement history class, even though it's not the primary textbook because the book is "un-American, leftist propaganda." Students in the advanced placement class also read an article titled, "Howard Zinn's Disappointing History of the United States," which criticizes Zinn's book.

Source: 11, May 2009, pp. 108–9.

1815 Zola, Emile
J'Accuse

1894 Listed on the *Index Librorum Prohibitorum* (List of Prohibited Books) in Rome, Italy.

1929 Banned in Yugoslavia.

1953 Banned in Ireland.

Source: 4, pp. 51–52.

1816 Zola, Emile
Nana

1888 An English court agreed that all of Zola's works must be withdrawn from circulation, making Zola the only writer to have his works outlawed in England in the nineteenth century. The major complaints centered on the perception that Zola had made a heroine of a prostitute and had discussed "debased man's nature" by uncovering the often sordid sexuality of the period.

1894 Listed on the *Index Librorum Prohibitorum* (List of Prohibited Books) in Rome, Italy.

1929 Banned in Yugoslavia.

1953 Banned in Ireland.

Source: 4, pp. 51–52; 6, pp. 2,718–20; 14, pp. 234–35.

1817 Zwerman, Gilda
Martina Navratilova

2000 CA Removed from the Anaheim school district because school officials said the book is too difficult for middle school students and that it could cause harassment against students seen with it. The American Civil Liberties Union (ACLU) of Southern California filed suit in *Doe v. Anaheim Union High School District* alleging that the removal is "a pretext for viewpoint-based censorship." The ACLU claims no other books have been removed from the junior high library for similar reasons, even though several, such as works by Shakespeare and Dickens, are more difficult reading. The ACLU contends that the school officials engaged in unconstitutional viewpoint discrimination by removing the book because it contains gay and lesbian material. In March 2001, the school board approved a settlement that restored the book to the high school shelves and amended the district's policy to prohibit the removal of books for subject matter involving sexual orientation, but the book will not be returned to the middle school.

Source: 11, Mar. 2001, p. 53; May 2001, p. 95; July 2001, p. 173.

Note: The bibliographic entries are numbered sequentially and the entry number, rather than the page number, is listed below.

Note: The bibliographic entries are numbered sequentially and the entry number, rather than the page number, is listed below.

Selected titles in this book have been indexed in the following categories: Art Books, Biographical Works, Black Literature, Children's Literature, Fiction, Folk Tales, Gay and Lesbian Literature, Nonfiction, Occult Books, Philosophical Treatises, Plays, Poetry, Political Works, Reference Books, Religious Titles, Sex Education Titles, Short Stories, Textbooks, and Young Adult Literature.

Neither this list nor any of the categories is all-inclusive and comprehensive. Rather, this index is meant to assist in the development of displays, articles, editorials, and presentations.

Thanks to both the American Library Association's Office for Intellectual Freedom—in particular, Barbara Jones, Deborah Caldwell-Stone, Angela Maycock, Nanette Perez, and Bryan Campbell—and the Illinois Library Association's staff, Cynthia M. Robinson and Kristy M. Mangel. Pat Scales contributed essential copy in two sections of the publication. All of these individuals offered valuable suggestions. They certainly tolerated my frequent monologues about improving the publication, and at the same time, graciously saved me from countless embarrassing errors by their fine editing skills.

Mary Huchting is a superb copy editor. As a First Amendment supporter, Mary reviewed the manuscript and corrected many errors. David Stone carefully proofed the designed copy, making sure that no new errors arose in the design phrase.

Decades ago, Mary Kane Trochim encouraged me to enter the incident descriptions for each title into a database. As a result, the bibliographic entries are numbered sequentially so that readers can find information by entry number, rather than by page number. Searching books by title, subject matter, or geographic location became much easier, and the value of this organization in a publication that builds on each year's history has been immeasurable. Readers looking for specific information on a book challenge, as well as this author, owe Mary their thanks for improving access to the publication's wealth of information.

Gary Sigman constructed, maintained, and refined the database to accommodate the ever-changing editorial and design needs for the comprehensive list of challenged titles. With his careful guidance, we made significant improvements this year to the database architecture.

Susan Friedman looked at the publication with fresh eyes and was the reader's advocate. With her ideas and vision, she strove to present the material in the most logical understandable manner.

Sam Silvio Design provided the thoughtful design for this year's publication. Sam's sophisticated design is clean and elegant. He is a most patient and gentle man.

Chris Watkins is a friend and colleague, and wonderful writer who served as a source of inspiration and a valuable sounding board. As a key strategic thinker, she assisted this publication in every aspect of its development.

Judith F. Krug, the creator of the ALA's Office for Intellectual Freedom, empowered me from the inception of Banned Books Week to produce the materials and resources necessary to make the event a reality and a continuing success. Her death last year was a great loss to the library community and the supporters of the First Amendment. All of us who knew her, worked with her, learned from her and loved her, know how much she would want this work to continue. Her spirit will forever inspire us to be forceful and eloquent in articulating this basic freedom.

The assistance and friendship of those individuals listed above and the friendship of many others unnamed here will be always be remembered and cherished by me.

In Memoriam
Patricia Ann Scarry
1949–2009